Exposition of the Psalms

Exposition of the Psalms

An Interpretation and Application
Volume Three: Psalms 101–150

Frank R. Shivers

LIGHTNING SOURCE
1246 Heil Quaker Blvd.
La Vergne, TN

Unless otherwise noted, Scripture quotations are from
The Holy Bible *King James Version*

Library of Congress Cataloging-in-Publication Data

Shivers, Frank R., 1949-
Exposition of the Psalms Vol. 3 / Frank Shivers
ISBN 978-1-878127-37-2

Library of Congress Control Number:
2018910734

Cover design by
Tim King of Click Graphics, Inc.

For Information:
Frank Shivers Evangelistic Association
P. O. Box 9991
Columbia, South Carolina 29290
www.frankshivers.com

Presented to

_____

By

_____

Date

_____

The law instructs, history informs, prophecy predicts, correction censures, and morals exhort. In the Book of Psalms, you find the fruit of all these, as well as a remedy for the salvation of the soul. The Psalter deserves to be called the praise of God, the glory of man, the voice of the church, and the most beneficial confession of faith.[1] ~ Ambrose

Here is a "Book of Devotion" for the ages. Here every heart chord is touched and tuned to holy melody. God is here in His natural and moral attributes. Christ is here in His divinity and humanity, humiliation and exaltation. The Gospel is here, sublime unfoldings of pardoning and purifying grace. Christian life is here: faith, hope, love—and even church history in outline.[2] ~ A. T. Pierson

If all the greatest excellences and most choice experience of all the true saints should be gathered from the whole church since it has existed and should be condensed into the focus of one book; if God, I say, should permit any most spiritual and gifted man to form and concentrate such a book, such a book would be what the Book of Psalms is, or like unto it. For in the Book of Psalms we have not the life of the saints only, but we have the experience of Christ Himself, the Head of all the saints. So that you may truly call the Book of Psalms a little Bible. Be assured that the Holy Spirit Himself has written and handed down to us this Book of Psalms as a Liturgy, in the same way as a father would give a book to his children. He Himself has drawn up this Manual for His disciples; having collected together, as it were, the lives, groans and experience of many thousands, whose hearts He alone sees and knows.[3] ~ James Hastings

There [Psalms] you look right down into the heart of saints and behold all manner of joys and joyous thoughts toward God and His love springing lustily into life! Again, you look into the heart of saints as into death and Hell! How gloomy and dark their mournful visions of God.[4] ~ Martin Luther

How varied and how splendid the wealth which this treasury [Psalms] contains it is difficult to describe in words; whatever I shall say, I know full well must fall far short of its worth.[5] ~ John Calvin

To

Joe Eudy
A loyal follower of Jesus Christ, ministry friend,
intercessor, and helper.

"Tychicus, a beloved brother and faithful minister in the Lord."

~ Ephesians 6: 21

Contents

According to legend, renowned Yosemite Ranger Carl Sharsmith was once asked by a visitor, "If you had only one day in Yosemite, what would you do?"

The veteran ranger and Yosemite lover looked solemn and replied "Madam, if I could only have one day in Yosemite, I'd sit by the Merced River and cry."[6]

Attempting to survey the Psalms in three volumes is even more formidable. Nonetheless, with due diligence, ever seeking to follow the divine guidance of the "pillar of fire" by night and the "pillar of a cloud" by day (Exodus 13:21), effort was exerted to enter the vast caverns of the Psalms, hewing out choice nuggets of pure gold to extract its invaluable and inexhaustible inspiration and instruction.

I join with Charles Haddon Spurgeon in saying, "In these busy days, it would be greatly to the spiritual profit of Christians if they were more familiar with the Book of Psalms, in which they would find a complete armory for life's battles and a perfect supply for life's needs. Here we have both delight and usefulness, consolation and instruction. For every condition there is a Psalm, suitable and elevating. The Book supplies the babe in grace with penitent cries and the perfected saint with triumphant songs. Its breadth of experience stretches from the jaws of Hell to the gate of Heaven."[7]

With regard to the vast works on the Psalms, one discovers various emphases. It has been my purpose in these three volumes to make understandable the "hidden" meaning of the original Hebrew words in which the Psalms were written; to simplify historical settings when known, making connection between the Psalm and the event; and to grant insight into the Psalm's personal devotional application. You, the reader, will render verdict whether or not that objective was achieved.

Words cannot describe or express the joy, challenge and enrichment to my soul derived in this journey through the Psalms. Its laborious but delightful task, that daily required hours upon hours in isolation in the study, will but be counted worthwhile if the reader is blessed in similar measure. Walter Brueggermann, in the Preface to

Spirituality of the Psalms, states, "Any comment upon them is inevitably partial and provisional. There is simply more than can be touched and handled. So one finishes with a sense of inadequacy, of not probing enough. That, of course, is why the Psalms continue to nourish and nurture long after our interpretation has run its course."[8] I couldn't agree more. This work at best but touches the hem of the garment of the treasure-filled Psalms. May the Lord favor this writing presently and then long after my departure unto His glory, honor and praise.

The Hebrew word for the Book of Psalms means "praises,"[9] whereas the Greek word means "songs of praise."[10] J. L. Crenshaw states that the word *Psalter* "comes from the title in Alexandrinus...and indicates a musical instrument, presumably to accompany the singing of Psalms."[11] Elwell and Comfort say the Psalter is a compilation of "poems sung to musical accompaniment, originally the harp."[12] Marvin Tate said, "The title probably respresents a stage in Israel's past when the Psalms were used as a general hymnal, suitable for all occasions."[13]

Augustine gave himself to a lifetime study of the Psalms; Henry Martyn was comforted and encouraged in times of tremendous stress through memorizing portions of the Psalms; Matthew Henry's father instructed him to read a Psalm a day, for it would bring him to love the whole of Scripture; to John Ruskin, Psalm 119 was the most precious because of its great emphasis on the Word of God.[14] Charles Haddon Spurgeon wrote in the introduction to his classical work on the Psalms, *The Treasury of David* (a work that took twenty years to compose), "More and more is the conviction forced upon my heart that every man must traverse the territory of the Psalms himself if he would know what a goodly land they are. They flow with milk and honey, but not to strangers; they are only fertile to lovers of their hills and vales."[15]

The chiefest treasure of the Psalms belongs to him that excavates its vast mines not casually but rigorously, not shallowly but thoroughly, and not merely academically but spiritually. John Stott has written, "The psalms...speak the universal language of the human soul....Whatever our spiritual mood may be, there is sure to be a Psalm which reflects it— whether triumph or defeat, excitement or depression, joy or sorrow, praise or penitence, wonder or anger. Above all, the Psalms declare the greatness of the living God as Creator, Sustainer, King, Lawgiver, Saviour, Father, Shepherd and Judge."[16] Matthew Henry says, "There is no one book of Scripture that is more helpful to the devotions of the saints than this, and it has been so in all ages of the church, ever since it was written....So rich, so well made, are these divine poems, that they can never be exhausted, can never be worn threadbare."[17]

Willem VanGemeren, in the introduction to his work on the Psalms in *The Expositor's Bible Commentary,* states, "The Book of Psalms is God's prescription for a complacent church, because through it He reveals how great, wonderful, magnificient, wise and utterly awe-inspiring He is!"[18] J. J. S. Perowne states, "No single Book of Scripture, not even of the New Testament, has, perhaps, ever taken such hold on the heart of Christendom. None, if we may dare judge, unless it be the Gospels, has had so large an influence in moulding the affections, sustaining the hopes, purifying the faith of believers. With its words, rather than with their own, they have come before God. In these they have uttered their desires, their fears, their confessions, their aspirations, their sorrows, their joys, their thanksgivings. By these their devotion has been kindled and their hearts comforted. The Psalter has been, in the truest sense, the Prayer Book both of Jews and Christians."[19]

The book of Psalms is a book for the spiritually thirsty and hungry. Isaiah well could have said of it, "Is anyone thirsty? Come and drink—even if you have no money!...Come to me with your ears wide open. Listen, and you will find life" (Isaiah 55:1a, 3a NLT). Max Lucado is right. "This collection of hymns and petitions are strung together by one thread—a heart hungry for God."[20] Mueller testified, "The Psalms teach one to prize a much tried life...David yields me every day the most delightful hour. There is nothing Greek, nothing Roman, nothing in the West, nor in the land towards midnight, to equal David, whom the God of Israel chose to praise Him higher than the gods of the nations. The utterance of His mind sinks deep into the heart, and never in my life, never have I thus seen God."[21]

But only the sanctified soul can reap such benefit and pleasure in their reading. W. S. Plumer is correct to say, "If to any man these songs are unsavory, the reason is found in the blindness and depravity of the human heart."[22] Hengstenberg said, "The Psalms are expressions of holy feeling, which can be understood by those only, who have become alive to such feeling."[23] The Psalms, as with all the Books of the Bible, must be read through the "lenses" of a sanctified mind and a heart hungry for God in order to discover their vast jewels of knowledge and wisdom and experience their inspirational, invigorating and instructional delight. C. H. Spurgeon wrote, "Whenever we look into David's Psalms, we may somewhere or other see ourselves. I never get into a corner but I find David in that corner. I think I was never so low that I could not find that David was lower, or I never climbed so high that I could not find that David was up above me, ready to sing his song upon his stringed instruments, even as I could sing mine."[24]

Authorship. Psalms is one of only two books in the Bible written by multiple authors (Proverbs being the other). Its many authors under the inspiration and direction of the Holy Spirit include David, Asaph, the sons of Korah, Heman, Ethan, Moses and Solomon. Of the 150 Psalms, authorship is unknown for 50[25] (see 2 Peter 1:21). Psalms that were composed by David ("the sweet psalmist of Israel," 2 Samuel 23:1) were Holy Spirit inspired (Acts 4:25), as were those that were not from David. A. F. Kirkpatrick wrote, "The widest diversity of opinion prevails as to the date and authorship of the Psalms, and we must often be content to acknowledge that a Psalm cannot be assigned to a definite period, still less to a particular author, with any degree of certainty."[26]

The title ascribed to various Psalms. The Psalms usually carry a heading or superscription that includes one or more of the following catergories: identification of the author, historical setting, musical and liturgical details, and genre.[27] The Psalms without a superscription are called "Orphan Psalms." These are Psalms 1; 2; 10; 33; 43; 71; 91; 93-97; 99; 104–107; 111–119; 135–137; 146–150.[28] With regard to the author and historical setting of these Psalms, man can make only a reasonable "guess."

Psalm titles are ascribed to 116 of the 150 psalms (eighty-seven of the first 100) in the Hebrew Psalter.[29] Uncertainity exists as to the time these titles were affixed to numerous Psalms—at the time of composition or later.[30] However, evidence abounds to prove they have long been included in the Psalter text (canonical text).[31]

These titles prove invaluable in determining a Psalm's historical setting and authorship. The title used in the superscription preceeding each Psalm associating names with the Psalm does not necessarily indicate authorship, as readers of the English text think. For example, "of David" is literally "to David." The Psalm therefore may possess one of three distinct meanings: (1) Davidic authorship; (2) attributed to David by the opinion of others; (3) connected with David's life and experiences.[32] This makes definitive authorship difficult if not impossible.

Chrysostom's view of the authorship of the Psalms is mine: "How does it concern me whether David was the author of all the Psalms or whether some of them were written by others, since it is certainly known that they were all written by the inspiration of the Holy Spirit?"[33] (See 2 Timothy 3:16–17 and 2 Samuel 23:2–3.) W. S. Plumer notes the absence of the historical setting in some of the Psalms is because it didn't have one. He states, "We are not bound to hold that David wrote all the Psalms to suit particular times and events."[34] A. F. Kirkpatrick wrote, "Important as it is for the full interpretation of many Psalms to know the circumstances under which they were written, and for the elucidation of the religious history of Israel to determine the age to which they belong, the Psalms as a whole suffer less from this uncertainty than might be expected. Their interest is human and universal. They appeal to the experience of all ages."[35]

When the Psalms were written. Historical data within the Psalms clearly suggest they were written over a span of a thousand years—from the time of Moses to the time of David, Asaph and Solomon to the time of the Ezrahites that lived most likely after the Babylonian captivity.[36] The final compilation of Psalms was not complete until the latter half of the fifth century B.C. (the time of Ezra and Nehemiah).[37]

Elwell and Comfort state, "Ezra is traditionally credited with the final grouping and editing of the psalms, a hypothesis that appears reasonable in light of his vital contribution to the systematic reshaping of the national religious life."[38]

Divine inspiration of the Psalms. George Horne writes, "The right of the Psalter to a place in the sacred canon [Holy Scriptures] hath never been disputed, and it is often cited by our Lord and His apostles in the New Testament as the work of the Holy Spirit."[39] Keil and Delitzsch wrote, "Jesus Christ's exposition of the Psalms is the beginning and the goal of Christian Psalm-interpretation. This began, as that of the Christian church, and in fact first of all that of the Apostles, at Pentecost when the Spirit, whose instrument David acknowledges himself to have been (2 Samuel 23:2), descended upon the apostles as the Spirit of Jesus, the fulfiller and fulfilment of prophecy....He opened up to the disciples the meaning of the Psalms."[40]

Tholuck says, "Hilary, Chrysostom and Augustine state that these Psalms were frequently sung by the congregation, sometimes recited by separate individuals and repeated by the rest."[41] A. F. Kirkpatrick agrees with Franz Delitzsch that there is nothing which comes to light in the New Testament which does not already exist in germ in the Psalms.[42]

Five books of the Psalms. The Psalms may be categorized as follows: "(1) penitential Psalms (6; 32; 38; 51; 102; 130; 143), (2) praise Psalms (113–118), (3) imprecatory Psalms, i.e., Psalms which invoke evil upon one's enemies (35; 52; 58; 59; 69; 79; 83; 109; 137; 140), (4) songs of ascents or songs of degrees (120–134), (5) messianic Psalms (2; 8; 16; 22–24; 40-41; 45; 68-69; 72; 89; 96–99; 102; 110; 118; 132)"[43] and hallelujah Psalms (146–150). The "Five Books" or divisions of the Psalter: Book 1 (Psalms 1–41); Book 2 (Psalms 42–72); Book 3 (Psalms 73–89); Book 4 (Psalms 90–106); Book 5 (Psalms 107–150). Many have seen a parallelism between these five books and the Pentateuch (the first five books of the Bible). *Genesis Section*, Psalms 1–41: The fall and restoration of man. *Exodus Section*, Psalms 42–72: Man's ruin and deliverance by God. *Leviticus Section*, Psalms 73–89: The Temple, holy sanctuary and house of God; and sanctification, holiness and communion with God. *Numbers Section*, Psalms 90–106: Man's testing, danger and protection. H. A. Ironside considers this book the "darkest" in the Psalter, for they deal with some of the most horrendously bitter and difficult experiences of the Christian.[44] *Deuteronomy Section*, Psalms 107–150: The absolute truthfulness of God's Word, praise of and adherence to it; and the believer's triumph over life's sorrows and hardships through Jehovah. David, who was gifted in spiritual poetry and music (1 Samuel 18:10; 2 Samuel 1:17–18; 6:5; 1 Chronicles 6:31; 16:7; 25:1; 2 Chronicles 7:6; 29:30; Ezra 3:10; Nehemiah 12:24, 36, 45; Amos 6:5) composed at least half of the Psalms (75). It is thought that he also wrote some of the "Orphan Psalms."

Theology of the Psalms. Oetinger states there is no essential New Testament truth not contained in the Psalms (according to its unfolded meaning).[45] Keil and Delizsch say, "The Old Testament barrier encompasses the germinating New Testament life, which at a future time shall burst it....Everywhere, where it begins to dawn in this eschatological darkness of the Old Testament, it is the first morning rays of the New Testament sunrise which is already announcing itself."[46]

In the Psalms Jesus Christ is presented as: the Anointed King (Psalms 2; 45; 72; 110), God's Son (Psalm 2), God (Psalms 45; 68; 97; 102), Servant (Psalms 69; 86), Son of Man (Psalm 8), Priest (Psalm 110), the Stone the Builders Rejected (Psalm 118), King of Glory (Psalm 24) and Suffering Savior (Psalms 22; 34; 38; 69).[47] Harry Ironside said, "If anybody has any doubt as to the divine inspiration of Scripture, it seems to me that a careful study of the Book of Psalms alone ought to make clear to him that God has ordered all these things, even to the arrangement of this wonderful book."[48]

Psalm singing. Eskew and McElrath summarize the use of the Psalms through history this way: "From one standpoint the entire history of the hymn could be delineated according to its varying relationship to the Scriptures. Generally speaking, the line of evolution in that story, if it were retold, is from the actual singing of parts of the Bible (the Psalms, for example) through the strict paraphrasing of extended passages and the dutiful use of biblical allusion, language and figures of speech to the free expression of scriptural thought and teaching in contemporary terms."[49] Psalm singing was customary in the church.

Tholuck writes, "When our Lord instituted the holy Supper, He sung Psalms with His apostles (Matthew 26:30). He testified to His disciples that the traits of His fate were delineated in the Psalms (Luke 24:44). He referred His opponents to a prophetic Psalm as inspired by the Holy Ghost (Matthew 22:43). The extent to which His humiliation and exaltation were, mirrorlike, beheld by Him in the Psalms may be illustrated by the fact that even on the cross, when expressing the desertion of His soul, He used not His own words, but adopted the language of His typical ancestor (Matthew 27:46). Paul and Silas, at dead of night, praise God in Psalms from the dungeon (Acts 16:25). Paul exhorts the Christian Church to sing Psalms (Colossians 3:16; Ephesians 5:19). Tertullian mentions, in the second century, that Christians were wont to sing Psalms at the Agapæ, and that pious husbands and wives repeated them antiphonically, i. e., by alternate responses. The Psalms have, ever since the first century, formed an essential portion of Christian worship."[50] Regretably that "essential portion" is growing less and less.

The Psalter (hymnal) has served as a model for the church's hymnology or hymnal. Martin Luther (1483–1546) composed "A Mighty Fortress Is Our God" (based on Psalm 46) while Isaac Watts (1674–1748) and Charles Wesley (1707–1788) attempted to use the content of various Psalms with distinctively New Testament teaching infused into them.[51] "Jesus Shall Reign" from Psalm 72 and "O God, Our Help in Ages Past" from Psalm 90 are examples of the composition of Isaac Watts. Wesley conversely based hymns upon the Psalms as he did other Scripture (not their translation as Watts did). "Oh, for a Heart to Praise My God" uses the ideas of Psalm 51, while "Jesu, Mighty to Deliver" is Psalm 70 expanded as a Christian song of praise.[52]

"Let the peace of Christ rule in your hearts, since as members of one body you were called to peace. And be thankful. Let the message of Christ dwell among you richly as you teach and admonish one another with all wisdom through psalms, hymns, and songs from the Spirit singing to God with gratitude in your hearts" (Colossians 3:15–16 NIV). Paul emphatically states that the "word of Christ" must dwell in us richly. Various types of Christian songs, including Psalms, are regarded as "Christ's word."[53] It is to take up abode within our hearts that it may build us up in the faith and be utilized to teach others.[54]

The gist of the Psalms. George Horne encapsulates the whole of the Psalms: "Composed upon particular occasions, yet designed for general use; delivered out as services for Israelites under the law, yet no less adapted to the circumstances of Christians under the Gospel, they present religion to us in the most engaging dress; communicating truths which philosophy could never investigate, in a style which poetry can never equal, while history is made the vehicle of prophecy, and creation lends all its charms to paint the glories of redemption. Calculated alike to profit and to please, they inform the understanding, elevate the affections, and entertain the imagination. Indited ["compose" or "put down in writing"[55]] under the influence of Him to whom all hearts are known and all events foreknown, they suit mankind in all situations, grateful as the manna which descended from above and conformed itself to every palate. The fairest productions of human wit, after a few perusals, like gathered flowers wither in our hands and lose their fragrancy; but these unfading plants of paradise become, as we are accustomed to them, still more and more beautiful; their bloom appears to be daily heightened; fresh odors are emitted and new sweets extracted from them. He who hath once tasted their excellences will desire to taste them yet again, and he who tastes them oftenest will relish them best."[56]

The Word of God in the Psalms. All who visit the Psalms soon discover the place of prominence it gives to the Word of God. The longest Psalm and chapter in the Bible, Psalm 119, alone ascribes honor and homage over and over again to the Word of God, saying that it is pure, is unmixed with error and lasts forever. Matthew Henry states regarding this emphasis, "What a high value does this Book put upon the Word of God, His statutes and judgments, His covenant and the great and precious promises of it; and how does it recommend them to us as our guide and stay, and our heritage forever!"[57]

Prophecy in the Psalms. Standing on equal footing alongside the emphasis on the Bible as inerrant and infallible are its messianic prophecies. J. Vernon McGee wrote, "The Book of Psalms is a hymnbook and a HIM book—it is all about Him....He is the object of praise in every one of them....Although all of them have Christ as the object of worship, some are technically called Messianic Psalms."[58] Joseph Exell said, "Nearly half of all Messianic references in the New Testament originate from the Psalms."[59] Harry Ironside wrote, "If you are thinking only of yourself as you read these Psalms, you will never see what the book is really taking up, but once you understand something of God's prophetic counsel, once you enter into His purpose in Christ Jesus for the people of Israel and the Gentile nations, you will realize how marvelously this book fits in with the divine program."[60]

Jesus, prior to His ascension, reminded the disciples that "all things must needs be fulfilled, which are written in the law of Moses, and the prophets, and the Psalms, concerning me" (Luke 24:44 ASV). A study of Genesis to Malachi reveals the progressive message of Messiah's coming primarily cited through prophecies. Note that Jesus includes the Psalms among the writings containing such prophecies. Andrew Bonar wrote, "There is in almost every one of all these Psalms something that fitted them for the use of the past generations of the church and something that fits them admirably for the use of the church now, while also there is diffused throughout a hint for the future. There is, we might say, *a past, a present* and *a future* element. Few of them can be said to have no prophetic reference, no reference to generations or events yet to arise—a circumstance that gives them a claim upon the careful study of everyone who searches into the prophetic records, in addition to the manifold other claims which they possess."[61] See Acts 13:33.

The Messianic Psalms may be divided into five categories: "(1) purely messianic Psalms—e.g., Psalm 110, which refers to a future Davidic king who is the Lord; (2) eschatological Psalms—e.g., Psalms 96–99, which are usually entitled enthronement Psalms and describe the coming of the Lord and His kingdom; (3) typological-prophetic Psalms—e.g., Psalm 22, where the writer describes his own experience which is transcended by that of Jesus the Messiah; (4) indirectly Messianic—e.g., Psalms 2; 45; 72 which were penned for a king of Israel or a royal occasion in general, but their ultimate and climactic fulfillment is realized in Christ; and (5) typical Messianic Psalms—these are less obvious: the psalmist in some sense is a type of Christ (Psalm 34:20), but not all aspects of the Psalm necessarily apply to the Messiah (see also Psalm 109:8; Acts 1:20)."[62] Keil and Delitzsch state, "The Old Testament, according to its very nature, tends toward and centers in Christ. Therefore the innermost truth of the Old Testament has been revealed in the revelation of Jesus Christ, but not all at once: His passion, resurrection and ascension are three steps of this progressive opening up of the Old Testament and of the Psalms in particular."[63]

B. H. Carroll said of the Psalmist's vision of the Messiah, "He saw the uncreated Son, the second Person of the Trinity, in counsel and compact with the Father, arranging in eternity for the salvation of men: Psalm 40:6–8; Hebrews 10:5–7. Then he saw this Holy One stoop to be the Son of Man: Psalm 8:4–6; Hebrews 2:7–9. Then He was the Son of David, and then he saw Him rise again to be the Son of God: Psalm 2:7; Romans 1:3–4."[64] Included in the Psalmist's prophecy was Christ's atoning sacrifice (Psalm 40:6–8; Hebrews 10:5–7); final judgment (Psalm 6:8; Matthew 25:41); visit from the Magi (Psalm 72:9–10; Matthew 2); wilderness temptations (Psalm 91:11–12; Luke 4:10–11); triumphant entry into Jersualem (Psalm 118; Matthew 21:9); corrupt trial (Psalms 27:12; 35:15–16; 38:13; 69:19 and Matthew 26:57–68; 27:26–31); crucifixion (Psalm 22:14–17; Luke 23:33); garments being parted and His vesture being gambled for (Psalm 22:18; Matthew 27:35); thirst and the gall and vinegar being offered (Psalm 69:21; Matthew 27:34); prayers for His enemies (Psalm 109:4; Luke 23:34) and resurrection, victory over death and Hell, ascension into Heaven and exaltation at God's right hand (Psalm 16:8–11; 24:7–10; 68:18; 2:6; 111:1–4; 8:4–6 and Acts 2:25–36; Ephesians 1:19–23; 4:8–10).[65]

The messianic Psalms were fulfilled explicitly in the person and life of Jesus Christ, proving to the gainsayers that He is in fact the long-awaited Savior of the world sent from God the Father. "With regard to the Jews, Bishop Chandler very pertinently remarks that 'they must have understood David their prince to have been a figure of Messiah. They would not otherwise have made his Psalms part of their daily worship; nor would David have delivered them to the church to be so employed, were it not to instruct and support them in the knowledge and belief of this fundamental article. Was the Messiah not concerned in the Psalms, it were absurd to celebrate twice a day in their public devotions the events of one man's life who was deceased so long ago as to have no relation now to the Jews and the circumstances of their affairs, or to transcribe whole passages from them into their prayers for the coming of the Messiah.'"[66]

Composition of the Psalms. With regard to composition, its most important characteristic is its parallelism (a statement that is emphasized or extended by repetition).[67] Within the Psalms there are three forms of paralleisms: synonymous parallelism (the same thought is expressed at least twice in a different way, as in Psalm 49:1); antithetic (contrasted) parallelism (the truth of the first sentence is stressed by contrast in its final clause, as in Psalm 1:6); synthetic (connecting) parallelism (the final teaching of the Psalm completes and expands that of the first sentence, as in Psalm 22:4).[68]

J. M. Boice wrote about the complexity of the Psalms: "I do not know of any book of the Bible that requires more knowledge, more experience of life and more skill of interpretation to understand it well than the Book of Psalms. It is because the Psalms are so diverse. They cover the vast range of biblical theology and the full scope of human experience—from doubt to faith, suffering to jubilation, defeat to victory—and they do so in an amazing variety of poetic forms. The Psalms are so deep, so diverse, so challenging that I do not believe anyone can ever really master them. Moreover, as soon as the student begins to get hold of one type of Psalm and thinks he understands it, he is suddenly confronted with another that is entirely different."[69] Harry Ironside writes, "It is very remarkable the way the Psalms are arranged. They are arranged in divine order. In many instances we find the last verses of the one introducing the theme of the next."[70]

The imprecatory Psalms. The imprecatory Psalms are prayers directed against enemies of David and the Jewish nation but "are not expressions of personal resentment."[71] B. H. Carroll explains: "They are vigorous expressions of righteous indignation against incorrigible enemies of God and His people and are to be interpreted in the light of progressive revelation....These imprecations do not teach that we, even in the worst circumstances, should bear personal malice, nor take vengenance on the the enemies of righteousness, but that we should live so close to God that we may acquiesce in the destruction of the wicked and leave the matter of vengeance in the hands of a just God, to whom vengeance belongs (Romans 12:19–21)."[72]

Profitabilty of the Psalms. The Psalter is a combination praisebook, "how-to" cope handbook, devotional exposition, moral and ethical compass for living life, duty manual and treatise on the infallibility of the Holy Scriptures. It is a book of praise, prayer, precept and promise. Psalms will benefit personal and corporate worship. The Book of the Psalms "can revolutionize our devotional life, our family patterns, and the fellowship and the witness of the church of Jesus Christ."[73] Max Lucado writes, "Worship is a daunting task. For that reason, God gave us the Psalms....Some [Psalms] are defiant. Others are reverent. Some are to be sung. Others are to be prayed. Some are intensely personal. Others are written as if the whole world would use them. Some were penned in caves, others in temples. But all have one purpose—to give us the words to say when we stand before God. The very variety should remind us that worship is personal. No secret formula exists. What moves you may stymie another. Each worships differently, but each should worship."[74]

To maximize the Psalms' effect and impact in worship, personalize them. Make them your own.

J. Vernon McGee stated, "Someone has said that there are 126 psychological experiences....all of them are recorded in the Book of Psalms. It is the only book which contains every experience of a human being. The Psalms run the psychological gamut. Every thought, every impulse, every emotion that sweeps over the soul is recorded in this book."[75] Athanasius, Bishop of Alexandria in the fourth century, wrote: "To me, indeed, it seems that the Psalms are to him who sings them as a mirror, wherein he may see himself and the motions of his soul, and with like feelings utter them. So also one who hears a psalm read takes it as if it were spoken concerning himself, and either, convicted by his own conscience, will be pricked at heart and repent, or else, hearing of that hope which is to God-wards, and the succour which is vouchsafed to them that believe, leaps for joy as though such grace were specially made over to him, and begins to utter his thanksgivings to God."[76] As we read, absorb, and personalize the Psalms, life is lifted to a higher plane spiritually. How wondrous is the thought that the same Psalms that profit us benefited David and others hundreds of years ago when they were first written, as they have myriads since. Though their blossom has been squeezed over and over again by kings and peasants, rich and poor, saint and sinner, their sweet fragrance remains untarnished and undepleted.

Exposition of the Psalms is written in three volumes: Vol. One: Psalms 1–50; Vol. Two: Psalms 51–100; and Vol. Three: Psalms 101–150.

Included with each entry is an *Exposition* of the text; a *Homily*, discourse based upon the Psalm with regard to its application, and *The Bottom Line*, a concise statement or paragraph summarizing the gist of the selected text. The task in selection of the verse(s) to exegete and expound in a homily in each Psalm was daunting and most challenging. In all the expositions I sought to be theologically sound and simple, thorough in exegesis and applicable in homily. To simplify navigation through the Psalms for specific subject matters, each are entitled according to its general or specific theme.

Conservative theological scholars were heavily leaned upon for interpretation of the Hebrew language and its theological and cultural meaning. Such word pictures and meanings opened up the Psalms to new truths and applications not before seen. Spurgeon's observation on the use of commentators in studying Scripture I found encouraging: "In order to be able to expound the Scriptures, and as an aid to your pulpit studies, you will need to be familiar with the commentators: a glorious army, let me tell you, whose acquaintance will be your delight and profit. Of course, you are not such wiseacres as to think or say that you can expound Scripture without assistance from the works of divines and learned men who have labored before you in the field of exposition. If you are of that opinion, pray remain so, for you are not worth the trouble of conversion and like a little coterie [inner circle of friends] who think with you, would resent the attempt as an insult to your infallibility. It seems odd that certain men who talk so much of what the Holy Spirit reveals to themselves should think so little of what he has revealed to others."[77]

My aim in this work was not to do a thorough treatise of the Psalms but to exegete a text from each that is paramount in importance while providing its practical doctrinal and devotional insight and inspiration. It is intended that the intensity of the work upon each text will provide both the minister and teacher inspiration and sufficient foundational exegetical basis for the building of sermons and studies, while providing knowledge and devotional insight to them and to others. Effort was made to limit the repetition of themes to facilitate entry of more subjects.

Why another commentary on the Psalms when hundreds have been written? The bottom line is that it was undertaken out of divine leadership. It was an inescapable work. *Exposition of the Psalms* is different from other commentaries in its focus upon a specific text(s) within each Psalm and in its 4,700 insights gleaned from some of the greatest theologians of history. It is to be viewed not as a replacement for traditional conservative commentaries on the Psalms, but as a supplement. The commentary is based upon the *King James Version* of the Holy Bible.

We are in danger of losing the Book of Psalms in the church. They are being read and sung less in the church. But even sadder, they are being preached less. I was heartbroken to read of a homiletics professor who stated that the Psalms "do not want" to be preached from. He that neglects preaching from the Psalter robs his people of what C. H. Spurgeon called *The Treasury of David*. The Book of Psalms contains many "pearls of great price" that beg to be preached! In this work the minister is presented with the necessary "lumber" with which to build sound expository sermons upon them.

Major contributing theologians to this work include Charles Haddon Spurgeon, W. S. Plumer, J. J. S. Perowne, A. F. Kirkpatrick, Albert Barnes, Matthew Henry, Matthew Poole, Joseph Benson, John Gill, W. A. Criswell, John MacArthur, J. Montgomery Boice, William A. VanGemeren, William Barclay, George Rawlinson, Adam Clarke, Martin Luther, John Calvin, Charles John Ellicott, Robert Jamieson, Andrew Robert Fausset, David Brown, Alexander Maclaren , Charles Bridges, Charles Simeon, Robert Bratcher, William Reyburn, Leslie C. Allen, John Walvoord, Roy Zuck, George Horne, Karl F. Keil, Franz Delitzsch, J. A. Alexander, P. C. Craigie, D. Williams, L. J. Ogilvie, William MacDonald, E. E. Hinson, W. M. Kroll, Warren Wierbe, Billy Graham, John Stott, W. A. Elwell, T. W. Comfort, Adrian Rogers, M. E. Tate, Herbert Lockyer, E. W. Bullinger, Derek Kidner, Allen Ross, John Trapp, James Coffman, R. Ellinsworth, Daniel Whedon, Thomas Watson, R. Whitaker, F. Brown, S. R. Driver, R. L. Harris, G. L. Archer, B. K. Waltke, W. P. Holladay, L. Kohler, M. D. Futato, W. Gesenius, S. P. Tregelles, J. Swanson, G. M. Landes, J. Strong, W. E. Vine, M. F. Unger, W. White, Jr., Joseph Parker and J. I. Packer.

Untranslated Hebrew Words Used in the Titles of Some of the Psalms

From *Handbook to the Old Testament*
W. Scott, page 238.

Aijeleth-Shahar (Psalm 22)	The hind of the morning
Alamoth (Psalm 46)	Virginals
Al-taschith (Psalm 57, 58, 59, 75)	Destroy not
Degree (Psalm 120–134)	To go up, ascend
Gittith (Psalm 8, 81, 84)	The wine-vat
Higgaion (Psalm 9:16)	Meditation
Jonath-Elem-Rechokim (Psalm 56)	Dove dumb (among) stranger
Mahalath (Psalm 53)	Disease
Mahalath Leannoth (Psalm 88)	Bitter disease
Maschil (Psalm 32, 42, 44, 45, 52, 53, 54, 55, 74, 78, 88, 89, 142)	To instruct
Michtam (Psalm 16, 56–60)	Golden (psalm)
Neginah (Psalm 61)	A stringed instrument
Neginoth (Psalm 4, 6, 54, 55, 67, 76)	The stringed instruments
Nehiloth (Psalm 5)	The pipes
Selah (Psalm 3:2, 4, 8, etc.)	Pause [meaning is uncertain]
Sheminith (Psalm 6, 12)	Eight-stringed instrument
Shiggaion (Psalm 7)	Wandering ode
Shoshannim (Psalm 45, 80)	The lilies
Shushan Eduth (Psalm 60)	The lily of the testimony[78]

Psalms Quoted in the New Testament[79]

Psalm 2:1–2	Acts 4:25–26
Psalm 2:7	Acts 13:33
Psalm 2:9	Revelation 2:27
Psalm 4:4	Ephesians 4:26
Psalm 5:9	Romans 3:13
Psalm 6:8	Matthew 7:23
Psalm 8:2	Matthew 21:16
Psalm 8:4–6	Hebrews 2:6–8
Psalm 8:6	1 Corinthians 15:27
Psalm 10:7	Romans 3:14
Psalm 14:3	Romans 3:10
Psalm 16:8	Acts 2:25
Psalm 16:10	Acts 13:35
Psalm 18:49	Romans 15:9
Psalm 19:4	Romans 10:18
Psalm 22:1	Matthew 27:46
Psalm 22:7	Matthew 27:39
Psalm 22:8	Matthew 27:43
Psalm 22:18	John 19:24
Psalm 22:18	Matthew 27:35
Psalm 22:22	Hebrews 2:12
Psalm 24:1	1 Corinthians 10:26
Psalm 31:5	Luke 23:46
Psalm 32:1–2	Romans 4:7–8
Psalm 34:8	1 Peter 2:3
Psalm 34:12	1 Peter 3:10
Psalm 34:20	John 19:36
Psalm 35:19	John 15:25
Psalm 36:1	Romans 3:18
Psalm 37:11	Matthew 5:5
Pslam 38:11	Luke 23:49
Psalm 40:6–8	Hebrews 10:5–7
Psalm 41:9	John 13:18
Psalm 41:13	Luke 1:68
Psalm 42:5	Matthew 26:38
Psalm 44:22	Romans 8:36

Psalm 45:6–7	Hebrews 1:8–9
Psalm 48:2	Matthew 5:35
Psalm 51:4	Romans 3:4
Psalm 53:1–3	Romans 3:10–12
Psalm 55:22	1 Peter 5:7
Psalm 62:12	Matthew 16:27
Psalm 68:18	Ephesians 4:8
Psalm 69:4	John 15:25
Psalm 69:9	Romans 15:3
Psalm 69:9	John 2:17
Psalm 69:22–23	Romans 11:9–10
Psalm 69:25	Acts 1:20
Psalm 72:18	Luke 1:68
Psalm 78:2	Matthew 13:35
Psalm 78:24	John 6:31
Psalm 82:6	John 10:34
Psalm 86:9	Revelation 15:4
Psalm 88:8	Luke 23:49
Psalm 89:10	Luke 1:51
Psalm 89:20	Acts 13:22
Psalm 90:4	2 Peter 3:8
Psalm 91:11–12	Matthew 4:6
Psalm 91:13	Luke 10:19
Psalm 94:11	1 Corinthians 3:20
Psalm 94:14	Romans 11:1–2
Psalm 95:7–11	Hebrews 3:7–11
Psalm 97:7	Hebrews 1:6
Psalm 98:3	Luke 1:54
Psalm 102:25–27	Hebrews 1:10–12
Psalm 103:17	Luke 1:50
Psalm 104:4	Hebrews 1:7
Psalm 105:8–9	Luke 1:72–73
Psalm 106:10	Luke 1:71
Psalm 106:45	Luke 1:72
Psalm 106:48	Luke 1:68
Psalm 107:9	Luke 1:53
Psalm 109:3	John 15:25

Psalm 109:8	Acts 1:20
Psalm 109:25	Matthew 27:39
Psalm 110:1	Matthew 22:44; Mark 12:36; Luke 20:42
Psalm 110:4	Hebrews 5:6
Psalm 111:9	Luke 1:68
Psalm 111:9	Luke 1:49
Psalm 112:9	2 Corinthians 9:9
Psalm 116:10	2 Corinthians 4:13
Psalm 117:1	Romans 15:11
Psalm 118:6	Hebrews 13:6
Psalm 118:22–23	Matthew 21:42
Psalm 118:26	Matthew 21:9
Psalm 132:5	Acts 7:46
Psalm 132:11	Acts 2:30
Psalm 132:17	Luke 1:69
Psalm 135:14	Hebrews 10:30
Psalm 140:3	Romans 3:13
Psalm 143:2	Romans 3:20
Psalm 146:6	Acts 4:24; 14:15

1. The Prince's Psalm (Resolutions of a Godly Man)   Psalm 101

"I will sing of mercy and judgment: unto thee, O LORD, will I sing. I will behave myself wisely in a perfect way. O when wilt thou come unto me? I will walk within my house with a perfect heart. I will set no wicked thing before mine eyes: I hate the work of them that turn aside; it shall not cleave to me. A froward heart shall depart from me: I will not know a wicked person. Whoso privily slandereth his neighbour, him will I cut off: him that hath an high look and a proud heart will not I suffer. Mine eyes shall be upon the faithful of the land, that they may dwell with me: he that walketh in a perfect way, he shall serve me. He that worketh deceit shall not dwell within my house: he that telleth lies shall not tarry in my sight. I will early destroy all the wicked of the land; that I may cut off all wicked doers from the city of the LORD."—Psalm 101.

"I will sing of mercy" (Vine, Unger and White say "loving-kindness; steadfast love; grace; mercy; faithfulness; goodness; devotion."[80] David is stating that in his rule of Israel he will manifest godlike love). AND "judgment" (David's reign would be based upon God's justice to the good and bad. Kirkpatrick says, "Lovingkindness and judgment are characteristics of the Divine rule [Psalm 89:14], which are to be reflected in the true human ruler [Isaiah 16:5]. They are the fundamental principles of right life and conduct, the bond of fellowship between man and God [Hosea 2:19], and between man and his fellowman [Hosea 12:6; Micah 6:8; Matthew 23:23]."[81] Spurgeon says, "He would extol both the love and the severity, the sweets and the bitters, which the Lord had mingled in his experience; he would admire the justice and the goodness of the Lord."[82] Benson says, "This was his fixed purpose. He consecrated this song to God, appealing hereby to Him for the sincerity of his intention, to make mercy and judgment the great rules of his administration; and agreeably hereto it is observed of him that he executed justice and judgment to all the people [2 Samuel 8:15]."[83] Simeon says, "Mercies, if unmixed, would 'exalt us above measure'; and judgments, if unmixed, would sink us into despondency. A ship needs both sails and ballast to carry it forward in safety; and so the Christian needs a diversity of dispensations in order to accomplish in him the purposes of God's grace....Mercies have a tendency to fill the soul with love to God and to make it pant for the full enjoyment of God in

1

Heaven. Judgments also operate to the same end, by weaning the soul from present things and causing it to long for that rest which remaineth for it in a better world"[84]).

Unto thee, O Lord, "will I sing" (Swanson says, "...i.e., use the voice as an instrument to voice, musical tones, rhythms, and often words."[85] He will make melody unto the Lord.[86]). "I will" (David asserts a manifestation of desire to rule rightly.) "behave" (Swanson says "innocent, i.e., pertaining to a person or condition of moral goodness, with a focus of being guiltless and not liable for sin or wrong."[87]) "myself wisely" (Swanson says "have insight, get wisdom, gain understanding, be prudent, be skilled, i.e., have a capacity for understanding, implying this state is a result of proper teaching."[88]) "in a perfect way" (Brown, Driver and Briggs say "completeness, integrity"[89]).

"O when wilt thou come unto me?" (Barnes says, "'When thou dost come unto me.'...The idea is that God would come to visit his habitation, and inspect his conduct; and that whenever this should occur, however often it might be, or however unexpectedly He might come, He should 'always' find these principles governing him in his family. A man should so live that 'whenever' God comes into his dwelling, or when anyone comes, or however narrow and searching may be the inspection, these principles shall be found to regulate his conduct."[90] Benson differs, saying, "David, having declared it to be his resolution to set his court and kingdom an example of true wisdom and unshaken integrity, shows, in these words, the sense he had of his need of a peculiar visitation of divine grace to enable him to put his resolution in practice, and accordingly expresses the passionate desire which he had for it in these words."[91] This seems to be the popular and proper interpretation.) "I will walk" (Vine, Unger and White say, "to go, walk, behave"[92]).

"Within my house" (Harris, Archer and Waltke say "house, household, home, place, temple, inward, family. The word is used of ordinary houses [Exodus 12:7], dwelling houses [Leviticus 25:29], houses of solid materials with doorposts [Deuteronomy 11:20], walls [Leviticus 14:37] of stones, wood, and mortar [Leviticus 14:45]."[93]) "with a perfect heart" (Swanson says "blamelessness, integrity, innocence, i.e., a state or condition of moral goodness in a life, with a focus of not having guilt or sin."[94] The psalmist's expression of innocence refers to a course of conduct in contrast with the wicked, not to original sin.[95] Carroll says, "The psalmists do not claim absolute, but relative sinlessness"[96]).

I will "set no wicked thing before mine eyes" (*Wicked*. Strong says "without profit, worthlessness; destruction, wickedness. Belial, evil, naughty, ungodly (men), wicked."[97]). I "hate" (scorn, detest) the work of them that "turn aside" (Brown, Driver and Briggs say "swerver, revolter, deeds that swerve [from the right]."[98]) it shall not "cleave to me" (Gesenius and Tregelles say "to cleave, to adhere specially firmly, as if with glue, TO BE GLUED"[99]).

"A froward heart" (Swanson says "perverse, morally crooked or warped, i.e., pertaining to what is distorted or perverted from a just, right condition"[100]) shall "depart from me" (Landes says "to turn aside, go off, retreat; to remove something or someone"[101]). I will "not know" (Vine, Unger and White say "to know, regard, recognize, pay attention to, be acquainted with"[102]) a "wicked person" (Swanson says "bad, evil, wicked, no good, i.e., pertaining to that which is not morally pure or good according to a proper standard, implying this evil hinders or severs a relationship to a person or principle which is proper"[103]).

Whoso privily "slandereth his neighbor" (Swanson says, "...i.e., speak words of insult to another or about another."[104]) him will I "cut off" (NLT says, "I will not tolerate." Landes says "to destroy; to silence; to disappear, vanish; be silenced"[105]) him that hath "a high look and a proud heart" (David would not tolerate him that was conceited and arrogant [puffed up with self-pride].) "will not I suffer" (Holladay and Kohler say "hold on to, endure"[106]).

Mine eyes shall be upon the "faithful of the land" (Swanson says "be faithful, be trustworthy, loyal, i.e., pertaining to reliability, so a state or condition of being dependable and loyal to a person or standard, and so not fail [Numbers 12:7]; trust, rely [Judges 11:20]"[107]) that they may "dwell with me" (Holladay and Kohler say "my company;...2. with me, in my presence"[108]). That he that "walketh in a perfect way" (Barnes says, "The phrase means an upright man; a man of integrity. It does not necessarily imply that he is absolutely holy, or free from all sin, but that he is upright, consistent, honest: a man whose moral character is developed in proper proportions, or is such that it may be relied on."[109])

"he shall serve me" (Rawlinson says, "...i.e. 'shall be promoted to office under my government'"[110]).

He that "worketh deceit" (Swanson says "deceit, treachery, i.e., the state or condition of causing something false to be believed as true [in word or action], and so mislead."[111]) "shall not dwell within my house" (Vine, Unger and White say "to dwell, sit, abide, inhabit, remain."[112] Rawlinson says, "It is the duty of a king to see, not only that his own ways are blameless, but that his entire household is well ordered, and consists of righteous persons."[113]) he that "telleth lies" (Vine, Unger and White say "falsehood; lie."[114] Speaking untruth.) "shall not tarry in my sight" (Rawlinson says "literally, shall not be established; i.e., shall not keep his position in my court, but be banished from it'[115]).

I will early "destroy all the wicked of the land" (Kirkpatrick says, "Day by day the king will hold his court of justice in the morning [2 Samuel 15:2; Jeremiah 21:12], that he may purge Jerusalem of evil and make it a holy city, worthy of its high title 'the city of Jehovah'"[116]).

That I may "cut off all wicked doers from the city of the Lord" (Benson says, "I will use my utmost diligence to reform the whole nation; but especially the place of my peculiar residence, which ought to be an example to the rest of my kingdom: taking care that all offenders be severely punished in the courts of justice; and, if there be no other remedy, cutting off those evil members, who have got an incurable habit of acting wickedly."[117] Rawlinson says, "So long as there were 'wicked doers' in the land, they would be sure to flock to Jerusalem, since the capital always attracts the criminal classes. David is especially anxious that Jerusalem, which he has made 'the city of the Lord' [2 Samuel 6:12–19] shall be kept free from the pollutions of evildoers, but to effect this object, he must purge the whole land. The spirit breathed is that of Psalm 15:1–5"[118]).

Homily

Psalm 101 is a Psalm of David. Spurgeon states, "This is just such a Psalm as the man after God's own heart would compose when he was about to become king in Israel. It is David all over, straightforward, resolute, devout; there is no trace of policy or vacillation. The Lord has appointed him to be king, and he knows it; therefore, he purposes in all things to behave as becomes a monarch whom the Lord Himself has chosen. If we call this THE PSALM OF PIOUS RESOLUTIONS, we shall perhaps remember it all the more readily. After songs of praise, a Psalm of practice not only makes variety, but comes in most fittingly. We never praise the Lord better than when we do those things which are pleasing in his sight."[119] In the Psalm, David pictures Christ Jesus, who lovingly ever looks upon the "faithful of the land" (the redeemed) and will ultimately banish the wicked from His presence at His coming in judgment.[120] A. F. Kirkpatrick wrote, "This Psalm has been called 'David's mirror for rulers,' 'the prince's Psalm,' 'a mirror for magistrates,' and the like."[121] Charles Simeon says, "David felt his responsibility in this respect [emphasis on virtue in his life]: and, either on his beginning to reign in Hebron after the death of Saul, or on his coming to the full possession of the kingdom at a subsequent period, he wrote this psalm, declarative of his determination to discountenance evil and encourage good, to the utmost extent of of his power, both amongst his courtiers and amongst his more immediate attendants in his household."[122]

Following God's judgment upon Uzzah, David declared, "How shall the Ark of Jehovah come unto me?" (2 Samuel 6:9 ASV), and it was taken into the house of Obed-Edom. Shortly thereafter, out of thirst for the presence of God in Jerusalem, he cries, "O when wilt thou come unto me?" And the ark was brought into the holy city. Psalm 101 *seems* to be a journal of that event, but such is speculation. A. F. Kirkpatrick concurs, stating, "This Psalm then may be regarded as the expression of David's solemn resolution to prepare himself and his city for Jehovah's coming to dwell in their midst. It is a companion piece to Psalms 15, which describes the character required in those who were to dwell in the immediate Presence of Jehovah, and Psalms 24, composed in all probability for the translation of the Ark; and it should further be compared with Psalm 18:20 ff., and with 'the last words of David' in 2 Samuel 23:1 ff."[123] Jennings and Lowe comment, "David, fearful and anxious with regard to the introduction of the Ark into his city, had exclaimed 'How shall the ark of the LORD come to me?' (2 Samuel 6:9). Now he is striving to become less unworthy of so great an honour and longing for the time when, by the resting of the Ark in the new city, God should 'record His Name' there 'and come unto him and bless him.'"[124]

The Psalm recounts David's holy resolves to prepare himself for the return of the Ark of Jehovah (the presence of God) to Jerusalem.

David states that he would embrace righteous and godly standards in governing Israel. The standards certainly are applicable for us with regard to our walk with God and relationship to others. *I will sing of mercy and judgment.* "It is of the LORD's mercies that we are not consumed, because his compassions fail not. They are new every morning: great is thy faithfulness" (Lamentations 3:22–23). David would rule with God's kind of loving-kindness and compassion and judge the good and bad based upon God's justice. As I write, there is a malicious devouring of a prominent leader in the Southern Baptist Convention with regard to a wrong committed. Though I do not justify that which he did (if indeed he is guilty of the charge), I am grieved by the lack of compassionate love and mercy manifested among many *brothers and sisters* toward him. When a brother falters, *we ought to shed tears instead of shouting with glee*. We ought to be the means for his deliverance, not his decimation. Christians need to be reminded of the words of Jesus: "And as ye would that men should do to you, do ye also to them likewise" (Luke 6:31). In the "shoes" of the fallen, how would you want to be treated? They that throw harsh and hurtful "stones" also need reminding that Jesus said, "He that is without sin among you, let him first cast a stone" (John 8:7).

Unto thee, O Lord, I will sing. Charles Simeon comments, "Where is the man under heaven, except the believer, who can adopt the language of the text or carry it into effect? Ungodly men may sing when all goes well with them, but where is he that will sing in the midst of his afflictions and make his afflictions themselves a ground of joy? Nowhere is that man to be found but in the church of Christ; for it is to His believing people only that God 'giveth songs in the night.' On the other hand, there is not an individual in the church of Christ who is not privileged to experience this joy and who does not actually possess it in proportion as he has made a progress in the divine life."[125] The prophet Habakkuk declares, "Although the fig tree shall not blossom, neither shall fruit be in the vines; the labour of the olive shall fail, and the fields shall yield no meat; the flock shall be cut off from the fold, and there shall be no herd in the stalls: Yet I will rejoice in the LORD, I will joy in the God of my salvation" (Habakkuk 3:17–18).

I will behave myself wisely. David resolved that he would walk in integrity, godly prudence and holiness ("perfect way"). Though well intended, he faltered. Manifest intentionality to walk uprightly in conduct before God and man, to be a person of wholehearted devotion to the Lord. Charles Simeon states, "Nothing can be more unreasonable than that men should condemn religion for the faults of those who profess it; but they will do so, and will take occasion from the misconduct of religious people to defame and decry all vital godliness."[126] Give no man reason to decry Christianity. Be a "steppingstone," not a "stumbling block," in their path to God. See Matthew 5:14–16. Simeon continues, "Those who behold the light that is set before them [are] constrained to acknowledge, that 'the righteous is more excellent than his neighbor.' A certain awe is impressed on the minds of the ungodly by the sight of 'a man of God.'"[127]

I will walk within my house with a perfect heart. David resolved as King that even in the privacy of his own home he would conduct himself rightly. Alexander Maclaren says, "The recesses of an Eastern palace were often foul with lust and hid extravagances of caprice and self-indulgence, but this ruler will behave there as one who has Jehovah for a guest."[128] Conduct at home privately and toward spouse and children reveals the true man or woman. Godliness begins first in the home. Resolve to exhibit holiness of life at home as you do at church. Matthew Henry wrote, "It is not enough to put on our religion when we go abroad and appear before men, but we must govern ourselves by it in our families. Those that are in public stations are not thereby excused from care in governing their families; nay, rather, they are more concerned to set a good example of ruling their own houses well (1 Timothy 3:5)."[129]

I will set no wicked thing before mine eyes. "Wicked" simply means "worthlessness," "vileness," or "wickedness."[130] To set "before mine eyes" means "to set before one as an end, or as a pattern."[131] David determined not to look at worthless, injurious, wicked things. That is, he would not "look upon it with deliberation and design, or with desire and delight."[132] If any ungodly or unjust thing was suggested to him, whatsoever specious pretenses it may be covered with, he would cast it out of his mind and thoughts.[133] The Christian is to resolve to monitor closely that which is consumed with the eyes on television or the internet, at the theater, or on the printed page. Pornography is the cause of shipwreck for many Christians, especially youth and young adult men. Fasten "I will set no wicked thing before mine eyes" to the computers and televisions in the home as a cautionary reminder. See Job 31:1 and Matthew 5:28. "Our mind's eye needs training as much as our physical vision. If we hang pictures in the halls of our brain that are not elevating, our moral perceptions will become lowered. The best thoughts are within our reach. Why should we choose, instead, thoughts that are flippant, vulgar, or worse? Every time we put an undesirable picture in our mind's eye, where it will be often in view, we deprave our own understanding. 'As [a man] thinketh in his heart, so is he.'"[134] *The work of them that turn aside; it shall not cleave to me.* They that turn away from the right and honorable path would not influence the Psalmist to do the same. As Christians we must not be lured away from the Lord by others. Spurgeon said, "I will disown their ways; I will not imitate their policy. Like dirt it may fall upon me, but I will wash it off and never rest till I am rid of it. Sin, like pitch, is very apt to stick."[135]

A froward heart shall depart from me. David resolves not to be crooked, neither to allow others of evil character to be employed within his household.[136] Align thyself with the righteous both in business and personal affairs.

I will not know a wicked person. David refused to be acquainted with (as in fellowship) or pay attention to the corrupt and morally impure. What heartache and havoc this resolution would save all that might make it. The wicked are the sowers of bad seed in the soil of the soul of the righteous. See Psalm 119:63.

He that slanders his neighbor I will cut off. David vows that he will not tolerate slander. Albert Barnes says, "Him will I cut off—that is, I will cut him off from me; I will not employ him. He would not have one in his house or in his service who did injustice to the character of others, who stabbed their reputation in the dark."[137] Give a deaf ear to slander. "We should form the habit of letting all slander and gossip go in one ear and out the other, instead of letting it go out our mouths."[138] The listening to and spreading of slanderous remarks makes one a coconspirator with the talebearer in the destruction they precipitate.

Him that hath an high look and a proud heart will not I suffer. The haughty, conceited and proud would have no place in David's government. Don't be impressed with yourself or personal abilities, skills, talents or accomplishments. Solomon cautions, "Pride goeth before destruction, and an haughty spirit before a fall" (Proverbs 16:18). Shun the arrogant and conceited.

Mine eyes shall be upon the faithful. It was the trustworthy and reliable man that would gain David's respect and trust. Spurgeon says, "He would seek them out, engage their services, take care of them and promote them to honor."[139] "Those who are not faithful to God will not be likely to be faithful to men."[140] Jennings and Lowe state, "Not only will he banish from his court all worthless characters, but also his eyes will scour the land to discover those that are trustworthy, and are, as himself, endeavouring to walk in the way of integrity, that he may attach them to his suite."[141] Seek out the righteous faithful for companionship and joint ventures. Be not unequally yoked with unbelievers and carnal believers. See 2 Corinthians 6:14.

He that worketh deceit shall not dwell (tarry) *within my house.* Albert Barnes says, "The man who is dishonest; who is full of tricks, false pretenses, and devices; who cannot be confided in as straightforward and sincere; one whose word cannot be relied on"[142] would not be allowed to remain in David's company. Jennings and Lowe state, "'Shall not be established,' i.e., shall not abide in undisturbed prosperity, before my eyes."[143]

He that telleth lies shall not tarry in my sight. David resolved to employ only him that was known for speaking truth. Spurgeon says, "Grace makes people truthful and creates in them an utter horror of everything approaching to falsehood. If David would not have a liar in his sight, much less will the Lord."[144] Be known as a person that speaks truth regardless of the consequence or cost. Solomon declared, "Lying lips are abomination to the LORD: but they that deal truly are his delight" (Proverbs 12:22). See Zephaniah 3:13; Acts 5:3 and Colossians 3:9.

I may cut off all wicked doers from the city of the Lord. "Judgment must begin at the house of God. How pure ought the church to be, and how diligently should all those who hold office therein labor to keep out and chase out people of unclean lives. Honorable offices involve serious responsibilities; to trifle with them will bring our own souls into guilt and injure beyond calculation the souls of others. Lord, come to us that we may walk before Thee with perfect hearts."[145] Matthew Henry states, "Not Jerusalem only, but the whole land was the city of the Lord; so is the Gospel-church. It is the interest of the city of the Lord to be purged from wicked doers, who both blemish it and weaken it; and it is therefore the duty of all to do what they can, in their places, towards so good a work and to be zealously affected in it. The day is coming when the Son of David shall cut off all wicked doers from the new Jerusalem, for there shall not enter into it any that do iniquity."[146]

The Bottom Line: David's vows or fixed rules regarding godly conduct (godliness, Christian piety) personally and professionally ought to be embraced by all believers at home, the office, school and marketplace, and in social outing. "The story is told of Ernest the Pious, Duke of Saxe-Gotha, that he sent an unfaithful minister a copy of this Psalm, and it became a proverbial saying in the country when a minister was guilty of misconduct, 'He will soon get the prince's Psalm to read' (Delitzsch).'"[147]

2. Changing Man, the Unchanging God   Psalm 102:25–28

"Of old hast thou laid the foundation of the earth: and the heavens are the work of thy hands. They shall perish, but thou shalt endure: yea, all of them shall wax old like a garment; as a vesture shalt thou change them, and they shall be changed: But thou art the same, and thy years shall have no end. The children of thy servants shall continue, and their seed shall be established before thee."—Psalm 102:25–28.

Of "old" (Barnes says, "It means here, long ago; of olden time; at the beginning."[148] Poole says, "The eternity of God looks both backward and forward; it is both without beginning and without end."[149]) hast thou "laid the foundation of the earth AND the heavens are the work of thy hands" (When there was nothing, the heavens and the earth and all that

10

therein consists derived their being from God by Christ Jesus. See John 1:1–3; Colossians 1:16; Ephesians 3:9 and Hebrews 1:2. "Plato declares that the wondrous order of the heavens is a proof of God's existence. Hafiz enlarges on the same topic, telling us how even the sweet scent and beauteous hue of the tiniest floweret that decks the field is but an efflux [flowing out] of the perfections of the Divinity. St. Paul shows how the heathen were not left without a witness of God, either in the external world or in their own conscience. Kant is said to have remarked that the two things which most forcibly impressed him with a feeling of the sublime were the starry heavens above him and the moral sense within him."[150]).

"They shall perish" (MacArthur says, "Eternal God created the heavens and earth, which will one day perish. Hebrews 1:10–12 applies this passage to the Lord Jesus Christ, who is superior to the angels because: 1) He is eternal, while they had a beginning; and 2) He created, but they were created. This passage clearly affirms the eternality and deity of Christ. The unchangeable God will outlast his creation, even into the new creation [Malachi 3:6; James 1:17; 2 Peter 3; Revelation 21, 22]."[151]).

But "thou shalt endure" (Gill says, "As the eternal God, from everlasting to everlasting, and even as Man, He will die no more; and, as Mediator, will ever remain. He will be King forever; His throne is forever and ever; His kingdom is an everlasting one; He is a priest forever, after the order of Melchizedek; His sacrifice is of an eternal efficacy, and He ever lives to make intercession for His people. He will always continue, as the Prophet, in His church, to teach by his Spirit, Word, and ordinances, in the present state; and hereafter will be the light of the New Jerusalem, and of His saints, forever."[152]).

"Yea, all of them shall wax old like a garment" (Rawlinson says, "With the perishable nature of the whole material creation, the Psalmist contrasts the absolute eternity of God. Yea, all of them shall wax old like a garment."[153]) as a "vesture shalt thou change them, and they shall be changed" (Benson says, "Isaiah tells us [Isaiah 51:6] that the heaven and earth shall wax old like a garment; but the Psalmist here goes one step further than the prophet and not only acquaints us that the heavens and earth shall wax old, but, like a worn-out garment, shall be changed for new. And what can he intend but the new heavens and new earth mentioned by St. Peter in the New Testament and said to be the expectation of believers according to God's promise? [2 Peter 3:13]."[154]).

But "thou art the same, and thy years shall have no end" (Rawlinson says, "It is by an accommodation to human modes of thought that God's 'years' are spoken of. An eternal existence is a unity—not made up of years and days."[155]). "The children of thy servants shall continue" (Barnes says, "The descendants of those that serve and obey thee. This represents the confident expectation of the Psalmist that, as God was unchangeable, all His promises toward His people would be fulfilled, even though the heavens and the earth should pass away. God was the same. His word would not fail. His promises were sure."[156]).

AND "their seed shall be established before thee" (Barnes says, "It means here that they would be firmly and permanently established; that is, the church of God would be permanent in the earth. It would not be like the generations of people that pass away. It would not be like the nomadic tribes of the desert that have no fixed habitation and that wander from place to place. It would not be even like the heavens that might put on new forms or wholly pass away. It would be as enduring and changeless as God himself; it would, in its proper form, endure forever. As God is eternal and unchangeable, so would the safety and welfare of his people be."[157] Benson says, "Though the heavens and the earth perish, and though we, Thy servants, pine away in our iniquities, according to Thy righteous sentence and threatening [Leviticus 26:39], and die in captivity; yet, by virtue of Thy eternal and unchangeable nature and Thy promises made to Abraham and his seed, we rest assured that our children, and their children after them, shall enjoy the promised mercies, even a happy restoration to and settlement in their own land, and the presence of our and their Messiah. And their seed shall be established before Thee—in the place of Thy gracious presence, either here in Thy church, or hereafter in Heaven."[158]).

Homily

The Psalm's unusual title reads *A Prayer of the afflicted when he is overwhelmed and poureth out his complaint before the Lord.* "Some think it was written by David. Hengstenberg and Alexander decidedly favor this view. If David was the author, the Psalm probably had no historic occasion, but is purely prophetic."[159] Dilday and Kennedy state, "The psalm originated near the close of the Babylonian exile. Allusions to prisoners, Zion's dust, and restoration make this dating virtually certain."[160] A. F. Kirkpatrick agrees: "We can hardly be wrong in assigning this Psalm to the closing years of the exile in Babylon. Zion is in ruins, but the appointed time for Jehovah to have compassion on her is come (Psalm 102:13–14). The Psalmist looks for the fulfilment of the prophecies of Jeremiah and Isaiah 40–66, and prays that he may be spared to witness the restoration of Israel with his own eyes (Psalm 102:23–24)."[161] Charles Simeon states it was "written at the return of the Jews from the Babylonish Captivity, and referring primarily to the restoration of the Jewish Church and polity, it evidently has respect to the Messiah and the establishment of his Church on the face of the whole earth, since it is said that 'the heathen shall fear the name of the Lord, and all the kings of the earth his glory.'"[162] The text (Psalm 102:25–28) is applied to Christ Jesus in Hebrews 1:10–12.

The Psalm cites the despair, loneliness and miserable condition of man and his resort to the Lord in prayer for help (Psalm 102:1–10); the frailty and brevity of life (Psalm 102:11, 23); God's merciful deliverance (Psalm 102:12–14, 17); the salvation of the heathen (Psalm 102:15); the unchangeable nature of God (Psalm 102:25–27) and the permanence of the redeemed, the church of the Lord Jesus Christ (Psalm 102:28). The Psalm is Messianic—prophecy of the coming of Jesus—for Psalm 102:25–27 is attributed to Jesus in Hebrews 1:10–12 which states He is Creator of the world, the everlasting and changeless Lord. W. S. Plumer wrote, "We cannot be mistaken in applying this language to Jesus. We have the authority of Heaven itself for so doing (Hebrews 1:10–12). Messianic ideas were very familiar to the prophets; and we are in more danger of not referring to the Redeemer all the passages in which He is spoken of than we are of applying to Him those which do not belong to Him (Acts 3:24). The English version here gives the complete sense as well as any. The three things ascribed to Christ are creative energy, eternity and immutability. In Christ his people to the end of the world have all their stability and certainty of triumph."[163]

Man's life is brief at best. It is as a "shadow" that "declineth." See Psalm 102:11. It is *stretched* out the furthest or longest as the sun sets when it's about to disappear (depart from the earth). "When it is the time of evening the shadows lengthen, but when it is dark they are no longer discernible, but come to an end and go."[164] Man's life is frail as grass that "withers." The metaphor of short-lived grass is used often in Scripture to depict life's frailty. See Psalm 90:6; Isaiah 40:6–7; James 1:10 and 1 Peter 1:24. The length or duration of life is uncertain, for sickness, accident or murder may unexpectedly, suddenly snatch it away. Every man, regardless of age, is only one heartbeat away from death and eternity. Knowing this, man ought to pray with Moses, "So teach us to number our days, that we may apply our hearts unto wisdom" (Psalm 90:12). Of the death of friends and loved ones, Tuck says, "Nothing so effectively convinces of the uncertainty of life. Nothing better pleads for the faithful doing of the duty of every hour. Nothing more effectively convinces that no man is necessary to God's work in the world. It teaches us that as our life-work may be 'rounded off' at any moment, it should always be ready for 'rounding off.'"[165]

But thou art the same, and thy years shall have no end. See Psalm 102:27. In the Hebrew the phrase is "But thou art He" which "denotes the essential characteristics of God, the attributes which belong to Him and no other. One of these attributes being Eternal Existence, the Psalmist's transition from the confession that the God he addresses bears this sacred title to the assertion that His 'years shall have no end' is perfectly natural."[166] See Ephesians 1:10–12 (reference to Jesus Christ). "It is very comfortable," writes Matthew Henry, "in reference to all the changes and dangers of the church, to remember that Jesus Christ is the same yesterday, today, and forever. And in reference to the death of our bodies and the removal of friends, to remember that God is an everlasting God. Do not let us overlook the assurance this Psalm contains of a happy end to all the believer's trials. Though all things are changing, dying, perishing like a vesture folding up and hastening to decay, yet Jesus lives, and thus all is secure, for he hath said, 'Because I live ye shall live also.'"[167] George Horne says, "Amidst the changes and chances of this mortal life one topic of consolation will ever remain, namely, the eternity and immutability of God our Savior, of Him who was, and is, and is to come. Kingdoms and empires may rise and fall; nay, the heavens and the earth, as they were originally produced and formed by the Word of God, the Son, or Second Person in the Trinity, to whom the Psalmist here addresses himself (see

Hebrews 1:10); so will they, at the day appointed, be folded up and laid aside, as an old and worn-out garment;...but Jehovah is ever the same; His years have no end, nor can His promise fail any more than Himself."[168] With man time changes things (sometimes suddenly), but the Lord is unchangeable—His promises, provision and protection to His children is the same today as yesterday and will be the same tomorrow. The same Jesus that is with us in health will be with us in sickness; in prosperity, with us in poverty; in tranquility, with us in sorrow; and in life, with us in death.

Matthew Henry states, "Christ will be the same in the performance that He was in the promise, the same to His church in captivity that He was to His church at liberty. Let not the church fear the weakening of her strength or the shortening of her days while Christ Himself is both her strength and her life; He is the same and has said, 'Because I live you shall live also.' Christ came in the fulness of time and set up His kingdom in spite of the power of the Old-Testament Babylon, and He will keep it up in spite of the power of the New-Testament Babylon."[169] Amen and Amen.

O God, our help in ages past,
Our hope for years to come,
Our shelter from the stormy blast,
And our eternal home,

Under the shadow of Thy throne
Thy saints have dwelt secure;
Sufficient is Thine arm alone,
And our defense is sure.

Before the hills in order stood
Or earth received her frame,
From everlasting Thou art God,
To endless years the same.

A thousand ages in Thy sight
Are like an evening gone,
Short as the watch that ends the night
Before the rising sun.

Time, like an ever-rolling stream,
> Bears all its sons away;

They fly forgotten, as a dream
> Dies at the opening day.

O God, our help in ages past,
> Our hope for years to come,

Be Thou our guard while life shall last
> And our eternal home. ~ Isaac Watts (1674–1748)

The Bottom Line: "He [God] is the only universal doctor; and the medicine He gives is the only true catholicon [Merriam-Webster says 'something that is a cure-all or panacea.'], healing in every instance. Whatever our spiritual malady may be, we should apply at once to this Divine Physician. There is no brokenness of heart which Jesus cannot bind up. 'His blood cleanseth from all sin.' We have but to think of the myriads who have been delivered from all sorts of diseases through the power and virtue of His touch, and we shall joyfully put ourselves in His hands. We trust Him, and sin dies; we love Him, and grace lives; we wait for Him, and grace is strengthened; we see Him as he is, and grace is perfected for eve."[170] Man's abiding comfort and security in a changing (and dying) body and world is in the eternal stability of the Lord. See Psalm 90:2.

3. Count Your Blessings and Give Thanks   Psalm 103:1–12

"Bless the LORD, O my soul: and all that is within me, bless his holy name. Bless the LORD, O my soul, and forget not all his benefits: Who forgiveth all thine iniquities; who healeth all thy diseases; Who redeemeth thy life from destruction; who crowneth thee with lovingkindness and tender mercies; Who satisfieth thy mouth with good things; so that thy youth is renewed like the eagle's. The LORD executeth righteousness and judgment for all that are oppressed. He made known his ways unto Moses, his acts unto the children of Israel. The LORD is merciful and gracious, slow to anger, and plenteous in mercy. He will not always chide: neither will he keep his anger for ever. He hath not dealt with us after our sins; nor rewarded us according to our iniquities. For as the heaven is high above the earth, so great is his mercy toward them that fear him. As far

as the east is from the west, so far hath he removed our transgressions from us."—Psalm 103:1–12.

"Bless" (Barnes says, "The word 'bless,' as applied to God, means to praise, implying always a strong affection for Him as well as a sense of gratitude."[171] Harman says, "The word translated 'praise' is literally 'bless,' a word used in the Old Testament to express thanks and gratitude...calls attention to God's loving and faithful character."[172]) "the LORD" (Henry says, "It is the Lord that is to be blessed and spoken well of; for He is the fountain of all good, whatever are the channels."[173]) "O my soul: and all that is within me" (Kirkpatrick says, *"My soul* is the Psalmist's self or personality: *all that is within me* are the various organs of the body, which were regarded by the Hebrews as the seat of thought will and emotion. The Psalmist summons all the faculties and powers of his being to unite in the praise of Jehovah."[174] Barnes says, "And all that is within me...—All my powers and faculties; all that can be employed in his praise: the heart, the will, the affections, the emotions. The idea is, that God is worthy of all the praise and adoration which the entire man can render."[175]).

"Bless his holy name" (Jamieson-Fausset-Brown say "His complete moral perfections."[176] Spurgeon says, "By the name we understand the revealed character of God, and assuredly those songs which are suggested, not by our fallible reasoning and imperfect observation, but by unerring inspiration, should more than any others arouse all our consecrated powers."[177]). "Bless the LORD, O my soul" (Nearly always, repetition in Scripture is for emphasis.[178]) and forget not all his "benefits" (Swanson says "what is done, performed; a kindness shown."[179] The goodness of God to man.).

Who "forgiveth all thine iniquities" (The foundational benefit to man from the gracious hand of God is divine pardon, the forgiveness of sins. Harman says, "The word translated 'forgives' *(solêach)* is never used of people forgiving one another, but it is used exclusively of God in the Old Testament, for it describes His gracious action in pardoning sinners."[180]) Who "healeth all thy diseases" (The recovery from sicknesses.) Who "redeemeth thy life from destruction" (Rescues, delivers. Benson says "both temporal and eternal; from deadly dangers and miseries."[181]). Who "crowneth thee" (Swanson says "surround,

17

envelope, close in upon, i.e., to completely be around a person or object, and so not allow an object or persons to pass in or out of an area."[182] God surrounds us with His unfailing love and faithfulness).

"With lovingkindness" (Vine, Unger and White say "loving-kindness; steadfast love; grace; mercy; faithfulness; goodness; devotion."[183]) and "tender mercies" (Swanson says "mercy, pity, favor, i.e., the state or condition of receiving favor, and so in some contexts, not be in judgment or deserved punishment, implying relationship."[184]). Who "satisfieth thy mouth with good things" (Poole says, "Who satisfieth all thy just desires and necessities."[185] Spurgeon says "or rather, 'filling with good thy soul.' No one is ever filled to satisfaction but a believer, and only God himself can satisfy even him."[186]).

So that thy "youth is renewed like the eagle's" (Rawlinson says, "So that thy youth is renewed like the eagle's; rather, like an eagle [see Isaiah 40:31]. The meaning is, not 'thy youth is renewed as an eagle's youth is,' for an eagle's youth is not renewed; but 'thy youth is renewed, and is become in its strength like an eagle.'"[187] Spurgeon says, "He who sat moping with the owl in the last Psalm here flies on high with the eagle. The Lord works marvelous changes in us, and we learn by such experiences to bless His holy name. To grow from a sparrow to an eagle, and leave the wilderness of the pelican to mount among the stars, is enough to make anyone bless the Lord."[188]).

The Lord "executeth" (performs, makes, gives) "righteousness" (Swanson says "righteousness, justice, rightness, i.e., the state of doing what is required according to a standard."[189]) and "judgment for all that are oppressed" (Barnes says "that is, 'justice.' He sees that justice is done to the oppressed. He is on their side. His law, His commands, His judicial decisions, His providential interpositions, are in their favor."[190]). He "made known his ways unto Moses" (Spurgeon says, "To him the Lord gave specially clear manifestations of His dispensations and modes of ruling among mankind, granting to him to see more of God than had before been seen by mortals, while he communed with Him upon the mount."[191] Also God revealed His "Law" to Moses, the governing means of man's life personally and corporately as a people.).

"His acts unto the children of Israel" (Gill says "His works, His wonderful works; His plagues on their enemies the Egyptians; His redemption of them out of the house of bondage; His leading them through the Red Sea as on dry land; His feeding them with manna in the wilderness, protecting them from their enemies, bringing them into the land of Canaan, and settling them there; see Psalm 78:11."[192]).

The Lord is "merciful and gracious" (compassionate, kind, gracious), "slow to anger" (patient, forbearing) AND "plenteous in mercy" (Swanson says "abundant, excess, i.e., pertaining to a relatively large collection or mass, with a focus that it is more than enough for a situation."[193] God's unfailing love toward man is more than enough, than will ever be needed.) He will not always "chide" (Barnes says "rebuke; contend; strive; for so the Hebrew word means. He will not always contend with people, or manifest His displeasure. This implies that He may chide or rebuke His people, but that this will not be forever. He will punish them; He will manifest His displeasure at their sins; He will show that He does not approve of their course, but He will show that He 'loves them,' and does not seek their ruin."[194]) neither will he keep his anger forever.

"He hath not dealt with us after our sins; nor rewarded us according to our iniquities." (Here is great cause for praise, for God hath not dealt with us as deserved. What might be our present and eternal condition had He not interposed His grace and mercy through Jesus in our behalf at Calvary?) "For as the heaven is high above the earth" (Gill says "which is the greatest distance known, or can be conceived of; the space between the heaven and the earth is seemingly almost infinite; and nothing can more illustrate the mercy of God, which reaches to the heavens, and is in Heaven; though this is but a faint representation of the largeness and abundance of it, and which indeed is boundless and infinite."[195]).

"So great is his mercy toward them that fear him" (Barnes says "to those who reverence and serve him. That is, His mercy is thus great in forgiving their offences; in imparting grace; in giving them support and consolation."[196]). "As far as the east is from the west so far hath he removed our transgressions from us" (Poole says "the guilt of our sins from our persons and consciences. The sense is, He hath fully pardoned them, so as never to remember them more, as He promiseth."[197] Barnes says "that is, He has put them entirely away. They are so removed that they cannot affect us anymore. We are safe from all condemnation for our sins, as if they had not been committed at all."[198] Spurgeon says, "He has removed them all, ALL! From the cradle to the tomb, they are all gone—sins in private, and sins in public, sins of thought, word, deed are all removed. The moment we believe in Jesus, they are all, all, all gone!"[199]).

Homily

The title ascribes the Psalm to David, but among scholars there is doubt. A. F. Kirkpatrick says, "The Psalm bears the name of David in the title, but it is impossible to suppose that it was written by him. The Aramaic coloring of the language, the allusions to Job, Jeremiah, and the later chapters of Isaiah, and the general style and matter of the Psalm, combine to make it certain that it belongs to a far later date. If Psalm 102 may be assigned to the close of the Exile, Psalm 103 may with equal probability be placed in the early years of the Return. It was written while the sense of the nation's forgiveness, of which that deliverance was the proof, was still fresh and vivid."[200] In contrast, Rosenmüller, "on account of the special mention of forgiveness of sin (vv. 3, 8–10), conceives that this Psalm was written by David, when after the death of Bathsheba's child (2 Samuel 12:19) he was assured that his great transgression had been pardoned."[201] Matthew Henry attributes the Psalm to David, as do I.

In capsule the Psalm is a recital of God's divine benefits or bless-ings to the redeemed. "This poem is one of the special treasures of the Psalter. Beautiful phrases, profound thought, and broad scope are distin-guishing features."[202] Spurgeon remarked, "As in the lofty Alps some peaks rise above all others, so among even the inspired Psalms there are heights of song which overtop the rest. This one hundred and third Psalm has ever seemed to us to be the Monte Rosa of the divine chain of moun-tains of praise, glowing with a ruddier light than any of the rest. It is as the apple tree among the trees of the wood, and its golden fruit has a flavor such as no fruit ever bears unless it has been ripened in the full sunshine of mercy."[203] He also remarked, "Our attempt at exposition is commenced under an impressive sense of the utter impossibility of doing justice to so sublime a composition....There is too much in the Psalm, for a thousand pens to write. It is one of those all-comprehending Scriptures which is a Bible in itself, and it might alone almost suffice for the hymn-book of the church."[204] Matthew Henry said, "This psalm calls more for devotion than exposition; it is a most excellent psalm of praise, and of general use."[205]

George Horne comments, "Thanksgiving cannot be sincere and hearty, unless a man bear impressed upon his mind, at the time, a quick sense of 'benefits' received; and 'benefits' we are most of us apt to 'forget'; those especially, which are conferred upon us by God. Therefore David repeateth his self-awakening call, and *summoneth all his powers of recollection*, that none of the divine favors might continue unnoticed and unacknowledged."[206] W. S. Plumer well states, "No man ever yet made a complete catalogue of the benefits he had received. Here we have an excellent beginning."[207]

"There is no prayer in this Psalm—it is all praise right through and through."[208] David cites five specific benefits for which the Christian ought to express heartfelt gratitude.

1. Who forgiveth all thine iniquities. In recital of the divine benefits afforded to man by God, the first named is the forgiveness of sins. To know that Christ forgives sin, yea to have experienced that pardon personally is man's foundational reason to praise Him. Not only doth He forgive the initial sin of disobedience that results in a reconciled relationship (salvation) but the "sins" committed afterward, enabling continual fellowship with Him. In contrast to this one other benefits are incomparable. John R. Rice writes, "In all of God's plan, nothing else in the universe is as important as forgiving, saving, restoring to God's fellowship those who are estranged from Him, who are fallen from His holiness, who are become His enemies, who have been captured and ruined by sin! Forgiveness is the highest aim of God."[209] Augustine remarks, "God's benefits will not be before our eyes unless our sins are also before our eyes."[210]

2. Who healeth all thy diseases. I believe in divine healing of sicknesses which may be wrought through doctors or without them. The man that has experienced divine healing and been raised from the sick bed or death bed has much cause to praise the Lord. He that is sickly has hope for recovery when medical science offers none. Obviously it is not God's plan to heal all, but it is for some. It also applies to the diseases of the soul. Scott said, "Sinful passions are the diseases of the soul."[211] W. S. Plumer wrote, "Did God's blessing stop at the forgiveness of sins and not go on to cure the madness in our hearts, we should be both vile and miserable forever."[212] See 1 John 1:7.

3. Who redeemeth thy life from destruction. J. A. Alexander remarks, "Redeeming means delivering, but with a strong implication of cost and risk."[213] See Matthew 27:27–50. Render praise to the Lord for deliverances from temporal dangers and troubles—but most especially from an eternity in Hell. John Gill states, "The people of God are redeemed from sin, the cause of it; and from the curse of the law, in the execution of which it lies; and from Satan, the executor of it; and all this by Christ, who is the Redeemer appointed and sent, and who being mighty, and so equal to the work, has obtained eternal redemption; through which the saints are secure from going down to the pit of destruction."[214]

Through many dangers, toils and snares
    We have already come.
T'was grace that brought us safe thus far,
    And grace will lead us home;
    And grace will lead us home. ~ John Newton (1779)

4. Who crowneth thee with lovingkindness and tender mercies. The meaning for "crowneth" is to "envelope or surround." The believer is ever enveloped in the loving-kindness (unfailing love, grace, faithfulness, goodness of God) and mercy (divine favor, pity; not receiving that which is justly deserved in way of punishment for sin and in the Hebrew is "expressive of the warmest and tenderest affection."[215]) of the Lord. Matthew Henry said, "What greater dignity is a poor soul capable of than to be advanced into the love and favor of God? This honor have all his saints. What is the crown of glory but God's favor?"[216]

Marvellous grace of our loving Lord,
    Grace that exceeds our sin and our guilt!
Yonder on Calvary's mount outpoured,
    There where the blood of the Lamb was spilt.
                        ~ Julia H. Johnston (1849–1919)

22

5. Who satisfieth thy mouth [soul] with good things. Praise the Lord for filling your life abundantly with things for your chief good. John Gill comments, "With the good things in the heart of God, with His favor and lovingkindness, as with marrow and fatness; with the good things in the hands of Christ, with the fullness of grace in Him, with pardon, righteousness, and salvation by Him; with the good things of the Spirit of God, His gifts and graces; and with the provisions of the Lord's house, the goodness and fatness of it; these He shows unto His people, creates hungerings and thirstings in them after them, sets their hearts alonging after them, and then fills and satisfies them with them."[217] Matthew Henry states, "It is only the favor and grace of God that can give satisfaction to a soul, can suit its capacities, supply its needs, and answer to its desires."[218] W. S. Plumer comments, "The blessing spoken of in this clause goes beyond the satisfying of the sensitive appetite. It embraces all the good that we receive for our nourishment, sustentation ["a sustaining or being sustained; maintenance, support, or preservation. something that sustains or supports"—Collins Dictionary] and comfort."[219] Spurgeon said, "Satisfaction. A rare word! It rings like a silver bell—satisfaction. The richest man in England [or the United States] has not found it. The greatest conqueror has never won it. The proudest emperor cannot command it....It is a spiritual blessing, a divine grace that comes from *the great satisfying God—the God who is himself all sufficient...to fill the heart of man.*"[220]

Thy youth is renewed like the eagle. J. A. Alexander states, "The only point of comparison with the eagle is its strength and vigor, as in 2 Samuel 1:23, Isaiah 40:31; and the whole verse may be paraphrased as follows: 'So completely does his bounty feed thy strength, that even in old age thou growest young again, and soarest like an eagle.'"[221] Tholuck said, "The glory of the old age of the godly consists in this, that while the faculties for sensuous, no less than mental enjoyment gradually decline, and the hearth of life gets thus deprived of its fuel, the blessings of godliness not only continue to refresh the soul in old age, but are not until then most thoroughly enjoyed. The sun of piety rises the warmer in proportion as the sun of life declines [2 Corinthians 4:16]."[222]

He knows how we are formed, he remembers that we are dust. See Psalm103:14. Frances Ridley Havergal said, "Think of that when you are tempted to question the gentleness of His leading. He remembers all the time and will never make you take even one step beyond what your feet are able to endure. Never mind if you think you are unable to take another step, for either He will strengthen you to make you able, or He will call a sudden halt, and you will not have to take it at all."[223]

In light of all that the Lord hath done for us, certainly the words of David ring from our lips, "Bless the LORD, O my soul: and all that is within me bless His holy name. Bless the LORD, O my soul, and forget not all his benefits" (Psalm 103:1–2). 'I will exhort my soul to remember the goodness of the Lord unto me and to give thanks unto Him in the totality of my being.' This praise certainly is generated from a time of silence at the footstool of God. Spurgeon remarks, "Some of the best moments of devotion I have ever been able to enjoy I have spent in entire silence, looking up. I sat still and wondered that God should ever love me and I found a dew gathering about my eyes. I thought of how He loved me and what that love had worked in me and for me, till, not venturing to speak, I have been content to be silent before the Lord in rapture inexpressible."[224]

How does man bless God? J. W. Walsh suggests:
"(1) By accepting the grace of God. To bless means to make holy.
"(2) By showing gratitude for the grace of God. To bless means to make happy.
"(3) By glorifying the grace of God. To bless means to glorify."[225]

James Smith's outline of Psalm 103:[226]
The *Quality* of His Mercies. Tender (v. 4).
The *Measure* of those Mercies. Plentous (v. 8).
The *Extent* of His Mercies. (v. 11).
The *Duration* of His Mercies. (v. 17).
The *Receivers* of those Mercies. "On them that fear Him" (v. 11).
The *Freeness* of His Mercies. They are to be received, and not earned (2 Corinthians 4:1).
The *Place* to receive His Mercies is at the Throne of Grace. (Hebrews 4:16).

The Bottom Line: W. S. Plumer said, "One of the saddest proofs of our fallen condition, is our propensity to forget God's benefits, especially his unspeakable gift, Jesus Christ (v. 2). Nothing but the basest ingratitude could chill our hearts or shut our lips."[227] John Piper says, "Genuine thankfulness is an act of the heart's affections, not an act of the lips' muscles."[228] Ironically we are prone to forget the many ways in which God is so good to us. Thus we, as David, must ever say, 'Soul, forget not His benefits.' Charles Simeon wrote, "It [gratitude unto the Lord] seems to be the principle that animates all the hosts of the redeemed in Heaven; who are incessantly occupied in singing praises to Him who loved them, and washed them from their sins in His own blood. By this also all the most eminent saints on earth have been distinguished."[229]

4. Creation's Song: the Handiwork of God　　　Psalm 104:24

"O LORD, how manifold are thy works! in wisdom hast thou made them all: the earth is full of thy riches."—Psalm 104:24.

"O Lord how manifold are thy works" (Kirkpatrick says, "This is a parenthetic ejaculation, from which the Psalmist cannot refrain, as he contemplates creation so far. It breaks the continuity of his description [Psalm 104: 2–32], but not unpleasingly."[230] *Manifold*. Swanson says "be many, i.e., increase a number or quantity of a collection or mass."[231] *Thy works*. Williams and Ogilvie say, "Since God is the Creator, the Psalmist continues, *'The earth is full of Your possessions.'* Paul speaks of Christ as the agent of creation and declares, 'all things were created through Him and for Him' [Colossians 1:16]. Everything is under His copyright. Everything is stamped with His trademark. Everything is signed with His name [see Job 41:11]."[232] Horne says, "[Therefore], transported with a survey of the wonders which present themselves in Heaven above and on earth below, the Psalmist breaks forth into an exclamation on the variety and magnificence, the harmony and proportion of the works of God in this outward and visible and perishable world. What then are the miracles of grace and glory? What are those invisible and eternal things which God hath for them that love Him in another and a better world, and of which the things visible and temporary are no more than shadows? Admitted to that place where we shall at once be indulged with a view of all the divine dispensations and of that beatitude in which they terminated, shall we not with angels and archangels cry out, *O Lord, how manifold are thy works.*"[233]).

"In wisdom hast thou made them all" (Gill says, "Some by 'wisdom' here understand Christ Himself, the wisdom of God; and not amiss, since without Him was not anything made (see Proverbs 3:19)."[234] Williams and Ogilvie say, "God's wisdom is seen in the way in which all of creation works together under His sovereign will."[235] Clarke says, "They are so constructed as to show the most consummate wisdom in their design and in the end for which they are formed. They are all God's property and should be used only in reference to the end for which they were created."[236]

Benson says, "When men undertake many works, and of different kinds, commonly some of them are neglected and not done with due care; but God's works, though many, and of different kinds, yet are all made in wisdom and with the greatest exactness: there is not the least flaw or defect in them. The most perfect works of art, the more narrowly they are viewed, (as, suppose, with the help of microscopes,) the more rough and imperfect they appear; but the more the works of God are examined (by these glasses), they appear the more fine and complete. God's works are all made in wisdom, for they are all made to answer the end designed, the good of the universe, in order to the glory of the universal King."[237]).

The earth is full of "thy riches" (Gesenius and Tregelles say "a creature, thing created."[238] Bratcher and Reyburn say, "It seems to mean possessions, property. Most translations have creatures or 'creations.' The verb related to creatures can mean either 'acquire' or 'create' [see Psalm 139:13a], and in Genesis 14:22 the verb is used to speak of God as the Creator."[239] Barnes says in the "Hebrew, 'possessions.' So the Septuagint and the Vulgate. That is, these various objects thus created are regarded as the 'possession' of God; or, they belong to him, as the property of a man belongs to himself. The Psalmist says that this wealth or property abounds everywhere; the earth is full of it."[240] Rawlinson says, "The earth is full of thy riches; or possessions (compare with Psalm 105:21). 'The earth is the Lord's and the fullness thereof' [Psalm 24:1]. Creation gives the right of ownership."[241]).

Homily

The author of the Psalm is unknown. Some think it was David since it seems to be a continuation of Psalm 103 (based upon its style in composition[242]) which he did write.

"Psalm 104 communicates certain information that is not well developed in Genesis 1, namely, God's purposeful, progressive plan of creation. Each of God's creative acts establishes the necessary conditions on Earth to allow for a subsequent act of creation. That is, what God did on creation day 2 sets the stage for what God did later, on creation days 3, 4, 5, and 6."[243] John MacArthur comments, "He refers to the original creation (Psalm 104:5) without forgetting the fall of man and the cursed earth (Psalm 104:23, 29, 35)....The flow of the Psalm loosely follows the order of creation as first reported in Genesis 1:1–31 but closes (Psalm 104:35) with an allusion to the end time events recorded in Revelation 20–22."[244] Jennings and Lowe state, "It need scarcely be said that this composition is one of the most beautiful in the Psalter, and has received the warmest eulogiums ["Type of: congratulations, extolment, kudos, praise; an expression of approval and commendation"[245]] from commentators of every time. The line of thought is one not frequently pursued in the Hebrew poetry; in fact, nowhere except in Job do we find the lessons of the natural world brought out in such ample detail. As regards the plan of the Poem, the order of Genesis 1 is evidently intentionally followed in the Poet's treatment of the works of creation; and once only does he deviate from that order, till the works of the sixth day have been described. Then (vv. 27–30) he expands that thought which has been more or less present throughout his enumeration of God's works—the absolute dependence of all of them on God, who is not only the cause but also the sustainer of life."[246]

I. The Heavens (Psalm 104:3–4)
II. The Earth and the Waters (Psalm 104:5–9)
III. The Springs and the Rain (Psalm 104:10–13)
IV. The Vegetation and the Hills (Psalm 104:14)
V. The Seasons and the Days (Psalm 104:19–23)
VI. The Sea (Psalm 104:24–26)
VII. Life and Death (Psalm 104:27–30)[247]

"The Lord by wisdom hath founded the earth; by understanding hath he established the heavens. By his knowledge the depths are broken up, and the clouds drop down the dew" (Proverbs 3:19–20). The "Lord" (Jehovah) by "wisdom" (Ross says, "The wisdom that directs life is the same wisdom that created the universe."[248]) hath "founded the earth" (God is the architect and builder of the earth). By His sovereign wisdom God *founded the earth* when there was nothing, upon nothing (Job 26:7). *"Creatio ex nihilo"* [creation out of nothing]—the best and only reasonable explanation for the existence of the universe and all within it is that an intelligent designer created it. The divine Designer (God) *established the heavens,* setting the stars, planets, moons, and suns in place. "He hath made the earth by his power, he hath established the world by his wisdom, and hath stretched out the heavens by his discretion" (Jeremiah 10:12). *He appointed the moon for seasons* (Psalm 104:19). The "moon is the perfect size and distance from the Earth for its gravitational pull. The moon creates important ocean tides and movement so ocean waters do not stagnate, and yet our massive oceans are restrained from spilling over across the continents."[249]

By His *knowledge the depths are broken up* (formation of oceans and rivers). See Proverbs 3:20. "Who laid the foundations of the earth, that it should not be removed forever. Thou coveredst it with the deep as with a garment: the waters stood above the mountains. At thy rebuke they fled; at the voice of thy thunder they hasted away. They go up by the mountains; they go down by the valleys unto the place which thou hast founded for them. Thou hast set a bound that they may not pass over; that they turn not again to cover the earth. He sendeth the springs into the valleys, which run among the hills. He watereth the hills from his chambers: the earth is satisfied with the fruit of thy works" (Psalm 104:5–10; 13).

Water from his chambers. The Architect of the world designed the clouds to soak up moisture only to return it to the earth ("the clouds drop down the dew"). "Water...colorless, odorless and without taste, and yet no living thing can survive without it. Plants, animals and human beings consist mostly of water (about two-thirds of the human body is water)....It has an unusually high boiling point and freezing point. Water allows us to live in an environment of fluctuating temperature changes, while keeping our bodies a steady 98.6 degrees."[250] God set oceanic boundaries to keep its waters in place ("set a bound that they may not pass over"); without which the earth would be flooded. "[E]very particle of the universe glitter[s] with infinite skill."[251] God not only set all that exists in nature into motion but constantly orchestrates its purposeful fulfillment. Williams and Ogilvie said, "God is not an absent clockmaker. He is the mainspring of all that He has made (Psalm 104:27)."[252]

> [E]very particle of the universe glitter[s] with infinite skill.
> Charles Bridges

In wisdom hast thou made them all. The earth is just the right size—any smaller, an atmosphere would be impossible, as with Mercury; any larger, its atmosphere would contain free hydrogen, like Jupiter's. Earth is the only known planet to possess the right combination of gases in its atmosphere to sustain animal, plant and human life. Earth is the perfect distance from the sun. The planets just on either side of Earth, Venus and Mars, are too close to the sun and too far from the sun, respectively, to support life as we see it on earth. Earth's faithful rotation on its axis enables it to be properly warmed and cooled each day. The uniformity and stability of nature is another mirror revealing the hand of intelligent design of the earth. Nature operates by inert, unchanging laws. The earth rotates the same distance every 24 hours, the speed of light is consistent, gravity remains the same, and day and night do not cease.[253]

The earth is full of thy riches. Spurgeon states, "It is not a poorhouse, but a palace; not a hungry ruin, but a well-filled storehouse. The Creator has not set His creatures down in a dwelling place where the table is bare and the buttery empty. He has filled the earth with food, and not with bare necessaries only, but with riches—dainties, luxuries, beauties, treasures. In the bowels of the earth are hidden mines of wealth, and on her surface are teeming harvests of plenty. All these riches are the Lord's; we ought to call them not 'the wealth of nations' but 'thy riches,' O Lord!"[254]

This is my Father's world,
  And to my list'ning ears
All nature sings, and round me rings
  The music of the spheres.

This is my Father's world;
　　I rest me in the thought
Of rocks and trees, of skies and seas,
　　His hand the wonders wrought.
　　　　　　　　　　　~ Maltbie D. Babcock (1858–1901)

Matthew Henry summarizes, "God has likewise established the heavens and directed all the motions of them in the best manner. The heavenly bodies are vast, yet there is no flaw in them—numerous, yet no disorder in them—the motion rapid, yet no wear or tear; the depths of the sea are broken up, and thence come the waters beneath the firmament, and the clouds drop down the dews, the waters from above the firmament, and all this by the divine wisdom and knowledge. Christ is that Wisdom, by whom the worlds were made and still consist."[255]

O Lord, my God, when I in awesome wonder
　　Consider all the worlds Thy Hands have made,
I see the stars; I hear the rolling thunder
　　Thy power throughout the universe displayed.

Then sings my soul, my Savior God, to Thee,
　　"How great Thou art; how great Thou art!"
Then sings my soul, my Savior God, to Thee,
　　"How great Thou art; how great Thou art!" ~ Carl Boberg (1885)

The Bottom Line: In considering God's handiwork in the world, we can only exclaim with the Psalmist, "O LORD, how manifold are thy works! in wisdom hast thou made them all: the earth is full of thy riches" (Psalm 104:24). In that He made all that exists, He is owner of all, demanding adherence to His Word and allegiance to Himself. As with nature, man was created with purposeful design. Utmost happiness and meaning is to live accordingly.

5. Thanksgiving for God's Wondrous Works　　　　　Psalm 105:1–5

　　"O give thanks unto the LORD; call upon his name: make known his deeds among the people. Sing unto him, sing psalms unto him: talk ye

of all his wondrous works. Glory ye in his holy name: let the heart of them rejoice that seek the LORD. Seek the LORD, and his strength: seek his face evermore. Remember his marvellous works that he hath done; his wonders, and the judgments of his mouth."—Psalm 105:1–5.

"O give thanks" (Swanson says "express praise, extol, i.e., make a public confession of the attributes and acts of power of a person. Note: there is a focus on the content of praise, spoken out-loud, usually in the context of the community; give thanks, i.e., give an expression of praise for a person, with a particular focus on the subject being engaged in the expression of thanks or praise."[256]) "unto the Lord" (Spurgeon says, "Jehovah is the author of all our benefits; therefore, let Him have all our gratitude."[257]).

"Call upon his name" (Barnes says, "More literally, 'Call Him by His name'; that is, address Him by His proper title; ascribe to Him the attributes which properly belong to Him; or, address Him in a proper manner."[258]) "make known his deeds" (Swanson says "deed, action, i.e., what is done as an activity or action."[259] Benson says, "Let each of you among his people, and even among the heathen, declare God's mighty acts as he has opportunity."[260] See Psalm 9:1.).

"Sing unto him" (Vine, Unger and White say *sing* "is often used to express joy, exultation, which seems to demand loud singing, especially when it is praise to God: 'Cry out and shout, thou inhabitant of Zion: for great is the Holy One of Israel in the midst of thee' [Isaiah 12:6]."[261]) "sing Psalms unto him" (Swanson says "i.e., praise as an act of worship to God in a chanting or melody, with the voice as the instrument; play notes on instrument, i.e., make music. Note: this may be only the accompaniment of an instrument to the main focus of singing words."[262]). "Talk ye of all his wondrous works" (Clarke says "of his miracles."[263]).

"Glory" (Swanson says "praise, cheer, brag on, extol, i.e., extol the greatness or excellence of a person."[264]) "ye in his holy name" (Clarke says, "Show [and share] the name Jesus: exult in it—praise it. His name was called Jesus, because He came to save His people from their sins."[265]). Let the heart of them rejoice that "seek the Lord" (Vine, Unger and White say "to seek, search, consult."[266] Swanson says "search, look for, i.e., try to learn information about an object, implying a diligence in the procurement of the information."[267]).

31

Seek the Lord, and His "strength" (Jamieson-Fausset-Brown say, "Seeking God's favor is the only true mode of getting true happiness, and His strength [Psalm 105:4] is the only true source of protection."[268] Spurgeon says, "Put yourselves under His protection. Regard Him not as a puny God, but look unto His omnipotence and seek to know the power of His grace. We all need strength; let us look to the strong place. Let us look to the Almighty Jehovah for it."[269]).

"Seek his face evermore" (Barnes says "His favor. His smiling upon us, His lifting up the light of His countenance is synonymous with His favor."[270] Benson says, "That is, His favor, or the light of His countenance; seek to enjoy this to eternity, and therefore continue seeking it to the end of the time of your probation. Seek it while you live in this world, and you shall have it while you live in the other world; and even then you shall be forever seeking it in an infinite progression, and yet be forever satisfied with it."[271]).

"Remember his marvelous works that he hath done" (Gill says, "They seem to design the works of Providence in favor of the children of Israel: best of all, works of grace done for His saints, none of which are to be forgotten, especially the great work of redemption and salvation, for the remembrance of which, under the New Testament, an ordinance is particularly appointed."[272] Plumer says, "It embraces all the amazing things done by God in the history of His people."[273]).

"His wonders" (Brown, Driver and Briggs say "be surpassing, extraordinary."[274] The supernatural works of God [miracles]. Plumer says, "If miracles and prodigies ['something extraordinary or inexplicable; an extraordinary, marvelous, or unusual accomplishment, deed, or event,' (Merriam-Webster)] could have converted the world, it would have been done long ago, vv. 5–27. The history of creation, of providence and of redemption abounds with them; and sometimes for a season cavillers have thus been silenced."[275]).

AND "the judgments of his mouth" (Rawlinson says "His sentences upon sinners, as upon the Egyptians [Psalm 105:28–38] and upon the Canaanites (Psalm105:11, 44)."[276] Kirkpatrick says "the judgments of His mouth. Not the precepts of the law, but the sentence pronounced and executed upon Pharaoh and the Egyptians [Exodus 6:6; Exodus 7:4; Exodus 12:12]."[277]).

Homily

It is evident that David was author of at least a portion of Psalm 105 for Psalm 105:1–8 is a recitation of David's words spoken to "Asaph and his brethren" (1 Chronicles 16:8–15) when the ark of God was brought to Jerusalem (1 Chronicles 16:1), but Adam Clark says, "It was probably enlarged and sung at the restoration of the people from the Babylonish captivity."[278] A. F. Kirkpatrick states, "The two historical Psalms [Psalms 105 and 106] which stand at the end of Book IV are closely related. Psalm 105 is a Psalm of thanksgiving, recapitulating the marvellous works by which Jehovah demonstrated His faithfulness to the covenant which He made with Abraham. Psalm 106 is a Psalm of penitence, reciting the history of Israel's faithlessness and disobedience. They present, so to speak, the obverse and reverse of Israel's history; the common prophetic theme of Jehovah's lovingkindness and Israel's ingratitude."[279] Jennings and Lowe say, "Both compositions may fairly be assigned to the concluding period of the seventy years' captivity."[280]

The Psalmist testifies to the goodness, mercy and loving-kindness of God to His people, not only in granting pardon, provision and protection, but also deliverance from trouble and oppressors. The Psalm recounts the goodness of God to Abraham, Isaac and Jacob (Psalm 105:9–16); Joseph (Psalm 105:17–22), Israel (Psalm 105:23–24), and Moses and the Israelites (Psalm 105:26–41).

God's wondrous works in history to Abraham, Isaac, Jacob; Joseph and his father; and Moses and the Israelites testify to His unfailing love, righteous judgment, faithfulness to promises, punishment of the bad, and reward of the good and holiness. David states that these historical marvelous works of God are grounds for jubilation and thanksgiving (see Psalm 105:1–3) and by implication for future obedience and faith.

Give thanks unto the Lord. See Psalm 105:1. Express gratitude unto the Lord with words and music, testifying and singing, for His goodness. See Psalm 106:1; Psalm 107:1; Psalm 111:1; Psalm 136:1 and Psalm 138:1. Above all, the redeemed ought to often give thanks for their salvation that was purchased at an exceedingly great cost.

Thank You, Lord, for saving my soul;
Thank You, Lord, for making me whole;
Thank You, Lord, for giving to me
Thy great salvation so rich and free. ~ Seth and Bessie Sykes (1945)

Christians are told to *talk of all his wondrous works*. See Psalm 105:2. Adam Clarke says, "Who have so many of these to boast of as Christians! Christianity is a tissue of miracles, and every part of the work of grace on the soul is a miracle. Genuine Christian converts may talk of miracles from morning to night, and they should talk of them and recommend to others their miracle-working God and Savior."[281] The Psalmist in Psalm 107:2 says, "Let the redeemed of the LORD say so, whom he hath redeemed from the hand of the enemy." John Gill comments, "Talk ye of all his wondrous works: all the works of the Lord are wonderful; what David elsewhere says of himself may be said of them, that they are wonderfully made, even the least and most inconsiderable of them; and especially his works of grace, when it is observed for whom they are performed, or on whom they are wrought; sinful creatures, enemies to God, and deserving of His wrath. These are to be talked of freely and frequently, in friendly conversation, in order to gain a further knowledge of them and warm each other's hearts with them, and to lead into adoring and admiring views of the love and grace of God in them."[282] See Deuteronomy 6:7. Make known His deeds. See Psalm 105:1. Spurgeon says, "Let the heathen hear of our God, that they may forsake their idols and learn to worship him."[283]

I love to tell the story;
    'Tis pleasant to repeat
What seems each time I tell it
    More wonderfully sweet.

I love to tell the story,
    For some have never heard
The message of salvation
    From God's own holy Word. ~ Katherine Hankey (1834–1911)

Remember his marvelous works that he hath done. See Psalm 105:5. This was a most needful reminder for the Jewish people, for Israel's history was one of forgetfulness. See Psalm 78:11. How prone man is to forget the bountiful mercies and blessings of God. Remembrances of former blessings (forgiveness, deliverance, help and provision) instill trust for new ones, especially in the hour of trial. See Psalm 103:1–6.

Are you ever burdened with a load of care?
Does the cross seem heavy you are called to bear?
Count your many blessings; ev'ry doubt will fly,
And you will be singing as the days go by.

Count your blessings; name them one by one.
Count your blessings; see what God hath done.
Count your blessings; name them one by one.
Count your many blessings; see what God hath done.

~ Johnson Oatman (1897)

The Bottom Line: The corporate recital of past personal blessings as well those of others keeps God's goodness in focus even while we are in the furnace of affliction. Divine blessings, especially that of salvation, ought to prompt praise and thanksgiving unto God and open our mouth to testify of His goodness unto the unsaved.

6. Divine Testing   Psalm 105:19

"Until the time that his word came: the word of the LORD tried him."—Psalm 105:19.

Until the time that "his word came" (Jennings and Lowes say, "The expression 'come,' as equivalent to 'come true' or 'come to pass,' is used in Judges 13:12, 17; 1 Samuel 9:6; Jeremiah 17:15."[284] Numerous interpretations are offered regarding the meaning of "his word." Kirkpatrick says, "The promise of Jehovah tried him. Two different Hebrew words are rendered *word* in the A.V. It seems best to understand them both of the word or promise of Jehovah communicated to Joseph in the dreams which excited the enmity of his brethren [Genesis 37:5 ff.]. The promise of Jehovah is as it were personified as Jehovah's agent

35

employed to fit Joseph for his high station [Psalm 119:50]."[285] Plumer differs, stating: "*The time,* perhaps predicted by Joseph. Some think the word means that by which he interpreted the dreams of his fellow-prisoners [Genesis 41:12–13]. From the time he left Canaan till he saw his father again was probably about twenty-four years."[286] Such is Adam Clarke's view: "This appears to refer to the completion of Joseph's interpretation of the dreams of the chief butler and baker." Jennings and Lowe say, "Or, again, 'His word came' may simply denote that Jehovah willed it, and immediately the king sent and released Joseph."[287]). When Scripture is silent, man can only speculate.

"The word of the Lord tried him" (Kirkpatrick says, "It tested him, purified and refined his character [Job 23:10], as it led him through dark ways of humiliation, till the time came for him to be raised to the honor for which Providence destined him."[288] Plumer says, "It is most probable that the Psalmist here refers to Joseph's being called on to interpret Pharaoh's dream, which was God's word to that wicked monarch, the explanation of which was a severe test, proof or trial of Joseph [Genesis 41:25–36]. Or it may be that he refers to the long delay of God in fulfilling His word."[289] Adam Clarke concurs, saying, "This seems to refer to the interpretation of Pharaoh's dreams."[290]

Homily

The Psalm is a historical song tracing Israel's history from God's Covenant with Abraham until later times in Caanan.

He sent a man before them, even Joseph....Until the time that his word came. See Psalm 105:17, 19. While a mere youth, Joseph received the "word of the LORD" regarding God's lofty plan for his life (Genesis 37:6–11). All of God's children have such a "word," though it may not be realized or understood. In fact, it may be dismissed or even ridiculed by family when it is known, as was the case with Joseph (Genesis 37:18–20). If you are patient by waiting before God in prayer for His divine plan, He will reveal what you seek. Pray with David, "Show me thy ways, O LORD; teach me thy paths. Lead me in thy truth, and teach me: for thou art the God of my salvation; on thee do I wait all the day" (Psalm 25:4–5). Believers have all been given the *royal* promise, that of eternal life in Heaven. See John 3:16 and John 14:1–3.

The word of the Lord tried [tested] *him.* Joseph's "dream" of royal exaltation over his brethren and people tarried in fulfillment. It probably seemed to Joseph at times that it was "only" a *dream*. Joseph was placed in a desert pit by his embittered brothers to die a painful death through starvation. Callously these brothers sat down near the pit to eat while Joseph was "in anguish of his soul" crying out for rescue (Genesis 42:21). As Joseph suffered, they rejoiced that the "dreamer" was finally disposed of. Talk about cold-heartedness! But Judah prevented the cold-blooded murder (Genesis 37:26–27) by suggesting the selling of Joseph into slavery, which they did (Genesis 37:28). The slave traders in turn sold Joseph to Potiphar, the captain of the guard in Pharaoh's government (Genesis 37:36; 39:1). Joseph had favor with Potiphar, who made him "overseer" of his house (Genesis 39:4). Potiphar's wife falsely accused Joseph of rape (Genesis 39:11–19). Upon being arrested for that of which he was not guilty (Genesis 39:20), his feet were put into shackles and his neck into an iron collar (a detail absent from the Genesis account, which is accurate as to the rest). See Psalm 105:18 NLT, HCSB, NIV. What horrendous torture this had to have been to Joseph!

During the imprisonment he interpreted dreams for the king's chief butler and baker (Genesis 40:5–13). The interpretation indicated that the chief butler would be restored to his former position while the baker would be hung. Prior to the release of the butler Joseph requested that he say a good word to Pharaoh in his behalf regarding his innocence (vv. 14–15). However, upon the butler's restoration, 'he did not remember Joseph, but forgot him' (v. 23). It was only "after two full years" that the butler recalled his broken promise to Joseph which led to his freedom and eventual realization of "the word of the Lord." See Genesis 41:38–41. Though the length of Joseph's imprisonment is unknown, some commentators suggest that it lasted around ten years.[291] Alexander Maclaren said, "His circumstances, judged by appearances, shattered his early visions and bade him believe them to be no more than the boyish aspirations which grown men dismiss or find melt away of themselves when life's realities wake the dreamer. We might either say that the non-fulfilment of the promise tested Joseph, or that the promise, by its non-fulfilment, tested him. The Psalmist chooses the latter more forcible and half paradoxical mode of speech. It proved the depth and vitality of his faith and his ability to see things that are not as though they were. Will this man be able continually through years of poverty and imprisonment to keep his eye on the light beyond, to see his star through clouds? Will he despise the 'light affliction,' in the potent and immovable belief that it is 'but for a moment?' Thus, for all these years the great blessed word, or the hope that was built upon it, tested Joseph in the very depths of his soul."[292]

The dream that was a "promise" tried or tested him in the furnace of affliction to purify him in preparation for its fulfillment in his exaltation to Pharaoh's second-in-command. God's promise of exaltation to His children (Heaven) likewise "tests" in order to "purify." "For our light affliction, which is but for a moment, worketh for us a far more exceeding and eternal weight of glory" (2 Corinthians 4:17). "Having therefore these promises, dearly beloved, let us cleanse ourselves from all filthiness of the flesh and spirit, perfecting holiness in the fear of God" (2 Corinthians 7:1). "'The word of the Lord tried him,' and because it tried him, it purified him. If we give credence, as we ought to, to that word, it will purify us, and it will test of what contexture our faith is."[293] The "testing" is merely a refining, purging of the dross or impurities from our life, that we may become "pure gold." "But the God of all grace, who hath called us unto his eternal glory by Christ Jesus, after that ye have suffered a while, make you perfect, stablish, strengthen, settle you" (1 Peter 5:10). "That the trial of your faith, being much more precious than of gold that perisheth, though it be tried with fire, might be found unto praise and honor and glory at the appearing of Jesus Christ" (1 Peter 1:7).

The believer possesses "the word of the Lord," or His promise, not only with regard to Heaven but also to divine assignments which just as surely shall come to pass, though at times delayed, as it was with Joseph. What is it that God hath called you to do or accomplish that has met with trouble and trials? "Though [the vision] tarry, wait for it; because it will surely come" (Habakkuk 2:3). Confidence or assurance that God always keeps His promises, despite the length of time from their pledge to their realization, enables perseverance. Knowledge that God tests ("the Lord tried him") believers to prepare them for their promised task or plan (not necessarily because of sin; Joseph was innocent of wrong) enhances faith when such is experienced. The knowledge that God's word to him, though it lingered, would be fulfilled, fueled Joseph's willingness to be the ridicule of his brothers, the Midianites' purchased "merchandise," Potiphar's slave, Potiphar's wife's falsely accused, and Pharaoh's prisoner.[294] Faith in God's promises or Word instills patience when fulfillment is delayed, enables endurance when we are tested through "light affliction," gives encouragement when there are "setbacks," and bestows willingness to suffer or be persecuted in the realization of them. See Hebrews 11:1, 6. Faith conquers doubts. Spurgeon wrote, "He [Joseph] believed the promise, but his faith was sorely exercised. A delayed blessing tests people and proves their metal, whether their faith is of that precious kind which can endure the fire. Of many a choice promise we may say with Daniel, 'the thing was true, but the time appointed was long.'"[295]

Matthew Henry summarizes, "He [Joseph] was exalted, highly exalted. He continued a prisoner, neither tried nor bailed, until the time appointed of God for his release (v. 19), when his word came, that is, his interpretations of the dreams came to pass, and the report thereof came to Pharaoh's ears by the chief butler. And then the word of the Lord cleared him; that is, the power God gave him to foretell things to come rolled away the reproach his mistress had loaded him with; for it could not be thought that God would give such a power to so bad a man as he was represented to be. God's word tried him, tried his faith and patience, and then it came in power to give command for his release."[296]

Joseph's "dreams" set in motion the adversity he experienced. Had he rejected, turned his back on God's call, it all would have been avoided. Every Christian has that option. Jesus said, "If any man will come after me, let him deny himself, and take up his cross daily, and follow me" (Luke 9:23). To follow Christ involves bearing a *cross*. It is unavoidable and inescapable. It's far better to bear affliction in obedience to God's will and plan than to avoid it through disobedience.

The Bottom Line: God is faithful and true to both His royal promise (eternal life) and the temporal promises. Be comforted and cheerful, for that which is promised shall come to past though it may be delayed. Divine testing or refining occurs at times to purify, ready the believer for the promised task. Suffering or affliction is designed to prepare the believer for success in the assignment. "It was a discipline indispensable if [Joseph] were to fitly fill the high station for which God had designed

39

him."[297] It is so for all Christians. Faith is indispensable in *possessing* the promises. Testing is a gift from God for our betterment and usefulness in His kingdom. Therefore count it all joy. See James 1:2–4.

7. Confession of Sin   Psalm 106:6–10

"We have sinned with our fathers, we have committed iniquity, we have done wickedly. Our fathers understood not thy wonders in Egypt; they remembered not the multitude of thy mercies; but provoked him at the sea, even at the Red sea. Nevertheless he saved them for his name's sake, that he might make his mighty power to be known. He rebuked the Red sea also, and it was dried up: so he led them through the depths, as through the wilderness. And he saved them from the hand of him that hated them, and redeemed them from the hand of the enemy."—Psalm 106:6–10.

We have "sinned" (Gesenius and Tregelles say "to miss, to err from the mark, speaking of an archer [the opposite idea to that of reaching the goal, to hit the mark]; to sin—to miss or wander from the way, or to stumble in the path of rectitude [uprightness]."[298] Kirkpatrick says, "often...Israel's sin is described as 'rebellion';—obstinate resistance to the revealed Will of God."[299] Barnes says, "We have sinned as 'they' did; we have followed their example. The illustration of the manner in which the nation had sinned occupies a considerable part of the remainder of the Psalm; and the idea here is, that, in the generation in which the Psalmist lived, there had been the manifestation of the same rebellious spirit which had so remarkably characterized the entire nation."[300]).

"With our fathers" (Rawlinson says, "The confession is as broad and general as possible, including all under sin—the 'fathers' from Moses downwards, the whole nation from the time of its settlement in Canaan, and even the afflicted exiles in Babylon."[301]). We have "committed iniquity" (Strong says "do amiss, bow down, make crooked, commit iniquity, pervert, do wickedly, do wrong."[302]).

Our fathers "understood not thy wonders in Egypt" (Swanson says "have insight, give attention, have regard, act with care, give heed

40

to, i.e., give thought for a person or situation, implying a proper response."[303] Barnes says, "They did not fully comprehend the design of the divine dealings. They did not perceive the greatness of the favor shown to them or the obligation to obey and serve God under which they were placed by these remarkable manifestations."[304] Rawlinson says "rather, considered not—did not give serious thought to them; took them as matters of course and so were not impressed by them."[305]).

"They remembered not" (forgetfulness) "the multitude" (Swanson says "many, large amount, i.e., a great number of countable items, often with a focus on being an impressive number; much, i.e., pertaining to a great mass or quantity of something."[306]) "thy mercies" (Swanson says "loyal love, unfailing kindness, devotion, i.e., a love or affection that is steadfast based on a prior relationship."[307]) but "provoked him" (They were obstinate, contentious and rebellious toward God at the Red sea. See Exodus 14:11–12.) at the sea, even at the Red sea.

Nevertheless he "saved them for his name's sake" (God delivered, rescued them not for their obedience toward Him but for His honor and glory. Poole says "that He might glorify His name and vindicate it from the blasphemous reproaches which the Egyptians and others would have cast upon it, if [Israel] had been destroyed."[308]) that he might make his "mighty power to be known" (Gill says "not only among the Israelites, but among the nations of the world; who, had He not saved them, might have thought and said that it was for want of power and that He could not do it [see Deuteronomy 9:28]."[309] See Exodus 7:5; Exodus 14:4, 18 and Exodus 15:11–16.).

"He rebuked the Red sea also, and it was dried up" (The NLT says "commanded." Spurgeon says, "A word did it. The sea heard his voice and obeyed. How many rebukes of God are lost upon us!"[310] At God's word the Red sea *dried up* to permit the Israelites passage of escape from the Egyptian army that pursued them. This was one of many "wonders" or "mercies" of the Lord Israel had forgotten.) "So he led them through the depths, as through the wilderness" (Rawlinson says, "*Midbar*, the word translated "wilderness," is properly a smooth stretch of down, very level, and suited for sheep walks."[311] Spurgeon says, "As if it had been the dry floor of the desert, the tribes passed over the bottom of the gulf; nor was their passage venturesome, for He bade them go; nor dangerous, for He led them. We also have under divine protection passed through many trials and afflictions, and with the Lord as our guide we have experienced no fear and endured no perils."[312]).

And he "saved them from the hand of him that hated them, and redeemed them from the hand of the enemy" (Rawlinson says, "The Pharaoh of the Exodus, whose 'hatred' had been shown by his oppression [Exodus 2:23; Exodus 3:9; Exodus 5:6–19], his prolonged refusal to let Israel go, and final pursuit of them, and attempt to destroy them on the western shore of the Red Sea [Exodus 14:5–10]. *And redeemed them from the hand of the enemy.* The deliverance from Egypt, typifying man's deliverance from sin, is constantly spoken of as a 'redemption' [Psalm 74:2; Psalm 107:2; Exodus 6:6, 7; Exodus 15:16, etc.]."[313] Gill says, "So the Lord Christ has saved and redeemed His people out of the hand of all their spiritual enemies and those that hate them and war against them, as sin, Satan, and the world [Luke 1:71]."[314]).

Homily

The author and time of composition of Psalm 106 are unknown, though it may have been written during or shortly after the Babylonian captivity. See Psalm 106:44–47. It is similar to Daniel 9. The Psalm opens with praise and confession (Psalm 106:1–6), followed by the listing of sins Israel committed due to their forgetfulness of God's mercies during the Exodus (Psalm 106:7–13). He then mentions their wilderness wanderings (Psalm 106:14–23; 28–32); their failure at Kadesh Barnea (Psalm 106:24–27); their time in Canaan (Psalm 106:34–39), and the Babylonian captivity (Psalm 106:44-47).

We have sinned. See Psalm 106:6. The primary purpose of the Psalm is to detail Israel's persistence in sin (obstinate rebellion) toward God despite His manifold mercies which were not "understood" and were "forgotten." See Psalm 106:7, 13, 21–22. Albert Barnes says, "It would have been sinful to have forgotten even one act of the divine favor; it was a great aggravation of their guilt that 'so many' acts were forgotten, or that they failed to make an impression on them."[315] The Psalmist states that the people of his day had repeated these same sins of their "fathers" (from Moses downward). The memories of God's goodness and faithfulness ought to have prompted praise, obedience, trust, devotion, and allegiance to Him, but they didn't. Kirkpatrick says, "So short were their memories, that at the first sign of danger, they rebelled against God's purpose to deliver them (Exodus 14:11–12). Again and again forgetfulness of past mercies is stigmatized as the source of sin. Psalm 106:13; Psalm 106:21; Psalm 78:11; Deuteronomy 32:18."[316] Yet even in their forgetfulness and rebellion, God remained faithful and merciful. See Psalm 106:8 and Psalm 106:43–46.

The Psalm yields at least six lessons.

1. A good memory of past blessings to self and others serves as a preventative for present sin and cause for hearty praise and devotion.

2. Recall of former interventions, deliverances, victories and provisions at God's hand instills faith that He is able and willing to do the same again.

3. As sin was graciously forgiven in the past, it may be in the present and future, for God changes not in His compassion and mercy. Our sins may be beyond measure, but never beyond grace.

4. God ultimately grants rescue and salvation to people "for his name's sake." Albert Barnes says "for the promotion of His own honor and glory; that it might be seen that He is powerful and merciful. This is constantly given as the reason why God saves people, why He forgives sin, why He redeems the soul, why He delivers from danger and from death."[317] The foundation for and basis of all prayer is "for his name's sake."

5. Wanton desires prove to be curses. God may give what is asked, but with it comes "leanness into the soul." See Psalm 106:15. "It may be that the worst thing that can happen to us is to secure (1) the bodily gratification or (2) the unhallowed ambition or (3) the unfavorable friendship on which we have set our hearts. God's truest kindnesses are often found in His withholding or His removing the objects of our regard."[318] Be careful what you request from the Lord. You may get it.

6. Confession of sin is to be made corporately and personally. "We have done wickedly." See Psalm 106:6; 1 John 1:9–10. The sins of the people against God are catalogued and confessed: forgetfulness of God's goodness (v. 13), tempting God (v. 14), envy (v. 16), idolatry (v. 19), unbelief or distrust in God (v. 24), worship to Baal-peor (v. 28), murmuring against God's provision (v. 32), disobedience to God's

commands (v. 34) and killing their children for a sacrifice (v. 38). It behooves us as well to name specific sins in times of confession.

Roll back the curtain of memory now and then;
Show me where you brought me from and where I could have been.
~ Dottie Rambo (1934–2008)

The Bottom Line: Thanksgiving is best expressed in "thanksliving," which is kindled by healthy spiritual remembering. See Psalm 103. Forget not nor take for granted the manifold goodness of the Lord. Oswald Chambers states, "'We have sinned with our fathers…[and]…did not remember" (Psalm 106:6–7). Then prod your memory and wake up immediately. Don't say to yourself, 'But God is not talking to me right now.' He ought to be. Remember whose you are and whom you serve. Encourage yourself to remember, and your affection for God will increase tenfold. Your mind will no longer be starved, but will be quick and enthusiastic, and your hope will be inexpressibly bright."[319]

8. Let the Redeemed Say So   Psalm 107:2

"*Let the redeemed of the LORD say so, whom he hath redeemed from the hand of the enemy.*"—Psalm 107:2.

Let the "redeemed" (Haman says, "The word for 'redeemed' comes from the verb 'redeem' used of God's deliverance of Israel from Egypt [Exodus 6:6; 15:13] and then of His redemption of exiled Israel from Babylon [See Psalms 74:2; 77:15; 78:35; 106:10]."[320] Swanson says "i.e., pertaining to an object or person who has been delivered from danger by being purchased from indenture [working for another] or slavery, with a focus on the relationship to the new master [Psalm 107:2; Isaiah 35:9; 51:10; 62:12], note: often in context this is a relationship of salvation to the Lord; buy back, redeem, i.e., purchase back an item or person, with money or goods, that had been sold at a prior time [Leviticus 25:25]."[321]).

"Of the LORD" (Salvation from sin or deliverance from danger that is solely wrought by God) "say so" (Vine, Unger and White say "to say, speak, tell, command, answer"[322]). Whom he hath "redeemed" (To be rescued, delivered. Barnes says, "It refers here not to a ransom from 'sin,' but to deliverance from 'danger.'"[323]) from the "hand of the enemy" (The redeemed in the context of the Psalm are those rescued from captivity and exile [perhaps Babylonian], and the enemy was the Babylonians. There is certainly a contrast in it to that of man's spiritual rescue from satanic captivity through Jesus Christ, the great liberator.).

Homily

The Five Books of the Psalms each have its counterpart in the Five Books of Moses. See the Introduction to this volume. The counterpart for Psalms 107–150 (Book V) is Deuteronomy which details God's ways with Israel. Though the authorship of the Psalm is unknown, it is generally ascribed to David.[324] Allan Harman states, "The fact that Book Five contains psalms attributed to David (Psalms 138–145) is not a problem, as the composition of a particular book was not contemporaneous with the writing of the songs."[325] Spurgeon states that the theme of the Psalm "is thanksgiving and the motives for it."[326] The Psalm may reference the Israelites' deliverance from Babylonian exile and captivity. See Psalm 107:2–3. The deliverance or rescue was divinely promised. See Isaiah 51:9–11. Regardless of whether our deliverance is eternal salvation or rescue from temporal danger, the Psalm encourages thanksgiving unto the Lord for that intervention. Give praise to the Lord for deliverance from captivity (Psalm 107:1–3), dangers related to travel (Psalm 107:4–9), prison (Psalm 107:10–16), sickness (Psalm 107:17–22), and storms upon the sea (Psalm 107:23–32). Charles Simeon wrote, "The intent of this psalm appears to be, not merely to display the providence of God as interposing in all the concerns of men, but especially the goodness of God in vouchsafing to hear the prayers of men, and to grant them deliverance in answer to their supplications. This is illustrated under a variety of interesting images. His interpositions are described in behalf of travellers lost, but conducted home in safety; of prisoners rescued from merited captivity; of persons sick and dying, restored to health; of mariners preserved, and brought to their desired haven."[327]

In this homily I want to relate the Psalm to man's rescue from the plight and power of sin by and through Jesus Christ.

Let the redeemed. The Lord hath rescued people "out of the lands, from the east, and from the west, from the north, and from the south" (Psalm 107:3). Salvation from sin is not exclusive to some but inclusive for all—from all points of the compass. All *may* be saved who *will* be saved. See Revelation 7:9.

Whom he hath redeemed. In, of and by Jesus Christ alone is man's deliverance from the power, presence and penalty of sin possible. "To the praise of the glory of his grace, wherein he hath made us accepted in the beloved. *In whom* we have redemption through his blood, the forgiveness of sins, according to the riches of his grace" (Ephesians 1:6–7). "Who gave *himself* for our sins, that he might deliver us from this present evil world, according to the will of God and our Father" (Galatians 1:4). God so loved the world (the inhabitants) that He sent His only Son to redeem it from the hand of the enemy, Satan. See John 3:16 and Ephesians 2:10–13.

Redeemed from the hand of the enemy. The archenemy of God and man is Satan. Of Satan Jesus said, "The thief cometh not, but for to steal, and to kill, and to destroy: I am come that they might have life, and that they might have it more abundantly" (John 10:10). Satan has supernatural strength to hold man captive, but Jesus has "super-duper-natural strength" that is exceedingly superior to set man free.

Let the redeemed of the Lord say so. W. S. Plumer said, "We must make proclamation of God's mercy. This is obligatory upon all, and especially upon them, *Whom he hath redeemed from the hand of the enemy*....Probably the prophet had in mind no particular temporal deliverance, but all such as might set forth the redemption of the soul."[328] Spurgeon wrote, "Whatever others may think or say, the redeemed have overwhelming reasons for declaring the goodness of the Lord. Theirs is a special redemption, and for it they ought to render special praise. The Redeemer is so glorious, the ransom price so immense, and the redemption so complete that they are under sevenfold obligations to give thanks unto the Lord, and to exhort others to do so. Let them not only feel so but say so; let them both sing and bid their fellows sing."[329] T. De Witt Talmage wrote, "An overture, an antiphon, a doxology is this psalm, and in my text the psalmist calls for an outspoken religion, and requests all who have been rescued and blessed no longer to hide the glorious facts, but to publish them, and, as far as possible, let all the world know about it. "Let the redeemed of the Lord say so." If you have in your heart the pearl of great price, why not let others see it? If you got off the wreck in the breakers, why not tell of the crew and the stout lifeboat that safely [rescued] you? If from the fourth story you are rescued in time of conflagration [raging inferno or blaze], why not tell of the fireman and the ladder down which he carried you? If you have a mansion in Heaven awaiting you, why not show the deed to those who may by the same process get a home on the same boulevard? By the last two words of my text the psalmist calls upon all of us who have received any mercy at the hand of God to stop impersonating the asylums for the dumb and, in the presence of men, women, angels, devils, and all worlds, *say so.*"[330]

The saved ought to tell how Jesus brought their meaningless wandering to an end, filling life with purpose (Psalm 107:4, 7); quenched their spiritual hunger and thirst (Psalm 107:5); satisfied their longing soul (Psalm 107:9); broke the chains of their darkness and eternal death (Hell) to set them free (Psalm 107:10, 14, 16); saved them out of their distresses or trouble (Psalm 107:13); healed them of the terminal sickness of sin (Psalm 107:20); calmed the raging storms pounding against the vessel of their life (Psalm 107:29) and granted them an abundant life complete with material as well as spiritual blessings (Psalm 107:38). In capsule, the redeemed ought to praise the Lord continuously for His "goodness, and...wonderful works" (Psalm 107:21) and proclaim that goodness to the unsaved world. Albert Barnes said, "What is here said is true in the most eminent sense of those who are redeemed by the blood of the Son of God, and who are made heirs of salvation. Every consideration makes it proper that they should praise the Lord. Of all on earth, they have most occasion for such praise; of all among people, it may be presumed that they will be best qualified to appreciate the goodness of the Lord."[331]

I'll tell the world how Jesus saved me
    And how He gave me a life brand new;
And I know that if you trust Him,
    That all He gave me, He'll give to you.

Oh, tell the world that you're a Christian;
    Be not ashamed His name to bear.
Oh, tell the world that you're a Christian
    And take Him with you anywhere. ~ Baynard L. Fox (1958)

Joseph Parker wrote, "A silent religion, or a speaking religion—which shall it be? David says, 'I will speak'—what do we say? Too often we resolve that we will keep silence. The theme on which David says he will speak is God's testimonies. Has he chosen a barren topic? Look at the range, the explicitness, and the emphasis of those testimonies, and you will say that never did man choose so fruitful, so abounding a theme. The fact is that there is not a single aspect of life which lies beyond the circumference of the Divine testimonies. God has anticipated everything, provided for everything. David, then, is ready for all occasions, for all men, at all times, and in all places."[332] See Psalm 119:46.

O give thanks unto the Lord, for he is good: for his mercy endureth for ever. See Psalm 107:1. This was Israel's expression of faith in the Lord during the times of David and Ezra, when the Temple's foundation was laid.[333] It was a well-known and rehearsed song among the Israelites.[334] See 1 Chronicles 16:34; 2 Chronicles 5:13; Psalm 118; 136:1; Jeremiah 33:11. Praise and thanksgiving are due unto the Lord for "He is good" to His people—blessing them faithfully with mercy (underserved forgiveness and benefits).

Charles Simeon provides an sermonic outline of Psalm 107:2–3.[335]

From whence you have been gathered ("The remotest ends of the earth are not so far from each other as ye were from God.")

By what means you have been redeemed ("It was by the precious blood of God's only dear Son. It was also by the effectual working of His power: for He, as a good Shepherd, sought you out and apprehended you and brought you home on His shoulders rejoicing.")

To what ye are brought ("As the Lord's redeemed people, ye are brought into a state of peace with God; ye have the privilege of constant communion with Him; ye may expect at His hands every blessing which your souls can desire; and ye shall finally posses all the glory and felicity of Heaven." See Ezekiel 34:12 and Luke 15:5.)

The Bottom Line: Matthew Henry summarizes, "God's works of mercy are wonderful works, works of wonderful power considering the weakness, and of wonderful grace considering the unworthiness of those He shows mercy to. It is expected of those who receive mercy from God that they return praise to Him. We must acknowledge God's goodness to the children of men as well as to the children of God."[336] W. S. Plumer writes, "If the redeemed remain silent, surely God will fail of His chief glory from earth."[337]

9. Morning Worship   Psalm 108:2

"Awake, psaltery and harp: I myself will awake early."—Psalm 108:2.

"Awake, psaltery and harp" (Exactly the same as Psalm 57:8. Henry says, "Let it not be done with a dull and sleepy tune, but let the airs be all lively."[338]). "I myself will awake early" (Kirkpatrick says, "Usually it is the dawn that awakes men; the Psalmist will awake the dawn by his praises before daybreak."[339]).

Homily

Psalm 108 was composed by David. It includes portions of his writings: Psalm 57:7–11 and Psalm 60:5–12.

Alexander Maclaren believed the Psalm was based upon the return from Babylon. "The hopes of conquest in the second part, the consciousness that while much has been achieved by God's help, much still remains to be won before Israel can sit secure, the bar or two in the minor key in verse 11, which heighten the exultation of the rest of the song, and the cry for help against adversaries too strong for Israel's unassisted might, are all appropriate to the early stages of the return."[340] Adam Clarke agrees, saying, "Their captivity being now ended, or nearly at an end, they look and pray for their restoration to their own land as amply as it was possessed in the most prosperous days of David."[341]

To be a developed (mature), not distorted (malformed), believer requires time spent regularly in the presence of God. Obviously a daily quiet time is not to be approached out of a legalistic spirit so as to escape guilt, but with a loving heart longing to "know him, and the power of his resurrection, and the fellowship of his sufferings, being made conformable unto his death" (Philippians 3:10). Practice a quiet time not *in order* to have a relationship with God, but because you *have* a relationship with God; not out of "have to," but out of "want to." David cites that reasons to *meet* with the Lord include praise for His bountiful mercy which is "great above the heavens"; eternal truth that "reacheth unto the clouds"; deliverances in times of "trouble"; and strength and power in time of battle. See Psalm 108:4, 12–13.

Six essential things need be observed to have a meaningful, beneficial quiet time.

The Rigid Schedule. David discovered the immense value of early rising to meet with the Lord prior to the business of the day. See Psalm 108:2 and Psalm 119:147. Jesus lived an intensely busy and crowded life, yet realized the need for soul-nourishment: "rising up a great while before day, he went out, and departed into a solitary place, and there prayed" (Mark 1:35). E. M. Bounds wrote, "He who fritters away the early morning, its opportunity and freshness, in other pursuits than seeking God will make poor headway seeking Him the rest of the day. If God is not first in our thoughts and efforts in the morning, He will be in the last place the remainder of the day. Behind this early rising and early praying is the ardent desire which presses us into this pursuit after God. Morning listlessness is the index to a listless heart. The heart which is behind in seeking God in the morning has lost its relish for God."[342] David's heart was "fixed" to worship the Lord privately, devotionally at a scheduled time ("I will awake early"). See Psalm 108:1–2. Our heart must likewise be established to do the same. The early morning is my scheduled time to meet with the Lord, the best part of the day to me. You may not be a morning person, but it is essential that the day begin with an encounter with the Lord in some measure (simply expand that time later in the day). Vance Havner said that orchestra members don't wait to tune their instruments after the concert; neither should the Christian wait to the end of day to tune his spiritual orchestra for the concert of life that is played in the course of the day.

The Right Spot. Select a place free from interruption where heart focus can be upon Holy God. Distraction is fatal.

The Ready Soul. Exercise discipline to enter this time alertly, not when you are tired or fatigued. Enter it rightly, with sin confessed and heart clean. Enter it receptively, with mind open to hear and receive from the Lord.

The Regular Span. How much time ought you to spend in the quiet time on a regular basis? It should be time enough to include adoration and exaltation of God, meditation upon and digestion of Scripture, and supplication and intercession at God's throne in a beneficial manner. The secret to an effective devotional time is not the quantity of time but the quality of time.

The Required Stuff. A Bible—that's all. A conservative, concise Bible commentary would prove beneficial.

The Routine Structure. Start the quiet time with a brief prayer of praise and petition for illumination of His Word. Next, read the predetermined Bible passage. George Müller, the great London evangelist, always gave precedence to the reading of the Word above time spent in prayer in his morning watches, and for good reason. Adrian Rogers stated, "It is more important for you to hear from God, than even for God to hear from you."[343] Read a Scripture passage repeatedly until its meaning and application are fully understood. A concise Bible commentary is recommended to keep at hand to aid in the understanding of difficult passages. Internalize the truth learned through meditation. "Our souls," states C. H. Spurgeon, "are not nourished merely by listening awhile to this and then to that and then to the other part of divine truth. Hearing, reading, marking, and learning all require inwardly digesting to complete their usefulness, and the inward digesting of the truth lies for the most part in meditating upon it. Why is it that some Christians, although they hear many sermons, make but slow advances in the divine life? Because they neglect their closets and do not thoughtfully meditate on God's Word. They love the wheat, but they do not grind it; they would have the corn, but they will not go forth into the fields to gather it; the fruit hangs upon the tree, but they will not pluck it; the water flows at their feet, but they will not stoop to drink it. From such folly deliver us, O Lord."[344]

Engage in a time of supplication and intercession; then depart with readiness to obey what was received from the Lord.

The Bottom Line: Spiritual growth hinges on daily communion with God—worship, intake of the Word, and prayer. And this takes discipline until it becomes a delight. In engaging the presence of God privately, soon you will say with David, "In thy presence is fulness of joy; at thy right hand there are pleasures for evermore" (Psalm 16:11).

10. The Wounded Spirit   Psalm 109:21–27

"But do thou for me, O GOD the Lord, for thy name's sake: because thy mercy is good, deliver thou me. For I am poor and needy, and my heart is wounded within me. I am gone like the shadow when it declineth: I am tossed up and down as the locust. My knees are weak through fasting; and my flesh faileth of fatness. I became also a reproach unto them: when they looked upon me they shaked their heads. Help me, O LORD my God: O save me according to thy mercy: That they may know that this is thy hand; that thou, LORD, hast done it."—Psalm 109:21–27.

"But do thou for me" (Barnes says "that is, interpose for me; exert Thy power in my behalf"[345]). "O GOD the Lord" (Kirkpatrick says, "God is printed in capitals in A.V., because it represents the sacred Name Jehovah, for which Elôhîm, 'God,' was substituted by the Jews in reading when Adônai, 'Lord,' the regular substitute, is joined with it...*Jehovah Adonai.*"[346]) "for thy name's sake" (Barnes says, "The phrase 'for thy name's sake' implies that the motive which prompted him was a desire that God might be honored. It was not primarily or mainly for his own happiness; it was that God might be glorified."[347]).

Because thy "mercy is good" (Gill says "or 'thy kindness'; meaning the loving-kindness of God to Christ, which He always bore to him, and was eminently and superlatively good; which he makes use of as an argument for his deliverance out of all his troubles, and from death itself."[348] God's mercy always exceeds man's sin. See Romans 5:20.) "deliver thou me" (Grant thy servant rescue, help in his troubles.).

"For I am poor" (Holladay and Kohler say "overwhelmed by want, poor, wretched."[349]) "and needy" (Gesenius and Tregelles say "oppressed, wretched...and I (am) afflicted and wretched"; Psalm 70:5; 86:1; 109:22.

Specially…used of one who suffers undeservedly, although a pious worshipper of God."[350]).

AND "my heart is wounded within me" (Rawlinson says, "The wound to David's heart was, on the former occasion, from the malignity of Saul; on the latter, especially from the desertion of his 'own familiar friend whom he trusted.'"[351] See Psalm 41:9. The friend most probably was Ahithophel. Bratcher and Reyburn say "to be pierced; this means distress, anguish, emotional turmoil and pain. The ancient versions presuppose another Hebrew verb, 'to writhe [in pain].'"[352] Swanson says "pierce, i.e., the penetration of a sharp object into the body, which can harm, wound, or even kill."[353] Barnes says, "I am as one that is prostrated by a weapon—as if my heart had been pierced. I have no courage, no strength. I am like one who lies wounded on a battlefield."[354] Poole says "wounded not slightly, but to the very heart with soul-piercing sorrows"[355]).

"I am gone like the shadow when it declineth" (Ellicott says, "Literally, a lengthened shade [Psalm 102:11; Song of Solomon 2:17]. When the day declines, the shadow lengthens; it becomes longer and longer, till it vanishes in the universal darkness. Thus does the life of the suffering generation pass away."[356] Rawlinson says, "When shadows 'decline,' they are just about to cease and disappear."[357] Anderson says, "As a shadow, when it is extended by the sun's setting, is approaching to evanescence, so, saith the speaker in this Psalm, I am fast disappearing; that is, I am approaching the end of mortal life."[358]).

"I am tossed up and down as the locust" (Holladay and Kohler say "be shaken off, out."[359] Gill says "or 'shaken out' by the wind, as the locust is by the east wind, and carried from place to place [Exodus 10:13], or when a swarm of them by a strong wind are crowded together and thrown upon one another; or like the grasshopper, which leaps from hedge to hedge, and has no certain abode."[360] The word may also refer to a locust being shaken off a plant by the farmer or off a garment.[361]).

"My knees are weak through fasting" (Gill says, "Either voluntary or forced, through want of food or refreshment."[362] Barnes says "hunger; want of food. Strength to stand is connected with firmness in the knee-joints, and hence, weakness and feebleness are denoted by the giving way of the knees."[363]) AND "my flesh faileth of fatness" (Kirkpatrick says, "hath grown lean and lost fatness may be the meaning. But more probably, is shrunken for want of oil. In his distress he had no appetite for food [Psalm 102:4], and like a mourner [2 Samuel 14:2] abstained from the use of oil."[364] Mourners abstained from anointing their body with olive oil.[365] See 2 Samuel 14:2.).

I became also a "reproach unto them" (Swanson says "disgrace, contempt, i.e., the state of dishonor and low status; 2. scorn, insult, taunt, slur, i.e., the act of speaking words which harm and insult another, a reproach, i.e., an object which has low status and dishonor."[366]) when they looked upon me they "shaked their heads" (Spurgeon says, "Words were not sufficient expression of their scorn, so they resorted to gestures which were meant both to show their derision and to irritate his mind. Though these things break no bones, yet they do worse, for they break and bruise far tenderer parts of us."[367]).

"Help me, O Lord my God: O save me according to thy mercy" (Grant rescue from my troubles and sorrows, for You are my only hope. Deliver; help me because Thou art a most kind and loving God rich in mercy to all that call upon you). "That they may know that this is thy hand; that thou, Lord, hast done it." Rawlinson says, "'Deliver me,' prays the Psalmist, 'in some signal way, so that my enemies may be forced to recognize Thy hand in my deliverance, and to confess that Thou, Lord, hast done it.'"[368]).

Homily

David composed the Psalm. The historical setting is uncertain. It may refer to David's persecution by Saul or the rebellion of Absalom, the treachery of Ahithophel (David's *Judas*) or to some other troublesome time. Calvin said, "Although David here complains of the injuries which he sustained, yet, as he was a typical character, everything that is expressed in the Psalm must properly be applied to Christ the head of the church, and to all the faithful, inasmuch as they are his members."[369] Matthew Henry wrote, "It is certain that in penning this Psalm David had an eye to Christ, his sufferings, and his persecutors."[370] W. S. Plumer agrees: "But why may we not regard it as wholly prophetic, borrowing perhaps its imagery from the history of David and of his enemies? This mode of explanation is simple, natural, free from unanswerable objections, and has been formally adopted in whole or in part by many."[371]

Psalm 109 is an *imprecatory Psalm*. Matthew Henry comments, "The imprecations here are very terrible—woe, and a thousand woes, to that man against whom God says *Amen* to them; and they are all in full force against the implacable enemies and persecutors of God's church and people, that *will not repent, to give Him glory.*"[372] Spurgeon wrote, "Truly this is one of the hard places of Scripture, a passage which the soul trembles to read; yet as it is a Psalm unto God, and given by inspiration, it is not ours to sit in judgment upon it, but to bow our ear to what God the Lord would speak to us therein."[373] A. P. Ross explains, "The Psalmists did not hesitate to avow their loyalty to God and His covenant. In their zeal to champion righteousness, their words frequently contain imprecations or curses [plea to God to send misfortunes upon another[374]]. They prayed that God would break the arms of the wicked (Psalm 10:15), smash their teeth (Psalm 58:6), and turn His wrath on them (Psalm 69:22–28). It must be remembered that the Psalmists were filled with zeal for God's theocracy. Thus these expressions were not indications of personal vendetta. The Psalmists, in fact, protested that their kindness to such people had been betrayed by treachery (Psalm 109:4–5). Their prayers represent their longing that God's cause be vindicated on earth, that sin would be judged—which God would do eventually."[375] "David," says Spurgeon, "would not smite the man who sought his blood, he frequently forgave those who treated him shamefully; and therefore these words cannot be read in a bitter, revengeful sense, for that would be foreign to the character of the son of Jesse."[376] Dodd said that these curses "in reality are mere prophetic denunciations."[377]

My heart is wounded within me. A wounded spirit is the injury to the emotions that manifests such horrendous pain and misery that it may feel as if we have been torn open and are bleeding from every orifice of the body. Tim Keller says, "What's a crushed spirit? A crushed spirit then is to look out at life and to have no desire for it, have little or no joy in it, have no passion to get out there and deal with it. Of course, there are degrees of a crushed spirit. It can be anywhere from listlessness and restlessness to discouragement to despondency to being very, very cast down and to losing all desire to live."[378] It is fueled by many things, including the unrelenting focus on the injuries, unforgiveness toward the offender and a desire to make him pay. Spurgeon states, "The Lord has always a tender regard to broken hearted ones, and such the Psalmist had become: the undeserved cruelty, the baseness, the slander of his remorseless enemies had pierced him to the soul, and this sad condition he pleads as a reason for speedy help. It is time for a friend to step in when the adversary cuts so deep. The case has become desperate without divine aid; now, therefore, is the Lord's time."[379]

Medical personnel talk of "weeping wounds," wounds which continue to fester, discharge and ooze, refusing to heal due to noxious matter. Emotionally, many people have "weeping wounds," wounds inflicted years earlier that refuse to heal due to the toxins of an unforgiving spirit, retaliatory spirit, bitterness, anger, blaming of God, fear, and pride. In the same way that doctors can close up wounds without their healing, we are good at doing the same with emotional or spirit wounds. The wound may be closed, but it is yet unhealed deep inside the body or mind, bearing grievous impact. Spirit wounding is such a sharp, crushing blow that it causes a person to spiritually stagger, finding it difficult to rise above it. No class of people is exempt from a broken spirit; black-tie and no-tie alike suffer from its painful stabbings. Sadly, many will live with a wounded spirit all their life and die with it when all the while help was available through Jesus Christ, Holy Scripture and the church.

David confesses that his heart had been pierced sharply and deeply, causing distress, turmoil upheaval, and horrendous pain. His wounded spirit was caused most likely by one counted a faithful friend, Ahithophel (perhaps the worst sort and most painful of wounding). See Acts 1:20. All that have been undermined and betrayed by a "friend" know something of the emotional anguish David experienced. But there are numerous other ways in which the spirit is wounded (slander, sin, bereavement, betrayal, disagreement, guilt, shame, sexual abuse, divorce, bullying, a child's rebellion and scorn, etc.).

Unlike physical wounds that are quite visible, spirit wounds are often concealed in the citadel of the heart due to shame or fear, undetected by others, hampering one's well-being and relationship to others and God. Included in this number are children who by verbal or sexual abuse are bearing deep hurt, and adults who yet bear painful wounds inflicted upon their spirit as a child (by parents, relatives, teachers). Concealment of a broken spirit may salve the wound, but it never will "solve" it. It may give relief from the wound but not grant release from it. Healing results when the hurt and its cause are presented unto the Lord and forgiveness is granted unto him who caused it (Proverbs 28:13).

The greatest cure for a wounded spirit is its prevention. Why? Spurgeon states, "Men may alleviate suffering, they may console the afflicted and cheer the distressed; but they cannot heal the broken in heart nor bind up their wounds. It is not human eloquence or mortal wisdom; it is not the oration of an Apollos nor the wondrous words of a prince of preachers; it is the 'still small voice' of God which alone confers the 'peace which passeth all understanding.' The binding of the heart is a thing done immediately by God, ofttimes without any instrumentality whatever; and when instrumentality is used, it is always in such a way that the man does not extol the instrument, but renders grateful homage to God."[380] Believers may play a role in its prevention in the life of another. Be sensitive not only to what you say but how you say it; refrain from talking behind another's back (it always gets back); abstain even from joking that degrades; be careful not to insinuate "between the lines" something you really didn't mean to say that would crush the spirit; keep confidences placed in you (don't parade them to others); use words that build up, not tear down; stop slander that may circulate; stop bullying; alert others to the believer's sensitivity or hypersensitivity to correction or criticism, etc., that such may be approached with extra grace and love; give affirmation to the person of their value and your love; and when the person is being verbally assaulted in a way that is sure to wound, run interference. What can be done to avoid a brother/sister's spirit wounding must be done. Believers should guard their heart against its wounding. Solomon states, "Keep your heart with all diligence, for out of it spring the issues of life" (Proverbs 4:23 NKJV). Don't be oversensitive or wear your feelings on your sleeve or harbor grudges or give place to that which may wound. Frankly, some things people say to or about us just don't matter.

It will be impossible to stop offensive things from occurring, but by applying God's Word you can stop them from inflicting hurt. Apply truths like "great peace have they which love thy law: and nothing shall offend them" (Psalm 119:165) and "thou wilt keep him in perfect peace, whose mind is stayed on thee: because he trusteth in thee" (Isaiah 26:3). "Tens of thousands of God's saints and sufferers," states Billy Graham, "through the ages have found their dark nights lightened and tortured souls strengthened because they found help from the Spirit in the Word of God."[381] *But do thou for me, O GOD the Lord, for thy name's sake. That they may know that this is thy hand; that thou, Lord, hast done it.* Pray for healing and rescue to the end that God will be glorified and honored by all that see His work in you. Spurgeon says, "Ungodly people will not see God's hand in anything if they can help it, and when they see good people delivered into their power, they become more confirmed than ever in their atheism; but all in good time God will arise and so effectually punish their malice and rescue the object of their spite that they will be compelled to say like the Egyptian magicians, 'This is the finger of God.'"[382]

The Bottom Line: Adrian Rogers wrote, "The Devil wants to blow out the light of hope in your heart, in your mind."[383] Don't let him. Earnestly pray with David, "Help me, O LORD my God: O save me according to thy mercy" (Psalm 109:26). David was confident that the Lord would come to his quick aid. See Psalm 109:30–31.

11. An Old Testament Proof-Text for the Deity of Jesus
Psalm 110

"The LORD said unto my Lord, Sit thou at my right hand, until I make thine enemies thy footstool. The LORD shall send the rod of thy strength out of Zion: rule thou in the midst of thine enemies. Thy people shall be willing in the day of thy power, in the beauties of holiness from the womb of the morning: thou hast the dew of thy youth. The LORD hath sworn, and will not repent, Thou art a priest for ever after the order of Melchizedek. The Lord at thy right hand shall strike through kings in the day of his wrath. He shall judge among the heathen, he shall fill the places with the dead bodies; he shall wound the heads over many countries. He shall drink of the brook in the way: therefore shall he lift up the head."—Psalm 110.

"The Lord said unto my Lord" (Jamieson-Fausset-Brown say, "That the Jews understood this term ['my Lord'] to denote the Messiah their traditions show, and Christ's mode of arguing on such an assumption [Matthew 22:44] also proves."[384] Rawlinson says, "Jehovah said unto him who is my [David's] Lord [King] and Master, i.e., to Messiah, who is my liege Lord, although about to be, in some mysterious way, my descendant."[385] Spurgeon says, "*Jehovah said unto my Adonai*: David in spirit heard the solemn voice of Jehovah speaking to the Messiah from of old. What wonderful intercourse there has been between the Father and the Son! From this secret and intimate communion spring the covenant of grace and all its marvelous arrangements."[386] Not only did David in spirit hear God speak the words "from of old," but also futuristically, following Christ's resurrection and ascension).

"Sit thou at my right hand" (Henry says, "The Lord, Jehovah, said unto him, *Sit as a king*. He receives of the Father this honor and glory [2 Peter 1:17], from Him who is the fountain of honor and power, and takes it not to Himself. He is therefore rightful Lord, and His title is incontestable; for what God has said cannot be gainsaid. He is therefore everlasting Lord; for what God has said shall not be unsaid. He will certainly take and keep possession of that kingdom which the Father has committed to Him, and none can hinder."[387] Plumer says, "In Scripture phrase *sitting* expresses quiet, repose. Jesus has entered into his rest....Sitting also denotes permanency of possession....Sitting denotes majesty and authority. The king sits on his throne, and does not stand in the presence of even his nobles."[388]).

"Until I make thine enemies thy footstool" (Rawlinson says, "To place the foot upon the neck or body of defeated enemies was a common practice of Oriental conquerors."[389] Spurgeon says, "The glorious Jehovah thus addresses the Christ as our Savior; for, says David, he said 'unto my Lord.' Jesus is placed in the seat of power, dominion, and dignity, and is to sit there by divine appointment while Jehovah fights for him and lays every rebel beneath his feet."[390]).

The Lord shall send "the rod of thy strength out of Zion" (Rawlinson says, "'The rod of thy strength,' or 'thy strong scepter,' is the same thing as 'thy ruling power' [see Jeremiah 48:17; Ezekiel 19:11]. The ruling power of Messiah was to go forth from Jerusalem [Acts 1:4–8; 2:1–4]."[391]).

"Rule thou in the midst of thine enemies" (Benson says "the imperative being put for the future, as is often the case elsewhere. Christ rules partly by His grace, converting some, and setting up His kingdom in their hearts, that kingdom which is righteousness, peace, and joy in the Holy Ghost; and partly by His powerful providence, whereby He defends His church and people, and subdues and punishes all their adversaries."[392] Gill says Christ rules "in the hearts of those who, in their unregenerate state, are enemies. But the arrows of His Word being sharp in them, they are brought to submit to Him; the everlasting doors are caused to open; He enters in, takes possession of their hearts, and rules there. Or this may be understood of His church in the world, which is His kingdom, and lies surrounded with enemies on all hands; but, in spite of them, and all their opposition, He will support His kingdom and interest."[393]).

"Thy people shall be willing in the day of thy power" (Benson says, "They shall offer and present unto thee, as their King and Lord, not oxen or sheep or goats, as Thy people did under the law, but themselves, their souls and bodies, as living sacrifices [Romans 12:1], and as free-will offerings, giving up themselves to Thee, to live to Thee and die to Thee. The sense is, Thou shalt have friends and subjects, as well as enemies, and Thy subjects shall not yield thee a false and feigned obedience, as those who are subjects to or conquered by earthly princes frequently do, but shall most willingly and readily obey all Thy commands without any dispute, delay, or reservation. And they shall not need to be pressed to Thy service, but shall voluntarily enlist themselves and fight under Thy banner against all Thy enemies."[394]).

"In the beauties of holiness from the womb of the morning" (Benson says "adorned with the beautiful and glorious robes of righteous-ness and true holiness, wherewith all new men, or true Christians, are clothed [Ephesians 4:24; Revelation 19:8, 14]; and with various gifts and graces of God's Spirit, which are beautiful in the eyes of God and of all good men.").

"Thou hast the dew of thy youth" (Jamieson-Fausset-Brown say, "The 'dew' is a constant emblem of whatever is refreshing and strength-ening [Proverbs 19:12; Hosea 14:5]. The Messiah, then, as leading His people, is represented as continually in the vigor of youth, refreshed and strengthened by the early dew of God's grace and Spirit."[395] Or as Hindson and Kroll say, "As the dew falls fresh every morning and is perpetually resupplied, so too are those who fall to the message of God's redeeming grace and join the ranks of the saved."[396]).

"The Lord hath sworn, and will not repent" (Rawlinson says, "'A fresh revelation' (Cheyne). David, admitted into the councils of the Most High, has been made aware that the Messiah is, by God's decree, to be both King and Priest. God has 'sworn' this, and will certainly not draw back from His oath."[397] It is an immutable decree.). "Thou art a priest for ever after the order of Melchizedek" (Hindson and Kroll say, "Whereas, the Messiah had been bidden to rule over His enemies from the right hand of God by God's decree, now, in similar decree, He is bidden to continue forever in His function as a priest. Thus, Jesus Christ is both King and Priest."[398] Benson says "or, after the manner; that is, so as he was a priest and also a king, and both without any successor and without end, in the sense intended [Hebrews 7:3]."[399] Spurgeon says, "Jesus is sworn in to be the priest of His people, and He must abide so even to the end, because His commission is sealed by the unchanging oath of the immutable Jehovah."[400]).

"The Lord at thy right hand shall strike through kings in the day of his wrath" (Barnes says, "The Hebrew word here rendered 'shall strike,' means 'to shake, to agitate'; and then, 'to shake in pieces, to dash in pieces, to crush'; and here it has the sense of dashing in pieces, smiting, wounding, crushing. The 'kings' referred to are the enemies of God and the Messiah; and the idea is that all would be subdued before Him, that He would set up a universal dominion, that none would be able to stand before Him, or that He would reign over all the earth."[401]).

"He shall judge among the heathen" (Rawlinson says "i.e., execute the royal office not only over Israel, but over the nations of the earth generally."[402]) "he shall fill the places with the dead bodies"(Spurgeon says, "In the terrible battles of his Gospel all opponents will fall till the field of fight is heaped high with the slain. This need not be understood literally, but as a poetical description of the overthrow of all rebellious powers and the defeat of all unholy principles. Yet should kings oppose the Lord with weapons of war, the result would be their overwhelming defeat and the entire destruction of their forces. Read in connection with this prophecy Revelation 19:17–21. Terrible things in righteousness will be seen ere the history of this world comes to an end."[403]).

"He shall wound the heads over many countries" (Gill says "not only strike at them, and strike them; but strike them through, utterly destroy them. This is to be understood of the kings and princes that stood up and set themselves against him [Psalm 2:2], which is interpreted of Herod and Pontius Pilate [Acts 4:26, 27], who both died shameful deaths, as did another Herod that set himself against the apostles and church of Christ [Acts 12:1–2, 23]; and also of heathens, kings and emperors who persecuted the Christians, as Diocletian, Maximilian, and others, who are represented as fleeing to rocks and mountains to hide them from the Lamb, the great day of His wrath being come [Revelation 6:15–17]; and also of the antichristian kings that shall be gathered together to the battle of the Lord God Almighty and shall be overcome and slain by Christ [Revelation 16:14], which will be a time of wrath."[404]).

"He shall drink of the brook in the way" (Henry says, "The wrath of God, running in the channel of the curse of the law, was the brook in the way, in the way of his undertaking, which must go through, or which ran in the way of our salvation and obstructed it, which lay between us and Heaven. Christ drank of this brook when He was made a curse for us, and therefore, when He entered upon His suffering, He went over the brook Kidron [John 18:1]. He drank deeply of this black brook (so *Kidron* signifies), this bloody brook, so drank of the brook in the way as to take it out of the way of our redemption and salvation."[405]) "therefore shall he lift up the head" (Kirkpatrick says "i.e., be triumphantly victorious."[406]).

Homily

This Messianic or Royal Psalm composed by David is quoted in the New Testament more than any other Old Testament text as referring to Jesus Christ.[407] See Matthew 22:41–46; Mark 12:35–37 and Luke 20:41–44. Its historical setting or time line is unknown.

Rawlinson says, "David has had revelations made to him concerning the kingdom, the priesthood, and the ultimate victory of the Messiah over the entire power of evil. In a grand burst of song, rough and rugged, no doubt, but full of energy and genius, he addresses Messiah, and sets forth His praise and glory, the mighty offices which He holds, and the wonderful triumph which awaits Him."[408] Jamieson-Fausset-Brown comment, "The explicit application of this Psalm to our Savior, by Him

(Matthew 22:42–45) and by the apostles (Acts 2:34; 1 Corinthians 15:25; Hebrews 1:13), and their frequent reference to its language and purport (Ephesians 1:20–22; Philippians 2:9–11; Hebrews 10:12–13), leave no doubt of its purely prophetic character."[409] George Horne wrote, "We are here informed of Jehovah's eternal and unchangeable decree concerning the kingdom of Messiah, its extension, power, and duration. That Messiah should, after His sufferings, be thus exalted, was determined in the divine counsel and covenant before the world began."[410] Jennings and Lowe state this psalm is nothing short of a direct Messianic prediction. They base this belief upon the fact that the "direct Messianic prophecies [are] proved (1) by the teaching of our Lord Himself and of His Apostles; (2) by the admissions of the early Jews; (3) by the requirements of the Psalm itself, which admits of no reasonable interpretation other than the Messianic....[M]any Jewish expositors since the time of Christ adopt the Messianic interpretation. This would lead us to infer that it was far more generally adopted before the time of Christ."[411] Charles Simeon says, "In some of the Psalms, David speaks of himself only; in others, of himself and of the Messiah too; but in this, of the Messiah exclusively: not a word is applicable to anyone else. The Jews have taken great pains to explain it away; but their attempts are, and ever must be, in vain. In the first verse, David relates the Father's address to His Son, when 'the council of peace was held between Them'; and the whole of the remainder is addressed by the Psalmist to the Messiah Himself. It altogether elucidates in a very striking manner the character of Christ."[412]

Spurgeon, in his introduction to the Psalm, wrote, "May the Spirit who spoke by the man after God's own heart give us eyes to see the hidden mysteries of this marvelous Psalm, in which every word has an infinity of meaning."[413] Martin Luther viewed Psalm 110 as the "crown of all the Psalms, worthy to be overlaid with precious jewels."[414] He wrote, "The 110th is very fine. It describes the kingdom and priesthood of Jesus Christ and declares Him to be the King of all things and the Intercessor for all men; to whom all things have been remitted by His Father, and who has compassion on us all. 'Tis a noble Psalm; if I were well, I would endeavor to make a commentary on it."[415] He further stated, "This is a peculiar and glorious prophecy concerning the kingdom of Christ...There is not a Psalm like it in the whole Scripture; and it ought to be very dear unto the church, seeing that it confirms that great article of faith—Christ sitting at the right hand of God the Father Almighty."[416]

Michael Wilcock comments, "To the modern reader, Psalm 110 is full of puzzles. To the early church, it was full of treasures."[417] Unlike the New Testament church that finds Psalm 23 the most precious of the Psalter, people during Old Testament times counted such to be Psalm 110. Donald M. Williams said, "It is enough simply to say that God revealed this prophetic Psalm to prepare for the coming of the Messiah.... What God promised in the Old Testament concerning His Son has been fulfilled in the New Testament. It is that simple. As we come to Psalm 110, then, we must accept it as predictive or violate both the worldview and the specific usage of Scripture. As we do this, the text will open up for us."[418]

Psalm 110 pointed not to David, but to another King greater than him and the angels, even King Jesus, the Messiah.[419] See Acts 2:34 and Hebrews 1:13. Jesus used the Psalm to prove His deity to the Pharisees.[420] See Matthew 22:41–45. The "Lord" refers to Jehovah God, while "my Lord" refers to the second person of the Trinity, Jesus Christ. See Psalm 110:1. David is hearing a heavenly conversation between God the Father and God the Son.

Until I make thine enemies thy footstool. God instructs the son (Jesus) to sit at His right hand (position of honor, dominion, sovereignty) *until* it was time to return to establish His rule of all the earth. (Jesus already had died upon the Cross, claiming victory over sin, Satan and death, and ascended back to Heaven.) F. B. Meyer said, "This was the welcome of the Ascension Day—the word with which the Father greeted Jesus. And all through the ages He has been engaged in making the foes of Christ the footstool of His feet. This is not accomplished yet, but it is sure."[421] Lockyer says, "As a footstool bears the entire weight of the body, so the enemies of the Lord are to bear the heavy weight His heavy and everlasting wrath upon their souls if they died unrepentant. The One sharing the throne also has a footstool."[422]

The rod of thy strength out of Zion: rule thou in the midst of thy enemies. The rule of Christ Jesus on earth will be culminated during the millennial kingdom. See Psalm 110:2; Psalm 72:7–11, 17–19. John F.

Walvoord says, "The millennial kingdom is primarily a political kingdom, though it has spiritual aspects and Jesus Christ is the King of Kings, who has come to reign over the earth. Because it is an earthly kingdom with Christ on the throne, it obviously cannot be fulfilled in the present age when Christ is in Heaven, though Christians form a part of the kingdom of God in a spiritual sense. Jesus Christ will serve as King of Kings and Lord of Lords in the millennial kingdom and will fulfill the promises that He will sit on David's throne over the house of Israel (2 Samuel 7:16; Psalm 89:20–37; Isaiah 11; Jeremiah 33:19–21). In His relationship to Israel as her King, He was born to rule over her (Luke 1:32–33). The people of Israel rejected Him as their King (Mark 15:12–13; Luke 19:14). In His death it was posted on the cross that He died as a King (Matthew 27:37). It is in keeping with this that when He comes again, He comes as the King who will fulfill prophecies of His ruling over the Davidic kingdom (Revelation 19:16). In addition to reigning over Israel as the Son of David, Christ is also King of Kings over the entire earth, and this includes, of course, the Gentile world. As Psalm 72:8 states, 'He will rule from sea to sea and from the river to the ends of the earth.'"[423] See Isaiah 2:1–4; 9:6–7; 11:1–10; 16:5; 24:23; 32:1; 40:1–11; 42:3–4; 52:7–15; 55:4; Daniel 2:44; 7:27; Micah 4:1–8; 5:2–5; Zechariah 9:9; 14:16–17. Walvoord states, "These verses demand a literal kingdom and a literal reign of Christ on earth."[424]

Thy people shall be willing in the day of thy power. Believers will rally *willingly* around Jesus in acknowledgement of His messiahship and rule (See Psalm 110:3) and priestly role after the order of Melchizedek (See Psalm 110:4). Alexander Maclaren says, "'The day of Thy power' is not a mere synonym for 'the time of Thy might,' but means specifically 'the day of Thine army,' that is, 'the day when Thou dost muster Thy forces and set them in array for the war.'"[425] During the interval between Christ's first and second coming, His people will volunteer ("shall be willing") to *fight* for His holy cause that His kingdom might be established on earth "as it is in heaven." This they will do in all holiness ("beauties of holiness"). See 1 Peter 1:15–16. The phrase often is used for the sacerdotal garments, the holy attire of God's priests in times of festivity or celebration.[426] With their conqueror, Jesus the High Priest, Christians (He "hath made us kings and priests" [Revelation 1:6]) will wear garments of holiness (figuratively) as they follow His commandments and serve His cause. They will be *separated* from the heathen in conduct. See 2 Corinthians 6:17.

Alexander Maclaren states, "The King is going forth to conquest. But He goes not alone. Behind Him come His faithful followers, all pressing on with willing hearts and high courage. Then, to begin with, the warfare which He wages is one not confined to Him. Alone He offers the sacrifice by which He atones; but, as we shall see, we too are priests. He rules, and His servants rule with Him. But ere that time comes, they are to be joined with Him in the great warfare by which He wins the earth for Himself. 'As Captain of the Lord's host am I now come.' He wins no conquests for Himself; and now that He is exalted at God's right hand, He wins none by Himself. We have to do His work; we have to fight His battles as good soldiers of Jesus Christ. By power derived from Him, but wielded by ourselves; with courage inspired by Him, but filling our hearts; not as though He needed us, but inasmuch as He is pleased to use us, we have to wage warfare for and to please Him who hath chosen us to be soldiers. The Captain of our salvation sits at the right hand of God, expecting till His enemies be made His footstool. He has bidden us to keep the field and fight the fight. From His height He watches the conflict—nay, He is with us while we wage it."[427]

After the order of Melchizedek. As Melchizedek was both a priest and king and "without father, without mother, without descent, having neither beginning of days, nor end of life" (see Hebrews 7:3), so also would the Messiah be. Spurgeon remarked, "Our Lord Jesus, like Melchizedek, stands forth before us as a Priest of divine ordaining; not made a priest by fleshly birth, as the sons of Aaron: He mentions neither father, mother, nor descent as His right to the sacred office; He stands upon His personal merits, by Himself alone; as no man came before Him in his work, so none can follow after; His order begins and ends in His own person, and in Himself it is eternal, 'having neither beginning of days nor end of years.' The King Priest has been here and left His blessing upon the believing, and now He sits in glory in His complete character, atoning for us by the merit of His blood, and exercising all power on our behalf."[428] *And will not repent.* "It is done, and done for ever and ever; Jesus is sworn in to be the Priest of His people, and He must abide so even to the end, because His commission is sealed by the unchanging oath of the immutable Jehovah."[429] "What the context," writes Allan Harman, "in Psalm 110 and the New Testament application both assert is that the psalmist is writing about a Person who is both King and Priest, something that never occurred in the Old Testament. The Testaments also agree that the promised Son of David would not be a Levitical priest but one after the order of Melchizedek. Priesthood would be his, not by ancestry, but by divine oath."[430]

In the day of his wrath. The battle of Armageddon will take place at the second coming of Jesus. See Psalm 110:5–6; Zechariah 14:1–15; Hebrews 10:13 and Revelation 19:11–21. Williams says, "This [Psalm 110:5–6] refers to the final battle which the Messiah will lead against the kings of this planet who, according to the New Testament, are under the rule of Satan and his earthly representative, Antichrist (see 2 Thessalonians 2:1–12; Revelation 13)....Destroying their power, "He shall judge among the nations" (Psalm 110:6). In His wrath, corpses will fill the earth, and the heads of state will be put on the block."[431]

Therefore shall he lift up the head. Albert Barnes says, "Therefore shall He triumph, or be successful. The head falls when we are faint and exhausted, when we are disappointed and are ashamed, when we are conscious of guilt. It is lifted up in conscious rectitude, in success and triumph, in the exuberance of hope. The idea here is that the Messiah would be triumphant. He would achieve the victory over all his foes; He would pursue, without exhaustion, His flying enemies; and He would return from the conquest joyous, exulting, triumphant. All this is under the image of a victorious hero; all this will be accomplished in the conquest of the world by the Gospel, in the subduing of the foes of God, in the final scene when the Redeemer shall deliver up the kingdom to God."[432]

The Bottom Line: Here in the midst of the Psalter, God provides hope both to the nation of Israel and His people of all time in promising the "establishment of the Messiah's (Jesus') rule over the nations and the final triumph of His kingdom. It is this hope that kept Israel facing the future with faith. It is this hope that began its fulfillment on a starlit night in Bethlehem. It is this hope that will take us through the trials and sufferings of our present life, as we look to our reigning, priestly King who will return in glory. All other hopes pale before Him."[433] Even so, come, Lord Jesus!

12. The First Thing Is to Get Wisdom   Psalm 111:10

"The fear of the LORD is the beginning of wisdom: a good understanding have all they that do his commandments: his praise endureth for ever."—Psalm 111:10.

The "fear of the Lord" (Barnes says "reverence for God; respect for His law, His will, His government, Himself; the fear of offending Him, which will lead us to do right."[434] Criswell says, "The 'fear' enjoined upon the wise in this psalm is not a shrinking, quaking effort to flee away. A sense of the awesomeness of God, as seen in His holiness, transcendence, and omniscience, and as viewed in the context of man's finiteness and moral degeneracy, creates an astonishment and a humble appreciation for God's mercies."[435]).

Is the "beginning" (Brown, Driver and Briggs say "beginning, chief."[436] Swanson says "what is first, the beginning, i.e., the initiation of an action, process, or state of being."[437] Plumer says *"beginning*, the same as the first word in the book of Genesis, also rendered *first, first fruits, chief, chiefest*. There is no wisdom in men till they fear God. When they do fear God, that is the wisest thing they do."[438]) "of wisdom" (Allen says, "'[W]isdom' is the ordering of life in accord with Yahweh's moral will, as interpreted by the Israelite tradition of wisdom teaching. And there is a great incentive for such a lifestyle: the secrets of a satisfying life are opened only to the willing practitioner of God's rulings [Matthew 7:24–27]."[439] Vine, Unger and White say "wise; skillful; practical;...a mastery of the art of living in accordance with God's expectations."[440]).

A "good understanding" (Swanson says "discretion, prudence, i.e., the capacity to understand and as a result act in accordance to a standard."[441] Plumer says, "The word rendered understanding is also rendered wisdom [Proverbs 12:8; 23:9.]"[442]) have all they "that do his commandments" (Spurgeon says, "Practical godliness is the test of wisdom. Men may know and be very orthodox, they may talk and be very eloquent, they may speculate and be very profound; but the best proof

68

of their intelligence must be found in their actually doing the will of the Lord."[443]).

"His praise" (Swanson says "adoration, thanksgiving, i.e., speak positive words about the excellence of another [2 Chronicles 20:22; Psalm 22:26]; note: often these words are in the context of being sung."[444]) "endureth forever" (Thomas says "perpetuity:—continually, eternal, forever, forevermore."[445] Allen says, "Doing and praising were ever to be the dual response to the revelation of what Yahweh had done, which was celebrated afresh at each of Israel's festivals."[446]).

Homily

J. A. Alexander states, "There is nothing in the psalm itself to determine its date or its historical occasion."[447] The most probable conjecture is that David penned it.

Psalm 111:10 sounds much like Proverbs 1:7. Throughout Proverbs, wisdom is presented as a spiritual quality, not secular or worldly. It's only source of acquisition is in a personal relationship with God made possible through Jesus Christ, His Son. "The fear of the LORD is the beginning of knowledge (wisdom)" (Proverbs 1:7). The placement of trust and allegiance in Jesus Christ is foundational to wisdom's possession. Wisdom's work primarily has to do with the development of character. It's fountainhead is God who through Holy Scripture instills in the heart the core governing principles of life, granting knowledge in their application in day-to-day life and challenges, that one may have happiness and success both in the spiritual and physical realm. Wisdom is "the skill of living in a way that honors God."[448] Wisdom is the imparting from God to man of the understanding or discernment to know the right and most prudent thing to do in any given situation in life. "Wisdom consists in two things: choosing a right end, and using right means to obtain it."[449] And only God enables both. Charles Simeon remarks, "Here he not only identifies the fear of the Lord with wisdom, but carries on the comparison from the beginning to the end, from the first formation of them in the soul to their final completion in Glory."[450]

Calvin said, "They are usually deemed wise who look well to their own interests, who can pursue a temporizing policy, who have the acuteness and artifice of preserving the favorable opinion of the world, and who even practice deception upon others. But even were I to grant that this character belongs to them, *yet is their wisdom unprofitable and perverse*, because true wisdom manifests itself in the observance of the law."[451]

Wisdom is important to acquire, for it clarifies right from wrong, truth from falsities, better from best, the pleasing in God's sight from the woeful, and the expedient from the less important. Wisdom benefits life with happiness, success, safety, confidence, peace, contentment, and added days (Proverbs 3:16–26).

In a nutshell, wisdom helps us make right choices. One of the greatest, if not the greatest, qualities of life is wisdom. Proverbs 19:8 says, "The one who acquires wisdom loves himself" (NET). In other words, if you really love yourself, help yourself out: Get Wisdom! It's not elusive but readily available upon diligent search (Proverbs 8:17). Wisdom is a lifelong pursuit that is completely possessed only in Heaven.

The fear of the Lord. The foundation to "wisdom" is the exhibition of holy awe and reverence toward the Lord and submissive obedience to Him as Lord and Savior. Tholuck said, "The fear of the Lord is the starting point of all true wisdom: any inquiry respecting things celestial or things terrestrial, if conducted in the fear of the Lord, is sure to lead to the right way; but it is no less the true source of the real wisdom of life."[452] George Horne wrote, "The 'fear of God' is the first step to salvation, as it exciteth a sinner to depart from evil, and to do good; to implore pardon, and to sue for [pursue] grace; to apply to a Saviour for the one, and to a Sanctifier for the other."[453] W. H. Alexander said, "They who evince this fear by doing His commandments give practical evidence of their wisdom, or good understanding; or the latter clause may be rendered as in the margin—*Good success, or prosperity*, have all they that do His commandments. The last word is not in the Hebrew, but is supplied by the sense and a reference to verse 7."[454] Oswald Chambers stated, "The remarkable thing about God is that when you fear God, you fear nothing else; whereas, if you do not fear God, you fear everything else."[455]

> There is no true wisdom where this fear is not; for without this fear, a man views nothing aright and does nothing aright.
> Charles Simeon

Charles Simeon wrote, "There is no true wisdom where this fear is not; for without this fear, a man views nothing aright and does nothing aright. Earthly things have in his eyes an importance which does not properly belong to them, and heavenly things are in no respect appreciated according to their real worth. But when 'God has put His fear into our hearts,' our misconceptions are removed, and our mistakes rectified."[456]

The Bottom Line: Matthew Henry said, "Men can never begin to be wise till they begin to fear God; all true wisdom takes its rise from true religion [truth as revealed by God] and has its foundation in it."[457] See Proverbs 4:7. He that possesses wisdom not only honors the Lord with his conduct but with his worship ("his praise endureth forever"). See Job 28:28; Proverbs 1:7; 9:10; 15:33.

13. Benefits of the Righteous   Psalm 112:1–9

"Praise ye the LORD. Blessed is the man that feareth the LORD, that delighteth greatly in his commandments. His seed shall be mighty upon earth: the generation of the upright shall be blessed. Wealth and riches shall be in his house: and his righteousness endureth for ever. Unto the upright there ariseth light in the darkness: he is gracious, and full of compassion, and righteous. A good man sheweth favour, and lendeth: he will guide his affairs with discretion. Surely he shall not be moved for ever: the righteous shall be in everlasting remembrance. He shall not be afraid of evil tidings: his heart is fixed, trusting in the LORD. His heart is established, he shall not be afraid, until he see his desire upon his enemies. He hath dispersed, he hath given to the poor; his righteousness endureth for ever; his horn shall be exalted with honour."—Psalm 112:1–9.

Praise ye the Lord. "Blessed" (happy) is the man that "feareth the Lord" (Swanson says "reverence, fear, i.e., pertaining to respect toward a superior."[458] It denotes reverential awe toward God and a heart that seeks to keep His commandments.) "that delighteth greatly"(Swanson says "desire, want, i.e., have a feeling or attitude to experience or possess an object; delight, take pleasure in, be eager, i.e., have a fondness or affection for an object or experience; be willing, i.e., to do something not by force, implying a voluntary choice."[459]).

71

"In his commandments" (Gesenius and Tregelles say "a command, a precept [2 Kings 18:36]; especially used of the precepts of God."[460] Hengstenberg says, "True obedience can only come from pleasure in the commandments of God."[461] Spurgeon says, "This man not only studies the divine precepts and endeavors to observe them, but rejoices to do so: holiness is his happiness; devotion is his delight; truth is his treasure."[462]).

"His seed shall be mighty upon earth" (Barnes says "his children; his posterity. That is, they shall be prospered; honored; distinguished among people: distinguished for their virtues, for their influence, for their success in life."[463] Henry says, "Blessings are laid up for the faithful and their children's children; and true riches are bestowed on them, with as much of this world's possessions as is profitable for them."[464]) "the generation of the upright shall be blessed" (Rawlinson says "i.e., shall receive blessing from the Most High, and shall therefore prosper. To be blessed in one's seed was, under the old covenant, the highest of blessings."[465]).

"Wealth and riches shall be in his house" (Jamieson-Fausset-Brown say, "Temporal blessings follow the service of God, exceptions occurring only as they are seen by God to be inconsistent with those spiritual blessings which are better."[466]).

AND "his righteousness endureth forever" (Spurgeon says, "Often when gold comes in, the Gospel goes out; but it is not so with the blessed person. Prosperity does not destroy holiness of life or humility of heart. The godly character stands the test of examination, overcomes the temptations of wealth, survives the assaults of slander, outlives the afflictions of time, and endures the trial of the last great day. The righteousness of a true saint endureth forever, because it springs from the same root as the righteousness of God and is indeed the reflection of it."[467] Barnes says, "That is, the effects of it shall be transmitted from age to age in the prosperity, the respectability, the wealth, the happiness of his descendants. It travels on from age to age, and blesses distant generations."[468]).

"Unto the upright there ariseth light in the darkness" (Benson says, "Although he may be subject to many of the troubles and calamities of life, as others are, yet they will be far from making him unhappy, for God will give him all the needful support and comfort in the midst of them, sanctifying them to him, and causing them, in many ways, to work together for his good, and in due time will grant him a happy issue out of them; whereas the wicked sink under their burdens, and their present miseries usher in their eternal destruction."[469]).

"He is gracious" (Benson says "the good or upright man, of whom he speaks both in the foregoing and following words. He exercises meekness, sweetness, and gentleness to those that provoke him; forgives offences, pities the instruments of his trouble, and shows mercy to persons in want and misery; while he acts justly and righteously toward all and will not be prevailed upon by any temptation to do anything dishonest, cruel, or unkind."[470]).

AND "full of compassion" (Swanson says "merciful, favorable, i.e., pertaining to showing favor, and not punishment as is often deserved, implying a forgiving relationship"[471]). AND "righteous" (Vine, Unger and White say "to be righteous, be in the right, be justified, be just"[472]). "A good man sheweth favor" (Vine, Unger and White say "to be gracious, considerate; to show favor; to favor someone."[473] To demonstrate kindness toward another—this is what Christ has done toward us, enabling our forgiveness and salvation.).

AND "lendeth" (Swanson says "i.e., to give money or goods...with the express intention of being paid back an equivalent or greater amount."[474] Barnes says, "It means that a good man will accommodate another—a neighbor—with money or with articles to be used temporarily and returned again. A man who always 'borrows' is not a desirable neighbor; but a man who never lends—who is never willing to accommodate—is a neighbor that no one would wish to live near, a crooked, perverse, bad man."[475]) "he will guide his affairs" (i.e., his business, conduct) "with discretion" (Barnes says "'judgment'; so the Hebrew. He would do it prudently, sensibly, economically, wisely"[476]).

"Surely he shall not be moved forever" (Rawlinson says, "God's blessing shall abide with him and make his happiness sure and stable."[477] Spurgeon says, "God has rooted and established him so that neither men nor devils will sweep him from his place. His prosperity will be permanent, and not like that of the gambler and the cheat, whose gains are evanescent; his reputation will be bright and lustrous from year to year, for it is not a mere pretense; his home will be permanent, and he will not need to wander from place to place as a bird that wanders from her nest; and even his memory will be abiding, for a good person is not soon forgotten."[478]).

"The righteous shall be in everlasting remembrance" (Poole says "shall be in everlasting remembrance, though whilst he lives he may be exposed to the censures and slanders and contradictions of sinners; yet after death his memory will be precious and honorable, both with God and with all men, his very enemies not excepted"[479]).

"He shall not be afraid of evil tidings" (Henry says, "It is the duty and interest of the people of God not to be afraid of evil tidings, not to be afraid of hearing bad news; and, when they do, not to be put into confusion by it and into an amazing expectation of worse and worse, but whatever happens, whatever threatens, to be able to say, with blessed Paul, *None of these things move me,* neither will *I fear, though the earth be removed,* [Acts 20:24]."[480] See Psalm 46:2.) "his heart is fixed" (Vine, Unger and White say "to be established, be readied, be prepared, be certain....Used abstractly, can refer to a concept as 'established,' or 'fixed' so as to be unchanging and unchangeable."[481]) "trusting in the Lord" (Gesenius and Tregelles say "to confide in any one, to set one's hope and confidence upon any one"[482]).

"His heart is established" (Barnes says, "Sustained; upheld....The word means to sustain; to support; and the idea is, that there is some basis of support—some strength—which is not his own."[483]) "he shall not be afraid" (Spurgeon says, "He is ready to face any adversary—a holy heart gives a brave face."[484]).

"Until he see his desire upon his enemies" (Poole says, "And although his enemies be many, and mighty, and terrible, yet he shall confidently and cheerfully wait upon God, until he see their ruin and his own deliverance and safety."[485] Barnes says, "This implies that he had nothing really to fear. He would certainly overcome his foes; and in the meantime he might look calmly on all their efforts to destroy him, for those efforts would be vain. So the believer now looks calmly on all his spiritual foes. He has nothing to fear, for he will overcome them all; he will certainly triumph; he will trample them all under his feet. He may well, therefore, endure these conflicts for a brief period, for the issue is certain, and the conflict will soon come to an end."[486]).

"He hath dispersed, he hath given to the poor" (Spurgeon says, "What he received, he distributed, and distributed to those who most needed it. He was God's reservoir, and forth from his abundance flowed streams of liberality to supply the needy."[487] Rawlinson says, "The only laudable 'dispersing' is that which has for its object the relief of distress, and which (it may be added) is wisely directed to that object."[488]).

"His righteousness endureth forever" (Poole says, "His charity [liberality] is not a transient or occasional act, but his constant course, of which he is not weary, but perseveres in it to the end of his life."[489] Barnes says, "His acts of charity are constant. His piety is not fitful, spasmodic, uncertain; it is steady principle; it is firm and solid; it may always be relied on."[490]).

"His horn shall be exalted with honor" (Poole says, "Though he may be reproached by ungodly men, yet his innocence shall be cleared, and his name and honor gloriously exalted."[491] Spurgeon says, "God will honor him, and even the wicked will feel an unconscious reverence of him. Let it be observed, in summing up the qualities of the God-fearing man, that he is described not merely as righteous, but as one bearing the character to which Paul refers as 'a good man.' Kindness, benevolence, and generosity are essential to the perfect character; to be strictly just is not good enough, for God is love, and we must act upon those same principles of grace which reign in the heart of God. The promises of prosperity are to souls who have proved their fitness to be stewards of the Lord by the right way in which they use their substance."[492]).

Homily

A Psalm of David, according to its title. The ending thought of Psalm 111 is expanded in Psalm 112 by stating seven benefits of the godly ("the man that feareth the LORD"). J. A. Alexander writes, "This formal agreement shows the intimate connection of the two compositions, and makes it highly probable that they belong not only to the same age but to the same author and were meant to form parts of one continued series or system."[493] Matthew Poole states, "This Psalm containeth a description of a good man's gracious disposition and carriage; as also of his blessed condition, even in this life as well as in the next."[494]

His seed shall be mighty upon the earth. See Psalm 112:2. The posterity (children) of the righteous will be richly blessed. Spurgeon says, "If the promise must be regarded as alluding to natural descendants, it must be understood as a general statement rather than a promise made to every individual, for the children of the godly are not all prosperous, nor all famous. Nevertheless, he who fears God and leads a holy life is, as a rule, doing the best he can for the future advancement of his house; no inheritance is equal to that of an unblemished name, no legacy can excel the benediction of a saint; and, taking matters for all in all, the children of the righteous man commence life with greater advantage than others, and are more likely to succeed in it, in the best and highest sense."[495] W. S. Plumer wrote, "The seed of the godly are valiant for the truth, for righteousness, for the glory of the Redeemer. Their influence is felt far and wide."[496]

Wealth and riches shall be in his house. See Psalm 112:3. The upright shall be prosperous, if not in gold, then certainly in grace (spiritual riches in Christ Jesus), which is the far better. Albert Barnes explains, "The two terms are used apparently to convey the idea that wealth or property in 'varied forms' would be in his house, that is, not merely gold and silver, but all that was understood to constitute wealth—variety of garments, articles of furniture, etc....*It pertains to a general truth* in regard to the influence of religion in promoting prosperity."[497] "Bishop Butler has well shown how, in God's moral government of the world, virtue [godliness, uprightness] tends to accumulate to itself the good things of this life, and vice to disperse and dissipate them."[498] Spurgeon remarked, "If we understand the passage spiritually, it is abundantly true. What wealth can equal that of the love of God? What riches can rival a contented heart? It matters nothing that the roof is thatched and the floor is of cold stone; the heart which is cheered with the favor of Heaven is 'rich to all the intents of bliss.'"[499] W. S. Plumer writes, "If any choose to refer the terms of this clause to the true riches and make them designate the infinite blessings of salvation, the sense is good, and the doctrine true. This view is favored by the next clause: And his righteousness endureth for ever."[500]

Unto the upright. W. S. Plumer says, "Those, who fear God, in their measure resemble Him. They have not omnipotence, omniscience, omnipresence, self-existence, independence, eternity, unchangeableness, nor any perfections in infinitude; but in their measure they are like Him in holiness, justice, goodness, mercy, truth and faithfulness."[501]

There ariseth light in the darkness. See Psalm 112:4. "Light is the emblem and sum of all good, as darkness is of all evil."[502] The rain falls upon the just as it does upon the unjust (raindrops of sickness, bereavement, suffering and trouble). Though not immune to similar adversities of the unbeliever, the Christian is assured that God will be with him in the midst of the storm to comfort, encourage and deliver. Albert Barnes wrote, "The peculiarity in regard to those who fear God is that these things will not always continue, that they shall not be overwhelmed by them, that it will not be uninterrupted and unmitigated gloom, that the sky shall not be always overcast."[503] What you trusted God for in the "light," don't doubt in the "dark." Ellicott says, "The Hebrew verb ["ariseth"] is commonly used of the sunrise [see Psalm 97:11; Isaiah 58:8]. For the good man the darkest night of trouble and sorrow will have a dawn of hope."[504]

Shall be in everlasting remembrance. See Psalm 112:6. John Gill says, "The righteous shall be in everlasting remembrance, with good men, and especially such whose names are recorded in Scripture; and even others are remembered after death, and for a long time after, their pious characters, sayings, actions, sufferings, works, and writings; and with God, who remembers His love to them, His covenant with them, His promises to them, has a book of remembrance for their thoughts, words, and actions, which will be remembered and spoken of at the last day, when forgotten by them."[505] J. A. Alexander wrote, "As long as he shall be remembered, he shall be remembered as a righteous man."[506] Solomon states that "the name of the wicked shall rot" (Proverbs 10:7). Man wants to forget the names of Hitler, Benedict Arnold, Mengistu Haile Mariam, Mao Zedong and Joseph Stalin. But there is interest in remembering the names (lives and works) of Billy Graham, D. L. Moody, C. H. Spurgeon, Henry Martyn and David Brainerd.

W. L. Watkinson wrote, "We think that when a man dies he has done with the world, and that the world has done with him. That view, however, needs revision. There is much about a man that cannot be put into a coffin....We cannot properly speak of the immortality of bad influence, yet that influence spreads and persists to a distressing extent. But we can speak confidently about the immortality of the influence of the good. Abel being dead yet speaketh; we are not told that Cain does. It is a reassuring thing to know that the good which men do is not buried with their bones. Not only do remarkable saints influence posterity beneficially; all saints do so, although it may be in a less degree. We find it easy to believe that the men influence posterity whose deeds are emblazoned in history, whose books are in the libraries, whose monuments are in the minster; but we are slow to believe in the posthumous life of the obscure and unknown. Yet *the immortality of influence* is just as true in regard to the humble as to the illustrious....The rolling pebble, the falling leaf, and the rippling water of...years ago left their sign in the rocks."[507] Just so, the Psalmist states, will it be regarding all the righteous, regardless of position or fame.

Surely he shall not be moved forever. J. A. Alexander said, "He shall not be moved from his prosperous condition, or from his position as a righteous man."[508] Morison wrote, "He shall not perish with ungodly men, nor shall he be deprived of the favor of his God."[509]

He shall not be afraid of bad news. See Psalm 112:7. William MacDonald says, "He doesn't have to live in constant fear of bad news, of business reverses, of natural calamities."[510] W. A. Alexander wrote, "The common version (*he shall not be afraid of evil tidings*) seems to confine the negation to the mere apprehension or anticipation of bad news, whereas the original expression comprehends, and indeed more properly denotes, being frightened when the evil tidings are heard."[511] The man whose heart is "fixed, trusting the Lord" has confidence that nothing can touch him that does not first pass through the hands of God. He knows that even in the darkest of days he stands beneath the umbrella of God's unfailing love and care. "There is no fear in love; but perfect love casteth out fear: because fear hath torment. He that feareth is not made perfect in love" (1 John 4:18). Spurgeon stated, "Christian, you ought not to dread the arrival of evil tidings; because if you are distressed by them, what do you more than other men? Other men have not your God to fly to; they have never proved His faithfulness as you have done, and it is no wonder if they are bowed down with alarm and cowed with fear. But you profess to be of another spirit; you have been begotten again unto a lively hope, and your heart lives in Heaven and not on earthly things. Now, if you are seen to be distracted as other men, what is the value of that grace which you profess to have received? Where is the dignity of that new nature which you claim to possess?"[512]

His heart is established. See Psalm 112:8. "A fixed heart is the negation both of fickleness and cowardice."[513] He is constantly sustained by the sovereign hand of Almighty God. Lockyer says, "He is no rolling stone, but firmly settled by experience and confirmed by years. Consequently, along with his holy heart, he has a brave face. He has no fear what men or demons may do."[514] John Gill says "with the doctrine of grace, which is food unto it, and by which it is strengthened and nourished. It is established in the faith of Christ, both in the grace of faith, and in the doctrine of faith, even in all the doctrines of the Gospel; so that he is not as a child, tossed to and fro with every wind. His heart is established in the exercise of grace, and he is steadfast and immovable in the discharge of duty."[515]

He shall not be afraid until. J. A. Alexander says, "*Until* does not imply that he shall then fear, but that there will then be no occasion so to do."[516] *He hath dispersed, he hath given to the poor.* See Psalm 112:9. Ross states, "He receives goodness in return for being generous (Psalm 112: 9) and just (Psalm 112:5)."[517] *His horn shall be exalted with honor.* See Psalm 112:9. Ross says, "'his horn will be lifted up,' that is, he will be made strong and honorable by the LORD."[518] The righteous (as herein depicted) will be honored by all men. Paul quotes this verse in 2 Corinthians 9:9 to emphaticize the temporal and eternal benefit of generosity.

The service of Jesus true pleasure affords;
    In Him there is joy without an alloy.
'Tis Heaven to trust Him and rest on His words;
    It pays to serve Jesus each day.

It pays to serve Jesus; it pays every day;
    It pays every step of the way.
Though the pathway to glory may sometimes be drear,
    You'll be happy each step of the way. ~ Frank C. Huston (1909)

The Bottom Line: The man that *fears the Lord* (the righteous, upright, saved) enjoys benefits beyond measure presently and eternally. He is more than a conqueror through Jesus Christ his Lord. See Romans 8:37. Such a man possess an immortality of influence.

14. The Incomparable Christ   Psalm 113:4–5

"The LORD is high above all nations, and his glory above the heavens. Who is like unto the LORD our God, who dwelleth on high."— Psalm 113:4–5.

The Lord is "high above all nations" (Bowling says "be high, lofty; rise up."[519] Benson says "superior to all princes and bodies of people in the world."[520] Rawlinson says "as being the great King over all the earth."[521] Jehovah is King not only of the United States but "all nations." See Psalm 47:2 and Psalm 99:2).

AND "his glory above the heavens" (The splendor, honor, magnificence of God. Poole says, "Whereas the glory of earthly monarchs is confined to this lower world and to small pittances of it, the glory of God doth not only fill the earth, but Heaven too, where it is celebrated by thousands and myriads of blessed angels; yea, it is far higher than Heaven, being infinite and incomprehensible."[522]).

"Who is like unto the Lord our God" (The Psalmist, in light of the awesomeness of God, asks a rhetorical question. "Who on earth and in the heavens is comparable to the Lord Jesus Christ?" The answer obviously is no one. Clarke says, "Those who are highly exalted are generally unapproachable; they are proud and overbearing or so surrounded with magnificence and flatterers that to them the poor have no access; but God, though infinitely exalted, humbleth Himself to behold even Heaven itself, and much more does He humble Himself when He condescends to behold earth and her inhabitants [Psalm 113:6]. But so does He love His creatures that He rejoices over even the meanest of them to do them good."[523]).

"Who dwelleth" (Strong says "to sit down; to dwell, to remain; cause to settle, abiding, continue, habitation."[524] God is enthroned on His permanent seat as sovereign King of the world.) "on high" (Gesenius and

Tregelles say "to be exalted, elevated to a greater degree of dignity and honor"[525]).

Homily

The Psalm, according to Adam Clarke, was probably composed following the Israelites' return from captivity.[526] Hengstenberg also favors that view. Its author is unknown. Psalms 113–118 are thanksgiving hymns sung by the Jews on solemn festive occasions, especially the Passover.[527] It is most probable that one or more of them was the hymn the disciples sang following the Last Supper. See Matthew 26:30 and Mark 14:26. Martin Luther wrote, "This is a most conspicuous and most blessed prophecy of the kingdom of Christ, and of its extension from the rising unto the setting of the sun throughout all the kingdoms of the earth."[528] L. C. Allen states, "In the *NT* the Magnificat (Luke 1:46–55) is the Psalm's counterpart; it too was inspired by Hannah's song. Yahweh is celebrated as the heavenly King who looks down in sympathy on human suffering and rejection and brings about surprising reversal."[529]

It is said that when Leonardo da Vinci was about to paint Christ's face in his *fresco* ["the art of painting on freshly spread moist lime plaster with water-based pigments"—*Merriam-Webster*] of the Last Supper that he spent time in meditation and prayer. Nonetheless, when he picked up the brush to paint, his hand trembled. This exposition and homily for Psalm 113 certainly has prompted my "hand to tremble" and my heart to quiver. It is holy ground, and I feel inadequate to even touch the hem of its garment in seeking to describe the incomparable Christ.

The Lord is high above all nations, and his glory above the heavens. See Psalm 113:4. "The two clauses are declaratory of His infinite superiority, both to the animate and inanimate creation, each being represented by its noblest part: the former by mankind, and that considered not as individuals but nations; the latter by the heavens."[530]

Who is like the Lord our God. See Psalm 113:5. All the kings of every nation, both past, present and yet to reign, together do not even touch the hem of His garment in comparison. John Gill well states, "Among the gods of the nations...or among the angels of Heaven or among any of the mighty monarchs on earth, there is none like Him for the perfections of His nature; for His wisdom, power, truth, and faithfulness; for His holiness, justice, goodness, grace, and mercy, who is eternal, unchangeable, omnipotent, omniscient, and omnipresent; nor for the works of His hands, His works of creation, providence, and grace. None ever did the like, and what makes this reflection the more delightful to truly good men is that this God is their God; and all this is true of our Immanuel, God with us, who is God over all and the only Savior and Redeemer; and there is none in Heaven and earth like Him or to be desired beside Him."[531] "He occupies His eternity with the intimate knowledge and practical government of each nation, province, family, individual soul. To the Infinite One nothing can be too small for His regard."[532]

Who dwelleth on high. J. A. Alexander states, "The verb denotes not merely *dwelling*, but *sitting enthroned*, sitting as a king."[533] J. J. S. Perowne says, "It denotes not merely the omniscience of God, but His greatness and His condescension."[534]

He is *the incomparable one*. The Lord Jesus Christ is incomparable in His virgin birth; virtuous (sinless) life; and vicarious death at Calvary to secure man's salvation over the power and penalty of sin, death and Satan; victorious resurrection three days following His crucifixion; and in His soon visible return for His "church." He is incomparable in His closeness, compassion, care, comfort and counsel to His followers. He is our Immanuel, "God with us." He is incomparable in His provision, protection and pardon to believers. Jesus Christ is incomparable in might, mercy, miracles and ministry. He is incomparable in His divine attributes.

He is *Omnipotent*. He is all-powerful. Spurgeon stated, "He is Himself the great central source and originator of all power."

He is *Omniscient*. He is all-knowing.

He is *Omnipresent*. He is present everywhere at the same time.

He is *immutable*. He remains ever the same. "Jesus Christ the same yesterday, and today, and forever." See Hebrews 13:8.

He is *love*. Jesus loves man and desires him to be saved. See John 3:16.

God is *holy* and *righteous,* incapable of doing wrong or failing to do as He declares. See Isaiah 6:3.

God is *merciful,* ever ready to forgive the sinner, reconciling him unto Himself. See 2 Corinthians 5:18–19 and Ephesians 2:4.

He is *creator, owner* and *sustainer* of all that exists. See Colossians 1:16–17.

He raiseth up the poor out of the dust and lifteth the needy out of the dunghill. See Psalm 113:7. J. A. Alexander states, "The mention of God's seeing far below Him suggests the idea of His condescension to the humblest objects which He thus beholds....Dust and dunghill [are] common figures in all languages for a degraded social state."[535] See Lamentations 4:5 and Psalm 7:5. L. C. Allen says, "The NT treats the grace of God in similar vein: God "chose what is weak,...low and despised in the world" (1 Corinthians 1:27–29 NRSV), and it is "the poor, the crippled, the blind, and the lame" who get invited to the heavenly banquet (Luke 14:15–24 NRSV). Likewise, the theme of vv. 4–9b finds a remarkable correspondence in God's raising and seating the church in a status parallel to the mighty acts wrought on behalf of the Son (Ephesians 1:19–2:7)."[536] The Christian, like his Lord and Master, is to invite the "the poor, the maimed (crippled), the lame, the blind" to their parties (Luke 14:12–14)."[537]

To answer the Psalmist's rhetorical question, there absolutely is no person or idol that compares with our God. Rawlinson says it best: "The highest created being does not approach within anything but an immeasurable distance of God."[538] Spurgeon agrees, saying, "None can be compared with Him for an instant; Israel's God is without parallel; our own God in covenant stands alone, and none can be likened unto Him."[539] Matthew Henry stated, "He is exalted above all blessing and praise, not only all ours, but all theirs. We must therefore say, with holy admiration, *Who is like unto the Lord our God?* who of all the princes and potentates of the earth? who of all the bright and blessed spirits above? None can equal Him; none dare compare with Him. God is to be praised as transcendently, incomparably, and infinitely great; for He dwells on high, and from on high sees all, and rules all, and justly attracts all praise to Himself."[540] Christ alone is therefore worthy of our acceptance, adoration and allegiance. *From the rising of the sun unto the going down of the same the Lord's name is to be praised.* See Psalm 113:3. Jennings and Lowe wrote " i.e., from East to West: throughout the world."[541]

Praise to the Lord, the Almighty, the King of creation!
O my soul, praise Him, for He is thy health and salvation!
    All ye who hear,
    Now to His temple draw near;
Sing now in glad adoration!

Praise to the Lord, who o'er all things so wondrously reigneth,
Who, as on wings of an eagle, uplifteth, sustaineth.
    Hast thou not seen
    How thy desires all have been
Granted in what He ordaineth?

Praise to the Lord, who hath fearfully, wondrously, made thee!
Health hath vouchsafed and, when heedlessly falling, hath stayed thee.
    What need or grief
    Ever hath failed of relief?
Wings of His mercy did shade thee. ~ Joachim Neander (1650–1680)

Praise ye the Lord, praise, O ye servants of the Lord, praise the name of the Lord. Calvin remarked, "Can there be anything more base than for us to magnify God's name but seldom and tardily, considering it ought to fill our thoughts with enrapturing admiration?"[542] In light of who God is, our lips ought to continuously render adoration unto Him regardless of circumstance. Morison said, "He who made the universe, and who sustains it in being, with all its innumerable tribes, is entitled to govern it, and claims this prerogative as His exclusive and inalienable right. He made all, He provides for all, He upholds all, He governs all; and therefore, let all unite in celebrating His glorious praise."[543] It is fitting that this Psalm, like Psalms 115–117, closes with a Hallelujah ("Praise ye the Lord").[544]

The Bottom Line: John Wesley said, "Bring me a worm that can comprehend a man, and then I will show you a man that can comprehend the Triune God."[545] God's greatness is unsearchable. A. W. Pink wrote, "Happy the soul that has been awed by a view of God's majesty."[546] See Psalm 93:1.

15. It Took a Miracle   Psalm 114

"When Israel went out of Egypt, the house of Jacob from a people of strange language; Judah was his sanctuary, and Israel his dominion. The sea saw it, and fled: Jordan was driven back. The mountains skipped like rams, and the little hills like lambs. What ailed thee, O thou sea, that thou fleddest? thou Jordan, that thou wast driven back? Ye mountains, that ye skipped like rams; and ye little hills, like lambs? Tremble, thou earth, at the presence of the Lord, at the presence of the God of Jacob; Which turned the rock into a standing water, the flint into a fountain of waters."—Psalm 114.

When "Israel went out of Egypt" (The Exodus.) "the house of Jacob" (Barnes says, 'The family of Jacob - a name appropriately used here, since it was the family of Jacob that had gone down into Egypt, and that had increased to these great numbers.'[547]) from a "people of strange language" (The Israelites were not able to understand the language of the Egyptians. See Genesis 42:23.). "Judah was his sanctuary" (Ross says, 'Judah became His sanctuary, which meant that Judah became the tribe in which He placed the temple.'[548] Poole says, 'Judah he mentions as the chief of all the tribes, not only in number and power, but also in dignity, in which the kingdom was to be seated, Genesis 49:10, as at this time it actually was, and from which the Messiah was to spring.'[549]).

AND "Israel his dominion" (Williams says, "Along with God's presence, Israel is unique because she is His 'dominion' or kingdom. God is King and the chosen people are His subjects where His rule and reign will be displayed."[550]). "The sea saw it, and fled" (Rawlinson says, "'The sea' is the Red Sea. It 'looked,' and saw God leading his people [Exodus 14:19–24], and then at once 'fled,' and left a dry channel as 'a way for the ransomed to passover.'"[551]).

"Jordan was driven back" (Benson says, "Although forty years intervened between the two events here mentioned, yet, as the miracles were of the same nature, they are spoken of together."[552] It refers to the dividing of the waters at the Jordan River to permit the Israelites to cross over into the Promised Land. See Joshua 3:13–17. Dilday and Kennedy say, "Apparently the crossing of the Red Sea (sea) and the crossing of the

'Jordan' (v. 3) were fused into one thought. Both events were dramatic responses of the physical creation to the act of God."[553]).

"The mountains skipped like rams, and the little hills like lambs" (Kirkpatrick says "a poetical description of the earthquake which accompanied the giving of the Law at Sinai [Exodus 19:18]."[554] The Plain Commentary says, "At the giving of the law at Sinai, Horeb and the mountains around, both great and small, shook with a sudden and mighty earthquake, like rams leaping in a grassy plain, with the young sheep frisking round them."[555]).

"What ailed thee, O thou sea, that thou fleddest? thou Jordan, that thou wast driven back?" (Barnes says, "That is, what influenced thee—what alarmed thee—what put thee into such fear and caused such consternation? Instead of stating the cause or reason why they were thus thrown into dismay, the Psalmist uses the language of surprise, as if these inanimate objects had been smitten with sudden terror, and as if it were proper to ask an explanation from themselves in regard to conduct that seemed so strange."[556]).

"Ye mountains, that ye skipped like rams; and ye little hills, like lambs?" (Spurgeon says, "What ailed ye, that ye were thus moved? There is but one reply: the majesty of God made you to leap. A gracious mind will chide human nature for its strange insensibility, when the sea and the river, the mountains and the hills, are all sensitive to the presence of God. Man is endowed with reason and intelligence, and yet he sees unmoved that which the material creation beholds with fear. God has come nearer to us than ever he did to Sinai, or to Jordan, for he has assumed our nature, and yet the mass of mankind are neither driven back from their sins nor moved in the paths of obedience."[557]).

"Tremble, thou earth, at the presence of the Lord, at the presence of the God of Jacob" (Rawlinson says, "The answer [to the question posed in Psalm 114:5] is given, but only indirectly given, in these words. Nothing less than 'the presence of the Lord—a miraculous and abnormal presence—can have produced the strange phenomena. The earth has felt the presence of God and has trembled, and has done right to tremble; but Israel may take comfort from the theophany, for it is a manifestation on her behalf. The presence that has made itself felt is the presence of the God of Jacob—the God who watches over Jacob and will succor and protect him constantly.'[558]).

"Which turned the rock into a standing water, the flint into a fountain of waters" (Delitzsch says "the flint into a fountain of waters. The causing of water to gush forth out of the flinty rock is a practical proof of unlimited omnipotence and of the grace which converts death into life. Let the earth then tremble before the Lord, the God of Jacob. It has already trembled before him, and before him let it tremble. For that which He has been He still ever is; and as He came once, He will come again."[559] The Psalmist refers to the rock Moses smote at Sinai that burst forth waters for the people to drink. See Exodus 17:6 and Numbers 20:11.).

Homily

Psalm 114 is one of the "finest lyrics in literature."[560] Historically it belongs to the period of the Israelites' Exodus from Egypt (captivity). Adam Clarke wrote, "As to the author of this Psalm, there have been various opinions: some have given the honor of it to Shadrach, Meshach, and Abed-nego; others, to Esther; and others, to Mordecai."[561] Drake says, "The exodus of Israel from Egypt, with some of its most remarkable accompanying and consequent miracles, are, in this brief Psalm, commemorated in the boldest style of poetry, with personifications, indeed, of inanimate nature of the utmost daring and sublimity."[562]

Spurgeon wrote that "This sublime SONG OF THE EXODUS is one and indivisible. True poetry has here reached its climax: no human mind has ever been able to equal, much less to excel, the grandeur of this Psalm. God is spoken of as leading forth His people from Egypt to Canaan, and causing the whole earth to be moved at His coming. Things inanimate are represented as imitating the actions of living creatures when the Lord passes by. They are apostrophized [accosted] and questioned with marvelous force of language, till one seems to look upon the actual scene. The God of Jacob is exalted as having command over river, sea, and mountain, and causing all nature to pay homage and tribute before his glorious majesty."[563] Poetically it details the miracles of God wrought during the Israelites' Exodus from Egyptian captivity at the Red Sea, Sinai (the rock) and at the Jordan River.

God caused nature to operate *strangely*—the Red Sea parting, forming walls of water to give the people a way of escape from the hands of Pharaoh; the rock at Mt. Horeb (Sinai) supplying water for the people to drink; and the Jordan River's rapid torrent reversed to go uphill to grant passage to the Israelites into the Promised Land. God utilized nature (His creation) working abnormally to facilitate Israel's deliverance. Poetically the Psalmist speaks of God's miraculous acts in nature in the salvation of the Israelites. The commotion in nature ("Ye mountains, that ye skipped [danced] like rams and ye little hills, like lambs.") surrounding their deliverance we are informed was caused by the presence of God. See Psalm 114:7. "The author of this Psalm designedly works for effect in pointing out the miraculous driving back the Red Sea and the river Jordan, and the commotion of the hills and mountains, without mentioning any agent. At last, when the reader sees the sea rapidly retiring from the shore, Jordan retreating to its source, and the mountains and hills running away like a flock of affrighted sheep, that the passage of the Israelites might be everywhere uninterrupted, then the cause of all is suddenly introduced, and the presence of God in His grandeur solves every difficulty."[564]

The Psalm presents a vivid picture of the sinner's deliverance from bondage in Egypt. He experiences liberty from the cruel taskmaster Satan; the chains and shackles of habitual sin; misery, despair and meaninglessness and "Egypt" (the world). See Psalm 107:14; Psalm 116:8 and John 15:19. The rescue or deliverance is secured by miracles (even as that of the Israelites was). It involves the miracle wrought by God at Calvary and the Empty Tomb in making provision for the deliverance. See Isaiah 53:5; Ephesians 1:7; 1 Peter 1:3 and 3:18. It takes the miracle of intervention over the powers of darkness (even as God had to change Pharaoh's mind to let the Israelites leave Egypt). See Acts 26:18. It takes the miracle of the New Birth. See John 3:3. The soul becomes the "dominion" of God. And it results in the miracle of a changed life forever. See 2 Corinthians 5:17. "The rocklike heart, so hard and barren and lifeless, becomes transformed as into a standing water, a very fountain of waters (John 7:37, 38)."[565] The new believer's life, like the Jordan River, is turned back from its natural course (repentance) in a complete opposite direction. That's a miracle! See Acts 20:21.

It took a miracle to put the stars in place;
It took a miracle to hang the world in space;
    But when He saved my soul,
    Cleansed and made me whole,
It took a miracle of love and grace! ~ John W. Peterson (1921-2006)

The Bottom Line: In salvation's conversion that which is *impossible* miraculously happens in an instant. In the Exodus that which had never happened occurred: the Red Sea parted; water flowed from the rock and the Jordan flowed backward uphill (not to mention that which has to do with the manna and quail, etc.). The point is that God loves the world so much that He will go to the furthest length, using even the most unexpected and miraculous means to awaken man to the need of deliverance from sin, and bring about divine reconciliation so that through Christ he might be saved. As there was a commotion in nature at the miraculous deliverance of the Israelites, just so there is an inner commotion within man at salvation. When God shows up, that's what happens.

16. The Greatest Thievery Is to Rob God of His Glory   Psalm 115:1

"Not unto us, O LORD, not unto us, but unto thy name give glory, for thy mercy, and for thy truth's sake."—Psalm 115:1.

"Not unto us, O Lord, not unto us" (Benson says, "By the repetition of these words the Psalmist humbly expresses his sense of the unworthiness of the Jews to receive the signal blessings with which the Lord had favored them, or rather, which they were now entreating Him to bestow upon them and which they expected to receive."[566]).

BUT "unto thy name give glory" (Landers says "reputation, importance; glory, splendor, distinction, honor."[567]) "for thy mercy" (Vine, Unger and White say "loving-kindness; steadfast love; grace; mercy; faithfulness; goodness; devotion."[568] The goodness of God in the time of trouble.[569]).

AND "for thy truth's sake" (Swanson says "faithfulness, reliability, trustworthiness, i.e., a state or condition of being dependable and loyal to a person or standard."[570]).

Homily

The author for Psalm 115 is unknown. It appears to be composed during a time of grave difficulty for the Israelites. See Psalm 115:9–14. Spurgeon thinks it was sung at the Passover and therefore relates to the Exodus (Israel's deliverance from Egypt).[571] Surprisingly, the subject of idolatry was not mentioned in the psalter before Psalm 96:5, and this is only the fifth mention of it. Based upon this J. M. Boice says, "This infrequency may indicate that Psalm 115 was written after the Jews' return from the Babylonian captivity, where they would have been able to witness the idol worship of the Babylonians firsthand."[572] Allan Harman agrees, saying it was written to contrast the worship of the supreme God with the worthless idols of the Gentiles.[573] Its historical occasion is simple speculation.

The Psalm is a plea unto God to vindicate His name, to hush the malicious, contemptuous and scorning sneers of the "heathen" ("people, nation; pagan peoples [as opposed to Israel]"[574]), specifically the idolaters in this case (see Psalm 115:4–8), by performance of great *wonders* as of old (perhaps as in the Exodus [Psalm 114 and Psalm 115:1–3]). If God does not intervene in divine favor (mercy, goodness) to help, the "heathen's" sneer and scorn of Him will only increase and bring dishonor to His holy name (reputation, glory, majesty). Though unworthy and underserving of the least of His favors, the Psalmist prays that for the sake of His name, mercy and truth, He would act. See Psalm 115:1. "The people undoubtedly wished for relief from the contemptuous insults of idolaters, but their main desire was that Jehovah Himself should no longer be the object of heathen insults. The saddest part of all their trouble was that their God was no longer feared and dreaded by their adversaries."[575] Sadly, such is the case presently in America. Pray that the "fear of the Lord" will be rekindled in the souls of evil men by whatever means necessary.

They that make them [idols] *are like unto them*. See Psalm 115:8. Charles Simeon states, "Great as is the stupidity of fallen man, one would not have imagined that it should ever enter into his mind to worship the works of his own hands. To come before those which cannot see and address ourselves to those that cannot answer and offer sacrifices to those who can smell no sweet savor from them, and to rely on those which have no operative or locomotive powers—all this seems to be a degree of infatuation beyond what one would conceive a creature possessed of reason should labor under. But so it is. There are millions of such persons who are, in fact, as senseless as the objects they worship. But there is one who is able either to save or to destroy, even Jehovah, 'who dwelleth in the heavens, and doth whatsoever pleaseth him.'"[576] *O Israel, trust in the LORD*. See Psalm 115:9. Not once or twice but three times is Israel instructed to trust in the Lord and not in idols made of human hands. See Psalm 115:9–11. "Why? Because he is our true 'help and shield.' The idols offer nothing; they are utterly impotent, as has just been described. [See Psalm 115:4–8.] By contrast, God lifts the down-trodden, helps us in our weakness, and shields us from our foes."[577]

The Lord has been mindful of us. See Psalm 115:12. Without exception, He has been minful of all of us. "To whom of those who ever trusted in him", wrote Charles Simeon, "has he not been both 'a help and a shield?' Whom has he not protected from innumerable dangers, and assisted in times of difficulty? Can any one doubt but that he would have long since perished from the assaults of sin and Satan, if God had not been with him to preserve and uphold him? But it is not *in time only* that God has been mindful of us: *from all eternity* has His eye been fixed upon us, and His infinite wisdom been occupied in our behalf. Long before we were in existence or the foundations of the earth were laid did He make provision for our happiness. He foresaw that we should fall, and he entered into covenant with His own Son to redeem us. He engaged also His Holy Spirit, to execute within us all the purposes of His love. Say, is not this a sufficient ground for trusting in Him? What greater encourage-ment can we have?"[578]

Idols once they won thee, charmed thee,
    Lovely things of time and sense;
Gilded thus does sin disarm thee,
    Honeyed lest thou turn thee thence.

What has stripped the seeming beauty
    From the idols of the earth?
Not a sense of right or duty,
    But the sight of peerless worth.

Not the crushing of those idols,
> With its bitter void and smart;

But the beaming of His beauty,
> The unveiling of His heart. ~ Ora Rowan (1834–1879)

The dead praise not the Lord. See Psalm 115:17. Adam Clarke comments, "Those dead men who worshipped as gods dumb idols, dying in their sins, worship not Jehovah; nor can any of those who go down into silence praise thee: earth is the place in which to praise the Lord for His mercies and get a preparation for His glory."[579] A. F. Kirkpatrick states, "The dead raise no Hallelujahs; they are cut off from communion with God and from the power of rendering Him service of lip and life. For this gloomy view of the state of the dead (Psalm 6:5; Psalm 30:9; Psalm 88:4–5, 10–12; Isaiah 38:11, 18)."[580] Spurgeon elucidates, "The dead do not praise the Lord, so far as this world is concerned. They cannot unite in the psalms and hymns and spiritual songs with which the church delights to adore her Lord. The preacher cannot magnify the Lord from his coffin, nor the Christian worker further manifest the power of divine grace by daily activity while he lies in the grave—neither any that go down into silence. The tomb sends forth no voice; from moldering bones and flesh-consuming worms there arises no sound of Gospel ministry nor of gracious song. One by one the singers in the consecrated choir of saints steal away from us, and we miss their music. Thank God, *they have gone above to swell the harmonies of the skies*, but as far as we are concerned, we have need to sing all the more earnestly because so many songsters have left our choirs."[581] And, I add, preachers left our churches.

Not unto us, O Lord, not unto us, but unto thy name give glory. See Psalm 115:1. Matthew Henry wrote, "Boasting is here forever excluded. Let no opinion of our own merits have any room either in our prayers or in our praises, but let both center in God's glory. Have we received any mercy, gone through any service, or gained any success? We must not assume the glory of it to ourselves, but ascribe it wholly to God....Say not, *The power of my hand has gotten me this wealth*, Deuteronomy 8:17. Say not, *For my righteousness the Lord has done these great and kind things for me*, Deuteronomy 9:4. No; all our songs must be sung to this humble tune, *Not unto us, O Lord!* and again, *Not unto us, but to thy name* let all the glory be given; for whatever good is wrought in us or wrought for us, it is for His mercy and His truth's sake, because He will glorify His mercy and fulfil His promise. All our crowns must be cast at the feet of Him that sits upon the throne, for that is the proper place for them."[582]

Not unto us, O Lord of Heav'n,
But unto Your Name be glory given;
In love and truth, Lord, You fulfil
The counsels of Your sovereign will.
Though nations fail Your pow'r to own,
Yet, Lord, You reign, and You alone. ~ Original Trinity Hymnal, #68

Spurgeon said in commemoration of his twenty-fifth anniversary as pastor of the Metroplolitan Tabernacle, "Whatever of acceptable service we have rendered and whatever of real success we have achieved has come from the Lord of hosts who has worked all our works in us. Whatever holy results may have followed from earnest efforts and whatever honor has redounded unto God from them is the Lord's doings and it is marvelous in our eyes. 'Not unto us, not unto us, O Lord, but unto Your name be glory for Your mercy and for Your truth's sake.' *Your goodness, not ours, has crowned the work.* Your goodness, indeed, makes every good work good and gives to every good its crown. From its first conception, even to its ultimate conclusion, all virtue is of You. From blade to full corn, all the harvest is of You, O Lord, and to You let it be ascribed. Let us, therefore, praise the Lord with all our hearts for twenty-five years of prayer and effort, of planning and working, of believing and rejoicing which He has crowned with His goodness."[583] "Thou crownest the year with thy goodness" (Psalm 65:11).

Boasting or bragging about spiritual accomplishments or successes, giftedness, academic achievement, position or personal ability or attraction, outside of being deceitfully arrogant and sinful is nauseating and despicable to God and man. See Psalm 52:1. Never have I encountered as many "conceited" young ministers as in this generation. See 2 Timothy 3:2. Watchman Nee wrote, "Many may boast in the depth of their Bible knowledge and in the excellency of their theological tenets, but those with spiritual discernment are aware that it is dead."[584] Pray that the haughty will be "brought down" (Luke 1:52) so as to hearken unto James' admonition to "humble yourselves in the presence of the Lord, and He will exalt you" (James 4:10 NASB). See Micah 6:8; 1 Peter 5:6a. John Maxwell says, "There are two kinds of pride, both good and bad. 'Good pride' represents our dignity and self-respect. 'Bad pride' is the deadly sin of superiority that reeks of conceit and arrogance."[585]

Guard thine heart from becoming like Jehu who, although he possessed some great virtues, was guilty of the sin of boastfulness. He says to Jehonadab "Come with me, and see my zeal for the LORD" (2 Kings 10:16). Jehu certainly is an Old Testament picture of the New Testament Pharisees who loved to showcase and parade their religious deeds by sounding the trumpet to bring attention to what they did. See Matthew 6:2, 5. It is wrong to "report" or make known church growth, converts won or personal accomplishments "to be seen of men" (Matthew 23:5). "Numbering" is a slippery slope that all leaders must tread cautiously upon lest it become mere *boasting* or reek with that smell. Intentional or not, we must do due diligence to assure that our reporting is not perceived as bragging, which robs the "glory and honor" from the Lord. Don't be a Jehu that says, "Come with me, and see my zeal for the LORD." See 1 Peter 5:5. Spurgeon said, "You are not mature if you have a high esteem of yourself. He who boasts in himself is but a babe in Christ, if indeed he be in Christ at all. Young Christians may think much of themselves. Growing Christians think themselves nothing. Mature Christians know that they are less than nothing. The more holy we are, the more we mourn our infirmities, and the humbler is our estimate of ourselves."[586]

Forbid it, Lord, that I should boast,
Save in the death of Christ, my God!
All the vain things that charm me most,
I sacrifice them through His blood. ~ Isaac Watts (1707)

Boastfulness is a sin that God judges severely. He will not share His glory with any man. See Isaiah 42:8. King David was "provoked" by Satan to number the people in order to boast of his great army. See 1 Chronicles 21:1. David's captain of the guard, Joab, opposed the numbering but obeyed. See 1 Chronicles 21:2–4. "And God was displeased with this thing; therefore he smote Israel" (1 Chronicles 21:7). David pleads with the Lord to withhold punishment upon the nation since it was his sin. "Is it not I that commanded the people to be numbered? even I it is that have sinned and done evil" (1 Chronicles 21:17). David acknowledged the grave sin committed against the glory of God.

Oswald Chambers wrote, "We have a tendency to look for wonder in our experience, and we mistake heroic actions for real heroes. It's one thing to go through a crisis grandly, yet quite another to go through every day glorifying God when there is no witness, no limelight, and no one paying even the remotest attention to us. If we are not looking for halos, we at least want something that will make people say, 'What a wonderful man of prayer he is!' or, 'What a great woman of devotion she is!' If you are properly devoted to the Lord Jesus, you have reached the lofty height where no one would ever notice you personally. All that is noticed is the power of God coming through you all the time."[587]

The Bottom Line: Many religious leaders and ministers are modern day "Jehu's." Arrogance and conceit, though nauseatingly apparent to others, is unseen to him that flaunts it. Spurgeon says, "Grace puts its hand on the boasting mouth, and shuts it once for all."[588] Clay Smith well said, "When image matters most, others matter least."[589]

17. Precious Is the Death of the Saints   Psalm 116:15

"Precious in the sight of the LORD is the death of his saints."— Psalm 116:15.

"Precious" (Gesenius and Tregelles say "dear, honored, magnificent, splendid."[590] Rawlinson says, "It is not a matter of indifference to God, when and under what circumstances each of his saints dies. Rather, it is a matter of deep concern to Him."[591] Jennings and Lowe say, "'*Weighty*,' i.e., it is no light matter to Jehovah that His pious worshippers perish."[592]) in the "sight of the Lord" (In life or death the born-again ones remain precious in his eyes. See Romans 14:8.) is the "death of his saints" (Swanson says "the godly, i.e., the ones faithful to God as a group."[593] Kirkpatrick says, "His beloved, or his godly ones."[594]).

Homily

The Psalm's date and authorship are uncertain, but it appears to have been written after Absalom's rebellion.[595] Adam Clarke wrote,

"Many think it relates wholly to the passion, death, and triumph of Christ. Most of the Fathers were of this opinion." [596] Fry is of the same opinion and argues for it from 2 Corinthians 4:10–14, where v. 10 is quoted.[597]

Death is not a matter of unconcern to God for either the saint who dies or their loved ones who remain. A. C. Dixon wrote, "As we see death, it means decay, removal, absence—things which we do not prize. But as God sees death, He beholds something really precious to Him and, we may justly infer, precious to us, for whatever is against us cannot be precious to our Father. We are looking at the wrong side of the tapestry, where all is tangle and confusion. God sees the right side, where the design is intelligent and the colours harmonious. We are without the veil and see but the dim light through the curtain; within is the Shechinah glory. We stand in the dark, believing and hoping; God is in the light, seeing and knowing."[598]

Precious in the sight of the LORD is the death of his saints (Psalms 116:15). He calls the death of a saint precious. "His saints"—those engraved upon the palms of His hands, endeared to His heart and fully justified by Calvary's blood. Certainly this strange epithet of death is not easy for us to grasp when it has snatched our loved one. Martin Luther renders this: "The death of his saints is held to be of value before the Lord."[599] Albert Barnes writes, "The idea here is that the death of saints is an object of value, that God regards it as of importance, that it is connected with His great plans, and that there are great purposes to be accomplished by it. The idea here seems to be that the death of a good man is in itself of so much importance, and so connected with the glory of God and the accomplishment of His purposes, that He will not cause it to take place except in circumstances, at times, and in a manner which will best secure those ends."[600] J. A. Alexander states, "God counts the death of His people too costly to be lightly or gratuitously suffered."[601] Spurgeon says the Lord "views the triumphant deaths of His gracious ones with sacred delight. If we have walked before Him in the land of the living, we need not fear to die before Him when the hour of our departure is at hand."[602] W. S. Plumer remarks, "He who gives grace to His chosen to live to His glory will not deny them grace to die in his peace."[603]

In earlier burial instructions, "Precious in the sight of the Lord is the death of his saints" with other verses was to be chanted.[604] The practice is worthy to imitate. Why is a saint's death precious in the sight of the Lord? It is precious due to its freeing power from suffering, sorrow, and sickness. Those who die in the Lord sing, "Free at last, free at last—praise God Almighty, I am free at last." It is precious in that it removes the saint from the present evil on earth and that which is yet to come. It is precious in that it puts on display the comforting grace of God as a witness to the world of how God sustains His children in the severest trial of sorrow, granting peace and solace. The death of a saint is precious in the sight of the Lord in that it means he/she is now with Him in Heaven. It is also precious in the fact that it may be the means of conversion of family and friends. Spurgeon states the Psalmist's declaration is truthful "because it [the death of a saint] is a precious sheep folded, a precious sheaf harvested, a precious vessel which had been long at sea brought into harbor, a precious child which had been long at school to finish his training brought home to dwell in the Father's house forever. God the Father sees the fruit of His eternal love at last ingathered; Jesus sees the purchase of His passion at last secured; the Holy Spirit sees the object of His continual workmanship at last perfected."[605]

However, the death of the unbeliever is not 'precious in His sight,' because he is eternally banished from God in the domain of Hell. See Revelation 20:15. Heaven is the eternal dwelling place of God reserved exclusively for the redeemed (the "born-again" ones). All are invited and welcome to enter this celestial city upon God's terms, which must be met prior to death. See John 3:3; John 10:9 and John 14:6.

Matthew Poole points out a second lesson from the text. "He sets a high price upon it [the life of the saint]; He will not readily grant it to those that greedily seek it; and if any son of violence procure it, He will make him pay very dearly for it; and when the saints suffer it [death] for God's sake, as they frequently do, it is a most acceptable sacrifice to God and highly esteemed by Him. Thus the blood of God's people is said to be precious in His sight [Psalms 72:14]."[606]

For thou hast delivered my soul from death, mine eyes from tears, and my feet from falling. See Psalm 116:8. David certainly had experienced jeopardy of life (hands of Saul), tears of bitterness and pain and physical and moral failure. But he states the Lord was gracious to deliver from them all. Charles Simeon states, "And are we at this time free from any great affliction? Surely we have reason to be thankful for it, for how numberless are the sources of grief from whence our whole souls may speedily be overwhelmed! In our own persons we are exposed to diseases and accidents every moment. In our relative connections too, how many occasions of sorrow are ever ready to arise! The misconduct of one, the unkindness of another, the misfortunes of a third, the death of one that was to us as our own souls—alas! alas! It is a vale of tears that we are passing through, moaning or bemoaned every hour. Our very pleasures not unfrequently become occasions of the bitterest pains. If then we have been kept for any time in a good measure of peaceful serenity, we may well account it a rich blessing for which we are bound to adore and magnify our God."[607]

He goes on to state, "Through His atoning blood you may look forward to death and judgment with far other eyes than they can be viewed by the ungodly world. You may regard death as the commencement of life and the very gate of Heaven. Only take care, therefore, that in your experience it be 'Christ to live,' and then you shall assuredly [know] that it will 'be gain to die.'"[608] See Philippians 1:21.

The Bottom Line: Whedon says, "The 'death of [God's] saints' is distinguished from death as the common lot of man, in the eyes of God, by rare excellence and honor, not physically, but morally considered. If there is any meaning in language, here is proof of a future life and of future rewards and punishments."[609] J. J. S. Perowne states, "PRECIOUS... IS THE DEATH, i.e., it is no light thing in the sight of God that His servants should perish. The more obvious form of expression occurs [in] Psalm 72:14: 'Precious is their blood in His eyes.'"[610] The death of the saint is counted precious—God so values their life that "God's servants are immortal, till their work is done." "No weapon that is formed against thee shall prosper" (Isaiah 54:17). See Zechariah 2:8.

18. A Missionary Call to Go to the Nations   Psalm 117

"O praise the Lord, all ye nations: praise him, all ye people. For his merciful kindness is great toward us: and the truth of the Lord endureth for ever. Praise ye the Lord."—Psalm 117.

"O praise the Lord" (Swanson says "cheer, brag on, extol, i.e., extol the greatness or excellence of a person, be praised, be worthy of praise, boast in, praise, glory in, i.e., express words of excellence, with a focus on the confidence one has in the object, person."[611] Ronald Allen says, "Praise is a choice, not a feeling. We are not to praise the Lord only when we feel warm and fuzzy inside. We are to praise Him even in our most troubled moments. For even during those times, He is still our God."[612]).

"All ye nations" (Clarke says, "Let all the Gentiles praise him, for He provides for their eternal salvation."[613] Lockyer says, "*Nations* consistently implies Gentile nations."[614] See Deuteronomy 32:43 and Luke 2:32). "Praise him, all ye people" (Clarke says, "All ye Jews, praise Him; for ye have long been His peculiar people. And while He sends His Son to be a light to the Gentiles, He sends Him also to be the glory of His people Israel.'[615]).

For His "merciful kindness" (Vine, Unger and White say "loving-kindness; steadfast love; grace; mercy; faithfulness; goodness; devotion."[616]) "is great" (Gesenius and Tregelles say "to show oneself strong." It will prevail.[617] Lockyer says "higher than we deserve."[618]) toward us: AND the "truth of the Lord" (Swanson says "faithfulness, reliability, trustworthiness, i.e., a state or condition of being dependable and loyal."[619] Ross says, "Because the Lord's Word is reliable, He is faithful. This term strengthens the concept of His covenant loyalty."[620]).

"Endureth forever" (Swanson says "everlasting, forever, eternity, i.e., pertaining to an unlimited duration of time."[621] Man's efforts throughout history to destroy God's "truth" (the Bible, Written Word, and Jesus, Living Word) have met with frustration and failure and always shall, for it is permanent. This is certainly reason to sing hallelujahs unto the Lord.) Praise ye the Lord.).

Homily

We know nothing with regard to the authorship of the Psalm. It is the shortest Psalm in the psalter and shortest chapter in the Bible. Spurgeon states, "This Psalm, which is very little in its letter, is exceedingly large in its spirit....The same divine Spirit which expatiates in the 119th, here condenses His utterances into two short verses, but yet the same infinite fullness is present and perceptible."[622] Martin Luther, in *Selected Psalms III, Vol. 14,* devoted 18 pages on each verse. Derek Kidner summarized Psalm 117: "The shortest Psalm proves, in fact, to be one of the most potent and most seminal [formative, important]."[623] Jennings and Lowe state, "This short composition is remarkable only as expressing a clear conviction that the Gentile world is destined to join in the worship of Jehovah."[624] See Romans 15:11. Charles Simeon wrote, "The psalm is in reality a prophecy, and so important a prophecy that St. Paul expressly quotes one part of it and gives, as it were, an explanation of the remainder."[625] See Romans 15:8–9.

In a nutshell the unknown Psalmist extols the Gentiles to join with the Jews in *worship* of God. God is not just for the Hebrews. He is for *all* and is to be universally *praised by all.* W. S. Plumer comments, "The call is indiscriminate to the whole world to come and give due praise to Jehovah. This verse is explained by the great commission given by Christ to his ministers [Matthew 28:19, 20; Mark 16:15, 16]."[626] Spurgeon says, "This is an exhortation to the Gentiles to glorify Jehovah, and a clear proof that the Old Testament spirit differed widely from that narrow and contracted national bigotry with which the Jews of our Lord's day became so inverately [a habit long and firmly established by long persistence that is unlikely to change—*Merriam-Webster*] diseased. The nations could not be expected to join in the praise of Jehovah unless they were also to be partakers of the benefits which Israel enjoyed; and hence the Psalm was an intimation to Israel that the grace and mercy of their God were not to be confined to one nation, but would in happier days be extended to all the race of man, even as Moses had prophesied when he said, 'Rejoice, O ye nations, his people."[627] See Deuteronomy 32:43.

Matthew Henry elucidates, "The sons of Levi and the seed of Israel praised Him, but the rest of the nations praised gods of wood and stone (Daniel 5:4), while there was no devotion at all paid, at least none openly, that we know of, to the living and true God. But here all nations are called to praise the Lord, which could not be applied to the Old-Testament times, both because this call was not then given to any of the Gentile nations, much less to all, in a language they understood, and because, unless the people of the land became Jews and were circumcised, they were not admitted to praise God with them."[628]

"And are not we ourselves evidences of its truth [the calling of the Gentiles to salvation]? Are not we Gentiles? and has not God's mercy reached unto us? Are not His promises also fulfilled to us? The promise to Abraham was that 'in him, and in his seed, should all the nations of the earth be blessed,' and this promise was made to him whilst he was yet uncircumcised in order that the interest which we uncircumcised Gentiles had in it might be more fully manifest. Behold then, we are living witnesses both of God's mercy and truth! His promises are fulfilled to us, yea, and are yet daily fulfilling before our eyes."[629]

From all that dwell below the skies
Let the Creator's praise arise;
Let the Redeemer's name be sung
Through every land, by every tongue.

Eternal are Thy mercies, Lord;
Eternal truth attends Thy word.
Thy praise shall sound from shore to shore
Till suns shall rise and set no more. ~ Isaac Watts (1719)

But here, the "gospel" is commanded to be preached to all "peoples." It was not just for the Jews or those compelled to practice Judaism. All are to be invited, though not all will accept. The "partition wall" must be torn asunder, opening the passage for every people group to enter, regardless of creed, culture or confession. Paul wrote, "God himself revealed his mysterious plan to me. And this is God's plan: Both Gentiles and Jews who believe the Good News share equally in the riches inherited by God's children. Both are part of the same body, and both enjoy the promise of blessings because they belong to Christ Jesus" (Ephesians 3:3, 6 NLT). The message of the Gospel, being sent to every people group in the world, would give them the opportunity equally to experience the unfailing kindness and mercy of God through Jesus Christ in salvation. And such tidings would generate "praise" among them. Paul quotes the text as validation for the Gospel to be preached to the Gentiles. See Romans 15:11.

Albert Barnes writes, "This doctrine [truth], however, was not fully made known until the coming of the Redeemer. The announcement of this was made by the Redeemer himself (Matthew 8:11; 12:21; 28:19); it was the occasion of no small part of the trouble which the Apostle Paul had with his countrymen (Acts 13:46; 18:6; 21:21; 22:21; 26:20, 23); it was one of the doctrines which Paul especially endeavored to establish as a great truth of Christianity, *that all the barriers between the nations were to be broken down and the Gospel proclaimed to all people alike*, Romans 3:29; 9:24, 30; 11:11; 15:9–11, 16, 18; Galatians 2:2; Ephesians 2:11–18; 3:1–9."[630]

Untold millions yet are untold. The IMB (International Mission Board of the Southern Baptist Convention) estimates that there are 11,741 people groups in the world. *People Group* is defined as "an ethno-linguistic group with a common self-identity that is shared by the various members."[631] Of these, 7,027 are *Unreached People Groups* (UPG— groups that are less than two percent evangelical Christian, that do not have indigenous believers who can carry the Gospel to the rest of their group). UPG's total 4.3 billion people, or 58.1 percent of the world's population. *Unengaged Unreached People Groups* (UUPG) number 3,179. These are those which have no access to the Gospel or church planting strategy. The population of the UUPG's are 220 million people.[632] It is God's desire that all unreached people groups of the world (consisting of over four billion people) not only hear about Him but worship Him through a personal relationship with Jesus Christ. John Piper says, "Missions is calling the world to do what they were created to do, namely, to enjoy making much of Christ forever."[633] And this is every Christian's job.

Christian persecution is horrific in certain regions. In Eritrea (East Africa), persecution of believers is twofold. The dictatorial regime routinely imprisons believers for conspiracy with the West. In North Korea believers are victimized severely in prison or labor camps where the worst of conditions exist. Christians in Pakistan also endure great persecution for their faith and conduct, due to the country's unjust blasphemy law. Likewise countries that embrace Buddhism, Islam and ethnic culture exact severe punishment upon the Christian church.[634] Pray for the persecuted church around the world and for wise spiritual laborers to be raised up in their midst or sent to render help in the mission of reaching the unreached for Christ.

We've a story to tell to the nations
    That shall turn their hearts to the right,
A story of truth and mercy,
    A story of peace and light,
    A story of peace and light.

For the darkness shall turn to dawning
    And the dawning to noonday bright;
And Christ's great kingdom shall come on earth,
    The kingdom of love and light. ~ H. Ernest Nichol (1862–1928)

C. E. Autrey wrote, "Why is the world blind? The world is blind because it has not faith in God. Why does it have no faith in God? It has no faith in God because it has not heard the Word of God. 'So then faith cometh by hearing, and hearing by the word of God' (Romans 10:17). The Word of God is the origin of faith, and by faith we have a definite, trans-forming experience with God, an experience which is spiritual. Much of the world is religious, but the religion consists largely of worshipping things and deified men."[635] How might the "darkness" turn to "dawning"? Through the proclaimation of the Word of God locally and globally, to which task the church is divinely charged. Autrey continued, "The church has the answer to the world's difficulties. Congress, Parliament, and the [White House] do not have the answer; therefore, the responsibility of the church is without parallel."[636] If the church fails to tell the Story to the nations, multitudes will die in sin only to be forever in Hell, separated from a loving God. Spurgeon candidly states, "If there be any one point in which the Christian church ought to keep its fervor at a white heat, it is concerning missions. If there be anything about which we cannot tolerate lukewarmness, it is in the matter of sending the Gospel to a dying world."[637] Faris Whitesell agrees: "The local church, then, is the keystone in the arch of evangelism. It must be spiritual, warm, friendly, full of good works and prayer, a radiating center of Christian influence ever influencing others for Christ and pointing the lost to the Lamb of God who taketh away the sin of the world."[638]

Are we stirred? "Now while Paul waited for them at Athens, *his spirit was stirred in him, when he saw the city wholly given to idolatry*" (Acts 17:16). Are you not *stirred* to go to the unreached people groups of the world with the Message that alone can set them free from their present despair and eternal doom, as Paul was "stirred" in Athens long ago? Then at once arise and go. Cease the delay. Time is fleeting. Opportunties are quickly passing. Doors are shutting.

If you had been to heathen lands,
Where weary ones with eager hands
Still plead, yet no one understands,
Would you go back? Would you?

If you had seen them in despair,
Beat on the breast and pull out the hair
While demon spirits filled the air,
Would you go back? Would you?

If you had seen the glorious sight
When heathen people, long in the night,
Are brought from darkness to the light,
Would you go back? Would you?

Yet still they wait, a weary throng;
They've waited, some, so very long.
When shall despair be turned to song?
I'm going back! Would you? ~ Eva Doerksen

> The Spirit of Christ is the spirit of missions, and the nearer we get to Him, the more intensely missionary we must become.
> Henry Martyn

Due to age, sickness or frailty perhaps you cannot go to the "regions beyond" as a vocational or volunteer missionary, but that which you can do you should do to assist those that can and do go. Assist financially. Encourage continuously. Pray fervently and steadfastly—"Ye also *helping* together by prayer for us" (2 Corinthians 1:11). All may be and should be missionaries in purse, prayer and person.

The Bottom Line: The Psalm is missionary in scope, exhorting believers to take the Gospel to all peoples of the world, bringing them to Christ that they may worship Him. John Piper is correct in stating, "Missions exist because worship doesn't."[639] Pray that Psalm 117 be fulfilled so that "all nations and peoples" will "Praise the LORD." It is then, and only then, that missionary efforts are no longer needed. See Matthew 9:38. Henry Martyn said, "The Spirit of Christ is the spirit of missions, and the nearer we get to Him, the more intensely missionary we must become."[640]

19. It's Best to Put Your Confidence in God   Psalm 118:8–9

"It is better to trust in the LORD than to put confidence in man. It is better to trust in the LORD than to put confidence in princes."—Psalm 118:8–9.

It is "better" (Swanson says "good, i.e., pertaining to the moral opposite of evil; pertaining to having good value."[641]) "to trust" (Gesenius and Tregelles say "properly TO FLEE, specially to take refuge, to flee somewhere for refuge, under the shadow (protection) of someone, under the shadow of the wings of God; hence to trust in someone, especially in God.'[642]).

In "the Lord" (Yahweh) "than to put confidence in man" (Swanson says "trust, rely on, put confidence in, i.e., believe in a person or object to the point of reliance upon."[643]). It is better to trust in the Lord than to "put confidence in princes" (Swanson says "leader, ruler, official, prince, i.e., one who is of great or noble status."[644]).

Homily

That David wrote this Psalm is attested by many. Patrick said, "There is nothing more probable than that David composed it."[645] Pool stated, "It most probably was composed by David."[646] Edwards said, "It is generally supposed to have been penned by David."[647] Matthew Henry wrote, "It is probable that David penned it."[648] Scott declared, "David is thought to have composed it."[649] Adam Clarke said, "Most probably David was the author of this Psalm, though many think it was done after the captivity. It partakes of David's spirit and everywhere shows the hand of a master. The style is grand and noble, the subject majestic."[650] It is Messianic in nature. Calvin states, "Let us remember that it was the design of the Spirit, under the figure of this temporal kingdom, to describe the eternal and spiritual kingdom of God's Son, even as David represented Christ."[651] Dodd said, "The learned Jews, both ancient and modern, confess it to speak of the Messiah."[652] Morison wrote, "It reaches forth in the spirit of prophecy to Messiah and to his spiritual kingdom."[653] A portion of the Psalm may have been incorporated in the hymn that Jesus and the disciples sang following the institution of the Lord's Supper. See Matthew 26:30.

The Israelites, upon their return from Captivity, began trusting in man (Cyrus, etc.) more than the Lord. See Ezra 1:4–6; 3:7. But this help proved futile and injurious. See Ezra 4:1–24. The Psalmist exhorts them to return to a trust in God.

These verses beckon man to place trust in God and not man (even the most influential, wealthy or prestigious) for peace, pardon, provision and protection. George Horne says, "Armies of men, however numerous and, to appearance, powerful may be routed and dispersed at once: princes may not be able to help us; if able, they may fail us, as not being willing to do it; if both able and willing, they may die ere they can execute their purpose. But that hope which is placed in God can never, by these or any other means, be disappointed."[654] Jamieson-Fausset-Brown said "Even the most powerful men are less to be trusted than God."[655]

It is better to trust in the Lord than to put confidence in man. W. S. Plumer states, "The same verses (Psalm 118:8–9) teach us that it is hard, though necessary, to withdraw trust from man. He is a poor, feeble, sinful worm. Though the wicked appear in great numbers, and enter into the most fearful alliances with one another, they are but grasshoppers."[656] Man is not always willing, available or able to help us. And some that do give help are "faithless" in doing so. Even the best of friends disappoint. Everyone needs to keep a big *cemetery* in his backyard to bury the faults and failures of his best friends! Plainly, there are issues in life in which man simply cannot grant help (emergency, crisis, death, sickness and suffering, sorrow, etc.) but none in which the Lord cannot. See 2 Chronicles 32:8. Additionally man's help at best ends at the grave, but God's will be commensurate with eternity. This is not to insinuate that all men are untrustworthy (for I personally bear proof some are dependable), just impotent to help in every need. The point of the text is that man ought to first look to Yahweh to supply his needs (spiritual, medical, emotional and material). See Psalm 20:7 and Jeremiah 17:5. Herbert

Lockyer said, "It is better in every way to trust in the Lord because He is wiser, seeing He is more able to help than the best of men, who are only frail men at the best."[657]

Stand up, stand up for Jesus!
    Stand in His strength alone.
The arm of flesh will fail you;
    Ye dare not trust your own. ~ George Duffield, Jr. (1858)

"Woe to them that go down to Egypt for help; and stay on horses, and trust in chariots, because they are many; and in horsemen, because they are very strong; but they look not unto the Holy One of Israel, neither seek the LORD" (Isaiah 31:1).

The Bottom Line: Spurgeon states, "Christians often look to man for help and counsel and mar the noble simplicity of their reliance upon their God....Is not God enough for thy need, or is His all-sufficiency too narrow for thy wants? Dost thou want another eye beside that of Him who sees every secret thing? Is His heart faint? Is His arm weary? If so, seek another God; but if He be infinite, omnipotent, faithful, true, and all-wise, why gaddest thou abroad so much to seek another confidence?"[658] "It is better," says Matthew Henry, "more wise, more comfortable, and more safe, there is more reason for it, and it will speed better, to trust in the Lord, than to put confidence in man, yea, though it be in princes. He that devotes himself to God's guidance and government, with an entire dependence upon God's wisdom, power, and goodness, has a better security to make him safe than if all the kings and potentates of the earth should undertake to protect him."[659]

20. Divine Chastening   Psalm 118:18

"The LORD hath chastened me sore: but he hath not given me over unto death."—Psalm 118:18.

The Lord hath "chastened me" (Swanson says "correct, discipline, i.e., punish in order to improve behavior, implying the training of the person."[660]) "sore" (severely). BUT He hath not "given me over to death" (Barnes says, "He had passed through great danger; he had been sorely afflicted; but he had been rescued and spared, and he came now to express his thanks to God for his recovery."[661]). Spurgeon selected Psalm 118:13–18 to be engraved upon a stone at the church's Jubliee House so all might understand the meaning of the house and its name. He stated the text was a truthful summary of his personal experience with regard to the faithfulness of God.

Homily

Most likely David composed the Psalm (Adam Clarke). William McDonald writes, "The occasion of this magnificent chorus of praise is the Second Coming of our Lord and Savior, Jesus Christ. The scene is Jerusalem where the crowds have gathered to celebrate the Advent of Israel's long-awaited Messiah."[662] Matthew Henry writes, "The account the Psalmist here gives of his troubles is very applicable to Christ: many hated Him without a cause; nay, the Lord Himself chastened Him sorely, bruised Him, and put Him to grief, that by His stripes we might be healed."[663] Martin Luther laid a personal claim to Psalm 118, saying he had "struck a very special relationship with the Psalm." He said, "This is my Psalm, my chosen Psalm. I love them all; I love all holy Scripture, which is my consolation and my life. But this Psalm is nearest my heart, and I have a peculiar right to call it mine. It has saved me from many a pressing danger, from which nor emperor, nor kings, nor sages, nor saints could have saved me. It is my friend; dearer to me than all the honors and power of the earth."[664] Using his own experience, David exhorts people to praise God for His mercy and deliverances.

Thou hast thrust sore at me. See Psalm 118:13. David's enemies were the means of his *severe* chastisement. The Lord's "rods" for exacting punishment are many and varied but all enveloped in love designed for our higher good. Spurgeon comments, "The Lord frequently appears to save His heaviest blows for His best-loved ones; if any one affliction be more painful than another it falls to the lot of those whom He most distinguishes in His service. The gardener prunes his best roses with most care. Chastisement is sent to keep successful saints humble, to make them tender towards others, and to enable them to bear the high honors which their heavenly Friend puts upon them."[665] Alexander Maclaren said, "Divine methods have one motive and one purpose, as the same motion of the earth brings summer and winter in turn. Since the desire of God is to make men partakers of His holiness, the root of chastisement is love, and hours of sorrow are not interruptions of the continuous favour which fills the life."[666] See Hebrews 12:10.

The Lord is my strength, and song, and is my salvation. See Psalm 118:14. Amidst the chastening the Lord was David's sure "strength" (God infused grace to bear it victoriously); and "song" (not necessarily in the chastening but certainly in its aftermath, for He puts a new song in the heart) and is "my salvation" (the Lord alone is responsible for his deliverance, for it was His right hand and strong arm that wrought it). Note, God is the subject of David's praise completely. Rawlinson says, "The deliverance was such that no words but those of the Song of Moses (Exodus 15:2) could fitly celebrate it."[667] John Gill states, "The Lord is the author and giver of strength, natural and spiritual; He is the "strength" of the hearts and lives of His people, and of their salvation; and therefore is their "song", the matter of it: they sing of His nature and perfections, of His works of providence and grace, of His righteousness and salvation."[668] David with joy is able to say following the chastening, "This is the day which the LORD hath made; we will rejoice and be glad in it" (Psalm 118:24). All will do likewise who submit to chastening, allowing it to purify, sanctify, detoxify, fortify and qualify (for one's post of service) to the end that Jesus is glorified.

> Submit to chastening, allowing it to purify, sanctify, detoxify, fortify and qualify (for one's post of service) to the end that Jesus is glorified.

For what specifically does the Lord correct (chastise)?

God chastises (corrects) *for stubbornness.* "You stubborn people! You are heathen at heart and deaf to the truth. Must you forever resist the Holy Spirit? That's what your ancestors did, and so do you!" (Acts 7:51 NLT). God longs to govern the whole of life, but the refusal to submit leaves Him no option but to exact loving strokes of discipline designed to prompt submission.

God chastises for negligence. The Lord corrects for neglect of the prayer closet (Psalm 27:8), Bible reading and study (Acts 17:11), church attendance (Hebrews 10:25), witnessing (Acts 1:8), keeping the heart with all diligence (Proverbs 4:23), worship (Psalm 95:6), rightful duty unto all men (Galatians 6:10) and charitable giving to kingdom work (Malachi 3:8).

God chastises for spiritual deafness or indifference. "But they refused to pay attention. They turned a cold shoulder and stopped listening" (Zechariah 7:11 CEB). To have the Lord speak through His sacred Word, sanctified conscience or holy saints, only to pay it no attention, spurs divine punishment.

God corrects for rebellion. King Saul is a prime example of rebellion in Scripture. See 1 Samuel 15:22–23. Rebellion is any act of opposition to the Lord's authority of rule or governorship of one's life. It is obstinate disobedience and refusal to bow in submission to God's plan. It is to 'grieve the Holy Spirit' (vex Him). See Ephesians 4:30.

God corrects for carnality or worldliness. Paul exhorted, "Be not conformed to this world" (Romans 12:2). John said, 'Love not the world, nor the things that are in the world, for if any man loves the world—the love of the Father is not in Him' (1 John 2:15). See James 4:4. It has been said that "we are called to be world changers, not world chasers." Philip Yancey correctly said, "All too often the church holds up a mirror reflecting back the society around it, rather than a window revealing a different way."[669]

Additionally *God chastises the saint for improper or immoral conduct and thoughts*. See Matthew 5:8 and Matthew 5:28.

Spurgeon said, "His chastening is the most severe with those whom He loves best: 'Whom the Lord tenderly loves He chastens, and scourges every son whom He receives.' Some of us know what it is to have this teaching by chastening. I have often told you that I am afraid I have never learned anything of God except by the rod; and, in looking back, I am afraid that I must confirm that statement. I have forgotten some of the gentle lessons; but when they have been whipped into me, I have remembered them."[670]

How are we to respond to chastening? W. A. Criswell gives the answer: "God sees and knows, and He is a loving Father who yearns over His children. These are the corrective disciplinary judgments of God by which He prepares us to be true sons of holiness, and if we belong to the household of faith we shall know His correction and discipline. Even our Lord, as this author writes in the fifth chapter of his book, 'though a Son, yet learned He obedience by the things which He suffered' (Hebrews 5:8). We are not to remonstrate [protest, complain] against God or to be displeased with God, much less lose faith in our Lord. We are to look to the ultimate end of the sorrow, of the affliction, of the chastening, of the instruction, of the discipline, for God has a great purpose in it: that we might be partakers of His holiness, that we might yield the peaceable fruit of righteousness. There is a design, a purpose that lies back of all of the trials and afflictions that come upon the children of God."[671]

The Bottom Line: If you are suffering under the rod of God, it is evidence of sonship. See Hebrews 12:8. Remember Hebrews 12:11 says, "Now no chastening for the present seemeth to be joyous, but grievous: nevertheless afterward it yieldeth the peaceable fruit of righteousness unto them which are exercised thereby." Allan Harman wrote, "Even fatherly acts of discipline are praiseworthy. God disciplines with justice (Jeremiah 30:11), and the New Testament develops the idea to say that the purpose of discipline is that we may share in God's holiness (Hebrews 12:10)."[672]

21. Jesus, the Cornerstone — Psalm 118:22

"The stone which the builders refused is become the head stone of the corner."—Psalm 118:22.

The "stone which the builders refused" (Vine, Unger and White say "to reject, refuse, despise."[673]) is become the "head stone of the corner" (Futato says "head, first, chief."[674]).

Homily

This messianic passage is quoted to one degree or another five times in the New Testament (Matthew 21:42; Mark 12:10, 11; Luke 20:17; Acts 4:11; 1 Peter 2:7) and alluded to in a sixth (Ephesians 2:20).[675] "The cornerstone (or foundation stone or setting stone) is the first stone set in the construction of a masonry foundation, important since all other stones will be set in reference to this stone, thus determining the position of the entire structure."[676] In the event the cornerstone was removed, the entire building would collapse. The Jews sought to build their "house" without the chief cornerstone (something the unsaved attempt to do presently).

Though David was rejected by those in authority, God raised him up to a position of prominence (king) in Israel, making him the chief cornerstone (Psalm 118:22). But a 'Greater than David' is seen here. Matthew Henry states, "But its principal reference is to Christ....He is the stone which the builders refused....He is a stone, not only for strength, and firmness, and duration, but for life, in the building of the spiritual temple [and] for the foundation of the gospel church....This stone was rejected by the builders, by the rulers and people of the Jews (Acts 4:8, 10, 11); they refused to own Him as the stone, the Messiah promised; they would not build their faith upon Him nor join themselves to Him; they would make no use of Him, but go on in their building without Him....They trampled upon this stone, threw it among the rubbish out of the city; nay, they stumbled at it. This was a disgrace to Christ, but it proved the ruin of those that thus made light of Him....He has become the *headstone of the corner*; He is advanced to the highest degree both of honor and usefulness, to be above all, and all in all. He is the chief top-stone in the corner, in whom the building is completed, and who must in all things have the pre-eminence, as the author and finisher of our faith."[677]

Spurgeon says, "The Lord Jesus Himself—He is the living stone, the tried stone, elect, precious, which God Himself appointed from of old. The Jewish builders—scribe, priest, Pharisee, and Herodian—rejected Him with disdain. They could see no excellence in Him that they should build upon Him; He could not be made to fit in with their ideal of a national church; He was a stone of another quarry from themselves, and not after their mind nor according to their taste; therefore they cast Him away and poured contempt upon Him, even as Peter said: 'This is the stone which was set at nought of you builders.' They reckoned Him as nothing, though He is Lord of all. In raising Him from the dead, the Lord God exalted Him to be the Head of His church."[678]

Jesus proclaimed Himself to be the *chief cornerstone*: "Because of God's grace to me, I have laid the foundation like an expert builder. Now others are building on it. But whoever is building on this foundation must be very careful. For no one can lay any foundation other than the one we already have—Jesus Christ" (1 Corinthians 3:10–11 NLT). Cornerstones often bear an inscription citing the occasion for the building's construction. The cornerstone of the church reads, "Christ also hath once suffered for sins, the just for the unjust, that he might bring us to God, being put to death in the flesh, but quickened by the Spirit" (1 Peter 3:18).

Christ is our cornerstone;
>On Him alone we build.
With His true saints alone
>The courts of Heaven are filled.
On His great love
>Our hopes we place
>Of present grace
And joys above. ~ John Darwall (1837)

The Bottom Line: The Messiah was prophesied to be the chief cornerstone (foundation stone on which the whole "house" is formed; by which it is strong and stands) of the "church" (His people; all the "sheep in His fold" that have been redeemed). The church stands with Christ or crumbles without Him, as does a person's life. W. S. Plumer states, "We need have no fear of the church. Her safety is secured by the exaltation of Christ (Psalm 118:22). He who raised her Head from the depths of humiliation will not leave His body to perish."[679]

22. An Introduction to the Longest Psalm   Psalm 119

Regarding Psalm 119, Adam Clarke remarked, "Several of the ancients, particularly the Greek fathers, have considered it as an abridgement of David's life, in which he expresses all the states through which he had passed, the trials, persecutions, succors, and encouragements he had received. The Latin fathers perceive in it all the morality of the Gospel and rules for a man's conduct in every situation of life."[680] Martin Luther wrote, "It contains prayers, consolations, doctrines, thanksgivings, and repeats all these with a varied fullness. It is given forth with a deep and blessed intent, namely, that by this repetition and fullness it may invite and exhort us to hear and diligently to treasure up the word of God."[681] Charles Bridges stated, "This Psalm may be considered as the journal of one who was deeply taught in the things of God—long practiced in the life and walk of faith. It contains the anatomy of experimental religion—the interior lineaments [distinctive features and characteristics] of the family of God. It is given for the use of believers in all ages as an excellent touchstone of vital godliness."[682]

Jennings and Lowe state, "It consists of one hundred and seventy-six verses, broken up into twenty-two divisions of eight verses each. Each division is appropriated by one of the twenty-two letters of the Hebrew alphabet, the eight lines of the first division opening each with a word beginning with the letter Aleph, the eight of the second with a word beginning with Beth, and so on throughout the alphabet. The number of the letters of the alphabet is also the number of times that the name of Jehovah occurs in the Psalm."[683] J. Brug wrote, "Although Psalm 119 seems rambling and disorganized to many present-day readers, it has a definite progression of thought. The psalmist moves from a concern for God's law to his own distress, then back to God's law, then to distress at the wickedness of God's enemies and finally to a closing pledge of obedience."[684]

The predominant theme in Psalm 119 is the Word of the Lord. Jamieson-Fausset-Brown state, "Its contents are mainly praises of God's Word, exhortations to its perusal and reverence for it, prayers for its proper influence, and complaints of the wicked for despising it."[685] Matthew Henry wrote, "The general scope and design of it is to magnify the law and make it honorable, to set forth the excellency and usefulness of divine revelation, and to recommend it to us, not only for the entertainment, but for the government, of ourselves."[686] The subject of Holy Scripture is addressed in every verse except for five (vv. 84, 90, 121, 122 and 132). Despite its numerous mentions (the Word of God), Spurgeon says the Psalmist "never repeats himself; for if the same sentiment recurs, it is placed in a fresh connection and so exhibits another interesting shade of meaning."[687] Matthew Henry agrees, stating, "If we duly meditate upon it, we shall find almost every verse has a new thought and something in it very lively."[688] J. M. Boice comments, "This Psalm praises God for His Word, the Bible, because God has given us the Bible and it is only through the Bible that we can come to know who God is and how to praise him."[689] Franz Delitzsch wrote, "Here we have set forth in inexhaustible fullness what the Word of God is to a man and how a man is to behave himself in relation to it."[690] Derek Kidner remarked: "This untiring emphasis [upon the Word of God] has led some to accuse the Psalmist of worshipping the Word rather than the Lord; but it has been well remarked that every reference here to Scripture, without exception, relates it explicitly to its Author; indeed, every verse from Psalm 119:4 to the end is a prayer for affirmation addressed to Him. This is true piety: a love of God not desiccated [devitalized, parched, depleted] by study but refreshed, informed and nourished by it."[691]

Warren Wiersbe wrote, "God is referred to in every verse. The number eight is stamped all over this Psalm. Each section has eight verses; there are eight special names for God's Word listed; there are eight symbols of the Word given; the believer has eight responsibilities to the Word. The word 'eight' in Hebrew literally means 'abundance, more than enough'; it is the number of new beginnings. It is as though the writer is saying, 'God's Word is enough. If you have the Scriptures that is all you need for life and godliness.'"[692] Donald Williams wrote, "Psalm 119 teaches that the living God is the God who speaks. He stands behind His written Word. Since it is God who has revealed Himself there, this Word is true....[I]t is settled in Heaven (v. 89); it comes with eternal and divine authority....The psalmist does not rely upon his unaided reason in order to understand God's Word; the God who speaks must illumine our hearts so that we can hear His speech (vv. 18, 33)."[693] Willem A. VanGemeren summarized the Psalm, saying, "This is a Psalm, not only of the law, but of love; not only of statute, but of spiritual strength; not only of devotion to precept, but of loyalty to the way of the Lord. The beauty of the Psalm resounds from the relationship of the Psalmist and his God."[694]

Regarding the author, Matthew Henry believed it to be "a collection of David's pious and devout ejaculations, the short and sudden breathings and elevations of his soul to God, which he wrote down as they occurred, and, towards the latter end of his time, gathered out of his day-book where they lay scattered, added to them many like words, and digested them into this Psalm, in which there is seldom any coherence between the verses; but, like Solomon's proverbs, it is a chest of gold rings, not a chain of gold links."[695] The great London pastor who wrote the classic work *The Treasury of David,* without apology or hesitation declared, "We believe that David wrote this Psalm. It is Davidic in tone and expression, and it tallies with David's experience in many interesting points."[696] Adam Clarke wrote of the Psalm's authorship and historical occasion, "There are so many things in it descriptive of David's state, experience, and affairs, that I am led to think it might have come from his pen; or if composed at or under the captivity, was formed out of his notes and memoranda."[697] Charles Bridges said, "Luther professed that he prized this Psalm so highly, that he would not take the whole world in exchange for one leaf of it."[698]

David in Psalm 119 refers to the Word of God by ten *synonyms* (i.e. they primarily mean the same thing [the "Law"] but with a slightly different slant). Matthew Henry elucidates, "There are ten different words by which divine revelation is called in this Psalm, and they are synonymous, each of them expressive of the whole compass of it (both that which tells us what God expects from us and that which tells us that we may expect from him) and of the system of religion which is founded upon it and guided by it."[699] An understanding of these terms enhances meditation, reflection and instruction upon the Psalm.

1. *Law.* The word occurs twenty-five times. The *Torah,* but also God's law in its widest sense.[700] The Law is designed to "direct, guide, teach, make straight, or even, point forward; because it guides, directs, and instructs in the way of righteousness; makes our path straight, shows what is even and right, and points us onward to peace, truth, and happiness. It is even our school master to bring us to Christ, that we may be justified through faith; and by it is the knowledge of sin."[701] VanGemeren notes it is "the godly instruction based on all revelation from God, Mosaic and prophetic."[702] Adam Clarke wrote, "It is called law because it guides, directs and instructs in the way of righteousness—makes our path straight, shows what is even and right, and points us onward to peace, truth and happiness. It is even our schoolmaster to bring us to Christ, that we may be justified through faith; and by it is the knowledge of sin."[703]

2. *Commandments.* The Torah ("The Ten Commandments") and other "orders" or directives from the Lord. The word occurs *twenty-two times* in the Psalm. Matthew Henry states, "God's commandments are so

called because given with authority and (as the word signifies) lodged with us as a trust."[704]

3. *Precepts.* The word occurs *twenty-one times* and appears only in the Book of Psalms. It refers to the "prescribed" instructions of the Lord. The term seems to be synonymous with "covenant" and with the revelation of God.[705] Adam Clarke comments, "They are called precepts from a word signifying to take notice or care of a thing, to attend, have respect to, to appoint, to visit; because they take notice of our way, have respect to the whole of our life and conversation, superintend, overlook and visit us in all the concerns and duties of life."[706]

4. *Word.* There are two different Hebrew words used for the "Word" in Psalm 119, bearing slightly different meanings. (1 The actual spoken or written utterances of the Lord.[707] "Any word that proceeds from the mouth of the Lord, whether it pertains to the Decalogue, the law of Moses, or the word revealed through the prophets."[708] (2 The promise of God; anything and everything that God has commanded, said or promised.[709] In one or the other form, it is found *forty-three times.* Matthew Henry says the Scripture is called "His word, or saying, because it is the declaration of his mind, and Christ, the essential eternal Word, is all in all in it."[710]

5. *Judgments.* The word is found *twenty-three times.* Judicial pronouncements of the Law upon conduct. "He is the Great Judge, and the verdicts rendered by him are authoritative and liberating (righteous laws)."[711] Matthew Poole wrote, "God's judgments are so called, because they proceed from the great Judge of the world and are His judicial sentence to which all men must submit."[712]

6. *Righteousness.* The word occurs *fourteen times.* God's Word is holy and just; a standard or rule for righteous living. Matthew Henry states, "His righteousness, because it is all holy, just, and good, and the rule and standard of righteousness."[713]

7. *Statutes.* The word is found *twenty times* in the Psalm. Swanson indicates they are a "regulation, decree, ordinance; i.e., a clear communicated prescription of what one should do."[714] Dickson says, "The word *statutes* signifies that this revealed will of God containeth the duties which God hath appointed and prescribed for our rule."[715]

8. *Way.* The word occurs *thirteen times.* The path (manner of conduct) authorized by God in which man must go to insure salvation and happiness. Matthew Poole states, "The word of God is called His way, as prescribed by Him for us to walk in."[716] See John 14:6.

9. *Truth.* It occurs in the Psalm *five times.* "The law," states Adam Clarke, "that is established steady, confirmed, and ordered in all things, and sure; which should be believed on the authority of God and trusted to as an infallible testimony from Him who cannot lie nor deceive."[717] Matthew Henry says, "His truth, or faithfulness, because the principles upon which the divine law is built are eternal truths."[718]

10. *Testimonies.* The word occurs *twenty-three times.* The commandments bear witness to the holy and righteous nature of God affirming as truth all that He has said. Matthew Poole states the Scripture is called God's testimony, "as it contains the witnesses of God's mind and will, and of man's duty."[719] John Gill says, "The whole Word of God, the Scriptures of truth, are his testimonies: they testify of the mind of God and of His love and grace in the method of salvation by Christ; they testify of Christ, His person, offices, and grace; of the sufferings of Christ, and the glory that should follow; and of all the happiness that comes to the people of God thereby."[720]

Thy Word is a lamp to my feet,
    A light to my path alway,
To guide and to save me from sin
    And show me the heav'nly way.

Forever, O Lord, is thy Word
    Established and fixed on high;
Thy faithfulness unto all men
    Abideth for ever nigh. ~ Ernest O. Sellers (1908)

The "I Will's in Psalm 119:

I Will Praise Thee (Psalm 119:7).
I Will Observe Thy Statutes (Psalm 119:8).
I Will Meditate in Thy Precepts (Psalm 119:15).
I Will Delight Myself in Thy Statutes (Psalm 119:16).

I Will Run the Way of Thy Commandments (Psalm 119:32).
I Will Walk at Liberty (Psalm 119:45).
I Will Speak of Thy Testimonies...and Not Be Ashamed (Psalm 119:46).
I Will Give Thanks at Midnight (Psalm 119:62).
I Will Never Forget Thy Precepts (Psalm 119:93).

The Bottom Line: God has given man divine instructions, commandments and promises (the Word of God) to establish his life upon the right "path" (upright, righteous, moral, good); enhance "fellowship" (personal relationship; communion) with Him and grant him prosperity (that which is necessary spiritually and physically for a full and meaningful life, abundant and overflowing with joy and delight).

23. The Word of God   Psalm 119:1–4

"Blessed are the undefiled in the way, who walk in the law of the LORD. *Blessed are they that keep his testimonies, and that seek him with the whole heart. They also do no iniquity: they walk in his ways. Thou hast commanded us to keep thy precepts diligently."*—Psalm 119:1–4.

"Blessed" (Happy) are the "undefiled" (Vine, Unger and White say "perfect; blameless; sincerity; entire; whole; complete; full."[721]) "in the way" (Swanson says "conduct, way of life, what is done, i.e., behave in a particular way, in the manner one conducts one's life, including habits, as a figurative extension of a thoroughfare."[722]) who "walk" (to follow, manner of conduct or behavior. Barnes says "who habitually obey His law."[723]) "in the law of the Lord" (Futato says "teaching, law, instruction."[724] Torah.). Blessed are they that "keep" [obey] His "testimonies" (Rawlinson says "a variant expression for keeping the Law, rather than the specification of a particular part of it."[725]).

AND that "seek him with the whole heart" (Swanson says "inquire, consult, find out, i.e., learn information not previously known."[726] Poole says "that seek His presence, and favor, and acquaintance."[727] Jamieson-Fausset-Brown say "that is, a knowledge of Him, with desire for conformity to His will."[728] Barnes says "with a sincere desire to know his will and to do it; without hypocrisy or guile; with no selfish or sinister aims."[729]).

They also do no "iniquity" (Swanson says "evil, injustice, crime, i.e., be in a state of not being right or just."[730] The NLT says they do not "compromise.") they "walk" (manner of conduct, behavior, activity.) "in his ways" (Clarke says, "They avoid all idolatry, injustice, and wrong; and they walk in God's ways, not in those ways to which an evil heart might entice them, nor those in which the thoughtless and the profligate [immoral, licentious] tread."[731] Spurgeon says, "This verse describes believers as they exist among us: although they have their faults and infirmities, yet they hate evil and will not permit themselves to do it; they love the ways of truth, right and true godliness, and habitually they walk therein. They do not claim to be absolutely perfect except in their desires, and there they are pure indeed, for they pant to be kept from all sin and to be led into all holiness."[732] First John 3:6 bears the same meaning.).

Thou hast "commanded" (Swanson says "order, tell, instruct, give direction, decree, i.e., state with force/authority what others must do."[733] Barnes says, "All this is here traced to the command of God, to the fact that He has required it. It is not mere human prudence; it is not mere morality; it is not because it will be for our interest; it is because God requires it. This is the foundation of all true virtue; and until a man acts from this motive, it cannot be said that he is in the proper sense a righteous man."[734]).

Us to "keep" (Vine, Unger and White say "to watch, to guard, to keep."[735]) "thy precepts" (Landes says "instructions, procedures."[736]) "diligently" (Gesenius and Tregelles say "in the highest degree."[737] Clarke says "'superlatively, to the uttermost.' God has never given a commandment, the observance of which He knew to be impossible. And to whatsoever He has commanded He requires obedience; and His grace is sufficient for us. We must not trifle with God."[738] Barnes says in the Hebrew it means "'very much'; that is, to do it constantly; faithfully. Each one of His laws is to be observed, and to be observed always, and in all circumstances."[739]).

Homily

David lays the foundation for the entire Psalm concisely in its first several verses. The happy or joyful man will be he who *habitually orders his lifestyle* in keeping with the sovereign commandments (instructions, the Law [Torah], orders) of the Lord and seeks wholeheartedly His holy presence and favor. See Psalm 119:1. He will live righteously, endeavoring to escape relapses into sin. See Psalm 119:2. His solemn heart cry is that of Robert Murray M'Cheyne: "Lord, make me as holy as a pardoned sinner can be." The righteous avoids sin like a mouse does the cat.

They also do no iniquity. J. A. Alexander wrote "do not practice wrong, (but) in His ways walk. This verse both limits and completes the one before it, by shewing that no zeal in seeking God can be acceptable, if coupled with a wicked life."[740] Spurgeon says, "Those who follow the Word of God do no iniquity; the rule is perfect, and if it be constantly followed no fault will arise....[N]o man can claim to be absolutely without sin, and yet we trust there are many who do not designedly, willfully, knowingly, and continuously do anything that is wicked, ungodly, or unjust. Grace keeps the life righteous as to act even when the Christian has to bemoan the transgressions of the heart."[741] Matthew Henry wrote, "They do not commit it as those do who are the servants of sin; they do not make a practice of it, do not make a trade of it."[742] Matthew Poole echoes the same interpretation, saying they "are not workers of iniquity, i.e., do not knowingly and resolvedly and industriously and customarily continue in sinful courses. So this phrase is understood (Job 31:3; 34:8; Psalm 5:5; 6:8; 125:5; Proverbs 10:29; and Luke 13:27); otherwise there is not a just man upon earth that sinneth not (Ecclesiastes 7:20)."[743]

They walk in his ways. See Psalm 119:3. Matthew Henry says "the ways which He has marked out to us and has appointed us to walk in."[744] The "ways" (paths on which one journeys through life) consist of God's written commandments and instructions and revealed *will* (mission, marriage, meticulous details of life). These are without hypocrisy for they walk in integrity. *Keep thy precepts diligently.* See Psalm 119:4. J. A. Alexander states, "The literal meaning is to keep very (much), i.e., not formally or superficially, but really and thoroughly."[745] The happy man also is he that "keeps" (obeys, preserves, guards) God's instructions "diligently" (carefully and constantly[746]) in every circumstance of life. He ever longs to keep God's "statutes" (God's prescribed rules or teachings) more faithfully. See Psalm 119:5.

Then shall I not be ashamed. See Psalm 119:6. Shame comes with sin: he that orders life after the counsel of the Lord will escape it. Ellicott says, "The Divine Law is as a mirror, which shows man his defects; the faithful, in looking in it, have no cause to blush."[747] John Gill suggests an additional meaning. He writes the man that is righteous will not be ashamed "of hope in God, of a profession of faith in Him, and of a conversation agreeable to it before men; nor of appearing before God in His house, worshipping Him there; nor at the throne of His grace, nor at the day of judgment, and before Christ at His coming."[748] J. A. Alexander says the righteous will not be "put to shame, defeated, frustrated, disappointed in one's highest hopes."[749]

The Bottom Line: The truly happy man is he that walks in the paths of the righteous (according to the directives of Holy Scripture and in holy communion with the Lord). He that walks in the way of God with all sincerity and devotion will not be ashamed of his conduct nor of his faith before others.

24. Victory over Sin   Psalm 119:9–11

"Wherewithal shall a young man cleanse his way? by taking heed thereto according to thy word. With my whole heart have I sought thee: O let me not wander from thy commandments. Thy word have I hid in mine heart, that I might not sin against thee."—Psalm 119:9–11.

"Wherewithal" (i.e., how) shall a "young man" (Vine, Unger and White say "youth; lad; young man."[750]) "cleanse" (Gesenius and Tregelles say "to be pure—always in a moral sense."[751]) "his way" (Clarke says "signifies a track, a rut, such as is made by the wheel of a cart or chariot."[752]). BY "taking heed" (Gesenius and Tregelles say "keep, to watch, to guard."[753] The NLT says "by obeying.") thereto "according to thy word" (Benson says "by diligently and circumspectly watching over himself, and examining and regulating all his dispositions and actions by the rule of thy word."[754]).

With my "whole" (Strong says "all, the whole of; totality, everything."[755]) heart have I "sought thee" (Swanson says "seek, inquire, consult, find out, i.e., learn information not previously known."[756]). O "let me not" (Barnes says "keep me in this steady purpose; this fixed design. This is the language of a heart where there is a consciousness of its weakness and its liability to err, strong as may be its purpose to do right."[757]) "wander" (Landes says "to stray; stagger; do wrong."[758] Allen says "stray, refers to deliberate, not unintended, sin."[759]) from thy "commandments" (Swanson says "order, commandment, i.e., an authoritative directive, either written or verbal, given as instruction or prescription to a subordinate."[760]).

"Thy word" (God's word of promise.) have I "hid in mine heart" (Holladay and Kohler say "shelter, store up, treasure up."[761] Barnes says, "The meaning here is that he had 'treasured' up the Word of God as the most valuable thing in his heart; it was 'there,' though unseen; it constituted the secret power by which he was governed; it was permanently deposited there as the most valuable of his treasures."[762]) "that I might not sin against thee" (The Bible will keep you from sin; sin will keep you from the Bible. God's Word is preventative medicine against sinning.).

Homily

R. C. Sproul stated, "When we sin, we not only commit treason against God, but we also do violence to each other. Sin violates people. There is nothing abstract about it. By my sin I hurt human beings. I injure their person; I despoil their goods; I impair their reputation; I rob from them a precious quality of life; I crush their dreams and aspirations for happiness. When I dishonor God, I dishonor all people who bear his image. Is it any wonder, then, that God takes sin so seriously?"[763]

Wherewithal shall a young man cleanse his way? See Psalm 119:9. That is, as Benson says "reform his life, or purge himself from all filthiness of flesh and spirit."[764] Of life's many questions for youth, few rise any higher than that posed by David. How might a youth be made clean from the defilement of sin and its addictiveness, to live a morally pure life? The question in itself does not necessarily infer that David was a young man at the time of its composition.[765] See Psalm 34:11–14. The teaching method set forth in the Book of Proverbs (Proverbs 1–7) may have been utilized.[766] A. Macleod wrote of the question: "It is something very deep and pure which is intended, or Job would never have said, 'What is man that he should be clean?' It is something very practical and searching, or Isaiah would not have begun his prophecies with the call, 'Wash you, make you clean,' etc. It is something intended to cover the whole area of life, or it never would have been made an ordinance in the old dispensation to have the vessels and persons clean that came into the presence of God; nor would Jesus in the new, in so solemn a way have washed the feet of His disciples to make them 'every whit clean.' It is the cleanness which is part of God's life which is intended. God is of purer eyes than to look upon sin. The fear of the Lord is clean, enduring for ever. It is the cleanness which is also the holiness of God—cleanness from sin, from evil, from guile, from insincerity; the very quality praised by the adoring angels when they cry, 'Holy, Holy, Holy,' in the presence of God. The question, therefore, means, 'Wherewithal shall a young man lead a holy life like the life of the Holy God? Wherewithal shall he make his way the way of a saint?'"[767]

By taking heed thereto according to thy word. To live victoriously, avoiding the dangerous snare and harm of immorality and other sins, requires diligent *watchfulness* ("take heed to thyself") over the soul regarding to whom it listens, in which acts it engages, what decisions it makes, and "hiding the Word of God in thine heart" (treasuring, storing up the Word in the coffin of the soul). See Psalm 119:11 and Proverbs 4:23. John Gill states, "The Word of God is a most powerful antidote against sin when it has a place in the heart; not only the precepts of it forbid sin, but the promises of it influence and engage to purity of heart and life."[768] W. S. Plumer comments, "A sinner is said to be cleansed, (1) when his guilt is pardoned; (2) when his pollution of heart is removed; (3) when he is preserved from falling into iniquity. Each of these is an unspeakable mercy."[769]

Upon the text (Psalm 119:9) Alexander Maclaren wrote describing the type of guide all, especially youth, need in order to transverse the pathway of life safely: "A guide of conduct must be plain—and whatever doubts and difficulties there may be about the doctrines of Christianity, there is none about its morality. A guide of conduct must be decisive—and there is no faltering in the utterance of the Book as to right and wrong. A guide of conduct must be capable of application to the wide diversities of character, age, circumstance—and the morality of the New Testament especially, and of the Old in a measure, secures that, because it does not trouble itself about minute details, but deals with large principles....A guide for morals must be far in advance of the followers, and it has taken generations and centuries to work into men's consciences, and to work out in men's practice, a portion of the morality of that Book. People tell us that Christianity is worn out. Ah! it will not be worn out until all its moral teaching has become part of the practice of the world, and that will not be for a year or two!"[770] No man can go wrong navigating life upon the Bible as his guide, chart and compass. "Thy word is a lamp unto my feet, and a light unto my path" (Psalm 119:105). Rawlinson states, "By looking to God's Word, and guiding himself thereby, the young man may 'cleanse his way'—not otherwise."[771]

> No man can go wrong navigating life upon the Bible as his guide, chart and compass.

Cleanse his way. The Word of God not only preserves from sin, but when sin is committed, it cleanses it. It is likened unto *water* that washes moral deformity away. See John 15:3 and Ephesians 5:25–27. When we meditate upon the Word, it reveals sin, prompting confession unto the Lord Jesus Christ, who in response *cleanses* it (washes it away) through His precious blood. See 1 John 1:7. It is a mirror that reflects the deformities in the heart, revealing the need of cleansing through His blood. See Hebrews 4:12.

Then shall I not be ashamed when I have respect unto all thy commandments. See Psalm 119:6. Holy Scripture protects from shame when it is shown "a due and true respect, which implies high valuation, hearty affection, diligent study, and common practice."[772]

There is a *shame* that is escapable. Shame follows sin; therefore, he that keeps God's commandments will escape it.[773] There is a *shame* that is unavoidable. See Hebrews 11:26. Bearing the "reproach of Christ" for holy conduct and faithful duty is a shame the Christian counts all joy. There is a *shame* that is cowardly and despicable. See Romans 1:16. To act opposite of Paul and thus by one's actions say, "I am ashamed of Christ and His teachings" is most hideous. See Luke 22:54–62.

I'm not ashamed to own my Lord
    Or to defend His cause,
Maintain the glory of His cross
    And honor all His laws.

Jesus, my Lord! I know His name;
>His name is all my boast.
Nor will he put my soul to shame,
>Nor let my hope be lost. ~ Isaac Watts (1674–1748)

When I shall have learned thy righteous judgments. Dutiful and disciplined study of God's Law precedes adherence to or practice of it. It must be *stored in the heart* with all understanding before it will be manifested in the life in all its ways. David says that knowledge of and obedience to God's holy and right judgments are essential to acceptable worship. John Chrysostom, A.D. 347–407, said, "To get the full flavor of an herb, it must be pressed between the fingers; so it is the same with the Scriptures: the more familiar they become, the more they reveal their hidden treasures and yield their indescribable riches."[774]

I will praise thee with uprightness. See Psalm 119:7. The "Word" enables righteous and honorable praise unto the Lord. Spurgeon comments, "There is such a thing as false and feigned praise, and this the Lord abhors; but there is no music like that which comes from a pure soul which stands in its integrity. Heart praise is required, uprightness in that heart, and teaching to make the heart upright. An upright heart is sure to bless the Lord, for grateful adoration is a part of its uprightness."[775]

Thy word have I hid in mine heart. David "hides God's Word in his heart—not merely in his memory, not in the intellectual powers of the mind, but in the city and citadel, where the affections dwell, where reason governs, the home of motive, of principle, and feeling. The memory should be the storehouse of the divine truth; it is often the very quiver of God from which He draws His arrows of conviction and the storehouse from which He draws comfort and peace for His people."[776] See Joshua 1:8. "Hid in the heart; laid up there; made secure there against the robbery of sin, Satan, scepticism, etc.—the Word of God, in its doctrines, precepts, promises, threatenings, examples, is a power in man which no other word can be. It teaches; it restrains; it warns; it guides; it saves. Things which we value, which are essential for certain ends, we preserve in the most secure places, as deeds, jewels, wills, etc. So a good man hides the Word of God in his heart so that in times of danger it is safe. A Roman priest once took a Bible from a boy and burnt it. The boy said to him, 'You cannot burn the Word which I have in my heart.' It was the Word of God hid in the heart that made the apostles so courageous in work and sufferings, that made martyrs so true and faithful, that now makes Christians so unyielding to the world's jeers, persecution, and atheism. Heaven and earth shall pass away, but God's Word, hid in the heart, endureth for ever."[777]

Understanding the value of the *Word,* David cries out, "Blessed art thou, O LORD: teach me thy statutes. I will meditate in thy precepts, and have respect unto thy ways. I will delight myself in thy statutes: I will not forget thy word" (Psalm 119:12, 15–16). All that treasure it will do likewise. Martin Luther advised, "Pause at every verse of Scripture and shake, as it were, every bough of it; that, if possible, some fruit at least may drop down."[778]

Herbert Lockyer suggests the following sermonic outline (Psalm 119:11).

1. The Best Possession—"Thy Word"
2. The Best Plan—"Have I hid"
3. The Best Place—"In mine heart"
4. The Best Purpose—"That I might not sin against thee."[779]

The Bottom Line: "Inward and unperceived, uncleanness will come upon you," wrote Charles Simeon, "if you be not always on your guard. A mariner may be drawn from his course by currents as well as driven by winds; therefore, from day to day he consults his compass and his chart to see whether there has been any deviation from his destined path. The same precautions must be used by you. You must not only 'examine yourselves, whether ye be in the faith,' but what progress you are making in the faith. Do this, beloved, daily and with all diligence; so shall ye 'be blameless und harmless, the sons of God, in the midst of a crooked and perverse nation, shining among them as lights in the world, and holding forth in your walk and conversation the word of life.'"[780] The *Word* prevents sin, points out sin, purges sin, purifies sin and protects from sin's shame. It is the cleanest "Book" and will enable him that fully embraces its truth to be clean. "Sanctify them through thy truth: thy word is truth" (John 17:17).

25. A Passion for God's Word—to Know It and Obey It
Psalm 119:33–38

"Teach me, O LORD, the way of thy statutes; and I shall keep it unto the end. Give me understanding, and I shall keep thy law; yea, I shall observe it with my whole heart. Make me to go in the path of thy commandments; for therein do I delight. Incline my heart unto thy testimonies, and not to covetousness. Turn away mine eyes from beholding vanity; and quicken thou me in thy way. Stablish thy word unto thy servant, who is devoted to thy fear."—Psalm 119:33–38.

"Teach me" (In Psalms, Harman says, "the verb *teach* always has as its object the word 'way' [here it points to statutes or decrees]."[781] It does not indicate any method about the instruction.[782] Barnes says "means properly to throw, to cast, to hurl; and then, to teach—as if truth were thrown and scattered abroad."[783] Swanson says "instruct, give guidance, direct, i.e., give information in a formal or informal setting, implying authority of the teacher or the content of the teaching [Exodus 4:12]"[784]). O Lord "the way" (Vine, Unger and White say "law; direction; instruction."[785] Kirkpatrick says "the verb from which tôrâh, 'instruction,' 'law,' is derived."[786]) "of thy statutes" (Vine, Unger and White say "statute; prescription; rule; law; regulation."[787]).

AND I shall "keep it" (Landes says "to keep watch, watch over, keep from; to observe, comply with."[788]) "unto the end" (Gesenius and Tregelles say "the end, the latter part of anything; also unto the end, continually [Psalm 119:33, 112]"[789]).

Give me "understanding" (Goldberg, Harris, Archer and Waltke say "consider, perceive, prudent, regard. The verb refers to knowledge which is superior to the mere gathering of data."[790] Cause me to consider. Simeon says, "A man may have the richest stores of human knowledge and the most discriminating faculty in various branches of science and yet be under the dominion, the allowed dominion, of his own lusts and passions."[791] Man needs spiritual knowledge and discernment which is under the dominion of God.). AND I shall "keep" (Strong says "to guard, in a good sense [to protect, maintain, obey, etc.]"[792]) "thy "law" (Brown, Driver and Briggs say "direction, instruction, law."[793]) yea, I shall "observe it" (Futato says "guard, watch, observe"[794]) with my whole heart.

"Make me" (Enable me. Barnes says "that is, incline me to it; so direct me that I shall thus walk. It is an acknowledgment of his dependence on God, that he might be able to carry out the cherished purposes of his soul."[795]) to go in the "path" (Swanson says "a means to do, formally, path, i.e., a means to do an act. or function as a figurative extension of a walkway or path to get from one place to another"[796]) of thy "commandments" (Swanson says "order, commandment, i.e., an authoritative directive, either written or verbal, given as instruction or prescription."[797]) for therein do I "delight" (Landes says "to take pleasure in, desire; to delight in; to be willing, to feel inclined."[798] Plumer says "it expresses a high degree of habitual pleasure"[799]).

"Incline my heart" (Brown, Driver and Briggs say "stretch out, spread out, extend, incline, bend."[800]) unto thy "testimonies" (Thomas says "admonitions, ordinance, warnings"[801]). AND "not to covetousness" (Swanson says "ill-gotten gain, dishonest gain, valuable things obtained by theft, deception, or other immoral actions."[802] Poole says "not to the inordinate love and desire of riches."[803] The Psalmist's feared sin specifically here was the lure of money.).

"Turn away mine eyes" (Swanson says "pass over, cross over, travel through, i.e., make linear motion often along a particular route or path; be crossed, lead, send, i.e., cause to pass or cross."[804] Jamieson-Fausset-Brown say "literally, 'Make my eyes to pass, not noticing evil.'"[805]). From "beholding vanity" (Landes says, "worthless, futile, inconsequential; unrestrained; deceitful, deceptive; [n.] destruction [destructive things]").[806] Jamieson-Fausset-Brown say "literally, 'falsehood'; all other objects of trust than God; idols, human power."[807] Clarke says "from beholding vanity—an idol, worldly pleasure, beauty, finery; any thing that is vain, empty, or transitory. Let me not behold it; let me not dwell upon it. Let me remember Achan: he saw—he coveted—he took—he hid his theft and was slain for his sin."[808]).

AND "quicken thou me" (Jamieson-Fausset-Brown say "make me with living energy to pursue the way marked out by Thee. Revive me from the death of spiritual helplessness."[809] Barnes says, "Endow me with life, energy, vigor, that I may walk in thy way."[810]) "in the way" (the righteous path; the way of thy Word and commandments).

"Stablish" (Spurgeon says "make me sure of Thy sure Word."[811] The NLT says, "Reassure me.") "word" (a promise[812]) unto thy "servant" (Swanson says "slave, bond servant, i.e., one who is owned by another for service"[813]) who is "devoted to thy fear" (Swanson says "reverence, fear, i.e., a state of piety and respect toward a superior."[814]).

Homily

The Psalmist personally prays for seven things of the Lord.

(1) *Teach me* (Psalm 119:33). David avails himself of the right Teacher (the Lord Jehovah) praying for spiritual enlightenment regarding the law (commandments) and how he might personally apply them. "We need no instruction in the way of sin. That has been our way, ever since Adam 'sought out his own invention.'"[815] See Isaiah 53:6. But we do constantly need instruction from the Lord. Matthew Henry says, "What he desires to be taught, not the notions or language of God's statutes, but the way of them—'the way of applying them to myself and governing myself by them; teach me the way of my duty which Thy statutes prescribe, and in every doubtful case let me know what Thou wouldst have me to do, let me hear the word behind me, saying, This is the way, walk in it' (Isaiah 30:21)."[816] Charles Bridges states, "The most clear instructions for the regulation of our conduct flow from single sentences or expressions in these 'statutes!' and this clearly proves an infinite wisdom in their distribution, a reference in the eternal mind to every detail of practical duty, and a divine power and unction applying the word to the several circumstances of daily conduct!"[817] Adam Clarke remarked, "To understand the spiritual reference of all the statutes under the law required a teaching which could only come from God."[818] See Psalm 119:12.

(2) *Give me* (Psalm 119:34). Albert Barnes wrote, "Give me right views of it, of its nature and obligation. It is not a prayer that God would give him the faculty of understanding or intelligence, but that He would enable him to take just views of the law."[819] Prior to obedience to the law a person must "understand" not only its teachings but purpose, requirement and profit. Divine wisdom is necessary for this understanding. See James 1:5. *With my whole heart.* Adam Clarke understands it to say, "I will not trifle with my God—I will not divide my affections with the world; God shall have all."[820]

(3) *Make me* (Psalm 119:35). Rawlinson states, "Keep me, i.e., from straying out of the right path, through ignorance or negligence."[821] Spurgeon says, "Thou hast made me to love the way; now make me to move in it. This is the cry of a child that longs to walk, but is too feeble; of a pilgrim who is exhausted. We shall not go into the narrow path till we are made to do so by the Maker's own power. O Thou who didst once make me, I pray Thee make me again: Thou hast made me to know; now make me to go. The Psalmist does not ask the Lord to do for him what he ought to do for himself; he wishes himself to go or tread in the path of the command."[822] To summarize, David pleads for added grace from God to do that which he passionately desires, for the "the spirit indeed is willing, but the flesh is weak" (Matthew 26:41).

Make me to walk in Thy commands;
    'Tis a delightful road.
Nor let my head or heart or hands
    Offend against my God. ~ Isaac Watts (1674–1748)

(4) *Incline me* (Psalm 119:36). It is God that must "incline" man's heart to faith, the distaste for sin and holiness of life, and desire to obey His commandments. This knowledge of man's depravity and utter weakness to do what is right (sin nature) prompts David to cry out for God to *bend* his heart in those directions. The apostle Paul possessed the same understanding, for he said, "Now then it is no more I that do it, but sin that dwelleth in me. For I know that in me (that is, in my flesh,) dwelleth no good thing: for to will is present with me; but how to perform that which is good I find not. For the good that I would I do not: but the evil which I would not, that I do" (Romans 7:17–19). W. S. Plumer remarked, "Divine grace and omnipotent power are necessary to bend the will, bow down the heart, and incline the affections to God. The reasons are (1 the heart is naturally wrong; (2 many things present themselves to allure us from God."[823]

(5) *Turn me* (Psalm 119:37). David prays for blinders upon his eyes to that which is wrong that he might not stray, that he may pass every sort of sin by without noticing it. The embryonic stage of any sin is the first look. See James 1:14–15. W. S. Plumer says, "It includes every kind of deception and delusion."[824] Matthew Henry comments,

"Beholding vanity deadens us and slackens our pace; a traveler that stands gazing upon every object that presents itself to his view will not rid ground; but, if our eyes be kept from that which would divert us, our hearts will be kept to that which will excite us."[825]

(6) *Stablish me* (Psalm 119:38). Albert Barnes says, "Confirm it; make it seem firm and true; let not my mind be vacillating or skeptical in regard to thy truth."[826] David prays, "Plant my feet solidly upon the assurance of Thy promise (the Word of God) that doubts may not jeopardize my walk." Matthew Henry wrote, "Those that are God's servants may, in faith and with humble boldness, pray that God would establish His Word to them, that is, that He would fulfil His promises to them in due time, and in the meantime give them an assurance that they shall be fulfilled. What God has promised we must pray for. We need not be so aspiring as to ask more; we need not be so modest as to ask less."[827] *Who is devoted to thy fear.* J. J. S. Perowne renders the words, "'Which (promise) is for Thy fear,' i.e., either (a) is given to them that fear Thee; or (b) which has the fear of Thee for its aim and object (Psalm 130:4), tends to cherish a holy fear."[828] W. S. Plumer states, "God's Word has so powerful a tendency to promote piety, that it is sometimes called His fear (Psalm 19:9)."[829]

Standing on the promises that cannot fail,
When the howling storms of doubt and fear assail,
By the living Word of God I shall prevail,
Standing on the promises of God. ~ Russell Kelso Carter (1849–1928)

(7) *Quicken me* (Psalm 119:37, 40). David prays for fresh or renewed strength to live the victorious life (to walk in righteousness and holiness of life). *I have longed after thy precepts.* J. A. Alexander says, "To long for God's precepts is to long for the knowledge of them and for grace to obey them."[830] It is a noble, expedient prayer for all that have grown lazy, slothful, sinfully indulgent and complacent. "Revive me again."

We've traveled together, my Bible and I,
Through all kinds of weather, with smile or with sigh.
In sorrow or sunshine, in tempest or calm,
Thy friendship unchanging, my lamp and my psalm.

We've traveled together, my Bible and I,
When life has grown weary, and death e'en was nigh.
But all through the darkness of mist or of wrong,
I found there a solace, a prayer, and a song.
So now who shall part us, my Bible and I?
Shall isms or schisms or "new lights" who try?
Shall shadow for substance, or stone for good bread
Supplant Thy sound wisdom, give folly instead?
Ah, no, my dear Bible, exponent of light!
Thou sword of the Spirit, put error to flight!
And still through life's journey, until my last sigh,
We'll travel together, my Bible and I. ~ Rose Benn, 1893

The Bottom Line: Knowledge alone of God's Word is not sufficient. We must have God's wisdom to grasp its intent and profit, and His power to adhere to it. Charles Bridges states, "The blind man must be led the plainest and most direct, as well as in the more difficult and rugged paths. And thus do we need the shining of light from above—not only in 'the deep things of God'—but for the reception of the most elementary truths."[831] Upon asking God to "teach" you His statutes, Adrian Rogers cites the four things that will happen:[832]

YOUR EYES WILL BE OPENED. *"Open Thou mine eyes, that I may behold wondrous things out of Thy law"* (v. 18). You may have 20/20 vision, but God must open your eyes for you to behold the wondrous things in His Word.

YOUR UNDERSTANDING WILL BE INCREASED. After His Resurrection, Jesus walked with two disciples on the road to Emmaus. He began to talk to them about the Old Testament, the Law, and the Prophets. *"Then opened He their understanding, that they might understand the scriptures"* (Luke 24:45). When you ask Him, God will do that for you.

YOUR HEART WILL BE STIRRED. *"Incline my heart unto Thy testimonies, and not to covetousness"* (v. 36). If you don't have a desire for the Word of God, ask, "O God, please incline my heart. Move my heart, open my eyes, stir my heart." When you pray over the Word, your heart will be stirred.

YOUR MIND WILL BE ENLIGHTENED. *"Thy hands have made me and fashioned me: give me understanding, that I may learn Thy commandments"* (v. 73). When your eyes are opened and your heart is stirred, your mind will be enlightened.

26. David's Sevenfold Promise about Scripture

Psalm 119:41–48

"Let thy mercies come also unto me, O LORD, even thy salvation, according to thy word. So shall I have wherewith to answer him that reproacheth me: for I trust in thy word. And take not the word of truth utterly out of my mouth; for I have hoped in thy judgments. So shall I keep thy law continually for ever and ever. And I will walk at liberty: for I seek thy precepts. I will speak of thy testimonies also before kings, and will not be ashamed. And I will delight myself in thy commandments, which I have loved. My hands also will I lift up unto thy commandments, which I have loved; and I will meditate in thy statutes."—Psalm 119:41–48.

Let thy "mercies" (Swanson says "loyal love, unfailing kindness, devotion"[833]) come also unto me" (Alexander says "come to me, or upon me, or into me, which are the ideas commonly expressed by this verb when construed directly with a noun"[834]). O Lord, even thy "salvation" (Swanson says "deliverance, safety, rescue, i.e., to be in a state of freedom from danger"[835]), according to thy "word" (Rawlinson says "thy promise [*imrah*]. God's Word was pledged, that He would grant mercy and salvation to all His faithful servants [Deuteronomy 28:1–13]."[836]).

So shall I have wherewith to "answer him that reproacheth me" (Poole says "that chargeth me with folly for my piety and trust in Thy promises."[837]) for I "trust" (Gesenius and Tregelles say "to confide in any one, to set one's hope and confidence upon any one."[838] Barnes says, "I believe it; I rely on it; I confide in that, as my only comfort and protection."[839]) "in thy word" (the promises of God. Jamieson-Fausset-Brown say "the possession of God's gift of 'salvation' (Psalm 119:41) will be the Psalmist's answer to the foe's 'reproach' that his hope was a fallacious one."[840]).

AND take not the "word of truth utterly out of my mouth" (Hengstenberg says "the 'well-grounded answer' that the Psalmist looks to make to those who reproach him."[841] See 1 Peter 3:15. But hypocrisy, indulgence of worldly lusts and pleasures or carnality "stops the utterance of the 'word of truth' and obscures our character as a 'saint of God' and a witness for His name. Justly indeed might He punish our unfaithfulness by forbidding us to speak anymore in His name."[842] Henry says, "We have need to pray to God that we may never be afraid or ashamed to own His truths and ways, nor deny Him before men. David found that he was sometimes at a loss, that the word of truth was not so ready to him as it should have been, but he prays, 'Lord, let it not be taken utterly from me; let me always have so much of it at hand as will be necessary to the due discharge of my duty.'"[843] "for I have hoped in thy judgments" (God's righteous regulations or rules.).

So shall I keep "thy law" (Thomas says "*torah*; direction, instruction, law."[844]) "continually forever and ever" (i.e., for eternity). AND I will "walk at liberty" (Barnes says, "The Hebrew word means 'wide, broad, large, spacious.' The reference is to that which is free and open; that in which there are no limits, checks, restraints."[845] Rawlinson says, "In obeying God's commandments, the Psalmist will not feel himself under constraint, but a wholly free agent."[846] Simeon says, "David accounted the service of his God to be perfect freedom. And so, indeed, it is for the man whom 'the truth of the Gospel has made free,' and who 'looks to God's precepts' as his only rule of conduct."[847]) for I seek thy "precepts" (Holladay and Kohler say "directions, orders."[848]).

I will "speak of thy testimonies also before kings, and will not be ashamed" (Barnes says, "I will not be ashamed to avow my belief in thy word before those in power—whether friendly or unfriendly to thee and to thy cause....I will not be intimidated from expressing my faith by any dread of their frowns."[849]). AND I will "delight" (take pleasure and joy in) myself in thy commandments, which I have "loved" (Gesenius and Tregelles say "to desire, to breathe after anything. The signification of breathing after, hence of longing."[850]).

My hands also will I "lift up unto thy commandments" (Kirkpatrick says, "The attitude of prayer, significant of an uplifted heart (Psalm 28:2), and here of reverence and devotion."[851] Jamieson-Fausset-Brown say "that is, I will prayerfully direct my heart to keep Thy commandments."[852]) which I have loved; and I will "meditate" (Swanson says "muse on, consider, think on, i.e., ponder and so give serious consideration to information, or a situation.") "in thy statutes" (Swanson says "regulation, decree, statute, ordinance, i.e., a clear communicated prescription of what one should do"[853]).

Homily

David promises the Lord eight things with regard to His holy Word. (1) *I will defend my belief* (Psalm 119:42). W. S. Plumer says, "If we are able to give any proper answer to the reproaches of our enemies, it is entirely through divine mercy which has restrained us, reformed us, forgiven us, and taught us heavenly wisdom."[854] The martyr slave said: "I cannot dispute for Christ, but I can burn for him."[855] "A holy life sustained by divine grace is a fair, logical answer to any cavil against religion."[856] See 1 Peter 3:15. Charles Bridges said, "What is the salvation which he had just been speaking of? The whole gift of the mercy of God—redemption from sin, death, and hell; pardon, peace, and acceptance with a reconciled God; constant communication of spiritual blessings; all that God can give or we can want; all that we are able to receive here or heaven can perfect hereafter. Now, if this 'comes to us'—comes to our hearts—surely it will furnish us at all times with 'an answer to him that reproacheth us.' The world casts upon us the reproach of the cross."[857]

That reproacheth me. W. S. Plumer wrote, "If we suffer reproach and persecution, nothing new has happened to us (v. 42). Saul hunted David like a partridge upon the mountains. Shimei cursed him as if he had been the vilest of malefactors. Christ's murderers reviled Him, and when dying taunted Him. Paul: 'We both labor and suffer reproach, because we trust in the living God' (1 Timothy 4:10)."[858]

(2) *I will keep thy law* (Psalm 119:44). In response to the unfailing kindness of God ("mercies") the Psalmist in gratitude pledges undying allegiance to the "torah" (the law; God's instructions and commandments to man on how to live righteously). Spurgeon says, "Nothing more effectually binds a man to the way of the Lord than an experience of the truth of his Word, embodied in the form of mercies and deliverances. Not only does the Lord's faithfulness open our mouths against His adversaries, but it also knits our hearts to His fear, and makes our union with

Him more and more intense."[859] Not only will the faithful and righteous "keep the law" but "keep it continually forever and ever" (permanently, eternally). He will honor it in unwavering obedience presently the best that a sinner saved by grace is able and then in perfection throughout eternity in Heaven. An *appetite* for the "word of God" and adherence to it is a mark of the truly redeemed of the Lord. See 1 John 2:3–5.

(3) *I will walk at liberty* (Psalm 119:45). The "word," instead of *shackling* (enslaving), actually emancipates (frees) man. Our adherence to it frees us from the chains of sin that dominate and destroy. "Its observance is no restraint, but the truest freedom."[860] Albert Barnes comments, "The meaning here is that he would feel he was free. He would not be restrained by evil passions and corrupt desires. He would be delivered from those things which seemed to fetter his goings. This does not here refer so much to external troubles or hindrances, to being oppressed and straitened by external foes, as to internal enemies—to the servitude of sin, to the slavery of appetite and passion."[861] Jesus affirms the liberating power of the Word in saying, "If ye continue in my word, then are ye my disciples indeed. And ye shall know the truth, and the truth shall make you free" (John 8:31–32). Knowing Jesus, who is the embodiment of "truth," and abiding in God's written holy utterances, that are the absolute truth, enable freedom. "It is for freedom that Christ has set us free" (Galatians 5:1 NIV). The "law" (word of God) enlarges and broadens the path for man to walk, through its purifying and liberating power. See Psalm 119:96. In Psalm 119:45, David says, "I will walk in freedom, for I have devoted myself to your commandments" (NLT). W. S. Plumer wrote, "Sin is slavery. Vice is bondage. Corruption loads us with fetters. Divine grace brings us out of prison, knocks off our chains, and sets us at large. The faculties of mind and heart and body never in so high a sense enjoy liberty as when renewed by God's Spirit."[862]

> They [the ungodly] will boast of liberty, and promise it to all who will conform to their ways; but they are altogether in a state of bondage.
> Charles Simeon

Charles Simeon correctly says, "They [the ungodly] will boast of liberty and promise it to all who will conform to their ways, but they are altogether in a state of bondage."[863] See 2 Peter 2:19.

(4) *I will seek thy precepts"* (Psalm 119:45). David not only promises to walk according to the commandments that are known but "seek" to know more. Spurgeon remarks, "Is not this the way to the highest form of liberty—to be always laboring to know the mind of God and to be conformed to it? Those who keep the law are sure to seek it, and bestir themselves to keep it more and more."[864]

(5) *I will speak of thy testimonies* (Psalm 119:46). The "word" infused into the Psalmist instills confidence in the Lord, which exhibits itself in courage and boldness in witnessing. J. A. Alexander said, "This passage seems to have been present to our Saviour's mind when he uttered the prediction in Matthew 10:18."[865] John Gill observes, "As very likely he did before Saul and his courtiers, before the king of Achish and the princes of the Philistines, when as yet he was not a king himself; and when he was come to the throne, such kings as came to visit him, instead of talking with them about affairs of state, he spoke of the Scriptures, and of the excellent things they bear witness of; and such a practice he determined to pursue and continue in."[866]

Martin Luther, who deeply loved this Psalm, undoubtedly was influenced by it to stand against the rulers of his day for Christ. Upon friends urging him not to see the king (when summoned to appear before him at Worms), Luther replied, "Go, I will surely go, since I am sent for, in the name of our Lord Jesus Christ; yea, though I knew that there were as many devils in Worms to resist me as there be tiles to cover the houses, yet I would go."[867] John the Baptist courageously condemned the adulterous relationship of Herod Antipas and Herodias, insisting they repent. See Matthew 14:1–13. Charles Bridges wrote, "To how many does 'the fear of man bring a snare?' Many a good soldier has faced the cannon's mouth with undaunted front, and yet shrunk away with a coward's heart from the reproach of the cross, and been put to blush even by the mention of the Savior's name. Far better—the Son of Man 'strengthening you'—to brave the fiery furnace or the den of lions in His service, than like Jonah, by flinching from the cross, to incur the sting of conscience and the frown of God."[868] Trust in God's Word (promises) opens the mouth to testify of the Gospel to the rich and poor; prince and peasant; friend and foe without trepidation.

And will not be ashamed. J. A. Alexander states, "Ashamed has here its strict sense, as denoting a painful feeling of humiliation."[869] Paul the apostle boldly declared, "For I am not ashamed of the gospel of Christ: for it is the power of God unto salvation to everyone that believeth; to the Jew first, and also to the Greek" (Romans 1:16). With David may we likewise say, 'I will not be ashamed' of Christ or His Gospel.

I am not ashamed of the Gospel,
>   The Gospel of Jesus Christ.
No, I am not afraid to be counted,
>   And I'm willing to give my life.
See, I'm ready to be all He wants me to be,
>   Give up the wrong for the right.
No, I am not ashamed of the Gospel
>   No, I am not ashamed of the Gospel of Jesus Christ.[870]

~ Janet Paschal

(6) *I will delight in thy commandments* (Psalm 119:47). The instructions of God instill joy, cheerfulness and happiness as they are absorbed and applied. Matthew Henry states, "*I will delight myself in thy commandments,* in conversing with them, in conforming to them. I will never be so well pleased with myself as when I do that which is pleasing to God."[871] J. A. Alexander wrote, "I will not obey them merely from a selfish dread of punishment or painful sense of obligation, but because I love them and derive my highest happiness from doing them."[872] Charles Bridges says, "If the Gospel separates the heart from sinful delights, it is only to make room for delights of a more elevated, satisfying, and enduring nature."[873]

(7) *I will revere thy word* (Psalm 119:48). David shows reverence to God's Word by the lifting of his hands. Perowne says, "The expression denotes the act of prayer."[874] Charles Bridges remarks, "Here we find him lifting up his hands with the gesture of one who is longing to embrace the object of his desire with both hands and his whole heart. Perhaps also in lifting up his hands unto the commandments, he might mean to express his looking upward for assistance to keep them, and to live in them."[875] See Psalm 38:2. Derek Kidner says this is "a bold expression of yearning for God's revelation in Scripture."[876] John Gill states, "Showing by such a

gesture his great esteem of them and affection for them, stretching out his hands and embracing them with both arms, as it were; and this being a praying gesture (2 Timothy 2:8), may signify his earnest desire and request that he might have grace and spiritual strength to enable him to observe them."[877] J. A. Alexander states, "As if he had said, I will derive my happiness from Thy commandments, which I love and have loved, and to these commandments, which I love and have loved, I will lift up my hands and heart together."[878] Calvin remarked, "It is a sure indication that we eagerly desire a thing when we stretch out the hands to grasp and enjoy it."[879] Let us imitate David by lifting up holy hands in honor, reverence and devotion to the Word of God and unto the Lord in praise and gratitude for it.

(8) *I will meditate in thy statutes* (Psalm 119:48). David pledges to muse (as a cow chews its cud) over the Word. George Mueller, a nineteenth-century pastor in England, stated, "I saw that the most important thing I had to do was give myself to the reading of the Word of God—not prayer, but the Word of God. Here again, not the simple reading of the Word of God so that it only passes through my mind just as water runs through a pipe, but considering what I read, pondering over it, and applying it to my heart. *To meditate on it*, that thus my heart might be comforted, encouraged, warned, reproved, instructed. And that thus, by means of the Word of God, while meditating on it, my heart be brought into experiencing communion with the Lord."[880] "Why then is the Bible read only—not meditated on? Because it is not loved. We do not go to it, as the hungry man to his food, as the miser to his treasure. The loss is incalculable."[881] Matthew Henry summarizes, "'I will meditate in thy statutes, not only entertain myself with thinking of them as matters of speculation, but contrive how I may observe them in the best manner.' By this it will appear that we truly love God's commandments, if we apply both our minds and our hands to them."[882] Note that twice in two verses David attests *love* for the commandments (Psalm 119:47, 48) which is the motivation for His meditation, memorization and adherence. "If ye love me keep my commandments" (John 14:15). W. S. Plumer wrote, "We never enter God's service aright till the lowest depths of our souls are moved. When our hearts go out after God's Word, then our feet run in the ways of His commandments, then our hands love to do what he requires, and the whole work of obedience is delightful."[883]

The Bottom Line: David's eightfold promise pertaining to the "Word" proceeded from gratitude for the Lord's underserved "mercy" and "salvation." See Psalm 119:41. In developing trust in the Lord, it was easy for him to place confidence in His Word. Lift up your hands as a sign of honor, reverence for God's Book (law, precepts, statutes, commandments, etc.) and yielded submission to its every word. George Müller said, "The strength of our faith is in direct proportion to our level of belief that God will do exactly what He has promised. Faith has nothing to do with feelings, impressions, outward appearances, nor the probability or improbability of an event. If we try to couple these things with faith, we are no longer resting on the Word of God, because faith is not dependent on them. Faith rests on the pure Word of God alone. And when we take Him at His Word, our hearts are at peace."[884] See Psalm 119:42.

27. The Scripture, an Indispensable Source of Comfort
Psalm 119:49–56

"Remember the word unto thy servant, upon which thou hast caused me to hope. This is my comfort in my affliction: for thy word hath quickened me. The proud have had me greatly in derision: yet have I not declined from thy law. I remembered thy judgments of old, O LORD; and have comforted myself. Horror hath taken hold upon me because of the wicked that forsake thy law. Thy statutes have been my songs in the house of my pilgrimage. I have remembered thy name, O LORD, in the night, and have kept thy law. This I had, because I kept thy precepts."—Psalms 119:49–56.

Remember "the word unto thy servant" (Gesenius and Tregelles say "a promise, something promised; a precept, an edict, a royal mandate."[885]) upon which thou hast caused me to "hope" (Harman says "points to enduring and expectant hope."[886] The hope is founded upon God's promises. Swanson says "wait for, i.e., extend a period of time in a place or state, implying a hope of resolution to some situation."[887]). This is my "comfort" (Swanson says "consolation, i.e., that which causes encouragement, implying hope [Job 6:10; Psalm 119:50]."[888]).

In my "affliction" (Landes says "misery; oppressed situation."[889]) for thy "word" (Kirkpatrick says, "Past experience of the life-giving sustaining power of God's promise is his comfort in affliction."[890]) for thy word hath "quickened me" (Holladay and Kohler say "be revived, get well, come back to life again."[891]).

The "proud" (Brown, Driver and Briggs say "insolent, presumptuous—wickedness; as term for godless, rebellious men; a haughty, insolent one, scorner is his name."[892]) have had me greatly in "derision" (Holladay and Kohler say "mock, ridicule, make fun of."[893] Opposition always comes to the man that aligns himself with God and His Word.) yet have I not "declined" (turned away, refrained from obeying) from thy "law" (Brown, Driver and Briggs say "direction, instruction, law."[894] Simeon says, "If any one could have escaped contempt, we should have supposed that David would be the happy man. His rank in society, as the king of Israel; his extraordinary prowess in arms; the services he had rendered to his country; and the marvellous sublimity of his piety must, we should have thought, have rendered him an object of universal love and admiration. But amongst his proud and envious subjects, this last quality neutralized, as it were, all his merits and reduced him to an object of hatred and contempt."[895]).

I remembered thy "judgments of old" (regulations, rules, promises of former times), O Lord; AND have comforted myself. "Horror hath taken hold upon me" (Thomas says "burning indignation."[896]) because of the "wicked that forsake the law" (Barnes says, "Their conduct alarms me. Their danger appalls me. Their condition overwhelms me. I see them rebelling against God. I see them exposed to His wrath. I see the grave just before them and the awful scenes of judgment near. I see them about to be cast off and to sink to endless woe, and my soul is transfixed with horror. The contemplation overwhelms me with uncontrollable anguish."[897] Similar is the psalmist's distress to that of Paul. See Acts 17:16.).

Thy "statutes" (God's law, commandments, regulations, rules) have been my "songs in the house of my pilgrimage" (Henry says, "David was the sweet singer of Israel, and here we are told whence he fetched his songs; they were all borrowed from the Word of God. God's statutes were as familiar to him as the songs which a man is accustomed to sing; and he conversed with them in his pilgrimage-solitudes. They were as pleasant to him as songs, and put gladness into his heart."[898]). I have remembered "thy name, O Lord" (Landes says "name; standing, reputation."[899]) in the night, and have "kept thy law" (I have obeyed thy commandments, orders, decrees, instructions.) "This I had, because I kept thy precepts" (The NLT says, "This is how I spend my life: obeying your commandments.").

Homily

Spurgeon summarizes Psalm 119:49–56 wondrously in stating: "This octrain ['a group or stanza of eight lines' *Oxford Dictionary*] deals with the comfort of the Word. It begins by seeking the main consolation, namely, the Lord's fulfilment of His promise, and then it shows how the Word sustains us under affliction, and makes us so impervious to ridicule that we are moved by the harsh conduct of the wicked rather to horror of their sin than to any submission to their temptations. We are then shown how the Scripture furnishes songs for pilgrims and memories for night watchers, and the Psalm concludes by the general statement that the whole of this happiness and comfort arises out of keeping the statutes of the Lord."[900]

Remember the word unto thy servant. See Psalm 119:49. Hengstenberg says it "is exactly the same as our phrase *to keep one's word.*"[901] David's experience with trial and trouble revealed over and over again that God was true to His promises, that God could be trusted regardless of the furious storm encountered. Matthew Henry said, "That God, who had given him the promise in the Word, had by His grace wrought in him a hope in that promise and enabled him to depend upon it, and had raised his expectations of great things from it."[902] Spurgeon remarked, "The Psalmist does not fear a failure in the Lord's memory, but he makes use of the promise as a plea, and this is the form in which he speaks after the manner of men when they plead with one another."[903] Put God in *remembrance of His Word* in times of distress, difficulty, death, defeat, discouragement and danger. In this God is pleased and faith is exhibited. "God will never disappoint expectations authorized and encouraged by his own promises."[904]

My Redeemer is faithful and true.
Everything He has said He will do,
And every morning His mercies are new.
My Redeemer is faithful and true. ~ Steven Curtis Chapman

This is my comfort in my affliction: for thy word has quickened me. See Psalm 119:50. God's Word (the promise ["the word unto thy servant"] to which he referred in the previous verse) was David's *only* healing and soothing medicine of "hope." See Psalm 119:49. Charles Bridges wrote, "One word of God, sealed to the heart, infuses more sensible relief than ten thousand words of man. When therefore the word assures us of the presence of God in affliction, of His continued pity and sympathy in His most severe dispensations and of their certain issue to our everlasting good, must not we say of it, 'This is our comfort in our affliction?'"[905] Paul testified to the "comfort" and "hope" that the Holy Scriptures instills: "For whatsoever things were written aforetime were written for our learning, that we through patience and comfort of the scriptures might have hope" (Romans 15:4). "The man whose hope comes from God feels the life-giving power of the Word of the Lord. Comfort in affliction is like a lamp in a dark place. Some are unable to find comfort at such times, but it is not so with believers, for their Savior has said to them, 'I will not leave you comfortless.'"[906] See John 14:18.

In the Catacombs of Rome where Christians hid in times of persecution, one symbol is found written upon the walls more than any other—that of an anchor.[907] Believers have always found strength and comfort in life's storms knowing that they have an Anchor that holds them safe and secure. The Anchor is the sure promises of God recorded in the Holy Scripture. "So God has given both his promise and his oath. These two things are unchangeable because it is impossible for God to lie. Therefore, we who have fled to him for refuge can have great confidence as we hold to the hope that lies before us. This hope is a strong and trustworthy anchor for our souls" (Hebrews 6:18–19 NLT). The text is an analogy of olden days when most ships had sails. When such a ship approached a harbor difficult to navigate, the captain would send a seaman ahead in a small boat with the anchor attached to a rope that extended back to the ship. Once in the bay the seaman would drop the anchor. The captain then would give orders to the crew to pull the rope little by little, drawing the ship safely into the harbor. In the Christian life, Christ has gone before us to drop the anchor within the harbor of Heaven.[908] The anchor is Scripture, God's promises, all of which insure security, strength and stability amidst life's storms until life's journey ends in the harbor of the Celestial City.

Hold fast to the Anchor's rope, for it is the griever's indispensable source of strength and comfort and prevents him from drifting off course, ever drawing you Heavenward. Regarding His promises, the famous evangelist D. L. Moody stated, "When a man says, 'I will,' it may not mean much. We very often say 'I will' when we don't mean to fulfill what we say. But when we come to the 'I will' of Christ, He means to fulfill it. Everything He promised to do, He is able and willing to accomplish. I cannot find any Scripture where He says 'I will' do this or 'I will' do that but that it will be done."[909]

For thy word hath quickened me. See Psalm 119:50. God's Word has reviving, renewing and reinvigorating strength to him who is cast down in soul and body. Spurgeon elucidates, "Troubles which weigh us down while we are half dead become mere trifles when we are full of life. Thus have we often been raised in spirit by quickening grace [through God's Word], and the same thing will happen again, for the Comforter is still with us."[910] "The word of God is quick and has a quickening power. It makes men both alive and lively in God's service."[911] See Hebrews 4:12.

Not only does it possess quickening power from despair and trouble but from the depravity and damnation of sin. Arthur Pink writes, "The writings of men may sometimes stir the emotions, search the conscience, and influence the human will, but in a manner and degree possessed by no other book the Bible convicts men of their guilt and lost estate. The Word of God is the Divine mirror, for in it man reads the secrets of his own guilty soul and sees the vileness of his own evil nature. In a way absolutely peculiar to themselves, the Scriptures discern the thoughts and intents of the heart and reveal to men the fact that they are lost sinners and in the presence of a Holy God."[912]

Most assuredly as Paul told Timothy the holy Scriptures infused with the power of the Holy Spirit "are able to make thee *wise unto salvation* through faith which is in Christ Jesus" (2 Timothy 3:14). Charles Bridges is correct in saying, "It is not, however, the Word without the Spirit, nor the Spirit generally without the Word; but the Spirit by the Word—first putting life into the Word, and then by the Word quickening the soul. The Word then is only the instrument. The Spirit is the Almighty agent."[913] Jesus declared, "It is the spirit that quickeneth; the flesh profiteth nothing: the words that I speak unto you, they are spirit, and they are life" (John 6:63).

It is therefore most imperative that in preaching and witnessing the Christian 'preach the word in season and out of season reprove, rebuke, exhort with all long suffering and doctrine' (2 Timothy 4:2) for "it is the power of God unto salvation to everyone that believeth; to the Jew first, and also to the Greek" (Romans 1:16).

The proud have had me greatly in derision. See Psalm 119:51. Matthew Henry wrote, "Though he [David] was a man of honour, a man of great prudence, and had done eminent services to his country, yet, because he was a devout conscientious man, the proud had him greatly in derision; they ridiculed him, bantered him, and did all they could to expose him to contempt. They laughed at him for his praying, and called it cant; for his seriousness, and called it *mopishness* ('the state of being foolish or silly' *Collins Dictionary*); for his strictness, and called it needless preciseness."[914] Scott writes, "Infidels, Pharisees, covetous men, libertines, and all the sons of pride and rebellion, will deride as visionaries and enthusiasts, those who speak of communion with God, and joy in him."[915] W. S. Plumer says, "It does not hurt the Christian pilgrim to have the dogs bark at him."[916] Matthew Henry said, "The traveller goes on his way though the dogs bark at him. Those can bear but little for Christ that cannot bear a hard word for Him."[917] Charles Simeon wrote, "You must not dream of honor from man; but be contented with the honor that cometh of God. You must expect to go through 'honor and dishonor, through evil report as well as good report.' Be not cast down when these trials come upon you; but submit to them, as sent of God for your good; and 'rejoice that you are counted worthy to endure them for the Lord's sake.'"[918]

I remembered thy judgments of old, and have comforted myself. See Psalm 119:52. That which God did yesterday in behalf of man He would be faithful to do for David since He ever remains the same in His nature and administration. See Hebrews 13:8. Albert Barnes states, "What God had done formerly He would do now; the favor which He had shown in times past He would continue to show now. In the trials of life, in the changes which occur, in the apparent wreck of things, in the fearful prospect of disaster and ruin at any time, it is well for us to think of the unchanging principles which mark the divine dealings. Under such an administration, all who put their trust in God must be safe."[919] *Thy statutes have been my songs.* See Psalm 119:54. "God's statutes form the theme of His songs; they calm his mind and refresh his spirit in this transitory life of trial (Genesis 47:9; 1 Chronicles 29:15), as songs beguile the night (Job 35:10), or cheer the traveler on his journey."[920] It is the Lord that gives the believer "songs in the night" (Job 35:10) to comfort and sustain. Jamieson-Fausset-Brown say, "As the exile sings songs of his home (Psalm 137:3), so the child of God, 'a stranger on earth,' sings the songs of Heaven, his true home (Psalm 39:12). In ancient times, laws were put in verse, to imprint them the more on the memory of the people. So God's laws are the believer's songs."[921]

Horror hath taken hold upon me because of the wicked that forsake thy law. See Psalm 119:53. W. S. Plumer wrote, "The emotion, which in English we call horror, is one of the strongest. It consists of terror mixed with detestation."[922] Calvin renders it, "Terror seized me."[923] Edwards: "Horror seizes me."[924] Michaelis: "A deadly east wind seizes me."[925] Cocceius: "Horror, as a tempest, has seized me."[926] "The fear and detestation which the prophet felt were not only on account of the doom of the ungodly, but chiefly for their wickedness, their forsaking the law of God."[927] Spurgeon: "My soul, feelest thou this holy shuddering at the sins of others? for otherwise thou lackest inward holiness. David's cheeks were wet with rivers of waters because of prevailing unholiness, Jeremiah desired eyes like fountains that he might lament the iniquities of Israel, and Lot was vexed with the conversation of the men of Sodom. Those upon whom the mark was set in Ezekiel's vision were those who sighed and cried for the abominations of Jerusalem. It cannot but grieve gracious souls to see what pains men take to go to Hell. They know the evil of sin experimentally, and they are alarmed to see others flying like moths into its blaze. Sin makes the righteous shudder, because it violates a holy law, which it is to every man's highest interest to keep....Sin in others horrifies a believer, because it puts him in mind of the baseness of his own heart; when he sees a transgressor he cries with the saint mentioned by Bernard, 'He fell today, and I may fall tomorrow.' Sin to a believer is horrible, because it crucified the Saviour; he sees in every iniquity the

147

nails and spear. How can a saved soul behold that cursed kill-Christ sin without abhorrence?"[928] The righteous ought to be horrified and distressed over the wickedness of the ungodly. See Psalm 119:136.

I have remembered thy name. See Psalm 119:55. Matthew Poole states under the title of God's name are "Thy holy nature and attributes, Thy blessed word, and Thy wonderful works."[929] *In the night.* See Psalm 119:55. John Gill said, "In the night of distress and affliction, or rather literally, in the night season, when on his bed and awake, while others were asleep, he revolved in his mind the greatness of the divine Being; the perfections of His nature; His wonderful works of creation, providence, and grace; His Word and ordinances, by which He was made known unto the sons of men; and these he called to mind and meditated upon in the night watches, to encourage his faith and hope in the Lord and draw out his love and affection to him."[930] The *name of the Lord* is a "strong tower"; the righteous run into it and are kept safe (Proverbs 18:10).

The Bottom Line: The sure source of comfort and hope for the believer is the memory of and meditation upon Holy Scripture and its divine Author. It is enabled by the Holy Spirit to bring consolation. "Banquet your faith upon God's own Word, and whatever your fears or wants, repair to the Bank of Faith with your Father's note of hand, saying, 'Remember the word unto Thy servant, upon which Thou hast caused me to hope.'"[931]

28. The Christian's Companions   Psalm 119:63

"I am a companion of all them that fear thee, and of them that keep thy precepts."—Psalm 119:63.

I am a "companion" (Swanson says "associate, i.e., one in close association as a companion, partner, or friend, with a focus on the elements that one has in common with the others in the association."[932] J. A. Alexander says "not merely a companion or frequenter of their company, but an associate, a congenial spirit, one of the same character."[933]) of all them that "fear thee" (Vine, Unger and White say "used of a person in an exalted position, 'standing in awe.' This is not simple fear, but reverence, whereby an individual recognizes the power and position of the individual revered and renders him proper respect. In this sense, the word may imply submission to a proper ethical relationship to God."[934]).

AND of them that "keep thy precepts" (Holladay and Kohler say "directions, orders."[935] The commandments or "Torah"; instructions of the Lord.).

Homily

David's avowal was to not associate (consort and socialize with or take to be a friend) with the wicked and profane, but only those (regardless of status) that loved God and obeyed His commandments. See 2 Corinthians 6:17. Allan Harman said, "Walking in the ways of the LORD means sharing companionship together, just like those in Malachi's day who 'talked with each other, and the LORD listened and heard' (Malachi 3:16)."[936] Matthew Henry comments, "He [David] was a companion of them. He had not only a spiritual communion with them in the same faith and hope, but he joined with them in holy ordinances in the courts of the Lord, where rich and poor, prince and peasant, meet together. He sympathized with them in their joys and sorrows (Hebrews 10:33); he conversed familiarly with them, communicated his experiences to them, and consulted theirs. He not only took such to be his companions as did fear God, but he vouchsafed himself to be a companion with all, with any, that did so, wherever he met with them. Though he was a king, he would associate with the poorest of his subjects that feared God (Psalm 15:4: James 2:1)."[937]

Drifting occurs due to wrong friends. Albert Barnes cautions, "A member of a church should regard it as a dark sign against himself in regard to his piety if his chosen friends are taken from the world and not from the professed friends of God; if he finds more pleasure in their society and in the scenes where they meet than he does in the society of Christians, however humble, or in places where they assemble for prayer and praise."[938] Friends will be an asset or a deficit, a plus or a minus, a help or a hindrance to your walk with God. Select friends cautiously and prayerfully, for no other factor outside of one's parents influences life to a greater degree. Friendships are so powerful an influence that they impact our lives in at least three ways. *First, we become like them.* Goethe said, "Tell me with whom thou art found, and I will tell thee who thou art." We become like those with whom we associate. Pure and clean water passing through a dirty pipe will become dirty. Does placing a good apple next to a rotten apple change the nature of that rotten apple? Certainly not, but the rotten apple changes the nature of the good one. Many clean and promising lives have fallen into the mire and filth of sin due to wrong associations. *Second, we become known as them*. A man is known by the company he keeps. People are prone to judge a person based upon the company he or she entertains. *Third, our future will be affected by them*. Go to any prison or drug rehab center, and it is doubtful that you will find one person who wouldn't say a friend played a role in his being there. Visit the graves in the cemeteries of the world, and an honest epitaph etched upon the tombstones of far too many would include the words: "I'm here due to a friend." Your future good or evil is affected by your friends. Now is the time to evaluate friendships and change them if they fail the biblical test. See Psalm 119:63 and Proverbs 13:20.

Make friends of God's children; help those who are weak,
Forgetting in nothing His blessing to seek. ~ William D. Longstaff (1882)

The Christian is not only to avoid the ungodly but to attach himself to the godly. *I am a companion of all them that fear thee*. Charles Bridges writes, "The calls of duty, or the leadings of providence, may indeed unavoidably connect us with those, who 'have no fear of God before their eyes.' Nor should we repel them from religiously affecting a sullen or uncourteous habit. But such men, whatever be their attractions, will not be the companions of our choice. Fellowship with them, is to 'remove the ancient landmark'; to forget the broad line of separation between us and them; and to venture into the most hazardous atmosphere."[939]

Scripture exhorts the Christian not to neglect corporate worship with other believers. See Hebrews 10:25. The Greek word for church is *ekklesia*, which comes from the Greek verb *kaleo* ("to call") and the preposition *ek* ("out"): "The called out ones." *Ekklesia* also may be translated to mean "assembly" because it was a word used to describe a people who were "called out to a meeting." The word church is found

115 times in the New Testament; 92 times it means the local congregation. The church is not brick and mortar but people of common faith who have been saved and called out to worship and serve God. See Colossians 1:13. Every believer needs the encouragement, instruction, correction, guidance, training and support that the church affords through the "Born Again" ones of which this "Bride of Christ" consists. Charles Bridges says, "To underrate therefore the privileged association with them that fear God, is to incur not only a most awful responsibility in the sight of God, but also a most serious hazard to our own souls."[940]

> It is not possible wholly to avoid civil intercourse with bad men, unless we go out of the world. But civility is a different thing from voluntarily making them our companions, our fellows.
> W. S. Plumer

W. S. Plumer wrote, "It is not possible wholly to avoid civil intercourse with bad men, unless we go out of the world, 1 Corinthians 5:9–10. But civility is a different thing from voluntarily making them our *companions*, our *fellows*."[941]

I love the thrill that I feel when I get together with God's wonderful people
Love the thrill that I feel when I get together with God's wonderful people
    What a sight just to see all the happy faces
    Praising God in heavenly places
What a thrill that I feel when I get together with God's wonderful people.
~ Lanny Wolfe

The Bottom Line: Those with whom you associate cast a long shadow of influence upon your life either for good or evil. W. S. Plumer comments, "The communion of saints mightily assists communion with God."[942]

29. The Benefit of Affliction (the Discipline of God)
Psalm 119:67–72

"Before I was afflicted I went astray: but now have I kept thy word. Thou art good, and doest good; teach me thy statutes. The proud have forged a lie against me: but I will keep thy precepts with my whole

heart. Their heart is as fat as grease; but I delight in thy law. It is good for me that I have been afflicted; that I might learn thy statutes. The law of thy mouth is better unto me than thousands of gold and silver."—Psalm 119:67–72.

Before I was "afflicted" (Coppes, Harris, Archer and Waltke say "afflict, oppress, humble. The primary meaning is 'to force,' or 'to try to force submission,' and 'to punish or inflict pain upon.'"[943] The NLT says "until you disciplined me." Ross says, "Knowing that in faithfulness God had afflicted him (vv. 67, 71), he asked God to comfort him."[944] This probably refers to the persecution and oppression he encountered.[945]). I went "astray" (Swanson says "err unintentionally, sin without intention, go astray, i.e., commit a sin or crime against God, so incurring guilt needing atonement, with a focus that the sin is a violation which does not have contemplated, thoughtful malice involved."[946]). BUT now have I "kept" (Landes says "to keep, watch over, observe; to take care of, preserve, protect; to save, retain; to do something carefully; to observe an order, stick to an agreement, keep an appointment; watchmen, guards; to be on one's guard."[947]).

"Thy word" (The commandment, instruction, promise of God. J. A. Alexander says, "*The saying* of God is what he says, including both commands and promises, which indeed are represented in the Old Testament, and especially in this psalm, as inseparable."[948]). Thou art "good, and doest good" (Swanson says "i.e., pertaining to the moral opposite of evil [2 Chronicles 30:18]; good, i.e., pertaining to having good value [Genesis 1:4]; generous, formally, good, i.e., pertaining to giving much in relation to one's possessions."[949] Alexander says "good, both essentially and actively or practically; good in thyself and good to others. The participle, as in v. 67, denotes habitual, constant action."[950]) "teach me" (Vine, Unger and White say "to teach, learn, cause to learn."[951]) "thy statutes" (God's prescribed instructions, law, commandments).

The "proud" (Holladay and Kohler say "presumptuous, arrogant."[952]) have "forged" (Brown, Driver and Briggs say "smear or plaster [over], stick, glue."[953]) "a lie against me" (Holladay and Kohler say "falsehood, deception what is wrong, false, pretended, unreal; without reason."[954]) but I will "keep" (obey, heed) thy precepts with "my whole heart" (its entirety, totality, everything[955]).

Their heart is as "fat as grease" (Swanson says "be unfeeling, calloused, i.e., lose all sense of shame, implying unresponsiveness to Torah."[956] Ellicott says "emblem of pride and insensibility."[957] Spurgeon says, "Their hearts, through sensual indulgence, have grown insensible, coarse and groveling; but Thou hast saved me from such a fate through Thy chastening hand. Proud men grow fat through carnal luxuries, and this makes them prouder still....The fat in such men is killing the life in them."[958]).

But I "delight in thy law" (J. A. Alexander says, "While they are utterly insensible to spiritual pleasures, and especially to those springing from the knowledge of thy law, I find therein my highest happiness."[959] While the ungodly indulge in the "fat" of the land without thought of God and His commandments David will continue to take pleasure, joy in obeying God's instructions, commandments refusing to yield to the same satanic lure.).

It is "good for me" (Holladay and Kohler say "joyous, glad: in good spirits; in good spirits; pleasing, desirable."[960] Rawlinson says, "'Sweet are the uses of adversity.' The Psalmist feels and confesses that the afflictions, which he has suffered, have been good for him. They have made him less apt to 'go astray' than he was."[961] Benson says, "He repeats what, in effect, he said before (Psalm 119:67), partly to intimate the certainty and importance of this truth, and partly because it is a great paradox to worldly men, who generally esteem afflictions to be evils, yea, the worst of evils."[962]).

That I have been "afflicted" (suffered) that I might "learn thy statutes" (Rawlinson says, "The whole nation 'learnt God's statutes' by the affliction of the Babylonish Captivity. Individuals 'learnt' them equally by their special chastisements."[963] *Statutes* are the prescribed instructions, commandments, ordinances of God.).

Homily

Thou art good, and doest good. "Wherever we look, we have no encouragement but in God. Indeed, if only we be acquainted with His goodness, we want no other encouragement: for, what will not He do, who is so good in Himself? and what will He refuse us, who has done so much for us already? Such considerations as these are sufficient to counterbalance every difficulty that the world, or the flesh, or the Devil can place in our way. Having this God for our God, we can want nothing for time or for eternity."[964]

Before I was afflicted. See Psalm 119:67. Coppes, Harris, Archer and Waltke wrote, "God uses affliction to prompt repentance; for example, the purpose of the wilderness wandering was to humble Israel (Deuteronomy 8:2–3). This is a recurrent theme in Scripture. The Exile is similarly viewed as to nature and end (Psalm 102:23; Isaiah 64:1; Zechariah 10:2). God is therefore thanked for affliction (Psalms 88:7; 90:15; 119:75; Lamentations 3:33). Onlookers are wrong to say that God afflicts the Messiah (Isaiah 53:4) because of His sin."[965] Jesus is the sinless One. The teaching of divine discipline or chastisement is echoed loudly in the New Testament. "FOR THOSE WHOM THE LORD LOVES HE DISCIPLINES, AND HE SCOURGES EVERY SON WHOM HE RECEIVES" (Hebrews 12:6 NASB). "Those whom I love, I reprove and discipline; therefore be zealous and repent" (Revelation 3:19). See James 1:12 and 2 Corinthians 12:7–10.

I went astray. See Psalm 119:67. Matthew Henry comments, "Sin is going astray; and we are most apt to wander from God when we are easy and think ourselves at home in the world."[966] "Often our trials act as a thorn hedge to keep us in the good pasture, but our prosperity is a gap through which we go astray." John Gill states, "*I went astray...*from God; from His Word, His ways and worship; like a lost sheep from the shepherd, the fold, the flock, and the footsteps of it (see Psalm 119:176); not that he willfully, wickedly, maliciously, and through contempt, departed from his God; this he denies (Psalm 18:21); but through the weakness of the flesh, the prevalence of corruption, and force of temptation, and very much through a careless, heedless, and negligent frame of spirit, he got out of the right way, and wandered from it before he was well aware. The word is used of erring through ignorance (Leviticus 5:18)."[967] Trials are a means which God uses to keep His children within "bounds" or to recover them upon their straying.

It is good that I have been afflicted. See Psalm 119:71. Charles Bridges paraphrases the Psalmist as saying, "I never prized it [the Word of God] before. I could, indeed, scarcely be said to know it. I never understood its comfort until affliction expounded it to me. I never till now saw its suitableness to my case."[968] David's attitude (joy in retrospect) toward his suffering was admirable, for it proved to be of great value and benefit to his walk with the Lord; it enabled greater knowledge and understanding of God's "law." David declared to the Lord with regard to his suffering, "Thou hast dealt well with thy servant, O LORD" (Psalm 119:65). May God give grace sufficient for us to say likewise while in the furnace of affliction or in its aftermath. Rawlinson says, "Notwithstanding all that he has suffered from the 'persecution' of princes (v. 161) and the 'contempt' (v. 22) and 'derision' of the wicked generally (v. 51), the Psalmist feels that God's dealings with him have, on the whole, been good and gracious." *Thou art good*. See Psalm 119:68. Spurgeon said, "Even in affliction God is good, and does good. This is the confession of experience. God is essential goodness in himself, and in every attribute of his nature he is good in the fullest sense of the term....His acts are according to his nature."[969] Matthew Henry says, "This is a reason why David reckoned that when by his afflictions he learned God's statutes, and the profit did so much counterbalance the loss, he was really a gainer by them; for God's law, which he got acquaintance with by his affliction, was better to him than all the gold and silver which he lost by his affliction."[970]

Man like a silly sheep doth often stray,
Not knowing of his way;
Blind deserts and the wilderness of sin
He daily travels in.
There's nothing will reduce him sooner than
Afflictions to his pen.
He wanders in the sunshine, but in rain
And stormy weather hastens home again.

Thou, the great Shepherd of my soul, O keep
Me, my unworthy sheep
From gadding; or if fair means will not do it,
Let foul, then, bring me to it.
Rather then I should perish in my error;
Lord bring me back with terror.
Better I be chastised with Thy rod
And Shepherd's staff, than stray from thee, my God.

Though for the present stripes do grieve me sore,
At last they profit more,
And make me to observe Thy Word, which I
Neglected formerly;
Let me come home rather by weeping cross
Than still be at a loss.
For health I would rather take a bitter pill,
Than eating sweet meats to be always ill.

~ Thomas Washbourne (1606–1687)

Charles Bridges said, "All have been taught in one school. All have known the power of affliction in some of its varied forms of inward conflict or outward trouble. All have found a time of affliction a time of love. All have given proof, that the pains bestowed upon them have not been in vain. Thus did Manasseh in affliction beseech the Lord, and humble himself greatly before the Lord God of his fathers. Thus also in afflictions the Lord heard Ephraim bemoaning himself and beheld Israel seeking Him early, and the forlorn wandering child casting a wishful, penitent look towards his Father's house, as if the pleasures that had enticed his heart from home, were now embittered to the soul."[971]

In my "storms" I will praise Him (not mock, ridicule, curse, deny Him as the ungodly do) for I know, as David did, that He has a divine purpose and plan in allowing them. See Romans 8:28.

Martin Luther chose as the motto for his personal Bible Psalm 119:92: "Unless thy law had been my delights, I should then have perished in mine affliction." May it likewise be etched boldly into ours.

The Bottom Line: "Affliction of any kind acts as a wholesome discipline in leading the pious more highly to value the truth and promises of God."[972] John Gill remarked, "Afflictions are sometimes as a school to the people of God, in which they learn much both of their duty and of their privileges; and when they are teaching and instructive, they are for good."[973] See Psalm 119:71 and Psalm 94:12.

30. Shameless Acts   Psalm 119:80

"Let my heart be sound in thy statutes; that I be not ashamed."—
Psalm 119:80.

Let my heart be "sound" (Vine, Unger and White say "perfect; blameless; sincerity; entire; whole; complete; full. [It] means 'complete,' in the sense of the entire or whole thing."[974]) in thy "statutes" (God's prescribed instructions, commandments.) that I be not "ashamed" (Swanson says "to have a painful feeling and emotional distress [sometimes to the point of despair], by having done something wrong, with an associative meaning of having the disapproval of those around them, note: this wrong can refer to a social mistake, or a serious sin; humiliate, bring shame, cause disgrace."[975]).

Homily

Let my heart be sound in thy statutes. See Psalm 119:80. David prays for grace and discipline to walk "blameless" (without hypocrisy, in spiritual health) with regard to the commandments (in their knowledge and practice) that he may not be shamed or disgraced ("ashamed") by sinful indulgences. Charles Bridges states, "He begs for soundness in the Lord's statutes. How many 'have made shipwreck of faith and of a good conscience' from an unsound heart! Ignorant of the spirituality of God's requirements, and resting in an outward obedience, they falsely conceive themselves to be 'alive without the law.'"[976] See Romans 7:9. Bridges states how one might "be sound in thy statutes": "Diligently improve all the means of grace for keeping your heart in a vigorous state. Be daily— yea continually—abiding in the vine and receiving life and health from its fulness. Be much conversant with the word of God—loving it for itself, its holiness, its practical influences. Be chiefly afraid of inward decays—of a barren, sapless notion of experimental truth; remembering, that except your profession be constantly watered at the root, 'the things that remain in you will be ready to die.' Specially 'commune with your own heart.' Watch it jealously, because of its proneness to live upon itself—its own graces or fancied goodness (a sure symptom of unsoundness)—instead of 'living by the faith of the Son of God.' Examine your settled judgment, your deliberate choice, your outgoing affections, your habitual allowed practice; applying to every detection of unsoundness the blood of Christ, as the sovereign remedy for the diseases of a 'deceitful and desperately wicked heart.'"[977]

That I be not ashamed. See Psalm 119:80. Benson says, "Namely, for my sins, which are the only just causes of shame, and for the disappointment of my hopes following upon them."[978] Pray that your conduct may never be cause for reproach to Christ and shame to His name and kingdom on earth. Pray that God will take you *Home before Dark*—prior to bearing disgrace to His name. The preventative for shameful acts is absorption of and adherence to God's Word. See Psalm 119:9–11.

Albert Barnes wrote, "A man has no occasion to be ashamed of a pure heart; and that which can alone keep us from being ultimately ashamed is sincerity, uprightness, and purity in the service of God."[979] Spurgeon said, "If the heart be sound in obedience to God, all is well, or will be well. If we be not sound before God, our name for piety is an empty sound. Only sincerity and truth will endure in the evil day. Whoever is right at heart has no reason for shame, and never will have any; hypocrites ought to be ashamed now, and they will one day be put to shame without end; their hearts are rotten, and their names will rot."[980]

Found among the papers of a young African pastor in Zimbabwe after he was martyred was discovered this brazen statement.

"I'm a part of the fellowship of the unashamed. The die has been cast. I have stepped over the line. The decision has been made. I'm a disciple of His, and I won't look back, let up, slow down, back away, or be still. My past is redeemed. My present makes sense. My future is secure. I'm finished with low living, sight walking, small planning, smooth knees, colorless dreams, tamed visions, mundane talking, cheap living, and dwarfed goals. I no longer need preeminence, prosperity, position, promotions, plaudits, or popularity. I don't have to be right or first or tops or recognized or praised or rewarded. I live by faith, lean on His presence, walk by patience, lift by prayer, and labor by the Holy Spirit's power. My face is set. My gait is fast. My goal is Heaven. My road may be narrow, my way rough, my companions few; but my Guide is reliable, and my mission is clear. I will not be bought, compromised, detoured, lured away, turned back, deluded, or delayed. I will not flinch in the face of sacrifice or hesitate in the presence of the adversary. I will not negotiate at the table of the enemy, ponder at the pool of popularity, or meander in the maze of mediocrity. I won't give up, shut up, or let up, until I have stayed up, stored up, prayed up, paid up, and preached up for the cause of Christ. I am a disciple of Jesus. I must give until I drop, preach until all know, and work until He comes. And when He does come for His own, He'll have no problems recognizing me. My colors will be clear!"[981]

Will you join the young African pastor and me in saying the same.

The Bottom Line: May no act you do bring shame unto Jesus' holy name. The preventative for shameless conduct is adherence to the Word of God.

31. The Unchanging Word of God   Psalm 119:89–91

"For ever, O LORD, thy word is settled in heaven. Thy faithfulness is unto all generations: thou hast established the earth, and it abideth. They continue this day according to thine ordinances: for all are thy servants."—Psalm 119:89–91.

"Forever" (Macrae, Harries and Archer say "forever, ever, everlasting, evermore, perpetual. [The word] is used more than three hundred times to indicate indefinite continuance into the very distant future."[982]). O Lord, "thy word" (the law, commandments of God) is "settled" (God's Word is established, firmly fixed, "rock-solid" without any possibility of change.) "in heaven" (Swanson says "i.e., the realm of God where God abides, similar to the area of the sky, but with a focus of where God abides, sometimes described as the upper regions above the upper sky."[983]).

Thy "faithfulness is unto all generations" (Kirkpatrick says, "The permanence of the earth which God has created is an emblem and guarantee of the permanence of His faithfulness."[984]) thou hast "established the earth and it abideth. They continue this day according to thine ordinances" (God created the earth by His Word and it continues its function wondrously.) for "all are thy servants" (Spurgeon says, "Created by the Word, they obey that Word, thus answering the purpose of their existence."[985]).

Homily

Forever thy word is settled in heaven. See Psalm 119:89. That is, it was "settled" in the secret counsel of the triune God in Heaven and is "far above out of our sight, and is immovable, as mountains of brass."[986] J. A. Alexander states "*settled*, literally made to stand, i.e., unalterably fixed. In Heaven, beyond the reach of all disturbing causes."[987] What was "settled" (eternally fixed, established) in Heaven can never be unsettled on earth. The decrees, statutes, commandments, promises, ordinances, instructions of God are forever unchangeable, despite man's attempt at their alteration and adulteration. Matthew 5:18 is the New Testament Psalm 119:18, wherein Jesus declared, "For verily I say unto you, Till heaven and earth pass, one jot or one tittle shall in no wise pass from the law, till all be fulfilled." See Revelation 22:18–19.

Last eve I passed beside a blacksmith's door
    And heard the anvil sing the vesper chime;
Then, looking in, I saw upon the floor
    Old hammers, worn with blasting years of time.

'How many anvils have you had,' said I,
    'To wear and batter all these hammers so?'
'Just one,' said he; and then, with twinkling eye,
    'The anvil wears the hammers out, you know.'

And so I thought, the anvil of God's Word
    For ages skeptic blows have beat upon.
Yet tho' the noise of falling blows was heard,
    The anvil is unharmed—the hammers gone." ~ John Clifford

Thou established the earth, and it continues. Psalm 119:90. "God's truth or faithfulness, upon which his laws are founded, is as fixed as the heaven and the earth; for they owe their durableness to the same truth."[988] L. C. Allen says, "The stable universe is a visible token of Yahweh's faithfulness. The results of the Word of God in its creative and sustaining role are seen in the ordered world, whose order is homage to its divine master."[989] Chalmers says, "The constancy of God in His works is an argument for the faithfulness of God in His Word."[990] "The fixedness of nature's laws, together with their subservience [serving or acting in a subordinate capacity; excessively submissive[991]] to God's purposes is a confirmation of the Christian's faith in the written Word."[992] Allan Harman wrote, "Creation is a witness to the power of God's Word, and generation after generation have a testimony, for nature confirms God's steadfastness."[993]

I have seen an end to all perfection. See Psalm 119:96. David testifies he was an eyewitness to the "end (refers not to the actual existence of 'perfection,' or to its duration, but its limitation or boundary or restriction)[994] of all perfection" (perfection or the claims to perfection [virtue] in oneself or in others)[995] finding that all such *claims* at best were limited. Benson speaks for David, saying, "I have observed that all human things, how complete soever they may seem, such as wisdom and power, glory and riches, and the greatest and most perfect accomplishments and enjoyments in this world, are exceeding frail, and soon come to an end."[996] In contrast, the *commandment of God is exceedingly broad*. "The bounds of created perfection may be defined, but those of God's law in its nature, application, and influence, are infinite. There is no human thing so perfect but that something is wanting to it; its limits are narrow, whereas God's law is of infinite breadth, reaching to all cases, perfectly meeting what each requires, and to all times."[997] Albert Barnes further elucidates, "He had examined all which claimed to be perfect; he had found it defective; he had so surveyed and examined the matter, as to be able to say that there could be no claim to perfection which would prove good."[998]

God's eternal, permanent, forever infallible and inerrant Word is sufficient and profitable for man's instruction in doctrine, devotion, deliverance and duty which alone bears the benefit of salvation, happiness, meaning and intimacy with the Lord through its application. It remains "perfect" (without fault or error) and will do so continuously "world without end," whereas the "perfection" of man (the best that man can be or do; his boasts of human perfection) pales in its contrast both in its *claim* and *continuance*. God's Holy Word "is useful to all persons, in all times and conditions, and for all purposes, to inform, direct, quicken, comfort, sanctify, and save me; it is of everlasting truth and efficacy; it will never deceive those who trust to it, as all worldly things will, but will make men happy both here and forever."[999] Amen!

Ultimately man's own righteousness will be revealed as but a filthy rag unfit for fellowship with God and Heaven. See Isaiah 64:6. *True* "perfection" (righteousness) is found only in Jesus Christ and it is in and of Him that man is counted "righteous," fit for communion with Holy God and an eternal abode in Heaven. See Matthew 5:20; Romans 5:17; 2 Corinthians 5:21 and Philippians 3:9.

The Bottom Line: D. L. Moody remarked, "When Christ said, 'The Scriptures cannot be broken,' He meant every word He said. Devil and man and Hell have been in league for centuries to try to break the Word of God, but they cannot do it. If you get the Word of God for your footing, you have good footing for time and eternity. 'Heaven and earth shall pass away, but my Word shall not pass away.' My friends, that Word is going to live, and there is no power in perdition or in earth to blot it out."[1000] See John 10:35.

32. Staying Away from Temptation   Psalm 119:101–104

"I have refrained my feet from every evil way, that I might keep thy word. I have not departed from thy judgments: for thou hast taught me. How sweet are thy words unto my taste! yea, sweeter than honey to my mouth! Through thy precepts I get understanding: therefore I hate every false way."—Psalm 119:101–104.

I have "refrained" (Strong says "to restrict, by act [hold back or in] or word [prohibit]:—finish, forbid, keep [back], refrain, restrain, retain, shut up, be stayed, withhold."[1001]) my "feet" (walk) from "every evil" (Swanson says "bad, evil, wicked, no good, i.e., pertaining to that which is not morally pure or good according to a proper standard, implying this evil hinders or severs a relationship to a person or principle which is proper."[1002]) "way" (path) that I might "keep" (Strong says "to hedge about as with thorns, i.e., guard; to protect, attend to, etc.:—beware, be circumspect, take heed to self."[1003]) "thy word" (God's law, promise, instruction).

I have not "departed" (Landes says "to turn aside, go off, retreat."[1004]) from thy "judgments" (God's judicial regulations, decrees) for thou hast "taught me" (Gesenius and Tregelles say "to cast, to lay foundations, for to lay the foundations of a city."[1005] As an arrow in the hand of the archer.[1006]).

How "sweet are thy words unto my taste" (Swanson says "be palatable, very eatable, i.e., something that is smooth-tasting and so pleasant to eat."[1007] This is the only place "sweet" is found in the Bible.) yea, sweeter than honey to my mouth. Through thy "precepts" (commandments, instructions, orders) I get "understanding" (Gesenius and Tregelles say "to distinguish, to separate, to stand apart, to be separate and distinct; to be easily distinguished, distinct, manifest; hence, to consider, to understand, which depends upon the power of discerning; to discern, to perceive."[1008]).

Therefore I "hate" (Holladay and Kohler say "be unable (or unwilling) to put up with, slight. Disdain for."[1009]) "every false way" (Holladay and Kohler say "what is wrong, false, pretended, unreal."[1010] Vine, Unger and White say "falsehood; lie; a way of life that goes contrary to the law of God."[1011]).

Homily

Out of pure motive (respect, honor for God's Word) David forbid himself ("restrained") from engaging in wanton conduct. See Psalm 119:101. He studiously avoided all places wherein he might stumble. Nonetheless, Scripture affirms he did not always succeed. In Psalm 119:67 and Psalm 119:176 he acknowledges failure to keep the commandments. However, greater would have been his going "astray" had it not been for the resolution not to "depart" from God's righteous standard and regulations. Albert Barnes paraphrases, "I [David] have avoided all those allurements which would turn me from obedience, and which would prevent a right observance of thy commands."[1012] He continued, "This indicates a purpose and a desire to keep the law of God and shows the method which he adopted in order to do this. That method was to guard against everything which would turn him from obedience; it was to make obedience to the law of God the great aim of the life."[1013] Spurgeon wrote, "There is no treasuring up the holy Word unless there is a casting out of all unholiness. David had zealously watched his steps and put a check upon his conduct."[1014] Man's love for God's Word is evidenced by the restraint of all that it opposes and reckless abandonment in obedience to all that it embraces. It is the pure and clean heart that says with David, "O how I love thy law! It is my meditation all the day" (Psalm 119:97).

I have not departed. See Psalm 119:102. Charles Bridges wrote, "So prone to depart—to be carried away by uncertain notions, by the oppositions of Satan, by the example or influence of the world—how is it that you are able to hold on your way?"[1015] It is by obeying the instruction of God's Word with unwavering perseverance (being "hedged in" by it on every side), which He endows with the strength necessary to that end. Kirkpatrick says, "The study of God's law gives him the power of discernment to 'prove the spirits' and reject all false teaching and laxity of conduct."[1016] See Psalm 119:104. "Communion with God in His Word and ordinances is not equal to communion with God in Heaven; but it is like it."[1017]

Oh, to grace how great a debtor
> Daily I'm constrained to be!
Let Thy goodness, like a fetter,
> Bind my wandering heart to Thee.

Prone to wander, Lord, I feel it,
> Prone to leave the God I love.
Here's my heart, oh, take and seal it;
> Seal it for Thy courts above. ~ Robert Robinson (1758)

I hate every false way. See Psalm 119:104. The "way" of sin is a "false way" (the way of deception, lies, pretending, and unreality). Its nature deceives man into thinking it is the right way to live. See Proverbs 14:12. With David, the believer must "hate" (exhibit disdain, distaste and abhorrence for) sin. Matthew Henry states, "Those who hate sin as sin will hate all sin, hate every false way, because every false way leads to destruction. And, *the more understanding we get by the Word of God,* the more rooted will our hatred of sin be (for to depart from evil, that is understanding [Job 28:28]), and the more ready we are in the Scriptures, the better furnished we are with answers to temptation."[1018] W. S. Plummer says, "All sin is a lie. By it we attempt to cheat God. By it we actually cheat our souls (Proverbs 14:12). There is no delusion like the folly of believing that a course of sin will conduce to our happiness."[1019]

Might you be able to say with David, "I have refrained my feet from every evil way" and have not "departed from His judgments"? If so, then unto God be all glory and praise. If not, take steps to make it so.

The Bottom Line: There is no reverence and respect for the Bible if that which it espouses is not obeyed. See Psalm 119:101. Resolve, as David did, to refrain your feet from every wicked way.

33. Man's Compass to Navigate Life   Psalm 119:105

"Thy word is a lamp unto my feet, and a light unto my path."— Psalm 119:105.

Thy "word" (Any word that proceeds from the Lord; the law, commandments, promises, etc.) is a "lamp" (Swanson says "i.e., a small container with olive oil with a wick, with the function to give light, often upon a lampstand."[1020] Landes says "light—from small clay lamp."[1021] Jamieson-Fausset-Brown say, "The allusion is to the lamps and torches carried at night before an Eastern caravan."[1022] Barnes says, "The Hebrew word means a light, lamp, candle."[1023]) "unto my feet" (It is a light that illuminates the way for the feet to walk to avoid stumbling in the dark.)

AND a "light" (Strong says "to make illuminous; illumination, luminary [in every sense, incl. lightning, happiness, etc.]:—bright, clear."[1024]) "unto my path" (Whitaker, Brown and Driver say "goers on paths, i.e., travelers; path through sea; of path to house, light and darkness. Often course of life; of path of God's appointment—of moral action, and character: paths of wisdom, justice; light."[1025] Solomon in Proverbs contrasts the path of the righteous with that of the wicked. See Proverbs 4:14–19.).

Homily

David who "hates every false way" (Psalm 119:104) and continuously "refrained his feet from every evil way" (Psalm 119:101) cites the enabling source of such conduct as the Word of God (the law, commandments, instructions, promises, etc.). See Psalm 119:105 and Proverbs 6:23.

The "Word" is as a candle or clay lamp (flashlight or torch) that illuminates a dark path preventing stumbling or falling as well as a guide that shows the way (gives direction) to go. We live in a "dark" world morally, politically and spiritually strewn with satanic "snares." See Psalm 141:9 and Ephesians 6:12. Satan, the adversary, is ever seeking our demise. See 1 Peter 5:8. Without the light of God's Word to reveal danger and give safe passage, stumbling is certain. See 2 Peter 1:19. God's "lamp" not only exposes that which ought to be avoided and the right "path" to go, but banishes fears, consoles the grieving heart, soothes the smitten conscience, supplies strength to face life's troubles, invigorates and nourishes the soul, and dispels doubts. Albert Barnes commented, "He who makes the word of God his guide, and marks its teachings, is in the right way. He will clearly see the path. He will be able to mark the road in which he ought to go, and to avoid all those bypaths which would lead him astray. He will see where those byroads turn off from the main path—often at a very small angle, and so that there seems to be no divergence. He will see any obstruction which may lie in his path, any declivity or precipice which may be near and down which in a dark night one might fall. Man needs such a guide, and the Bible is such a guide."[1026]

John Gill said, "The whole Scripture is a light shining in a dark place, a lamp or torch to be carried in the hand of a believer while he passes through this dark world and is in the present state of imperfection, in which he sees things but darkly. This is the standard of faith and practice. By the light of this lamp the difference between true and false doctrine may be discerned; error and immorality may be reproved and made manifest; the way of truth and godliness, in which a man should walk, is pointed out; and by means of it he may see and shun the stumbling blocks in his way and escape falling into pits and ditches. It is a good light to walk and work by."[1027] The "work" of the "Word" should prompt every believer to say with David, "How sweet are thy words unto my taste! yea, sweeter than honey to my mouth!" (Psalm 119:103), and, "More to be desired are they than gold, yea, than much fine gold: sweeter also than honey and the honeycomb" (Psalm 19:10).

But the "Word" (lamp) without the "oil" (the Holy Spirit's illumination, understanding and application) is futile. Charles Bridges explains, "But except the lamp be lighted—except the teaching of the Spirit accompany the Word—all is darkness, thick darkness. Let us not then be content to read the Word without obtaining some light from it in our understanding, in our experience, in our providential path."[1028] John Gill further elucidates, "The Word of God is only so to a man whose eyes are opened and enlightened by the Spirit of God, which is usually done by means of the Word; for a lamp, torch, candle, or any other light are of no use to a blind man."[1029] Seek illumination of God's Word from Him that inspired it. See 2 Peter 1:20–21.

No lamp or candle is helpful unless taken in hand and utilized. Obviously, the same is true with the "lamp" of God's Word. "It is a lamp which we may set up by us, and take into our hands for our own particular use."[1030] If we habitually used the "light" we would not find the path traveled perplexing or difficult to navigate. Matthew Henry wrote, "The use we should make of it: it must be not only a light to our eyes, to gratify them, and fill our heads with speculations, but a light to our feet and to our path, to direct us in the right ordering of our conversation [conduct], both in the choice of our way in general and in the particular steps we take in that way, that we may not take a false way nor a false step in the right way."[1031]

Thy Word is a lamp. Its distance (It is a divine light—shines from Heaven to earth and earth to Heaven). Its duration (It has been shining for thousands of years and will continue to until the return of Christ). Its direction (It points or guides from darkness [sin] into the light [righteousness]). Its dividend (It gives knowledge of God and His design for man's life that leads to abundant and eternal life). Its delight (It is "sweeter than honey to my mouth" when it is put to use). Its durability (Heaven and earth shall pass away, but God's Word lasts forever; no bad weather can ever put it out, for it is powered by the "everlasting" Holy Spirit of the Living God).

The Bottom Line: The Israelites in the Wilderness Wandering were guided by a "pillar of fire" toward God's determined destination. Without it they would have "shipwrecked." See Exodus 13:21. Holy Scripture is that fire or light by which God guides believers toward their destination (presently and eternally) happily and safely. To shun it results in sure disaster and devastation. W. S. Plumer wrote of God's Holy Word,

"It alone can solve a thousand doubts. It alone gives effectual comfort in the day of distress. It alone preserves our feet from forbidden paths."[1032]

34. It's Time for God to Work and the Saint to Work for God
Psalm 119:126

"It is time for thee, LORD, to work: for they have made void thy law."—Psalm 119:126.

It is "time" (Gesenius and Tregelles say "a fit, or proper time, an opportunity"[1033]) for thee, Lord, "to work" (Swanson says "perform or act."[1034] It is time for God to vindicate His Word and name. Barnes says, "literally, 'Time to do for Yahweh'; and the construction might be either that it is time to do [something] for Yahweh; or, that it is time for Yahweh Himself to do [something]."[1035]) for "they" (the wicked and ungodly) have "made void" (Holladay and Kohler say "break, destroy, put an end to, frustrate, invalidate."[1036]) "thy law" (the instructions, commandments, promises, statutes of God).

Homily

The text may bear two interpretations, both extremely valid. *It is time for thee, LORD, to work.* Matthew Henry wrote, "A desire that God would appear, for the vindication of His own honor: 'It is time for Thee, Lord, to work, to do something for the effectual confutation of atheists and infidels and the silencing of those that set their mouth against the heavens.'"[1037] "There is a wonderful boldness, I might say audacity, in this language of the Psalmist—a summons of God to the rescue of His own world. And yet such challenge is the privilege of earnest men. It is the violence which takes Heaven by force. God does not resent it; He hears it; He invites it; He answers it."[1038] See Isaiah 24:5; 33:8 and Jeremiah 11:10; 31:32.

This first rendering of the text is a timely prayer for *revival,* for as it was in David's time, so in ours there is opposition to and a blasphemous attempt to "nullify" (not just disobey it or ignore it but destroy it) God's holy and infallible "law" (Holy Scriptures). Disbelief in and denial of the Word (as "inspired", sacred, authoritative), deceitful treatment of it by false teachers (the corruption, contradiction, twisting of it by altering the truth it states), disdain for it by *scoffers* (mockery and profane jesting [2 Chronicles 36:16 and 2 Peter 3:3]), defiance of it by the wicked and even disobedience and indifference to it by the saints (Daniel 9:10–11 and Luke 6:46) beckon the Christian to cry out more earnestly than ever, "It's time for thee, Lord, to work." They 'sigh and cry for all the abominations that be done in the midst thereof' (Ezekiel 9:4). Charles Bridges states, "This pleading does not contradict the law of love, which requires us to love, pray for, and to bless our enemies; for the Lord's people are not angry for their own cause, but for His. David had no regard to his own honor, but to God's law."[1039] Revival always begins first with mourning (brokenness over sin and its consequences), godly repentance, and cries unto the Lord to intervene for one personally and then to work at large (in the church, community, country, world). See Psalm 119:136.

Revive me, according to thy word. See Psalm 119:25. Donald M. Williams wrote, "This prayer for revival is based upon God's Word, God's promise to give life. This revival will also be biblical; it will be consistent with God's Word. True revival in the history of the church is always 'according to Your word.'"[1040] Counterfeit revivals abound, deceiving many. They are far more destructive than constructive, personally and corporately. Hank Hanegraaff, author of *The Counterfeit Revival*, wrote, "First, when followers finally catch on to the manipulations of revival leaders, they often become disillusioned and disenchanted. They no longer know what to believe or whom to trust and secretly fear that the untrustworthiness of those who claim to be God's representatives translates into the untrustworthiness of God Himself. Furthermore, these testimonies leave believers with a watered-down understanding of miracles that cheapens their appreciation of the biblical reality."[1041] Jesus Himself warned that outward, visible manifestations of "revival" accompanied the false shepherd—decisions wrought by the manipulation of the flesh which would deceive many. See Matthew 7:22 and 1 John 4:1. Sadly, among these are ministers that are sincere and genuine in what they proclaim, and in the pressure (manipulation) they constrain decisions. They just are wrong. Instead of allowing the Holy Spirit to ignite the match with His Word to spur conviction of sin unto salvation, they rely upon their own matches (personality, persuasion, power, position and pressure). Such preachers and soul winners need to be reminded of Jesus' words: "No man can come to me, except the Father which hath sent me draw him" (John 6:44). This *holy prompting* to be converted or change conduct is delivered by the Holy Spirit. Schaff said, "Religion [Christianity] is voluntary, and cannot and ought not to be forced."[1042] A man convinced against his will is unconvinced still, regardless of "decision" made. The renowned evangelist D. L. Moody correctly said, "A man, to be converted, has to give up his will, his ways, and his thoughts."[1043] The test of the true evangelist or pastor is not only an unalterable stance on God's Word as authoritative but wholehearted adherence to it in practice and preaching. Revival must be "according to thy Word."

It is time for God to work. Note, David simply prescribes unto the Lord the "work" to be done, not the manner for its execution. Man's part is to pray earnestly and persistently for God to vindicate His name, Word and cause in the ways He deems best, as He deems best and when He deems best. We pray, expressing the need, realizing it is He that writes the prescription.

Often when He does arise to "work," its form and fashion surprises and astonishes. Spurgeon said, "The Lord can work either by judgments which hurl down the ramparts of the foe, or by revivals which build up the walls of his own Jerusalem. How heartily may we pray the Lord to raise up new evangelists, to quicken those we already have, to set his whole church on fire, and to bring the world to his feet. God's work is ever honorable and glorious; as for our work, it is as nothing apart from him."[1044]

It is time, to work for thee, O Lord. "Darkness" is increasingly permeating the world. The righteous must no longer sit idly by without lifting voice and hand in God's behalf while the world like a runaway freight train on a high mountain spirals downward into greater degeneracy, debauchery, and destruction. It is time to go to work for the Lord. It's time for the saints to "arouse themselves to efforts to stay the tide of wickedness, and to secure the ascendancy of religion, of virtue, and of law."[1045]

Rise up, O men of God!
　　Have done with lesser things.
Give heart and soul and mind and strength
　　To serve the King of kings.

Rise up, O men of God!
  His kingdom tarries long.
Bring in the day of brotherhood,
  And end the night of wrong. ~ William Pierson Merrill (1911)

For they have made void thy law. "They make it void—denying its power to rule, to annul its power to punish."[1046] Thomas Coke states they "have made void thy law, by not only transgressing, but also rejecting it; as if they could wholly lay aside not only the duties, but also the penalties annexed to the breach of it."[1047] Nonetheless, the Word of God (commandments) remains the inalterable, eternal moral code of God for mankind.

The person that orders life by its instructions will be divinely favored and blessed. He that does not will experience the severe judgment and punishment of God. "Note, those are mistaken who think that when they have robbed us of our Bibles, and our ministers, and our solemn assemblies, they have robbed us of our God; for, though God has tied us to them when they are to be had, He has not tied Himself to them."[1048]

Spurgeon gives words of hope when all is *gloomy* spiritually and morally: "When Israel in Egypt was reduced to the lowest point, and it seemed that the covenant would be void, then Moses appeared and wrought mighty miracles; so, too, when the church of God is trampled down, and her message is derided, we may expect to see the hand of the Lord stretched out for the revival of religion, the defense of the truth, and the glorifying of the divine name."[1049]

Not until the people of God sigh and cry out for God (in mourning, fasting, brokenness, repentance) to "do something"—to bring back His glory, reveal His holy presence, awesome power and judgment—will He act. See 2 Chronicles 7:14. And that *time* is now!

The Bottom Line: Matthew Henry said, "God's time to work is when vice has become most daring and the measure of iniquity is full."[1050] Likewise, that is also the time for the saint to work. "Oh, for another Pentecost with all its wonders, to reveal the energy of God to gainsayers, and make them see that there is a God in Israel! Man's extremity, whether of need or sin, is God's opportunity."[1051] Man's antagonism toward the Word makes it even the more precious to the saint.

35. Wonderful Words of Life   Psalm 119:129

"Thy testimonies are wonderful: therefore doth my soul keep them."—Psalm 119:129.

Thy "testimonies" (the commandments, statutes, law of the Lord) are "wonderful" (Kirkpatrick says "superhuman in their excellence: lit. wonders, the term often used of God's revelation of His power in miraculous acts [Exodus 15:11; Psalm 77:11, 14; Psalm 119:18].[1052] Harman says, "It is a word exclusively used of God's actions or words, and marks out what cannot be produced by human effort."[1053]).

"Therefore doth my soul keep them" (Rawlinson says, "I obey Thy Law, not only because it is Thy Law, but still more because it is intrinsically 'holy, just, and good' [Romans 7:12.]"[1054] Barnes says "because they are so surpassingly wise and benevolent; because they are so manifestly the work of wisdom and goodness."[1055] Gill says "as a rich treasure, which he laid up in the cabinet of his heart, and preserved as what was most rare and valuable: and such are the wonderful things in the Word of God; and such is the efficacy of its doctrines, and the influence the truths of it have upon the minds of gracious persons"[1056]).

Homily

David declares that all of God's "testimonies are wonderful." W. S. Plumer writes, "For light, truth, purity, wisdom, righteousness, consolation, doctrine, precept, history, poetry, promise, warning, threatening and saving power, God's word is full of marvels. It abounds in prodigies ("an extraordinary, marvelous, or unusual accomplishment, deed, or event" *Merriam-Webster*). It is a paragon of excellence."[1057] Writing of the wonderfulness of God's Word, Spurgeon said "full of wonderful revelations, commands and promises. Wonderful in their nature, as being free from all error, and bearing within themselves overwhelming self-evidence of their truth; wonderful in their effects as instructing, elevating, strengthening, and comforting the soul. Jesus, the eternal Word, is called Wonderful, and all the uttered words of God are wonderful in their degree. Those who know them best wonder at them most. It is wonderful that God should have borne testimony at all to sinful men, and more wonderful still that His testimony should be of such a character, so clear, so full, so gracious, so mighty."[1058] Matthew Henry states, "The Word of God gives us admirable discoveries of God, and Christ, and another world; admirable proofs of divine love and grace."[1059]

It was because of the "wonder" of God's Word that David obeyed them ("therefore doth my soul keep them"). Of this Spurgeon remarked, "Their wonderful character so impressed itself upon his mind that he kept them in his memory; their wonderful excellence so charmed his heart that he kept them in his life."[1060] See Psalm 119:11.

Matthew Henry echoes the same, stating, "'Therefore doth my soul keep them, as a treasure of inestimable value, which I cannot be without.' We do not keep them to any purpose unless our souls keep them. There they must be deposited, as the tables of testimony in the ark; there they must have the innermost and uppermost place."[1061]

Sing them over again to me,
> Wonderful words of life;
Let me more of their beauty see,
> Wonderful words of life;

Words of life and beauty
Teach me faith and duty.
Beautiful words, wonderful words,
Wonderful words of life. ~ Philip P. Bliss (1874)

The Word of God is prized in the heart when it is obeyed in life. The two are inseparable. "Note that his religion was soul work; not with head and hand alone did he keep the testimonies, but his soul, his truest and most real self, held fast to them."[1062]

The Bottom Line: Holy Scripture is wonderful with regard to its author, preservation, proclamation, promises, power, permanence (unchangeableness), plainness, profit and purity. The "wonder" of it ought to instill passionate desire to embrace and obey it. Upon the *unfolding* (opening up) of God's Word unto the "simple" (see Psalm

119:30), the Light of divine revelation shines forth to the soul with knowledge, wisdom, direction, consolation, understanding and hope. See Psalm 119:105 and Psalm 119:130.

36. The Illumination of Holy Scriptures   Psalm 119:130

"The entrance of thy words giveth light; it giveth understanding unto the simple."—Psalm 119:130.

The "entrance" (Jamieson-Fausset-Brown say "literally, 'opening'; God's words, as an open door, let in light, or knowledge. Rather, as Hengstenberg explains it, 'The opening up,' or, 'explanation of thy word.' To the natural man the doors of God's Word are shut."[1063] Kirkpatrick says, "R.V. the opening of thy words, the setting forth or unfolding of them."[1064] Gesenius and Tregelles say "declaration, opening, open and perspicuous [plain to the understanding especially because of clarity and precision of presentation statement *Merriam-Webster*]."[1065] Strong says "opening, unfolding, entrance, doorway."[1066] Apart from divine illumination many wonderful truths and things remain hidden.).

Of thy "words" (the statutes, commandments, promises, precepts of the Lord) "giveth light" (Gesenius and Tregelles say "to enlighten, i.e., to imbue ['permeate, saturate, diffuse, pervade, bathe, drench' Google.com Dictionary] with wisdom."[1067] Swanson says "shine, i.e., be in a state of light [Job 33:30]; give light, shine, light up, i.e., shine forth light rays from a source or a reflective source, sufficient to see and hear; give sight, i.e., cause the eyes to see"[1068]).

It "giveth understanding" (discernment, comprehension) "unto the simple" (J. A. Alexander says "not the foolish, in the strong sense in which that term is applied to the ungodly [Psalm 14:1]—but those imperfectly enlightened and still needing spiritual guidance, a description applicable, more or less, to all believers."[1069] Spurgeon says, "Those whom the world dubs as fools are among the truly wise if they are taught of God. What a divine power rests in the Word of God, since it not only bestows light, but gives that very mental eye by which the light is received."[1070] Henry says "to the weakest capacities; for it shows us a way to Heaven so plain that the wayfaring men, though fools, shall not err therein."[1071]).

Homily

In the previous verse David extols the Word for its "wonder," in this verse for its "light." Matthew Henry states "the great use for which the Word of God was intended, to give light, that is, to give understanding, to give us to understand that which will be of use to us in our travels through this world; and it is the outward and ordinary means by which the Spirit of God enlightens the understanding of all that are sanctified."[1072]

The entrance of thy words giveth light. The word means an "opening" or "doorway" or "disclosure." The word is used in Joshua 20:4 in reference to the Cities of Refuge ("He that doth flee unto one of those cities shall stand at the entering of the gate."); in Genesis 18:1 with regard to the Lord appearing to Abraham at Mamre ("He [Abraham] sat in the tent door in the heat of the day."); in 1 Kings 6:8 concerning the construction of the Temple ("The door for the middle chamber..."). God's Word is an open *gate* and *door* through which we may enter into the "wonderful testimonies" of the Lord to discover "true truth" about God, the Holy Spirit, Jesus, sin, forgiveness, salvation, eternity, morality, ethics, meaning and purpose in life, happiness, success and Satan. The benefits that await us through its open door are incalculable and indescribable but ever so wonderful. See Psalm 119:129. The treasures within the "house" of God's Word are esteemed by David as far more valuable than "gold; yea, above fine gold" (Psalm 119:127). All that enter its "door" in reverence and sincerity declare the same.

It giveth understanding to the simple. The Holy Spirit is the "oil" in the "lamp of the Word," enabling its illumination, comprehension and application to the most ignorant, unlearned, naive, and foolish that are willing to learn. Therefore no man has an excuse for not obeying it. Charles Bridges wrote, "So astonishing is the power of this heavenly light, that from any one page of this holy book, a child...under heavenly teaching, may draw more instruction than the most acute philosopher could ever obtain from any other fountain of light!...For very possible is it to be possessed of all the treasures of literature, and yet to remain in total ignorance of everything that is most important for a sinner to know."[1073]

175

The Word must be allowed entrance to shine forth its light of truth. Treasures within a house that are freely yours cannot be of profit until you enter its "door" to take possession. My soul is grieved over the squandered "light" (treasure) of so many simply because they refuse to enter the "door." Man's love for the "darkness" prevents his entering the door of the "light." See Psalm 119:155. Jesus said, "If therefore the light that is in thee be darkness, how great is that darkness!" (Matthew 6:23). "As soon as the Word of God enters into us, and has a place in us, it enlightens us."[1074] Spurgeon remarks, "The Word finds no entrance into some minds because they are blocked up with self-conceit, or prejudice, or indifference; but where due attention is given, divine illumination must surely follow upon a knowledge of the mind of God."[1075] Charles Bridges says, "Not only the pride of human reason, but the love of sin, shuts out the light: 'Men love darkness rather than light, because their deeds are evil.'"[1076]

Satan is the great hinderer of man's entering the "door" of both the *written Light* (Holy Scriptures) and the *personified Light* (Jesus Christ). See John 8:12. Paul wrote, "In whom the god of this world hath blinded the minds of them which believe not, lest the light of the glorious gospel of Christ, who is the image of God, should shine unto them" (2 Corinthians 4:4). See 1 Corinthians 2:14. The Christian is to pray that the "darkness" will be thwarted by the "light," that he that is blind may clearly see and be saved. "To open their eyes, and to turn them from darkness to light, and from the power of Satan unto God, that they may receive forgiveness of sins, and inheritance among them which are sanctified by faith that is in me" (Acts 26:18).

The Bottom Line: The Word must be proclaimed loudly, broadly, plainly, persistently locally and globally to all peoples, regardless of race or face, for it is the *illumination of God's plan* (will) in their salvation, service and satisfaction. See Psalm 119:18 and Psalm 119:46.

37. A Prayer for Mercy   Psalm 119:132–133

"Look thou upon me, and be merciful unto me, as thou usest to do unto those that love thy name. Order my steps in thy word: and let not any iniquity have dominion over me."—Psalm 119:132–133.

"Look" (Gesenius and Tregelles say "to turn oneself."[1077]) thou upon me, and be "merciful unto me" (Swanson says "be gracious, take pity, be kind, i.e., show an act. of kindness, compassion, or benefice to another."[1078] To be gracious in treatment to another.) "as thou usest to do" (Benson says "as thou hast been wont to do unto Thy people in all former ages. Do not deny me the common privilege of all the faithful."[1079] Barnes says, "The idea is, treat me according to the rules which regulate the treatment of Thy people. Let me be regarded as one of them, and be dealt with accordingly."[1080]) "unto those that love thy name" (Kirkpatrick says, "The plea is a bold one, but not too bold. The covenant gives those who love Jehovah's revelation of Himself [Psalm 5:11; Psalm 69:36] the right to claim His grace."[1081]).

"Order" (Vine, Unger and White say "to be established, be readied, be prepared, be certain....[Its] root used concretely connotes being firmly established, being firmly anchored and being firm."[1082]) "my steps" (Swanson says "conduct one's life, formally, step or footstep, i.e., the patterns of behavior as a figurative extension of a stepping of a foot forward."[1083]) in thy word.

AND let not "iniquity" (Livingston, Harris, Archer and Waltke say "trouble, sorrow, idolatry, wickedness, iniquity, emptiness. [RSV and NEB prefer "evil," and "mischief" over KJV's favorite, "iniquity."] The primary meaning of the word seems to have two facets: a stress on trouble which moves on to wickedness, and an emphasis on emptiness which moves on to idolatry."[1084]) have "dominion over me" (Strong says "to dominate, i.e., govern; have rule, have dominion, have power—have the mastery, be ruler."[1085]).

Homily

No Christian has prayed his last prayer for "mercy," regardless of godliness. All have feet of clay with a never ending pull and enticement toward sin that occasionally causes stumbling. In such times it is wondrous to know that the Lord stands ready to be *merciful unto us, as thou usest to do*. In the same way in which the Lord treats all the saints (from the ages past unto the present and forever more) when they "fall," He will be faithful to treat you.

Such knowledge spurs praise and rejoicing, for though it is highly undeserved and unmerited, Christ Jesus freely gives it unto man. T. De Witt Talmage wrote, "Oh, this mercy of God! I am told it is an ocean. Then I place on it four swift-sailing craft, with compass, and charts, and choice rigging, and skilful navigators, and I tell them to launch away, and discover for me the extent of this ocean. That craft puts out in one direction, and sails to the north; this to the south; this to the east; this to the west. They crowd on all their canvas, and sail ten thousand years, and one day come up the harbour of Heaven; and I shout to them from the beach, 'Have you found the shore?' and they answer: 'No shore to God's mercy.' Swift angels, despatched from the throne, attempt to go across it. For a million years they fly and fly; but then come back and fold their wings at the foot of the throne, and cry: 'No shore; no shore to God's mercy!'"[1086]

Order my steps in thy word. Psalm 119:133. David is confident of God's mercy in times of failure, but his intention is to not fall. Therefore he prays, "Establish and anchor my feet in your commandments that my conduct ('steps') may be righteous, free from wickedness and its mastery."

Matthew Henry states, "We ought to walk by rule; all the motions of the soul must not only be kept within the bounds prescribed by the Word, so as not to transgress them, but carried out in the paths prescribed by the Word, so as not to trifle in them."[1087] Spurgeon comments, "'He keepeth the feet of his saints.' By His grace he enables us to put our feet step by step in the very place which his Word ordains. This does not stop short of perfect holiness; neither will the believer's desires be satisfied with anything beneath that blessed consummation."[1088]

Let not any iniquity have dominion over me. See Psalm 119:133. Charles Bridges wrote, "He [David] had been used to 'hide the word in his heart' as his safeguard against sin, and from his own experience of its power he had recommended it to the especial attention of the young. Yet the recollection of his continual forgetfulness and conscious weakness leads him to turn his rule into a matter of prayer—*order my steps in Your word*—implying that if his steps were not ordered, from want of their keeping, iniquity would regain its dominion. And who of us have not daily need of this ruling discipline?"[1089]

Benson says, "The dominion of sin is to be dreaded and deprecated by every one of us; and if in sincerity we pray against it, we shall receive, as an answer of our prayers, the accomplishment of that promise (Romans 6:14), sin shall not have dominion over you."[1090] Adam Clarke said, "Let me have no governor but God; let the throne of my heart be filled by Him and none other."[1091]

> Let me have no governor but God; let the throne
> of my heart be filled by him and none other.
> Adam Clarke

W. S. Plumer assures that, "The prayer against the dominion of sin, if offered in faith, shall surely be answered."[1092] See Romans 6:14 and Psalm 19:13.

The Bottom Line: Mercy is the free gift of the Lord Jesus Christ to all that seek it in heart-felt contrition and repentance. Adherence to the Word of God protects from sin and its domination, therefore the believer ought to pray for enabling power to "walk" in it.

38. Tears for the Lost   Psalm 119:136

"Rivers of waters run down mine eyes, because they keep not thy law."—Psalm 119:136.

"Rivers of waters run down mine eyes" (Barnes says, "It is not a gentle weeping, but my eyes are like a fountain which pours out full-flowing streams."[1093]) because "they" (the ungodly, wicked) "keep not thy law" (David is deeply broken and burdened over the wicked that trample beneath their feet God's Word, treating both it and God with disdain. See Psalm 119:53).

Homily

As Jesus looked upon the multitude, He was moved with compassion (Matthew 9:36). Oswald J. Sanders said, "Oh, to realize that souls, precious, never dying souls, are perishing all around us, going out into the blackness of darkness and despair, eternally lost, and yet to feel no anguish, shed no tears, know no travail! How little we know of the compassion of Jesus!"[1094] And of David's.

A famous surgeon was asked, "Do you fear a day when your hands will no longer be able to operate?"

He replied, "No, I fear the day when my heart no longer feels the suffering of those I operate on."

Believer, that's the day you must fear! Fear the day when your heart becomes callous and indifferent to those dying and going to Hell. Heinrich Heine, the German philosopher and poet, in a time of distress stood before the statue of Venus of Milo and cried, "Ah, yes! I suppose you would help me if you could, but you can't. Your lips are still, and your heart is cold."[1095]

I wonder how many look to Christians for direction to Jesus Christ saying the exact same thing.

Rivers of water run down mine eyes. David had a compassionate heart toward the wicked. W. S. Plumer wrote, "The word *rivers* indicates much more than an occasional tear or a slight uncomfortable sensation. Lot cannot live in Sodom without having his righteous soul vexed from day to day (2 Peter 2:8)."[1096]

Spurgeon said, "He [David] wept in sympathy with God to see the holy law despised and broken. He wept in pity for men who were thus drawing down upon themselves the fiery wrath of God."[1097] Matthew Poole paraphrases David's words: "Rivers of waters; plentiful and perpetual tears, witnesses of my deep sorrow for God's dishonor and displeasure, and for the miseries which sinners bring upon themselves and others."[1098] See Lamentations 3:48.

We must exhibit the same sympathy, pity, and compassion for the lost. Hyman J. Appelman wrote, "The passion of the soul winner is twofold: a burning passion of love for the blessed Redeemer; a burdening compassion of longing for the souls of men....Our passion for Christ will generate within us a compassion for the souls of men. The two are inseparable. They ever go together....Dry-eyed, dry-hearted, dry-tongued preaching, praying and personal work will never win souls for Christ. Someone has well said, 'It takes a broken heart to preach a bleeding cross.' Cry unto God, beloved. Cry unto God for the gift of passion, the gift of tears. Compassion for souls must be developed, or our work will become matter-of-fact and mechanical....A passionless Christian is a bitter anomaly. A passionless Christian is the heartache of Heaven. A passionless Christian is the laughingstock of Hell."[1099]

Set my soul afire, Lord, for the lost in sin.
Give to me a passion as I seek to win.
Help me not to falter; never let me fail.
Fill me with Thy Spirit; let Thy will prevail. ~ Gene Bartlett (1965)

They keep not the law. The mother of the famed preacher William Burns, in seeing him weeping, inquired, "Why those tears?" He answered, "I am weeping at the sight of the multitudes in the streets, so many of whom are passing through life unsaved." Burns was consumed, as was David, with a burden for souls that was expressed with "rivers of waters flowing down mine eyes."

Oh, for eyes that are fountains of tears that flow unbidden in wake of man's callousness to the Gospel, moral corruption, disdain for the sacred (for God, His Word, church), persecution of the saints, the murder of the innocent unborn, and "political correctness." See Psalm 119:139 (David's grief over those that "forget" (neglect) God's law again expressed). Oh, for tears that flow from a broken heart because of man's certain and eternal doom. Oh, that we might have tears over our *grief* for not having tears because of their *disbelief*.

> Oh, that we might have tears over our *grief*
> For not having tears because of their *disbelief*.

Albert Barnes correctly states, "There is nothing for which we should be excited to deeper emotion in respect to our fellowmen than for the fact that they are violators of the law of God and exposed to its fearful penalty. There is nothing which more certainly indicates true piety in the soul than such deep compassion for people as sinners, or because they are sinners. There is nothing which is more certainly connected with a work of grace in a community, or revival of true religion, than when such a feeling pervades a church."[1100]

Charles Bridges wrote, "Do we lay to heart the perishing condition of fellow-sinners? Could we witness a house on fire, without speedy and practical evidence of our compassion for the inhabitants? And yet, alas! how often do we witness souls on the brink of destruction—unconscious of danger, or bidding defiance to it—with comparative indifference! How are we Christians, if we believe not the Scripture warnings of their danger? or if, believing them, we do not bestir ourselves to their help? What hypocrisy is it to pray for their conversion, while we are making no effort to promote it! Oh! let it be our daily supplication that this indifference concerning their everlasting state may give place to a spirit of weeping tenderness; that He may not be living as if this world were really what it appears to be, a world without souls; that we may never see the Sabbaths of God profaned, His laws trampled underfoot, the ungodly 'breaking their bands asunder, and casting away their cords from them,' without a more determined resolution ourselves to keep these laws of our God, and to plead for their honor with these obstinate transgressors."[1101] Amen and Amen.

Absence of passion and power. Students attending Elisha's School of the Prophets, while working in the field, lost the axe head from the axe. The work was halted (for it could not continue until the axe head was found) and Elisha was informed. Elisha frankly asked, "Where fell it?" (2 Kings 6:5–6). Sadly many Christians are doing the work of soul winning with a lost "axe head," the power of the Holy Spirit is absent. This accounts for much labor but little fruit, or cessation of labor altogether. How might the lost axe head be recovered?

Realize its absence. The road to recovery of divine power begins with awareness it is missing. Many are like those of Hosea's day: "Worshiping foreign gods has sapped their strength, but they don't even know it. Their hair is gray, but they don't realize they're old and weak" (Hosea 7:9 NLT). Face the fact honestly that you have become a dry shadow of the former self that was overflowing with Holy Spirit power.

Recognize its cause. "Where fell it?" Return to the place where the power was lost. Was it in neglect of the prayer closet or intake of the Word or worship with the saints or an impure act or some other form of disobedience? It is expedient you acknowledge the place in the "water" it fell that it may be restored.

Restore its use. Don't keep swinging the axe without the axe head, for such is futile. Get the power back. How? (1) Acknowledge to God the attitude or action that quenched or grieved the Holy Spirit that prompted His withdrawal of power. (2) Confess it as sin. (3) Turn away from the grievous act. (4) Ask the Holy Spirit to infill you with His presence and power for the glory of God's sake and that of lost souls.

The students found the lost axe head, reattached it to the axe, and the work resumed successfully. Go and do likewise for the sake of those on the death-march to Hell.

Rescue the perishing; care for the dying.
　　Snatch them in pity from sin and the grave.
Weep o'er the erring one; lift up the fallen.
　　Tell them of Jesus the mighty to save.
　　　　　　　　　　　　　~ Fanny Jane Crosby (1820–1915)

W. S. Plumer states, "We cannot mourn too much for sin; that is impossible. One of the darkest signs of any age is when the people weep but little for sin."[1102] See Deuteronomy 9:18–19; Jeremiah 9:1 and Ezekiel 9:4. Matthew Henry said, "The sins of sinners are the sorrows of saints. We must mourn for that which we cannot mend."[1103] Dickson said, "Two things in sin chiefly move the godly to mourn for it. One is the dishonor it brings on God. The other is the perdition it brings on the sinner."[1104]

Charles Simeon wrote, "However men may labor to disprove it, Hell must be the portion of all that forget God. And who can form any adequate conception of the torments that shall be there endured? To spend an eternity in such a furnace as that which Nebuchadnezzar kindled for the destruction of the Hebrew youths would be beyond measure dreadful, but what must it be to lie down in that lake of fire which the breath of the Almighty hath kindled? And can we view sinners hastening to that place of torment and not weep over them? Our blessed Lord wept over Jerusalem on account of the temporal calamities that should come upon it, and shall not we weep over the eternal miseries which men are bringing on themselves? Must not our hearts be harder than adamant if they do not melt into tears at such a sight? Can we weep at the recital of a story we know to be fictitious and not mourn over such awful realities."[1105]

   The Bottom Line: "If the Lord teaches us the privileges of His statutes, He will teach us compassion for those who keep them not."[1106] We just need to listen and obey. May we see sinners as did Jesus, as "brands in the fire" that must be "pulled" (delivered) out before it's too late. See Jude 23.

39. Straying Sheep   Psalm 119:176

   "I have gone astray like a lost sheep; seek thy servant; for I do not forget thy commandments."—Psalm 119:176.

   I have "gone astray" (Gesenius and Tregelles say "to err, to wander, to go astray."[1107]) like a "lost sheep" (Gesenius and Tregelles say "to be lost, to lose oneself, to wander, especially used of a lost and wandering sheep, to flee away in the desert, as a wild beast, and there to disappear as it were."[1108]); "seek thy servant" (David prays that the Great Shepherd will look for him that he might be returned to the fold. See Luke 15:4–6.) for I do not "forget thy commandments" (the law, instructions, precepts, promises of God).

   Homily

   Albert Barnes, in summarizing Psalm 119, wrote, "This Psalm, more than any other, abounds in confident statements respecting the life of the author, his attachment to the law of God, the obedience which he rendered to that law, and his love for it—as well as with appeals to God, founded on the fact that he did love that law, and that his life was one of obedience."[1109] Barnes continues, "The Psalm would not have been complete as a record of religious experience, or as illustrating the real state of the human heart, without a distinct acknowledgment of sin, and hence, in its close, and in view of his whole life, upright as in the main it had been, the Psalmist confesses that he had wandered; that he was a sinner; that his life had been far from perfection, and that he needed the gracious interposition of God to seek him out, and to bring him back."[1110] J. J. S. Perowne says, "According to the accents, the rendering would rather be, 'I have gone astray; seek Thy servant as a lost sheep.' In what sense can one who has so repeatedly declared his love of God's word, who has asserted that he has kept God's precepts, make this confession? The figure cannot be employed here in the same sense, for instance, in which it is employed in our Lord's parable. He who is the lost sheep here is one who does not forget God's commandments. The figure, therefore, seems in this place to denote the helpless condition of the Psalmist, without protectors, exposed to enemies, in the midst of whom he wanders, not knowing where to find rest and shelter. But in the 'I have gone astray,' there is doubtless the sense of sin as well as of weakness, though there is also the consciousness of love to God's law, 'I do not forget Thy commandments.' The word rendered 'lost' may be rendered 'ready to perish.'[1111]

I have gone astray like lost sheep. W. S. Plumer writes, "Lost sheep are always in danger, and often in distress. Sin both imperils and embitters life. As a sheep is a silly and helpless thing, and, when lost, never finds itself, but wanders on, till the shepherd seeks it; so the soul of man must be brought back from its errors and miseries by the Lord Himself. Such is the common view taken by expositors."[1112] David confesses to the Lord that he was guilty of wandering, straying off the righteous path like a "lost sheep" into sin, and needed restoration. He accepted full blame for the transgression. This is almost the only time in the entire Psalm that David actually confesses his sin.[1113]

Despite the Christian's ardent and fervent commitment to the Lord, at times during the pilgrimage to Heaven, like David, he will wander away from the fold as a *sheep,* inapt to find his way back home. The saint, as the lost sinner, cannot recover himself from the pigpen of sin; he is dependent upon the Lord, the supreme Shepherd, for restoration. Regrettably, when we sing, "I have ceased from my wandering and going astray, since Jesus came into my heart," it is an untruth, for in us "dwelleth no good thing." See Romans 7:18. Salvation doesn't mean instant perfection. We all stray, drift at times in deed or thought in keeping God's law. In *straying,* the saint not only forfeits happiness, peace and fellowship with the Lord, but also exposes himself to numerous dangers and harms (as did the prodigal son in Luke 15:13). The true believer *bemoans* departure from the path of uprightness and *groans* for restoration, recovery and renewal.

Prone to wander, Lord, I feel it;
    Prone to leave the God I love.
Here's my heart; oh, take and seal it,
    Seal it for Thy courts above. ~ Robert Robinson (1758)

Wondrously the Good Shepherd *pursues* the wandering sheep until it is "found" through conviction, chastisement, conscience and the church, in loving-kindness. Though we abandon Him, He loves us too much to abandon us.

I do not forget thy commandments. Albert Barnes paraphrases David: "In all my wandering; with my consciousness of error; with my sense of guilt, I still do feel that I love thy law—thy service—thy commandments. They are the joy of my heart, and I desire to be recalled from all my wanderings, that I may find perfect happiness in Thee and in Thy service evermore."[1114]

Spurgeon makes application for the believer, saying, "Now, if the grace of God enables us to maintain in our hearts the loving memory of God's commandments, it will surely yet restore us to practical holiness. We cannot be utterly lost if our heart is still with God. If we be gone astray in many respects, yet still, if we be true in our soul's inmost desires, we shall be found again, and fully restored."[1115] In times of failure, it is good for the believer to remember "thy commandments"—especially the "promises" that assure forgiveness, mercy and restoration—to retard the fiery darts of doubts of Satan hurled upon the soul. Heaven only knows how many a wayward saint and sinner in *rescue missions* or upon *skid row* were spiritually rescued by remembering the "Word" that was instilled in their heart as a youngster upon their mother's lap or in Sunday School.

The Father, in seeing the prodigal son on the road home, runs to meet him. It's the only time in the Bible where God is pictured in a hurry. Jesus so readily receives the wandering saint back home that He runs to meet him with open arms and compassion. See Luke 15:20. Spurgeon well said, "It is blessed to know that the grace of God is free to us at all times, without preparation, without fitness, without money, and without price! 'I will love them freely.' These words invite backsliders to return: indeed, the text (Hosea 14:4) was specially written for such—'I will heal their backsliding; I will love them freely.'"[1116]

Backslider! surely the generosity of the promise will at once break your heart, and you will return and seek your injured Father's face.

Backsliding souls, return to God;
>Your faithful God is gracious still.
Leave the false ways ye long have trod,
>And he will all backsliding heal.

Poor, famish'd prodigal, come home;
>Thy father's house is open yet.
Much greater mercy bids thee come
>Than all thy sins, though these are great.

The blood of Christ (a precious blood!)
>Cleanses from all sin (doubt it not)
And reconciles the soul to God
>From every folly, every fault. ~ Joseph Hart (1832)

Stay mindful of the purpose for which Jesus came into the world—"to seek and to save that which was lost." See Luke 19:10. The unsaved are utterly dependent upon the Lord for rescue and deliverance from sin's domination and penalty. "Look unto me, and be ye saved, all the ends of the earth: for I am God, and there is none else" (Isaiah 45:22).

The Bottom Line: All we like sheep do go astray, but the Good Shepherd (Jesus) will always restore upon our confession and repentance ("I have gone astray"). See 1 John 1:9. The believer longs for that day (Heaven) in which he may sing truthfully and with exuberant joy, "I have ceased from my wanderings and going astray."

40. Lying Lips (False Accusations)   Psalm 120:1–4

"In my distress I cried unto the Lord, and he heard me. Deliver my soul, O Lord, from lying lips, and from a deceitful tongue. What shall be

given unto thee? or what shall be done unto thee, thou false tongue? Sharp arrows of the mighty, with coals of juniper."—Psalm 120:1–4.

In my "distress" (Strong says "adversary, adversity, affliction, anguish, distress, tribulation, trouble"[1117]) I "cried unto the Lord" (Landes says "to call, shout, summon, proclaim, announce"[1118]). And he "heard me" (answered). "Deliver my soul" (Swanson says "saved, delivered, be spared, i.e., pertaining to being safe from danger, and so be in a more favorable circumstance; deliver, save, rescue, defend, ease, i.e., cause one to be safe and out of danger"[1119]). O Lord, from "lying lips" (Brown, Driver and Briggs say "deception, disappointment, falsehood; deception, what deceives, disappoints, and betrays one."[1120]).

AND from a "deceitful tongue" (Swanson says "deceit, treachery, i.e., the state or condition of causing something false to be believed as true (in word or action), and so mislead."[1121] Poole says "which covereth mischievous designs with pretenses of kindness"[1122]). What shall be given unto thee? Or what shall be done unto thee, thou false tongue? (The Psalmist addresses the slanderer. In the next verse he answers his own question.).

"Sharp arrows of the mighty" (Kirkpatrick says, "He has shot his arrows of slander or false accusation at the innocent, but a mightier than he, even God Himself, will pierce him with the arrows of His judgement: he has kindled the fire of strife by his falsehoods, but the lightnings of Divine wrath will consume him."[1123]) with "coals of juniper" (Kirkpatrick says "metaphor for divine judgments"[1124]).

Homily

Psalms 120–134 are entitled "Songs of Degrees." It is most likely they were sung by the Israelites in their pilgrimage to Jerusalem on festival occasions, three times a year.[1125] See Deuteronomy 16:16 and 1 Kings 12:27–28. David is the author of four (Psalm 122, Psalm 124, Psalm 131 and Psalm 133), Solomon of one (Psalm 127), while the authors of the other ten are unknown. The Psalms were probably composed following the captivity.[1126] "Their very name—'Songs of Degrees'—denotes that they were sung as the people went up towards their land, their city, and the sanctuary of the Lord. But the frequent allusions to the Exile [captivity in Babylon], to its degradation and sorrow, to the almost complete destruction which had there all but overtaken them, and then to their preservation and restoration, all show that in these fifteen Psalms we have the devout utterances of those whom God had once suffered to be in exile, but whom he had not only graciously preserved therein, but now had wonderfully restored. So that we may picture the long line of the returning captives as they journeyed on over the weary waste of rock and sand which stretched between the place of their exile and their beloved home. We listen to them refreshing and cheering their hearts from time to time by singing one or other of these holy Psalms. After their return, these Psalms appear to have been collected together, and to have formed part of their national liturgy, and were sung, as they well deserved to be, when their city and temple were again built and dedicated to the Lord."[1127] A. F. Kirkpatrick agrees, saying, "On the title, *A song of ascents*, or A song for the goings up, prefixed to this and the next fourteen Psalms. They are probably taken from a collection of the songs sung by pilgrims as they went up to the Feasts at Jerusalem."[1128]

The Psalmist, overwhelmed with "distress" (soul anguish, disturbance) about those that spoke lies about him (slanderers, betrayers), pleads for divine rescue ("Deliver my soul, O Lord."). Matthew Henry said, "They smiled in his face and kissed him, even when they were aiming to smite him under the fifth rib. The most dangerous enemies, and those which it is most hard to guard against, are such as carry on their malicious designs under the color of friendship. The Lord deliver every good man from such lying lips."[1129] A slanderer is a person who gives an untrue report (verbal, gestures, writing, pictures, etc.) about another. W. S. Plumer wrote, "Innocence is no shield against the slanders invented by the father of lies, and spread abroad by his children."[1130]

The Old Testament condemns slandering: "Do not spread false rumors, and do not help a guilty person by giving false testimony" (Exodus 23: 1 GNT), as does the New Testament: "Brothers, do not slander one another. Anyone who speaks against his brother or judges him speaks against the law and judges it. When you judge the law, you are not keeping it, but sitting in judgment on it" (James 4: 11 NIV). An old writer has said about slander, "This is an accursed thing! It works oftentimes by other means than words: by a look or a shrug of the shoulders it levels its poisoned arrows; it has broken many a virtuous heart and stained many a virtuous reputation. It has nodded away many a good name, and winked into existence a host of suspicions, that have gathered round and crushed the most chaste and virtuous of our kind. It often works in the dark, and generally under the mask of truthfulness and love."[1131]

William Barclay wrote, "In these terrible days men will be *slanderers*. The Greek for *slanderer* is *diabolos,* which is precisely the English word *devil.* The devil is the patron saint of all slanderers and of all slanderers he is chief. There is a sense in which slander is the most cruel of all sins. If a man's goods are stolen, he can set to and build up his fortunes again; but if his good name is taken away, irreparable damage has been done."[1132] "Tongues are more terrible instruments than can be made with hammers and anvils, and the evil which they inflict cuts deeper and spreads wider."[1133] The average person speaks 11,000,000 words in a year. That's 715,000,000 words by the age 65. Our words may be kind, gracious, polite, courteous, godly, uplifting, edifying; or debasing, deflating, profane, damaging, cruel, insensitive and destructive. Paul admonishes, "No foul language should come from your mouth, but only what is good for building up someone in need, so that it gives grace to those who hear" (Ephesians 4:29 CSB). God commanded, "Do not bear false witness against your neighbor" (Exodus 20:16 TLV). Many are they that bear the scar and pain caused by lying lips (false accusations). Marriages have been shipwrecked, ministries ruined, reputations irreparably marred, friendships abolished, innocence stolen, freedom forfeited (incarceration in prison) and lives ended (suicide) all because of an untruth propagated. It is because of the irreparable damage and harm of lying that God judges it severely and harshly.

> Tongues are more terrible instruments than can be made with hammers and anvils, and the evil which they inflict cuts deeper and spreads wider.
> William Barclay

As Shakespeare had it:
Good name in man and woman, dear my lord,
Is the immediate jewel of their souls:
Who steals my purse steals trash; 'tis something, nothing;
Twas mine, 'tis his, and has been slave to thousands:
But he that filches from me my good name
Robs me of that which not enriches him
And makes me poor indeed.

"Many men and women who would never dream of stealing, think nothing—even find pleasure—in passing on a story which ruins someone else's good name, without even trying to find out whether or not it is true."[1134]

What shall be done unto thee, thou false tongue? George Horne states, "The purport of the question plainly is this: What profit or advantage do you expect to reap from this practice of lying and slandering? what will at last be its end and its reward?"[1135] The Psalmist answers his own question. The slanderous liar will experience divine pun-ishment. See Psalm 120:4. J. A. Alexander writes, "The general idea of severe and painful punishment is here expressed by the obvious and intelligible figures of keen arrows and hot coals."[1136] *Sharp arrows of the mighty.* W. S. Plumer says, "The arrows of a mighty man were used in war and shot from powerful crossbows, inflicting death or exquisite agony."[1137] *With coals of juniper.* Spurgeon says, "The slanderer will feel woes comparable to coals of juniper, which are quick in flaming, fierce in blazing, and long in burning. Juniper coals long retain their heat, but Hell burneth ever, and the deceitful tongue may not deceive itself with the hope of escape from the fire which it has kindled. What a crime is this to which the Almighty allots a doom so dreadful!"[1138] Solomon said, "A false witness shall not be unpunished, and he that speaketh lies shall not escape" (Proverbs 19:5). See Psalm 5:6. Matthew Henry remarked, "They set God at a distance from them, but from afar his arrows can reach them."[1139] See Psalm 64:7. False accusations may boomerang. Haman devised a plot to frame Mordecai (false accusations about him) that he might be hung on a gallows fifty cubits high. But the plot was discovered, and he, not Mordecai, was hung on those very gallows. See Esther 5:9–14; 6:4.

R. A. Torrey identifies four kinds of slanderers. "The slanderous liar slanders his fellowman, the atheistical liar slanders God, the infidel liar slanders the Word of God and the God who is the author of it, and the Unitarian liar slanders the Son of God. The apostle John tells us that the Unitarian liar is the liar of liars. See 1 John 2:22."[1140] "The slanderer wounds three at once—himself, him he speaks of, and him that hears."[1141]

The Bottom Line: "Lying is Satan's work. And when we engage in lying, we let our hearts become Satan's workshop."[1142] See John 8:44.

Slanderous lying is like opening the cage of a venomous snake upon another. Its posionous fangs destroys the life. Slanderous lying is like throwing a lit match upon a keg of dynamite. Its explosion may be far more devastating than intended or imagined. Slanderous lying is like gutting a feather pillow in the face of hurricane force winds. Despite regret in the aftermath, the "feathers" can never be retrieved. Lying is like playing dominos. The words, for the immediate future at least, keep impacting lives.

41. A Psalm of Hope in the Time of Trial   Psalm 121

"I will lift up mine eyes unto the hills, from whence cometh my help. My help cometh from the LORD, which made heaven and earth. He will not suffer thy foot to be moved: he that keepeth thee will not slumber. Behold, he that keepeth Israel shall neither slumber nor sleep. The LORD is thy keeper: the LORD is thy shade upon thy right hand. The sun shall not smite thee by day, nor the moon by night. The LORD shall preserve thee from all evil: he shall preserve thy soul. The LORD shall preserve thy going out and thy coming in from this time forth, and even for evermore."— Psalm 121.

"I will lift up mine eyes" (In distress often one "looks down" at the feet in gloom and despair. The Psalmist exclaims that he will "look up" in confident assurance to the Lord for hope and help. Gill says, "The lifting up of the eyes is a prayer gesture [John 11:41] and is expressive of boldness and confidence in prayer, and of hope and expectation of help and salvation [Job 11:15]; when, on the contrary, persons abashed and ashamed, hopeless and helpless, cannot look up, or lift up their eyes or face to God [Ezra 9:6]."[1143] Simeon says, "It represents the Psalmist as expressing his conviction of the utter insufficiency of all earthly powers to assist him, and his determination to confide in God alone."[1144]).

"Unto the hills" (Rawlinson says, "The 'holy hills' that stand round about Jerusalem are intended [Psalm 87:1; Psalm 125:2]."[1145] The "holy hills" were Moriah and Zion where the ark of God was housed, the symbol of His holy presence, or he was lifting his eyes to Heaven and God who dwelled there [Psalm 3:2].[1146] In light of the Psalm being *The Traveler's Psalm,* chanted or sung by the people in route to the holy feast (one of

192

three annual) in Jerusalem, the former interpretation is most likely. The point is that the Jews did not look for help to the hills where the graven idols stood or to the people that dwelt among them for assistance, but alone unto their mighty Deliverer from captivity and Holy Warrior, Defender and Helper, the Lord God Almighty who made the mountains.).

"From whence cometh my help" (The clause should be read as a question.[1147] But, Cheyne says, "the question is only asked to give more effect to the answer."[1148] Kirkpatrick says, "The question of the second line (which cannot be taken as a relative clause) is not one of doubt or despondency, but is simply asked to introduce the answer which follows in Psalm 121:2. That answer gives a deeper turn to the thought of the question. It is not from the mountains of Zion, but from Jehovah Who has fixed His earthly dwelling-place there that help comes."[1149]).

"My help" (Swanson says "helper, assistant, i.e., one who assists and serves another with what is needed."[1150] Ellicott says "not as the superstition of the Canaanite said, from the sacred summits themselves, but from their Creator's Lord."[1151]) "cometh from the Lord, which made heaven and earth" (Kirkpatrick says "is a frequent epithet of Jehovah in the later Psalms [Psalm 115:15; Psalm 124:8; Psalm 134:3; Psalm 146:6]. It is the guarantee of His power to help. It contrasts His omnipotence with the impotence of the heathen gods 'that have not made the heavens and the earth' [Jeremiah 10:11]."[1152]).

He will not "suffer thy foot to be moved" (Brown, Driver and Briggs say "remove, retire; deviate from right course; repel, push, thrust; dwindle, diminish, grow weak."[1153] The Psalmist assures himself that Jehovah will enable his feet to stand firm, preventing stumbling, and be his able Protector.) "he that keepeth" (watches over as a guardian) thee will not slumber. Behold, he that keepeth Israel "shall neither slumber nor sleep" (His sleepless vigilance. Barnes says, "He will be ever watchful and wakeful. Compare Isaiah 27:3. All creatures, as far as we know, sleep; God never sleeps. Compare Psalm 139:11–12. His eyes are upon us by day and in the darkness of the night—the night literally; and also the night of calamity, woe, and sorrow."[1154] MacArthur says, "The living God is totally unlike the pagan gods/dead idols [1 Kings 18:27]."[1155]).

"The Lord is thy keeper" (Landes says "to keep, watch over, observe; to take care of, preserve, protect; to save, retain; to do something carefully; watchmen, guards."[1156] Barnes says "thy Preserver; thy Defender. He will keep thee from danger; He will keep thee from sin; He will keep thee unto salvation."[1157]) the Lord is "thy shade" (Kirkpatrick says, "'Shade' seems simply to denote 'protection' generally, the idea of the metaphor being lost [Psalm 91:1; Numbers 14:9]; hence it can be joined with 'upon thy right hand,' that being the usual position of the champion or protector (Psalm 16:8; Psalm 109:31)."[1158] Rawlinson says, "'*Thy shade*' means 'thy protection; thy defense.'"[1159]).

"Upon thy right hand" (Rawlinson says, "Protection was especially needed on the right hand, as the side which no shield guarded."[1160] In other places in Scripture God's right hand of protection and power is said to be the believer's defender. Of this, Vine, Unger and White say, "The Bible speaks anthropomorphically, attributing to God human parts and, in particular, a 'right hand' [Exodus 15:6]. The Bible teaches that God is a Spirit and has no body or bodily parts [Exod. 20:4; Deut. 4:15–19]. This figure is used of God's effecting His will among men and of His working in their behalf [showing His favor]."[1161] Jennings and Lowe say, "What is true of Israel is true of the individual believer also. All that is meant is that Jehovah is a shelter to the believer and is ever at his right hand to forestall his need." [1162]).

"The sun shall not smite thee by day" (Barnes says, "The Hebrew word means to smite, to strike, as with a rod or staff, or with the plague or pestilence; and then, to kill, to slay. The allusion here is to what is now called a 'sunstroke'—the effect of the burning sun on the brain. Such effects of the sun are often fatal now, as doubtless they were in the time of the Psalmist."[1163] Jennings and Lowe say *smite* is "used with reference to the injurious effects of."[1164] See Jonah 4:8.) "nor the moon by night" (Clarke says, "I believe the Psalmist simply means, they shall not be injured by heat nor cold; by a *sunstroke* by day nor a *frostbite* by night."[1165] Barnes says, "The Psalmist here refers to some prevalent opinion about the influence of the moon, as endangering life or health. Some have supposed that he refers to the sudden cold which follows the intense heat of the day in Oriental countries."[1166] The point of both "sun" and "moon" is that God protects His children from harm day and night.)

The Lord shall "preserve thee" (Gesenius and Tregelles say "to keep, to watch, to guard; to guard from anything."[1167]) from "all evil" (Swanson says "bad, evil, wicked, no good, i.e., pertaining to that which is not morally pure or good according to a proper standard, implying this evil hinders or severs a relationship to a person or principle which is proper."[1168]) he shall "preserve thy soul" (Matthew Henry says, "All souls are His; and the soul is the man, and therefore He will with a peculiar care preserve them, that they be not defiled by sin and disturbed by affliction. He will keep them by keeping us in the possession of them; and He will preserve them from perishing eternally."[1169]).

"The Lord shall preserve thy going out and thy coming in" (Kirkpatrick says "all thy undertakings and occupations."[1170] Jennings and Lowe say, "This phraseology is borrowed from the blessing for obedience in Deuteronomy 28:6: "Blessed art thou when thou comest in, and blessed art thou when thou goest out" [see also Deuteronomy 31:2; 1 Samuel 29:6]. What is meant is 'Jehovah shall bless thee in all the actions of thy life.'"[1171]) "from this time forth, and even for evermore" (Without ceasing, until the end when the saint is with Jesus in Heaven.).

Homily

J. A. Alexander wrote, "The whole Psalm is a description of Jehovah as the Guardian or Protector of His people."[1172] Its author is uncertain.

As the Jews traveled to Jerusalem (to attend one of the three annual feasts of celebration to the Lord) over rugged terrain (no roads, merely paths at best) where robbers might easily hide for attack, they found joy and peace in singing this Psalm. The Psalm is not just for the traveling Jew to sing in journey to Jerusalem, but for every believer to sing in the pilgrimage to Heaven. Life is encompassed with many troubles, trials, and tribulations, prompting fear and anxiety and hidden "snares" to cause stumbling. Recitation and application of this Psalm in such times proffers peace, hope and consolation, as it did for the Israelites.

I will lift up mine eyes. The Psalmist reminds the believer that in time of trouble, anxiety or sorrow, he should look up, not out or in or down. "A man duly sensible of his dependence on God abhors the idea of trusting in an arm of flesh. He would not so dishonor God; he would not so invade His unalienable prerogative. He loves the very thought of being a pensioner on the Divine bounty. The habit of committing every concern to God, and of receiving every blessing from God, is truly delightful to him."[1173] *To look out* unto man or to *look in* unto self for help or to look down in hopeless despondency and paralyzing fear is futile. Help is found in *looking up*. *My help cometh from the Lord.* Matthew Henry remarks, "Shall I depend upon the strength of the hills? upon princes and great men? No; my confidence is in God only....[W]e must lift up our eyes above the hills. We must see all our help in God; from Him we must expect it, in His own way and time....It is almighty wisdom that contrives, and almighty power that works the safety of those that put themselves under God's protection."[1174]

> *To look out* unto man or *to look in* unto self for help or *to look down* in hopeless despondency and paralyzing fear is futile. Help is found in *looking up*.

Who made heaven and earth. Matthew Henry said, "He that made heaven and earth is sovereign Lord of all the hosts of both, and can make use of them as He pleases for the help of His people, and restrain them when He pleases from hurting His people."[1175] God will move all "heaven and earth" (go to the utter limits) to care for His children. That's how much He loves us! *He that keepeth thee.* Jehovah is the believer's Protector, Defender, Deliverer, Guardian, and Preserver. He keeps you from all sorts of evil (bad and wicked things) and the fear associated with it. He keeps you from harm (injury, sickness, suffering, loss) except that designed for your good and His glory. See 1 Peter 1:6–7; Romans 5:3–5; Psalm 34:19 and Romans 8:18, 28. He keeps you from sin and mischief. See Psalm 19:13. He keeps you from stumbling, staggering or falling in the faith. See Jude 24. He keeps you secure in salvation. See John 10:28–29. He keeps you from temptation. See Matthew 6:13.

He will not suffer thy foot to be moved. Whatever the storm that assails and the hurt it inflicts, the believer's footing will be firm, "steadfast, unmoveable, always abounding in the work of the Lord" (1 Corinthians 15:58), for his feet are fixed, established upon the "the Solid Rock." John Gill remarks, "The Lord keeps the feet of his saints from falling: he will not suffer them to be moved out of the spiritual estate in which they stand; nor off of the Foundation and Rock of ages, on which their feet are set, and their goings established."[1176] Calvin said, "He will not suffer thee to stumble."[1177] Edwards states, "He will not suffer thy foot to slip."[1178] *The Lord is thy keeper.* "Jehovah's work is all perfect. His guardian, preserving care is all we need."[1179] *Thy shade at thy right hand.* J. J. S. Perowne wrote, "Jehovah standing upon thy right hand to defend thee is thy shade."[1180] J. A. Alexander states, "A shade or shadow is a common figure for protector, and the right hand often mentioned as the place of a protector."[1181] See Psalm 110:5 and Numbers 14:9.

My hope is built on nothing less
Than Jesus Christ, my righteousness;
I dare not trust the sweetest frame,
But wholly lean on Jesus' name.

On Christ, the solid Rock, I stand.
All other ground is sinking sand;
All other ground is sinking sand.

When darkness veils His lovely face,
I rest on His unchanging grace;
In every high and stormy gale,
My anchor holds within the veil. ~ Edward Mote (1797–1874)

He shall preserve thy going out and thy coming in. God's umbrella of protection *forever* envelops the saint, from the moment of departure from home to work or for errand until his return. He safekeeps His child in sickness or health, peace or adversity, gain or loss, joy or sorrow.

Every pious Jew, in departure from and return to home, touches the *Mezuza*—a small metal cylinder attached to the right-hand doorpost. It contains parchment inscribed with Deuteronomy 6:4–9 and Deuteronomy 11:13–21. He then recites Psalm 121:8.[1182] It might do believers good to practice this formal ritual so as to forge in the heart and mind the promise of God's sovereign protection to both them and their families.

George Horne comments, "The good man, during his journey through life, shall be under God's protection at all seasons, as Israel in the wilderness was defended from the burning heat of the sun, by the moist and refreshing shadow of the cloud; and secured against the inclement influences of the nocturnal heavens, by the kindly warmth and splendour diffused from the pillar of fire."[1183]

Be not dismayed whate'er betide;
 God will take care of you.
Beneath his wings of love abide;
 God will take care of you.

God will take care of you,
 Through ev'ry day,
 O'er all the way.
He will take care of you;
God will take care of you.

Through days of toil when heart does fail,
 God will take care of you;
When dangers fierce your path assail,
 God will take care of you.

No matter what may be the test,
 God will take care of you.
Lean, weary one, upon his breast;
 God will take care of you. ~ Civilla D. Martin (1904)

Knowing God's promises, trust Him to care for you or those that you love. In faith, cry out unto Him for help, as the Psalmist did. It takes faith to pray for what we want, but it takes more faith to take what God gives.[1184]

Approach, my soul, the mercy seat
 Where Jesus answers pray'r;
There humbly fall before His feet,
 For none can perish there.

Thy promise is my only plea;
 With this I venture nigh.
Thou callest burdened souls to Thee,
 And such, O Lord, am I. ~ John Newton (1779)

Charles Simeon wrote, "You should never forget what an Almighty Friend you have. How many times in this psalm are you reminded, that the Lord, even the Almighty God, is your Helper and Deliverer! Were He less powerful or less vigilant or less worthy of credit, you might well fear. But what ground can he have for fear who has God Himself for his refuge?...Only rely on God, and you are safe."[1185]

> Only rely on God, and you are safe.
> Charles Simeon

George W. Truett cautions, "Mind, when trouble comes, how you behave. No matter what the trouble is, mind how you behave. Many a man has dishonored God when trouble came. No matter what the trouble is, no matter what brought it, no matter who brought it, no matter how it came about, God is dishonored if a Christian does not bear his fiery trial like he ought to bear it. You are being tested for God, and you will dishonor Him egregiously, or you will honor Him gloriously, according to your behavior when trouble is on. Remember that."[1186]

The Bottom Line: J. M. Boice says, "The point of Psalm 121 is not that we will not have problems, but that God will keep us safe as we go through them."[1187] Spurgeon summarizes the Psalm, "Jehovah will keep thy soul....If the soul be kept, all is kept....Our soul is kept from the dominion of sin, the infection of error, the crush of despondency, the puffing up of pride; kept from the world, the flesh, and the Devil;...kept in the love of God; kept unto the eternal kingdom and glory. What can harm a soul that is kept of the Lord?"[1188] Whatever happens to the *shell* in which the soul is housed (the body) is "not worthy to be compared with the glory which shall be revealed in us" (Romans 8:18).

42. Why Going to Church Makes Us Glad   Psalm 122:1

"I was glad when they said unto me, Let us go into the house of the LORD."—Psalm 122:1.

"I" (David, the Psalm's composer, but also the words (song) of the Jews as they traveled to Jerusalem to worship) was glad" (Swanson says "rejoice, be glad, delight in, be elated, i.e., have a feeling or attitude of joy and happiness, with a possible focus of making an outward expression of that joy [Deuteronomy 27:7]."[1189] Jennings and Lowe say "lit. 'I had joy in those who said to me'"[1190]).

When "they said unto me" (David's friends) "Let us go" (An invitation was extended to David to join "us," not "you go into." Benson says "or, we will go, into the house of the Lord."[1191] Plumer says, "Literally, I was glad in those saying to me, To the house of Jehovah we will go."[1192]) "into the house of the Lord" (Barnes says "up to the place where God dwells; the house which He has made His abode."[1193] Mount Zion, (Jerusalem) the first chosen city by God wherein He would record His name.).

Homily

A Psalm composed by David and sung by the Israelites in their journey to attend one of the three annual great festivals in Jerusalem (The Feast of Unleavened Bread; The Feast of Pentecost; The Feast of Tabernacles). Jerusalem was their *spiritual center*. David testifies to the awesome joy it was to be invited by others to join them in the journey to "church" to worship. Matthew Henry states, "In singing this Psalm we must have an eye to the gospel church, which is called the 'Jerusalem that is from above.'"[1194]

I was glad. That which was of wondrous joy and gladness to David sadly is a joy for most, for they do not darken the doors of the church. The decline in church attendance by the masses prompts the sincere Christian to ask with Nehemiah, "Why is the house of God forsaken?" (Nehemiah 13:11). It is forsaken due to its inner turmoil and faction; inconsistencies in talk and walk among its members; inefficiency or lack of proficiency in the programs offered (failure to prepare adequately for preaching, teaching and singing; just throwing things together at the last minute); unfriendly reception; compromise of Biblical truth; absence of evangelism; liturguical formality; unwillingness to change methods—to think outside the box (not compromise of biblical message); disunity; dullness or "coldness"; and loss of focus (failure to keep the main thing, the main thing [Proverbs 29:18]). Hindering "walls" (personally and corporately as a body) erected must be pulled down regardless of tradition, preference or culture.

The reasons that David found gladness in going to church reveal why it likewise should be an awesome pleasure for every believer. He found gladness in going to church because of *the people who would gather there.* "Let us go into the house of the Lord." To intertwine with fellow saints that have had a taste out of the same fountain of Living Water is soul enriching and life enhancing. Believers "spur" or encourage each other forward in the faith, in its belief, steadfastness and practice. The author of Hebrews exhorted, "And let us consider *how we may spur one another on toward love and good deeds,* not giving up meeting together, as some are in the habit of doing, but encouraging one another—and all the more as you see the Day approaching" (Hebrews 10:24-25 NIV).

You will notice we say "brother and sister" 'round here;
It's because we're a family and these are so near.
When one has a heartache, we all share the tears
And rejoice in each victory in this family so dear.

I'm so glad I'm a part of the Family of God;
I've been washed in the fountain, cleansed by His blood!
Joint heirs with Jesus as we travel this sod,
For I'm part of the family, the Family of God. ~ Bill and Gloria Gaither

The praise that would occur there. "To give thanks unto the name of the LORD" (Psalm 122:4). David said, "Praise waiteth for thee, O God, in Zion" (Psalm 65:1). See Psalm 100:4. It is joyous to attend church to render unto the Lord the sacrifice of praise and thanksgiving for all His benefits and blessings.

The precepts that would be taught there. David said, "Thy testimonies have I taken as an heritage forever: for they are the rejoicing of my heart" (Psalm 119:111). Again David declared, "I rejoice at thy word, as one that findeth great spoil" (Psalm 119:162). It is a joy to hear and receive the Word of the Lord as it is proclaimed from church pulpit and classroom rostrum. It is delightful "medicine" to the soul. Martin Luther wrote, "Our Jerusalem is the church, and our temple is Christ. Wheresoever Christ is preached...there we are sure God dwells; and there

201

is our temple, our tabernacle, our cherubim, and our mercy-seat; for there God is present with us by His Word."[1195]

The peace that would be manifest there. David found comfort in the "church" in the aftermath of his baby son's death. See 2 Samuel 12:20–21. He often pined for or resorted to the church for comfort and consolation. The church provides an oasis from the trouble, anxiety and conflict of the world.

The power that had been experienced there. David's joy in "church" attendance was also based upon the power of God that wrought his deliverance from the chains of sin, fear, guilt and anxiety. In and through His church the Lord works miracles, rescuing souls from spiritual bondage and eternal damnation. He that has been saved within her walls during a revival, VBS, church service or other event exhibits a special connection with and pleasure for her. All who experience the touch of Jesus (pardon) love the church which He founded.

The person that would be worshipped there. "Let us go into the house of the LORD" (Psalm 122:1). It is His "house." And we enter it to glorify Him with all the mind, soul and strength. The Psalmist declared "Then will *I go unto the altar of God, unto God my exceeding joy*: yea, upon the harp will I praise thee, O God my God" (Psalm 43:4). God is the "exceeding joy" of the redeemed, who find great delight in the worship and adoration of Him. W. S. Plumer states, "The great end and aim of religious assemblies are not merely the promotion of decency and morality among men, but obedience to the command of God and the due celebration of *His* worship, of which thanksgiving is an important part."[1196] Going to church is a pleasure (awesome gladness) because of the people that gather there, the precept that is taught there, the praise that is lifted up there, the peace that is manifest there; but all would be futile were it not for the Person that is worshipped there. The fundamental reason to go to church is to experience the presence and power of the Lord.

They said unto me, let us go into the house of the Lord. David was grateful for the encouragement of other believers to attend church. He didn't resent it or chide them for it. Spurgeon remarks, "Good children are pleased to go home and glad to hear their brothers and sisters call them thither. David's heart was in the worship of God, and he was delighted when he found others inviting him to go where his desires had already gone: it helps the ardor of the most ardent to hear others inviting them to a holy duty. The word was not 'go,' but 'let us go'; hence the ear of the Psalmist found a double joy in it. He was glad for the sake of others: glad that they wished to go themselves, glad that they had the courage and liberality to invite others."[1197] May the day be soon that "many people shall go and say, Come ye, and let us go up to the mountain of the LORD, to the house of the God of Jacob; and he will teach us of his ways, and we will walk in his paths: for out of Zion shall go forth the law, and the word of the LORD from Jerusalem" (Isaiah 2:3). The saint must no longer bite his tongue but boldly invite saint and sinner to attend worship in the house of the Lord on a regular basis.

The Bottom Line: Going to church ought to be a delight, not a dread. Believers ought to constantly extol others to join them in attending church. At times there must be an adjustment of methodology to avoid stagnation and decline. The seven last words of the church are "we never did it that way before." W. S. Plumer said, "If a converted man who did not love the worship of God could be found, he would be such a monster as the world has never seen."[1198]

43. Pray for the Peace of Jerusalem   Psalm 122:6–7

"Pray for the peace of Jerusalem: they shall prosper that love thee. Peace be within thy walls, and prosperity within thy palaces."— Psalm 122:6–7.

"Pray" (Harris, Archer and Waltke say "ask, inquire, beg."[1199] Plumer says, "In asking for the peace of the Holy City, they sought all that could make it great."[1200] Kirkpatrick says, "This is probably the right rendering; but the phrase might also be rendered 'Inquire for the welfare of Jersualem,' greet or salute her, the customary salutation being 'Is it well (lit. peace) with thee?' or 'Peace be unto thee.'"[1201]) for the "peace" (*Shalom*. Landes says "prosperity, success; intactness; welfare, state of health, peace; friendliness; deliverance, salvation."[1202]) of "Jerusalem" (Whitaker, Brown, Driver and Briggs say "renowned as capital of all Israel, afterwards of southern kingdom, seat of central worship in temple, first named as city of Canaanite Adoni-Ṣedek; inhabited by Jebusites;

captured by Judah; first named in connection with David; taken possession of by David as king; David's royal seat; it remained the capital until taken by Nebuchadnezzar, 588 B.C.; it became the chief home of the returned exiles."[1203] Perowne says, 'PEACE...PROSPER, and in the next verse PEACE...PROSPERITY, with a play on words in the original (*shâlōm*, *shalvah*), with an allusion to the name of Jerusalem (*Yerushalaim*).'[1204]

They shall "prosper" (Swanson says "be at ease, be secure, have peace, i.e., be in a favorable circumstance, and so have lack of strife or trouble, implying peace, prosperity, and ease of life."[1205]) that "love thee" (Gesenius and Tregelles say "to desire, to love; to breathe after, to be inclined."[1206]).

Peace be within "thy walls" (Barnes says "refers here to the fortifications or defenses around Jerusalem.'[1207] Jamieson-Fausset-Brown say, "Let peace—including prosperity, everywhere prevail."[1208] Plumer says, "A term expressing the defences of the city; while palaces or courts point to the internal improvements of Jerusalem, particularly her public buildings [Psalm 48:3, 13]. The verse is a prayer that in all respects the Holy City may have the divine blessing."[1209]) AND "prosperity" (Gesenius and Tregelles say "tranquility, security [Psalm 30:7]"[1210]) "within thy palaces" (Poole says "especially in the court and the dwellings of the princes and rulers, whose welfare is a public blessing to all the people.'[1211]).

Homily

The Psalm may be biblically applied in three different ways—the actual city of Jerusalem, the church (Hebrews 12) and Heaven (the New Jerusalem).[1212]

Pray for the peace of Jerusalem. David beckons the Jews to pray for a state of tranquility and rest from conflict in Jerusalem, especially among her rulers, for the people's welfare and God's glory. Rawlinson says, "The prayer, which he would have others offer, the Psalmist now offers himself. The prayer embraces, first, the whole community; then, especially those who have the direction and government of it."[1213] Jerusalem has been attacked and overcome time and again throughout history. Yet God has preserved her. The Christian still is to pray for peace to dwell "within her walls and palaces."

Peace shall be upon Israel. The psalmist in Psalm 125:5 evokes a prayer or benediction for the peace of Israel. Franz Delitzsch states, "He means 'the Israel of God.' In these words the Psalmist gathers up all his hopes and prayers and wishes, as it were stretching out his hands over Israel in priestly benediction. Peace is the end of tyranny, hostility, division, disquiet, alarm: peace is freedom and harmony and security and blessedness. Upon this Israel he calls down peace from above."[1214] See Galatians 6:16. Archaeologists have discovered *Shalom al Yisrael* ("Peace be with Israel") inscribed in the mosaic floors of ancient synagogues in Israel.[1215]

But it extends beyond that, as Albert Barnes observes: "This is the language which those who were going up to the city—to the house of the Lord—addressed to each other, expressing the joyful feelings of their hearts at their own near approach to the city. It breathes the desire that all would pray for the peace and prosperity of a city so dear to their own souls; where the worship of God was celebrated; where God Himself dwelt; where justice was administered: a city of so much importance and so much influence in the land. To us now it inculcates the duty of praying for the church: its peace; its unity; its prosperity; its increase; its influence on our country and on the world at large."[1216]

"The church of Jesus Christ is for us what Jerusalem was for ancient Israel."[1217] See Hebrews 12:22–24.

Pray for the peace of our Jerusalem, the church. The church, like ancient and present Jerusalem, is in continuing battle from without and within (faction, disunity, division). Murdoch Campbell says, "One great evidence of our being in the way to that glorious City is that there is nothing in this world that commands our concern or interest more than the prosperity of God's Zion [church] and of all those who seek its good in every part of the world."[1218]

Spurgeon wrote, "Peace is prosperity; there can be no prosperity which is not based on peace, nor can there long be peace if prosperity be gone, for decline of grace breeds decay of love. We wish for the church rest from internal dissension and external assault: war is not her element (Acts 9:31)....Our Jerusalem is a city of palaces: kings dwell within her walls, and God himself is there. The smallest church is worthy of higher honor than the greatest confederacies of nobles....For the sake of all the saintly spirits which inhabit the city of God we may well entreat for her the boons of lasting peace and abounding prosperity."[1219]

George Horne wrote, "What that church was, the Christian church militant upon earth now is, and demandeth, in like manner, the prayers of all Christian people for its peace and welfare in a troublesome and contentious world. Its increase here below is in reality the increase of Jerusalem above, of which it is a part and ought to be a resemblance. Heaven has therefore decreed that they who contribute their labours, as well as their prayers, to promote so good and so glorious an end shall enjoy its protection, and its blessing shall be upon the work of their hands; 'They shall prosper that love thee.'"[1220]

Thankful we are for Jerusalem (the homeland of the Jews), the church (our new Jerusalem on earth) but also for the heavenly Jerusalem that is the saint's eternal abode with the Lord. John describes that city in Revelation: "Having the glory of God: and her light was like unto a stone most precious, even like a jasper stone, clear as crystal; And had a wall great and high, and had twelve gates, and at the gates twelve angels, and names written thereon, which are the names of the twelve tribes of the children of Israel: On the east three gates; on the north three gates; on the south three gates; and on the west three gates. And the wall of the city had twelve foundations, and in them the names of the twelve apostles of the Lamb" (Revelation 21:11–14).

John continues, "And I saw no temple therein: for the Lord God Almighty and the Lamb are the temple of it. And the city had no need of the sun, neither of the moon, to shine in it: for the glory of God did lighten it, and the Lamb is the light thereof. And the nations of them which are saved shall walk in the light of it: and the kings of the earth do bring their glory and honour into it. And the gates of it shall not be shut at all by day: for there shall be no night there. And they shall bring the glory and honour of the nations into it. And there shall in no wise enter into it any thing that defileth, neither whatsoever worketh abomination, or maketh a lie: but they which are written in the Lamb's book of life" (Revelation 21:22–27).

And once again the scene was changed, new earth there seem'd to be;
I saw the Holy City beside the tideless sea.
The light of God was on its streets; the gates were open wide,
And all who would might enter, and no one was denied.
No need of moon or stars by night, or sun to shine by day;
It was the new Jerusalem, that would not pass away
It was the new Jerusalem, that would not pass away.

Jerusalem! Jerusalem! Sing, for the night is o'er!
Hosanna in the highest; hosanna for evermore!
Hosanna in the highest; hosanna for evermore!

~ Frederick Edward Weatherly (1892)

The New Jerusalem (Heaven) is the homeland of the redeemed of the Lord. Only they that have experienced the new birth through Jesus Christ will be permitted within its domain.

The Bottom Line: The Christian is in pilgrimage to the New Jerusalem. As he journeys, he is to be personally involved in the advancement of the prosperity of the present Jerusalem (church), praying for her peace and welfare. Additionally, believers are to pray for the historical city of Jerusalem, the homeland of God's chosen people, that it may experience peace (rest from conflict and war).

44. Looking unto Jesus   Psalm 123:2–3

"Behold, as the eyes of servants look unto the hand of their masters, and as the eyes of a maiden unto the hand of her mistress; so our eyes wait upon the LORD our God, until that he have mercy upon us. Have mercy upon us, O LORD, have mercy upon us: for we are exceedingly filled with contempt."—Psalm 123:2–3.

Behold, as "the eyes of servants look unto the hand of their masters" (Rawlinson says "watch, i.e., for the slightest sign that he may give of his will. Such signs were usually given by some movement of the 'hand.'"[1221] Jamieson-Fausset-Brown say, "Deference, submission, and trust are all expressed by the figure. In the East, servants in attending on their masters are almost wholly directed by signs, which require the closest observance of the hands of the latter."[1222] Spurgeon says, "Orientals speak less than we do and prefer to direct their slaves by movements of their hands; hence, the domestic must fix his eyes on his master, or he might miss a sign and so fail to obey it."[1223])

AND "as the eyes of a maiden" (Holladay and Kohler say "female slave, maidservant"[1224]) "unto the hand" (Rawlinson says, "Masters were waited on by male slaves; their wives by handmaids—both equally anxious to do their will, and therefore equally watchful of all the signs that indicated it."[1225]) of her "mistress" (Swanson says "i.e., a female lord in authority or possession of another"[1226]).

So "our eyes wait upon the Lord our God" (In like manner the believer looks unto the Lord.) "until that he have mercy upon us" (Henry says, "Our eyes wait on the Lord—the eye of desire and prayer; the begging eye; and the eye of dependence, hope, and expectation; the longing eye. Our eyes must wait upon God as the Lord, and our God, until that He have mercy upon us.'[1227]).

"Have mercy upon us, O Lord, have mercy upon us" (Vine, Unger and White say "'to be gracious, considerate; to show favor.' This word is found in ancient Ugaritic with much the same meaning as in biblical Hebrew. But in modern Hebrew *chanan* seems to stress the stronger meaning of 'to pardon or to show mercy.'"[1228]).

For we are "exceedingly filled with contempt" (Dilday and Kennedy say, "The entire Israelitish community was the object of scorn and mockery. Who were those who held the people in 'contempt' (vv. 3, 4)? Perhaps they were their own public officials, cruel and corrupt at the time. Or possibly they were pagan nations and rulers."[1229] J. A. Alexander says, "The contempt is that of heathen neighbours, and especially that of the Samaritans, which is expressly mentioned in the history."[1230] See Nehemiah 1:3 and Nehemiah 2:19. Perowne says "'has long been filled,' lit. 'has been filled to itself,' the reflexive pronoun marking the depth of the inward feeling (Compare with Psalm 120:6). This expression, together with the earnestness of the repeated prayer 'Be gracious unto us,' shows that the 'scorn' and 'contempt' have long pressed upon the people, and their faith accordingly been exposed to a severe trial."[1231] Henry says, "Those who are owned of God are often despised and trampled on by the world. Some translate the words which we render *those that are at ease* and *the proud* so as to signify the persons that are scorned and contemned. 'Our soul is troubled to see how those that are at peace, and the excellent ones, are scorned and despised.' The saints are a peaceable people and yet are abused (Psalm 35:20), the excellent ones of the earth and yet undervalued, Lamentations 4:1–2."[1232]

Spurgeon says, "*Contempt is bitterness*; the person who feels it may well cry for mercy to God. Filled with contempt, as if the bitter wine had been poured in till it was up to the brim. This had become the chief thought of their minds, the peculiar sorrow of their hearts. Excluding all other feelings, a sense of scorn monopolized the soul and made it unutterably wretched. Another word is added—*exceedingly filled*. Filled to running over. A little contempt they could bear, but now they were satiated with it, and weary of it. Nothing is more wounding, embittering, festering than disdain. When our companions make little of us we are far too apt to make little of ourselves and of the consolations prepared for us. Oh, to be filled with communion, and then contempt will run off from us and never be able to fill us with its biting vinegar."[1233] It is imperative in such times of repression and persecution from the heathen or irreligious not to seek vindication for convictions and conduct, for it distracts. St. Augustine prayed, "O Lord, deliver me from this lust of always vindicating myself." Oswald Chambers states, "Such a need for constant vindication destroys our soul's faith in God. Don't say, 'I must explain myself,' or, 'I must get people to understand.' Our Lord never explained anything—He left the misunderstandings or misconcep-tions of others to correct themselves."[1234] Matthew Henry says, "*Have mercy upon us, O Lord! have mercy upon us.* We find little mercy with men; their tender mercies are cruel; there are cruel mockings. But this is our comfort, that with the Lord there is mercy and we need desire no more to relieve us, and make us easy, than the mercy of God. Whatever the troubles of the church are, God's mercy is a sovereign remedy."[1235]).

Homily

A Psalm of David composed to be sung by the Jews in their pilgrimage to the three annual big feasts in Jerusalem. A. F. Kirkpatrick speculates, "The Psalm may have been written about the time of Nehemiah's first visit to Jerusalem. It was a report of the miserable plight of the remnant of the returned exiles which induced him to go there (Nehemiah 1:3); and he speaks repeatedly of the contempt and scorn with which the Samaritans and the heathen neighbours of the Jews viewed his efforts for the restoration of the city, until the success of those efforts provoked them to measures of active hostility. See Nehemiah 2:19; Nehemiah 4:1–4; Nehemiah 4:7ff."[1236]

As the eyes of servants (slaves) look to the hand of their masters and as the eyes of the maiden (slave girl) unto the hand of her mistress (authoritative owner). Albert Barnes explains, "The true idea seems to be that they look to them with deference and respect; that they attentively mark every expression of their will; that they are ready to obey their commands on the slightest intimation of their wishes—standing in a waiting posture, with no will of their own—their own wills absorbed in the will of the master or the mistress."[1237] Savary in his letters on Africa states, "The slaves, having their hands crossed on their chest, stand silently at the end of the hall. With their eyes fastened on their Master, they seek to anticipate his every wish."[1238]

So our eyes wait upon the Lord our God. "Looking unto Jesus the author and finisher of our faith; who for the joy that was set before him endured the cross, despising the shame, and is set down at the right hand of the throne of God" (Hebrews 12:2). Spurgeon remarks, "True saints, like obedient servants, look continuously, for there is never a time when they are off duty. Upon the Lord they look expectantly, looking for supply, succor, and safety from His hands, waiting that He may have mercy upon them. They have no other confidence, and they learn to look submissively, waiting patiently for the Lord, seeking both in activity and suffering to glorify His name."[1239]

Jamieson-Fausset-Brown say, "Servants of God should look (1) to His directing hand, to appoint them their work; (2) to His supplying hand (Psalm 104:28), to give them their portion in due season; (3) to His protecting hand, to right them when wronged; (4) to His correcting hand (Isaiah 9:13; 1Peter 5:6); (5) to His rewarding hand."[1240] "Hypocrites have their eye to the world's hand; thence they have their reward (Matthew 6:2); but true Christians have their eye to God as their rewarder."[1241] Matthew Henry adds that believers ought to also look to "His assisting hand."

Thomas Manton (1620–1677) says, "The lifting up the eyes implies faith and confident persuasion that God is ready and willing to help us. The very lifting up of the bodily eyes toward Heaven is an expression of this inward trust."[1242] Spurgeon (1834–1892) explains, "The uplifted eyes naturally and instinctively represent the state of heart which fixes desire, hope, confidence, and expectation upon the Lord."[1243] Alexander Maclaren (1826–1910) says, "They should stand where they can see him; they should have their gaze fixed upon him; they should look with patient trust, as well as with eager willingness to start into activity when he indicates his commands."[1244]

> Look up, my brother and sister, to the guiding hand, providing hand, correcting hand, protecting hand, helping hand and imploring hand of the Lord attentively, continuously, submissively and expectantly.

We lift up our eyes to God—to him "that dwelleth in the heavens." See Psalm 123:1. Look up, my brother and sister, to the guiding hand, providing hand, correcting hand, protecting hand, helping hand and imploring hand of the Lord attentively, continuously, submissively and expectantly. He alone has the strength (power) to help in trouble, comfort in sorrow, heal in sickness, point the way to go in confusion and ignorance and secure in conflict. It is futile to look to man for that which the Lord alone can do.

Looking unto Jesus, never need we yield!
Over all the armor, faith the battle shield!
Standard of salvation in our hearts unfurled,
Let its elevation overcome the world.

Look away to Jesus; look away from all!
Then we need not stumble; then we shall not fall.
From each snare that lureth, foe or phantom grim,
Safety this ensureth, look away to Him.

Looking up to Jesus on the emerald throne;
Faith shall pierce the heavens where our King is gone.
Lord, on Thee depending now continually,
Heart and mind ascending, let us dwell with Thee.
~ Frances Ridley Havergal (1836–1879)

The Bottom Line: The believer's focus must be upon the *hand* of the Lord continuously lest he miss marching orders (instruction, guidance, approval) from the Lord. Spurgeon writes, "We must use our eyes with resolution, for they will not go upward to the Lord of themselves, but they incline to look downward, or inward, or anywhere but to the Lord."[1245] Oswald Chambers wrote, "This verse is a description of total reliance on God. Just as the eyes of a servant are riveted on his master, our eyes should be directed to and focused on God. This is how knowledge of His countenance is gained and how God reveals Himself to us (see Isaiah 53:1). Our spiritual strength begins to be drained when we stop lifting our eyes to Him."[1246]

45. "If" God Was Not on Our Side   Psalm 124

"If it had not been the LORD who was on our side, now may Israel say; If it had not been the LORD who was on our side, when men rose up against us: Then they had swallowed us up quick, when their wrath was kindled against us: Then the waters had overwhelmed us, the stream had gone over our soul: Then the proud waters had gone over our soul. Blessed be the LORD, who hath not given us as a prey to their teeth. Our soul is escaped as a bird out of the snare of the fowlers: the snare is broken, and we are escaped. Our help is in the name of the LORD, who made heaven and earth."—Psalm 124.

"If it had not been the Lord who was on our side, now may Israel say; If it had not been the Lord who was on our side" (Barnes says, "The idea is that Someone had been with them and had delivered them, and that such was the nature of the interposition that it could be ascribed to no one but Yahweh. It bore unmistakable evidence that it was His work."[1247]) "when men rose up against us" (The identity of the enemy that rose up in opposition and oppression David does not specify.)

"Then they had swallowed us up quick" (Swanson says "to be consumed, formally, be swallowed, i.e., pertaining to being in a state of ruin or destruction; devour, consume, formally, swallow up, gulp down, i.e., cause destruction and ruin, be devoured, formally, be swallowed up."[1248] Barnes says, "There was no other help, and ruin—utter ruin—would have soon come upon us. The word *quick* here means alive; and the idea is derived from persons swallowed up in an earthquake, or by the opening of the earth, as in the case of Korah, Dathan, and Abiram. Numbers 16:32–33. Compare Psalm 106:17. The meaning here is that they would have been destroyed as if they were swallowed up by the opening of the earth; that is, there would have been complete destruction."[1249]).

"When their wrath was kindled against us" (Rawlinson says "or, 'blazed out against us.' The comparison of anger to fire is an almost universal commonplace."[1250]). "Then the waters had overwhelmed us" (Swanson says "overflow, flood, engulf, be a torrent, i.e., a movement of water which has considerable force as in a flooding river, potentially sweeping an object away in its flow."[1251]) "the stream" (Brown, Driver and Briggs say "torrent."[1252]) "had gone over our soul" (Kirkpatrick says "overwhelmed us and put an end to our existence."[1253]).

"Then the proud waters had gone over our soul" (Barnes says, "The word *proud* here is applied to the waters as if raging, swelling, rolling, tumultuous; as if they were self-confident, arrogant, haughty."[1254]

Jamieson-Fausset-Brown say "the epithet proud added to waters denotes insolent enemies."[1255]).

"Blessed" (Thomas says "to kneel, bless:—abundantly bless."[1256]) be the Lord, who hath not given us as a "prey to their teeth" (Barnes says, "The figure is here changed, though the same idea is retained. The image is now that of destruction by wild beasts—a form of destruction not less fearful than that which comes from overflowing waters. Such changes of imagery constantly occur in the Book of Psalms, and in impassioned poetry everywhere."[1257] Jamieson-Fausset-Brown say, "The figure is changed to that of a rapacious wild beast and then of a fowler, and complete escape is denoted by breaking the net."[1258] See Psalm 3:7 and Psalm 91:3.).

Our soul is "escaped" (Swanson says "save, deliver, rescue, spare, i.e., deliver one from danger and so cause one to be safe, often with a focus of physically leaving an area."[1259]) "as a bird out of the snare" (Gesenius and Tregelles say "a net, a snare [Job 18:9]; especially of a fowler."[1260]) of the "fowlers" (the hunter, i.e., enemy) the snare is "broken" (Swanson says "break, destroy, crush, maul."[1261]).

AND we are "escaped" (Landes says "to flee to safety; to save someone; to leave undisturbed, at rest."[1262] Rawlinson says, "We have been like birds taken in the 'snare,' or net, of a fowler. But now we are escaped—not, however, of our own strength or of our own cleverness."[1263]).

"Our help" (Jamieson-Fausset-Brown say, "He thus places over against the great danger the omnipotent God, and drowns, as it were in an anthem, the wickedness of the whole world and of Hell, just as a great fire consumes a little drop of water [Luther]."[1264]) is in the "name of the Lord" (Rawlinson says "i.e., in the manifested might—'of the Lord.'"[1265] Spurgeon says, "Jehovah's revealed character is our foundation of confidence, His person is our sure fountain of strength."[1266]) "who made heaven and earth" (See Psalm 121:2 and Psalm 134:3).

Homily

Matthew Henry says, "David penned this Psalm (we suppose) upon occasion of some great deliverance which God wrought for him and his people from some very threatening danger, which was likely to have involved them all in ruin, whether by foreign invasion, or intestine insurrection [internal war], is not certain."[1267] J. J. Stewart Perowne believes the event was Israel's deliverance from Babylonian captivity.[1268] A. F. Kirkpatrick differs, saying, "The language of the Psalm points rather to some sudden danger which had been providentially averted, than to a blow which had actually fallen. Israel's enemies had threatened them; and if Jehovah had not fought for them, Israel might easily have been annihilated. But He had not suffered the wild beast to seize its victim; He had broken the snare and baulked the fowler of his prey. Such a danger menaced the restored community when Nehemiah was rebuilding the walls of Jerusalem. The contempt described in Psalm 123 was succeeded by hostility."[1269] Whatever the occasion of rescue, it was unforgettable.[1270] In Psalm 123 the Israelites were in captivity praying (looking) to the Lord for deliverance. In Psalm 124 they celebrate that deliverance. It is one of the fifteen Psalms that were sung by the Jews in their ascent to Jerusalem to attend one of the three annual feasts. S. Davies wrote, "To this writer the nation's life had been full of 'ifs' and 'thens'—its saddening possibilities with their dreary consequences. If we had stood alone, if God had not been round about us, if unerring wisdom had not thought for us and worked for us when the calamity threatened—then had we been as the bird in the snare of the fowler; then had we been overwhelmed!"[1271]

If it had not been the Lord who was on our side. "It is tantamount to saying, what if the Lord had not been for us?—leaving the answer to the imagination of the reader."[1272] The Lord has done great things for the redeemed. He has snatched them (salvation, deliverance) from the hand of the enemy (Satan), giving him a crushing defeat at Calvary by dying for man's sin (substitutionary death [1 John 2:2]); thoroughly washed away the defilement and ugliness of their sin (justification), casting it into the 'sea of forgetfulness' (Micah 7:19) to remember it no more, making them "the righteousness of God" (2 Corinthians 5:21); eternally secured their soul for Himself (His ransom for the sinner paid at Calvary is eternally binding; Satan never again can take his soul "captive" [John 10:28]); sustained them without interruption (protection, provision, pardon); walked with them in holy communion (John 15:4); enabled victory in life's battles over the enemy (1 John 4:4; 1 Corinthians 15:57 and Romans 8:37); directed their steps that they may not drift into unrighteousness or defeat (Psalm 37:23; Proverbs 3:5–6 and Proverbs 16:9); flooded their heart with joy, comfort and contentment in all circumstances (1 Thessalonians 5:18; John 7:38 and Philippians 4:11); lifted up their head following sin through mercy and grace (Psalm 3:3); and prepared them a Home in Heaven (John 14:1–3). And the list yet continues without end, for His goodness unto those that love Him is indescribable, immeasurable and incalculable.

Spurgeon says, "The glorious Lord became our ally; He took our part and entered into treaty with us. If Jehovah were not our protector, where should we be? Nothing but His power and wisdom could have guarded us from the cunning and malice of our adversaries; therefore, let all his people say so, and openly give Him the honor of His preserving goodness. Here are two 'ifs,' and yet there is no 'if' in the matter. The Lord was on our side, and *is* still our defender, and will be so from henceforth, even forever. Let us with holy confidence exult in this joyful fact."[1273] Alexander Maclaren wrote, "Being in Christ, it is safe to forget the past; it is possible to be sure of the future; it is important to be diligent in the present."[1274]

Now let Israel say. Had it not been for the Lord "on our side," where might we be today? As with David and the Israelites, we have great reason to praise the Lord for His hand of goodness upon us. Spurgeon observes, *"We are far too slow in declaring our gratitude, hence the exclamation which should be rendered, 'O let Israel say.'* We murmur without being stirred up to it, but our thanksgiving needs a spur, and it is well when some warmhearted friend bids us say what we feel. Imagine what would have happened if the Lord had left us, and then see what has happened because he has been faithful to us. Are not all the materials of a song spread before us? Let us sing unto the Lord."[1275]

How sovereign, wonderful, and free
Is all his love to sinful me!
He plucked me as a brand from Hell;
My Jesus has done all things well.

And since my soul has known His love,
What mercies has He made me prove,
Mercies which all my praise excel;
My Jesus has done all things well. ~ Samuel Medley (1776)

The Bottom Line: John Bunyan said, "A sensible thanksgiving for mercies received is a mighty prayer in the Spirit of God. It prevails with Him unspeakably."[1276] Abraham Lincoln once said, "Sir, my concern is not whether God is on our side; my greatest concern is to be on God's side, for God is always right."[1277]

46. The Promise of Perpetual Preservation   Psalm 125:1–2

"They that trust in the LORD shall be as mount Zion, which cannot be removed, but abideth for ever. As the mountains are round about Jerusalem, so the LORD is round about his people from henceforth even for ever."—Psalm 125:1–2.

They that "trust in the Lord" (Swanson says "trust, rely on, put confidence in, i.e., believe in a person or object to the point of reliance upon."[1278] Simeon says, "The person who trusts in the Lord must see Him as a Covenant-God in Christ Jesus, engaged to accomplish for His chosen people all that their necessities can require....Viewing Him as both a God of providence and of grace, we must fully expect His attention to our every request, to order every thing for our good, and to save us in Christ Jesus with an everlasting salvation."[1279]) shall be as "mount Zion" (Barnes says, "A mountain is an emblem of firmness and stability; and it is natural to speak of it as that which could not be removed."[1280] Jamieson-Fausset-Brown say "as an emblem of permanence, and locality of Jerusalem as one of security, represent the firm and protected condition of God's people, supported not only by Providence, but by covenant promise. Even the mountains shall depart, and the hills be removed, but God's kindness shall not depart, nor His covenant of peace be removed [Isaiah 54:10]."[1281] Kirkpatrick says, "Mount Zion is here named in particular, partly because the Psalm concerns the inhabitants of Jerusalem, partly because it was so intimately connected with an irrevocable Divine purpose [Isaiah 14:32; Isaiah 28:16]. It is the confidence of Israel, rather than its prosperity, which is as firm as the rock of Zion. No storms of trial can shake it."[1282]).

Which "cannot be removed but abideth forever" (Kirkpatrick says, "Mountains in general, as the most solid part of the solid earth, were to the Israelite the symbol of all that was immovable and unchangeable [Psalm 93:1; Isaiah 54:10]."[1283] Plumer says, "Abideth, dwelleth, sitteth, tarryeth, hath a fixed abode. What is here said of believers in general is true of each of them. They have stability and shall ever have it because they confide in Jehovah."[1284]).

"As the mountains are round about Jerusalem" (Gill says, "There was Mount Zion on the side of the north, and the mount of Olives on the east, and other mountains on the other sides of it; so that it was encompassed with them, and was naturally as well as artificially fortified. Tacitus describes Jerusalem as inaccessible, walls and mountains, rocks and towers, surrounding it....so the Lord is round about His people from henceforth even forever."[1285]).

"So the Lord is round about his people from henceforth even forever" (Benson says, "Defending it, not only from stormy winds and tempests, the force of which these mountains broke, but from the assaults of its enemies. And such a defense is God's providence to His people. His protection is round about them on every side and is constant and persevering, from henceforth, says the Psalmist, even forever. Mountains may molder and come to naught, and the rocks be removed out of their place (Job 14:18), but God's covenant with His people, with those who persevere in faith, love, and obedience, cannot be broken, nor His care of them cease [Isaiah 54:10]."[1286]).

Homily

The composer of the Psalm is unknown. Alexander Maclaren wrote, "The so-called 'Songs of Degrees,' of which this Psalm is one, are probably a pilgrim's songbook, and possibly date from the period of the restoration of Israel from the Babylonish captivity. In any case, this little Psalm looks very much like a record of the impression that was made on the pilgrim as he first topped the crest of the hill from which he looked on Jerusalem."[1287] Jennings and Lowe summarize the Psalm: "The long domination of a heathen power during the recent exile, and the present molestations of the semi-idolatrous Samaritans, must doubtless have had their effects on the weak-hearted among the Psalmist's countrymen. In the present Poem therefore words of consolation and of threatening are naturally blended. The faithful, says the Psalmist, need not be terrified, for calamity shall not endure; they have a firm foundation which cannot totter, and Jehovah is to them as it were a bulwark, deterring the oppressive foe who would pervert them from their holy faith."[1288]

They that trust in the Lord. Alexander Maclaren says, "It literally means to 'hang upon' something, and so, beautifully, it tells us what faith is—just hanging upon God. Whoever has laid his tremulous hand on a fixed something, partakes, in the measure in which he does grasp it, of the fixity of that on which he lays hold; so 'they that trust in the Lord shall be as Mount Zion,' that stands there summer and winter, day and night, year out and year in, with its strong buttresses and its immovable mass, the very emblem of solidity and stability."[1289] Matthew Henry said "who trust in the Lord, who depend upon His care and devote themselves to His honor. All that deal with God must deal upon trust, and He will give comfort to those only that give credit to Him, and make it to appear they do so by quitting other confidences....The closer our expectations are confined to God, the higher our expectations may be raised from Him."[1290] "The steadfastness of the trustful soul is the consequence of the encircling defense of Jehovah's power."[1291] George Horne cautions, "Let not our 'trust in God' be a presumptuous, ungrounded assurance; but let it be a confidence springing from faith unfeigned, out of a pure heart, a good conscience, and fervent charity. Then shall our situation, whether as a church or as individuals, resemble that of the holy mount in the beloved city, and our God will be unto us a fortress, and a wall round about."[1292] *Shall be as Mount Zion.* Charles Simeon explains, "Mount Zion was a place of so much strength, that, from the days of Joshua to the time of David, the Israelites could never take it. They occupied Jerusalem: but Mount Zion was too strong for them; insomuch that the Jebusites who inhabited it laughed them to scorn, vaunting, that if there were none left but blind and lame to defend the fortress, the Jews should never be able to prevail against it. But far more impregnable is the fortress in which they dwell who trust in the Lord: 'The name of the Lord is a strong tower: the righteous runneth to it, and is safe.' They may be assaulted both by men and devils; but they are assured, that 'God will keep them by His own power, through faith, unto everlasting salvation.' They are in the Saviour's hands; and He has pledged Himself that 'none shall ever pluck them out of His hands.'"[1293]

Which cannot be removed. These words are echoed to the believer in Romans 8:31–39. Nothing in Heaven or earth can separate the Christian from the love of Christ. Eternal security, the preservation of the saint, clearly is espoused. W. S. Plumer wrote, "So effectually was Jerusalem surrounded by mountains, that one prophet speaks of it as a *caldron* (Ezekiel 11:3). These mountains stood there from age to age. They stand there still.....Jehovah is a bulwark and a defence that has never failed His people. What the mountains seemed to be, the Lord is, an impregnable wall to His true people, who are not faithless but believing, sincere not hypocritical. *From henceforth even for ever*, literally, from now and unto eternity."[1294] Matthew Henry well states, "They [the redeemed] cannot be removed by the prince of the power of the air, nor by all his subtlety and strength. They cannot be removed from their integrity nor from their confidence in God."[1295] John Gill wrote, "They can never be removed from the Lord, though they may be removed from His house and ordinances, as sometimes David was, and from His gracious presence, and sensible communion with Him, and out of the world by death; yet never from His heart's love, nor out of the covenant of His grace, which is sure and everlasting; nor out of His family, into which they are taken; nor from the Lord Jesus Christ, nor out of His hands and arms, nor from off His heart; nor from off Him, the foundation on which they are laid; nor out of a state of grace, either regeneration or justification; but such abide in the love of God, in the covenant of His grace, in the hands of His Son, in the grace wherein they stand, and in the house of God for evermore."[1296]

As the mountains are round about Jerusalem. "This girdle of mountains is an ever present symbol to the dweller in Jerusalem of Jehovah's guardianship of His people."[1297] J. A. Alexander remarked, "As in verse 1, the permanent security of the church itself is likened to the firmness of mount Zion on its base, so here the protecting care, which causes this security, is likened to the heights by which the city is surrounded upon all sides."[1298]

In the same way the Lord is round about his people from henceforth even forever. Spurgeon remarks, "The hill of Zion is the type of the believer's constancy, and the surrounding mountains are made emblems of the all-surrounding presence of the Lord. The mountains around the holy city, though they do not make a circular wall, are nevertheless set like sentinels to guard her gates. God does not enclose His people within ramparts and bulwarks, making their city to be a prison; but yet He so orders the arrangements of His providence that His saints are as safe as if they dwelt behind the strongest fortifications....It is not said that Jehovah's power or wisdom defends believers, but He Himself is round about them: they have His personality for their protection, His Godhead for their guard."[1299] Adam Clarke states, "The Lord is round about his people—He is above, beneath, around them; and while they keep within it, their fortress is impregnable, and they can suffer no evil."[1300]

Martin Luther wrote, "It is much easier to learn than to believe that we who have by us the Word of God and receive it are surrounded with divine aid. If we were surrounded by walls of steel and fire, we should feel secure and defy the Devil. But the property of faith is not to be proud of what the eye sees, but to rely on what the Word reveals."[1301] W. H. J. Page writes: "Some persons are like the sand—ever shifting and treacherous (Matthew 7:26). Some are like the sea—restless and unsettled (Isaiah 57:20; James 1:6). Some are like the wind—uncertain and inconstant (Ephesians 4:14). Believers are like a mountain—strong, stable and secure."[1302]

The Bottom Line: The Psalm is a promise of perpetual preservation. The child of God (the born-again) is completely and continuously protected by the presence of Almighty God (*the Lord is round about them*). Nothing can touch the believer without passing through His custodial hands. Andrew Bonar said, "Milton celebrates 'the inviolable saints,' the holy hosts that guard the throne of God. But the family of saints on earth may claim that title equally with them, being invincible and inviolable in their King."[1303]

47. Weeping, Sowing and Reaping   Psalm 126:5–6

"They that sow in tears shall reap in joy. He that goeth forth and weepeth, bearing precious seed, shall doubtless come again with rejoicing, bringing his sheaves with him."—Psalm 126:5–6.

They that "sow" (Kaiser, Harris, Archer and Waltke say "scatter seed, sow."[1304]) in tears shall "reap" (Holladay and Kohler say "reap the harvest."[1305]) in "joy" (Strong says "i.e. shout:—cry, gladness, joy, proclamation, rejoicing, shouting, sing(-ing), triumph."[1306]).

He that goeth forth and weepeth, "bearing" (Brown, Driver and Briggs say "lift, carry, take."[1307]) "precious seed" (Jesus is the altogether precious and wondrous One that transforms lives.) shall doubtless come again with "rejoicing" (jubilation) bringing his "sheaves" (harvest) with him. Jesus' words in John 4:36–38 may echo this psalm.[1308]

Homily

The Psalm's author is unknown. Matthew Henry states, "Probably this psalm was penned by Ezra, or some of the prophets that came up with the first."[1309] Henry continues, "It was with reference to some great and surprising deliverance of the people of God out of bondage and distress that this psalm was penned, most likely their return out of Babylon in Ezra's time. Though Babylon be not mentioned here (as it is in Psalm 137) yet their captivity there was the most remarkable captivity both in itself and as their return out of it was typical of our redemption by Christ."[1310] Charles Simeon wrote, "The great body of the Psalms was composed by David; but some were written many hundred years before his time, as the 90th was by Moses, and others many hundred years after him, as that before us, which was evidently written after the Babylonish captivity. It relates in the first instance to the delivery of Israel from their sore bondage and their restoration to their long desolated country, but it is well applicable to that redemption which is vouchsafed to the souls of men and which was shadowed forth by that great event."[1311] W. S. Plumer wrote, "Whatever was its authorship, or the occasion of its composition, it was designed for the edification of the church in all coming time."[1312]

The first year of the Israelites' return following exile would be difficult agriculturally. Hard and gruesome work to prepare the fields for sowing would be necessary. The agonizing ("in tears") task however would prove profitable (harvest) and joyful. W. S. Plumer said, "After the night of weeping comes the morning of joy. There is no more precious fruit gathered from earth than that which springs from seed sown in tears, and pain, and sighing, and persecution. Yet how often do we misinterpret providence and question the divine faithfulness?"[1313] See Isaiah 35:10 and Isaiah 66:20.

A spiritual application that pictures the saints as soul winners sowing the Gospel seed with compassion in the harvest field is often made of this passage. Hyman J. Appelman said, "This is the soul winner's text—the simplest, the most definite in the world. Its directions are positive; its assurances encouraging. God, Christ and the Holy Spirit are behind it. The testimony of nineteen hundred years supports its assertion. The witness of the great soul winners through the ages sustains its direct promise. It is universal, unqualified, to be accepted and made concrete by all who have made soul winning the ultimate aim of their Christian experience and existence."[1314] Soul winning is a heart work ("sow in tears"); a hard work ("sow"); a huge work ("goeth forth" into the entire world); a happy work ("with rejoicing") and a harvest work ("bringing his sheaves with him"). The text further cites the soul winner's passion ("sow in tears"); proclamation ("precious seed"); plan ("goeth" and "sows") and promise ("with rejoicing, bringing his sheaves with him").

They that sow in tears. General William Booth was notified by one of his captains that the work was so difficult that no progress had been made. Booth replied with two words: "Try tears." Success soon was known in the work. Spurgeon remarks, "It is not every sowing which is thus insured against all danger, and guaranteed a harvest; but the promise specially belongs to sowing in tears. When a man's heart is so stirred that he weeps over the sins of others, he is elect to usefulness. Winners of souls are first weepers for souls. As there is no birth without travail, so is there no spiritual harvest without painful tillage. When our own hearts are broken with grief at man's transgression, we shall break other men's hearts; tears of earnestness beget tears of repentance."[1315] *Shall reap in joy.* The work of the farmer is so demanding, difficult and discouraging that at times he "weeps," but its result or return causes "rejoicing." Just so with him that works in the harvest field sowing the seed of the Gospel and reaping it. The difficulties and tears incurred in that work are more than worthwhile upon seeing souls birthed into the family of God.

He that goeth forth. Intentionality about the rescue of and compassion for the eternally lost must be accompanied with "going." You have to "go" in order to "tell." Ours is a *seedless generation* due to the church's failure to "sow" the "precious seed," which is Jesus Christ crucified, buried and raised for the salvation of the world.

How do you spell "go"? Do you spell it "pray"? Clearly the saint is to pray for the unsaved, but there comes a time when he must leave off praying and begin telling. Do you spell it "giving"? Financially investing in evangelism is of tremendous need, something the believer ought to do, but he must remember this command cannot be obeyed by proxy. Do you spell it "visitation"? Extending a kind invitation to another to attend church is commendable, but this in itself does not replace personal witnessing of the death, burial and resurrection of Jesus Christ and man's need to be saved. Do you spell it "pastor"? Witnessing is every man's responsibility, not just that of the ministerial staff.

"Go" can only be spelled "g-o"; that is, get out and get telling people about the wonderful Savior, Jesus Christ, endeavoring to bring them to Him. You may not be comfortable with the word *go*. You may wish Jesus had excluded it. But it is what it is, and therefore you must do what it commands. Encompassed in the word *go* is the promise that 'lo I will be with you always, even until the end of the earth.'

Bearing precious seed. The harvest always is determined by the seed planted. To "reap" the harvest of the unsaved for Jesus Christ, the "gospel" seed (the death, burial and resurrection of Jesus and its meaning with regard to man's unregenerate state) must be sown. It is the only seed that convicts and converts the soul. Its absence in preaching and witnessing explains the absence of souls saved. Peter underscores my point in saying, "Being born again, not of corruptible seed, but of incor-ruptible, by the word of God, which liveth and abideth forever" (1 Peter 1:23). See Mark 4:1–20.

Shall doubtless come again...bringing his sheaves with him. The promise is "doubtless" (to be taken as a sure and certain thing) that the labor practiced as prescribed in soul winning will result in the harvest of souls. William MacDonald says, "Those who live sacrificially for the spread of the Gospel may endure present privation, but what is that compared to the joy of seeing souls saved and in Heaven worshiping the Lamb of God forever and forever?"[1316]

Going forth with weeping, sowing for the Master,
    Though the loss sustained our spirit often grieves.
When our weeping's over, He will bid us welcome;
    We shall come rejoicing, bringing in the sheaves.

Bringing in the sheaves, bringing in the sheaves,
We shall come rejoicing, bringing in the sheaves,
Bringing in the sheaves, bringing in the sheaves,
We shall come rejoicing, bringing in the sheaves. ~ Knowles Shaw (1874)

A second implication of the text relates to weeping prompted by adversity, suffering, persecution or trial in Christian duty. Horne states, "Here, O disciple of Jesus, behold an emblem of thy present labor, and thy future reward. Thou sowest, perhaps, in tears; thou dost thy duty amid persecution and affliction, sickness, pain, and sorrow; thou labourest in the church, and no account is made of thy labors; no profit seems likely to arise from them....Yet the day is coming when thou shalt reap in joy; and plentiful shall be thy harvest."[1317] Matthew Henry exhorts, "Suffering saints are often in tears; they share the calamities of human life, and commonly have a greater share than others. But they sow in tears; they do the duty of an afflicted state. *Weeping must not hinder sowing*; we must get good from times of affliction. And they that sow, in the tears of godly sorrow, to the Spirit, shall of the Spirit reap life everlasting; and that will be a joyful harvest indeed."[1318] Henry continues, "The troubles of the saints will not last always, but, when they have done their work, shall have a happy period. The captives in Babylon were long sowing in tears, but at length they were brought forth with joy, and then they reaped the benefit of their patient suffering, and brought their sheaves with them to their own land, in their experiences of the goodness of God to them. Job and Joseph and David, and many others, had harvests of joy after a sorrowful seedness. Those that sow in the tears of godly sorrow shall reap in the joy of a sealed pardon and a settled peace."[1319] "If we sow tears, shall we reap tears? No, never, never, never. Far different shall be the fruit arising from that seed! even joy, yea, "joy unspeakable and glorified."[1320]

> If we sow tears, shall we reap tears? No, never, never, never. Far different shall be the fruit arising from that seed! even joy, yea, "joy unspeakable and glorified."
> Charles Simeon

The Bottom Line: You reap according to that which is sown. To win souls, the Word of God must be sown compassionately in the power of the Holy Spirit upon the "field" of the lost despite hostility or persecution.

48. Children as Arrows   Psalm 127:4

"As arrows are in the hand of a mighty man; so are children of the youth."—Psalm 127:4.

As "arrows" (Swanson says "i.e., a shooting missile shot with a bow, as a weapon"[1321]) are in the hands of a "mighty man" (Futato says "mighty man, warrior"[1322]) "so are" (in the same way) "the children of thy youth" (Rawlinson says "i.e. children born to a man in his youth."[1323] Harman says, "The illustration here is from Near Eastern society, with the thought of the children providing protection in time of trouble and old age [to their parents]."[1324]).

Homily

The author is uncertain. Some think David, others Solomon. B. H. Carroll believes the Psalm was written when Solomon built the Temple. Assuming Solomon is the composer, it is quite interesting to note that though he wrote 1,005 songs, only one or perhaps two psalms (Psalm 72 and Psalm 127) are attributed to him. See 1 Kings 4:32. B. H. Carroll states, "A brief interpretation of it is as follows: The house here means household. It is a brief lyric, setting forth the lessons of faith and trust. This, together with Psalm 128, is justly called 'A Song of Home.'"[1325]

The Psalmist states children are "as arrows" in the hand of a mighty man. *Children, like arrows, must be developed* with the right components (biblical values, convictions, beliefs, and discipline) *and shaped correctly* (by discipline, example, and instruction). It is far better for parents to shape their children than for them to be shaped by the White House, schoolhouse or playhouse. *Children, like arrows (with some exceptions), go where they are aimed.* The primary reason why some children turn out bad is because a parent's aim was bad. *Children, like arrows, are purposed for battle*. The apostle Paul states that we are in a constant war against Satan and his cohorts. As parents, equip your child to fight the good fight of faith, driving the enemy back in the name of Jesus Christ. *Children, like arrows, are message bearers.* Children are to take the message of King Jesus into the entire world, seeking to bring the lost to a saving knowledge of Him. As gospel arrows, they are able to go where you may never go and do so more swiftly (some as missionaries, evangelists, church planters, pastors). *Children, like arrows, must be taken out the quiver.* Arrows, though pretty to look at, must be withdrawn from the quiver and "shot" to bear intended impact. Children in the "quiver" are safe but unproductive. It's only when they are "shot" into the world that they may have impact for Christ.

As overwhelming as the truth is that your hand is upon the bow-string that delivers the arrow (child) into this spiritually dark world, find hope in knowing that God's hand is upon your hand directing and empowering it inasmuch as is allowed. Matthew Henry writes that children, "with prudence, may be directed aright to the mark, God's glory and the service of their generation; but afterwards, when they have gone abroad into the world, they are arrows out of the hand; it is too late to bend them then. But these arrows in the hand too often prove arrows in the heart, a constant grief to their godly parents, whose gray hairs they bring with sorrow to the grave."[1326]

Children are an heritage of the Lord. See Psalm 127:3. W. A. Criswell states, "Children must always be looked upon as belonging to the Lord. They are a sacred trust, a holy heritage. The rabbis of old declared that a child has three parents: God, his father, and his mother (Genesis 20:17–18; 30:1–2). Parents, then, are held accountable unto God for their stewardship of parenthood."[1327]

Children, as arrows, have responsibilities toward their parents. "You are to protect them in their old age and be to them as arrows in the hands of the warrior. Protect them from the assaults of poverty, should they require your assistance in this respect. Poverty and old age are unsuitable companions: let it be your pleasure to alleviate this distressing yoke as far as you can. They did not leave you to the cold charity of strangers when you were more feeble than they now are. Why should you act differently towards them and pay back your debt with an immense ingratitude? You are to protect them under all the infirmities of declining years."[1328]

A slightly different application may be made with regard to training schools for ministers—colleges and seminaries ("households" that send forth the preachers, as her children, as mighty "arrows" into the world for Jesus Christ).[1329] Biblical theological institutions have been entrusted by the Lord with the task of sharpening minds and abilities (as "arrows") of the called out ones for effective ministry. Woe be unto them that form crooked and bent arrows (liberalism).

Except the Lord build the house. May I relate the words to the building of a sermon. Only if God works in the minister in the study and writing of sermons will they be blessed in their preaching. Spurgeon's grandfather said to him about the preparation of sermons, "I study my sermon as much as if the work of preaching depended entirely upon myself. And I go into the pulpit relying upon the Spirit of God, knowing that it does not depend upon myself but upon Him." *Unless the Lord builds the house its laborers labor in vain.* Unless the construction of a sermon from its foundation up is orchestrated by the Holy Spirit, he that "labors" in building it will find his labor futile.

The Bottom Line: How well a job are you doing in fabricating a *good* arrow with the right components to insure it will not be warped? A Chinese proverb says, "When a son is born into a family, a bow and arrow are hung before the gate."[1330] As children, are you fulfilling the role as "bow and arrow" to your parents?

49. The Reward of the Holy Man   Psalm 128:1–3

"Blessed is every one that feareth the LORD; that walketh in his ways. For thou shalt eat the labour of thine hands: happy shalt thou be, and it shall be well with thee. Thy wife shall be as a fruitful vine by the sides of thine house: thy children like olive plants round about thy table."—Psalm 128:1–3.

"Blessed" (Henry says, "Those who are truly holy are truly happy."[1331] Harman says, "The word 'blessings' [lit. 'your blessings'] may be a deliberate echo of Deuteronomy 33:29: 'Blessed are you, O Israel!'"[1332]) is "everyone" (Henry says, "Whoever he be; in every nation he that fears God and works righteousness is accepted of Him, and therefore is blessed whether he be high or low, rich or poor;...if religion rule him, it will protect and enrich him."[1333]) that "feareth" (To show reverence, awe for the Lord by honoring and obeying Him. Dilday and Kennedy say, "Fear of the Lord affects human conduct, so the psalmist was convinced. The 'one that feareth the Lord' is the one 'that walketh in his ways.'"[1334] Jennings and Lowe say, "According to the Rabbis (Ibn Ezra and Kimchi), "fearing the LORD" here denotes abstaining from breaches of the prohibitory commandments of the Decalogue; and "walking in His ways," the performance of the positive commandments."[1335]) the Lord; that "walketh" (travels) in his "ways" (Futato says "way, road, journey, conduct."[1336] Barnes says "the ways which God commands or directs."[1337] Harman says, "Where true reverence towards the Lord exists, there will also be a life of obedient attention to his ways."[1338]).

For thou "shalt eat the labor of thine hands" (Rawlinson says, "This is the first point of the 'blessedness.' God's faithful servant shall enjoy the fruits of his own industry, and not have them devoured by strangers."[1339] Jennings and Lowe say, "The meaning of the verse is that the God-fearing man shall find a successful issue in the labours of husbandry."[1340]) "happy shalt thou be" (joyful). AND "it shall be well with thee" (Brown, Driver and Briggs say "be pleasant, delightful, delicious, cheerful, happy."[1341]).

Thy wife shall be as a "fruitful vine by the sides of thine house: thy children like olive plants round about thy table" (Harman says, "The use of vine and olive tree as illustrations is probably because both were so central to daily life in Israel, and both were well known for the fact that they live for a long time."[1342] Poole says "numerous, growing and flourishing, good both for ornament and manifold uses, as olive trees are. Round about thy table; where they shall sit at meat with thee, for thy comfort and safety."[1343] Jennings and Lowe say, "Here perhaps are meant the sides of the inner court, where the women's apartments lay. It is generally assumed that these words have no connection with the metaphor of the vine, just as that of the 'olive plants' has no connection with the 'table'; but if the above view is taken, we may perhaps suppose that it was customary to grow vines on the walls of these inner courts. The Midrash Tillim remarks that the wife is as the fruitful vine when she is modest and remains in the sides of the house, like Sarah, who was 'in the tent' when inquired for."[1344]).

Homily

W. S. Plumer writes, "Commentators are remarkably silent respecting the authorship of this Psalm. We find no historic occasion for its composition."[1345] Matthew Henry states, "This is a psalm for families."[1346] The Psalm is encapsulated by A. F. Kirkpatrick: "Prosperity and domestic happiness will be the lot of him who fears Jehovah and obeys His laws."[1347]

The person that walks (orders his conduct) in the "fear of" (reverence for and obedience unto) the Lord is truly "blessed" (happy) and rewarded by the Lord. J. A. Alexander states, "However things may now seem to an eye of sense, it is still a certain truth that the truly happy man is he who fears Jehovah, not in mere profession, but who testifies his fear of Him by walking in His ways or doing His commandments."[1348]

The holy saint is rewarded for allegiance and devotion to the Lord. However, the *when and how* of that reward is an unknown. It may be administered spiritually, physically or materialistically now or in the future. Commonly, the Lord rewards believers in all of these ways.[1349] The Psalmist states the holy saint will be industrious in work, making provision for his family. Matthew Henry says "that they shall succeed in their employments."[1350] He will be happy and joyous. Domestically his wife will bear him children and be a good homemaker. Spurgeon says, "Good wives are also fruitful in kindness, thrift, helpfulness, and affection: if they bear no children, they are by no means barren if they yield us the wine of consolation and the clusters of comfort....*By the sides of thine house*....She is a fruitful vine, and a faithful housekeeper."[1351] His children will flourish about the table, enjoying meals with him, providing comfort and care. "Children should be treated as the most sacred charge placed in the hand of man by the hand of God. No one can tell the capacities and possibilities that are folded in the form and hidden in the heart of a little child."[1352] Children are the blessing of the Lord and need to be treated as such.

In summarizing the reward of the Lord upon the holy man, the Psalmist makes a sweeping statement. He says, *It shall be well with thee*. Benson wrote "both in this world and in the world to come. Whatever befalls thee, good shall be brought out of it; and "it shall be well with thee while thou livest, better when thou diest, and best of all in eternity."'[1353]

Behold, that thus shall the man be blessed that feareth the Lord. See Psalm 128:4. Spurgeon remarked, "It is not to be inferred that all blessed men are married and are fathers, but that this is the way in which the Lord favors godly people who are placed in domestic life. He makes their relationships happy and profitable. In this fashion does Jehovah bless God-fearing households, for he is the God of all the families of Israel. Family blessedness comes from the Lord, and is a part of his plan for the preservation of a godly race, and for the maintenance of His worship in the land. To the Lord alone we must look for it. The possession of riches will not insure it; the choice of a healthy and beautiful bride will not insure it; the birth of numerous comely children will not insure it: there must be the blessing of God, the influence of piety, the result of holy living."[1354]

The Bottom Line: God rewards the man that loves, honors, reveres and obeys Him. He will experience from the hand of God that which the unholy and ungodly cannot. The family that reveres God and obeys His Word shall forever prosper regardless of storms that assail.

50. Ploughmen of Slander   Psalm 129

"Many a time have they afflicted me from my youth, may Israel now say: Many a time have they afflicted me from my youth: yet they have not prevailed against me. The plowers plowed upon my back: they made long their furrows. The LORD is righteous: he hath cut asunder the cords of the wicked. Let them all be confounded and turned back that hate Zion. Let them be as the grass upon the housetops, which withereth afore it groweth up: Wherewith the mower filleth not his hand; nor he that bindeth sheaves his bosom. Neither do they which go by say, The blessing of the LORD be upon you: we bless you in the name of the LORD."—Psalm 129.

Many a time have they "afflicted" (Holladay and Kohler say "be hostile toward, be in state of conflict."[1355]) me from my "youth" (Benson says "from the time that I was a people; when I was in Egypt, and after I came out of it, which is called the time of Israel's youth [Jeremiah 2:2; Ezekiel 23:3]."[1356] Kirkpatrick says, "The history of Israel is often compared to the life of an individual. Israel's life began in Egypt [Hosea 2:3, 15; 11:1; Jeremiah 2:2]. From the Egyptian bondage onward it has repeatedly been oppressed by enemies."[1357]) may "Israel now say" (Kirkpatrick says "i.e. let Israel thankfully recall the lessons of its history [Psalm 118:2; Psalm 124:1]"[1358]).

"Many a time have they afflicted me from my youth" (Barnes says, "This repetition is designed to fix the thoughts on the fact, and to impress it on the mind....The idea is that it is no new thing to be thus afflicted. It has often occurred. It is a matter of long and almost constant experience. Our enemies have often attempted to destroy us, but in vain. What we experience now we have often experienced, and when thus tried we have been as often delivered, and have nothing now therefore to fear."[1359]) "yet they have not prevailed against me" (Rawlinson says, "Israel has not been given as a prey to the heathen's teeth [Psalm 124:6]. She is still a nation, unsubdued; she holds her own; the struggle is not ended."[1360]).

"The plowers plowed" (Brown, Driver and Briggs say "cut in, engrave, plough."[1361]) upon my back: they made their long "furrows" (Swanson says "plow path, i.e., a ploughing line which appears as a groove in the dirt, made in cultivated dirt for beginning the planting process, note: in context it refers to a wounding of the body."[1362] Jesus Christ's back was wounded by the beating with the Roman whip. See John 19:1). The Lord is "righteous" (Just, upright, holy. See Psalm 145:17.) He hath "cut asunder the cords of the wicked" (Metaphor of Israel as an ox to which the plough of the Egyptians was fastened. *Cords.* Jamieson-Fausset-Brown say "that is, which fasten the plough to the ox; and cutting denotes God's arresting the persecution."[1363] God delivered His people, set them "free.").

Let them all be "confounded" (Swanson says "be ashamed, i.e., to have a painful feeling and emotional distress [sometimes to the point of despair], by having done something wrong."[1364]). AND "turned back" (Holladay and Kohler say "draw back, shrink back, recoil."[1365]) that hate Zion. Let them be as the "grass upon the housetops" (Kirkpatrick says, "Grass or corn springs up quickly on the flat roofs of oriental houses, but having no depth of soil, it withers prematurely away, and yields no joyous harvest."[1366]).

Which "withereth afore it groweth up" (Jamieson-Fausset-Brown say, "The ill-rooted roof grass, which withers before it grows up and procures for those gathering it no harvest blessing, sets forth the utter uselessness and the rejection of the wicked."[1367]). Wherewith "the mower filleth not his hand" (Gill says, "Such grass never rises high enough to be mowed, nor is of that account to have such pains taken with it; nor the quantity so large as to fill a mower's hand, and carry it away in his arms."[1368] Perowne says, "The flat roofs of the Eastern houses 'are plastered with a composition of mortar, tar, ashes, and sand,' in the crevices of which grass often springs. The houses of the poor in the country were formed of a plaster of mud and straw, where the grass would grow still more freely: as all the images are taken from country life."[1369]).

Nor he that "bindeth sheaves his bosom" (Swanson says "i.e., one who ties grain stalks into bundles and transports out of the field."[1370] The "grass" is not enough to be mowed and certainly not enough to bundle.)

"Neither do they which go by say, The blessing of the Lord be upon you: we bless you in the name of the Lord" (The usual greeting to harvesters in the field, "we bless you in the name of the Lord," was not to be extended to the wicked who hated Zion. See 2 John 10–11).

Homily

The author is unknown. "The persecution and deliverance which are prominent in the Psalmist's mind are perhaps not to be connected with the Babylonish Captivity and its consummation, so much as with the troublous interval immediately succeeding."[1371] Matthew Henry speculates, "It is not certain when it was penned, probably when they were in captivity in Babylon or about the time of their return."[1372] Kirkpatrick thinks it perhaps was written with regard to the dangers that threatened Israel in the time of Nehemiah, while Allan Harman states it was written after the return from exile in Babylon. The bottom line is, its setting isn't known. See Psalm 129:4.

The plowers ploughed upon my back. Walford writes, "The persecutors of Israel are compared to ploughmen; because as they cut up and, as it were, torture the surface of the earth, so did the adversaries greatly and grievously distress these afflicted people."[1373] Allan Harman says, "The 'ploughmen' are the soldiers who have attacked her, and her 'back,' scarred with long furrows, is the whole period of history during which she was at the mercy of her attackers."[1374] Matthew Poole's paraphrase is: "They have not only thrown me down and trod me under foot, but have cruelly tormented me, wounded and mangled me, and had no more pity upon me than the ploughman hath upon the earth which he cuts up at his pleasure."[1375]

Spurgeon remarked, "The scourgers tore the flesh as plowmen furrow a field. The people [Israelites] were maltreated like a criminal given over to cruel whips; the back of the nation was scored and furrowed by oppression. It is a grand piece of imagery condensed into few words....The afflicted nation was, as it were, lashed by her adversaries so cruelly that each blow left a long red mark, or perhaps a bleeding wound, upon her back and shoulders, comparable to a furrow which tears up the ground from one end of the field to the other."[1376] W. S. Plumer states, "Persecutors have always been cruel. They have plowed the back of the church and made long their furrows. Lying, reviling, slander, blasphemy, whipping, scourging, burning, hanging, crucifying, casting to the wild beasts, and every conceivable form of cruelty has been exhausted from age to age in trying to erase from the earth the last vestige of true piety."[1377]

They made long their furrows. J. J. S. Perowne states "deep wounds, such as those made by the lash on the back of slaves."[1378]

Spurgeon makes a spiritual application, "Many a heart has been in like case, smitten and sore wounded by them that use the scourge of the tongue, so smitten that their whole character has been cut up and scored by calumny ["the act of uttering false charges or misrepresentations maliciously calculated to harm another's reputation" *Merriam-Webster*]."[1379] These "plowers" (slanderers) are often friends.

Guard against plowing a furrow upon someone's back with a venomous tongue. Paul exhorts, "Watch the way you talk. Let nothing foul or dirty come out of your mouth. Say only what helps, each word a gift" (Ephesians 4:29, MSG).

Prior to sharing something about another, let it pass through the filter of four gates for approval. If all four gates sanction it, then share it.[1380]

Gate 1: Is it confidential? If so, never mention it.
Gate 2: Is it true? This may take some investigation.
Gate 3: Is it necessary? So many words are useless.
Gate 4: Is it kind? Does it serve a wholesome purpose?[1381]

How to respond to "plowers" of slander upon your back? Spurgeon suggests, "The best way to deal with slander is to pray about it: God will either remove it, or remove the sting from it. Our own attempts at clearing ourselves are usually failures; we are like the boy who wished to remove the blot from his copy, and by his bungling made it ten times worse."[1382]

The Bottom Line: Slander cuts deeper and inflicts more pain than any sword. Don't *plow* upon another's back.

51. The Assurance of God's Forgiveness   Psalm 130:3–4

"If thou, LORD, shouldest mark iniquities, O Lord, who shall stand? But there is forgiveness with thee, that thou mayest be feared."—Psalm 130:3–4.

"If thou" (Rawlinson says "if thou didst not 'hide our transgressions.'"[1383]) Lord, shouldest "mark iniquities" (Swanson says "keep, i.e., cause a state or condition to remain; guard, watch."[1384] Benson says "observe them accurately, and punish them severely, as they deserve.'[1385]) "iniquities" (Holladay and Kohler say "activity that is crooked or wrong: — conscious, intentional offense, sin; guilt incurred by offense, sin."[1386] Gesenius and Tregelles say "a depraved action, a crime, a sin."[1387]).

"O Lord, who shall stand?" (Benson says "in Thy presence, or at Thy tribunal. No man could acquit himself, or escape the sentence of condemnation, because all men are sinners. *To stand* is a judicial phrase and imports a man being absolved or justified upon a fair trial."[1388] Jamieson-Fausset-Brown say, "Standing is opposed to the guilty sinking down in fear and self-condemnation. The question implies a negative, which is thus more strongly stated."[1389] See Malachi 3:2 and Revelation 6:15–16.).

But there is "forgiveness" (Strong says "pardon."[1390]) with "thee" (Only God has the authority, right and power to forgive the sinner).

Homily

Psalm 130 is a Penitential Psalm, the sixth of seven (Psalms 6, 32, 38, 51, 102, 130 and 143). The author is unknown. Charles Simeon states, "The more holy any man is, the more enlarged will be his views of the spirituality of God's Law, and the more painful his sense of his shortcomings and defects: and it should seem that David was permitted to sustain great anguish of mind on this account, that so he might be the better fitted to instruct and comfort God's tempted people to the very end of time."[1391]

John Wesley was saved while attending a service at a chapel on Aldersgate Street in London (May 24, 1738) where he heard someone reading from the *Introduction to Romans* by Martin Luther. What is mostly unknown is that on the afternoon of that day he attended a vesper service at St. Paul's Cathedral where Psalm 130 was sung as an anthem.

He was deeply moved by the anthem and it became one of the factors that led to his salvation.[1392]

Martin Luther, pressed to identify his favorite Psalms, included in the listing Psalm 130 (Psalms 32, 51, 130 and 143).[1393] He called it one of the "Pauline Psalms" (*Psalmi Paulini*) because it taught forgiveness by grace without human effort or works. J. M. Boice states that Luther's exposition on Psalm 130 is one of the best in the Old Testament "of the way of salvation by grace on the basis of Christ's atonement."[1394] Upon Luther's death (February 18, 1546), his version of the Psalm was read by Justus Jonas to the throngs who sang it by the bier ("A bier is a stand on which a corpse, coffin, or casket containing a corpse, is placed to lie in state or to be carried to the grave" Wikipedia.).[1395]

The Psalm unfolds the gist of divine forgiveness solely based upon grace apart from man's work. See Ephesians 2:8–9. Clearly and forthrightly it indicates the "who, what, why, when and how" of personal forgiveness.

The subject of the forgiveness. "Who shall stand?" The "who" is all mankind—depraved and guilty sinners deserving punishment, not forgiveness, at the hands of God. "All have sinned, and come short of the glory of God" (Romans 3:23). Man is totally hopeless to exonerate himself at the tribunal of God's judgment. Apart from God's compassion and mercy, none can "stand" justified and clean, acceptable in His holy presence. Albert Barnes says, "The Hebrew word ['stand'] means properly to keep, to watch, to guard. The word, as used here, refers to that kind of vigilance or watchfulness which one is expected to manifest who is on guard; who keeps watch in a city or camp by night. The idea is, If God should thus look with a scrutinizing eye; if He should try to see all that He could see; if He should suffer nothing to escape His observation; if He should deal with us exactly as we are; if He should overlook nothing, forgive nothing, we could have no hope."[1396]

The scope or sphere of the forgiveness. "But." This is the "Whisper of Hope" for the sinner.[1397] "There is forgiveness." God's forgiveness encompasses all manner of sin, regardless of its hideousness. Spurgeon says, "Where God draws no limit, do not you draw any. If God sets the door wide open, and says, 'There is forgiveness,' then come along, you

sinners, whoever you may be, from gaols [jail; reformatory] and peni-
tentiaries, come along from your Pharisaic places of boasting and self-
righteousness, come along with you, for there is forgiveness even for you.
Ye rich, ye poor, ye learned, ye ignorant, ye that know nothing, know at
least this, 'There is forgiveness.'"[1398] None are exempt from the need or
the means of salvation.

The source of the forgiveness. W. S. Plumer wrote, "Human merits
are excluded from the whole scheme of salvation."[1399] Man, inapt to right
himself with Holy God and deserving eternal damnation, is thrown a
rescue line in the person of Jesus Christ. God loved the world so much
that He sent His only son to die upon a cross to make possible sin's
forgiveness. See John 3:16. Albert Barnes remarked, "God is a Being who
does pardon sin, and...this is the only ground of hope. When we come
before God, the ground of our hope is not that we can justify ourselves;
not that we can prove we have not sinned; not that we can explain our
sins away; not that we can offer an apology for them; it is only in a frank
and full confession, and in a hope that God will forgive them. He who
does not come in this manner can have no hope of acceptance with
God."[1400] Spurgeon states, "Free, full, sovereign pardon is in the hand of
the great King: it is his prerogative to forgive, and He delights to exercise
it. Because His nature is mercy, and because He has provided a sacrifice
for sin, therefore forgiveness is with Him for all that come to Him
confessing their sins."[1401]

What can wash away my sin?
    Nothing but the blood of Jesus.
What can make me whole again?
    Nothing but the blood of Jesus.

Oh! precious is the flow
That makes me white as snow;
No other fount I know,
    Nothing but the blood of Jesus.

For my cleansing this I see:
    Nothing but the blood of Jesus!
For my pardon this my plea:
    Nothing but the blood of Jesus!

Nothing can my sin erase,
>Nothing but the blood of Jesus!
Naught of works, 'tis all of grace;
>Nothing but the blood of Jesus!

This is all my hope and peace:
>Nothing but the blood of Jesus!
This is all my righteousness:
>Nothing but the blood of Jesus! ~ Robert Lowry (1826–1899)

The splendor of forgiveness. It is completely free, without cost. "Ho, every one that thirsteth, come ye to the waters, and he that hath no money; come ye, buy, and eat; yea, come, buy wine and milk without money and without price" (Isaiah 55:1). The "free" cleansing of sin (it's based upon Jesus' tender love, grace and compassion) and the restoration to God it provides are incomparable in the joy, peace and satisfaction they afford. This is the "wonder of wonders." See Ephesians 2:8–9 and Revelation 22:17.

He paid a debt He did not owe;
I owed a debt I could not pay.
>I needed someone to wash my sins away.
And now I sing a brand new song:
"Amazing Grace."
>Christ Jesus paid a debt that I could never pay.
>   ~ Ellis J. Crum (1977)

The supply of forgiveness. "With him is *plenteous* redemption" (Psalm 130:7). "The LORD is merciful and gracious, slow to anger, and plenteous in mercy" (Psalm 103:8). The supply of God's mercy to grant forgiveness to sinners is as great as it was at the first. There will never be a shortage of God's mercy, grace, love or forgiveness, regardless of the numerous times it is extended to man at large or personally. Benson says the forgiveness of the Lord is "abundantly sufficient for all persons who will accept it upon God's terms, and for the remission of, and deliverance from, all sins; and therefore here is good ground of hope for all contrite and returning sinners."[1402]

The surety of forgiveness. "There is." The immediacy of forgiveness is sure to all that desire it and who through repentance (confession of sin) request it. This moment there is forgiveness; in all of life's tomorrows there is forgiveness. "The power of pardon is permanently resident with God: He has forgiveness ready to his hand at this instant."[1403]

Matthew Henry says, "We are to humble ourselves before God, as guilty in His sight. Let us acknowledge our sinfulness; we cannot justify ourselves or plead not guilty. It is our unspeakable comfort that there is forgiveness with him, for that is what we need. Jesus Christ is the great Ransom; He is ever an Advocate for us, and through Him we hope to obtain forgiveness."[1404] Upon full and earnest confession of sin (repentance), Jesus forgives the sinner.

Alec Motyer comments, "Everything else flows from that inexplicable basis: He loves us (Deuteronomy 7:7–8), and because He loves us, He himself provides and pays the ransom price, so that forgiveness full and free floods over our guilty souls. If it occurred to you to wonder how we could ever rest, unworried, calm, content, in the Lord's presence, as in Psalm 131, ask the Lord's three companions—forgiveness (Psalm 130:4); unfailing and committed love (Psalm 130:7) and full and complete redemption and ransom (Psalm 130:7). And what needs of ours do these three wonderful gifts from God meet? They meet our deepest need of a restored relationship with God, of a trusting intimacy with the Lord, and of the assurance that we are fully accepted, welcomed and adopted in Jesus Christ and His work on the cross. This combining of 130 and 131 points us to Christ."[1405]

The Bottom Line: Matthew Henry says, "It is our unspeakable comfort, in all our approaches to God, that there is forgiveness with Him, for that is what we need. He has put Himself into a capacity to pardon sin; He has declared Himself gracious and merciful and ready to forgive. He has promised to forgive the sins of those that do repent."[1406] Although God does not *mark* the iniquities of the "redeemed," He does for the unbeliever (sees them; records them and will punish them).

52. Be Humble, Not Haughty   Psalm 131:1

"Lᴏʀᴅ, my heart is not haughty, nor mine eyes lofty: neither do I exercise myself in great matters, or in things too high for me."—Psalm 131:1.

Lord, my heart is not "haughty" (Strong says "i.e., be lofty; to be haughty:—exalt, be haughty, be (make) high (-er), be proud, raise up great height, upward; arrogance."[1407]) nor mine eyes "lofty" (proud, arrogant).

"Neither do I exercise myself in great matters or in things too high for me" (Benson says, "It neither is, nor hath been my practice to attempt, or arrogate to myself, anything above my degree, place, and calling, or to affect worldly glory or domination."[1408] *Or in things too high for me.* Spurgeon says, "High things may suit others who are of greater stature, and yet they may be quite unfit for us. A man does well to know his own size. Ascertaining his own capacity, he will be foolish if he aims at that which is beyond his reach, straining himself, and thus injuring himself. Such is the vanity of many men that if a work be within their range they despise it, and think it beneath them: the only service which they are willing to undertake is that to which they have never been called, and for which they are by no means qualified. What a haughty heart must he have who will not serve God at all unless he may be trusted with five talents at the least!"[1409]).

Homily

Calvin, Poole, Dodd, Scott, Tholuck, Hengstenberg and Alexander credit David as composer of the Psalm.

John Gill conjectures: "This Psalm was written by David in his younger days, before he came to the throne, while he was in Saul's court."[1410] George Horne wrote, "It is most probably a Psalm of David, and is eminently applicable to Messiah, in His state of humiliation on earth. Happy would it be for the world, if all His disciples could imbibe the spirit of this short but lovely Psalm, and copy after the example which it setteth before them."[1411]

"This Psalm, while expressive of David's pious feelings on assuming the royal office, teaches the humble, submissive temper of a true child of God."[1412] Spurgeon states, "It is both by David and of David: he is the author and the subject of it, and many incidents of his life may be employed to illustrate it. Comparing all the Psalms to gems, we should liken this to a pearl: how beautifully it will adorn the neck of patience. It is one of the shortest Psalms to read, but one of the longest to learn. It speaks of a young child, but it contains the experience of a man in Christ. Lowliness and humility are here seen in connection with a sanctified heart, a will subdued to the mind of God, and a hope looking to the Lord alone. Happy is the man who can without falsehood use these words as his own; for he wears about him the likeness of his Lord, who said, "I am meek and lowly in heart." The Psalm is in advance of all the Songs of Degrees which have preceded it; for loveliness is one of the highest attainments in the divine life. There are also steps in this Song of Degrees: it is a short ladder, if we count the words; but yet it rises to a great height, reaching from deep humility to fixed confidence. Le Blanc thinks that this is a song of the Israelites who returned from Babylon with, humble hearts, weaned from their idols. At any rate, after any spiritual captivity let it be the expression of our hearts."[1413]

My heart is not haughty. David attests to his own humility without losing it. Cox explains, "To claim this virtue is as a rule to forfeit it, but David contrives to claim humility with humility. His words have no taint of pride in them; they are not like the prayer of the Pharisee: 'God, I thank Thee that I am not as other men are.' There is no comparison with others. We feel that he is alone with God; that he is showing God his heart as it really is; that he is virtually thanking God for the meek and quiet spirit which He has given."[1414] He was not possessed with selfish ambition or desires for worldly advancement or fame (which his life bears out). He did not elevate himself or push for that to happen. In fact, he had to be sought out by Samuel while tending his father's sheep. See 1 Samuel 16:11.

Despite a lengthy delay following being anointed by Samuel to be king, he did not violently seek occupancy of the throne, but patiently waited for God to dethrone Saul. He that was a "king" assumed the role of the servant to Saul. During the interval, persecution from the hands of Saul was experienced (about ten years) which he handled admirably (he refused to harm God's anointed).[1415] He resigned in humble submission to allow God to work it all out when and how He deemed best, calmly resting upon His promise that it would happen. Robert Murray M'Cheyne (1813–1843) did the same. He said, "It has always been my aim, and it is my prayer, to have no plan as regards myself, well assured as I am that the place where the Savior sees meet to place me must ever be the best place for me."[1416] Franz Delitzsch said of David, "Submission to God's guidance, resignation to His dispensations, contentment with that which was allotted to him, are the distinguishing traits of his noble character."[1417]

Andrew Murray in *Humility* defines humility as "the displacement of self by the enthronement of God."[1418] He continues, "It is to expect nothing, to wonder at nothing that is done to me, to feel nothing done against me. It is to be at rest when nobody praises me, and when I am blamed or despised."[1419]

He that has been forgiven mercifully by the Lord (as was David) ought to exhibit humility. Herbert Lockyer wrote, "Being graciously delivered from the judgment of our iniquities truly deserved should humble us. Having shed our filthy garments we should be clothed in the garment of humility."[1420]

"Until a humility," states Andrew Murray, "that rests in nothing less than the end and death of self, and which gives up all the honor of men, as Jesus did, to seek the honor that comes from God alone (which absolutely makes and counts itself nothing) that God may be all, that the Lord alone may be exalted—until such a humility is what we seek in Christ above our chief joy, and welcome at any price, there is very little hope of a faith that will conquer the world."[1421]

De Burgh says, "Humility is with Him the title to honor. As our Lord—Himself the great example of this truth—has taught us, saying, 'Except ye be converted, and become as little children, ye shall not enter into the kingdom of heaven' (Matthew 18:3): as void of pretension, as free from worldly ambition, as humble and mistrustful of self, as confiding, and as simply dependent on its parent, as 'a little child.'"[1422] Humility is the foundation stone to the building of a virtuous (righteous) life. See Psalm 138:6 and Isaiah 57:15.

The opposite of humility is sinful pride. See Proverbs 16:18 and Proverbs 18:12. It is an ugly sin that goes neither unnoticed nor unpunished by God. It is counted an abomination unto the Lord (Proverbs 16:5).

McKane says, "The nose is in the heavens, the seat is in the mire" (Arabic proverb).[1423] Arrogance and pride are the demeaning and destructive sins of the day, both among the clergy and laity. Deflation of the ego is imperative to rise to usefulness to man and God. Scott said, "The proud man is insolent in his deportment, and despises mean persons, situations, and occupations; he is vain-glorious and ambitious, aspiring after great connections and important employments, engaging in deep schemes and speculations, and courting observation and applause."[1424] John W. Stott declared, "Pride is your greatest enemy; humility is your greatest friend."[1425] The way *up* is *down*.

W. S. Plumer writes, "We cannot too carefully guard against all the motions and effects of pride and haughtiness. They are contrary to God's entire nature. It is better to be an humble beggar than a proud prince, a lowly penitent than a haughty angel."[1426]

The Bottom Line: William Law states, "You can have no greater sign of confirmed pride than when you think you are humble enough."[1427] Matthew Henry said, "Humble saints cannot think so well of themselves as others think of them, are not in love with their own shadow, nor do they magnify their own attainments or achievements. The love of God reigning in the heart will subdue all inordinate self-love."[1428]

53. The Weaned Child   Psalm 131:2–3

"Surely I have behaved and quieted myself, as a child that is weaned of his mother: my soul is even as a weaned child. Let Israel hope in the LORD from henceforth and for ever."—Psalm 131:2–3.

Surely I have "behaved" (Rawlinson says "rather, I have stilled and quieted my soul. I have brought my soul into a state of peacefulness and content."[1429] Ross says, "David...testified to his humility. His soul was not disturbed by selfish ambition and passion."[1430]). AND "quieted myself" (Strong says "forbear, hold peace, quiet self, rest, be silent, keep (put to) silence, be (stand) still, tarry, wait."[1431]) "as a child that is weaned of his mother" (Rawlinson says, "The weaned child is quiet and content; the suckling always impatient and restless."[1432] Dilday and Kennedy say, "The child gave up the mother's breast and learned contentment and security without it. Similarly, in his maturing process the psalmist turned from his own ambitions and learned to wait on God."[1433]).

"My soul is even as a weaned child" (Benson says "as void of all that ambition and malice, wherewith I am charged, as a child newly weaned; or, rather, as wholly depending upon God's providence, as the poor helpless infant, when it is deprived of its accustomed food, the milk of the breast, takes no care to provide for itself, but wholly relies upon its mother for support. I have levelled my mind to an equality with my condition and resolved to acquiesce in the present state of things, committing myself wholly to Thy care, being content to be disposed of as Thou pleasest."[1434] Plumer says, "The simile of the weaned child supposes the child not in the process of weaning, but effectually weaned."[1435]).

"Let Israel hope in the Lord from henceforth and forever" (Poole says, "Let all Israelites learn by my [David's] example to commit themselves to God in well-doing, and to fix all their hope and trust upon him alone."[1436]).

Homily

The title ascribes the Psalm to David. Matthew Henry says, "This Psalm is David's profession of humility, humbly made, with thankfulness to God for His grace, and not in vain-glory. It is probable enough that (as most interpreters suggest) David made this protestation in answer to the calumnies of Saul and his courtiers, who represented David as an ambitious aspiring man, who, under pretense of a divine appointment, sought the kingdom, in the pride of his heart."[1437]

My soul is even as a weaned child. John Gill says, "This is to be understood not of a child while weaning, when it is usually peevish, fretful, and froward; but when it is weaned, and is quiet and easy in its mother's arms."[1438] David's humility and restraint not to crave "things too high for me" (selfish and worldly ambition) enabled him to be as calm and peaceful "as a weaned child" upon its mother's lap. Picture the "breast" of the mother as worldly ambition and acclaim and David as a "baby." David "weaned" himself off the "breast" (milk of worldly ambition), though difficult—the time when the suckling stage must end meets with great fretting and tantrum, for that which is the baby's comfort and reliance is "removed"—through the soothing caresses of his "mother"

(God). Spurgeon says, "He is weaned *of* his mother rather than *from* her."[1439] No longer craving the milk of the world to satisfy, David was content to wholly depend upon the Lord for nourishment, which enabled a state of calm and peace. "It is not the helplessness of the child—children in the East were sometimes not weaned till the age of three—but its contentment in spite of the loss of what once seemed indispensable, that is the point of the comparison."[1440]

J. J. S. Perowne contrasts spiritual weaning with that of the baby. "The figure is graceful, touching, original, beautifully expressive of the humility of a soul chastened by disappointment. It expresses both the cost at which he gained rest, for the child is not weaned without much pain and strife, and also the purity and unselfishness of the rest he gained. As the weaned child, when its first fretfulness and uneasiness are past, no longer cries and frets and longs for the breast, but lies still and is content because it is with its mother; so my soul is weaned from all discontented thoughts, from all fretful desires for earthly good, waiting in stillness upon God, finding its satisfaction in His presence, resting peacefully in His arms."[1441] George Horne wrote: "A child newly weaned *mourneth because of the favourite aliment which is withdrawn from him*, but depending absolutely on the mother for every thing, learneth to acquiesce in her treatment of him, and quietly to accept what it shall please her to give."[1442]

The Christian is to "wean" himself not only from worldly ambition but its sinful desires and pleasures. See 2 Corinthians 6:17. The weaning is initiated at conversion, but because the Adamic nature yet remains, continues throughout life. It takes inward struggle, battle and discipline to kill the old man and its lusts. As the baby fights to regain and retain the milk of the breast, the believer battles the return (the pull) to fleshly "appetites." This is why even the godly Apostle Paul said, "I die daily" (1 Corinthians 15:31). Every day we must climb into the *electric chair of fleshly cravings* and die to their desire (wean ourselves from them). Spurgeon observes, "When we think ourselves safely through the weaning, we sadly discover that the old appetites are rather wounded than slain, and we begin crying again for the breasts which we had given up. It is easy to begin shouting before we are out of the woods, and no doubt hundreds have sung this Psalm long before they have understood it."[1443]

The fact is, though we long to be a "weaned child," we are yet a "weaning" child. What ought you to wean yourself from in order to be more like Jesus (alcohol consumption, drug usage, pornography, lust, sexual misconduct, anger, worldly ambition and pursuit, etc.)? As long as we pine for and/or yield to the *bottle* of the "world" as the weaning child to its mother's breast, there will be anxiety, worry, unrest and difficulty. But, says Spurgeon, "When your desires are held within bounds, your temptations to rebel are ended. You wasted this and you wanted that, and so you quarreled with God, and your Lord and you were seldom on good terms. He did not choose to pamper you, and you wanted that He should, and so you fretted like a weaning child. Now you leave it to His will, and you have peace. The strife is over. Your soul is quieted, and behaves itself becomingly."[1444]

Let Israel hope in the Lord from henceforth and forever. David's confidence in God, humility, patience and contentment despite affliction and trouble was to serve as an example to all Israel. By David's example they were to walk in faith, waiting upon the Lord for his crowning as King (and not force it with violence) and deliverance.

My heart is not haughty. Matthew Henry wrote, "Consciousness of our integrity. This was David's rejoicing, that his heart could witness for him that he had walked humbly with his God, notwithstanding the censures he was under and the temptations he was in. He aimed not at a high condition, nor was he desirous of making a figure in the world but, if God had so ordered, could have been well content to spend all his days, as he did in the beginning of them, in the sheep-folds."[1445] Blessed is the man that may make the same attestation.

The Bottom Line: At the time of this writing, a friend informed me that the past seven to eight days had been most difficult as they took the pacifier from their child ("weaned"). As with his child, the believer has to be delivered ("weaned") from carnal pleasurable things by his loving Father (God) throughout life, which causes grave protest of the *Adamic nature.* Paul addresses this battle in Romans 7:21–25, as does the author of Hebrews in Hebrews 12:1. Christians are bridges under construction, in a continu-ous state of weaning from the fleshly appetites and attitudes of the world. Every day there must be a conscious decision to deny fleshly desires and lusts that "war against the soul" (1 Peter 2:11). See 1 Corinthians 15:31. "There is not any thing, not health, nor friends, nor liberty, nor life itself, that we should value any further than as it may be improved to the glory of God. Our hearts must be weaned from all, so as to be ready to part with every thing, whenever God, in his providence, shall call for it."[1446]

> There is not any thing, not health, nor friends, nor liberty, nor life itself, that we should value any further than as it may be improved to the glory of God. Our hearts must be weaned from all, so as to be ready to part with every thing, whenever God, in his providence, shall call for it.
> Charles Simeon

54. The Minister Must Be Holy   Psalm 132:9

"Let thy priests be clothed with righteousness; and let thy saints shout for joy."—Psalm 132:9.

Let thy "priests" (Swanson says "cleric, minister, i.e., one who performs religious rites and rituals to God on behalf of others [1 Samuel 1:3], note: the OT priests had other functions that included medical diagnosis, policing functions and teaching, but as related to the service to the Lord."[1447]) be "clothed" (Gesenius and Tregelles say "to put on a garment, to clothe oneself with a garment."[1448]) with "righteousness" (Vine, Unger and White say "to be righteous, be in the right, be justified, be just."[1449]).

AND let thy "saints" (Thomas says "pious:—godly, godly ones."[1450]) "shout for joy" (Vine, Unger and White say "to sing, shout, cry out. *Ranan* is often used to express joy, exultation, which seems to demand loud singing, especially when it is praise to God."[1451]).

Homily

The Psalm's writer is uncertain. Some suggest David; others, Solomon. The occasion seems to be the return of the Ark to Jerusalem (its location was God's presence among the people) and the resultant celebration and worship to the Lord among the saints. See Psalm 132:7–8; 1 Samuel 6:21–7:2 and 2 Samuel 6:2. "It is called 'the ark of your might' because it represented the very presence of the God of power."[1452] See Psalm 132:8b. Exodus 25:10–22 describes the Ark.

Spurgeon says, "No garment is so resplendent as that of a holy character. In this glorious robe our great High Priest is evermore arrayed, and he would have all his people adorned in the same manner. Then only are priests fit to appear before the Lord, and to minister for the profit of the people, when their lives are dignified with goodness. They must ever remember that they are God's priests, and should therefore wear the livery [a special uniform worn by a servant *Oxford Dictionary*] of their Lord, which is holiness: they are not only to have righteousness, but to be clothed with it, so that upon every part of them righteousness shall be conspicuous. Whoever looks upon God's servants should see holiness if they see nothing else."[1453] L. R. Scarborough said, "Those who handle the vessels of the Lord must have pure hearts and clean hands. 'Holiness unto the Lord' must be on the skirts of God's spiritual priesthood today."[1454]

> Beloved, if you stand behind this holy desk and your life isn't pure, if your life isn't absolutely holy as far as you know it, if you are not walking under an unclouded sky with the ungrieved, unquenched Holy Spirit in your life, then, my friend, you've absolutely blocked the message from any authority whatsoever.
> Stephen Olford

The apostle Paul, though clean in deed and motive in his own eyes, before the Lord found it imperative to *persuade* the Corinthians of his integrity—not simply to vindicate himself, but so the Gospel he proclaimed would be received freely (2 Corinthians 5:11). William Barclay comments, "A man's message will always be heard in the context of his character. That is why the preacher and the teacher must be beyond suspicion. We have to avoid, not only evil, but the very appearance of evil, lest anything make others think less, not of us, but of the message which we bring."[1455] It has been said, "Never do anything that makes God look bad." This is especially true for the preacher. Stephen Olford, in a lecture series at New Orleans Baptist Theological Seminary, said, "Beloved, if you stand behind this holy desk and your life isn't pure, if your life isn't absolutely holy as far as you know it, if you are not walking under an unclouded sky with the ungrieved, unquenched Holy Spirit in your life, then, my friend, you've absolutely blocked the message from any authority whatsoever."[1456]

George Whitefield liked always to have his preaching attire scrupulously clean. He would say, "These are not trifles; a minister must be without spot, even in his garments, if he can." Spurgeon to this declared, "Purity cannot be carried too far in a minister."[1457] John MacArthur, commenting on 1 Timothy 6:11, stated, "A man of God is a lifelong fugitive, fleeing those things that would destroy him and his ministry....He not only does right but also thinks right; he not only behaves properly but also is properly motivated. He is a man who serves God with reverence and awe (Hebrews 12:28)."[1458]

The apostle Paul is an exemplary pattern for the preacher in regard to holiness of conduct in that no man could accuse him of unethical or immoral conduct privately or publicly (Acts 20:18). Psalm 24:3–5 should ring in the minister's ear as he prepares to preach to the unsaved: "Who shall ascend into the hill of the LORD? or who shall stand in his holy place? He that hath clean hands, and a pure heart; who hath not lifted up his soul unto vanity, nor sworn deceitfully. He shall receive the blessing from the LORD, and righteousness from the God of his salvation." Clean hands and a pure heart in the minister are a must to communicate God's Word of salvation effectively. Phillips Brooks said, "It does not take great men to do great things; it only takes consecrated men."[1459] Spurgeon cautioned, "Take care, dear reader, that you do not forsake the path of duty by leaving your occupation, and take care you do not dishonor your profession while in it. Think little of yourselves, but do not think too little of your callings."[1460]

Ministers "must be men in whom is the Spirit, and in whose lives are found the principles of Jesus Christ. It is vain to commend him with the lip when the life bears no confirming witness; but when lip and life speak the same truth, there is power and fruitage. They will be men whose word will be of divine redemption, whose work will be the healing, the strengthening, and the saving of the souls of men; and this plenitude of salvation will overflow to the life of those they serve."[1461]

The Bottom Line: The minister must be clothed with the garment of holiness in the totality of his being. He must be adorned with the robe of unassailable holiness (purity of life), soundness (incorrupt) of theology and ministerial *alacrity* [denotes physical quickness coupled with eagerness or enthusiasm *Merriam-Webster*[1462]]. "Laugh at ministers all you want; they have the words we need to hear, the ones the dead have spoken" (Rabbit in John Updike, *Rabbit Is Rich*). Fuller wrote, "Surely that preaching which comes from the soul works most on the soul."[1463]

55. Unity in the Church (Essential to Revival)   Psalm 133

"Behold, how good and how pleasant it is for brethren to dwell together in unity! It is like the precious ointment upon the head, that ran down upon the beard, even Aaron's beard: that went down to the skirts of his garments; As the dew of Hermon, and as the dew that descended upon the mountains of Zion: for there the LORD commanded the blessing, even life for evermore."—Psalm 133.

"Behold" (Spurgeon says, "It is a wonder seldom seen; therefore behold it! It may be seen, for it is the characteristic of real saints; therefore fail not to inspect it! It is well worthy of admiration; pause and gaze upon it! It will charm you into imitation; therefore note it well."[1464]) "good" (Thomas says "pleasant, agreeable, good:—beautiful, beneficial."[1465]).

AND "pleasant" (Swanson says "i.e., pertaining to being acceptable and favorable; beautiful, i.e., pertaining to the lovely and attractive appearance of an object."[1466]) it is for "brethren" (brothers; blood-relatives which describes the redeemed. Barnes says, "All the people of God—all the followers of the Redeemer—are brethren, members of the same family, fellow-heirs of the same inheritance [Matthew 23:8.]"[1467] Plumer says, "All pious men are brethren, being born of God, having one Lord, one faith, one baptism, one hope, one aim, one end, one God and Father. How good and how delightful it is for men as human beings or for citizens of the same country to live in peace and harmony!"[1468]) to "dwell" (Vine, Unger and White say "to dwell, sit, abide, inhabit, remain. The word has the sense of 'to remain.'"[1469]) together in "unity" (Swanson says "wholly, in unity, with each other, i.e., pertaining to being whole and in a state of oneness"[1470]).

It is like the "precious ointment" (Rawlinson says, "The anointing oil of the sanctuary was an ointment composed of many 'precious' ingredients, as myrrh, cinnamon, sweet calamus, and cassia, besides oil olive, which was its basis [Exodus 30:23, 24]. Not only Aaron [Leviticus 8:12], but all later high priests, were anointed with it [Exodus 30:30]."[1471] Simeon says, "A full account of this ointment is given us in the book of Exodus. The ingredients of which it was composed were of the most odoriferous kind: the proportions of each were minutely specified by God himself: and its use, when properly compounded, was solely confined to the things or persons connected with the service of the sanctuary. It was strictly forbidden to the whole nation to form any other ointment like unto it, or to use any part of it for any other purpose than that which was ordained by God. It was itself most holy; and it made every thing holy that came in contact with it."[1472] Benson says that "unity" "is no less grateful and refreshing than that holy anointing oil, which was strongly perfumed, and diffused its fragrance all around, to the great delight of all present, when it was poured upon the head of Aaron, at the time of his con-secration to the priestly office, so plentifully, that it ran down his face, even to the collar or binding of his garment."[1473]).

"Upon the head, that ran down upon the beard, even Aaron's beard: that went down to the skirts of his garments" (Kirkpatrick says, "This sacred oil was poured upon Aaron's head [Exodus 29:7; Leviticus 8:12; Leviticus 21:10] when he was consecrated to the office of high-priest, whereas the ordinary priests were only sprinkled with it [Exodus 29:21]. It would flow down upon his beard and onto his shoulders and his breast, upon which he bore the names of the Twelve Tribes [Exodus 28:9–12, 17–21], symbolizing thereby the consecration of the whole nation of which he was the representative. The stream of perfumed oil, carefully compounded with aromatic spices, would diffuse its fragrance all around, symbolizing the holy influence which should emanate from the chief religious representative of Israel, and from the nation which he represented. The point of the simile then seems to be, that as the sacred oil flowed down over Aaron's shoulders, so the harmonious unity of those who dwell in Jerusalem will influence the whole nation for good. The same spirit will be diffused throughout the whole community."[1474] Barnes says, "There is no other resemblance between the idea of anointing with oil and that of harmony among brethren than this which is derived from the gladness—the joyousness—connected with such an anointing. The Psalmist wished to give the highest idea of the pleasantness of such harmony; and he, therefore, compared it with that which was most beautiful to a pious mind—the idea of a solemn consecration to the highest office of religion."[1475])

As the "dew of Hermon, and as the dew that descended upon the mountains of Zion" (Spurgeon says, 'From the loftier mountains the moisture appears to be wafted to the lesser hills: the dews of Hermon fall on Zion. The Alpine Lebanon ministers to the minor elevation of the city of David; and so does brotherly love descend from the higher to the lower, refreshing and enlivening in its course. Holy concord is as dew, mysteriously blessed, full of life and growth for all plants of grace. It brings with it so much benediction that it is as no common dew, but as that of Hermon which is especially copious [in large amounts; more than enough says the *Cambridge Dictionary*], and far reaching."[1476] Benson says, "Union, in any nation, is the gift of God; and therefore unity among brethren, beginning from the king, is like the dew of heaven, which, falling first upon the higher summits of Hermon [refreshing and enriching wherever it falls] naturally descends to a lower; and thence even to the humble valleys."[1477]).

"For there" (Benson says "where brethren live in peace and unity; or, in Zion, last mentioned, that is, in God's church, or among his people."[1478] Jamieson-Fausset-Brown say "is, in Zion, the Church; the material Zion, blessed with enriching dews, suggests this allusion the source of the influence enjoyed by the spiritual Zion."[1479]) "the Lord commanded the blessing" (Poole says "ordained, promised, conferred, and established His blessing, to wit, all manner of blessedness for His people that sincerely worship Him in that place. Life, to wit, a happy and pleasant life; for to live in misery is accounted and oft called death, both in Scripture and in other authors."[1480]).

"Even life for evermore" (Gill says, "The great blessing of all, which includes all others, and in which they issue, the promise of the covenant, the blessing of the Gospel; which is in the hands of Christ, and comes through Him to all His people; to the peacemakers particularly, that live in love and peace; these shall live forever in a happy eternity, and never die, or be hurt of the second death."[1481]).

Homily

A Psalm of David probably sung during the Israelites' journey to one of the three major feasts annually in Jerusalem. See Psalm 122. Allan Harman states, "A suitable setting for this psalm would be the period after David became king not only of Judah but also of Israel (see 2 Samuel 5:1–5)."[1482] J. J. S. Perowne wrote, "Nowhere has the nature of true unity—that unity which binds men together, not by artificial restraints, but as brethren of one heart—been more faithfully described, nowhere has it been so gracefully illustrated, as in this short Ode."[1483]

W. S. Plumer well remarks "The highest unity is that of *brethren in Christ*, animated with love and pity to one another, with a common, pious zeal for truth and holiness, with joyful hopes all centered in Christ. Among these discord, wrath, bitterness and contention are odious just in proportion as they are under the highest obligations to dwell together in love and unity."[1484] Unity among the "brethren" in the church of Jesus Christ consists of several elements.

(1) Doctrine. Intellectually or mentally believers "agree" to sameness of truth expounded in the Word of God and its ethical, moral and spiritual application. J. C. Ryle wrote, "Unity without the gospel is a worthless unity; it is the very unity of hell."[1485]

(2) Direction. Believers manifest sameness of purpose and vision for the church's primary task of extending the kingdom of God on earth locally and globally and the promotion of His glory and honor.

(3) Disposition. Believers love and respect one another despite differences in face or race and work together (cooperate, teamwork) in the fulfillment of the basis for the church's existence (the exaltation of Christ; evangelism of the lost; edification of the saint). Apart from hearty cooperation, the uniting of the giftedness, godliness and guidance (wisdom) of "all" the saints God's work will suffer (be greatly impeded).

(4) Duty. Believers assume the roles or tasks in the church according to their giftedness and abilities for the furtherance of the Gospel and the glory of God. They don't park on someone else's "nickel." It's not somebody doing everything but everybody doing something. In a day when it is stated that eighty percent of church work is performed by

twenty percent of the membership, this aspect of "unity" must be again emphasized in preaching and teaching.

(5) Demeanor. In the ideal church, the members' walk, thought and talk are similar, for its fountainhead is the Holy Scriptures. Churches are greatly injured and hindered when their members walk outside the church in ways contrary to the teachings within the church.

(6) Deference. M. R. DeHaan said, "We need not all agree, but if we disagree, let us not be disagreeable in our disagreements."[1486] At times the believer must set aside personal "preferences" (not theological dogma) and defer to that of others in the body. "No leader or teacher can overestimate the value of the spirit of unity in the Church of Christ. No surrender of our own preferences can be too great to secure it."[1487]

(7) Dependence. Believers ought to exhibit dependence upon the Lord Jesus Christ for guidance in church planning (strategy), policies, procedures, practice and *power*. The church as the body of Christ looks to its "head" for direction in every aspect of its operation. See Colossians 1:18. It is ultimately in Him the church triumphs over bad and evil.

We will walk with each other; we will walk hand in hand,
And together we'll spread the news that God is in our land,
And they'll know we are Christians by our love, by our love.
They will know we are Christians by our love. ~ Peter Scholtes (1966)

Like a mighty army moves the church of God;
Brothers, we are treading where the saints have trod.
We are not divided, all one body we,
One in hope and doctrine, one in charity.
~ Sabine Baring-Gould (1834–1924)

Unity is like "precious ointment." George Horne says, "Oil is, without question, the finest emblem of union that ever was conceived. It is a substance consisting of very small parts, which yet, by their mutual adhesion, constitute one uniform, well-united, and useful body."[1488] Thus, David uses the metaphor of "oil" to describe the chemistry of the church. Unity is a "precious ointment" (oil symbolizing joy, happiness, oneness, harmony) that diffuses a pleasant and delightful aroma that appeals and attracts. People avoid churches filled with discord, disunity and division. The famed evangelist D. L. Moody said, "I have never yet known the Spirit of God to work where the Lord's people were divided."[1489]

> I have never yet known the Spirit of God to work where the Lord's people were divided.
> Dwight Moody

It is there. God commands His people (His body, the church) to dwell in unity. It is only in such churches that His chiefest blessings will be manifest and His message will be met with the greatest success (soul salvation). Therefore, the church must experience a revival that, as it rights them with Christ, merges them together as "one" and then, at all expense (apart from theological or moral compromise), maintains it. John F. Walvoord remarks, "The only way it is possible to have one mind is to have the mind of God derived from the unity of the Spirit of God, a unity which comes only when believers find the will of God and give themselves unselfishly and unstintingly to its fulfillment."[1490]

George Horne said, "Many things are good which are not pleasant; and many pleasant which are not good. But unity among brethren, whether civil or religious, is productive both of profit and pleasure. Of profit, because therein consisteth the welfare and security of every society; of pleasure, because mutual love is the source of delight, and the happiness of one becomes, in that case, the happiness of all."[1491]

"Do you know," writes Adrian Rogers, "what God wants from you today? Reconciliation. That's far more important than singing in the choir, preaching a sermon, serving in the nursery, or giving an offering. When we learn this, God is going to bring great revival to our churches. Revival always begins when people begin to confess their faults one to another, pray for one another, and forgive one another. Revival isn't raising the roof with a lot of emotion. It is getting the walls down. It is not just saying, 'I am going to get right with God.' It is saying, 'I want to get right with my brothers and sisters.' When we are reconciled, revival will come."[1492]

The Bottom Line: "Whatever disunites man from God also disunites man from man."[1493] The Holy Spirit is the source of unity in the body. As He is allowed to rule in man's heart, the harmonic connection with others occurs. Imagine a chair (God seated) encircled by chairs (saints seated). As the chairs draw closer to the center chair they draw closer to each other.

56. The Encouragement of God's Servant   Psalm 134

"Behold, bless ye the LORD, all ye servants of the LORD, which by night stand in the house of the LORD. Lift up your hands in the sanctuary, and bless the LORD. The LORD that made heaven and earth bless thee out of Zion."—Psalm 134.

"Behold" (Plumer says "equivalent to see, come now, give heed."[1494]) "bless ye the Lord" (Brown, Driver and Briggs say "kneel, bless; praise."[1495]) all ye "servants of the Lord" (Plumer says "a term that does sometimes embrace all the creatures of God; sometimes, all Israel; sometimes, God's loving, obedient people; but it is here limited to those who officially serve in the temple."[1496]) which by "night stand in the house of the Lord" (Maclaren says, "That is to say, the priests or Levites whose charge it was to patrol the Temple through the hours of night and darkness, to see that all was safe and right there, and to do such other priestly and ministerial work as was needful; they are called upon to 'lift up their hands in'—or rather *towards*—'the Sanctuary, and to bless the Lord.'"[1497] Barnes says, "There was a class of singers in the Temple who devoted the night, or a part of the night, to praise; and it is possible that this service may have been, as it was subsequently in some of the monasteries, continued by succeeding choirs, during the entire night."[1498] Plumer says, "The sacred fire was kept burning on the altar all night, the lamps also burned all night, and songs were sung in the temple by night. Fry: 'We know generally that there was a nightly service in the temple.'"[1499] See 1 Chronicles 9:33; Luke 2:37; Acts 26:7.). *"stand* in the house" (Perowne says "a common word for the service of the Priests and Levites [Deuteronomy 10:8; 1 Chronicles 23:30; 2 Chronicles 29:11]."[1500]).

"Lift up your hands" (Barnes says, "The lifting up of the hands is properly expressive of prayer, but the phrase may be used to denote praise or worship in general."[1501]) "in the sanctuary" (Poole says "in the sanctuary; in that holy house of God where you stand [Psalm 134:1]."[1502]).

AND "bless the Lord" (Gill says "which is repeated, to show the importance of the work, that it might not be forgotten and neglected; this being a principal part of spiritual service, and greatly acceptable to God."[1503]).

"The Lord that made heaven and earth bless thee" (Spurgeon says, 'This last verse is the answer from the Temple to the pilgrims preparing to depart as the day breaks. It is the ancient blessing of the high priest condensed, and poured forth upon each individual pilgrim....You are scattering and going to your homes one by one; may the benediction come upon you one by one. You have been up to Jehovah's city and Temple at His bidding; return each one with such a benediction as only He can give—divine, infinite, effectual, eternal. You are not going away from Jehovah's works or glories, for He made the heaven above you and the earth on which you dwell. He is your Creator, and He can bless you with untold mercies; He can create joy and peace in your hearts, and make for you a new heaven and a new earth. May the Maker of all things make you to abound in blessings.'[1504] See Numbers 6:24.).

"Out of Zion" (Barnes says, "That is, may God speak to you out of Zion; may He confer on you such blessings as properly go out of Zion; or such as Zion [or His church] can furnish. Go not away unblessed; go not without a token of divine favor—for God will bless you."[1505]).

Homily

The author and historical occasion of the Psalm are unknown. It probably was sung by the Jews as they departed home after attending one of the three annual feasts in Jerusalem. In the first two verses, the people speak to the priests; in the third verse, the priests speak to the people as they depart. It is one of the two shortest Psalms (with Psalm 117). Three things are clear with regard to this Psalm, according to Delitzsch: "This Psalm consists of a greeting (vv. 1–2) and the reply thereto (v.3). The greeting is addressed to those priests and Levites who have the night watch in the Temple; and this *psalm* is purposely placed at the end of the collection of Songs of degrees in order to take the place of a final blessing."[1506]

The servants that ministered in the Temple "at night" were not the Jewish people but the Levites or priests. The Targum describes the first verse of the Temple Watch. "The custom in the second Temple appears to have been this: After midnight the chief of the doorkeepers took the key of the inner Temple and went with some of the Priests through the small postern of the Fire Gate. In the inner court, this watch divided itself into two companies, each carrying a burning torch; one company turned west, the other east; and so they compassed the court to see whether all were in readiness for the Temple service on the following morning. In the bakehouse, where the mincha (meat offering) of the High Priest was baked, they met with the cry, 'All well!' Meanwhile the rest of the Priests arose, bathed themselves, and put on their garments. They then went into the stone chamber (one half of which was the hall of session of the Sanhedrin), and there, under the superintenddence of the officer who gave the watchword and one of the Sanhedrin, surrounded by the Priests clad in their robes of office, their several duties for the coming day were assigned to each of the Priests by lot (Luke 1:9)."[1507]

It is the task of the church member to encourage the *servants of the Lord* to maintain hearty worship ("Bless ye the Lord"), continued faithfulness to their lofty duty and the church ("which by night stand in the house of the Lord") and holiness in life ("Lift up your hands in the sanctuary"; to lift the hands both in prayer and praise toward the *Holy of Holies,* ministers must be holy.) In such a time as ours in which 1,500 ministers quit the ministry monthly, the laity must step up to lighten the load, bear part of the burden, and infuse with healthy doses of encouragement.

The Lord that made heaven and earth bless thee out of Zion. George Horne says, "The two preceding verses (Psalm 134:1–2) seem directed to the priests of the temple, by some person, probably of consequence, come up to pay his devotion. This third verse is therefore returned, as from the priests."[1508] Those that encourage the minister and endeavor to promote his effectiveness in ministry shall of them and the Lord be richly blessed. Of this Paul is an example in the blessing of Onesiphorus for his encouragement and help. He declared, "May the Lord show special kindness to Onesiphorus and all his family because he often visited and *encouraged me.* He was never ashamed of me because I was in chains. When he came to Rome, he searched everywhere until he found me. May the Lord show him special kindness on the day of

Christ's return. And you know very well how helpful he was in Ephesus" (2 Timothy 1:16–18 NLT).

Junior Hill said, "As far as the Bible reveals...Onesiphorus never preached a sermon. He never did a miracle. He never taught a class. He never wrote a Bible book. All we know about Onesiphorus is that his epitaph reads: he oft refreshed the Apostle Paul. The word 'refreshed' literally means 'to cool something down with the breath of your mouth.' And it is an illustration of somebody who is ministering to you in a way that calms or edifies you" (by presence, pen, purse).[1509] Every minister needs an Onesiphorus.

Literally 1 Samuel 23:16 reads, "Jonathan helped David strengthen his grip on God." Ultimately this defines Christian friendship—the act of instilling in the life of another the words of God that will encourage in times of grave difficulty; enlighten in times of spiritual darkness; enhance one's joy, peace and hope, strengthening their grip on God.

The Bottom Line: The minister is sorely in need of encouragement and help. Help stave off the burnout, dropout and even suicide of your pastor by befriending, encouraging and helping him.

57. The Name of Jesus   Psalm 135:13

"*Thy name, O LORD, endureth for ever; and thy memorial, O LORD, throughout all generations.*"—Psalm 135:13.

Thy "name" (Yahweh), O Lord, "endureth forever" (Swanson says "everlasting, forever, eternity, i.e., pertaining to an unlimited duration of time, usually with a focus on the future."[1510] See Exodus 3:15.).

AND thy "memorial" (Poole says, "These wonderful works of Thine shall never be forgotten. The land which Thou gavest us [Psalm 135:12], and which we yet enjoy, is an everlasting monument of Thy power and goodness, and an obligation and encouragement to trust in Thee in all our present or future difficulties."[1511] Plumer says, "There is no land where, and there is no time when, Jehovah does not evince His existence, His perfections, and His government over the world. The two clauses of the verse are parallel. Patrick's paraphrase is: 'O Lord, how astonishing is this Thy omnipotent goodness! the fame of which shall never be forgotten.'"[1512]).

O Lord, "throughout all generations" (Spurgeon says, "This verse must be construed in its connection, and it teaches us that the honor and glory gained by the Lord in the overthrow of the mighty kings would never die out."[1513]).

Homily

W. S. Plumer wrote, "The authorship of this Psalm is not settled, nor have we any clue to the occasion of its composition."[1514] J. J. S. Perowne states, "The Psalm is almost entirely composed of passages taken from other sources. Compare v. 1 with Psalm 134:1; v. 3 with Psalm 147:1; vv. 6 and 15–20 with Psalm 115; v. 7 with Jeremiah 10:13; v. 14 with Deuteronomy 32:36; v. 8–12 with Psalm 136:10–22."[1515] Jennings and Lowe say, "The theme is the supreme preeminence of Jehovah, the God of Nature and the God of Sacred History, over all other deities; His relation to Israel as Protector, and Israel's reciprocal relation as pledged to offer to Him the sacrifice of praise and blessing."[1516]

Thy name O Lord, endureth forever. Spurgeon states, "God's name is eternal and will never be changed. His character is immutable; His fame and honor also will remain to all eternity. There will always be life in the name of Jesus, and sweetness and consolation. Those upon whom the Lord's name is named in verity and truth will be preserved by it, and kept from all evil, world without end. Jehovah is a name which will outlive the ages, and retain the fullness of its glory and might forever."[1517] *And thy memorial throughout all generations.* "Jehovah's Name is called His memorial, as bringing to mind all that He is and does. Such as He has once revealed Himself to be He will continue forever."[1518] See Psalm 102:12. Matthew Henry summarizes the text, "God is, and will be, always the same to His church, a gracious, faithful, wonder-working God; and His church is, and will be, the same to Him, a thankful praising people; and thus His name endures forever."[1519]

The same is applicable to the name of Jesus. *In His name* forever there is healing for hurt; solace in sorrow; forgiveness in fault; deliverance in domination (sin's); protection in peril; triumph in temptation; rescue in rebellion and pardon in punishment (eternal damnation).

> *In His name* forever there is healing for hurt; solace in sorrow; forgiveness in fault; deliverance in domination (sin's); protection in peril; triumph in temptation; rescue in rebellion and pardon in punishment (eternal damnation).

John Gill says, "The name of Christ endures forever; His person and offices, His Gospel, which is His name; His children and people, who are called by His name, and in whom His name is perpetuated; the fame of His wondrous works in nature, providence, and grace; and especially of His great work of redemption and salvation."[1520] Christ's name, like the ringing of a bell, sends out its chimes through the ages, assuring His people that He will keep His promises (to exhibit mercy and grace, forgiveness, salvation and deliverance from sin's cruel bondage and give them entrance at the last into Canaan (Heaven). While the names of the great men of history have perished or are perishing, Christ's name remains unchanged in its fame and glory. It will be forever perpetuated.

T. DeWitt Talmage (1832–1902) in the sermon *The Name of Jesus* said, "*It [the name of Jesus] will be perpetuated in art,* for there will be other Bellinis to depict the Madonna; there will be other Ghirlandaios to represent Christ's baptism; there will be other Bronzinos to show us Christ's visiting the spirits in prison; other Giottos to appall our sight with the crucifixion. The name will be preserved in song, for there will be other Handels to write *Messiah;* other Dr. Young's to portray His triumph; other Cowpers to sing His love. *It will be preserved in costly and magnificent architecture,* for Protestantism as well as Catholicism is yet to have its St. Marks and its St. Peters. *That name will be preserved in the literature of the world,* for already it is embalmed in the best books. There will be other Dr. Paley's to write *Evidences of Christianity,* other Richard Baxters to describe the Savior's coming to judgment. But above all, and more than all, that name will be *embalmed in the memory of all the good of earth and all the great ones of Heaven.*"[1521] For certain, Christ's name will be perpetuated by those He snatched as brands from the burning, transforming their lives forever. "Will the delivered bondman of earth ever forget who freed him? Will the blind man of earth forget who gave him sight? Will the outcast of earth forget who brought him home? No! No!"[1522] Spurgeon wrote, "Grateful hearts will forever beat to Thy praise, and enlightened minds will continue to marvel at all Thy wondrous works. Human memorials decay, but the memorial of the Lord abides evermore."[1523]

Talmage concludes, "To destroy the memory of that name of Christ, you would have to burn up all the Bibles and all the churches on earth, then, in a spirit of universal arson, go through the gate of Heaven, put a torch to the temples and the towers and the palaces; and after all that city was wrapped in awful conflagration, and the citizens came out and gazed on the ruin, even then they would hear that name in the thunder of falling tower and the crash of crumbling wall and see it wrought in the flying banners of flame; and the redeemed of the Lord on high would be happy yet and cry out, 'Let the palaces and temples burn; we have Jesus left!'"[1524]

Hallelujah, Christ's name endureth forever!

The kingdom of this world
Is become the kingdom of our Lord
And of His Christ, and of His Christ;
And He shall reign for ever and ever.
King of kings, and Lord of lords,...
And He shall reign forever and ever,
King of kings, forever and ever,
And Lord of lords,
Hallelujah! Hallelujah! ~ George Frideric Handel, *Messiah*

George Horne summarizes, "By the destruction of Pharaoh, with his Egyptians, and by the battles and victories of Joshua; much more, by the overthrow of the spiritual Pharaoh [Satan], with his infernal host, and by the battles and victories of the true Joshua [Jesus Christ]; Jehovah hath gotten him glory, and his 'name is magnified' in the church from age to age."[1525]

The Bottom Line: Bow in submission to the wonderful, precious, powerful and eternal name of Jesus, acclaiming and accepting Him as Lord and Savior. It is "the name above all names" and the only name that saves man from his sin. "Wherefore God also hath highly exalted him, and given him a name which is above every name: That at the name of Jesus every knee should bow, of things in heaven, and things in earth, and things under the earth; And that every tongue should confess that Jesus Christ is Lord, to the glory of God the Father" (Philippians 2:9–11).

58. The Mercy of God Endures Forever   Psalm 136:1

"O give thanks unto the Lᴏʀᴅ; for he is good: for his mercy endureth for ever."—Psalm 136:1.

O give "thanks" (Vine, Unger and White say "to confess, praise, give thanks. An affirmation or confession of God's undeserved kindness throws man's unworthiness into sharp relief. Hence, a confession of sin may be articulated in the same breath as a confession of faith or praise and thanksgiving."[1526]) unto the Lord; for he is "good" (Holladay and Kohler say "good in every variety of meaning"[1527]).

His "mercy" (Vine, Unger and White say "loving-kindness; steadfast love; grace; mercy; faithfulness; goodness; devotion."[1528]) "endureth forever" (It is eternal without change).

Homily

The composer of the Psalm is unknown but likely the same as in the previous Psalm. Jennings and Lowe comment, "In precisely the same method as Psalm 135, the present Psalm first extols the God of nature, then the God of Jewish history. It borrows freely, as does Psalm 135, from earlier compositions, more especially from the Book of Deuteronomy."[1529] Its composition is similar to that of the responsive readings found in many hymnals. "The first [part of the verse] would be sung by some of the Levites, the second by the choir as a body, or by the whole congregation together with the Levites."[1530] It was written after the captivity. Martin Luther said, "In this repeated expression ["for His mercy endureth forever"] the Psalmist looks to the promise of Christ to come."[1531] Every verse in the Psalm is the same with the exception of a variance to the name of God ("Lord," "God of gods," "Lord of lords"). George Horne states, "The attributes here mentioned are those of 'goodness' and 'power'; the one renders Him willing, the other able, to save."[1532]

The Psalmist cites reasons to render praise to the Lord.

(1) For His goodness and kindness. See Psalm 136:1.

(2) For He is superior to all other gods. See Psalm 136:2.

(3) For His mighty works and miracles. See Psalm 136:4.

(4) For His acts in creation. He cites the wonders of the first three days of creation—the heavens; dry land and the sun and moon to give light. See Psalm 136:5–9.

(5) For His deliverance of the Israelites from Egyptian bondage. He smote the firstborn in Egyptian homes while sparing the Israelites' firstborn (provided blood was sprinkled on their doorposts). See Psalm 136:10. When they were pursued by Pharaoh's army (the Exodus), the Lord divided the Red Sea to provide an escape route over dry ground. Upon their safe passage to the other side, the Lord caused the waters to return upon Pharaoh's army, destroying them utterly. See Psalm 136:11–15.

(6) For His protection and provision for His people during their forty years in the wilderness before entering into Canaan. See Psalm 136:16. Thanks rendered unto God for the conquest of Peraea. See Psalm 136:17–22.

(7) The Psalmist finally gives a blanket statement as to why God ought to be forever exalted and praised. *He remembered us* in our low estate. *He hath redeemed us* from our enemies. *He hath provided for us* (food). See Psalm 136:23–25.

Spurgeon says, "The exhortation is intensely earnest: the Psalmist pleads with the Lord's people to give thanks, three times repeated. Thanks are the least that we can offer, and these we ought freely to give. The inspired writer calls us to praise Jehovah for all His goodness to us, and all the greatness of His power in blessing His chosen."[1533]

For his mercy endureth forever. Twenty-six times this phrase is repeated in the Psalm. Matthew Henry remarks, "This most excellent sentence, that God's mercy endureth forever, is magnified above all the truths concerning God."[1534] Scott wrote, "By 'mercy' we understand the Lord's disposition to be compassionate and relieve those whom sin has rendered miserable and base; His readiness to forgive and be reconciled to the most provoking of transgressors, and to bestow all blessings upon them; together with all the provision which He has made for the honor of His name, in the redemption of sinners by Jesus Christ."[1535] In every favor (goodness) of God's hand extended toward us we ought to remember it came undeserved and unmerited completely based upon the mercy of God. *Endureth forever.* W. S. Plumer writes, "There is no better word. *Forever, to eternity, everlasting.*"[1536] Believers must constantly contemplate the unchangeableness of the mercy of God which makes Him willing to act graciously toward the unsaved and them. Jeremiah reminds us that "it is of the LORD's mercies that we are not consumed, because his compassions fail not. They are new every morning: great is thy faithfulness" (Lamentations 3:22–23).

Who remembered us in our low estate and hath redeemed us. See Psalm 136:23–24. In the greater work of soul salvation (He regarded our low sinful estate and need of pardon) has the Lord demonstrated mercy unto us through His sufferings in Gethsemane, ridicule and rejection by man, torture by the Roman soldiers prior to the cross and then great mental and physical anguish and torment upon the cross. Matthew Henry stated, "Forgetful as we are, things must be often repeated to us. By mercy we understand the Lord's disposition to save those whom sin has rendered miserable and vile, and all the provision He has made for the redemption of sinners by Jesus Christ. The counsels of this mercy have been from everlasting, and the effects of it will endure forever, to all who are interested in it. The Lord continues equally ready to show mercy to all who seek for it, and this is the source of all our hope and comfort."[1537] Thank God He remembered us in our sinful estate and intervened in undeserved "mercy." See Titus 3:5.

When nothing else could help
Love lifted me. ~ James Rowe (1866–1933)

The Bottom Line: Thomas Watson said, "God is more willing to pardon than to punish. Mercy does more multiply in Him than sin in us. Mercy is His nature."[1538] Give thanks unto God for He is "rich in mercy, for his great love wherewith he loved us, Even when we were dead in sins, hath quickened us together with Christ, (by grace ye are saved;) And hath raised us up together, and made us sit together in heavenly places in Christ Jesus: That in the ages to come he might shew the exceeding riches of his grace in his kindness toward us through Christ Jesus" (Ephesians 2:4–7).

59. The Lord's Song in a Strange Land   Psalm 137:1–4

"By the rivers of Babylon, there we sat down, yea, we wept, when we remembered Zion. We hanged our harps upon the willows in the midst thereof. For there they that carried us away captive required of us a song; and they that wasted us required of us mirth, saying, Sing us one of the songs of Zion. How shall we sing the Lord's *song in a strange land?"—* Psalm 137:1–4.

By the "rivers of Babylon" (Kirkpatrick says "not only the Euphrates and, its tributaries, such as the Chebar (Ezekiel 1:1; 3:15), but the numerous canals with which the country was intersected. Babylonia was characteristically a land of streams, as Palestine was a land of hills; it was the feature of the country which would impress itself upon the mind of the exiles."[1539]).

"There we sat down" ("Among the poets, sitting on the ground is a mark of misery or captivity."[1540] Benson says their distress arose "from their reflecting on Zion, and their banishment from it: and that they seated themselves down by the rivers from [by] choice, retiring thither from the noise and observation of their enemies, as they had opportunity, in order that they might unburden their oppressed minds before the Lord, and to one another."[1541] Rawlinson says, "The exiles had their leisure hours—they were not kept by their masters at hard work continually. During these leisure hours they naturally 'sat down' by the rivers of Babylon, as the most pleasant and attractive places. They brought their harps with them [v. 2], with some idea, perhaps, of indulging in mournful strains. Grief, however, overpowered them—Zion came to their recollection—and they could do nothing but weep."[1542]).

"Yea, we wept" (Brown, Driver and Briggs say "weep, bewail; grief."[1543] Benson says, "Driven from their native country, stripped of every comfort and convenience, in a strange land among idolaters, wearied and brokenhearted, they sit in silence by those hostile waters [and weep]."[1544]).

When we "remembered Zion" (Jerusalem, the city of David. Gill says, "They imitated the flowing stream by which they sat, and swelled it with their tears; they wept for their sins, which brought them thither; and it increased their sorrow, when they called to mind what privileges they had enjoyed in Zion, the city of their solemnities; where they had often seen the tribes of Israel bowing before and worshipping the God of Israel; the daily sacrifices and others offered up; the solemn feasts kept; the songs of Zion, sung by the Levites in delightful harmony; and, above all, the beauty of the Lord their God, His power and glory, while they were inquiring in His sanctuary: and also when they reflected upon the sad condition and melancholy circumstances in which Zion now was; the city, Temple, and altar, lying in heaps of rubbish; no worship and service performed; no sacrifices offered, nor songs sung; nor any that came to her solemn feasts [Lamentations 1:2]."[1545]).

"We hanged our harps" (Swanson says "stringed instrument: translated as; harp, lyre, lute, zither [or cither], kithara [or cithara], i.e., a musical instrument with a strong frame to place tension on strings as a tone, then plucked to make music, though some could be quite large, generally of a portable size."[1546] Barnes says "the harps once used to accompany the songs of praise and the service of God in the Temple; the harps with which they had sought to beguile their weary hours, and to console their sad spirits in their captivity."[1547]).

"Upon the willows in the midst thereof" (Barnes says, "It is probable that the weeping willow—the willow with long pendulous branches—is here referred to. Trees in desert lands spring up along the courses of the streams, and appear, in the wide desolation, as long and waving lines of green wherever the rivers wind along. The course of a stream can thus be marked by the prolonged line of meandering green in the desert as far as the eye can reach....The willow may be less abundant there now than it was in former times, as is true of the palm tree in Palestine, but there is no reason to doubt that it grew there."[1548]).

For there "they that carried us away captive" (the Babylonians) "required" (Gesenius and Tregelles say "to ask, to demand."[1549]) of us a "song" (Swanson says "i.e., music including lyrics and instrumental elements"[1550]). AND "they" (captors) "that wasted us" (Gesenius and Tregelles say "a vexer, tormentor; properly vexation, vexing, or the act of him who causes others to lament, forces the expression of grief from others"[1551]) "required" (Rawlinson says "demand roughly and rudely to be entertained with the foreign music, which is perhaps sweeter than their own, or at any rate more of a novelty"[1552]) of us "mirth" (Brown, Driver and Briggs say "joy, gladness, mirth"[1553]).

Saying, "Sing us one of the songs of Zion" (Gill says "which used to be sung in Zion in the Temple, called the songs of the Temple [Amos 8:3]; this demand they made either out of curiosity, that they might know something of the Temple songs and music they had heard of; or rather as jeering at and insulting the poor Jews in their miserable and melancholy circumstances; as if they had said, now sing your songs if you can: or in order to make themselves sport and diversion with them, as the Philistines with Samson.

The spiritual songs of Zion are the songs of electing, redeeming, calling, pardoning, and justifying grace; which natural men neither understand, nor can learn, but scoff at and despise."[1554] Poole says "such songs as you used to sing in the temple at Zion; which they required either out of curiosity, or to delight their ears, or rather by way of scoffing and insultation over them, and their temple and religion."[1555]).

"How shall we sing the Lord's song in a strange land?" (Spurgeon says, "How shall they sing at all? Sing Jehovah's song among the uncircumcised? With one voice they refuse, but the refusal is humbly worded by being put in the form of a question. If the men of Babylon were wicked enough to suggest the defiling of holy things for the gratification of curiosity, or for the creation of amusement, the men of Zion had not so hardened their hearts as to be willing to please them at such a fearful cost."[1556] Perowne says, "This verse tells of the mocking taunt of their captors: 'Sing us one of the songs of Zion'; and the half sad, half proud answer of the heart, strong in its faith and unconquerable in its patriotism: 'How shall we sing Jehovah's song in a strange land?' It were a profanation; it were a treachery. Sooner let the tongue fail to sing than sing to make the heathen mirth; sooner let the hand lose her cunning than tune the harp to please the stranger."[1557]).

Homily

W. S. Plumer wrote, "The theme of this Psalm is the captivity in Babylon. Expositors are not agreed as to the relation it bears to the time of the captivity. Some think it prophetic and written even as early as the time of David and by him."[1558] It is thought to have been written while the Israelites were in Babylonian captivity or shortly thereafter. It depicts the Israelites' grief and sorrow in a hostile land, their affliction and the taunting of their captors. The Psalm spiritually pictures the world (Babylon), church (earthly Zion), the Christian (the Israelites in their oppression) and Heaven (Zion, the city of God).

Babylon (the evil world) is ravaging Zion (the church) through false doctrine, compromise of biblical truth, unbelief and conformity to its likeness. As the Israelites moaned and groaned (literally, "howled") over the destruction and ruination of Jerusalem (earthly Zion)—not their personal oppression and adversity—the Christian does likewise for the state of the church. In contrasting the former days of the church with her present condition, saints cannot help but weep bitter tears over her great decline. We cry, "O Lord, restore the church's former 'glory.'"

Spurgeon comments, "Be it ours to weep in secret for the hurt of our Zion: it is the least thing we can do; perhaps in its result it may prove to be the best thing we can do. Be it ours also to sit down and deeply consider what is to be done. Be it ours, in any case, to keep upon our mind and heart the memory of the church of God which is so dear to us. The frivolous may forget, but Zion is graven on our hearts, and her prosperity is our chief desire."[1559] We must not hang our "harps" upon the willows despite the "darkness" and "disdain." We must keep on singing and praising. Matthew Henry says that the Israelites were probably faulty in hanging their harps on the trees, "for praising God is never out of season; it is His will that we should in everything give thanks."[1560] See 1 Thessalonians 5:18.

The second spiritual implication of the text relates to the believer in exile (Babylon, type of the evil world) under great oppression and perse-cution. He, like the Israelites, remembers the glory and beauty of Zion (but his is Heaven, the eternal Zion) and longs for it. See John 14:1–3. The holy saint can never be "happy" or satisfied in the world, for it is antago-nistic to God and himself.

Believers must remember that they are in spiritual exile, that their homeland is Zion (the New Jerusalem, Heaven). "For our conversation [citizenship] is in heaven; from whence also we look for the Savior, the Lord Jesus Christ" (Philippians 3:20). See Hebrews 13:14.

This world is not my home; I'm just passing through.
My treasures are laid up somewhere beyond the blue.
The angels beckon me from Heaven's open door,
And I can't feel at home in this world anymore.

~ Albert E. Brumley (1905–1977)

The third spiritual implication relates to the sinner that is exiled from Zion (the church, representing the presence of God) due to sinful disobedience. The wages of sin is "death" (present and eternal separation from God). See Romans 6:23. Bound in chains by the cruel captor of the soul (Satan), he moans for deliverance and salvation. Jesus Christ is the sinner's Redeemer and Rescuer from satanic captivity and the penalty for sin. See John 8:36.

The fourth spiritual implication relates to the backslidden saint who by sinful conduct "exiles" himself from Zion (the church, the sweet fellowship with the Lord and His people). His song is quenched and joy departed. He pines and cries for restoration, as did the prodigal in the swine pen. With bitter tears he laments the sin that stole him away from his "Beloved Lord" and the wonderful people of "Zion," and its painful consequences (anguish, guilt, distress, unhappiness and restlessness). Without a "song" to sing (in a "strange land," a hostile, sinful place, the believer's song is silenced), he hangs his "harp" upon the willows at the river bank (for he has no heart to use it) and tearfully inquires of the Lord as to when he might "enter [thy] gates with thanksgiving and [thy] courts with praise" (Psalm 100:4). The Christian may lapse into sin but will not be content to wallow in it. He, like Job, will pine for the former days when he walked in sweet fellowship with the Lord (Job 29:2–5), and, like the prodigal son, long to go home to his Father (Luke 15:13–18).

I have returned to the Father of Abraham,
The shepherd of Moses who called Him the great I am.
He's Jesus to me, Eternal Deity.
Praise His name, I have returned. ~ Marijohn Wilkin (1974)

The Bottom Line: The "song" of Zion is a sacred song that must be sung with holy lips. When the heart is clean and right with Jesus, the song automatically springs forth from the lips. Otherwise there is no spirit or heart or good in singing it. The Christian and church, though existing in a non-Christian world, must keep playing their "harps" and singing His "song" despite persecution, oppression or discrimination. Keep looking up, my brother and sister, for the hour is at hand when the Lord will vindicate not only His name but His church and people. Soon Jesus will "snatch" the saints away to Zion (the New Jerusalem, Heaven).

60. There Is Power in Prayer   **Psalm 138:2b–3**

"Thou hast magnified thy word above all thy name. In the day when I cried thou answeredst me, and strengthenedst me with strength in my soul."—Psalm 138:2b–3.

"Thou hast magnified thy word above all thy name" (Simeon says "that is, above every thing whereby He has made Himself known to mortal man. He has revealed himself in part, by his works of Creation and Providence; but far more abundantly by His Word."[1561] Henry says, "God has made Himself known to us in many ways in creation and providence, but most clearly by His Word. The judgments of His mouth are magnified even above those of His hand, and greater things are done by them. The wonders of grace exceed the wonders of nature; and what is discovered of God by revelation is much greater than what is discovered by reason."[1562] Barnes says, "The word *name* here would refer properly to all that God had done to make Himself known—since it is by the name that we designate or distinguish anyone; and, thus understood, the meaning would be, that the Word of God—the revelation which He has made of Himself and of His gracious purposes to mankind—is superior in clearness, and in importance, to all the other manifestations which He has made of Himself; all that can be known of Him in His works. Beyond all question there are higher and clearer manifestations of Himself, of His being, of His perfection, of His purposes, in the volume of revelation, than any which His works have disclosed or can disclose."[1563]).

"In the day" (Gill says "when in distress through Saul's persecution, he cried to the Lord, and He immediately answered him, and delivered him out of his troubles; and such immediate answers of prayer are to be remembered with thankfulness"[1564]) when I "cried" (Landes says "to call, shout, summon"[1565] To pray.) "thou answeredst me" (Landes says "to

271

reply, answer; to give evidence."[1566] Rawlinson says, "Thy answer came to my prayer almost as soon as it was out of my mouth."[1567] Barnes says, "In the very day when I called, Thou gavest me the answer: that is, immediately."[1568]).

AND "strengthenedst me with strength in my soul" (Barnes says "literally, 'Thou didst embolden—or, didst make me courageous with strength.' Thou didst enable me to meet danger, and to overcome fear."[1569] *Strengthenedst*. Kirkpatrick says "thou didst encourage me."[1570] Jamieson-Fausset-Brown say, "That promise, as an answer to his prayers in distress, revived and strengthened his faith."[1571] Plumer says "strengthenedst with strength."[1572] Calvin says "hast abundantly administered strength."[1573] Edwards says "invigoratedst with much strength."[1574] Street says "strengthenest with courage."[1575] The verb might be rendered *enlargedst*.[1576]).

Homily

A Psalm composed by David. Plumer states, "Many think this ode was written not long after the ten years of David's persecution were terminated by the death of Saul."[1577] Calvin said, "In this Psalm, David, in remembrance of the singular help which had always been vouchsafed him by God—the experience he had enjoyed of His faithfulness and goodness—takes occasion to stir himself up to gratitude; and from what he had known of the divine faithfulness, he anticipates a continuance of the same mercy. If dangers must be met, he confidently looks for a happy issue."[1578]

In the day that I cried. Spurgeon states, "It is the distinguishing mark of the true and living God that He hears the pleadings of His people and answers them. What answer can there be to a cry—to a mere inarticulate wail of grief? Our Heavenly Father is able to interpret tears, and cries, and He replies to their inner sense. The answer came to David in the same day as the cry ascended: so speedily does prayer rise to Heaven; so quickly does mercy return to earth. This also is our defense against modern heresies: we cannot forsake the Lord, for He has heard our prayers."[1579]

He answeredst me. Matthew Henry comments, "It was a speedy answer: *In the day when I cried*. Note, those that trade with Heaven by prayer grow rich by quick returns."[1580] It was a spiritual answer. "If God give us strength in our souls to bear the burdens, resist the temptations, and do the duties of an afflicted state, if he strengthen us to keep hold of

Himself by faith, to maintain the peace of our own minds and to wait with patience for the issue, we must own that He has answered us, and we are bound to be thankful."[1581] Spurgeon remarks, "This was a true answer to his prayer. If the burden was not removed, yet strength was given wherewith to bear it....It may not be best for us that the trial should come to an end; it may be far more to our advantage that by its pressure we should learn patience....Strength imparted to the soul...means courage, fortitude, assurance, heroism."[1582] W. S. Plumer states, "The whole battle of the believer's life calls for intrepidity ["resolute fearlessness, fortitude, and endurance, *Merriam-Webster*"]. The enemy is fierce; the child of God must be heroic. In this warfare natural courage avails nothing. It must come from God, and be imparted to the soul."[1583]

Does prayer work? James states, "The earnest prayer of a righteous person has great power and produces wonderful results" (James 5:16 NLT). Sometimes prayer results are seen instantly, while at other times they are delayed. Sometimes we receive exactly that for which we pray, while at other times God provides something far better (though we may not think so at the time). Henry Drummond tells of a little girl aboard a ship en route across the ocean that dropped her doll overboard. She ran to the captain asking if he might stop the ship to rescue her doll. His refusal led her to count him insensitive and cruel. Upon reaching port, the captain purchased the finest doll available and gave it to the girl. He had refused her request but gave her something far better.[1584] God always can be trusted "to do exceeding abundantly above all that we ask or think" (Ephesians 3:20).

There is power in prayer; this we know from practice, observation and Holy Scripture. Joshua prayed, and Achan's sin was exposed. Hannah prayed, and Samuel was born. Daniel prayed, and the lions became closed-mouthed. Hezekiah prayed, and a hundred eighty-five thousand Assyrians were killed. Nehemiah prayed, and the King granted him a leave of absence to help his people. Elisha prayed, and a child that was dead was raised. Knox prayed, and all of Scotland trembled. Taylor prayed, and the China Inland Mission was birthed. Mueller prayed, and provision was sent to feed the orphans. Luther prayed, and the Reformation occurred. God assures man of the effectiveness of prayer. See James 5:16. Sadly, we don't put enough confidence in prayer. We don't really believe what

God said about its power. E. M. Bounds said that the man who prays gets from God that which the man that does not pray cannot get.

He answered prayer so sweetly that I stand
Amid the blessings of His wondrous hand
And marvel at the miracle I see,
The favors that His love hath wrought for me.

Pray on for the impossible and dare
Upon thy banner this brave motto bear:
"My Father answers prayer." ~ Unknown

The prayer of the saint is always heard by God, and He either grants the healing, resolves the trouble, removes the difficulty or grants *grace sufficient* to patiently and courageously bear the trial by instilling and fortifying the soul "with strength [courage, boldness, faith] in my soul." *Though I walk in the midst of trouble, thou wilt revive me.* See Psalm 138:7. David seemingly so walked continuously all his life. The text means to be surrounded by trouble or be in the center of trouble. Albert Barnes says it means, "Though I am in the low vale of sorrow, I shall not be overlooked or forgotten."[1585] Alphra White wrote, "Although His answer seems so long in coming and we continue to 'walk in the midst of trouble,' *'the center of trouble' is the place where He preserves us, not the place where He fails us.*"[1586] George Horne writes, "In troublous times, and the days of affliction, we must look back on that which God hath already done for us, and from thence draw an argument, that he will 'perfect' that which remains, and not leave his work unfinished: we must remember, that His mercies fail not after a time, but 'endure for ever' the same; and when we call to mind that we are 'the work of His own hands,' how can we think He will 'forsake us,' unless we utterly and finally forsake Him?"[1587]

The Lord will perfect that which concerneth me. See Psalm 138:8. Spurgeon wrote, "All my interests are safe in Jehovah's hands. God is concerned in all that concerns His servants. He will see to it that none of their precious things shall fail of completion; their life, their strength, their hopes, their graces, their pilgrimage, shall each and all be perfected. Jehovah Himself will see to this and therefore it is most sure."[1588] "We have three things here. First, the believer's confidence—'The Lord will fulfill His purpose for me.' Second, the ground of that confidence—'Lord, Your faithful love endures forever.' And third, the result and outgrowth of His confidence expressed in the prayer—'Do not abandon the work of your hands.'[1589]

> All things and everything are dependent
> on the measure of men's praying.
> E. M. Bounds

The Bottom Line: Timothy Keller writes, "Prayer is awe, intimacy, struggle—yet the way to reality. There is nothing more important, or harder, or richer, or more life-altering. There is absolutely nothing so great as prayer."[1590] E. M. Bounds said, "In all God's plans for human redemption, He proposes that men pray. The men are to pray in every place, in the church, in the closet, in the home, on sacred days and on secular days. All things and everything are dependent on the measure of men's praying. Prayer is the genius and mainspring of life. We pray as we live; we live as we pray. Life will never be finer than the quality of the closet. The mercury of life will rise only by the warmth of the closet."[1591]

61. The Divine Inspection   Psalm 139:23–24

"Search me, O God, and know my heart: try me, and know my thoughts: And see if there be any wicked way in me, and lead me in the way everlasting."—Psalm 139:23–24.

"Search me, O God" (Gesenius and Tregelles say "to search, to investigate. The primary idea is perhaps that of searching in the earth by digging, so that kindred roots are [exposed]; to the inmost depth. That which is known by investigation, hidden, secret."[1592]). AND "know" (Plumer says "the same form of the same verb in both cases. It is very comprehensive and implies intimate acquaintance."[1593] Vine, Unger and White say "to know, regard, recognize, pay attention to, be acquainted with."[1594]) "my heart" (Swanson says "mind, soul, spirit, self, i.e., the source of the life of the inner person in various aspects, with a focus on feelings, thoughts, volition, and other areas of inner life."[1595]).

"Try me" (test, examine) AND know "my thoughts" (Barnes says, "The idea is, Search me thoroughly; examine not merely my outward

275

conduct, but what I think about; what are my purposes; what passes through my mind; what occupies my imagination and my memory; what secures my affections and controls my will."[1596] Gill says, "He had tried him, and knew every thought in him [Psalm 139:1]. This therefore is not said for the sake of God; who, though He is the trier of hearts, and the searcher of the reins, is indeed a discerner of the thoughts and intents of the heart at once, and knows immediately what is in man; and needs no testimony of him, nor to make use of any means in order to know him and what is within him: but David said this for his own sake, that God would search and make known to him what was in his heart, and try him by His Word, as gold is tried in the fire; or by anything difficult and self-denying, as he tried Abraham; or by any afflictive providence; or in any way he thought fit to make him acquainted thoroughly with himself."[1597]).

AND "see" (The NLT says "point out." To reveal. Bratcher and Reyburn say, "This is more than a request; it is a way of claiming innocence of any wrong. The psalmist is confident that Yahweh will find nothing in him that deserves punishment."[1598]) "if there be any wicked way in me" (Plumer says "wicked way; way of pain or grief, that is a way that grieves God's Spirit, grieves good men, and must finally grieve me."[1599] Gill says, "Some render it, 'the way of an idol' because a word from the same root signifies an idol: every carnal lust in a man's heart is an idol; and whatsoever engrosses the affections, or has more of them than God Himself has, or is preferred to Him."[1600] Bratcher and Reyburn say, "It seems best to understand the word to mean a sin, or fault, that is harmful to the psalmist."[1601] Based on this interpretation of the word, Barnes says, "The prayer is that God would search him and see if there was anything in him that partook of the nature of idolatry, or of defection from the true religion; any tendency to go back from God, to worship other gods, to leave the worship of the true God. As idolatry compre-hends the sum of all that is evil, as being alienation from the true God, the prayer is that there might be nothing found in his heart which tended to alienate him from God."[1602]).

AND "lead me" (Swanson says "lead, guide, i.e., direct the movements...implying leadership and rulership."[1603] Williams and Ogilvie say, "Having come from God, he wants to go to God. The way everlasting is the way home to the Father's heart."[1604]) "in the way everlasting"

(Plumer says, "The way everlasting is the one good old path trodden by pious patriarchs, prophets and saints of all ages, and leading to eternal life."[1605] Barnes says "the way which leads to eternal life; the path which I may tread forever. In any other way than in the service of God his steps must be arrested."[1606] Kirkpatrick says "the opposite to the way of ruin and death. See Psalm 1:6; Psalm 25:4–5; Jeremiah 21:8."[1607]).

Homily

A Psalm of David.

Search me, O Lord. Alexander Maclaren comments, "It means to dig deep. God is prayed, as it were, to make a cutting into the man, and lay bare his inmost nature, as men do in a railway cutting, layer after layer, going ever deeper down till the bed-rock is reached. 'Search me'— dig into me, bring the deep-lying parts to light—'and know my heart'; the center of my personality, my inmost self. That is the prayer, not of fancied fitness to stand investigation, but of lowly acknowledgment. In other words, it is really a form of confession. 'Search me. I know Thou wilt find evil, but still—search me!'"[1608] George Horne says, "He [David] concludes with a petition, that his proceedings, and even his thoughts, might be still scrutinized by his Maker, in order to their perfect purification from any evil which might be in them, or adhere to them. Should the hottest furnace of adversity be found necessary to purge the dross from the silver, he refuseth not to be dissolved in it, and new-formed, so that he might only become a vessel of honor fitted for the Master's use here below, and vouchsafed a place afterwards in his temple above."[1609]

Based upon David's prayer, note ten practical and doctrinal observations.

(1) Man's searching is not sufficient, for it's not thorough. None are capable to fully "dig deep" enough to uncover all sin. See 1 Corinthians 4:4. Williams and Ogilvie write, "Have his cares led to sin? Is there something he doesn't know about that needs to be changed in him? David does not only want to know his deviations, however. If they are there, he wants to be corrected and restored."[1610]

(2) Deceit conceals the awareness of sin. Satan deceives man into believing "bitter is sweet" and "sweet is bitter" and is the master in hiding from man's consciousness unrecognized sin. See Jeremiah 17:9–10.

(3) Conceit prevents the investigation of sin. Spiritual arrogance and pride prompts a person to think that he is "better" than he actually is.

(4) Prejudicial bias unconsciously yields a "false reading" regarding sin.

(5) It is impossible to hide sin from God. See Psalm 139:1–3. Tholuck said, "The thought of the omniscience [all knowing] of God ought in every prayer to purify our souls, while that of His omnipresence [everywhere at the same moment] ought to sanctify it."[1611]

(6) It takes a heart in "hot pursuit" of God to pray for divine searching. David was willing to discover the worst about himself that he might become his best for the Lord. "That man must have a rare confidence," says Calvin, "who offers himself so boldly to the scrutiny of God's righteous judgement."[1612] Alexander Maclaren states, "Oh! it is a prayer easily offered; hard to stand by. It is a prayer often answered in ways that drive us almost to despair. It means, 'Do anything with me; put me into any sevenfold heated furnace of sorrow; do anything that will melt my hardness and run off my dross, which Thy great ladle ["dipper, scoop, spoon," *Merriam-Webster*] will then skim away, that the surface may be clear and the substance without alloy.'"[1613]

(7) "Thoughts" are concealed from man's view but not the Lord's. Henry Ward Beecher said, "Before men we stand as opaque beehives. They can see the thoughts go in and out of us, but what work they do inside of a man they cannot tell. Before God we are as glass beehives, and all that our thoughts are doing within us He perfectly sees and understands."[1614] It is essential that the believer pray that God might "test" his every thought, revealing that which is wrong and harmful (lustful, impure, selfish, arrogant, vengeful, etc.) to their spiritual walk. A man is nothing but the sum and total of his thoughts. That's why it is so important they be noble, admirable, honorable, clean and holy. Solomon said, "For as he thinketh in his heart, so is he" (Proverbs 23:7), and, "Keep thy heart with all diligence; for out of it are the issues of life" (Proverbs 4:23).

(8) The hypocrite cannot withstand the inspection of God. W. S. Plumer states, "False pretenses have no power to hide anything from God. The hope of the hypocrite shall both justly and terribly perish."[1615]

(9) Indifference toward God regarding sin doesn't alter His judgment. Calvin said, "We are ashamed to let men know and witness our delinquencies; but we are as indifferent to what God may think of us, as if our sins were covered and veiled from His inspection."[1616]

(10) To avoid "the wicked way" of grief and pain, man must depend upon God to "guide him" in the "way everlasting." The "everlasting way" is the *ancient way* (in contrast to the way of sin that results in ruin, devastation, destruction), the path which God has set from time eternal for His people to go in.[1617] See Jeremiah 6:16 and Jeremiah 18:15. Spurgeon says, "It is a way which Thou hast set up of old; it is based upon everlasting principles."[1618] Matthew Henry said, "The way of godliness is an everlasting way; it is everlastingly true and good, pleasing to God and profitable to us."[1619]

O Thou, to whose all-searching sight
The darkness shineth as the light,
Search, prove my heart; it pants for thee;
Oh, burst these bands and set it free.

Wash out its stains; refine its dross;
Nail my affections to the cross.
Hallow each thought; let all within
Be clean, as Thou, my Lord, art clean.

If in this darksome wild I stray,
Be Thou my Light; be Thou my Way.
No foes, no violence I fear,
No harm, while Thou, my God, art near.

Savior, where'er Thy steps I see,
Dauntless, untired, I follow thee;
Oh, let Thy hand support me still
And lead me to Thy holy hill.

~ Nicolaus Ludwig, Graf von Zinzendorf (1721);
Translator: John Wesley (1738)

Allan Harman writes, "Irrespective of our immediate situation, He knows us absolutely, and even the inmost recesses of our minds are like an open book before Him."[1620] Williams and Ogilvie state, "He formed us in the womb. He knows our frame. He sees our embryo. He fashions our days. He knows our thoughts. He hears our words. He knows when we sit down and when we stand up. He protects us. His hand is upon us. He who inhabits all things is near to us. We cannot escape His presence. In the light He sees us. In the dark He sees us. We are the continual object of His thoughts. He searches us. He changes us."[1621] And He does all this that we might walk in intimacy with Him.

Nothing between my soul and the Savior,
>Naught of this world's delusive dream;
I have renounced all sinful pleasure.
>Jesus is mine; there's nothing between.

Nothing between my soul and the Savior,
>So that His blessed face may be seen.
Nothing preventing the least of His favor;
>Keep the way clear! Let nothing between.

Nothing between, like worldly pleasure;
>Habits of life, though harmless they seem,
Must not my heart from Him e'er sever.
>He is my all; there's nothing between.

Nothing between, like pride or station;
>Self-life or friends shall not intervene.
Though it may cost me much tribulation,
>I am resolved; there's nothing between.

Nothing between, e'en many hard trials,
>Though the whole world against me convene;
Watching with prayer and much self-denial,
>I'll triumph at last, with nothing between.
>~ Charles Albert Tindley (1905)

O God, thou knowest my foolishness; and my sins are not hid from thee. See Psalm 69:5. "Though we should climb to the top of Carmel in the pride of our hearts or go down with Jonah to the bottoms of the mountains in our deceit, He will find us out, strip us, unmask us, and set us in the sunlight to be despised by all intelligent beings. My sins cannot be hid from Him since He reads the secrets of the heart, and the *tortuous* ["Twisting, twisty, twisting and turning, winding; excessively lengthy and complex"[1622]] passages of the soul are easily threaded by His unerring wisdom."[1623]

Oswald Chambers wrote, "Bind the sacrifice with cords to the horns of the altar" (Psalm 118:27). You must be willing to be placed on the altar and go through the fire; willing to experience what the altar represents— burning, purification, and separation for only one purpose— the elimination of every desire and affection not grounded in or directed toward God. But you don't eliminate it, God does. You "bind the sacrifice...to the horns of the altar" and see to it that you don't wallow in self-pity once the fire begins. After you have gone through the fire, there will be nothing that will be able to trouble or depress you."[1624]

Let us pray with a heart of sincerity: O Lord, enter with Thy candle into the cellar of my heart and reveal the *explosives* of sin that must be emptied out through acknowledgement and repentance. Amen.

The Bottom Line: "The prayer of the text is in fact the yearning of the devout soul for purity."[1625]

Spurgeon summarizes the prayer, "See whether there be in my heart, or in my life, any evil habit unknown to myself. If there be such an evil way, take me from it; take it from me. No matter how dear the wrong may have become, nor how deeply prejudiced I may have been in its favor, be pleased to deliver me therefrom altogether, effectually, and at once, that I may tolerate nothing which is contrary to Thy mind."[1626]

> It is useless to ask God to search us if we lock our hearts against His searching.
> Alexander Maclaren

Alexander Maclaren wrote, "It is useless to ask God to search us if we lock our hearts against His searching....By His natural omniscience, He knows them altogether, but the seeing which is preparatory to destroying them depends on our willingness to submit ourselves to the often painful process by which He drags our sins to light."[1627]

62. The Scorner's Coming Demise   Psalm 140:11

"Let not an evil speaker be established in the earth: evil shall hunt the violent man to overthrow him."—Psalm 140:11.

Let not an "evil speaker" (Plumer says "literally the man of tongue, meaning one of lawless speech, who slanders man and reproaches God."[1628] Dilday and Kennedy say, "Pointed, poisonous tongues were the weapons of the enemies. Vicious slander, secretly plotted, was intended to inflict deadly wounds."[1629]) be "established" (Barnes says "be successful or prosperous; let him not carry out his designs"[1630]) in the earth.

"Evil shall hunt the violent man to overthrow him" (Spurgeon says, "He hunted the good, and now his own evil will hunt him. He tried to overthrow the goings of the righteous, and now his own unrighteousness will prove his overthrow."[1631] *Overthrow*. Brown, Driver and Briggs say "evil, distress, misery, injury, calamity"[1632]).

Homily

Spurgeon said, "The life of David wherein he comes in contact with Saul and Doeg is the best explanation of this Psalm; and surely there can be no reasonable doubt that David wrote it, and wrote it in the time of his exile and peril."[1633]

Let not an evil speaker. John Gill said that the "evil speaker" is "one that sets his mouth against the heavens, and speaks evil of God; of His being, perfections, purposes, and providences: whose tongue walks through the earth, and speaks evil of all men, even of dignities; and especially of the saints of the most High, and of the Gospel and ways of Christ."[1634] Jennings and Lowe say "not merely a babbler, but a malicious slanderer."[1635] *Evil shall hunt the violent man.* The slanderer and scorner of holy things will not escape divine retribution. He may spew forth blasphemous statements about the Christian faith, laughing at its claims and mocking its God, but the day will come when the laughter and mockery will turn into bitter weeping.

T. De Witt Talmage wrote: "The laugh of skepticism in all the ages is only the echo of Sarah's laughter. God says He will accomplish a thing, and men say it cannot be done. A great multitude laugh at the miracles.

They say they are contrary to the laws of nature. What is a law of nature? It is God's way of doing a thing. You ordinarily cross the river by the bridge; tomorrow you change for one day and you go across the ferry. You made the rule; have you not the right to change it?...If He (God) makes the law, has He not the right to change it at any time He wants to change it?...God says the Bible is true....Herbert Spencer laughs. John Stuart Mills laughs. All great German universities laugh—softly! A great many of the learned institutions of this country, with long rows of professors *seated on the fence* between Christianity and infidelity, laugh softy. They say, "We didn't laugh." That was Sarah's trick. God thunders from the heavens: "But thou didst laugh!"...The Garden of Eden was only a fable. There never was any ark built; or, if it was built, it was too small to hold two of every kind. The pillar of fire by night is only the northern lights, the ten plagues of Egypt only a brilliant specimen of jugglery. The sea parted because the wind blew violently a great while from one direction. The sun and moon did not put themselves out of the way for Joshua. Jacob's ladder was only horizontal and picturesque clouds. The destroying angel smiting the firstborn in Egypt was only cholera infantum become epidemic. The gullet of the whale, by positive measurement, is too small to swallow a prophet; the lame, the dumb, the blind, the halt cured by mere human surgery. The resurrection of Christ's friend only a beautiful tableau, Christ and Lazarus and Mary and Martha acting their parts well....There is not a doctrine or statement of God's Holy Word that has not been derided by the skepticism of this day....Oh, what an awful thing it is to laugh in God's face and hurl His revelation back at Him! After a while the day will come when they will say they did not laugh. Then all the hypercriticisms, all the caricatures, and all the learned sneers...will be brought to judgment, and...God will thunder, "But thou didst laugh!"...The meanest laughter ever uttered is the laughter of the skeptic."[1636] But it will be silenced!

Evil shall hunt the slanderer. Jennings and Lowe say "i.e., misfortunes, ceaseless and unrelenting, shall continually dog his steps."[1637] Matthew Henry states, "Evildoers must expect to be destroyed. Evil shall hunt the violent man [the slanderer and mocker] as the bloodhound hunts the murderer to discover him, as the lion hunts his prey to tear it to pieces. Mischievous men will be brought to light and brought to ruin; the destruction appointed shall run them down and overthrow them."[1638]

George Horne says, "Those tongues, which have contributed to set the world on fire, shall be tormented with the hot burning coals of eternal vengeance; and they who, with so much eagerness and diligence, have prepared pits for the destruction of their brethren shall be cast into a deep and bottomless pit, out of which they will not rise up again any more forever. Evil speakers and false accusers shall gain no lasting establishment, but punishment shall hunt sin through all its doubles and seize it at last as its legal prey."[1639] *Let the evil speaker not be established*. Spurgeon frankly says, "Men of false and cruel tongues are of most use when they go to fatten the soil in which they rot as carcasses: while they are alive they are the terror of the good, and the torment of the poor. God will not allow the specious orators of falsehood to retain the power they temporarily obtain by their deceitful speaking. They may become prominent, but they cannot become permanent. They shall be disendowed and disestablished in spite of all that they can say to the contrary."[1640]

The Christian must pray that God will silence the tongue that defames His name, defies His person, desecrates His House, discredits His Word and utters disdain for His people. "Pray that God would not grant the desires of the wicked, nor further their evil devices."[1641] Pray for and work for their conversion. Converted atheists, agnostics and other pronounced enemies of God become some of His greatest evangels.

> Pray that God will silence the tongue that defames
> His name, defies His person, desecrates His House,
> discredits His Word and utters disdain for His people.

The Bottom Line: Pray that God will not allow the venomous tongue that opposes truth, good and Himself to prosper or succeed.

63. The Old Testament Matthew 6:13   Psalm 141:1–4; 9–10

"LORD, I cry unto thee: make haste unto me; give ear unto my voice, when I cry unto thee. Let my prayer be set forth before thee as incense; and the lifting up of my hands as the evening sacrifice. Set a watch, O LORD, before my mouth; keep the door of my lips. Incline not my heart to any evil thing, to practise wicked works with men that work

iniquity: and let me not eat of their dainties….Keep me from the snares which they have laid for me, and the gins of the workers of iniquity. Let the wicked fall into their own nets, whilst that I withal escape."—Psalm 141:1–4; 9–10.

Lord, I "cry unto thee" (Vine, Unger and White say "'to call, call out.'…To 'call' on God's name is to summon His aid.…The sense of 'summoning' God to one's aid was surely in Abraham's mind when he 'called upon' God's name (Genesis 12:8). 'Calling' in this sense constitutes a prayer prompted by recognized need and directed to One who is able and willing to respond [Psalm 145:18; Isaiah 55:6]."[1642]) "make haste unto me" (Gesenius and Tregelles say "hasty, quick, alert. To excite to speed; swift."[1643]).

"Give ear unto my voice, when I cry unto thee" (Barnes says, "The meaning here is, David prayed that God would be attentive to or would regard his prayer. This form of the petition is, that He would attend to his 'words'—to what he was about to 'express' as his desire. He intended to express only what he wished to be granted."[1644]).

"Let" (Vine, Unger and White say "to be established, be readied, be prepared, be certain, be admissible."[1645] Alexander says, "He prays not only for acceptance, but for constant or perpetual acceptance, as the offerings referred to were the stated daily services of the Mosaic ritual."[1646]) my "prayer" (Swanson says "plea, request, petition, i.e., the act. of speaking to or making requests to God."[1647]) be set forth before thee as "incense" (Swanson says "burning perfumes, i.e., material used to produce a fragrant smoke [Exodus 25:6], note: usually used for incense offerings; [2] smoke offering, i.e., an offering of incense burned on an altar to worship deity [Psalm 66:15; 141:2; Isaiah 1:13]."[1648] Rawlinson says "with the regularity of the incense, and with its acceptableness."[1649]).

AND "the lifting up of my hands" (Kirkpatrick says "the gesture of prayer [Psalm 28:2; Psalm 63:4; 1 Timothy 2:8], the outward symbol of an uplifted heart [Psalm 25:1]."[1650]) as the "evening sacrifice" (Perowne says, "The sacrifice here meant is strictly the offering consisting of fine flour with oil and frankincense, or of unleavened cakes mingled with oil, which was burnt upon the altar."[1651] *Evening.* "perhaps because in the evening it was reckoned the main offering, whereas in the morning it was merely an appendage to the animal sacrifice."[1652]).

"Set a watch, O Lord, before my mouth" (Ellicott says, "The image drawn from the guard set at city gates at night seems to indicate the evening as the time of composition of the Psalm."[1653]) "keep the door of my lips" (Rawlinson says, "David's was a hasty, impetuous temper, which required sharp control. He strove to 'keep his own mouth with a bridle'—to 'be dumb with silence, and hold his peace'—but this was not always possible for him of his own unassisted strength. He therefore makes his prayer to God for the divine help."[1654] This prayer may specifically refer to his speech about Saul. Spurgeon says, "We are ennobled by being doorkeepers for Him, and yet He deigns to be a doorkeeper for us.").

"Incline not my heart to any evil thing" (Spurgeon says, "This is equivalent to the petition, 'Lead us not into temptation.'"[1655] Barnes says, "The expression 'incline not' is not designed to mean that God exerts any 'positive' influence in leading the heart to that which is wrong; but it may mean 'do not place me in circumstances where I may be tempted; do not leave me to myself; do not allow any improper influence to come over me by which I shall be led astray.'"[1656]) "to practice wicked works with men that work iniquity" (Barnes says, "literally, to practice practices in wickedness with people....to be united or associated with people who do wrong; to do the things which wicked and unprincipled people do."[1657]).

AND "let me not eat of their dainties" (Swanson says, "i.e., food which is considered very fine and luxurious, the eating of these implying indulgence as well as participation."[1658] Here it refers to sinful luxury.[1659]). "Keep me" (Brown, Driver and Briggs say "keep, watch, preserve."[1660] Jennings and Lowe say, "lit. 'keep me from the hands of the snare, etc.,' 'the hands' representing the closing and grasping apparatus of the snare."[1661]) "from the snares" (Harris, Archer and Waltke say "bird trap [Hosea 5:1; Amos 3:5]. Often used figuratively for calamities and plots."[1662]) "which they" (David's enemies; specifically King Saul) "have laid for me" (Holladay and Kohler say "catch [birds] with a snare; be caught; let oneself get entangled."[1663]).

AND "the gins" (Whitaker, Brown and Driver say "snare. Bait or lure, in a net for birds; figure of what allures and entraps anyone to disaster or ruin"[1664]) of the workers of "iniquity" (Swanson says "wickedness, iniquity, i.e., an act [of many kinds] which is morally evil and corrupt, and damaging to one's relationship to God and others, according to a standard."[1665]).

"Let" (Gesenius and Tregelles say "to cause to fall, to supplant. It is used of a man falling on the ground [Psalm 37:24]; or falling from a horse or a seat [Genesis 49:17; 1 Samuel 4:18]; into a ditch [Psalm 7:16]; falling into a snare [Amos 3:5], etc.; falling in battle."[1666]) "the wicked" (the unrighteous, ungodly) "fall" (Holladay and Kohler say "bring down, make fall; make something fall to ruin."[1667]) "into their own nets" (Swanson says "deadly captivity, i.e., the state of being a prisoner to some as a figurative extension of a hunt and capturing device, i.e., a net or snare."[1668] whilst that I "withal escape" (Alexander says "change of *withal* to the synonymous but less ambiguous expression, *at the same time*. The transpositions of this clause are unusual, even in Hebrew—at the same time I until (or while) I pass, i.e., pass by uninjured or escape."[1669]).

Homily

Commentators are unsure as to the historical occasion of the Psalm. Two prevailing thoughts are that David composed the Psalm in a time of persecution by King Saul or during Absalom's rebellion. He prays for preservation from the temptation to do wickedly or become like the wicked.

Lord, I cry unto thee. "His crying denotes fervency in prayer; he prayed as one in earnest. His crying to God denotes faith and fixedness in prayer."[1670] Spurgeon wrote, "Others trust to themselves, but I cry unto thee. The weapon of all-prayer is one which the believer may always carry with him, and use in every time of need."[1671] *Let my prayer be set before thee.* David's request that his prayer be acceptable reveals that not all prayer is. The prayer of the Pharisee (Parable of the Pharisee and Tax Collector [Luke 18:9–14]) was denied, whereas that of the humble tax collector was heard. "Acceptable" prayer flows from a heart attuned ("in tune") with the heart of God. It is humble, not haughty; contrite, not callous; remorseful, not remorseless; repentant, not unrepentant and exhibits belief, not disbelief. *The lifting up of my hands.* Matthew Henry said "the lifting up of his hands in prayer, which denotes both the elevation and enlargement of his desire and the out-goings of his hope and expectation, the lifting up of the hand signifying the lifting up of the heart, and being used instead of lifting up the sacrifices which were heaved and waved before the Lord. Prayer is a spiritual sacrifice; it is the offering up of the soul, and its best affections, to God."[1672]

Jesus forthrightly issues the imperative of prayer in saying, "Men ought always to pray, and not to faint" (Luke 18:1). Believers live in an evil, polluted society. The only escape from its toxic fumes which promote spiritual fainting (drifting, backsliding, and worldliness) is the intake of "pure air" from the atmosphere of Heaven, which occurs in prayer. Prayer is to the believer what an oxygen mask is to those who work in hazardous waste facilities, an absolute essential to survival. Obviously, then, this oxygen mask for believers ought to be worn continuously ("always to pray"). The apostle Paul similarly states, "Pray without ceasing" (1 Thessalonians 5:17).

Set a watch, before my mouth. David begs God to help him control his tongue. See Psalm 141:3. "The special point of the prayer is that he may be guarded from adopting the profane language of the ungodly men by whom he is surrounded."[1673] Certain employments especially prompt the expediency of the prayer. Next, David prays for abstinence from sinful acts. *Incline not my heart to any evil thing.* See Psalm 141:4. That is, lead me not into temptation. Prevent my feet from entering the arena of temptation to do wrong. God doesn't prompt temptation but certainly grants power to resist it. *Incline not my heart...to practice wicked works.* Keep me from identifying with the unrighteous in their wanton "practice" and being counted as "one of them." See Obadiah 11. Sadly far too many Christians look more like their "worldly" counterparts rather than resembling their Christian brothers and sisters. Such compromise is injurious to the cause of Christ and the church. Paul exhorted, "Wherefore come out from among them, and be ye separate, saith the Lord, and touch not the unclean thing; and I will receive you" (2 Corinthians 6:17).

Let me not eat of their dainties. Albert Barnes says, "The word here rendered 'dainties' properly refers to things which are pleasant, lovely, and attractive; which give delight or pleasure. It may embrace 'all' that the world has to offer as suited to give pleasure or enjoyment. It refers here to what those in more elevated life have to offer; what they themselves live for."[1674] Few temptations are more enticing and persuasive than those that surround the pleasures of this present age. The pursuit of wealth, clamor for status and success, lust for wanton "fun" and accumulation of worldly goods shipwreck the best of Christians. The believer, realizing vulnerability to the pull of the world, must adopt David's prayer, lest he stumble. Demas incautiously was victimized by the temptation. See 2 Timothy 4:10.

With men that work iniquity. Solomon admonishes strenuously, without reservation, that a person refrain from fellowship with the wicked ("walk not"; "enter not"; "go not"; "avoid it"; "turn from it") due to the horrendous danger lurking on the evil path (Proverbs 4:16). He warns the believer not even to put one foot on it ("enter not"), but if that has happened to immediately get off it ("turn from it") and stay off it ("avoid it"). A key to staying off the unrighteous path is not to "pass by it" (don't allow Satan the chance to lure you onto it; avoid people and places that entice unto wrong). Spurgeon states, "Alas, there is great power in company: even good men are apt to be swayed by association; hence the fear that we may practice wicked works when we are with wicked workers. We must endeavor not to be with them lest we sin with them. It is bad when the heart goes the wrong way alone, worse when the life runs in the evil road alone; but it is apt to increase unto a high degree of ungodliness when the backslider runs the downward path with a whole horde of sinners around him."[1675]

Keep me from the snares. David closes the prayer begging the Lord for awareness of and deliverance from the enemies' snares (hidden entrapments; enticing baits and lures). See notes on Psalm 57:6. The land is strewn with "landmines" designed to cause spiritual shipwreck. Locations of the landmines are undetectable to man but known unto the Lord. It therefore is expedient to pray for divine illumination regarding their whereabouts. Benson says, "Keep me from being taken in it: give me to discover and evade it."[1676] Matthew Henry remarked, "Be the gin [snare] placed with ever so much subtlety, God can and will secure His people from being taken in it."[1677] Spurgeon said, "Brave men do not dread battle, but they hate secret plots. We cannot endure to be entrapped like unsuspecting animals; therefore we cry to God for protection."[1678]

But should we fall prey to one of Satan's snares, God is able to grant deliverance. *Pull me out of the net...for thou art my strength*. See Psalm 31:4. "This is a proper petition, and one which can be granted: from between the jaws of the lion, and out of the belly of Hell, can eternal love rescue the saint. It may need a sharp pull to save a soul from the net of temptations, and a mighty pull to extricate a man from the snares of malicious cunning, but the Lord is equal to every emergency, and the most skilfully placed nets of the hunter shall never be able to hold His chosen ones."[1679]

The Bottom Line: "A Christian, living among unbelievers and sensualists in the world, hath abundant reason to put up the same prayers, and to use the same precautions."[1680] Jonathan Swift wrote, "Human brutes, like other beasts, find snares and poison in the provision of life, and are allured by their appetites to their destruction."[1681]

64. No Man Cared for My Soul   Psalm 142:4

"I looked on my right hand, and beheld, but there was no man that would know me: refuge failed me; no man cared for my soul."— Psalm 142:4.

"I" (David) "looked" (Strong says "to scan, i.e., look intently at."[1682] Plumer says, "Hengstenberg, Alexander, French and Skinner all have the imperative, *look and see*. This is best. David calls on the Lord to employ His omniscience in looking into his helpless condition."[1683]) on my "right hand" (Barnes says, "The 'right hand' is referred to here as the direction where he might look for a protector."[1684] Kirkpatrick says "where his protector would be standing if he had one."[1685] Perowne says "the direction in which he would naturally look for succor."[1686] See Psalm 16:8 and Psalm 121:5.).

AND beheld, but there was no man that would "know me" (Strong says "i.e., look intently at; hence with recognition, to acknowledge, be acquainted with, care for, respect, revere."[1687]). "Refuge failed me" (Swanson says "fortress, i.e., a place to flee or escape to for safety."[1688] Plumer says "refuge, as in Psalm 59:16, literally [means] a place to fly to, or flight itself, not the word rendered refuge in the next verse."[1689]). No man "cared for my soul" (Landes says "to care for; to inquire about."[1690] Barnes says, "that is, no one sought to save my life; no one regarded it as of sufficient importance to attempt to preserve me."[1691] Plumer says, "The clause is literally, *There is none caring*, so rendered also in Deuteronomy 11:12."[1692]).

Homily

The title says, 'A Prayer when he was in the cave.' There were at least two instances when David was in a cave—the cave of Adullam to which he fled from Achish (1 Samuel 22), the King of Gath, and En-gedi where he took refuge from King Saul (1 Samuel 24). Adam Clarke thinks that of the two, the latter is the most probable for the Psalm's writing. See Psalm 57 and Psalm 142 (the two "cave" Psalms).

Of Psalm 57 Warren Wiersbe wrote "Your own 'cave' may be a sickroom, a difficult place of ministry, or even a home where there is tension or trouble. If you do what David did, you will experience peace and victory even in the cave. David's faith transformed his cave into a Holy of Holies (v. 1)! His confidence was not in the rocks but 'under His wings.' In spite of sharp teeth (v. 4), nets and pits (v. 6), David was sure of God's help."[1693]

David was in sore distress ("my spirit overwhelmed within me") and "looked" in vain for someone to *care for my soul*. He had known many, but none at this time "knew him." It appears that even Jonathan at this time was not to be found or at least didn't come forward for fear of reprisal by David's enemies. Spurgeon paraphrases David: "'Whether I lived or died was no concern of anybody's. I was cast out as an outcast. No soul cared for my soul. I dwelt in no-man's-land, where none cared to have me, and none cared about me.' This is an ill plight—no place to lay our head, and no head willing to find us a place. How pleased were his enemies to see the friend of God without a friend! How sad was he to be utterly deserted in his utmost need! Can we not picture David in the cave, complaining that even the cave was not a refuge for him, for Saul had come even there? Hopeless was his looking out; we shall soon see him looking up."[1694]

Isn't it often the case that when we get "down on our luck" or become afflicted with a serious illness or overcome by a besetting sin or plagued with problems, that friends abandon us. Spurgeon well said, "The fact is that in times of desertion it is not true that no man did know us, but no man would know us. Their ignorance is willful."[1695] Matthew Henry writes, "None of all his old friends would give him a night's lodging, or direct him to any place of secresy and safety. How many good men have been deceived by such swallow-friends, who are gone when winter comes! David's life was exceedingly precious, and yet, when he was unjustly proscribed [condemned; denounced; criticized], no man cared for it, nor would move a hand for the protection of it."[1696]

Real friends surface in our times of crisis. When Jim Bakker, founder of PTL, was asked about the fall of PTL and the scattering of all the people close to him, including his friends, he commented, "I didn't lose any friends....I just discovered who my true friends are." In reality, at best we have only a few friends and many acquaintances. *I cried unto thee, O Lord: I said, Thou art my refuge.* The desertion of friends drives David to Him that never abandons His children. See Psalm 46:1 and Proverbs 18:24.

God is our refuge and our strength,
     Our ever-present aid;
And therefore, though the earth be moved,
     We will not be afraid.

Though hills into the seas be cast,
     Though foaming billows roar,
Yea, though the mighty billows shake
     The mountains on the shore. ~ Scottish Psalter (1650)

John Gill says of Psalm 142:4, "This is an emblem of a soul under first awakenings and convictions, inquiring the way of salvation, and where to find help, but at a loss for it in the creature."[1697] What a vivid "picture" of the lost soul in dire distress, hounded by Satan, looking for a believer, any believer to "care" enough for his soul to tell him the way to salvation. How sad that his search is so often in vain, for many Christians show no concern for the eternally damned. Though believers rub shoulders with the lost at work, school, play, neighborhood, and in errands of the day, they never "tell" of Christ. And the lost die in their sin, crying out to God at the Judgment, "No man cared for my soul." See Matthew 9:36 and Ezekiel 22:30.

The president of a college told W. A. Criswell a story about one of his students. The student was a new convert. This young student asked an older man at a bus stop, "Are you a Christian?" The man replied, "Yes, sir, I have been a Christian for over forty years." The student then said in response, "If you have been a Christian for over forty years, how is it that you did not ask me if I was a Christian?" Criswell relates a second story that is similar. In talking to a businessman in Dallas, the name of a deacon came up. Criswell said, "That man is a deacon in our church and one of our finest men. He is a superintendent of one of our Sunday school departments." The businessman replied, "I did not know that. I have done business with him for twenty-five years, and I did not even know he was a Christian."[1698] To know Christ and not tell of Christ is the sin that often is committed plainly because of woeful apathy with regard to the lost.

Porter M. Bales wrote: "Sadly, the last question man is ever asked is with regard to his soul, making the statement of David woefully true. *We should care for the souls of men* because Jesus Christ and Him crucified is the world's only hope. The world is sick and feverish and restless and tossing. There are many remedies prescribed for the world's ills. The teacher says that more knowledge is the remedy, but we will never know enough. The artists say that more beauty is the remedy, but a bouquet of flowers will not ease the cutting pains of blood poison. The philosopher says we need a new theory of life, but we do not now live perfectly the theories we have. The supreme need of the world is Jesus. He will cure every ill of every individual, of every home, of every community anywhere. He will cool the fever of the restless world, soothe its nerves, bring order out of chaos and peace to a troubled soul. He and He alone is the remedy for the world's ills."[1699]

Who Cares for the unsaved? *God the Father cares* (John 3:16); *the Lord Jesus Cares* (Philippians 2:5–8); *the Holy Spirit cares* (Revelation 22:17); *the saved ones in Heaven care* (Luke 15:10); *the lost ones in Hell care* (Luke 16:27–28).[1700] And Christians and the church care (or at least they should).

People lost in darkness, searching for the way;
But do you know of someone, that you can help today?

Do you really care? Do you know how to share
With people everywhere, do you really care? ~ Bill Cates (1967)

Matthew Henry comments, "Herein he was a type of Christ, who, in his sufferings for us, was forsaken of all men, even of his own disciples, and trod the winepress alone, for there was none to help, none to uphold [Isaiah 63:5]."[1701] See John 1: 11.

The Bottom Line: Let none with whom you are acquainted say to the Lord at the Judgment, "No man cared for my soul."

Rescue the perishing;
Care for the dying;
Snatch them in pity from sin and the grave.
Weep o'er the erring one;
Lift up the fallen;
Tell them of Jesus the mighty to save.~ Fanny Jane Crosby (1869)

65. The Prayer of Prayers   Psalm 143:8–10

"Cause me to hear thy lovingkindness in the morning; for in thee do I trust: cause me to know the way wherein I should walk; for I lift up my soul unto thee. Deliver me, O LORD, from mine enemies: I flee unto thee to hide me. Teach me to do thy will; for thou art my God: thy spirit is good; lead me into the land of uprightness."—Psalm143:8–10.

"Cause" (let) me to "hear" (Plumer says, "To hear in this verse is equivalent to enjoy or possess."[1702]) thy "lovingkindness" (Vine, Unger and White say "loving-kindness; steadfast love; grace; mercy; faithfulness; goodness; devotion."[1703] Unfailing or loyal love. See Lamentations 3:23.) "in the morning" (Gesenius and Tregelles say "morning, daybreak, dawn"[1704]) for in thee do I "trust" (Oswalt, Harris, Archer and Waltke say "trust in, feel safe, be confident. [It] expresses that sense of well-being and security which results from having something or someone in whom to place confidence."[1705]).

"Cause me to know" (To clearly know, comprehend, discover, acknowledge, awareness.[1706]) the "way" (path, course) wherein I should "walk" (Vine, Unger and White say "to go, walk, behave....This verb can also be used of one's behavior, or the way one 'walks in life.' So he who 'walks' uprightly shall be blessed of God [Isaiah 33:15]. This does not refer to walking upright on one's feet but to living a righteous life."[1707] Alexander says *the way I must go*, "not merely to be right, but to be safe and happy; the way of safety as well as that of duty"[1708]) for I "lift up my soul unto thee" (Ellicott says "my desire."[1709] Gill says it is a reference to prayer.[1710] Thus, David lifts up his burden and desire unto the Lord early in the morning in prayer.)

"Deliver me" (Swanson says "saved, delivered, be spared, i.e., pertaining to being safe from danger, and so be in a more favorable circumstance."[1711]) O Lord, from mine enemies: "I flee unto thee to hide me" (Barnes says, "The Hebrew is, I hide myself with Thee; that is, I take refuge with Thee; I put myself under Thy protection; I make myself thus secure, as Thou art secure."[1712]).

"Teach me to do thy will" (Learn. Barnes says "to do that which will be agreeable or pleasing to Thee"[1713]) for thou art my God: "thy spirit is good" (Barnes says "the spirit which guides those who trust in Thee; the spirit with which 'Thou' dost guide people. That spirit is wise, prudent, judicious, reliable."[1714] See Nehemiah 9:20. The Holy Spirit. See John 16:12–15. Spurgeon says, "God is all spirit and all good. His essence is goodness, kindness, holiness: it is His nature to do good, and what greater good can He do to us than to hear such a prayer as that which follows."[1715]).

"Lead me" (guide me) into "the land of uprightness" (Holladay and Kohler say "level ground; straightness, fairness, righteousness."[1716] Spurgeon says, "David would fain be among the godly, in a land of another sort from that which had cast him out. He sighed for the upland meadows of grace, the tablelands of peace, the fertile plains of communion. He could not reach them of himself; he must be led there. God, who is good, can best conduct us to the goodly land."[1717]).

Homily

A Psalm composed by David perhaps on the occasion of Absalom's rebellion. Simeon suggests it better fits the time of David's persecutions at the hand of Saul.[1718] It is the seventh and final Penitential Psalm.

Psalm 143:8–10 may be called "The Prayer of Prayers" for the Christian. In it David encapsulates man's greatest need—knowledge of God's will and Word and the necessary illumination to understand and apply both to life. See Psalm 90:14.

Cause me to know the way wherein to walk. Matthew Henry comments, "Sometimes those that are much in care to walk right are in doubt, and in the dark, which is the right way. Let them come boldly to the throne of grace and beg of God, by His Word, and Spirit, and providence, to show them the way and prevent their missing it. A good man does not ask what is the way in which he must walk, or in which is the most pleasant walking, but what is the right way, the way in which he should walk."[1719] Raleigh summarizes the verse: "The text may be said to comprise every other prayer. If God gives His servant to 'know the way wherein he should walk,' and strength to walk in it, peace, and order, and liberty, and joy will soon come. Life is a daily difficulty....Think of the number of things that are to be believed, that are to be renounced, that are to be examined, that are to be distinguished in themselves and from other things, that are to be tentatively dealt with, that are to be done, that are to be left undone, that are to be waited for, that are to be suffered. All these are included in the 'way wherein we should walk.'"[1720]

Teach me to do thy will. Alexander Maclaren wrote, "That practical conformity to the will of God requires divine teaching, but yet that teaching must be no outward thing. It is not enough that we should have communicated to us, as from without, the clearest knowledge of what we ought to be. There must be more than that. Our Psalmist's prayer was a prophecy. He said, 'Teach me to do Thy will.' And he thought, no doubt, of an inward teaching which should mold his nature as well as enlighten it; of the communication of impulses as well as of conceptions; of something which should make him love the divine will, as well as of something which should make him know it."[1721] *Lead me into the land of uprightness.* "The way is long, and steep, and he who goes without a divine leader will faint on the journey; but with Jehovah to lead, it is delightful to follow, and there is neither stumbling nor wandering."[1722]

Thy Spirit is good. George Horne remarked, "But conscious of his own inability to do the will of Jehovah, even when known, he [David] entreateth the good Spirit of God to 'lead' him out of the mazes of error and the pollutions of vice, into the pleasant 'land' of truth and holiness."[1723] The enabling and illuminating power source of the Christian's life is the Holy Spirit. See Acts 1:8. The Holy Spirit is the third Person of the Trinity and resides in the believer. See 1 Corinthians 3:16–17; 6:19–20. The Holy Spirit helps the believer pray (Romans 8:26–27); avoid doing wrong (Galatians 5:16); tell others of Jesus (Acts 1:8); understand the Bible (1 Corinthians 2:6–16); live in peace and joy (Romans 5:5); know comfort in sorrow and difficulty (John 14:16–17); and discern the Will of God (Job 32:8; 33:4). There is but one baptism of the Holy Spirit, and that occurs at conversion, but there can and should be many infillings of the Holy Spirit throughout the Christian's life. See Ephesians 5:18. The Baptism of the Holy Spirit is when the Holy Spirit takes up residence in the Christian at salvation; the infilling of the Holy Spirit is when the Christian yields to His control, allowing Him not only to be resident but President in his life. See Galatians 5:16, 25. Referring to the infilling of the Holy Spirit in the believer's life, Leonard Ravenhill stated, "An automobile will never move until it has ignition—fire; so some men are neither moved nor moving because they have everything but fire."[1724]

The Holy Spirit ignites the Christian and "fires the engine" in the Christian's devotion, duty, and discipline. Corrie Ten Boom said, "Trying to do the Lord's work in your own strength is the most confusing, exhausting, and tedious of all work. But when you are filled with the Holy Spirit, then the ministry of Jesus just flows out of you."[1725]

> If the Holy Spirit can take over the subconscious with our consent and cooperation, then we have almighty Power working at the basis of our lives. Then we can do anything we ought to do, go anywhere we ought to go, and be anything we ought to be.
> E. Stanley Jones

Silently now I wait for Thee,
Ready, my God, Thy will to see;
Open my eyes, illumine me, Spirit Divine! ~ Clara H. Scott (1895)

The Bottom Line: Thirsty souls lift their hands unto the Lord in prayer begging for divine guidance (illumination) that they may not drift off course out of God's will and way. E. Stanley Jones said, "If the Holy Spirit can take over the subconscious with our consent and cooperation, then we have almighty Power working at the basis of our lives. Then we can do anything we ought to do, go anywhere we ought to go, and be anything we ought to be."[1726] *"Teach me!* How practical—teach me to do! How undivided in obedience—to do *thy will!* To do all of it, let it be what it may. This is the best form of instruction, for its source is God, its object is holiness, its spirit is that of hearty loyalty."[1727]

66. The Vanity and Brevity of Life   Psalm 144:1–4

"Blessed be the Lord *my strength, which teacheth my hands to war, and my fingers to fight: My goodness, and my fortress; my high tower, and my deliverer; my shield, and he in whom I trust; who subdueth my people under me.* Lord, *what is man, that thou takest knowledge of him! or the son of man, that thou makest account of him! Man is like to vanity: his days are as a shadow that passeth away."*—Psalm 144:1–4.

"Blessed" (Oswalt, Harris, Archer and Waltke say "to kneel, bless, praise"[1728]) be the Lord "my strength" (i.e., my rock) "which teacheth my hands to war and my fingers to fight" (Barnes says "that is, he teaches my fingers so that I can skillfully use them in battle. Probably the immediate reference here is to the use of the bow—placing the arrow, and drawing the string."[1729] See 2 Samuel 22:35.). "My goodness" (Vine, Unger and White say "loving-kindness; steadfast love; grace; mercy; faithfulness; goodness; devotion."[1730]).

AND "my fortress" (Swanson says "stronghold, mountain or rock fortress, i.e., a place where one resides as a hiding or defensive position."[1731]) "my high tower" (Landes says "high point for a refuge."[1732]); AND "my deliverer" (i.e., rescuer); "my shield" (protector). AND he in whom I "trust" (In whom I take refuge) "who subdueth my people under me" (Barnes says, "It is to be remarked that David 'here' refers to his people—"who subdueth my people"—meaning that those over whom God had placed him had been made submissive by the divine power."[1733] Plumer says, "The word *subdued* is not to be taken in a bad sense. Calvin: 'When a people yields a cordial and willing obedience to the laws, all subordinating themselves to their own place peaceably, this signally proves the divine blessing.'"[1734]).

Lord, what is man, that thou "takest knowledge of him" (Barnes says, "The word rendered 'that thou takest knowledge of him' means here to take notice of; to regard. The idea is, It is amazing that a being so insignificant as man should be an object of interest to God, or that One so great should pay any attention to him and to his affairs."[1735]) or "the son of man" (all mankind) that "thou makest account of him" (Barnes says, "The word here means that Thou shouldest 'think' of him, that he should ever come into Thy thought at all."[1736]).

Man is like to "vanity" (Swanson says "meaninglessness, emptiness, futility, uselessness, i.e., what is of no use on the basis of being futile and lacking in content"[1737]) "his days are as a shadow that passeth away" (Poole says "or, that declineth, as Psalm 102:11 and Psalm 109:23; that groweth less and less, till it be quite out of sight, and lost."[1738] Jennings and Lowe say, "In 102:11, the figure is more expanded, becoming that of a lengthening shadow, disappearing because merged in the dusk of evening."[1739] Even so, God yet is mindful of him. God's concern for man is a human puzzlement.).

Homily

It is thought that David wrote the Psalm following the death of Absalom and Israel's restoration to peace.[1740] J. A. Alexander stated, "The Davidic origin of this Psalm is as marked as that of any in the psalter."[1741] Jennings and Lowe summarize the Psalm: "In peaceful strains, he prays for the blessings of an unmolested thriving Constitution; he demands that the young generation of his country may grow up full of hope and full of promise; that blessings of the field and of the flock may be multiplied; that the rulers may have the hearty support of the populace; that the nation may escape the annoyances of invasions and depredations."[1742]

The Psalm opens with thunderous praise unto the Lord for being David's rock of strength; faithful friend that always shows unfailing love and mercy; fortress of defense; high tower of escape; rescuer from difficulty, trouble and enemies; shield of protection against the fiery darts of the enemy; and dependable refuge. He marvels at the condescension of God in light of the nothingness of man and in the final section begs for deliverance from present dangers. In the midst of that final appeal David again breaks out into spontaneous praise saying, "I will sing a new song unto thee, O God: upon a psaltery and an instrument of ten strings will I sing praises unto thee" (Psalm 144:9). Henry Lockyer well wrote, "David was pleading for new mercies and these demand new songs. He wanted to give God freshly baked loaves for His table. See 1 Samuel 21:6. The song of others may be empty and false, but as for *me*, I will adore thee with a new, true song. And it was a song for salvation given to *Kings*."[1743]

What is man, that thou takest knowledge of him! See Psalm 144:3. Jennings and Lowe state, "The same thought as in Psalm 8:4: the language is varied chiefly by the use of other verbs. Literally, the verse runs 'Jehovah, what is man that Thou shouldest know him, the son of frail-man that Thou shouldest take him into consideration?' The connection with the preceding is—'What am I, a mere mortal, that Thou shouldest thus befriend me?'"[1744] Spurgeon says, "The Psalmist's wonder is that God should stoop to know him....'Why and wherefore is this? What has man done? What has he been? What is he now that God should know him, and make Himself known to him as his goodness, fortress, and high tower?' This is an unanswerable question. Infinite condescension can alone account for the Lord stooping to be the friend of man."[1745] Though man may not understand God's gracious care and intervention (with regard to eternal salvation through His Son, Jesus Christ), he must not ignore it or count it lightly, but at once embrace it through faith and repentance. See Acts 20:21.

Man is like to vanity. See Psalm 144:4. Man's existence is "vanity" (futility, emptiness, weakness, transitoriness, frailty). Matthew Henry says, "Man's days have little substance, considering how many thoughts and cares of a never dying soul are employed about a poor dying body."[1746] W. S. Plumer said, "*Is like*, in the preterite ["A past action or state." [1747]] *has been like* in all generations, and up to this time. Neither intrinsic worth, nor permanence of existence on earth can be the cause of God's tenderness to man, but only the divine kindness."[1748]

Thomas Raffles, 1788–1863, wrote: "With what idle dreams, what foolish plans, what vain pursuits, are men for the most part occupied! They undertake dangerous expeditions and difficult enterprises in foreign countries, and they acquire fame; but what is it?—*Vanity*! They pursue deep and abstruse speculations, and give themselves to that 'much study which is a weariness to the flesh,' and they attain to literary renown, and survive in their writings; but what is it?—*Vanity*! They rise up early, and sit up late, and eat the bread of anxiety and care, and thus they amass wealth; but what is it?—*Vanity*! They frame and execute plans and schemes of ambition; they are loaded with honors and adorned with titles; they afford employment for the herald, and form a subject for the historian; but what is it?—*Vanity*! In fact, all occupations and pursuits are worthy of no other epithet, if they are not preceded by, and connected with, a deep and paramount regard to the salvation of the soul, the honor of God, and the interests of eternity....Oh, then, what phantoms, what airy nothings are those things that wholly absorb the powers and occupy the days of the great mass of mankind around us! Their most substantial good perishes in the using, and their most enduring realities are but 'the fashion of this world that passeth away.'"[1749]

His days are as a shadow that passeth away. See notes on Psalm 102 and Psalm 115. Albert Barnes says, "It is, that as a shadow has no substance, and that as it moves along constantly as the sun declines, until it vanishes altogether, so man has nothing substantial or permanent, and so he is constantly moving off and will soon wholly disappear."[1750] Matthew Henry remarks, "Man's life is as a shadow that passes away. In their highest earthly exaltation, believers will recollect how mean, sinful, and vile they are in themselves; thus they will be preserved from self-importance and presumption."[1751]

Man is prone to take life for granted without serious thought about its transitoriness. James speaks of man's life as a mere "vapor" that vanishes quickly. "Whereas ye know not what shall be on the morrow. For what is your life? It is even a vapor, that appeareth for a little time, and then vanisheth away" (James 4:14). The word "vapor" in comparison to life is common in Scriptures.[1752] It means "a mist, an exhalation, a smoke; such a vapor as we see ascending from a stream, or as lies on the mountainside in the morning, or as floats for a little time in the air, but which is dissipated by the rising sun, leaving not a trace behind."[1753] Peter likens man's life to a blade of grass that grows up only to wither away. "For all flesh is as grass, and all the glory of man as the flower of grass. The grass withereth, and the flower thereof falleth away" (1 Peter 1:24). Life is a mere "shadow," "vapor" and "blade of grass," requiring preparation to make the best of its brief days and for eternity. See notes on Psalm 90.

David told Jonathan there was but a step between him and death. See 1 Samuel 20:3. He realized that at any moment Saul or one of his soldiers could slay him. The same is applicable to us, for the step of death is an ever present reality.

It Is a Certain Step (all will take it should Jesus tarry)
It Is an Uncertain Step (when, where, how are unknowns)
It Is a Final Step (an end to opportunity to be saved, service, etc.)
It Is a Solitary Step (it is but one and must be taken alone)
It Is a Sad Step (for the unsaved but joyous and peaceful for God's child)
Are you prepared for your next step?[1754] (2 Kings 20:1; Hebrews 9:27)

The Bottom Line: Man's insignificance, nothingness, unworthiness, emptiness and transitoriness ought to cause him to seek the Lord who has demonstrated unfailing love, care and kindness toward him, that he might have life abundantly and eternally. See John 10:9–10. It is a hidden unknown as to when a person will take his last "step" on earth and step into eternity. See James 4:14; 1 Peter 1:24 and Psalm 103:15.

67. The Goodness of God (Part One)   Psalm 145:8–13

"The LORD is gracious, and full of compassion; slow to anger, and of great mercy. The LORD is good to all: and his tender mercies are over all his works. All thy works shall praise thee, O LORD; and thy saints shall bless thee. They shall speak of the glory of thy kingdom, and talk of thy power; To make known to the sons of men his mighty acts, and the glorious

majesty of his kingdom. Thy kingdom is an everlasting kingdom, and thy dominion endureth throughout all generations."—Psalm 145:8–13.

The Lord is "gracious" (Swanson says "gracious, compassionate, i.e., pertaining to being merciful to the needy and repentant"[1755]) AND "full of compassion" (Strong says "full of compassion, merciful"[1756]); "slow to anger" (Plumer says "literally long of anger, i.e., it is commonly long before God becomes so angry as to cut men down"[1757]).

AND of "great" (Gesenius and Tregelles say "great, of magnitude and extent."[1758] Barnes says, "The manifestation of that mercy is great: great, as on a large scale; great, as manifested toward great sinners; great, in the sacrifice made that it may be displayed; great, in the completeness with which sin is pardoned—pardoned so as to be remembered no more."[1759]) "mercy" (The unfailing love and kindness of God).

The Lord is "good to all" (Landes says "good; merry; pleasant; desirable; beautiful; friendly, kind"[1760]) AND his "tender mercies" (Holladay and Kohler say "loving feeling, compassion"[1761]) are over all his "works" (Landes says "work, labor, deed, accomplishment, achievement"[1762]; God's work in creation and rule of the universe, salvation, etc.). All thy works shall "praise thee, O Lord" (Alexander, Harris, Archer and Waltke say "confess, praise, give thanks, thank."[1763] All Thy works "thank You.").

AND thy "saints" (Swanson says "the godly, i.e., the ones faithful to God as a group"[1764]) shall "bless thee" (to kneel down; praise). They shall speak of the "glory of thy kingdom and talk of thy power" (Benson says "of which they are loyal subjects, and the blessings and glories of which they make it their business to publish to the world, that mankind may be thereby induced to submit their hearts and lives to so gracious a scepter as that of the Messiah, and that His dominion may become 'as universal in its extent as it is everlasting in its duration.'"[1765]).

"To make known to the sons of men his mighty acts, and the glorious majesty of his kingdom." (*Mighty acts.* J. A. Alexander says "literally mights or powers, but always used, like greatness, in an active, not an abstract sense."[1766] See Psalm 106:2. Patrick's paraphrase of the verse is: "It is their duty to discourse of the incomparable wisdom and goodness, and care, which Thou exercisest in the government of the whole world; especially of us; and to recount the memorable acts of Thy invincible power among us; that all mankind, who regard not such things so much as they ought, may be made sensible how mighty the Lord is: and adore the amazing splendor of His illustrious works; and the admirable order He observes in His government of all things."[1767]).

"Thy kingdom is an everlasting kingdom, and thy dominion endureth throughout all generations." (Plumer says, "The rendering is excellent....Jehovah will never give up the world to the reign of devils or the sovereign sway of finite agents."[1768]).

Homily

The Psalm is attributed to David (his last in the psalter) and is titled *David's Psalm of Praise*. W. S. Plumer says, "It has no known historic occasion."[1769] Matthew Henry states, "The entitling of this *David's Psalm of Praise* may intimate not only that he was the penman of it, but that he took a particular pleasure in it and sung it often; it was his companion wherever he went."[1770]

They shall abundantly utter the memory of thy great goodness. See Psalm 145:4. Augustine of Hippo wrote, "The highest good, than which there is no higher, is God, and consequently He is unchangeable good, hence truly eternal and truly immortal. All other good things are only from Him."[1771] "To His care the insect owes its hour of pleasure, and to His goodness the strong beast of the forest its strength and swiftness, and to His skill and His remembrance the bird of the air its flight and its song. We, too, ascribe our life, our health, our comforts, our domestic joys, our social happiness, our intellectual delights, our spiritual satisfactions, to the bounties of His hand and the kindness of His heart of love. There is no living thing whose powers and whose pleasures do not testify of the goodness of the beneficent Creator. 'All his works praise him.'"[1772] Matthew Henry wrote, "God's goodness is great goodness; the treasures of it can never be exhausted, nay, they can never be lessened, for He ever will be as rich in mercy as He ever was. It is memorable goodness; it is what we ought always to lay before us, always to have in mind and preserve the memorials of, for it is worthy to be had in everlasting remembrance; and the remembrance we retain of God's goodness we should utter, we should abundantly utter, as those who are full of it, very full of it, and desire that others may be acquainted and affected with it."[1773]

The Lord is good to all. See Psalm 145:9. God is *so* good to His children. He manifests to them (utterly underserved) unfailing love ("compassion"), patience ("slow to anger"), gentleness ("tender mercies"), "great mercy" (abundance of pardon to forgive the worst of sins and the worst of sinners), restoration to him that "falls" (stumbles into sin) and readiness to hear and answer their prayer (v. 18). "But His 'great' goodness has to do with eternal life; and when we think of what He has done for that, we can see that His goodness is indeed great. Whether we contemplate the depths of sin and misery from which His grace has brought us up; or whether we tell of the glorious heights of joy, sanctity, and service, to which He is bringing us; or of the pure beauty and grace which prompted Him thus to deal with us so utterly undeserving; or of the fearful cost at which He purchased us—even the precious blood; or of the present blessed help of His Holy Spirit, which we daily enjoy, and by which we are enabled to serve and glorify Him, and to become channels of blessing to others—when we think of all this, or of any part of it, our souls are lost in wonder as we gaze with awe and unspeakable gratitude on His great goodness."[1774]

It is this "goodness" that prompts the Christian to say, "Every day will I bless thee; and I will praise thy name forever and ever. Great is the Lord and greatly to be praised" (Psalm 145:2–3). It is this "goodness" that the saint must hold in constant "memory." See Psalm 145:7. Saints "pray" but often fail to give "praise." Mortals take God's goodness for granted (thus withhold due gratitude) because it is so abundantly, consistently and generously given. A. W. Pink said, "Gratitude is the return justly required from the objects of His beneficence; yet it is often withheld from our great Benefactor simply because His goodness is so constant and so abundant. It is lightly esteemed because it is exercised toward us in the common course of events. It is not felt because we daily experience it."[1775] Spurgeon wrote, "When others behave badly to us, it should only stir us up the more heartily to give thanks unto the Lord, because He is good; and when we ourselves are conscious that we are far from being good, we should only the more reverently bless Him that He is good. We must never tolerate an instant's unbelief as to the goodness of the Lord; whatever else may be questionable, this is absolutely certain, that Jehovah is good; His dispensations may vary, but His nature is always the same."[1776]

> Whatever else may be questionable, this is absolutely certain, that Jehovah is good.
> Charles Spurgeon

"God inhabits the praises of Israel [His people]" (Psalm 22:3). May the saint declare with David, "His praise shall continually be in my mouth" (Psalm 34:1). Praise Him, for He is good and does good for you.

God is so good;
God is so good;
God is so good;
He's so good to me. ~ Paul Makai (1970)

One great end of God's goodness is to bring man to repentance.[1777] Paul said, "Don't you see how wonderfully kind, tolerant, and patient God is with you? Does this mean nothing to you? Can't you see that his kindness is intended to turn you from your sin [lead you to repentance]?" (Romans 2:4 NLT). Albert Barnes remarks, "The tendency, the design of the goodness of God is to induce people to repent of their sins, and not to lead them to deeper and more aggravated iniquity."[1778] Barnes gives four ways in which God's goodness, patience, and mercy toward the sinner works "repentance":

(1) It shows the wrongness or evil of sin when it is seen to be committed against so good and merciful a God.

(2) It softens and melts the rebellious heart. The goodness of God lavished upon the sinner even in his stubborn rebellion, over time can subdue it.

(3) It overwhelms the profane sinner who from childhood to youth to adulthood to old age often profanes His name, violates His every law and treats Him with disdain without experiencing the "wrath" of God. "If there is anything that can affect the heart of man, it is this; and when he is brought to see it, and contemplate it, it rushes over the soul and overwhelms it with bitter sorrow."

(4) "The mercy and forbearance of God are constant. The manifestations of His goodness come in every form: in the sun, and light, and air; in the rain, the stream, the dew-drop; in food, and raiment, and home; in friends, and liberty, and protection; in health, and peace; and in the Gospel of Christ, and the offers of life; and in all these ways God is appealing to His creatures each moment and setting before them the evils of ingratitude, and beseeching them to turn and live."[1779]

Matthew Poole states, "God's goodness is abused when it is not used and improved to this end."[1780] See Hosea 11:4 and 2 Peter 3:9.

The Bottom Line: The "memory" of the goodness of God ought to prompt gratitude that is expressed in "repentance" (turning from sin unto the Lord Jesus Christ in faith), praise and faithful devotion.

68. The Goodness of God (Part Two)—Pass It On   Psalm 145:4

"One generation shall praise thy works to another, and shall declare thy mighty acts."—Psalm 145:4.

One generation shall "praise" (Plumer says "praise, not the same word as in v. 2, but one rendered commend, glory, triumph"[1781]) thy "works" (deeds) to another, AND shall "declare" (Poole says, "The people that live in one age shall relate them to their posterity, and so success-sively in all ages."[1782]) thy "mighty acts" (Plumer says, "The word rendered *acts* here and in v. 12 is often rendered power, also might, strength, mastery. Alexander renders it *mighty doings*."[1783]).

Homily

One generation shall praise thy works to another. See Psalm 145: 4. As this generation was handed the "baton" of the knowledge of the goodness of the works of God by the previous, even so must we faithfully pass it on to the next. Each generation amasses "fresh" witnesses (testimony and knowledge) to the glory and honor and goodness of God that must be preserved for future generations. Horne says, "And as the greatness of God our Savior hath no bounds, so His praises should have no end, nor should the voice of thanksgiving ever cease in the church. As 'one generation' drops it, 'another' should take it up, and prolong the delightful strain, till the sun and the moon shall withdraw their light, and the stars fall extinguished from their orbs."[1784]

The task is not assigned just to a segment of a generation, but to all of it. Parents are to instill biblical truth into the hearts of their children. Politicians are to insure the continuance of biblical values, principles and precepts and protection for the followers of Christ. Bible colleges and seminaries must not digress from teaching the Scripture in its "purity" to young minds preparing for the task of vocational ministry. Religious authors (theologians, ministers, etc.) must continue to record for future generations biblical knowledge, truth and godly wisdom. Thankful and spiritually enriched I am for past generations of godly men that wrote down their biblical insights and knowledge, preserving them for "future generations." Christians at large must proclaim the Gospel from the mountaintop to the valley until society is saturated with its good news and the last lost person saved. See Psalm 145:5;11. Pray that this generation does not commit injurious and devastating harm to the next by failure "to preserve the truth" and to "pass it on."

> The generation that is rising up shall follow the example of that which is going off: so that the death of God's worshippers shall be no diminution of His worship, for a new generation shall rise up in their room to carry on that good work, more or less, to the end of time, when it shall be left to that world to do it in which there is no succession of generations.
> Matthew Henry

Oh, may all who come behind us find us faithful;
>   May the fire of our devotion light their way.
May the footprints that we leave lead them to believe,
>   And the lives we live inspire them to obey. ~ Jon Mohr

Matthew Henry summarizes the text, "The generation that is going off shall tell them to that which is rising up, shall tell what they have seen in their days and what they have heard from their fathers; they shall fully and particularly declare Thy mighty acts (Psalm 78:3); and the generation that is rising up shall follow the example of that which is going off: so that the death of God's worshippers shall be no diminution of His worship, for a new generation shall rise up in their room to carry on that good work, more or less, to the end of time, when it shall be left to that world to do it in which there is no succession of generations."[1785]

The Bottom Line: The believer's duty is to saturate society with the "works" of God, embedding it so deeply and profoundly that it is preserved for the next generation. (We are only one generation away from being a heathen nation.) May the generation that comes behind us find us "faithful" to this task.

69. God's Care for the Defenseless, Desolate and Helpless
Psalm 146:9

"The LORD preserveth the strangers; he relieveth the fatherless and widow: but the way of the wicked he turneth upside down."—Psalm 146:9.

The Lord "preserveth" (Landes says "to keep, watch over, observe; to take care of, preserve, protect; to save, retain; to do something carefully."[1786] J. A. Alexander says "relieves, restores, raises up from their low condition."[1787]) the "strangers" (Gesenius and Tregelles say "a sojourner, stranger, foreigner, a person living out of his own country."[1788]). He "relieveth" (Plumer says "relieves, or lifts up, i.e., shows His friendship to the widow and the fatherless is declared in all His Word [Psalm 68:5; Proverbs 15:25; Jeremiah 49:11; Hosea 14:3].'[1789] Upholdeth. Jennings and Lowe say "'stablisheth,' sets on a firm footing"[1790]).

The "fatherless" (orphan) and widow: BUT the "way" (The NLT says "plans") of the "wicked" (the ungodly; unrighteousness) he "turneth upside down" (Barnes says, "The Hebrew word here means to bend, to curve, to make crooked, to distort; then, to overturn, to turn upside down."[1791] Jennings and Lowe say "'Turneth upside down,' or more correctly, 'turneth aside,' i.e., so as to lead the ungodly into destruction."[1792]).

Homily

The final five Psalms (Psalm 146–150) are called *Hallelujah Psalms*. No author is identified. Psalm 146 likely was written following the captivity and may refer to when Cyrus ceased the rebuilding of the walls of Jerusalem.[1793] Jennings and Lowe state, "The joyousness which characterizes Psalm 145 is intensified throughout the little group of Psalms 146–150, till the climax is reached, in Psalm 150, in the glorious charge, 'Let every thing that hath breath praise the LORD.'"[1794]

The Lord preserveth the strangers; he relieveth the fatherless and widow. J. J. S. Perowne says, "The STRANGERS...The WIDOW...The FATHERLESS, the three great examples of natural defencelessness."[1795] A. F. Kirkpatrick states, "The sojourners or resident aliens who had no rights of citizenship, orphans, and widows are typical examples of defenselessness. They are therefore specially under Jehovah's protection, and are commended in the Law to the care of the Israelites."[1796] W. S. Plumer comments, "The terms rendered *widow and fatherless* are sometimes used to denote in general the desolate, the helpless, and so we learn God is always ready to give help to those that have no friend or protector."[1797] Jesus Himself declared, "Beware of the scribes, which desire to walk in long robes, and love greetings in the markets, and the highest seats in the synagogues, and the chief rooms at feasts; *Which devour widows' houses*, and for a shew make long prayers: the same shall receive greater damnation" (Luke 20:46–47). Widows had no legal standing in New Testament times, therefore they would have to employ an attorney to go to court in their behalf. These attorneys charged exorbitant fees, creating even greater hardship for the widow. Such lawyers Jesus promised would *receive a greater damnation* for taking advantage of the defenseless. See Psalm 68:5.

J. A. Alexander states, "The stranger, the widow, and the orphan are constantly presented in the Law as objects of compassion and beneficence."[1798] Matthew Henry notes, "It ought not to pass without remark that the name of Jehovah is repeated here five times in five lines, to intimate that it is an almighty power (that of Jehovah) that is engaged and exerted for the relief of the oppressed, and that it is as much the glory of God to succor [relief, assistance] those that are in misery."[1799]

He cares (upholdeth) *for the stranger* (alien, immigrant, non-citizen). Albert Barnes wrote, "The stranger—away from home and friends; with no one to feel an interest in him or sympathy for him; with the feeling that he is forsaken; with no one on whom he can call for sympathy in distress—may find in God one who will regard his condition; who will sympathize with him; who is able to protect and befriend him."[1800] Citizens of the domain of Heaven (the kingdom of God) are to do likewise. Jesus said with regard to caring for strangers, "Inasmuch as ye have done it unto one of the least of these my brethren, ye have done it unto me" (Matthew 25:40). John Gill states, "In a spiritual sense, He [God] preserves the lives and saves the souls of His people among the Gentiles, who are aliens from the commonwealth of Israel, and strangers to the covenant of promise; for these He laid down His life a ransom, and became the propitiation for their sins; to these He sends his Gospel, which is the power of God to salvation unto them."[1801] See Ephesians 2:12–13. We (the redeemed) were "strangers" that Jesus Christ in loving care "took in" to make citizens of the kingdom of God. He awaits to do the same for all that are "afar off."

He cares for (upholdeth) *the fatherless.* "In thee [Jehovah God] the fatherless findeth mercy" (Hosea 14:3). God cares for the orphan and opposes all who deal with him mischievously (Deuteronomy 10:18; Psalm 10:14, 17–18; 68:5; 82:3; 146:9). He is their defender ("pleads their cause") against injustice. He is their protector, watching over them lest they are taken advantage of in some way or mistreated (stealing their fields). And how may the orphan know that God will so care for him? Solomon states that "their redeemer is mighty." He is the Almighty God and "His omnipotence is engaged and employed for their protection, and their proudest and most powerful oppressors will not only find themselves an unequal match for this, but will find that it is at their peril to contend with it."[1802] Be careful not to harm orphans or invade their rights or steal their possessions. Pray for the orphans' welfare morally, physically and spiritually. Intervene in their behalf when they are being abused or misused or neglected.

He cares for (upholdeth) *the widow.* God cares for and over-watches widows with protection. Our gracious and compassionate Lord draws a circle of fire about the confines of the widow, keeping injurious intruders out. The widow can assuredly depend upon the Lord for help (Jeremiah 49:11). None who seek to take advantage of a defenseless widow (unjust dealings, robbery, and deceit) will escape God's fury; he will be brought to "ruin." Care for the widow is the believers' task. James

1:27 says, "Pure religion and undefiled before God and the Father is this: to visit the fatherless and widows in their affliction." In 1 Timothy 5:3–16 the Lord gives specific guidelines for their care. Moses stood up for the widow: "You shall not afflict any widow or orphan" (Exodus 22:22 NASB). He also warned, "Cursed is he who distorts the justice due an alien, orphan, and widow" (Deuteronomy 27:19 NASB). J. Vernon McGee cautions, "The early church took care of widows, but they didn't do it in some haphazard, sentimental way. The deacons were to make an investigation to see who were truly widows, where the need was, and how much need there was."[1803] W. D. Mounce clarifies that a true widow "is not simply a woman whose husband is dead but one who deserves to be supported by the church."[1804]

The way of the wicked he turneth upside down. God will overthrow the ungodly—thwart, impede and interfere with their plans.[1805] "His merciful protection of His saints leads Him to overthrow the goings of the wicked, who are their enemies."[1806] W. S. Plumer says, "The most dreadful disasters that have overtaken the wicked in past ages are but feeble tokens of their ruin, the utter disappointment of all their hopes, the perfect defeat of all their plans in the world to come."[1807] Albert Barnes writes, "The idea here is, that their path is not a straight path; that God makes it a crooked way; that they are diverted from their design; that through them He accomplishes purposes which they did not intend; that He prevents their accomplishing their own designs; and that He will make their plans subservient to a higher and better purpose than their own."[1808] See Psalm 147:6.

Defeat may serve as well as victory
To shake the soul and let the glory out.
When the great oak is straining in the wind,
The limbs drink in new beauty, and the trunk
Sends down a deeper root on the windward side.
Only the soul that knows the mighty grief
Can know the mighty rapture. Sorrows come
To stretch out spaces in the heart for joy. ~ Edwin Markham (1852–1940)

The Bottom Line: God promises caring protection and provision for the weak and destitute of life without regard to *race or face.* See

Psalm 55:22. "God wins His greatest victories through apparent defeats. Very often the enemy seems to triumph for a season, and God allows it. But then He comes in and upsets the work of the enemy, overthrows the apparent victory, and as the Bible says, "frustrates the ways of the wicked" (Psalm 146:9)."[1809]

70. The Bars of Thy Gates (Home, Church and Life)   Psalm 147:13

"For he hath strengthened the bars of thy gates; he hath blessed thy children within thee."—Psalm 147:13.

For he hath "strengthened" (Vine, Unger and White say "to be strong, strengthen, harden, take hold of."[1810] Kirkpatrick says, "The same word is used in Nehemiah 3:4 ff. of repairing or fortifying the wall and gates. All through Nehemiah's narrative appears the conviction that 'this work was wrought of our God.'"[1811]) the "bars of thy gates" (Barnes says, "He has made thee safe and secure—as if He had given additional strength to the fastenings of the gates of the city. Cities were surrounded by walls. They were entered through gates. Those gates were fastened by bars passed across them, to which the gates were secured."[1812] Perowne says, "But as the Psalm so evidently refers to the return from the Captivity and the rebuilding of Jerusalem (v. 2), there can be little doubt that there is here a direct and literal reference to the setting up of the gates as described in Neh. 7:1–4."[1813]).

He hath "blessed thy children within thee" (The inhabitants within the gates of Jerusalem God blessed with peace and safety.[1814] Rawlinson says, "Under Nehemiah's government, when he had firmly established it, Israel enjoyed a period of repose and of great prosperity, which, at the date of the Psalm, was probably just commencing."[1815]).

Homily

Psalm 147 is the second of the five Hallelujah Psalms. The author is unknown. Adam Clarke states, "It was probably penned after the captivity, when the Jews were busily employed in rebuilding Jerusalem, as may be gathered from the second and thirteenth verses."[1816] Charles Simeon is of the same opinion. Jennings and Lowe summarize the Psalm: "The redeemed nation is here summoned to extol the many-sided

313

wisdom and love of Jehovah. It is He who has built up Jerusalem, strengthened the bars of her gates, blessed her children within her, made peace within her borders. He it is, if the thoughts range over His dealings with mankind generally, who everywhere confirms the humble, overthrows the wicked, comforts the afflicted. He too it is that provides for the needs of irrational life. And He it is that orders the conduct of things inanimate, that knows and names the myriad stars, that sends rain, wind, frost, ice, snow, at His pleasure."[1817]

Though this text refers historically to the walls and gates Nehemiah constructed, no harm is done to apply it to the home. As the "bars of the gates" were built around Jerusalem by those under Nehemiah's leadership for their protection, so must both husband and wife under God's leadership erect such about the home for security. See Nehemiah 7:1–4. Note that the text states God "strengthened the bars of thy gates" upon the completion of the task. It was not Nehemiah who strengthened them, but God; He only was able to construct them as required.

Build the "bars of the gates" about the home with the lumber of prayer, the Word of God, worship (private and corporate), submission to God, and abstinence from things that defile and damage (alcohol, drugs, pornography, gambling, etc.) and God will so strengthen them that no enemy will be able to make entry.

A second adaptation of the text may be made with regard to the church ("the body of Christ"). All that are "saved" are safe within the "bars of the gates" (Christ's sovereign protection) from Satan and the demons of Hell, evil, fear of death and uncertainty about eternal destiny, persecution and whatever or whoever else may assail. Christ Jesus "in me" is my shield and buckler, mighty warrior, strong and high Tower of refuge and strength, regardless of the enemies' assault. See 1 John 4:4. Spurgeon describes the believer's security in Christ Jesus: "They are not only His by choice, but by purchase. He has bought and paid for them to the utmost farthing; hence, about His title there can be no dispute. Not with corruptible things, as with silver and gold, but with the precious blood of the Lord Jesus Christ, the Lord's portion has been fully redeemed. There is no mortgage on His estate. No suits can be raised by opposing claimants; the price was paid in open court, and the Church is the Lord's freehold forever. See the blood-mark upon all the chosen, invisible to human eye, but known to Christ, for 'the Lord knoweth them that are His'; He forgetteth none of those whom He has redeemed from among men; He counts the sheep for whom He laid down His life, and remembers well the Church for which He gave Himself."[1818] See Romans 8:35–39.

The anchor holds, though the ship's been battered;
    The anchor holds, though the sails are torn.
I have fallen on my knees as I face the raging seas.
    The anchor holds in spite of the storm. ~ Ray Boltz

A third adaptation may be made in reference to the "church" (the gathering place of the saints). With Jesus as its "gates," the church is fortified against the onslaught of opposition from atheists, agnostics, libertarians, Universalists, liberal theologians and ministers and every "high thing that exalteth itself against the knowledge of God." See 2 Corinthians 10:5. The church may be battered and rammed, but her anchor will eternally "hold." The promise of Christ is sure that "the gates of hell shall not prevail against it" (Matthew 16:18). Certainly the "way" the church "looks" today (with regard to meeting place, décor and way of worship) is ever changing, but be ever confident that she (the true, uncompromising body of Christ that stands upon His infallible Word) will not "go away." That is an eternal guarantee.

Spurgeon says, "Modern libertines would tear down all gates and abolish all bars; but so do not we, because of the fear of the Lord."[1819]

The Bottom Line: Whether it is the home, church or personal life, if it be in submissiveness to Jesus, He will strengthen its "bars upon the gates," making it invulnerable to the enemy.

71. The Praise Voices of God's Creation   Psalm 148:1–13

"Praise ye the LORD. Praise ye the LORD from the heavens: praise him in the heights. Praise ye him, all his angels: praise ye him, all his hosts. Praise ye him, sun and moon: praise him, all ye stars of light. Praise him, ye heavens of heavens, and ye waters that be above the heavens. Let them praise the name of the LORD: for he commanded, and they were created. He hath also stablished them for ever and ever: he hath made a

decree which shall not pass. Praise the LORD from the earth, ye dragons, and all deeps: Fire, and hail; snow, and vapour; stormy wind fulfilling his word: Mountains, and all hills; fruitful trees, and all cedars: Beasts, and all cattle; creeping things, and flying fowl: Kings of the earth, and all people; princes, and all judges of the earth: Both young men, and maidens; old men, and children: Let them praise the name of the LORD: for his name alone is excellent; his glory is above the earth and heaven."—Psalm 148:1–13.

"Praise" (Swanson says "cheer, brag on, extol, i.e., extol the greatness or excellence of a person"[1820]) ye the Lord. Praise ye the Lord from the "heavens" (Rawlinson says "i.e., beginning at the heavens, making them the primary source from which the praises are to be drawn"[1821]): praise him in the "heights" (Rawlinson says "in the upper tenons, or the most exalted regions of His creation"[1822]). Praise ye him, all his angels: praise ye him, all his "hosts" (Holladay and Kohler say "army, warriors."[1823] Plumer says "hosts, a term applied both to angels and to the heavenly bodies. It here may include both."[1824] Horne says, "From the heavens and those unutterable heights where hosts of immortal spirits, admitted to a sight of their King, enjoy unfading pleasures, the song is to begin."[1825]).

Praise ye him, sun and moon: praise him, all ye stars of light. Praise him, ye "heavens of heavens" (Plumer says, "It is more probable that the phrase corresponds to third heavens in the New Testament, the abode of saints and angels—Paradise."[1826]). AND ye "waters be above the heavens" (Plumer says "the clouds which are ordinarily above the lower heavens in which the birds soar"[1827]).

"Let them praise the name of the Lord: for he commanded, and they were created." (Plumer says, "These things praise God now and shall continue to do so; or we may read it as in the English. These wonderful things are created to glorify God, and they shall certainly answer that end. It is only sinful men and apostate angels who of all God's creatures fail to put honor upon their Maker."[1828] *Name.* Jamieson-Fausset-Brown say "as representing His perfections."[1829] *He commanded.* Jamieson-Fausset-Brown say, "'He' is emphatic, ascribing creation to God alone."[1830] *Created.* Benson says, "They owe their existence wholly to His will and pleasure."[1831]).

He hath also "stablished" (Gesenius and Tregelles say "to stand; to set firmly, to sustain"[1832]) them "forever and ever" (Barnes says, "He has made them firm, stable, enduring. That they may be eternal is possible; that they will not be, no one can prove. Matter, when created, has no necessary tendency to decay or annihilation; and the universe—the stars, and suns, and systems—which have endured so many...ages may continue to exist any number of...ages to come. Of course, however, all this is dependent on the will of God."[1833] Jamieson-Fausset-Brown say, "Perpetuity of the frame of nature is, of course, subject to Him who formed it."[1834] Poole says "either absolutely, as to the substance of them, or at least to the end of the world."[1835] Henry says "that is, to the end of time, a short ever, but it is their ever; they shall last as long as there is occasion for them"[1836]).

He hath made a "decree which shall not pass" (Brown, Driver and Briggs say "prescribed task, assigned to."[1837] Poole says, "He hath made them constant and incorruptible, not changeable and perishing, as the things of the lower world are."[1838]). Praise the Lord from the earth, "ye dragons" (Swanson says "sea creatures, i.e., very large, impressive-looking creatures of the oceans, including very large fish and large marine mammals (Genesis 1:21). Note: possibly referring to a sea monster."[1839]).

AND "all deeps" (Barnes says "all that are in the depths of the sea. Not merely the 'dragons' or sea monsters, but all that inhabit the oceans."[1840]).

"Fire, and hail; snow, and vapors; stormy wind fulfilling his word" (Plumer says, "The *fire* here is the lightning, which attends the hail. See Psalm 18:12. The *snow* is but frozen vapors falling to the earth. Either as breeze or tempest, the *wind* fulfils God's *word*, i. e., does his will; for he holds the winds in his fist. All these illustrate the grandeur of the scale on which Jehovah works and the control of the Almighty over all causes and agents, however far beyond the power of mortals."[1841] *Fire and hail.* Rawlinson says, "By 'fire,' in this combination, we must understand 'lightning,' or rather the various electrical phenomena accompanying storms in the East, which are sometimes very strange and terrible."[1842] *Stormy wind.* Spurgeon says, "Though rushing with incalculable fury, the storm wind is still under law, and moves in order due, to carry out the designs of God."[1843]).

"Mountains, and all hills" (Benson says, "These are of great use in the earth. From them descend the running streams into the valleys, without which animals could not live. On the mountains grow those vast trees which are necessary for daily use in various ways; and on the hills and mountains is herbage for vast multitudes of cattle, whereby men are supplied with food and clothing."[1844]) "fruitful trees and all cedars" (Jamieson-Fausset-Brown say "or, 'trees of fruit,' as opposed to forest trees."[1845]).

"Beasts, and all cattle; creeping things, and flying fowl" (Spurgeon says, "No one can become familiar with insect and bird life without feeling that they constitute a wonderful chapter in the history of divine wisdom. The minute insect marvelously proclaims the Lord's handiwork: when placed under the microscope it tells a wondrous tale. So, too, the bird which soars aloft displays in its adaptation for an aerial life an amount of skill which our balloonists have in vain attempted to emulate. True devotion not only hears the praises of God in the sweet song of feathered minstrels, but even discovers it in the croaking from the marsh, or in the buzz of "the blue fly which singeth in the window pane." More base than reptiles, more insignificant than insects, are songless [people]."[1846]

"Kings of the earth, and all people; princes, and all judges of the earth: Both young men, and maidens; old men, and children" (Jamieson-Fausset-Brown say "all rational beings, from the highest in rank to little children."[1847] Horne says, "After the whole creation hath been called upon to praise Jehovah; man, for whom the whole was made; man, the last and more perfect work of God; man, that hath been since redeemed by the blood of the Son of God incarnate, is exhorted to join and fill up the universal chorus of Heaven and earth, as being connected with both worlds, that which now is, and that which is to come. *Persons of every degree, of each sex, and of every age*; 'kings,' whose power God hath made an image of his own, and who are the suns of their respective systems; 'judges,' and magistrates of all kinds, who derive their power, as the moon and planets do their light, from its original source; 'young men and maidens,' in the flower of health, strength, and beauty; 'old men,' who have accomplished their warfare, and are going out of life; 'children,' who are just come into it, and see everything new before them; all these have their several reasons for 'praising the Lord, whose name is excellent, and His glory above Heaven and earth.'"[1848]

Henry says, "God is to be praised also in the constitution of families, for He is the founder of them; and for all the comfort of relations, the comfort that parents and children, brothers and sisters, have in each other, God is to be praised."[1849]).

"Let them praise the name of the Lord" (Benson says, "Let them acknowledge and celebrate the wisdom, goodness, and power of the Lord."[1850]) "for his name alone is excellent" (Exalted. Gill says excellent "in power, wisdom, goodness, truth, and faithfulness, and in all other perfections of His nature; His works, by which He is known, are excellent, both of nature and of grace, and proclaim His glory; His Son, in whom His name is, and by whom He has manifested Himself, is excellent as the cedars....The Lord's name is alone excellent; all creature excellences are nothing in comparison of Him, in Heaven or in earth, those of angels and men; and therefore should be praised by all, and above all."[1851]).

"His glory is above the earth and heaven" (Gill says, "There is the glory of celestial and terrestrial bodies, which differ; the glory of the sun, moon, and stars, and of one star from another; but the glory of the divine Being, the Creator of them, infinitely exceeds the glory of them all: His glorious Majesty resides above Heaven and earth; the Heaven is the throne He sits upon, and the earth the footstool He stands on; and Christ, who is sometimes called His glory, and is the brightness of it [Psalm 63:2]; is exalted above every name on earth, and is made higher than the heavens, and so is exalted above all blessing and praise."[1852]).

Homily

The author (some count it as David) and date of the Psalm are uncertain. Adam Clarke says, "As a hymn of praise, this is the most sublime in the whole book."[1853] The Psalm is the third of the five Hallelujah Psalms.

J. J. S. Perowne wrote, "Things with and things without life, beings rational and irrational, are summoned to join the mighty chorus. The Psalm is an expression of the loftiest devotion, and embraces at the same time the most comprehensive view of the relation of the creature to the Creator."[1854]

The Psalmist calls for the entirety of creation to in unison raise their "voices" in praise to God. George Horne summarizes the Psalm: "The various parts [of choral praise to God] are to be performed by the angelic hosts; material heavens, and the luminaries placed in them; the ocean, with its inhabitants; the meteors of the air; the earth, as divided into hills and valleys, with the vegetables that grow out of it; the human race of every degree, of each sex, and of every age; more especially the...church of God [the redeemed purchased by the blood of Christ]."[1855]

Matthew Henry similarily states, "This psalm is a most solemn and earnest call to all the creatures, according to their capacity, to praise their Creator, and to show forth His eternal power and Godhead, the invisible things of which are manifested in the things that are seen."[1856]

The Angels in heaven are to praise the Lord. "They, with their loftier intelligence, their nearer access, and their larger experience of the Divine goodness, must have a deeper and fuller sense than we have of the greatness and excellency of God."[1857] *The heavens are to praise the Lord.* "The material heavens, through all their various regions, with the luminaries placed in them, and the waters sustained by them, though they have neither speech nor language, and want the tongue of men, yet by their splendor and magnificence, their motions and their influences, all regulated and exerted according to the ordinance of their Maker, do, in a very intelligible and striking manner, declare the glory of God; they call upon us to translate their actions into our language, and copy their obedience in our lives; that so we may, both by word and deed, glorify, with them, the Creator and Redeemer of the universe."[1858]

The mountains and hills are to render praise. John Gill says "which are originally formed by the Lord, and set fast by His power and strength; these are the highest parts of the earth, and are very ornamental and useful; they include all in them and upon them, the trees and herbage that grow upon them, gold, silver, brass, and iron in them; all very beneficial to mankind, and afford matter of praise to God for them."[1859]

Fruitful trees and all cedars are to render praise. John Gill comments, "Trees bearing fruit are the fig trees, pomegranates, vines, and olives, with which the land of Canaan abounded; and such as bear lemons, oranges, plums, pears, apples, cherries, which produce fruit for

320

the use, pleasure, and delight of man, and so a means of praising God; and 'cedars,' the trees of the Lord which He hath planted; though they bear no fruit, yet very useful in building, and were of great service in the Temple at Jerusalem; and which are put for all others of like usefulness, and minister just occasion of praise."[1860]

The animals and insects of creation are to praise the Lord. W. S. Plumer says, "*Beasts*, living creatures, from the connection supposed to be those which are wild, in contrast with cattle, a term commonly denoting domestic animals. *Creeping things*...includes lesser land animals even down to insects. *Flying fowl*, literally bird of wing, all the feathered tribes. *All living* things from the elephant to the ant, the bear, the boar, the beaver and the beetle, the ostrich, the condor, the eagle, the sparrow and the hummingbird should join the chorus of universal praise."[1861]

The entirety of mankind is to praise the Lord. Matthew Henry states, "Let all manner of persons praise God. Those of each rank, high and low. The praises of kings, and princes, and judges, are demanded; those on whom God has put honor must honor Him with it, and the power they are entrusted with, and the figure they make in the world, put them in a capacity of bringing more glory to God and doing Him more service than others. Yet the praises of the people are expected also, and God will graciously accept of them; Christ despised not the hosannas of the multitude."[1862]

Begin, my soul, th' exalted lay;
Let each enraptur'd thought obey
    And praise the Almighty's name.
Lo! heaven and earth, and seas and skies
In one melodious concert rise
    To swell th' inspiring theme.

Ye fields of light, celestial plains,
Where gay transporting beauty reigns,
    Ye scenes divinely fair,
Your Maker's wondrous power proclaim;
Tell how He form'd your shining frame
    And breath'd the fluid air.

Ye angels, catch the thrilling sound
While all th' adoring thrones around
     His boundless mercy sing.
Let every listening saint above
Wake all the tuneful soul of love
     And touch the sweetest string.

Join, ye loud spheres, the vocal choir;
Thou, dazzling orb of liquid fire,
     The mighty chorus aid.
Soon as grey evening gilds the plain,
Thou, moon, protract the melting strain
     And praise Him in the shade.

Thou heaven of heavens, His vast abode,
Ye clouds, proclaim your forming God
     Who call'd yon worlds from night.
"Ye shades, dispel!"—th' Eternal said;
At once th' involving darkness fled
     And nature sprung to light.

Whate'er a blooming world contains
That wings the air, that skims the plains,
     United praise bestow;
Ye dragons, sound His awful name
To Heaven aloud; and roar acclaim,
     Ye swelling deeps below.

Let every element rejoice:
Ye thunders, burst with awful voice
     To Him who bids you roll;
His praise in softer notes declare,
Each whisp'ring breeze of yielding air,
     And breathe it to the soul.

To Him, ye graceful cedars, bow;
Ye tow'ring mountains, bending low,
     Your great Creator own.
Tell, when affrighted nature shook,
How Sinai kindled at His look
     And trembled at His frown.

Ye flocks that haunt the humble vale,
Ye insects flutt'ring on the gale,
    In mutual concourse rise;
Crop the gay rose's vermeil bloom
And waft its spoils, a sweet perfume,
    In incense to the skies.

Wake, all ye mountain tribes, and sing;
Ye plumy warblers of the spring,
    Harmonious anthems raise
To Him who shap'd your finer mould,
Who tipp'd your glitt'ring wings with gold
    And tun'd your voice to praise.

Let man, by nobler passions sway'd,
The feeling heart, the judging head,
    In heav'nly praise employ;
Spread His tremendous name around
Till Heav'n's broad arch rings back the sound,
    The gen'ral burst of joy.

Ye whom the charms of grandeur please,
Nurs'd on the downy lap of ease,
    Fall prostrate at His throne.
Ye princes, rulers, all adore;
Praise him, ye kings, who makes your pow'r
    An image of His own.

Ye fair, by nature form'd to move,
Oh, praise th' eternal source of love
    With youth's enliv'ning fire.
Let age take up the tuneful lay;
Sigh his blest name—then soar away
    And ask an angel's lyre.[1863] ~ Ogilvie

The Bottom Line: Man is to join his "voice" with the rest of creation in ascribing praise to God.

72. God Delights in His People   Psalm 149:4

"For the Lord *taketh pleasure in his people: he will beautify the meek with salvation."*—Psalm 149:4.

For the Lord "taketh pleasure" (Swanson says "pleased, delight in, enjoy, favor, i.e., have a feeling or attitude of fondness and finding pleasure in an object, implying it to be delightful and favorable in the opinion of the speaker"[1864]) in "his people" (Gill says "not all mankind; though they are all His people by creation, and are under the care of His providence; yet they are not all acceptable to Him; some are abhorred by Him for their sins and transgressions: but these are a special and peculiar people, whom He has foreknown and chosen, taken into the covenant of His grace, and provided in it blessings for them; whom He has given to Christ, and He has redeemed; and who are called by the Spirit and grace of God, whereby they appear to be His people."[1865]).

He will "beautify" (Barnes says, "The word here rendered beautify means to adorn, to honor, as the sanctuary [Isaiah 60:7—rendered glorify]; and it here means that the salvation which God would bestow upon them would be of the nature of an ornament, as if they were clothed with costly or splendid raiment."[1866]) the "meek" (Holladay and Kohler say "be low, humble, gentle before God."[1867] Spurgeon says, "They are humble, and feel their need of salvation; He is gracious, and bestows it upon them. They lament their deformity, and He puts a beauty upon them of the choicest sort. He saves them by sanctifying them, and thus they wear the beauty of holiness, and the beauty of a joy which springs out of full salvation. He makes His people meek, and then makes the meek beautiful. Herein is grand argument for worshiping the Lord with the utmost exultation: He who takes such a pleasure in us must be approached with...exceeding joy."[1868]).

"With salvation" (Kirkpatrick says, "Salvation is not to be limited to victory, but denotes welfare and prosperity generally."[1869] Poole says "both temporal, in delivering them from, and setting them above, all their enemies; and afterwards, with everlasting salvation and glory."[1870] Henry says "but especially with eternal salvation. The righteous shall be beautified in that day when they shine forth as the sun. In the hopes of this, let them now, in the darkest day, sing a new song."[1871]).

Homily

Psalm 149 is the fourth of the five Hallelujah Psalms. "It is more probable that it was written by David, as many think. The author of Psalm 148 probably wrote this. But on these points we have no knowledge."[1872] Matthew Henry encapsulates the Psalm saying, "It is a psalm of triumph in the God of Israel, and over the enemies of Israel. Probably it was penned upon occasion of some victory which Israel was blessed and honoured with. Some conjecture that it was penned when David had taken the stronghold of Zion, and settled his government there. But it looks further, to the kingdom of the Messiah, who, in the chariot of the everlasting Gospel, goes forth conquering and to conquer."[1873]

God takes pleasure in His children ("God has a favor to His people, delights in them, sets His affection on them."[1874]). He takes pleasure in their likeness unto Himself. He takes pleasure in their faith. He takes pleasure in their regeneration. He takes pleasure in their fellowship. He takes pleasure in their service. He takes pleasure in their worship. He takes pleasure in their repentance. He takes pleasure in what they yet shall be. He takes pleasure in their prayers and praise. Spurgeon said, "I believe that every true sculptor can see in the block of marble the statue that he means to make....And the Lord takes pleasure in His people because He can see us as we shall be. "It doth not yet appear what we shall be," but it does appear to Him. In the case of His mind and the shaping of His eternal purpose He knows, dear sister, though you are now struggling with your fears, what you will be when you shall stand before the blazing lamps of the eternal throne. He knows, young man, though you have but a few days turned from sin, and begun to struggle with vice, what you will be when, with all the blood-washed host, you shall cast your crown before His throne. Yes, the Lord takes delight in His people as knowing what they are yet to be."[1875]

"Jesus remembers that He died for us; the Holy Spirit remembers that He strove with us; the great Father remembers how He has preserved us; and because of all this goodness in the past, He takes pleasure in us."[1876]

J. I. Packer said, "What condescension is this on Jehovah's part, to notice, to love, and to delight in His chosen! Surely there is nothing in our persons, or our actions, which could cause pleasure to the Ever-blessed One, were it not that He condescends to people of low estate."[1877] Certainly God's delight in us prompts a "new song" to be sung. See Psalm 149:1. J. M. Boice wrote, "We love old songs, just as we love old doctrines; but each generation has fresh lessons of God's grace, and new experiences of God's grace call for new songs."[1878]

Let the high praises of God be in the mouth, and a two-edged sword in their hand. See Psalm 149:6. Dilday and Kennedy said, "A song in the mouth (vv. 1–5) and a sword in the hand (vv. 6–9) were two expressions of victory. The first was marked by joy, the second by heroic action. Together they offered praise to the God who gives victory."[1879]

The Bottom Line: Spurgeon wrote, "It is delightful that God takes pleasure in us who are His people. We feel that this is a great stoop of condescending grace. What is there in us in which the Lord can take pleasure? Nothing, unless He has put it there! If He sees any beauty in us, it must be the reflection of His own face."[1880] God's pleasure toward the saint ought to prompt joyful praise and gratitude even upon "their beds." See Psalm 149:5. "There are some here who never praised Him in all their lives. What wretched creatures you are! God has been blessing you all this while, and you have never praised Him....Oh, begin to praise God, begin to·thank God at once!...Always praise Him. Always praise Him. When nobody hears you, in the silence of your bedchamber, still sing aloud unto your God."[1881]

73. The Sum and Total of the Psalms: Praise God   Psalm 150

"Praise ye the LORD. Praise God in his sanctuary: praise him in the firmament of his power. Praise him for his mighty acts: praise him according to his excellent greatness. Praise him with the sound of the trumpet: praise him with the psaltery and harp. Praise him with the timbrel and dance: praise him with stringed instruments and organs. Praise him upon the loud cymbals: praise him upon the high sounding cymbals. Let every thing that hath breath praise the LORD. Praise ye the LORD."—Psalm 150.

"Praise" (Swanson says "cheer, brag on, extol, i.e., extol the greatness or excellence of a person"[1882]) ye the Lord. Praise God in his "sanctuary" (Futato says "holiness, sacredness"[1883]): praise him in the "firmament" (Rawlinson says "i.e., in the broad expanse of heaven."[1884] Dilday and Kennedy say, "The terms 'in His sanctuary' and 'firmament of His power' (v. 1) possibly were parallel designations of the heavenly source of praise. Or, they contrasted the earthly and the heavenly sources."[1885]) "of his power" (Barnes says, "It is called 'the expanse of His power' because it is in the heavens—in the sun, the moon, the stars— that the power of God seems to be principally displayed."[1886]).

Praise him for his "mighty acts" (Benson says in Hebrew, "mightinesses."[1887] Barnes says, "The reference is to that which displays the power of God; the things which manifest His omnipotence."[1888]). Praise him according to his "excellent greatness" (Kirkpatrick says "the abundance of his greatness."[1889] Gill says "or, 'according to the multitude of His greatness'; which appears in His nature, perfections, and work, and these both of providence and grace; and in proportion hereunto, and according to the abilities of creatures, angels, and men, is He to be praised; which is giving Him the honor due unto His name."[1890]).

Praise him with the "sound of the trumpet" (Alexander says, "Here begins an enumeration of the instruments employed in public worship, and therefore necessarily associated with the idea of divine praise. The *trumpet* was used to assemble the people, and would therefore excite many of the same associations with our church bells. The other instruments were used as actual accompaniments of the Psalms performed in public worship."[1891] Swanson says "i.e., a curved animal horn used as a bugling and trumpeting device for signaling."[1892] Plumer says, "There seem to have been two kinds of trumpets in use among the Hebrews, the straight and the crooked; but of the size, or power of these instruments we know nothing."[1893]).

Praise him with the "psaltery and harp" (Swanson says "stringed instrument, lyre, harp, kithara, i.e., a musical instrument consisting of a strong frame, taut strings of animal or plant material, plucked to make melodic sounds, usually of a portable size"[1894]).

Praise him with the "timbrel" (Holladay and Kohler say "tambourine."[1895] See Exodus 15:20.). AND "dance" (Swanson says "circle-dancing, round-dancing, i.e., a series of rhythmic body movements, likely segregated by sex, possibly accompanied by rhythm instruments and/or musical instruments, with the associative meaning of being joyful"[1896]). Praise him with "stringed instruments" (Plumer says "a general term not determining the form or shape, but only that they had strings"[1897]). AND "organs" (Harris, Archer and Waltke say "flute, reed-pipe"[1898]).

Praise him upon the "loud cymbals: praise him upon the high sounding cymbals." (Plumer says "cymbals, the same word in both clauses. It does not occur very often, and is variously rendered. It is generally agreed that cymbals were instruments which produced a loud clanging noise. Probably they were metallic plates [struck together]. The Jews themselves confess that they have lost the knowledge, by which they might reproduce these several instruments."[1899] Percussion instrument.).

"Let everything that hath breath praise the Lord" (Benson says, "Every living creature in Heaven and earth [Revelation 5:13], according to their several capacities, some objectively, as manifesting His glorious perfections in their formation, qualities, and endowments, and giving men and angels just occasion to praise Him; and others actively, with hearts and voices, words and actions, showing forth His praise. Mankind, especially, are under peculiar and indispensable obligations to comply with the Psalmist's exhortation."[1900]). Praise ye the Lord.).

Homily

Jamieson-Fausset-Brown state, "This is a suitable doxology for the whole book, reciting the 'place, theme, mode, and extent of God's high praise.'"[1901] Psalm 150 is the fifth and final Hallelujah Psalm. Its author and occasion are unknown. Jennings and Lowe wrote, "This the final Hallelujah (in which every verse but the last commences with *hal'loo*) sets forth where, why, and how the eulogy of Jehovah is to be offered. It is to be offered in the heavens, and on the earth; in recognition both of His inherent power, and of its manifestation in mighty acts; with every external appliance expressive of joyousness, with wind-instruments and stringed-instruments, with tabrets, cymbals, and dances (vv. 1–5)."[1902] Charles Simeon wrote, "In all the five last psalms he speaks the language of praise. Every one of them begins and ends with Hallelujah, that is, 'Praise ye the Lord.' In the psalm before us, short as it is, he repeats his exhortation no less than thirteen times. Oh, that he might not repeat it in vain! Oh, that we might 'drink into his spirit,' and be transported, like him, with love and gratitude, with adoration and thanksgiving!"[1903]

William W. Hamilton wrote, "Blessed are they who find delight in thanksgiving, and who recognize and appreciate the individual mercies, who see and are grateful for the national strength and prosperity, who know truly the soul's hope of eternity and deliverance from Hell, who bless likeness to God, and who anticipate full satisfaction. Did ever mortal pen write down such expressions of true gratitude and thanksgiving as are found in the psalms, and can we read them over without having our hearts say, 'Praise ye the Lord' (Psalm 150:1); 'Praise ye the name of the Lord; praise him, O ye servants of the Lord' (Psalm 135:1)?"[1904]

Regarding resounding praise, note: *Its What*. "Praise God..." The Lord God Almighty is alone worthy of man's adoration and worship.

Its Where. "Praise God in his sanctuary: praise him in the firmament of his power" (Psalm 150:1). John R. W. Stott says Psalm 150:1 is "an invitation to both humans and angels to worship God—humans in earth's sanctuary, and angels in Heaven."[1905] Praise God in His "holy place." John MacArthur writes, "'Sanctuary' most likely refers to the Temple in Jerusalem, so the sense would be 'Praise God on earth and in heaven.'"[1906] Spurgeon comments, "Praise begins at home. 'In God's own house pronounce His praise.' The holy place should be filled with praise; just as of old the high priest filled the Holy of Holies with the smoke of sweet-smelling incense. In His church below and in His courts above hallelujahs should be continually presented. In the person of Jesus, God finds a holy dwelling or sanctuary, and there He is greatly to be praised."[1907] Praise ought also to ascend unto the Lord in the "firmament of his power." Tuck says, "It is quite true that praise is to be offered in those buildings which are set apart for God's worship; but we must always regard them as representative of God's great temple of nature and of human history."[1908] Matthew Henry says, "Praise Him because of His power and glory which appear in the firmament, its vastness, its brightness, and its splendid furniture; and because of the powerful influences it has upon this earth. Let those that have their dwelling in the firmament of His power, even the holy angels, lead in this good work."[1909]

Its Why. "Praise him for his mighty acts: praise him according to his excellent greatness" (Psalm 150:2). Ellsworth wrote, "Worlds of meaning are folded into those terms! The former includes His works of creation, providence and redemption. The latter refers to God's person—that is, all the attributes that make Him the unspeakably glorious God he is."[1910] Benson says render praise unto the Lord for, "the power He hath exerted in creating, upholding, and governing the world, and in redeeming and saving the human race."[1911]

Its How. Utilize all manners of instruments (trumpet, psaltery and harp, stringed instruments, tambourine) in extoling the glorious name of the Lord. See Psalm 150:3–5. Matthew Henry writes, "That *in serving God we should spare no cost nor pains.* That the best music in God's ears is devout and pious affections."[1912] "Whoever despises music," says Luther, "I am displeased with him. Next to theology, I give a place to music, for thereby all anger is forgotten; the Devil is driven away; melancholy, many tribulations, and evil thoughts are expelled. It is the solace of a desponding mind."[1913] Paul exhorts the saint to use stringed instruments in worship in Ephesians 5:19. John MacArthur says, "'Making melody,' literally 'to pluck a stringed instrument,' so it could refer primarily to instrumental music while including vocal also."[1914] Henry Ward Beecher gives warning about "music" in the church: "There is a provision, even in our churches, for the excitation and expression of praise. It is the song service of the church. But the first and most fatal difficulty in this is that we have no religious music; or, rather, that the music of the church is for the sake of music, and not for the sake of praise. It expresses the aesthetic or art feeling about praise—not heart feeling. It is aimed at a wholly different thing from that which music was designed to be in the sanctuary."[1915] (Beecher was a preacher during our nation's Civil War long before the modern era of "church" music.) W. A. Criswell states, "It is obvious from this list of instruments [Psalm 150:3–5] that the religious music of ancient Israel was both loud and rhythmic. Music was an important part of both O.T. and N.T. worship (Ephesians 5:19; Colossians 3:16), and the same ought to be true in the church today."[1916]

Its Who. "Let everything that hath breath praise the Lord" (See Psalm 150:6). Albert Barnes states, "All living things in the air, the earth, the waters. Let there be one universal burst of praise. Let his praises be celebrated not only with instruments of music, but let all living beings unite in that praise; let a breathing universe combine in one solemn service of praise."[1917] Spurgeon said, "The Gospel meaning is that all powers and faculties should praise the Lord—all sorts of persons, under all circumstances, and with differing constitutions, should do honor unto the Lord of all. If there be any virtue, if there by any talent, if there be any influence, let all be consecrated to the service of the universal Benefactor. Harp and lyre—the choicest, the sweetest—must be all our Lord's."[1918]

Its When. "Praise ye the Lord" (Psalm 150:6). Perpetually on earth and then eternally in Heaven saints will praise Him. Jamieson-Fausset-Brown say, "Living voices shall take up the failing sounds of dead instruments, and as they cease on earth, those of intelligent ransomed spirits and holy angels, as with the sound of mighty thunders, will prolong eternally the praise, saying: 'Alleluia! Salvation, and Glory, and Honor, and Power, unto the Lord our God'; 'Alleluia! for the Lord God omnipotent reigneth.' Amen!"[1919] See Revelation 4:8 and Revelation 7:15.

Matthew Henry exhorts, "Having our breath in our nostrils, let us consider that it is still going forth, and will shortly go and not return. Since therefore we must shortly breathe our last, while we have breath let us praise the Lord, and then we shall breathe our last with comfort, and, when death runs us out of breath, we shall remove to a better state to breathe God's praises in a freer better air."[1920]

The Bottom Line: "It is required that every human creature praise the Lord. What have we our breath, our spirit, for, but to spend it in praising God; and how can we spend it better?"[1921] "The chief end of man is to glorify God and to enjoy Him forever"(The Westminster "Shorter Catechism"). The Psalmist closes the Psalter saying, "Let everything that hath breath praise the Lord. Praise ye the Lord" (Psalm 150:6). What a fitting conclusive appeal this is to the *Book of Praises!*

In Heaven, "prayers will there be swallowed up in everlasting praises; there will be no intermission in praising God, and yet no weariness—hallelujahs forever repeated, and yet still new songs.... Hallelujah is the word there (Revelation 19:1, 3); let us echo to it now, as those that hope to join in it shortly. Hallelujah, praise you the Lord."[1922] Amen and Amen!

"Blessed be the Lord God of Israel for ever and ever. And all the people said, Amen, and praised the Lord" (1 Chronicles 16:36).

[1] Plumer, W. S. *Studies in the Book of Psalms: Being a Critical and Expository Commentary, with Doctrinal and Practical Remarks on the Entire Psalter.* (Philadelphia; Edinburgh: J. B. Lippincott Company; A & C Black, 1872), 7.

[2] Hamilton, William W. *Sermons on Books of the Bible: Vol. 2.* (Nashville: Broadman Press, 1925), 35–36.

[3] Hastings, James. *The Great Texts of the Bible: Job to Psalm 23.* (New York: Charles Scribner's Sons, 1913), Psalm 1:1.

[4] Bonar, A. A. *Christ and His Church in the Book of Psalms.* (New York: Robert Carter & Brothers, 1860), v.

[5] Perowne, J. J. S. *The Book of Psalms: A New Translation, with Introductions and Notes, Explanatory and Critical, Fifth Edition, Revised, Vol. 1.* (London; Cambridge: George Bell and Sons; Deighton Bell and Co., 1883), 29.

[6] https://www.yosemite.com/yosemite-in-two-days/, accessed November 21, 2018. The author adapted an illustration shared by Craig C. Broyles in *Psalms: New International Biblical Commentary,* Vol. 11, p. 1.

[7] Spurgeon, C. H. *Psalms.* (Wheaton, IL: Crossway Books, 1993), 11.

[8] Brueggemann, W. *Spirituality of the Psalms.* (Minneapolis: Fortress Press, 2002), vii.

[9] Criswell, W. A. Ed., *The Criswell Study Bible,* Psalms (Introduction). (Nashville: Thomas Nelson Publishers, 1979), 640.

[10] Freedman D. N., A. C. Myers, & A. B. Beck, Eds. *Eerdmans Dictionary of the Bible.* (Grand Rapids, MI: W. B. Eerdmans, 2000), 1093. (J. L.Crenshaw, in Psalms, Book of)

[11] Ibid.

[12] Elwell, W. A. and P. W. Comfort. *Tyndale Bible Dictionary.* (Wheaton, IL: Tyndale House Publishers, 2001), 1093.

[13] Mills, Watson and Richard Wilson, Eds., *Mercer Commentary on the Bible.* (Macon, GA: Mercer University Press, 1995), 431.

[14] Lockyer, Herbert, Sr. *Psalms: A Devotional Commentary,* Psalm 119. (Grand Rapids: Kregel Publications, 1993), 535, 537.

[15] Spurgeon, C. H. *Psalms.* (Wheaton, IL: Crossway Books, 1993), 8–9.

[16] Stott, John. *Favorite Psalms.* (Grand Rapids: Baker Books, 1988), 5.

[17] Henry, M. *Matthew Henry's Commentary on the Whole Bible: Complete and Unabridged in One Volume.* (Peabody: Hendrickson, 1994), 743.

[18] VanGemeren, Willem A. *The Expositor's Bible Commentary,* Psalms. (Grand Rapids: Zondervan, 1991), Introduction.

[19] Perowne, J. J. S. *The Book of Psalms: A New Translation, with Introductions and Notes, Explanatory and Critical, Fifth Edition, Revised, Vol. 1.* (London; Cambridge: George Bell and Sons; Deighton Bell and Co., 1883), 22.

[20] Lucado, M. *Life Lessons from the Inspired Word of God*: Book of Psalms. (Dallas, TX: Word Pub., 1997), 7–9.

[21] Plumer, W. S. *Studies in the Book of Psalms: Being a Critical and Expository Commentary, with Doctrinal and Practical Remarks on the Entire Psalter.* (Philadelphia; Edinburgh: J. B. Lippincott Company; A & C Black, 1872), 8.

[22] Ibid., 5.

[23] Ibid.

[24] *The Spurgeon Study Bible.* (Nashville: Holman Bible Publishers, 2017), 689.

[25] Coffman's Commentaries on the Bible, Psalms, (Introduction).

[26] Kirkpatrick, A. F. (Ed.). *The Cambridge Bible for Schools and Colleges,* Psalms. (Cambridge: Cambridge University Press, 1914), xi.

[27] VanGemeren, Willem A. *The Expositor's Bible Commentary,* Psalms. (Grand Rapids: Zondervan, 1991), 18.

[28] Ibid.

[29] Mills, Watson and Richard Wilson, Eds., *Mercer Commentary on the Bible.* (Macon, GA: Mercer University Press, 1995), 331.

[30] Fraser, James H. *The Authenticity of the Psalm Titles.* Submitted in partial fulfillment of requirements for the degree of Master of Theology in Grace Theological Seminary, May 1984. https://faculty.gordon.edu/hu/bi/ted_hildebrandt/otesources/19-psalms/text/books/frazer-pstitles/frazer-pstitles.pdf, accessed November 24, 2018.

[31] Ibid.

[32] Watts, J. Walsh. *Old Testament Teaching.* (Nashville: Broadman Press, 1967), 150–151.

[33] Plumer, W. S. *Studies in the Book of Psalms: Being a Critical and Expository Commentary, with Doctrinal and Practical Remarks on the Entire Psalter.* (Philadelphia; Edinburgh: J. B. Lippincott Company; A & C Black, 1872), 11.

[34] Ibid., 78.

[35] Kirkpatrick, A. F. (Ed.). *The Cambridge Bible for Schools and Colleges,* Psalms. (Cambridge: Cambridge University Press, 1914), 37.

[36] Swindoll, Chuck. "Psalms." https://www.insight.org/resources/bible/the-wisdom-books/psalms, accessed November 24, 2018.

[37] Criswell, W. A. Ed., *The Criswell Study Bible,* Psalms (Introduction). (Nashville: Thomas Nelson Publishers, 1979), 640.

[38] Elwell, W. A. and P. W. Comfort. *Tyndale Bible Dictionary.* (Wheaton, IL: Tyndale House Publishers, 2001), 1093–1094.

[39] Horne, G. *A Commentary on the Book of Psalms.* (New York: Robert Carter & Brothers, 1856), 12.

[40] Keil & Delitzsch. Commentary on the Old Testament: Volume 5. (Peabody, Massachusetts: Hendrickson Publishers, 2006), 28.

[41] Tholuck, A. *A Translation and Commentary of the Book of Psalms: For the Use of the Ministry and Laity of the Christian Church,* (J. I. Mombert, Trans.). (Philadelphia: William S. & Alfred Martien, 1858), 2.

[42] Kirkpatrick, A. F. (Ed.). *The Cambridge Bible for Schools and Colleges,* Psalms. (Cambridge: Cambridge University Press, 1914), xcvi.

[43] Criswell, W. A., P. Patterson, E. R. Clendenen, D. L. Akin, M. Chamberlin, D. K. Patterson, and J. Pogue (Eds.). Believer's Study Bible, (electronic ed.). (Nashville: Thomas Nelson, 1991), Ps. 1:1.

[44] Ironside, H. A. Studies in Book One of the Psalms. (New York: Loizeaux Brothers, 1951), Introduction.

[45] Keil & Delitzsch. Commentary on the Old Testament: Volume 5. (Peabody, Massachusetts: Hendrickson Publishers, 2006), 46.

[46] Ibid.

[47] "Psalms of Trust: Living Real Life in the Real World," 7. https://docplayer.net/88840979-Psalms-of-trust-living-real-life-in-the-real-world.html, accessed October 2, 2018.

[48] Ironside, H. A. Studies in Book One of the Psalms. (New York: Loizeaux Brothers, 1951), Psalm 2:1–12.

[49] Eskew, Harry and Hugh T. McElrath, *Sing With Understanding.* (Nashville: Broadman Press, 1980), 45.

[50] Tholuck, A. *A Translation and Commentary of the Book of Psalms: For the Use of the Ministry and Laity of the Christian Church,* (J. I. Mombert, Trans.). (Philadelphia: William S. & Alfred Martien, 1858), 2.

[51] Harman, A. *Psalms: A Mentor Commentary (Vol. 1–2).* (Ross-shire, Great Britain: Mentor, 2011), 92–93.

[52] Ibid., 93.

[53] Ibid.

[54] Ibid.

[55] https://www.vocabulary.com/articles/chooseyourwords/indict-indite/, accessed August 19, 2018.

[56] Plumer, W. S. *Studies in the Book of Psalms: Being a Critical and Expository Commentary, with Doctrinal and Practical Remarks on the Entire Psalter.* (Philadelphia; Edinburgh: J. B. Lippincott Company; A & C Black, 1872), 5.

[57] Henry, M. *Matthew Henry's Commentary on the Whole Bible: Complete and Unabridged in One Volume.* (Peabody: Hendrickson, 1994), 743.

[58] McGee, J. V. *Thru the Bible Commentary: Poetry* (Psalms 1–41) (electronic ed., Vol. 17). (Nashville: Thomas Nelson, 1991), ix.

[59] https://www.studylight.org/commentaries/isn/psalms.html, accessed March 28, 2019.

[60] Ironside, Harry. *Notes on Selected Books*, 16.

[61] Bonar, A. A. *Christ and His Church in the Book of Psalms*. (New York: Robert Carter & Brothers, 1860), xi.

[62] Criswell, W. A., P. Patterson, E. R. Clendenen, D. L. Akin, M. Chamberlin, D. K. Patterson, and J. Pogue (Eds.). Believer's Study Bible, (electronic ed.). (Nashville: Thomas Nelson, 1991), Ps. 1:1.

[63] Keil & Delitzsch. Commentary on the Old Testament: Volume 5. (Peabody, Massachusetts: Hendrickson Publishers, 2006), 28.

[64] Carroll, B. H. *An Interpretation of the English Bible: The Poetical Books of the Bible*. (Nashville: Broadman Press, 1948), 138.

[65] Ibid., 139–143.

[66] Horne, G. *A Commentary on the Book of Psalms*. (New York: Robert Carter & Brothers, 1856), 19.

[67] Exell, Joseph S. Ed. *The Biblical Illustrator,* Introduction to the Psalms.

[68] Ibid.

[69] Boice, J. M. *Psalms 1–41: An Expositional Commentary*. (Grand Rapids, MI: Baker Books, 2005), 254.

[70] Ironside, H. A. *Studies on Book One of the Psalms*. (Neptune, NJ: Loizeaux Brothers, 1952), 195–196.

[71] Carroll, B. H. *An Interpretation of the English Bible: The Poetical Books of the Bible*. (Nashville: Broadman Press, 1948), 123.

[72] Ibid.

[73] VanGemeren, Willem A. *The Expositor's Bible Commentary,* Psalms. (Grand Rapids: Zondervan, 1991), 5.

[74] Lucado, M. *Life Lessons from the Inspired Word of God*: Book of Psalms. (Dallas, TX: Word Pub., 1997), 7–9.

[75] McGee, J. V. *Thru the Bible Commentary: Poetry* (Psalms 1–41) (electronic ed., Vol. 17). (Nashville: Thomas Nelson, 1991), viii.

[76] Perowne, J. J. S. *The Book of Psalms: A New Translation, with Introductions and Notes, Explanatory and Critical, Fifth Edition, Revised, Vol. 1*. (London; Cambridge: George Bell and Sons; Deighton Bell and Co., 1883), 25.

[77] Spurgeon, C. H. *Commenting and Commentaries*. (London: Passmore & Alabaster, 1890), 1.

[78] Nichols, J. W. H. *Musings in the Psalms*. (Galaxie Software, 2005), 12.

[79] Kirkpatrick, A. F. (Ed.). *The Cambridge Bible for Schools and Colleges,* Psalms. (Cambridge: Cambridge University Press, 1914), appendix. (Several passages

included are not formally introduced as quotations though taken straight from the Psalms.)

[80] Vine, W. E., M. F. Unger, & W. White, Jr. *Vine's Complete Expository Dictionary of Old and New Testament Words (Vol. 1).* (Nashville, TN: T. Nelson, 1996), 142.

[81] Kirkpatrick, A. F. (Ed.). *The Cambridge Bible for Schools and Colleges,* Psalms. (Cambridge: Cambridge University Press, 1914), Psalm 101:1.

[82] Spurgeon, C. H. *The Treasury of David.* (Grand Rapids, Michigan: Kregel Publications, 2004), Psalm 101:1.

[83] Benson, Joseph. *The Holy Bible With Notes, Critical, Explanatory and Practical.* (London: J. Kershaw, 1825), Psalm 101:1.

[84] Simeon, C. *Horae Homileticae: Psalms, LXXIII–CL* (Vol. 6). (London: Samuel Holdsworth, 1836), 184.

[85] Swanson, J. *Dictionary of Biblical Languages with Semantic Domains: Hebrew (Old Testament)* (electronic ed.). (Oak Harbor: Logos Research Systems, Inc., 1997).

[86] Spence-Jones, H. D. M. (Ed.). *Psalms,* (Vol. 2). (London; New York: Funk & Wagnalls Company, 1909), 360.

[87] Swanson, J. *Dictionary of Biblical Languages with Semantic Domains: Hebrew (Old Testament)* (electronic ed.). (Oak Harbor: Logos Research Systems, Inc., 1997).

[88] Ibid.

[89] Brown, F., S. R. Driver, and C. A. Briggs. *Enhanced Brown-Driver-Briggs Hebrew and English Lexicon.* (Oxford: Clarendon Press, 1977), 1070.

[90] Barnes, Albert. Notes on the Psalms, Critical, Explanatory and Practical. (New York: Harper & Brothers, 1868), Psalm 101:2.

[91] Benson, Joseph. *The Holy Bible With Notes, Critical, Explanatory and Practical.* (London: J. Kershaw, 1825), Psalm 101:2.

[92] Vine, W. E., M. F. Unger, and W. White, Jr. *Vine's Complete Expository Dictionary of Old and New Testament Words* (Vol. 1). (Nashville: T. Nelson, 1996), 279.

[93] Goldberg, L., R. L. Harris, G. L. Archer Jr., and B. K. Waltke (Eds.). *Theological Wordbook of the Old Testament,* 241 בַּיִת, (electronic ed.). (Chicago: Moody Press, 1999), 105.

[94] Swanson, J. *Dictionary of Biblical Languages with Semantic Domains: Hebrew (Old Testament)* (electronic ed.). (Oak Harbor: Logos Research Systems, Inc., 1997).

[95] Carroll, B. H. *An Interpretation of the English Bible: The Poetical Books of the Bible.* (Nashville: Broadman Press, 1948), 122.

[96] Ibid.

[97] Strong, J. *The New Strong's Dictionary of Hebrew and Greek Words.* (Nashville: Thomas Nelson, 1996).

[98] Brown, F., S. R. Driver, and C. A. Briggs. *Enhanced Brown-Driver-Briggs Hebrew and English Lexicon.* (Oxford: Clarendon Press, 1977), 962.

[99] Gesenius, W., and S. P. Tregelles. *Gesenius' Hebrew and Chaldee Lexicon to the Old Testament Scriptures.* (Bellingham, WA: Logos Bible Software, 2003), 185.

[100] Swanson, J. *Dictionary of Biblical Languages with Semantic Domains: Hebrew (Old Testament)* (electronic ed.). (Oak Harbor: Logos Research Systems, Inc., 1997).

[101] Landes, G. M. *Building Your Biblical Hebrew Vocabulary: Learning Words by Frequency and Cognate* (Vol. 41). (Atlanta, GA: Society of Biblical Literature, 2001), 57.

[102] Vine, W. E., M. F. Unger, and W. White, Jr. *Vine's Complete Expository Dictionary of Old and New Testament Words* (Vol. 1). (Nashville: T. Nelson, 1996), 130.

[103] Swanson, J. *Dictionary of Biblical Languages with Semantic Domains: Hebrew (Old Testament)* (electronic ed.). (Oak Harbor: Logos Research Systems, Inc., 1997).

[104] Ibid.

[105] Landes, G. M. *Building Your Biblical Hebrew Vocabulary: Learning Words by Frequency and Cognate* (Vol. 41). (Atlanta, GA: Society of Biblical Literature, 2001), 116.

[106] Holladay, W. L., and L. Köhler. A Concise Hebrew and Aramaic Lexicon of the Old Testament. (Leiden: Brill, 2000), 134.

[107] Swanson, J. *Dictionary of Biblical Languages with Semantic Domains: Hebrew (Old Testament)* (electronic ed.). (Oak Harbor: Logos Research Systems, Inc., 1997).

[108] Holladay, W. L., and L. Köhler. A Concise Hebrew and Aramaic Lexicon of the Old Testament. (Leiden: Brill, 2000), 276.

[109] Barnes, Albert. Notes on the Psalms, Critical, Explanatory and Practical. (New York: Harper & Brothers, 1868), Psalm 101:6.

[110] Spence-Jones, H. D. M. (Ed.). *Psalms,* (Vol. 2). (London; New York: Funk & Wagnalls Company, 1909), 360.

[111] Swanson, J. *Dictionary of Biblical Languages with Semantic Domains: Hebrew (Old Testament)* (electronic ed.). (Oak Harbor: Logos Research Systems, Inc., 1997).

[112] Vine, W. E., M. F. Unger, and W. White, Jr. *Vine's Complete Expository Dictionary of Old and New Testament Words* (Vol. 1). (Nashville: T. Nelson, 1996), 64.

[113] Spence-Jones, H. D. M. (Ed.). *Psalms,* (Vol. 2). (London; New York: Funk & Wagnalls Company, 1909), 360.

[114] Vine, W. E., M. F. Unger, and W. White, Jr. *Vine's Complete Expository Dictionary of Old and New Testament Words* (Vol. 1). (Nashville: T. Nelson, 1996), 77.

[115] Spence-Jones, H. D. M. (Ed.). *Psalms,* (Vol. 2). (London; New York: Funk & Wagnalls Company, 1909), 360.

[116] Kirkpatrick, A. F. (Ed.). *The Cambridge Bible for Schools and Colleges,* Psalms. (Cambridge: Cambridge University Press, 1914), Psalm 101:8.

[117] Benson, Joseph. *The Holy Bible With Notes, Critical, Explanatory and Practical.* (London: J. Kershaw, 1825), Psalm 101:8.

[118] Spence-Jones, H. D. M. (Ed.). *Psalms,* (Vol. 2). (London; New York: Funk & Wagnalls Company, 1909), 361.

[119] Spurgeon, C. H. *The Treasury of David.* (Grand Rapids, Michigan: Kregel Publications, 2004), Psalm 101 (Introduction).

[120] Brooks, K. *Summarized Bible: Complete Summary of the Old Testament.* (Bellingham, WA: Logos Bible Software, 2009), 132.

[121] Kirkpatrick, A. F. (Ed.). *The Cambridge Bible for Schools and Colleges,* Psalms. (Cambridge: Cambridge University Press, 1914), Psalm 101 (Introduction).

[122] Simeon, C. *Horae Homileticae: Psalms, LXXIII–CL* (Vol. 6). (London: Samuel Holdsworth, 1836), 194.

[123] Kirkpatrick, A. F. (Ed.). *The Cambridge Bible for Schools and Colleges,* Psalms. (Cambridge: Cambridge University Press, 1914), Psalm 101 (Introduction).

[124] Jennings, A. C., and W. H. Lowe. *The Psalms, with Introductions and Critical Notes* (Second Edition, Vol. 2). (London: Macmillan and Co., 1885), 170.

[125] Simeon, C. *Horae Homileticae: Psalms, LXXIII–CL* (Vol. 6). (London: Samuel Holdsworth, 1836), 186.

[126] Ibid., 188.

[127] Ibid., 189.

[128] Kirkpatrick, A. F. (Ed.). *The Cambridge Bible for Schools and Colleges,* Psalms. (Cambridge: Cambridge University Press, 1914), Psalm 101:2.

[129] Henry, M. *Matthew Henry's Commentary on the Whole Bible: Complete and Unabridged in One Volume.* (Peabody: Hendrickson, 1994), 887.

[130] Jennings, A. C., and W. H. Lowe. *The Psalms, with Introductions and Critical Notes* (Second Edition, Vol. 2). (London: Macmillan and Co., 1885), 170.

[131] Ibid.

[132] https://biblehub.com/commentaries/psalms/101-3.htm.

[133] Ibid.

[134] Exell, Joseph S. Ed. *The Biblical Illustrator,* Psalm 101:3. From the Free Church Record.

[135] Spurgeon, C. H. *The Treasury of David.* (Grand Rapids, Michigan: Kregel Publications, 2004), Psalm 101:3.

[136] Ibid.

[137] Barnes, Albert. Notes on the Psalms, Critical, Explanatory and Practical. (New York: Harper & Brothers, 1868), Psalm 101:5.

[138] Baggarly, H. M. *Tulia Herald*, Tulia, Texas, Feb. 4, 1954.

[139] Spurgeon, C. H. *The Treasury of David.* (Grand Rapids, Michigan: Kregel Publications, 2004), Psalm 101:6.

[140] Ibid.

[141] Jennings, A. C., and W. H. Lowe. *The Psalms, with Introductions and Critical Notes* (Second Edition, Vol. 2). (London: Macmillan and Co., 1885), 172.

[142] Barnes, Albert. Notes on the Psalms, Critical, Explanatory and Practical. (New York: Harper & Brothers, 1868), Psalm 101:7.

[143] Jennings, A. C., and W. H. Lowe. *The Psalms, with Introductions and Critical Notes* (Second Edition, Vol. 2). (London: Macmillan and Co., 1885), 172.

[144] Spurgeon, C. H. *The Treasury of David.* (Grand Rapids, Michigan: Kregel Publications, 2004), Psalm 101:7.

[145] Ibid.

[146] Henry, M. *Matthew Henry's Commentary on the Whole Bible: Complete and Unabridged in One Volume.* (Peabody: Hendrickson, 1994), 888.

[147] Kirkpatrick, A. F. (Ed.). *The Cambridge Bible for Schools and Colleges,* Psalms. (Cambridge: Cambridge University Press, 1914), Psalm 101 (Introduction).

[148] Barnes, Albert. Notes on the Psalms, Critical, Explanatory and Practical. (New York: Harper & Brothers, 1868), Psalm 102:1.

[149] https://biblehub.com/commentaries/psalms/102-25.htm.

[150] Jennings, A. C., and W. H. Lowe. *The Psalms, with Introductions and Critical Notes* (Second Edition, Vol. 1). (London: Macmillan and Co., 1884), 77.

[151] MacArthur, J., Jr. (Ed.). *The MacArthur Study Bible,* (electronic ed.). (Nashville, TN: Word Pub, 1997), 832.

[152] Gill, John. *The John Gill Exposition of the Entire Bible,* Psalm 102:26.

[153] Spence-Jones, H. D. M. (Ed.). *Psalms,* (Vol. 2). (London; New York: Funk & Wagnalls Company, 1909), 372.

[154] Benson, Joseph. *The Holy Bible With Notes, Critical, Explanatory and Practical.* (London: J. Kershaw, 1825), Psalm 102:26.

[155] Spence-Jones, H. D. M. (Ed.). *Psalms,* (Vol. 2). (London; New York: Funk & Wagnalls Company, 1909), 372.

[156] Barnes, Albert. Notes on the Psalms, Critical, Explanatory and Practical. (New York: Harper & Brothers, 1868), Psalm 102:28.

[157] Ibid.

[158] Benson, Joseph. *The Holy Bible With Notes, Critical, Explanatory and Practical.* (London: J. Kershaw, 1825), Psalm 102:28.

[159] Plumer, W. S. *Studies in the Book of Psalms: Being a Critical and Expository Commentary, with Doctrinal and Practical Remarks on the Entire Psalter.* (Philadelphia; Edinburgh: J. B. Lippincott Company; A & C Black, 1872), 905.

[160] Dilday, R. H., Jr., and J. H. Kennedy. *Psalms.* In H. F. Paschall and H. H. Hobbs (Eds.). *The Teacher's Bible Commentary.* (Nashville: Broadman and Holman Publishers, 1972), 335–336.

[161] Kirkpatrick, A. F. (Ed.). *The Cambridge Bible for Schools and Colleges,* Psalms. (Cambridge: Cambridge University Press, 1914), Psalm 102 (Introduction).

[162] Simeon, C. *Horae Homileticae: Psalms, LXXIII–CL* (Vol. 6). (London: Samuel Holdsworth, 1836), 203.

[163] Plumer, W. S. *Studies in the Book of Psalms: Being a Critical and Expository Commentary, with Doctrinal and Practical Remarks on the Entire Psalter.* (Philadelphia; Edinburgh: J. B. Lippincott Company; A & C Black, 1872), 909–910.

[164] Spence-Jones, H. D. M. (Ed.). *Psalms,* (Vol. 2). (London; New York: Funk & Wagnalls Company, 1909), 380.

[165] Ibid., 381.

[166] Jennings, A. C., and W. H. Lowe. *The Psalms, with Introductions and Critical Notes* (Second Edition, Vol. 2). (London: Macmillan and Co., 1885), 181.

[167] Henry, Matthew. *Matthew Henry's Concise Bible Commentary,* Psalm 102:23–28.

[168] Benson, Joseph. *The Holy Bible With Notes, Critical, Explanatory and Practical.* (London: J. Kershaw, 1825), Psalm 102:27.

[169] Henry, M. *Matthew Henry's Commentary on the Whole Bible: Complete and Unabridged in One Volume.* (Peabody: Hendrickson, 1994), 890.

[170] Spurgeon, C. H. *Morning and Evening,* May 31 (Evening).

[171] Barnes, Albert. Notes on the Psalms, Critical, Explanatory and Practical. (New York: Harper & Brothers, 1868), Psalm 103:1.

[172] Harman, A. *Psalms: A Mentor Commentary (Vol. 1–2).* (Ross-shire, Great Britain: Mentor, 2011), 735–736.

[173] Henry, M. *Matthew Henry's Commentary on the Whole Bible: Complete and Unabridged in One Volume.* (Peabody: Hendrickson, 1994), 890.

[174] Kirkpatrick, A. F. (Ed.). *The Cambridge Bible for Schools and Colleges,* Psalms. (Cambridge: Cambridge University Press, 1914), Psalm 103:1.

[175] Barnes, Albert. Notes on the Psalms, Critical, Explanatory and Practical. (New York: Harper & Brothers, 1868), Psalm 103:1.

[176] Jamieson, R., A. R. Fausset, & D. Brown. *Commentary Critical and Explanatory on the Whole Bible* (Vol. 1). (Oak Harbor, WA: Logos Research Systems, Inc., 1997), Psalm 103:1.

[177] Spurgeon, C. H. *The Treasury of David.* (Grand Rapids, Michigan: Kregel Publications, 2004), Psalm 103:1.

[178] Spence-Jones, H. D. M. (Ed.). *Psalms,* (Vol. 2). (London; New York: Funk & Wagnalls Company, 1909), 382.

[179] Swanson, J. *Dictionary of Biblical Languages with Semantic Domains: Hebrew (Old Testament)* (electronic ed.). (Oak Harbor: Logos Research Systems, Inc., 1997).

[180] Harman, A. *Psalms: A Mentor Commentary (Vol. 1–2).* (Ross-shire, Great Britain: Mentor, 2011), 736.

[181] Benson, Joseph. *The Holy Bible With Notes, Critical, Explanatory and Practical.* (London: J. Kershaw, 1825), Psalm 103:4.

[182] Swanson, J. *Dictionary of Biblical Languages with Semantic Domains: Hebrew (Old Testament)* (electronic ed.). (Oak Harbor: Logos Research Systems, Inc., 1997).

[183] Vine, W. E., M. F. Unger, and W. White, Jr. *Vine's Complete Expository Dictionary of Old and New Testament Words* (Vol. 1). (Nashville: T. Nelson, 1996), 142.

[184] Swanson, J. *Dictionary of Biblical Languages with Semantic Domains: Hebrew (Old Testament)* (electronic ed.). (Oak Harbor: Logos Research Systems, Inc., 1997).

[185] https://biblehub.com/commentaries/psalms/103-5.htm.

[186] Spurgeon, C. H. *The Treasury of David.* (Grand Rapids, Michigan: Kregel Publications, 2004), Psalm 103:5.

[187] Spence-Jones, H. D. M. (Ed.). *Psalms,* (Vol. 2). (London; New York: Funk & Wagnalls Company, 1909), 382.

[188] Ibid.

[189] Swanson, J. *Dictionary of Biblical Languages with Semantic Domains: Hebrew (Old Testament)* (electronic ed.). (Oak Harbor: Logos Research Systems, Inc., 1997).

[190] Barnes, Albert. Notes on the Psalms, Critical, Explanatory and Practical. (New York: Harper & Brothers, 1868), Psalm 105:6.

[191] Spurgeon, C. H. *The Treasury of David.* (Grand Rapids, Michigan: Kregel Publications, 2004), Psalm 103:7.

[192] Gill, John. *The John Gill Exposition of the Entire Bible,* Psalm 103:7.

[193] Swanson, J. *Dictionary of Biblical Languages with Semantic Domains: Hebrew (Old Testament)* (electronic ed.). (Oak Harbor: Logos Research Systems, Inc., 1997).

[194] Barnes, Albert. Notes on the Psalms, Critical, Explanatory and Practical. (New York: Harper & Brothers, 1868), Psalms 103:9.

[195] Gill, John. *The John Gill Exposition of the Entire Bible,* Psalm 103:11.

[196] Barnes, Albert. Notes on the Psalms, Critical, Explanatory and Practical. (New York: Harper & Brothers, 1868), Psalm 103:11.

[197] https://biblehub.com/commentaries/psalms/103-12.htm.

[198] Barnes, Albert. Notes on the Psalms, Critical, Explanatory and Practical. (New York: Harper & Brothers, 1868), Psalm 103:12.

[199] The Spurgeon Study Bible. (Nashville: Holman Bible Publishers, 2017), 777.

[200] Kirkpatrick, A. F. (Ed.). The Cambridge Bible for Schools and Colleges, Psalms. (Cambridge: Cambridge University Press, 1914), Psalm 103 (Introduction).

[201] Jennings, A. C., and W. H. Lowe. The Psalms, with Introductions and Critical Notes (Second Edition, Vol. 2). (London: Macmillan and Co., 1885), 182.

[202] Dilday, R. H., Jr., and J. H. Kennedy. Psalms. In H. F. Paschall and H. H. Hobbs (Eds.). The Teacher's Bible Commentary. (Nashville: Broadman and Holman Publishers, 1972), 336.

[203] Spurgeon, C. H. The Treasury of David. (Grand Rapids, Michigan: Kregel Publications, 2004), Psalm 103 (Introduction).

[204] Ibid.

[205] Henry, M. Matthew Henry's Commentary on the Whole Bible: Complete and Unabridged in One Volume. (Peabody: Hendrickson, 1994), 890.

[206] Horne, G. A Commentary on the Book of Psalms. (New York: Robert Carter & Brothers, 1856), 363.

[207] Plumer, W. S. Studies in the Book of Psalms: Being a Critical and Expository Commentary, with Doctrinal and Practical Remarks on the Entire Psalter. (Philadelphia; Edinburgh: J. B. Lippincott Company; A & C Black, 1872), 914.

[208] Spurgeon, C. H. "The Keynote of the Year" (Sermon delivered March 7, 1889).

[209] Hutson, Curtis. Great Preaching on Thanksgiving. (Murfreesboro: Sword of the Lord Publishers, 1987), 67–68.

[210] Benson, Joseph. The Holy Bible With Notes, Critical, Explanatory and Practical. (London: J. Kershaw, 1825), Psalm 103:2.

[211] Plumer, W. S. Studies in the Book of Psalms: Being a Critical and Expository Commentary, with Doctrinal and Practical Remarks on the Entire Psalter. (Philadelphia; Edinburgh: J. B. Lippincott Company; A & C Black, 1872), 914.

[212] Ibid.

[213] Alexander, J. A. The Psalms Translated and Explained. (Edinburgh: Andrew Elliot; James Thin, 1864), 415.

[214] Gill, John. The John Gill Exposition of the Entire Bible, Psalm 103:4.

[215] Alexander, J. A. The Psalms Translated and Explained. (Edinburgh: Andrew Elliot; James Thin, 1864), 415.

[216] Henry, M. Matthew Henry's Commentary on the Whole Bible: Complete and Unabridged in One Volume. (Peabody: Hendrickson, 1994), 890.

[217] Gill, John. The John Gill Exposition of the Entire Bible, Psalm 103:5.

[218] Henry, M. *Matthew Henry's Commentary on the Whole Bible: Complete and Unabridged in One Volume.* (Peabody: Hendrickson, 1994), 890.

[219] Plumer, W. S. *Studies in the Book of Psalms: Being a Critical and Expository Commentary, with Doctrinal and Practical Remarks on the Entire Psalter.* (Philadelphia; Edinburgh: J. B. Lippincott Company; A & C Black, 1872), 914–915.

[220] *The Spurgeon Study Bible.* (Nashville: Holman Bible Publishers, 2017), 776.

[221] Alexander, J. A. *The Psalms Translated and Explained.* (Edinburgh: Andrew Elliot; James Thin, 1864), 416.

[222] Plumer, W. S. *Studies in the Book of Psalms: Being a Critical and Expository Commentary, with Doctrinal and Practical Remarks on the Entire Psalter.* (Philadelphia; Edinburgh: J. B. Lippincott Company; A & C Black, 1872), 918.

[223] Cowman, L. B. *Streams in the Desert,* (Grand Rapids: Zondervan, 1999), January 3.

[224] Spurgeon. C. H. "The Keynote of the Year" (Sermon delivered March 7, 1889).

[225] Walsh, J. W. *Old Testament Teaching.* (Nashville: Broadman Press, 1967), 171.

[226] Smith, James. *Handfuls on Purpose,* Vol. 4, Series Twelve, 257.

[227] Plumer, W. S. *Studies in the Book of Psalms: Being a Critical and Expository Commentary, with Doctrinal and Practical Remarks on the Entire Psalter.* (Philadelphia; Edinburgh: J. B. Lippincott Company; A & C Black, 1872), 917.

[228] "30 Christian Quotes about Thankfulness." https://www.crosswalk.com/faith/spiritual-life/inspiring-quotes/30-christian-quotes-about-thankfulness.html, accessed June 22, 2018.

[229] Simeon, C. *Horae Homileticae: Psalms, LXXIII–CL* (Vol. 6). (London: Samuel Holdsworth, 1836), 206.

[230] Kirkpatrick, A. F. (Ed.). *The Cambridge Bible for Schools and Colleges,* Psalms. (Cambridge: Cambridge University Press, 1914), Psalm 104:24.

[231] Swanson, J. *Dictionary of Biblical Languages with Semantic Domains: Hebrew (Old Testament)* (electronic ed.). (Oak Harbor: Logos Research Systems, Inc., 1997).

[232] Williams, D., and L. J. Ogilvie. *Psalms 73–150* (Vol. 14). (Nashville: Thomas Nelson Inc., 1989), 239.

[233] Benson, Joseph. *The Holy Bible With Notes, Critical, Explanatory and Practical.* (London: J. Kershaw, 1825), Psalm 104:24.

[234] Gill, John. *The John Gill Exposition of the Entire Bible,* Psalm 104:24.

[235] Williams, D., and L. J. Ogilvie. *Psalms 73–150* (Vol. 14). (Nashville: Thomas Nelson Inc., 1989), 239.

[236] Clarke, Adam. *Clarkes' Commentary and Critical Notes,* Psalm 104:24.

[237] Benson, Joseph. *The Holy Bible With Notes, Critical, Explanatory and Practical.* (London: J. Kershaw, 1825), Psalm 104:24.

[238] Gesenius, W., and S. P. Tregelles. *Gesenius' Hebrew and Chaldee Lexicon to the Old Testament Scriptures.* (Bellingham, WA: Logos Bible Software, 2003), 735.

[239] Bratcher, R. G. and W. D. Reyburn. *A Translator's Handbook on the Book of Psalms.* (New York: United Bible Societies, 1991), 886.

[240] Barnes, Albert. Notes on the Psalms, Critical, Explanatory and Practical. (New York: Harper & Brothers, 1868), Psalm 104:24.

[241] Spence-Jones, H. D. M. (Ed.). *Psalms,* (Vol. 2). (London; New York: Funk & Wagnalls Company, 1909), 399.

[242] Jennings, A. C., and W. H. Lowe. *The Psalms, with Introductions and Critical Notes* (Second Edition, Vol. 2). (London: Macmillan and Co., 1885), 187.

[243] Bontrager, Krista Kay with Fazale Rana. "Psalm 104: A Poetic View of Creation," excerpted from "Psalm 104: In Wisdom You Made Them All." http://www.reasons.org, accessed December 11, 2013.

[244] MacArthur, J., Jr. (Ed.). *The MacArthur Study Bible,* (electronic ed.). (Nashville, TN: Word Pub, 1997), 834.

[245] https://www.vocabulary.com/dictionary/eulogium, accessed November 11, 2018.

[246] Jennings, A. C., and W. H. Lowe. *The Psalms, with Introductions and Critical Notes* (Second Edition, Vol. 2). (London: Macmillan and Co., 1885), 188.

[247] Williams, D., and L. J. Ogilvie. *Psalms 73–150* (Vol. 14). (Nashville: Thomas Nelson Inc., 1989), 232.

[248] Ross, A. P. in Gaebelein, Frank E., ed. *The Expositor's Bible Commentary,* (Vol. 5), Proverbs. (Grand Rapids: Zondervan, 1991), 919.

[249] Marilyn Adamson. Is there a God?, http://www.leaderu.com/everystudent/isthere/isthere2.html, accessed June 23, 2018.

[250] Ibid.

[251] Bridges, Charles. *Exposition of the Book of Proverbs.* (New York: Robert Carter, 1847), 32.

[252] Williams, D., and L. J. Ogilvie. *Psalms 73–150* (Vol. 14). (Nashville: Thomas Nelson Inc., 1989), 233.

[253] Adapted. Source unknown.

[254] Spurgeon, C. H. *The Treasury of David.* (Grand Rapids, Michigan: Kregel Publications, 2004), Psalm 104:24.

[255] Henry, M. *Matthew Henry's Commentary on the Whole Bible: Complete and Unabridged in One Volume.* (Peabody: Hendrickson, 1994), 961.

[256] Swanson, J. *Dictionary of Biblical Languages with Semantic Domains: Hebrew (Old Testament)* (electronic ed.). (Oak Harbor: Logos Research Systems, Inc., 1997).

[257] Spurgeon, C. H. *The Treasury of David.* (Grand Rapids, Michigan: Kregel Publications, 2004), Psalm 105:1.

[258] Barnes, Albert. Notes on the Psalms, Critical, Explanatory and Practical. (New York: Harper & Brothers, 1868), Psalm 105:1.

[259] Swanson, J. *Dictionary of Biblical Languages with Semantic Domains: Hebrew (Old Testament)* (electronic ed.). (Oak Harbor: Logos Research Systems, Inc., 1997).

[260] Benson, Joseph. *The Holy Bible With Notes, Critical, Explanatory and Practical.* (London: J. Kershaw, 1825), Psalm 105:1.

[261] Vine, W. E., M. F. Unger, and W. White, Jr. *Vine's Complete Expository Dictionary of Old and New Testament Words* (Vol. 1). (Nashville: T. Nelson, 1996), 234.

[262] Swanson, J. *Dictionary of Biblical Languages with Semantic Domains: Hebrew (Old Testament)* (electronic ed.). (Oak Harbor: Logos Research Systems, Inc., 1997).

[263] Clarke, Adam. *Clarkes' Commentary and Critical Notes*, Psalm 105:2.

[264] Swanson, J. *Dictionary of Biblical Languages with Semantic Domains: Hebrew (Old Testament)* (electronic ed.). (Oak Harbor: Logos Research Systems, Inc., 1997).

[265] Clarke, Adam. *Clarkes' Commentary and Critical Notes*, Psalm 105:3.

[266] Vine, W. E., M. F. Unger, and W. White, Jr. *Vine's Complete Expository Dictionary of Old and New Testament Words* (Vol. 1). (Nashville: T. Nelson, 1996), 220.

[267] Swanson, J. *Dictionary of Biblical Languages with Semantic Domains: Hebrew (Old Testament)* (electronic ed.). (Oak Harbor: Logos Research Systems, Inc., 1997).

[268] Jamieson, R., A. R. Fausset, & D. Brown. *Commentary Critical and Explanatory on the Whole Bible* (Vol. 1). (Oak Harbor, WA: Logos Research Systems, Inc., 1997), Psalm 105:3–4.

[269] Spurgeon, C. H. *The Treasury of David.* (Grand Rapids, Michigan: Kregel Publications, 2004), Psalm 105:4.

[270] Barnes, Albert. Notes on the Psalms, Critical, Explanatory and Practical. (New York: Harper & Brothers, 1868), Psalm 105:4.

[271] Benson, Joseph. *The Holy Bible With Notes, Critical, Explanatory and Practical.* (London: J. Kershaw, 1825), Psalm 105:1–4.

[272] Gill, John. *The John Gill Exposition of the Entire Bible,* Psalm 105:5.

[273] Plumer, W. S. *Studies in the Book of Psalms: Being a Critical and Expository Commentary, with Doctrinal and Practical Remarks on the Entire Psalter.* (Philadelphia; Edinburgh: J. B. Lippincott Company; A & C Black, 1872), 932.

[274] Brown, F., S. R. Driver, and C. A. Briggs. *Enhanced Brown-Driver-Briggs Hebrew and English Lexicon.* (Oxford: Clarendon Press, 1977), 810.

[275] Plumer, W. S. *Studies in the Book of Psalms: Being a Critical and Expository Commentary, with Doctrinal and Practical Remarks on the Entire Psalter.* (Philadelphia; Edinburgh: J. B. Lippincott Company; A & C Black, 1872), 937.

[276] Spence-Jones, H. D. M. (Ed.). *Psalms,* (Vol. 2). (London; New York: Funk & Wagnalls Company, 1909), 414.

[277] Kirkpatrick, A. F. (Ed.). *The Cambridge Bible for Schools and Colleges,* Psalms. (Cambridge: Cambridge University Press, 1914), Psalm 105:5.

[278] Clarke, Adam. *Clarkes' Commentary and Critical Notes,* Psalm 105 (Introduction).

[279] Kirkpatrick, A. F. (Ed.). *The Cambridge Bible for Schools and Colleges,* Psalms. (Cambridge: Cambridge University Press, 1914), Psalm 105 (Introduction).

[280] Jennings, A. C., and W. H. Lowe. *The Psalms, with Introductions and Critical Notes* (Second Edition, Vol. 2). (London: Macmillan and Co., 1885), 200.

[281] Clarke, Adam. *Clarkes' Commentary and Critical Notes,* Psalm 105:3.

[282] Gill, John. *The John Gill Exposition of the Entire Bible,* Psalm 105:2.

[283] Spurgeon, C. H. *The Treasury of David.* (Grand Rapids, Michigan: Kregel Publications, 2004), Psalm 105:1.

[284] Jennings, A. C., and W. H. Lowe. *The Psalms, with Introductions and Critical Notes* (Second Edition, Vol. 2). (London: Macmillan and Co., 1885), 203.

[285] Kirkpatrick, A. F. (Ed.). *The Cambridge Bible for Schools and Colleges,* Psalms. (Cambridge: Cambridge University Press, 1914), Psalm 105:19.

[286] Plumer, W. S. *Studies in the Book of Psalms: Being a Critical and Expository Commentary, with Doctrinal and Practical Remarks on the Entire Psalter.* (Philadelphia; Edinburgh: J. B. Lippincott Company; A & C Black, 1872), 933.

[287] Jennings, A. C., and W. H. Lowe. *The Psalms, with Introductions and Critical Notes* (Second Edition, Vol. 2). (London: Macmillan and Co., 1885), 203.

[288] Kirkpatrick, A. F. (Ed.). *The Cambridge Bible for Schools and Colleges,* Psalms. (Cambridge: Cambridge University Press, 1914), Psalm 105:19.

[289] Plumer, W. S. *Studies in the Book of Psalms: Being a Critical and Expository Commentary, with Doctrinal and Practical Remarks on the Entire Psalter.* (Philadelphia; Edinburgh: J. B. Lippincott Company; A & C Black, 1872), 933–934.

[290] Clarke, Adam. *Clarkes' Commentary and Critical Notes,* Psalm 105:19.

[291] Maclaren, Alexander. *The Expositor's Bible:* The Psalms. (New York: Scriptura Press, 2015), Psalm 105:19.

[292] Ibid.

[293] Ibid.

[294] Ibid.

[295] Spurgeon, C. H. *The Treasury of David.* (Grand Rapids, Michigan: Kregel Publications, 2004), Psalm 105:19.

[296] Henry, M. *Matthew Henry's Commentary on the Whole Bible: Complete and Unabridged in One Volume.* (Peabody: Hendrickson, 1994), 895.

[297] Spence-Jones, H. D. M. (Ed.). *Psalms,* (Vol. 2). (London; New York: Funk & Wagnalls Company, 1909), 420.

[298] Gesenius, W., and S. P. Tregelles. *Gesenius' Hebrew and Chaldee Lexicon to the Old Testament Scriptures.* (Bellingham, WA: Logos Bible Software, 2003), 271.

[299] Kirkpatrick, A. F. (Ed.). *The Cambridge Bible for Schools and Colleges,* Psalms. (Cambridge: Cambridge University Press, 1914), Psalm 106:7.

[300] Barnes, Albert. Notes on the Psalms, Critical, Explanatory and Practical. (New York: Harper & Brothers, 1868), Psalm 106:6.

[301] Spence-Jones, H. D. M. (Ed.). *Psalms,* (Vol. 2). (London; New York: Funk & Wagnalls Company, 1909), 426.

[302] Strong, J. *The New Strong's Dictionary of Hebrew and Greek Words.* (Nashville: Thomas Nelson, 1996).

[303] Swanson, J. *Dictionary of Biblical Languages with Semantic Domains: Hebrew (Old Testament)* (electronic ed.). (Oak Harbor: Logos Research Systems, Inc., 1997).

[304] Barnes, Albert. Notes on the Psalms, Critical, Explanatory and Practical. (New York: Harper & Brothers, 1868), Psalm 106:7.

[305] Spence-Jones, H. D. M. (Ed.). *Psalms,* (Vol. 2). (London; New York: Funk & Wagnalls Company, 1909), 426.

[306] Swanson, J. *Dictionary of Biblical Languages with Semantic Domains: Hebrew (Old Testament)* (electronic ed.). (Oak Harbor: Logos Research Systems, Inc., 1997).

[307] Swanson, J. *Dictionary of Biblical Languages with Semantic Domains: Hebrew (Old Testament)* (electronic ed.). (Oak Harbor: Logos Research Systems, Inc., 1997).

[308] https://biblehub.com/commentaries/psalms/106-8.htm.

[309] Gill, John. *The John Gill Exposition of the Entire Bible,* Psalm 107:8.

[310] Spurgeon, C. H. *The Treasury of David.* (Grand Rapids, Michigan: Kregel Publications, 2004), Psalm 107:9.

[311] Spence-Jones, H. D. M. (Ed.). *Psalms,* (Vol. 2). (London; New York: Funk & Wagnalls Company, 1909), 426.

[312] Spurgeon, C. H. *The Treasury of David.* (Grand Rapids, Michigan: Kregel Publications, 2004), Psalm 107:9.

[313] Spence-Jones, H. D. M. (Ed.). *Psalms,* (Vol. 2). (London; New York: Funk & Wagnalls Company, 1909), 426.

[314] Gill, John. *The John Gill Exposition of the Entire Bible,* Psalm 106:10.

[315] Barnes, Albert. Notes on the Psalms, Critical, Explanatory and Practical. (New York: Harper & Brothers, 1868), Psalm 106:7.

[316] Kirkpatrick, A. F. (Ed.). *The Cambridge Bible for Schools and Colleges,* Psalms. (Cambridge: Cambridge University Press, 1914), Psalm 106:7.

[317] Barnes, Albert. Notes on the Psalms, Critical, Explanatory and Practical. (New York: Harper & Brothers, 1868), Psalm 106:8.

[318] Spence-Jones, H. D. M. (Ed.). *Psalms,* (Vol. 2). (London; New York: Funk & Wagnalls Company, 1909), 431.

[319] Chambers, Oswald. *My Utmost For His Highest,* February 11.

[320] Harman, A. *Psalms: A Mentor Commentary (Vol. 1–2).* (Ross-shire, Great Britain: Mentor, 2011), 774.

[321] Swanson, J. *Dictionary of Biblical Languages with Semantic Domains: Hebrew (Old Testament)* (electronic ed.). (Oak Harbor: Logos Research Systems, Inc., 1997).

[322] Vine, W. E., M. F. Unger, and W. White, Jr. *Vine's Complete Expository Dictionary of Old and New Testament Words* (Vol. 1). (Nashville: T. Nelson, 1996), 216.

[323] Barnes, Albert. Notes on the Psalms, Critical, Explanatory and Practical. (New York: Harper & Brothers, 1868), Psalm 107:2.

[324] Plumer, W. S. *Studies in the Book of Psalms: Being a Critical and Expository Commentary, with Doctrinal and Practical Remarks on the Entire Psalter.* (Philadelphia; Edinburgh: J. B. Lippincott Company; A & C Black, 1872), 953.

[325] Harman, A. *Psalms: A Mentor Commentary (Vol. 1–2).* (Ross-shire, Great Britain: Mentor, 2011), 774.

[326] Spurgeon, C. H. *The Treasury of David.* (Grand Rapids, Michigan: Kregel Publications, 2004), (Introduction).

[327] Simeon, C. *Horae Homileticae: Psalms, LXXIII–CL* (Vol. 6). (London: Samuel Holdsworth, 1836), 238–239.

[328] Plumer, W. S. *Studies in the Book of Psalms: Being a Critical and Expository Commentary, with Doctrinal and Practical Remarks on the Entire Psalter.* (Philadelphia; Edinburgh: J. B. Lippincott Company; A & C Black, 1872), 954.

[329] Spurgeon, C. H. *The Treasury of David.* (Grand Rapids, Michigan: Kregel Publications, 2004), Psalm 107:2.

[330] Exell, Joseph S. Ed. *The Biblical Illustrator,* Psalm 107:2. T. De Witt Talmage ("Say So").

[331] Barnes, Albert. Notes on the Psalms, Critical, Explanatory and Practical. (New York: Harper & Brothers, 1868), Psalm 107:2.

[332] Exell, Joseph S. Ed. *The Biblical Illustrator,* Psalm 119:46. Joseph Parker ("Guilty Silence").

[333] Nichols, J. W. H. *Musings in the Psalms.* (Galaxie Software, 2005), 71.

[334] Ibid.

[335] Simeon, C. *Horae Homileticae: Psalms, LXXIII–CL* (Vol. 6). (London: Samuel Holdsworth, 1836), 240.

[336] Henry, M. *Matthew Henry's Commentary on the Whole Bible: Complete and Unabridged in One Volume.* (Peabody: Hendrickson, 1994), 899.

[337] Plumer, W. S. *Studies in the Book of Psalms: Being a Critical and Expository Commentary, with Doctrinal and Practical Remarks on the Entire Psalter.* (Philadelphia; Edinburgh: J. B. Lippincott Company; A & C Black, 1872), 960.

[338] Henry, M. *Matthew Henry's Commentary on the Whole Bible: Complete and Unabridged in One Volume.* (Peabody: Hendrickson, 1994), 901.

[339] Kirkpatrick, A. F. (Ed.). *The Cambridge Bible for Schools and Colleges,* Psalms. (Cambridge: Cambridge University Press, 1914), Psalm 108:2.

[340] Boice, J. M. *Psalms 107–150: An Expositional Commentary.* (Grand Rapids, MI: Baker Books, 2005), 878.

[341] Clarke, Adam. *Clarkes' Commentary and Critical Notes,* Psalm 108 (Introduction).

[342] Bounds, E. M. *Power through Prayer.* (Scotts Valley, Cal.: CreateSpace, 2009), 50.

[343] Rogers, Adrian. "How to Have a Meaningful Quiet Time." Lwf.org, accessed March 12, 2011.

[344] Spurgeon, C. H. *Morning and Evening,* October 12.

[345] Barnes, Albert. Notes on the Psalms, Critical, Explanatory and Practical. (New York: Harper & Brothers, 1868), Psalm 109:21.

[346] Kirkpatrick, A. F. (Ed.). *The Cambridge Bible for Schools and Colleges,* Psalms. (Cambridge: Cambridge University Press, 1914), Psalm 109:21.

[347] Barnes, Albert. Notes on the Psalms, Critical, Explanatory and Practical. (New York: Harper & Brothers, 1868), Psalm 109:21.

[348] Gill, John. *The John Gill Exposition of the Entire Bible,* Psalm 109:21.

[349] Holladay, W. L., and L. Köhler. A Concise Hebrew and Aramaic Lexicon of the Old Testament. (Leiden: Brill, 2000), 278.

[350] Gesenius, W., and S. P. Tregelles. *Gesenius' Hebrew and Chaldee Lexicon to the Old Testament Scriptures.* (Bellingham, WA: Logos Bible Software, 2003), 5.

[351] Spence-Jones, H. D. M. (Ed.). *Psalms,* (Vol. 3). (London; New York: Funk & Wagnalls Company, 1909), 22.

[352] Bratcher, R. G. and W. D. Reyburn. *A Translator's Handbook on the Book of Psalms.* (New York: United Bible Societies, 1991), 944.

[353] Swanson, J. *Dictionary of Biblical Languages with Semantic Domains: Hebrew (Old Testament)* (electronic ed.). (Oak Harbor: Logos Research Systems, Inc., 1997).

[354] Barnes, Albert. Notes on the Psalms, Critical, Explanatory and Practical. (New York: Harper & Brothers, 1868), Psalm 109:22.

[355] https://biblehub.com/commentaries/psalms/109-22.htm.

[356] https://biblehub.com/psalms/109-23.htm.

[357] Spence-Jones, H. D. M. (Ed.). *Psalms,* (Vol. 2). (London; New York: Funk & Wagnalls Company, 1909), 22.

[358] Plumer, W. S. *Studies in the Book of Psalms: Being a Critical and Expository Commentary, with Doctrinal and Practical Remarks on the Entire Psalter.* (Philadelphia; Edinburgh: J. B. Lippincott Company; A & C Black, 1872), 968.

[359] Holladay, W. L., and L. Köhler. A Concise Hebrew and Aramaic Lexicon of the Old Testament. (Leiden: Brill, 2000), 241.

[360] Gill, John. *The John Gill Exposition of the Entire Bible,* Psalm 109:23.

[361] Bratcher, R. G. and W. D. Reyburn. *A Translator's Handbook on the Book of Psalms.* (New York: United Bible Societies, 1991), 944.

[362] Gill, John. *The John Gill Exposition of the Entire Bible,* Psalm 109:24.

[363] Barnes, Albert. Notes on the Psalms, Critical, Explanatory and Practical. (New York: Harper & Brothers, 1868), Psalm 109:24.

[364] Kirkpatrick, A. F. (Ed.). *The Cambridge Bible for Schools and Colleges,* Psalms. (Cambridge: Cambridge University Press, 1914), Psalm 109:24.

[365] Bratcher, R. G. and W. D. Reyburn. *A Translator's Handbook on the Book of Psalms.* (New York: United Bible Societies, 1991), 944–945.

[366] Swanson, J. *Dictionary of Biblical Languages with Semantic Domains: Hebrew (Old Testament)* (electronic ed.). (Oak Harbor: Logos Research Systems, Inc., 1997).

[367] Spurgeon, C. H. *The Treasury of David.* (Grand Rapids, Michigan: Kregel Publications, 2004), Psalm 109:25.

[368] Spence-Jones, H. D. M. (Ed.). *Psalms,* (Vol. 3). (London; New York: Funk & Wagnalls Company, 1909), 22.

[369] Plumer, W. S. *Studies in the Book of Psalms: Being a Critical and Expository Commentary, with Doctrinal and Practical Remarks on the Entire Psalter.* (Philadelphia; Edinburgh: J. B. Lippincott Company; A & C Black, 1872), 964–965.

[370] Henry, M. *Matthew Henry's Commentary on the Whole Bible: Complete and Unabridged in One Volume.* (Peabody: Hendrickson, 1994), 901.

[371] Plumer, W. S. *Studies in the Book of Psalms: Being a Critical and Expository Commentary, with Doctrinal and Practical Remarks on the Entire Psalter.* (Philadelphia; Edinburgh: J. B. Lippincott Company; A & C Black, 1872), 964.

[372] Henry, M. *Matthew Henry's Commentary on the Whole Bible: Complete and Unabridged in One Volume.* (Peabody: Hendrickson, 1994), 902.

[373] Spurgeon, C. H. *The Treasury of David.* (Grand Rapids, Michigan: Kregel Publications, 2004), Psalm 109 (Introduction).

[374] Bratcher, R. G. and W. D. Reyburn. *A Translator's Handbook on the Book of Psalms.* (New York: United Bible Societies, 1991), 942.

[375] Ross, A. P. In Walvoord, J. F. and R. B. Zuck (Eds.). *The Bible Knowledge Commentary: An Exposition of the Scriptures* (Vol. 1, Psalms). (Wheaton, IL: Victor Books, 1985), 788.

[376] Spurgeon, C. H. *The Treasury of David.* (Grand Rapids, Michigan: Kregel Publications, 2004), Psalm 109 (Introduction).

[377] Plumer, W. S. *Studies in the Book of Psalms: Being a Critical and Expository Commentary, with Doctrinal and Practical Remarks on the Entire Psalter.* (Philadelphia; Edinburgh: J. B. Lippincott Company; A & C Black, 1872), 965.

[378] Keller, Tim. "THE WOUNDED SPIRIT," Preached in Manhattan, N.Y., on December 5, 2004. https://verticallivingministries.com/2014/01/08/tim-keller-on-the-wounded-spirit-proverbs-series/, accessed June 30, 2018.

[379] Spurgeon, C. H. *The Treasury of David.* (Grand Rapids, Michigan: Kregel Publications, 2004), Psalm 109:22.

[380] Spurgeon, C.H. "Healing for the Wounded." November 11, 1855. http://www.spurgeon.org, accessed June 28, 2014.

[381] Graham, Billy. *Storm Warning.* (Dallas: Word, 1992), 40.

[382] Spurgeon, C. H. *Psalms.* (Wheaton, IL: Crossway Books, 1993), 127.

[383] https://www.lwf.org/products/b122, accessed June 30, 2018.

[384] Jamieson, R., A. R. Fausset, & D. Brown. *Commentary Critical and Explanatory on the Whole Bible* (Vol. 1). (Oak Harbor, WA: Logos Research Systems, Inc., 1997), Psalm 110:1.

[385] Spence-Jones, H. D. M. (Ed.). *Psalms,* (Vol. 3). (London; New York: Funk & Wagnalls Company, 1909), 29.

[386] Spurgeon, C. H. *The Treasury of David.* (Grand Rapids, Michigan: Kregel Publications, 2004), Psalm 110:1.

[387] Henry, M. *Matthew Henry's Commentary on the Whole Bible: Complete and Unabridged in One Volume.* (Peabody: Hendrickson, 1994), 903.

[388] Plumer, W. S. *Studies in the Book of Psalms: Being a Critical and Expository Commentary, with Doctrinal and Practical Remarks on the Entire Psalter.* (Philadelphia; Edinburgh: J. B. Lippincott Company; A & C Black, 1872), 973.

[389] Spence-Jones, H. D. M. (Ed.). *Psalms,* (Vol. 3). (London; New York: Funk & Wagnalls Company, 1909), 29.

[390] Spurgeon, C. H. *The Treasury of David.* (Grand Rapids, Michigan: Kregel Publications, 2004), Psalm 110:1.

[391] Spence-Jones, H. D. M. (Ed.). *Psalms,* (Vol. 3). (London; New York: Funk & Wagnalls Company, 1909), 29.

[392] Benson, Joseph. *The Holy Bible With Notes, Critical, Explanatory and Practical.* (London: J. Kershaw, 1825), Psalm 110:2.

[393] Gill, John. *The John Gill Exposition of the Entire Bible,* Psalm 110:2.

[394] Benson, Joseph. *The Holy Bible With Notes, Critical, Explanatory and Practical.* (London: J. Kershaw, 1825), Psalm 110:2.

[395] Jamieson, R., A. R. Fausset, & D. Brown. *Commentary Critical and Explanatory on the Whole Bible* (Vol. 1). (Oak Harbor, WA: Logos Research Systems, Inc., 1997), Psalm 110:3.

[396] Hindson, E. E., and W. M. Kroll, (eds.). *KJV Bible Commentary.* (Nashville: Thomas Nelson, 1994), 1136.

[397] Spence-Jones, H. D. M. (Ed.). *Psalms,* (Vol. 3). (London; New York: Funk & Wagnalls Company, 1909), 29.

[398] Hindson, E. E., and W. M. Kroll, (eds.). *KJV Bible Commentary.* (Nashville: Thomas Nelson, 1994), 1136.

[399] Benson, Joseph. *The Holy Bible With Notes, Critical, Explanatory and Practical.* (London: J. Kershaw, 1825), Psalm 110:4.

[400] *The Spurgeon Study Bible.* (Nashville: Holman Bible Publishers, 2017), 786.

[401] Barnes, Albert. Notes on the Psalms, Critical, Explanatory and Practical. (New York: Harper & Brothers, 1868), Psalm 110:5.

[402] Spence-Jones, H. D. M. (Ed.). *Psalms,* (Vol. 3). (London; New York: Funk & Wagnalls Company, 1909), 29.

[403] Spurgeon, C. H. *The Treasury of David.* (Grand Rapids, Michigan: Kregel Publications, 2004), Psalm 110:6.

[404] Gill, John. *The John Gill Exposition of the Entire Bible,* Psalm 110:6.

[405] Henry, M. *Matthew Henry's Commentary on the Whole Bible: Complete and Unabridged in One Volume.* (Peabody: Hendrickson, 1994), 904.

[406] Kirkpatrick, A. F. (Ed.). *The Cambridge Bible for Schools and Colleges,* Psalms. (Cambridge: Cambridge University Press, 1914), Psalm 110:7.

[407] Bratcher, R. G. and W. D. Reyburn. *A Translator's Handbook on the Book of Psalms.* (New York: United Bible Societies, 1991), 947.

[408] Spence-Jones, H. D. M. (Ed.). *Psalms,* (Vol. 3). (London; New York: Funk & Wagnalls Company, 1909), 29.

[409] Jamieson, R., A. R. Fausset, & D. Brown. *Commentary Critical and Explanatory on the Whole Bible* (Vol. 1). (Oak Harbor, WA: Logos Research Systems, Inc., 1997), Psalm 110:1–7.

[410] Horne, G. *A Commentary on the Book of Psalms.* (New York: Robert Carter & Brothers, 1856), 403.

[411] Jennings, A. C., and W. H. Lowe. *The Psalms, with Introductions and Critical Notes* (Second Edition, Vol. 2). (London: Macmillan and Co., 1885), 240.

[412] Simeon, C. *Horae Homileticae: Psalms, LXXIII–CL* (Vol. 6). (London: Samuel Holdsworth, 1836), 251.

[413] Spurgeon, C. H. *The Treasury of David.* (Grand Rapids, Michigan: Kregel Publications, 2004), Psalm 110 (Introduction).

414 Lockyer, Herbert, Sr. *Psalms: A Devotional Commentary,* Psalm 110. (Grand Rapids: Kregel Publications, 1993), Introduction.

415 Luther's Table Talk. "Of God's Word," Section XXVII. https://www.ccel.org/ccel/luther/tabletalk.v.i.html, accessed July 1, 2018.

416 Plumer, W. S. *Studies in the Book of Psalms: Being a Critical and Expository Commentary, with Doctrinal and Practical Remarks on the Entire Psalter.* (Philadelphia; Edinburgh: J. B. Lippincott Company; A & C Black, 1872), 973.

417 Wilcock, Michael. *The Message of Psalms 73–150.* (Downers Grove, IL: InterVarsity Press, 2001), 163.

418 Ogilvie, Lloyd J. (General Editor). *The Preacher's Commentary: Psalms 73 – 150.* (Nashville: Thomas Nelson Publishers, 1989), 289.

419 Hughes, R. B., and J. C. Laney. *Tyndale Concise Bible Commentary.* (Wheaton, IL: Tyndale House Publishers, 2001), 223.

420 Ibid.

421 Lockyer, Herbert, Sr. *Psalms: A Devotional Commentary,* Psalm 110. (Grand Rapids: Kregel Publications, 1993), Psalm 110:1.

422 Ibid.

423 Walvoord, John F. "The Second Coming of Christ and the Millennial Kingdom," January 1, 2008. https://bible.org/seriespage/15-second-coming-christ-and-millennial-kingdom, accessed July 1, 2018.

424 Ibid.

425 Maclaren, Alexander. *The Expositor's Bible:* The Psalms. (New York: Scriptura Press, 2015), Psalm 110:3.

426 Lockyer, Herbert, Sr. *Psalms: A Devotional Commentary,* Psalm 110. (Grand Rapids: Kregel Publications, 1993), Psalm 110:3.

427 Maclaren, Alexander. *The Expositor's Bible:* The Psalms. (New York: Scriptura Press, 2015), Psalm 110:3.

428 Spurgeon, C. H. *The Treasury of David.* (Grand Rapids, Michigan: Kregel Publications, 2004), Psalm 110:4.

429 Ibid.

430 Harman, A. *Psalms: A Mentor Commentary (Vol. 1–2).* (Ross-shire, Great Britain: Mentor, 2011), 793–794.

431 Ogilvie, Lloyd J. (General Editor). *The Preacher's Commentary: Psalms 73 – 150.* (Nashville: Thomas Nelson Publishers, 1989), 292–293.

432 Barnes, Albert. Notes on the Psalms, Critical, Explanatory and Practical. (New York: Harper & Brothers, 1868), Psalm 110:7.

433 Ogilvie, Lloyd J. (General Editor). *The Preacher's Commentary: Psalms 73 – 150.* (Nashville: Thomas Nelson Publishers, 1989), 293.

434 Barnes, Albert. Notes on the Psalms, Critical, Explanatory and Practical. (New York: Harper & Brothers, 1868), Psalm 111:10.

[435] Criswell, W. A., P. Patterson, E. R. Clendenen, D. L. Akin, M. Chamberlin, D. K. Patterson, and J. Pogue (Eds.). Believer's Study Bible, (electronic ed.). (Nashville: Thomas Nelson, 1991), Ps. 111:10.

[436] Brown, F., S. R. Driver, and C. A. Briggs. *Enhanced Brown-Driver-Briggs Hebrew and English Lexicon.* (Oxford: Clarendon Press, 1977), 912.

[437] Swanson, J. *Dictionary of Biblical Languages with Semantic Domains: Hebrew (Old Testament)* (electronic ed.). (Oak Harbor: Logos Research Systems, Inc., 1997).

[438] Plumer, W. S. *Studies in the Book of Psalms: Being a Critical and Expository Commentary, with Doctrinal and Practical Remarks on the Entire Psalter.* (Philadelphia; Edinburgh: J. B. Lippincott Company; A & C Black, 1872), 980.

[439] Allen, L. C. *Psalms 101–150* (Revised) (Vol. 21). (Dallas: Word, Incorporated, 2002), 126.

[440] Vine, W. E., M. F. Unger, and W. White, Jr. *Vine's Complete Expository Dictionary of Old and New Testament Words* (Vol. 1). (Nashville: T. Nelson, 1996), 290.

[441] Swanson, J. *Dictionary of Biblical Languages with Semantic Domains: Hebrew (Old Testament)* (electronic ed.). (Oak Harbor: Logos Research Systems, Inc., 1997).

[442] Plumer, W. S. *Studies in the Book of Psalms: Being a Critical and Expository Commentary, with Doctrinal and Practical Remarks on the Entire Psalter.* (Philadelphia; Edinburgh: J. B. Lippincott Company; A & C Black, 1872), 980.

[443] Spurgeon, C. H. *The Treasury of David.* (Grand Rapids, Michigan: Kregel Publications, 2004), Psalm 111:10.

[444] Swanson, J. *Dictionary of Biblical Languages with Semantic Domains: Hebrew (Old Testament)* (electronic ed.). (Oak Harbor: Logos Research Systems, Inc., 1997).

[445] Thomas, R. L. *New American Standard Hebrew-Aramaic and Greek Dictionaries: updated edition.* (Anaheim: Foundation Publications, Inc., 1998).

[446] Allen, L. C. *Psalms 101–150* (Revised) (Vol. 21). (Dallas: Word, Incorporated, 2002), 126.

[447] Alexander, J. A. *The Psalms Translated and Explained.* (Edinburgh: Andrew Elliot; James Thin, 1864), 461.

[448] *The Quest Study Bible.* (Grand Rapids: Zondervan, 2011), 907.

[449] Exell, Joseph S. Ed. *The Biblical Illustrator,* Psalm 11:10. S. Davies ("Religion the Highest Wisdom").

[450] Simeon, C. *Horae Homileticae: Psalms, LXXIII–CL* (Vol. 6). (London: Samuel Holdsworth, 1836), 261.

[451] Plumer, W. S. *Studies in the Book of Psalms: Being a Critical and Expository Commentary, with Doctrinal and Practical Remarks on the Entire Psalter.* (Philadelphia; Edinburgh: J. B. Lippincott Company; A & C Black, 1872), 982.

[452] Ibid.

[453] Horne, G. *A Commentary on the Book of Psalms.* (New York: Robert Carter & Brothers, 1856), 408.

[454] Alexander, W. H. *The Book of Praises: Being the Book of Psalms, according to the Authorized Version, with Notes Original and Selected.* (London: Jackson, Walford, and Hodder, 1867), 380.

[455] Chambers, Oswald. *My Utmost For His Highest,* January 19.

[456] Simeon, C. *Horae Homileticae: Psalms, LXXIII–CL* (Vol. 6). (London: Samuel Holdsworth, 1836), 261–262.

[457] Henry, M. *Matthew Henry's Commentary on the Whole Bible: Complete and Unabridged in One Volume.* (Peabody: Hendrickson, 1994), 905.

[458] Swanson, J. *Dictionary of Biblical Languages with Semantic Domains: Hebrew (Old Testament)* (electronic ed.). (Oak Harbor: Logos Research Systems, Inc., 1997).

[459] Ibid.

[460] Gesenius, W., and S. P. Tregelles. *Gesenius' Hebrew and Chaldee Lexicon to the Old Testament Scriptures.* (Bellingham, WA: Logos Bible Software, 2003), 501.

[461] Spence-Jones, H. D. M. (Ed.). *Psalms,* (Vol. 3). (London; New York: Funk & Wagnalls Company, 1909), 42.

[462] Spurgeon, C. H. *The Treasury of David.* (Grand Rapids, Michigan: Kregel Publications, 2004), Psalm 112:1.

[463] Barnes, Albert. Notes on the Psalms, Critical, Explanatory and Practical. (New York: Harper & Brothers, 1868), Psalm 112:2.

[464] Henry, Matthew. *Concise Commentary on the Bible.* Psalm 112:2.

[465] Spence-Jones, H. D. M. (Ed.). *Psalms,* (Vol. 3). (London; New York: Funk & Wagnalls Company, 1909), 43.

[466] Jamieson, R., A. R. Fausset, & D. Brown. *Commentary Critical and Explanatory on the Whole Bible* (Vol. 1). (Oak Harbor, WA: Logos Research Systems, Inc., 1997), Psalm 112:3.

[467] Spurgeon, C. H. *The Treasury of David.* (Grand Rapids, Michigan: Kregel Publications, 2004), Psalm 112:3.

[468] Barnes, Albert. Notes on the Psalms, Critical, Explanatory and Practical. (New York: Harper & Brothers, 1868), Psalm 112:3.

[469] Benson, Joseph. *The Holy Bible With Notes, Critical, Explanatory and Practical.* (London: J. Kershaw, 1825), Psalm 112:4.

[470] Ibid. Psalm 112:5.

[471] Swanson, J. *Dictionary of Biblical Languages with Semantic Domains: Hebrew (Old Testament)* (electronic ed.). (Oak Harbor: Logos Research Systems, Inc., 1997).

[472] Vine, W. E., M. F. Unger, and W. White, Jr. *Vine's Complete Expository Dictionary of Old and New Testament Words* (Vol. 1). (Nashville: T. Nelson, 1996), 205.

[473] Ibid., 100.

[474] Swanson, J. *Dictionary of Biblical Languages with Semantic Domains: Hebrew (Old Testament)* (electronic ed.). (Oak Harbor: Logos Research Systems, Inc., 1997).

[475] Barnes, Albert. Notes on the Psalms, Critical, Explanatory and Practical. (New York: Harper & Brothers, 1868), Psalm 112:5.

[476] Ibid.

[477] Spence-Jones, H. D. M. (Ed.). *Psalms,* (Vol. 3). (London; New York: Funk & Wagnalls Company, 1909), 43.

[478] Spurgeon, C. H. *The Treasury of David.* (Grand Rapids, Michigan: Kregel Publications, 2004), Psalm 112:6.

[479] https://biblehub.com/commentaries/psalms/112-6.htm.

[480] Henry, M. *Matthew Henry's Commentary on the Whole Bible: Complete and Unabridged in One Volume.* (Peabody: Hendrickson, 1994), 906.

[481] Vine, W. E., M. F. Unger, and W. White, Jr. *Vine's Complete Expository Dictionary of Old and New Testament Words* (Vol. 1). (Nashville: T. Nelson, 1996), 186.

[482] Gesenius, W., and S. P. Tregelles. *Gesenius' Hebrew and Chaldee Lexicon to the Old Testament Scriptures.* (Bellingham, WA: Logos Bible Software, 2003), 112.

[483] Barnes, Albert. Notes on the Psalms, Critical, Explanatory and Practical. (New York: Harper & Brothers, 1868), Psalm 112:8.

[484] Spurgeon, C. H. *The Treasury of David.* (Grand Rapids, Michigan: Kregel Publications, 2004), Psalm 112:8.

[485] https://biblehub.com/commentaries/psalms/112-8.htm.

[486] Barnes, Albert. Notes on the Psalms, Critical, Explanatory and Practical. (New York: Harper & Brothers, 1868), Psalm 112:8.

[487] Spurgeon, C. H. *The Treasury of David.* (Grand Rapids, Michigan: Kregel Publications, 2004), Psalm 112:9.

[488] Spence-Jones, H. D. M. (Ed.). *Psalms,* (Vol. 3). (London; New York: Funk & Wagnalls Company, 1909), 43.

[489] https://biblehub.com/commentaries/psalms/112-9.htm.

[490] Barnes, Albert. Notes on the Psalms, Critical, Explanatory and Practical. (New York: Harper & Brothers, 1868), Psalm 112:9.

[491] https://biblehub.com/commentaries/psalms/112-9.htm.

[492] Spurgeon, C. H. *The Treasury of David.* (Grand Rapids, Michigan: Kregel Publications, 2004), Psalm 112:9.

[493] Alexander, J. A. *The Psalms Translated and Explained.* (Edinburgh: Andrew Elliot; James Thin, 1864), 463.

[494] https://biblehub.com/commentaries/psalms/112-1.htm.

[495] Spurgeon, C. H. *The Treasury of David.* (Grand Rapids, Michigan: Kregel Publications, 2004), Psalm 112:2.

[496] Plumer, W. S. *Studies in the Book of Psalms: Being a Critical and Expository Commentary, with Doctrinal and Practical Remarks on the Entire Psalter.* (Philadelphia; Edinburgh: J. B. Lippincott Company; A & C Black, 1872), 983.

[497] Barnes, Albert. Notes on the Psalms, Critical, Explanatory and Practical. (New York: Harper & Brothers, 1868), Psalm 112:3.

[498] Spence-Jones, H. D. M. (Ed.). *Psalms,* (Vol. 3). (London; New York: Funk & Wagnalls Company, 1909), 43.

[499] Spurgeon, C. H. *The Treasury of David.* (Grand Rapids, Michigan: Kregel Publications, 2004), Psalm 112:3.

[500] Plumer, W. S. *Studies in the Book of Psalms: Being a Critical and Expository Commentary, with Doctrinal and Practical Remarks on the Entire Psalter.* (Philadelphia; Edinburgh: J. B. Lippincott Company; A & C Black, 1872), 983.

[501] Plumer, W. S. *Studies in the Book of Psalms: Being a Critical and Expository Commentary, with Doctrinal and Practical Remarks on the Entire Psalter.* (Philadelphia; Edinburgh: J. B. Lippincott Company; A & C Black, 1872), 983.

[502] Ibid.

[503] Barnes, Albert. Notes on the Psalms, Critical, Explanatory and Practical. (New York: Harper & Brothers, 1868), Psalm 112:4.

[504] https://biblehub.com/psalms/112-4.htm.

[505] Gill, John. *The John Gill Exposition of the Entire Bible,* Psalm 112:6.

[506] Alexander, J. A. *The Psalms Translated and Explained.* (Edinburgh: Andrew Elliot; James Thin, 1864), 464.

[507] Exell, Joseph S. Ed. *The Biblical Illustrator,* Psalm 112:6 ("The Immortality of Influence").

[508] Alexander, J. A. *The Psalms Translated and Explained.* (Edinburgh: Andrew Elliot; James Thin, 1864), 464.

[509] Plumer, W. S. *Studies in the Book of Psalms: Being a Critical and Expository Commentary, with Doctrinal and Practical Remarks on the Entire Psalter.* (Philadelphia; Edinburgh: J. B. Lippincott Company; A & C Black, 1872), 984.

[510] MacDonald, W. *Believer's Bible Commentary: Old and New Testaments,* (A. Farstad, Ed.) (Nashville: Thomas Nelson, 1995), 727.

[511] Alexander, J. A. *The Psalms Translated and Explained.* (Edinburgh: Andrew Elliot; James Thin, 1864), 464.

[512] Spurgeon, C. H. *Morning and Evening,* September 15 (Morning).

[513] Alexander, J. A. *The Psalms Translated and Explained.* (Edinburgh: Andrew Elliot; James Thin, 1864), 464.

[514] Lockyer, Herbert, Sr. *Psalms: A Devotional Commentary,* Psalm 110. (Grand Rapids: Kregel Publications, 1993), Psalm 112:8.

[515] Gill, John. *The John Gill Exposition of the Entire Bible,* Psalm 112:8.

[516] Alexander, J. A. *The Psalms Translated and Explained.* (Edinburgh: Andrew Elliot; James Thin, 1864), 465.

[517] Ross, A. P. In Walvoord, J. F. and R. B. Zuck (Eds.). *The Bible Knowledge Commentary: An Exposition of the Scriptures* (Vol. 1, Psalms). (Wheaton, IL: Victor Books, 1985), 875.

[518] Ibid.

[519] Goldberg, L., R. L. Harris, G. L. Archer Jr., and B. K. Waltke (Eds.). *Theological Wordbook of the Old Testament,* 2133 רום, (electronic ed.). (Chicago: Moody Press, 1999), 837

[520] Benson, Joseph. *The Holy Bible With Notes, Critical, Explanatory and Practical.* (London: J. Kershaw, 1825), Psalm 113:4.

[521] Spence-Jones, H. D. M. (Ed.). *Psalms,* (Vol. 3). (London; New York: Funk & Wagnalls Company, 1909), 51.

[522] https://biblehub.com/commentaries/psalms/113-4.htm.

[523] Clarke, Adam. *Clarkes' Commentary and Critical Notes,* Psalm 113:5.

[524] Strong, J. *The New Strong's Dictionary of Hebrew and Greek Words.* (Nashville: Thomas Nelson, 1996).

[525] Gesenius, W., and S. P. Tregelles. *Gesenius' Hebrew and Chaldee Lexicon to the Old Testament Scriptures.* (Bellingham, WA: Logos Bible Software, 2003), 153.

[526] Clarke, Adam. *Clarkes' Commentary and Critical Notes,* Psalm 113 (Introduction).

[527] Ibid.

[528] Plumer, W. S. *Studies in the Book of Psalms: Being a Critical and Expository Commentary, with Doctrinal and Practical Remarks on the Entire Psalter.* (Philadelphia; Edinburgh: J. B. Lippincott Company; A & C Black, 1872), 988.

[529] Allen, L. C. *Psalms 101–150* (Revised) (Vol. 21). (Dallas: Word, Incorporated, 2002), 137.

[530] Alexander, J. A. *The Psalms Translated and Explained.* (Edinburgh: Andrew Elliot; James Thin, 1864), 466.

[531] Gill, John. *The John Gill Exposition of the Entire Bible,* Psalm 113:5.

[532] Spence-Jones, H. D. M. (Ed.). *Psalms,* (Vol. 3). (London; New York: Funk & Wagnalls Company, 1909), 51.

[533] Alexander, J. A. *The Psalms Translated and Explained.* (Edinburgh: Andrew Elliot; James Thin, 1864), 466.

[534] Perowne, J. J. S. *The Book of Psalms; A New Translation, with Introductions and Notes, Explanatory and Critical* (Fifth Edition, Revised, Vol. 1). (London; Cambridge: George Bell and Sons; Deighton Bell and Co., 1883), 323.

[535] Plumer, W. S. *Studies in the Book of Psalms: Being a Critical and Expository Commentary, with Doctrinal and Practical Remarks on the Entire Psalter.* (Philadelphia; Edinburgh: J. B. Lippincott Company; A & C Black, 1872), 989.

[536] Allen, L. C. *Psalms 101–150* (Revised) (Vol. 21). (Dallas: Word, Incorporated, 2002), 137.

[537] Ibid.

[538] Spence-Jones, H. D. M. (Ed.). *Psalms,* (Vol. 3). (London; New York: Funk & Wagnalls Company, 1909), 51.

[539] Spurgeon, C. H. *The Treasury of David.* (Grand Rapids, Michigan: Kregel Publications, 2004), Psalm 113:5.

[540] Henry, M. *Matthew Henry's Commentary on the Whole Bible: Complete and Unabridged in One Volume.* (Peabody: Hendrickson, 1994), 907.

[541] Jennings, A. C., and W. H. Lowe. *The Psalms, with Introductions and Critical Notes* (Second Edition, Vol. 2). (London: Macmillan and Co., 1885), 260.

[542] Plumer, W. S. *Studies in the Book of Psalms: Being a Critical and Expository Commentary, with Doctrinal and Practical Remarks on the Entire Psalter.* (Philadelphia; Edinburgh: J. B. Lippincott Company; A & C Black, 1872), 990.

[543] Ibid.

[544] Jennings, A. C., and W. H. Lowe. *The Psalms, with Introductions and Critical Notes* (Second Edition, Vol. 2). (London: Macmillan and Co., 1885), 262.

[545] https://www.christianquotes.info/top-quotes/16-awe-inspiring-quotes-about-gods-majesty/#ixzz5KD5vScTE, accessed July 3, 2018.

[546] Ibid.

[547] Barnes, Albert. Notes on the Psalms, Critical, Explanatory and Practical. (New York: Harper & Brothers, 1868), Psalm 114:1.

[548] Ross, A. P. In Walvoord, J. F. and R. B. Zuck (Eds.). *The Bible Knowledge Commentary: An Exposition of the Scriptures* (Vol. 1, Psalms). (Wheaton, IL: Victor Books, 1985), 876.

[549] https://biblehub.com/commentaries/psalms/114-2.htm.

[550] Ogilvie, Lloyd J. (General Editor). *The Preacher's Commentary: Psalms 73 – 150.* (Nashville: Thomas Nelson Publishers, 1989), 312.

[551] Spence-Jones, H. D. M. (Ed.). *Psalms,* (Vol. 3). (London; New York: Funk & Wagnalls Company, 1909), 56.

[552] Benson, Joseph. *The Holy Bible With Notes, Critical, Explanatory and Practical.* (London: J. Kershaw, 1825), Psalm 114:3.

[553] Dilday, R. H., Jr., and J. H. Kennedy. *Psalms.* In H. F. Paschall and H. H. Hobbs (Eds.). *The Teacher's Bible Commentary.* (Nashville: Broadman and Holman Publishers, 1972), 341.

[554] Kirkpatrick, A. F. (Ed.). *The Cambridge Bible for Schools and Colleges,* Psalms. (Cambridge: Cambridge University Press, 1914), Psalm 114:4.

[555] Spurgeon, C. H. *The Treasury of David.* (Grand Rapids, Michigan: Kregel Publications, 2004), Psalm 114:4. Explanatory notes and quaint sayings.

[556] Barnes, Albert. Notes on the Psalms, Critical, Explanatory and Practical. (New York: Harper & Brothers, 1868), Psalm 114:5-6.

[557] Spurgeon, C. H. *The Treasury of David.* (Grand Rapids, Michigan: Kregel Publications, 2004), Psalm 114:6.

[558] Spence-Jones, H. D. M. (Ed.). *Psalms,* (Vol. 3). (London; New York: Funk & Wagnalls Company, 1909), 57.

[559] Spurgeon, C. H. *The Treasury of David.* (Grand Rapids, Michigan: Kregel Publications, 2004), Psalm 114:8. Explanatory notes and quaint sayings.

[560] Lockyer, Herbert, Sr. *Psalms: A Devotional Commentary,* Psalm 114. (Grand Rapids: Kregel Publications, 1993), Introduction.

[561] Plumer, W. S. *Studies in the Book of Psalms: Being a Critical and Expository Commentary, with Doctrinal and Practical Remarks on the Entire Psalter.* (Philadelphia; Edinburgh: J. B. Lippincott Company; A & C Black, 1872), 991.

[562] Ibid.

[563] Spurgeon, C. H. *The Treasury of David.* (Grand Rapids, Michigan: Kregel Publications, 2004), Psalm 114. Overview.

[564] Clarke, Adam. *Clarkes' Commentary and Critical Notes*, Psalm 114:3.

[565] Spence-Jones, H. D. M. (Ed.). *Psalms,* (Vol. 3). (London; New York: Funk & Wagnalls Company, 1909), 58.

[566] Benson, Joseph. *The Holy Bible With Notes, Critical, Explanatory and Practical.* (London: J. Kershaw, 1825), Psalm 115:1.

[567] Landes, G. M. *Building Your Biblical Hebrew Vocabulary: Learning Words by Frequency and Cognate* (Vol. 41). (Atlanta, GA: Society of Biblical Literature, 2001), 63.

[568] Vine, W. E., M. F. Unger, and W. White, Jr. *Vine's Complete Expository Dictionary of Old and New Testament Words* (Vol. 1). (Nashville: T. Nelson, 1996), 142.

[569] Barnes, Albert. Notes on the Psalms, Critical, Explanatory and Practical. (New York: Harper & Brothers, 1868), Psalm 115:1.

[570] Swanson, J. *Dictionary of Biblical Languages with Semantic Domains: Hebrew (Old Testament)* (electronic ed.). (Oak Harbor: Logos Research Systems, Inc., 1997).

[571] Spurgeon, C. H. *The Treasury of David.* (Grand Rapids, Michigan: Kregel Publications, 2004), Psalm 115:1.

[572] Boice, J. M. *Psalms 107–150: An Expositional Commentary.* (Grand Rapids, MI: Baker Books, 2005), 936.

[573] Harman, A. *Psalms: A Mentor Commentary (Vol. 1–2).* (Ross-shire, Great Britain: Mentor, 2011), 817.

[574] Landes, G. M. *Building Your Biblical Hebrew Vocabulary: Learning Words by Frequency and Cognate* (Vol. 41). (Atlanta, GA: Society of Biblical Literature, 2001), 160.

[575] Spurgeon, C. H. *The Treasury of David.* (Grand Rapids, Michigan: Kregel Publications, 2004), Psalm 115:1.

[576] Simeon, C. *Horae Homileticae: Psalms, LXXIII–CL* (Vol. 6). (London: Samuel Holdsworth, 1836), 269–270.

[577] Boice, J. M. *Psalms 107–150: An Expositional Commentary.* (Grand Rapids, MI: Baker Books, 2005), 937.

[578] Simeon, C. *Horae Homileticae: Psalms, LXXIII–CL* (Vol. 6). (London: Samuel Holdsworth, 1836), 271–272.

[579] Clarke, Adam. *Clarkes' Commentary and Critical Notes*, Psalm 115:17.

[580] Kirkpatrick, A. F. (Ed.). *The Cambridge Bible for Schools and Colleges,* Psalms. (Cambridge: Cambridge University Press, 1914), Psalm 115:17.

[581] Spurgeon, C. H. *The Treasury of David.* (Grand Rapids, Michigan: Kregel Publications, 2004), Psalm 115:17.

[582] Henry, M. *Matthew Henry's Commentary on the Whole Bible: Complete and Unabridged in One Volume.* (Peabody: Hendrickson, 1994), 908.

[583] Spurgeon, C. H. "Crowning Blessings Ascribed to God" (Sermon #1475), May 18, 1879. (The second sermon in commemoration of the completion of 25 years of his ministry in the midst of the church assembling in the Tabernacle).

[584] https://www.christianquotes.info/quotes-by-topic/quotes-about-boasting/#ixzz5KOmtiAxV, accessed July 5, 2018.

[585] https://www.brainyquote.com/topics/arrogance, accessed January 29, 2018.

[586] https://www.christianquotes.info/quotes-by-topic/quotes-about-boasting/#ixzz5KOmZseHx, accessed July 5, 2018.

[587] Chambers, Oswald. *My Utmost For His Highest,* November 16.

[588] https://www.christianquotes.info/quotes-by-topic/quotes-about-boasting/#ixzz5KOnMhrkD, accessed July 5, 2018.

[589] Smith, Clay. "Grow Character" (Sermon, November 18, 2018), Alice Drive Baptist Church, Sumter, SC.

[590] Gesenius, W., and S. P. Tregelles. *Gesenius' Hebrew and Chaldee Lexicon to the Old Testament Scriptures.* (Bellingham, WA: Logos Bible Software, 2003), 363.

591 Spence-Jones, H. D. M. (Ed.). *Psalms,* (Vol. 3). (London; New York: Funk & Wagnalls Company, 1909), 72.
592 Jennings, A. C., and W. H. Lowe. *The Psalms, with Introductions and Critical Notes* (Second Edition, Vol. 2). (London: Macmillan and Co., 1885), 271.
593 Swanson, J. *Dictionary of Biblical Languages with Semantic Domains: Hebrew (Old Testament)* (electronic ed.). (Oak Harbor: Logos Research Systems, Inc., 1997).
594 Kirkpatrick, A. F. (Ed.). *The Cambridge Bible for Schools and Colleges,* Psalms. (Cambridge: Cambridge University Press, 1914), Psalm 116:15.
595 Simeon, C. *Horae Homileticae: Psalms, LXXIII–CL* (Vol. 6). (London: Samuel Holdsworth, 1836), 288.
596 Plumer, W. S. *Studies in the Book of Psalms: Being a Critical and Expository Commentary, with Doctrinal and Practical Remarks on the Entire Psalter.* (Philadelphia; Edinburgh: J. B. Lippincott Company; A & C Black, 1872), 1000.
597 Ibid.
598 Exell, Joseph S. Ed. *The Biblical Illustrator,* Psalm 116:15. A. C. Dixon ("Precious Death").
599 Barnes, Albert. Notes on the Psalms, Critical, Explanatory and Practical. (New York: Harper & Brothers, 1868), Psalm 116:15.
600 Ibid.
601 Alexander, J. A. *The Psalms Translated and Explained.* (Edinburgh: Andrew Elliot; James Thin, 1864), 474.
602 Spurgeon, C. H. *The Treasury of David.* (Grand Rapids, Michigan: Kregel Publications, 2004), Psalm 116:15.
603 Plumer, W. S. *Studies in the Book of Psalms: Being a Critical and Expository Commentary, with Doctrinal and Practical Remarks on the Entire Psalter.* (Philadelphia; Edinburgh: J. B. Lippincott Company; A & C Black, 1872), 1006.
604 Lockyer, Herbert. "The Death of the Saints" *Sword of the Lord.* (Murfreesboro, TN.: Sword of the Lord Publishers, March 29, 2013), 11.
605 Exell, Joseph S. Ed. *The Biblical Illustrator,* Psalm 116:15.
606 https://biblehub.com/commentaries/psalms/116-15.htm.
607 Simeon, C. *Horae Homileticae: Psalms, LXXIII–CL* (Vol. 6). (London: Samuel Holdsworth, 1836), 279.
608 Ibid., 291.
609 Whedon, Daniel, (ed.). *Commentary on the Old Testament.* (New York: Phillips and Hunt, 1882), 383.
610 Perowne, J. J. S. *The Book of Psalms; A New Translation, with Introductions and Notes, Explanatory and Critical* (Fifth Edition, Revised, Vol. 1). (London; Cambridge: George Bell and Sons; Deighton Bell and Co., 1883), 335.

[611] Swanson, J. *Dictionary of Biblical Languages with Semantic Domains: Hebrew (Old Testament)* (electronic ed.). (Oak Harbor: Logos Research Systems, Inc., 1997).

[612] Akin, Daniel. "A Little Psalm With A Big Message." http://www.danielakin.com/wp-content/uploads/2008/10/Psalm-117-a-little-Psalm-with-a-big-message-manuscript-kh.pdf, accessed July 7, 2018.

[613] Clarke, Adam. *Clarkes' Commentary and Critical Notes*, Psalm 117:1.

[614] Ibid.

[615] Lockyer, Herbert, Sr. *Psalms: A Devotional Commentary,* Psalm 110. (Grand Rapids: Kregel Publications, 1993), Psalm 117:1.

[616] Vine, W. E., M. F. Unger, and W. White, Jr. *Vine's Complete Expository Dictionary of Old and New Testament Words* (Vol. 1). (Nashville: T. Nelson, 1996), 142.

[617] Gesenius, W., and S. P. Tregelles. *Gesenius' Hebrew and Chaldee Lexicon to the Old Testament Scriptures.* (Bellingham, WA: Logos Bible Software, 2003), 156.

[618] Lockyer, Herbert, Sr. *Psalms: A Devotional Commentary,* Psalm 110. (Grand Rapids: Kregel Publications, 1993), Psalm 117:2.

[619] Swanson, J. *Dictionary of Biblical Languages with Semantic Domains: Hebrew (Old Testament)* (electronic ed.). (Oak Harbor: Logos Research Systems, Inc., 1997).

[620] Ross, A. P. In Walvoord, J. F. and R. B. Zuck (Eds.). *The Bible Knowledge Commentary: An Exposition of the Scriptures* (Vol. 1, Psalms). (Wheaton, IL: Victor Books, 1985), 878.

[621] Swanson, J. *Dictionary of Biblical Languages with Semantic Domains: Hebrew (Old Testament)* (electronic ed.). (Oak Harbor: Logos Research Systems, Inc., 1997).

[622] Spurgeon, C. H. *The Treasury of David.* (Grand Rapids, Michigan: Kregel Publications, 2004), Psalm 117 (Introduction).

[623] Kidner, Derek. *Psalms 73–150: A Commentary on Books III–V of the Psalms.* (Downers Grove, Ill.: InterVarsity, 1975), 412.

[624] Jennings, A. C., and W. H. Lowe. *The Psalms, with Introductions and Critical Notes* (Second Edition, Vol. 2). (London: Macmillan and Co., 1885), 272o.

[625] Simeon, C. *Horae Homileticae: Psalms, LXXIII–CL* (Vol. 6). (London: Samuel Holdsworth, 1836), 293.

[626] Plumer, W. S. *Studies in the Book of Psalms: Being a Critical and Expository Commentary, with Doctrinal and Practical Remarks on the Entire Psalter.* (Philadelphia; Edinburgh: J. B. Lippincott Company; A & C Black, 1872), 1006.

[627] Spurgeon, C. H. *The Treasury of David.* (Grand Rapids, Michigan: Kregel Publications, 2004), Psalm 117:1.

[628] Henry, M. *Matthew Henry's Commentary on the Whole Bible: Complete and Unabridged in One Volume.* (Peabody: Hendrickson, 1994), 911.

[629] Simeon, C. *Horae Homileticae: Psalms, LXXIII–CL* (Vol. 6). (London: Samuel Holdsworth, 1836), 293.

[630] Barnes, Albert. Notes on the Psalms, Critical, Explanatory and Practical. (New York: Harper & Brothers, 1868), Psalm 117:1.

[631] http://www.peoplegroups.org, accessed September 25, 2017. IMB updated figures as of September 24, 2017.

[632] Ibid.

[633] Piper, John. "Everlasting Truth for the Joy of All Peoples," Psalm 117. October 26, 2003. https://www.desiringgod.org/messages/everlasting-truth-for-the-joy-of-all-peoples, accessed July 7, 2018.

[634] Carmicheal, Rich, (ed.). *Herald of His Coming.* (Gospel Revivals: Seelyville, IN). September, 2018, 11.

[635] Autrey, C. E. *Evangelistic Sermons.* (Grand Rapids: Zondervan Publishing House, 1962), 77.

[636] Ibid., 79.

[637] https://gracequotes.org/quote/if-there-be-any-one-point-in-which-the-christian-c/, accessed July 7, 2018.

[638] Whitsell, Faris. *Basic New Testament Evangelism.* (Grand Rapids: Zondervan Publishing House, 1949), 146.

[639] Piper, John. "Everlasting Truth for the Joy of All Peoples," Psalm 117. October 26, 2003. https://www.desiringgod.org/messages/everlasting-truth-for-the-joy-of-all-peoples, accessed July 7, 2018.

[640] *The Church Missionary Review*, Volume 43. (London: Church Missionary Society, Salisbury Square, Jan. 1892), 65.

[641] Swanson, J. *Dictionary of Biblical Languages with Semantic Domains: Hebrew (Old Testament)* (electronic ed.). (Oak Harbor: Logos Research Systems, Inc., 1997).

[642] Gesenius, W., and S. P. Tregelles. *Gesenius' Hebrew and Chaldee Lexicon to the Old Testament Scriptures.* (Bellingham, WA: Logos Bible Software, 2003), 294.

[643] Swanson, J. *Dictionary of Biblical Languages with Semantic Domains: Hebrew (Old Testament)* (electronic ed.). (Oak Harbor: Logos Research Systems, Inc., 1997).

[644] Ibid.

[645] Plumer, W. S. *Studies in the Book of Psalms: Being a Critical and Expository Commentary, with Doctrinal and Practical Remarks on the Entire Psalter.* (Philadelphia; Edinburgh: J. B. Lippincott Company; A & C Black, 1872), 1008–1009.

[646] Ibid.

[647] Ibid.

[648] Ibid.

[649] Ibid.

[650] Ibid.

[651] Ibid., 1009.

[652] Ibid.

[653] Ibid.

[654] Benson, Joseph. *The Holy Bible With Notes, Critical, Explanatory and Practical.* (London: J. Kershaw, 1825), Psalm 118:8.

[655] Jamieson, R., A. R. Fausset, & D. Brown. *Commentary Critical and Explanatory on the Whole Bible* (Vol. 1). (Oak Harbor, WA: Logos Research Systems, Inc., 1997), Psalm 118:8–9.

[656] Plumer, W. S. *Studies in the Book of Psalms: Being a Critical and Expository Commentary, with Doctrinal and Practical Remarks on the Entire Psalter.* (Philadelphia; Edinburgh: J. B. Lippincott Company; A & C Black, 1872), 1015.

[657] Lockyer, Herbert, Sr. *Psalms: A Devotional Commentary,* Psalm 110. (Grand Rapids: Kregel Publications, 1993), Psalm 118: 8.

[658] Spurgeon, C. H. *Morning and Evening,* March 7 (Evening).

[659] Henry, M. *Matthew Henry's Commentary on the Whole Bible: Complete and Unabridged in One Volume.* (Peabody: Hendrickson, 1994), 912.

[660] Swanson, J. *Dictionary of Biblical Languages with Semantic Domains: Hebrew (Old Testament)* (electronic ed.). (Oak Harbor: Logos Research Systems, Inc., 1997).

[661] Barnes, Albert. Notes on the Psalms, Critical, Explanatory and Practical. (New York: Harper & Brothers, 1868), Psalm 118:18.

[662] MacDonald, W. *Believer's Bible Commentary: Old and New Testaments,* (A. Farstad, Ed.) (Nashville: Thomas Nelson, 1995), 733.

[663] Henry, Matthew. *Matthew Henry's Concise Bible Commentary,* Psalm 118:18.

[664] Luther, Martin, from his Dedication of his Translation of Psalm CXVIII to the Abbot Frederick of Nuremberg.

[665] Spurgeon, C. H. *The Treasury of David.* (Grand Rapids, Michigan: Kregel Publications, 2004), Psalm 118:18.

[666] Maclaren, Alexander. *The Psalms.* (New York: A. C. Armstrong and Son, 1904), 284.

[667] Spence-Jones, H. D. M. (Ed.). *Psalms,* (Vol. 3). (London; New York: Funk & Wagnalls Company, 1909), 89.

[668] Gill, John. *The John Gill Exposition of the Entire Bible,* Psalm 118:14.

[669] https://www.christianquotes.info/quotes-by-topic/quotes-about-carnality/#ixzz5KgcQBBbZ, accessed July 8, 2018.

[670] Spurgeon, C. H. "Blessed Discipline" (Sermon # 2374). A Sermon Delivered On Thursday Evening, May 24, 1888, The Metropolitan Tabernacle, Newington.

[671] Criswell, W. A. The Daily Word, "Constructive Correction," November 23, 2018.

[672] Harman, A. *Psalms: A Mentor Commentary (Vol. 1–2)*. (Ross-shire, Great Britain: Mentor, 2011), 837.

[673] Vine, W. E., M. F. Unger, and W. White, Jr. *Vine's Complete Expository Dictionary of Old and New Testament Words* (Vol. 1). (Nashville: T. Nelson, 1996), 58.

[674] Futato, M. D. *Beginning Biblical Hebrew*. (Winona Lake, IN: Eisenbrauns, 2003), 288.

[675] Criswell, W. A., P. Patterson, E. R. Clendenen, D. L. Akin, M. Chamberlin, D. K. Patterson, and J. Pogue (Eds.). Believer's Study Bible, (electronic ed.). (Nashville: Thomas Nelson, 1991), Ps. 118:22.

[676] https://en.wikipedia.org/wiki/Cornerstone, accessed July 8, 2018.

[677] Henry, M. *Matthew Henry's Commentary on the Whole Bible: Complete and Unabridged in One Volume*. (Peabody: Hendrickson, 1994), 913.

[678] Spurgeon, C. H. *The Treasury of David*. (Grand Rapids, Michigan: Kregel Publications, 2004), Psalm 118:22.

[679] Plumer, W. S. *Studies in the Book of Psalms: Being a Critical and Expository Commentary, with Doctrinal and Practical Remarks on the Entire Psalter*. (Philadelphia; Edinburgh: J. B. Lippincott Company; A & C Black, 1872), 1016.

[680] Ibid.

[681] Ibid.

[682] Ibid.

[683] Jennings, A. C., and W. H. Lowe. *The Psalms, with Introductions and Critical Notes* (Second Edition, Vol. 2). (London: Macmillan and Co., 1885), 279.

[684] Brug, J. F. *Psalms 73–150*. (2nd ed.). (Milwaukee, WI: Northwestern Pub. House, 1989), 194.

[685] Jamieson, R., A. R. Fausset, & D. Brown. *Commentary Critical and Explanatory on the Whole Bible* (Vol. 1). (Oak Harbor, WA: Logos Research Systems, Inc., 1997), Psalm 119:1–176 (Introduction).

[686] Henry, M. *Matthew Henry's Commentary on the Whole Bible: Complete and Unabridged in One Volume*. (Peabody: Hendrickson, 1994), 913.

[687] Spurgeon, C. H. *The Treasury of David*. (Grand Rapids, Michigan: Kregel Publications, 2004), Psalm 119 (Introduction).

[688] Henry, M. *Matthew Henry's Commentary on the Whole Bible: Complete and Unabridged in One Volume*. (Peabody: Hendrickson, 1994), 914.

[689] Boice, J. M. *Psalms 107–150: An Expositional Commentary*. (Grand Rapids, MI: Baker Books, 2005), 970.

[690] Keil & Delitzsch. Commentary on the Old Testament: Volume 5. (Peabody, Massachusetts: Hendrickson Publishers, 2006), 243.

[691] Kidner, Derek. *Psalms 73–150: A Commentary on Books III–V of the Psalms.* (Downers Grove, Ill.: InterVarsity, 1975), 455.

[692] Wiersbe, W. W. *Wiersbe's Expository Outlines on the Old Testament.* (Wheaton, IL: Victor Books, 1993), Ps. 119.

[693] Ogilvie, Lloyd J. (General Editor). *The Preacher's Commentary: Psalms 73 – 150.* (Nashville: Thomas Nelson Publishers, 1989), 341.

[694] VanGemeren, Willem A. *The Expositor's Bible Commentary,* Psalms. (Grand Rapids: Zondervan, 1991), 736–737.

[695] Henry, M. *Matthew Henry's Commentary on the Whole Bible: Complete and Unabridged in One Volume.* (Peabody: Hendrickson, 1994), 913.

[696] Spurgeon, C. H. *The Treasury of David.* (Grand Rapids, Michigan: Kregel Publications, 2004), Psalm 119 (Introduction).

[697] Clarke, Adam. *Clarkes' Commentary and Critical Notes*, Psalm 119 (Introduction).

[698] Bridges, Charles. *Exposition of Psalm CXIX.* (London: Seeley, Burnside and Seeley, 1846), Preface.

[699] Henry, M. *Matthew Henry's Commentary on the Whole Bible: Complete and Unabridged in One Volume.* (Peabody: Hendrickson, 1994), 913.

[700] Spence-Jones, H. D. M. (Ed.). *Psalms,* (Vol. 3). (London; New York: Funk & Wagnalls Company, 1909), 102.

[701] Clarke, Adam. *Clarkes' Commentary and Critical Notes*, Psalm 119 (Introduction).

[702] VanGemeren, Willem A. *The Expositor's Bible Commentary,* Psalms. (Grand Rapids: Zondervan, 1991), 737.

[703] Clarke, Adam. *Clarkes' Commentary and Critical Notes*, Psalm 119 (Introduction).

[704] Henry, M. *Matthew Henry's Commentary on the Whole Bible: Complete and Unabridged in One Volume.* (Peabody: Hendrickson, 1994), 913.

[705] VanGemeren, Willem A. *The Expositor's Bible Commentary,* Psalms. (Grand Rapids: Zondervan, 1991), 737.

[706] Clarke, Adam. *Clarkes' Commentary and Critical Notes*, Psalm 119 (Introduction).

[707] Spence-Jones, H. D. M. (Ed.). *Psalms,* (Vol. 3). (London; New York: Funk & Wagnalls Company, 1909), 102.

[708] VanGemeren, Willem A. *The Expositor's Bible Commentary,* Psalms. (Grand Rapids: Zondervan, 1991), 737.

[709] Ibid.

[710] Henry, M. *Matthew Henry's Commentary on the Whole Bible: Complete and Unabridged in One Volume.* (Peabody: Hendrickson, 1994), 913.

[711] VanGemeren, Willem A. *The Expositor's Bible Commentary,* Psalms. (Grand Rapids: Zondervan, 1991), 737.

[712] Plumer, W. S. *Studies in the Book of Psalms: Being a Critical and Expository Commentary, with Doctrinal and Practical Remarks on the Entire Psalter.* (Philadelphia; Edinburgh: J. B. Lippincott Company; A & C Black, 1872), 1020.

[713] Henry, M. *Matthew Henry's Commentary on the Whole Bible: Complete and Unabridged in One Volume.* (Peabody: Hendrickson, 1994), 913–914.

[714] Swanson, J. *Dictionary of Biblical Languages with Semantic Domains: Hebrew (Old Testament)* (electronic ed.). (Oak Harbor: Logos Research Systems, Inc., 1997).

[715] Plumer, W. S. *Studies in the Book of Psalms: Being a Critical and Expository Commentary, with Doctrinal and Practical Remarks on the Entire Psalter.* (Philadelphia; Edinburgh: J. B. Lippincott Company; A & C Black, 1872), 1020.

[716] Ibid., 1021.

[717] Clarke, Adam. *Clarkes' Commentary and Critical Notes,* Psalm 119 (Introduction).

[718] Henry, M. *Matthew Henry's Commentary on the Whole Bible: Complete and Unabridged in One Volume.* (Peabody: Hendrickson, 1994), 914.

[719] Plumer, W. S. *Studies in the Book of Psalms: Being a Critical and Expository Commentary, with Doctrinal and Practical Remarks on the Entire Psalter.* (Philadelphia; Edinburgh: J. B. Lippincott Company; A & C Black, 1872), 1019–1020.

[720] Gill, John. *The John Gill Exposition of the Entire Bible,* Psalm 119:2.

[721] Vine, W. E., M. F. Unger, and W. White, Jr. *Vine's Complete Expository Dictionary of Old and New Testament Words* (Vol. 1). (Nashville: T. Nelson, 1996), 176.

[722] Swanson, J. *Dictionary of Biblical Languages with Semantic Domains: Hebrew (Old Testament)* (electronic ed.). (Oak Harbor: Logos Research Systems, Inc., 1997).

[723] Barnes, Albert. Notes on the Psalms, Critical, Explanatory and Practical. (New York: Harper & Brothers, 1868), Psalm 119:1.

[724] Futato, M. D. *Beginning Biblical Hebrew.* (Winona Lake, IN: Eisenbrauns, 2003), 290.

[725] Spence-Jones, H. D. M. (Ed.). *Psalms,* (Vol. 3). (London; New York: Funk & Wagnalls Company, 1909), 103.

[726] Swanson, J. *Dictionary of Biblical Languages with Semantic Domains: Hebrew (Old Testament)* (electronic ed.). (Oak Harbor: Logos Research Systems, Inc., 1997).

[727] https://biblehub.com/commentaries/psalms/119-2.htm.

[728] Jamieson, R., A. R. Fausset, & D. Brown. *Commentary Critical and Explanatory on the Whole Bible* (Vol. 1). (Oak Harbor, WA: Logos Research Systems, Inc., 1997), Psalm 119:2.

[729] Barnes, Albert. Notes on the Psalms, Critical, Explanatory and Practical. (New York: Harper & Brothers, 1868), Psalm 119:2.

[730] Swanson, J. *Dictionary of Biblical Languages with Semantic Domains: Hebrew (Old Testament)* (electronic ed.). (Oak Harbor: Logos Research Systems, Inc., 1997).

[731] Clarke, Adam. *Clarkes' Commentary and Critical Notes*, Psalm 119:3.

[732] Spurgeon, C. H. *The Treasury of David.* (Grand Rapids, Michigan: Kregel Publications, 2004), Psalm 119:3.

[733] Swanson, J. *Dictionary of Biblical Languages with Semantic Domains: Hebrew (Old Testament)* (electronic ed.). (Oak Harbor: Logos Research Systems, Inc., 1997).

[734] Barnes, Albert. Notes on the Psalms, Critical, Explanatory and Practical. (New York: Harper & Brothers, 1868), Psalm 119:4.

[735] Vine, W. E., M. F. Unger, & W. White, Jr. *Vine's Complete Expository Dictionary of Old and New Testament Words (Vol. 1).* (Nashville, TN: T. Nelson, 1996), Psalm 119:4.

[736] Landes, G. M. *Building Your Biblical Hebrew Vocabulary: Learning Words by Frequency and Cognate* (Vol. 41). (Atlanta, GA: Society of Biblical Literature, 2001), 58.

[737] Gesenius, W., and S. P. Tregelles. *Gesenius' Hebrew and Chaldee Lexicon to the Old Testament Scriptures.* (Bellingham, WA: Logos Bible Software, 2003), 444.

[738] Clarke, Adam. *Clarkes' Commentary and Critical Notes*, Psalm 119:4.

[739] Barnes, Albert. Notes on the Psalms, Critical, Explanatory and Practical. (New York: Harper & Brothers, 1868), Psalm 119:4.

[740] Alexander, J. A. *The Psalms Translated and Explained.* (Edinburgh: Andrew Elliot; James Thin, 1864), 482.

[741] Spurgeon, C. H. *The Treasury of David.* (Grand Rapids, Michigan: Kregel Publications, 2004), Psalm 119:3.

[742] Henry, M. *Matthew Henry's Commentary on the Whole Bible: Complete and Unabridged in One Volume.* (Peabody: Hendrickson, 1994), 914.

[743] https://biblehub.com/commentaries/psalms/119-3.htm.

[744] Henry, M. *Matthew Henry's Commentary on the Whole Bible: Complete and Unabridged in One Volume.* (Peabody: Hendrickson, 1994), 914.

[745] Alexander, J. A. *The Psalms Translated and Explained.* (Edinburgh: Andrew Elliot; James Thin, 1864), 482.

[746] Henry, M. *Matthew Henry's Commentary on the Whole Bible: Complete and Unabridged in One Volume.* (Peabody: Hendrickson, 1994), 914.

[747] https://biblehub.com/psalms/119-6.htm.

[748] Gill, John. *The John Gill Exposition of the Entire Bible,* Psalm 119:6.

[749] Alexander, J. A. *The Psalms Translated and Explained.* (Edinburgh: Andrew Elliot; James Thin, 1864), 482–483.

[750] Vine, W. E., M. F. Unger, and W. White, Jr. *Vine's Complete Expository Dictionary of Old and New Testament Words* (Vol. 1). (Nashville: T. Nelson, 1996), 299.

[751] Gesenius, W., and S. P. Tregelles. *Gesenius' Hebrew and Chaldee Lexicon to the Old Testament Scriptures.* (Bellingham, WA: Logos Bible Software, 2003), 244.

[752] Clarke, Adam. *Clarkes' Commentary and Critical Notes,* Psalm 119:9.

[753] Gesenius, W., and S. P. Tregelles. *Gesenius' Hebrew and Chaldee Lexicon to the Old Testament Scriptures.* (Bellingham, WA: Logos Bible Software, 2003), 837.

[754] Benson, Joseph. *The Holy Bible With Notes, Critical, Explanatory and Practical.* (London: J. Kershaw, 1825), Psalm 119:9.

[755] Strong, J. *Enhanced Strong's Lexicon.* (Ontario: Woodside Bible Fellowship, 1995).

[756] Swanson, J. *Dictionary of Biblical Languages with Semantic Domains: Hebrew (Old Testament)* (electronic ed.). (Oak Harbor: Logos Research Systems, Inc., 1997).

[757] Barnes, Albert. Notes on the Psalms, Critical, Explanatory and Practical. (New York: Harper & Brothers, 1868), Psalm 119:10.

[758] Landes, G. M. *Building Your Biblical Hebrew Vocabulary: Learning Words by Frequency and Cognate* (Vol. 41). (Atlanta, GA: Society of Biblical Literature, 2001), 106.

[759] Allen, L. C. *Psalms 101–150* (Revised) (Vol. 21). (Dallas: Word, Incorporated, 2002), 186.

[760] Swanson, J. *Dictionary of Biblical Languages with Semantic Domains: Hebrew (Old Testament)* (electronic ed.). (Oak Harbor: Logos Research Systems, Inc., 1997).

[761] Holladay, W. L., and L. Köhler. A Concise Hebrew and Aramaic Lexicon of the Old Testament. (Leiden: Brill, 2000), 309.

[762] Barnes, Albert. Notes on the Psalms, Critical, Explanatory and Practical. (New York: Harper & Brothers, 1868), Psalm 119:11.

[763] Sproul, R. C. "40 Quotes From R. C. Sproul." https://www.thegospelcoalition.org/article/40-quotes-rc-sproul/, accessed November 15, 2018.

[764] Benson, Joseph. *The Holy Bible With Notes, Critical, Explanatory and Practical.* (London: J. Kershaw, 1825), Psalm 119:9.

[765] Harman, A. *Psalms: A Mentor Commentary (Vol. 1–2).* (Ross-shire, Great Britain: Mentor, 2011), 845.

[766] Ibid.

[767] Exell, Joseph S. Ed. *The Biblical Illustrator,* Psalm 110:9 ("A Young Man's Way).

[768] Gill, John. *The John Gill Exposition of the Entire Bible,* Psalm 119:11.

[769] Plumer, W. S. *Studies in the Book of Psalms: Being a Critical and Expository Commentary, with Doctrinal and Practical Remarks on the Entire Psalter.* (Philadelphia; Edinburgh: J. B. Lippincott Company; A & C Black, 1872), 1026.

[770] Maclaren, Alexander. *The Expositor's Bible:* The Psalms. (New York: Scriptura Press, 2015), Psalm 119:9.

[771] Spence-Jones, H. D. M. (Ed.). *Psalms,* (Vol. 3). (London; New York: Funk & Wagnalls Company, 1909), Psalm 119:9.

[772] https://biblehub.com/commentaries/psalms/119-6.htm.

[773] Spence-Jones, H. D. M. (Ed.). *Psalms,* (Vol. 3). (London; New York: Funk & Wagnalls Company, 1909), 103.

[774] http://www.bible-researcher.com/hermeneutics2.html, accessed July 13, 2018.

[775] Spurgeon, C. H. *The Treasury of David.* (Grand Rapids, Michigan: Kregel Publications, 2004), Psalm 119:7.

[776] Exell, Joseph S. Ed. *The Biblical Illustrator,* Psalm 119:11. C. J. Phipps Eyre ("God's Word in the Heart").

[777] Exell, Joseph S. Ed. *The Biblical Illustrator,* Psalm 119:11. Anonymous ("The Word of God in the Heart").

[778] Plumer, W. S. *Studies in the Book of Psalms: Being a Critical and Expository Commentary, with Doctrinal and Practical Remarks on the Entire Psalter.* (Philadelphia; Edinburgh: J. B. Lippincott Company; A & C Black, 1872), 1063.

[779] Lockyer, Herbert, Sr. *Psalms: A Devotional Commentary,* Psalm 110. (Grand Rapids: Kregel Publications, 1993), Psalm 119:11.

[780] Simeon, C. *Horae Homileticae: Psalms, LXXIII–CL* (Vol. 6). (London: Samuel Holdsworth, 1836), 305–306.

[781] Harman, A. *Psalms: A Mentor Commentary (Vol. 1–2).* (Ross-shire, Great Britain: Mentor, 2011), 851.

[782] Ibid.

[783] Barnes, Albert. Notes on the Psalms, Critical, Explanatory and Practical. (New York: Harper & Brothers, 1868), Psalm 119:33.

[784] Swanson, J. *Dictionary of Biblical Languages with Semantic Domains: Hebrew (Old Testament)* (electronic ed.). (Oak Harbor: Logos Research Systems, Inc., 1997).

[785] Vine, W. E., M. F. Unger, and W. White, Jr. *Vine's Complete Expository Dictionary of Old and New Testament Words* (Vol. 1). (Nashville: T. Nelson, 1996), 133.

[786] Kirkpatrick, A. F. (Ed.). *The Cambridge Bible for Schools and Colleges,* Psalms. (Cambridge: Cambridge University Press, 1914), Psalm 119:33.

787 Vine, W. E., M. F. Unger, and W. White, Jr. *Vine's Complete Expository Dictionary of Old and New Testament Words* (Vol. 1). (Nashville: T. Nelson, 1996), 244.

788 Landes, G. M. *Building Your Biblical Hebrew Vocabulary: Learning Words by Frequency and Cognate* (Vol. 41). (Atlanta, GA: Society of Biblical Literature, 2001), 79.

789 Gesenius, W., and S. P. Tregelles. *Gesenius' Hebrew and Chaldee Lexicon to the Old Testament Scriptures.* (Bellingham, WA: Logos Bible Software, 2003), 649.

790 Goldberg, L., R. L. Harris, G. L. Archer Jr., and B. K. Waltke (Eds.). *Theological Wordbook of the Old Testament,* 239 בִּין, (electronic ed.). (Chicago: Moody Press, 1999), 103.

791 Simeon, C. *Horae Homileticae: Psalms, LXXIII–CL* (Vol. 6). (London: Samuel Holdsworth, 1836), 318.

792 Strong, J. *The New Strong's Dictionary of Hebrew and Greek Words.* (Nashville: Thomas Nelson, 1996).

793 Brown, F., S. R. Driver, and C. A. Briggs. *Enhanced Brown-Driver-Briggs Hebrew and English Lexicon.* (Oxford: Clarendon Press, 1977), 435.

794 Futato, M. D. *Beginning Biblical Hebrew.* (Winona Lake, IN: Eisenbrauns, 2003), 289.

795 Barnes, Albert. Notes on the Psalms, Critical, Explanatory and Practical. (New York: Harper & Brothers, 1868), Psalm 119:35.

796 Swanson, J. *Dictionary of Biblical Languages with Semantic Domains: Hebrew (Old Testament)* (electronic ed.). (Oak Harbor: Logos Research Systems, Inc., 1997).

797 Ibid.

798 Landes, G. M. *Building Your Biblical Hebrew Vocabulary: Learning Words by Frequency and Cognate* (Vol. 41). (Atlanta, GA: Society of Biblical Literature, 2001), 72.

799 Plumer, W. S. *Studies in the Book of Psalms: Being a Critical and Expository Commentary, with Doctrinal and Practical Remarks on the Entire Psalter.* (Philadelphia; Edinburgh: J. B. Lippincott Company; A & C Black, 1872), 1036.

800 Brown, F., S. R. Driver, and C. A. Briggs. *Enhanced Brown-Driver-Briggs Hebrew and English Lexicon.* (Oxford: Clarendon Press, 1977), 639.

801 Thomas, R. L. *New American Standard Hebrew-Aramaic and Greek Dictionaries: updated edition.* (Anaheim: Foundation Publications, Inc., 1998).

802 Swanson, J. *Dictionary of Biblical Languages with Semantic Domains: Hebrew (Old Testament)* (electronic ed.). (Oak Harbor: Logos Research Systems, Inc., 1997).

803 https://biblehub.com/commentaries/psalms/119-36.htm.

[804] Swanson, J. *Dictionary of Biblical Languages with Semantic Domains: Hebrew (Old Testament)* (electronic ed.). (Oak Harbor: Logos Research Systems, Inc., 1997).

[805] Jamieson, R., A. R. Fausset, & D. Brown. *Commentary Critical and Explanatory on the Whole Bible* (Vol. 1). (Oak Harbor, WA: Logos Research Systems, Inc., 1997), Psalm 119:37.

[806] Landes, G. M. *Building Your Biblical Hebrew Vocabulary: Learning Words by Frequency and Cognate* (Vol. 41). (Atlanta, GA: Society of Biblical Literature, 2001), 140.

[807] Jamieson, R., A. R. Fausset, & D. Brown. *Commentary Critical and Explanatory on the Whole Bible* (Vol. 1). (Oak Harbor, WA: Logos Research Systems, Inc., 1997), Psalm 119:37.

[808] Clarke, Adam. *Clarkes' Commentary and Critical Notes*, Psalm 119:37.

[809] Jamieson, R., A. R. Fausset, & D. Brown. *Commentary Critical and Explanatory on the Whole Bible* (Vol. 1). (Oak Harbor, WA: Logos Research Systems, Inc., 1997), Psalm 119:37.

[810] Barnes, Albert. Notes on the Psalms, Critical, Explanatory and Practical. (New York: Harper & Brothers, 1868), Psalm 119:37.

[811] Spurgeon, C. H. *The Treasury of David.* (Grand Rapids, Michigan: Kregel Publications, 2004), Psalm 119:38.

[812] Swanson, J. *Dictionary of Biblical Languages with Semantic Domains: Hebrew (Old Testament)* (electronic ed.). (Oak Harbor: Logos Research Systems, Inc., 1997).

[813] Ibid.

[814] Ibid.

[815] Bridges, C. *Exposition of Psalm 119: As Illustrative of the Character and Exercises of Christian Experience* (Seventeenth Edition). (New York: Robert Carter and Brothers, 1861), 56.

[816] Henry, M. *Matthew Henry's Commentary on the Whole Bible: Complete and Unabridged in One Volume.* (Peabody: Hendrickson, 1994), 917.

[817] Bridges, C. *Exposition of Psalm 119: As Illustrative of the Character and Exercises of Christian Experience* (Seventeenth Edition). (New York: Robert Carter and Brothers, 1861), 57.

[818] Plumer, W. S. *Studies in the Book of Psalms: Being a Critical and Expository Commentary, with Doctrinal and Practical Remarks on the Entire Psalter.* (Philadelphia; Edinburgh: J. B. Lippincott Company; A & C Black, 1872), 1036.

[819] Barnes, Albert. Notes on the Psalms, Critical, Explanatory and Practical. (New York: Harper & Brothers, 1868), Psalm 119:34.

[820] Plumer, W. S. *Studies in the Book of Psalms: Being a Critical and Expository Commentary, with Doctrinal and Practical Remarks on the Entire Psalter.* (Philadelphia; Edinburgh: J. B. Lippincott Company; A & C Black, 1872), 1036.

[821] Spence-Jones, H. D. M. (Ed.). *Psalms,* (Vol. 3). (London; New York: Funk & Wagnalls Company, 1909), 105.

[822] Spurgeon, C. H. *The Treasury of David.* (Grand Rapids, Michigan: Kregel Publications, 2004), Psalm 119:35.

[823] Plumer, W. S. *Studies in the Book of Psalms: Being a Critical and Expository Commentary, with Doctrinal and Practical Remarks on the Entire Psalter.* (Philadelphia; Edinburgh: J. B. Lippincott Company; A & C Black, 1872), 1036.

[824] Ibid.

[825] Henry, M. *Matthew Henry's Commentary on the Whole Bible: Complete and Unabridged in One Volume.* (Peabody: Hendrickson, 1994), 917.

[826] Barnes, Albert. Notes on the Psalms, Critical, Explanatory and Practical. (New York: Harper & Brothers, 1868), Psalm 119:38.

[827] Henry, M. *Matthew Henry's Commentary on the Whole Bible: Complete and Unabridged in One Volume.* (Peabody: Hendrickson, 1994), 917.

[828] Perowne, J. J. S. *The Book of Psalms; A New Translation, with Introductions and Notes, Explanatory and Critical* (Fifth Edition, Revised, Vol. 1). (London; Cambridge: George Bell and Sons; Deighton Bell and Co., 1883), 353.

[829] Plumer, W. S. *Studies in the Book of Psalms: Being a Critical and Expository Commentary, with Doctrinal and Practical Remarks on the Entire Psalter.* (Philadelphia; Edinburgh: J. B. Lippincott Company; A & C Black, 1872), 1037.

[830] Alexander, J. A. *The Psalms Translated and Explained.* (Edinburgh: Andrew Elliot; James Thin, 1864), 487.

[831] Bridges, C. *Exposition of Psalm 119: As Illustrative of the Character and Exercises of Christian Experience* (Seventeenth Edition). (New York: Robert Carter and Brothers, 1861), 56.

[832] Rogers, Adrian. "How to Make Your Bible Come Alive." https://www.lightsource.com/ministry/love-worth-finding/articles/how-to-make-your-bible-come-alive-15542.html, accessed October 24, 2018.

[833] Swanson, J. *Dictionary of Biblical Languages with Semantic Domains: Hebrew (Old Testament)* (electronic ed.). (Oak Harbor: Logos Research Systems, Inc., 1997).

[834] Alexander, J. A. *The Psalms Translated and Explained.* (Edinburgh: Andrew Elliot; James Thin, 1864), 487.

[835] Swanson, J. *Dictionary of Biblical Languages with Semantic Domains: Hebrew (Old Testament)* (electronic ed.). (Oak Harbor: Logos Research Systems, Inc., 1997).

[836] Spence-Jones, H. D. M. (Ed.). *Psalms,* (Vol. 3). (London; New York: Funk & Wagnalls Company, 1909), 105.

[837] https://biblehub.com/commentaries/psalms/119-42.htm.

[838] Gesenius, W., and S. P. Tregelles. *Gesenius' Hebrew and Chaldee Lexicon to the Old Testament Scriptures.* (Bellingham, WA: Logos Bible Software, 2003), 112.

[839] Barnes, Albert. Notes on the Psalms, Critical, Explanatory and Practical. (New York: Harper & Brothers, 1868), Psalm 119:42.

[840] Jamieson, R., A. R. Fausset, & D. Brown. *Commentary Critical and Explanatory on the Whole Bible* (Vol. 1). (Oak Harbor, WA: Logos Research Systems, Inc., 1997), Psalm 119:42.

[841] Spence-Jones, H. D. M. (Ed.). *Psalms,* (Vol. 3). (London; New York: Funk & Wagnalls Company, 1909), 105.

[842] Bridges, Charles. *Exposition of Psalm CXIX.* (London: Seeley, Burnside and Seeley, 1846), 113.

[843] Henry, M. *Matthew Henry's Commentary on the Whole Bible: Complete and Unabridged in One Volume.* (Peabody: Hendrickson, 1994), 917.

[844] Thomas, R. L. *New American Standard Hebrew-Aramaic and Greek Dictionaries: updated edition.* (Anaheim: Foundation Publications, Inc., 1998).

[845] Barnes, Albert. Notes on the Psalms, Critical, Explanatory and Practical. (New York: Harper & Brothers, 1868), Psalm 119:45.

[846] Spence-Jones, H. D. M. (Ed.). *Psalms,* (Vol. 3). (London; New York: Funk & Wagnalls Company, 1909), 105.

[847] Simeon, C. *Horae Homileticae: Psalms, LXXIII–CL* (Vol. 6). (London: Samuel Holdsworth, 1836), 327.

[848] Holladay, W. L., and L. Köhler. A Concise Hebrew and Aramaic Lexicon of the Old Testament. (Leiden: Brill, 2000), 296.

[849] Barnes, Albert. Notes on the Psalms, Critical, Explanatory and Practical. (New York: Harper & Brothers, 1868), Psalm 119:46.

[850] Gesenius, W., and S. P. Tregelles. *Gesenius' Hebrew and Chaldee Lexicon to the Old Testament Scriptures.* (Bellingham, WA: Logos Bible Software, 2003), 15.

[851] Kirkpatrick, A. F. (Ed.). *The Cambridge Bible for Schools and Colleges,* Psalms. (Cambridge: Cambridge University Press, 1914), Psalm 119:48.

[852] Jamieson, R., A. R. Fausset, & D. Brown. *Commentary Critical and Explanatory on the Whole Bible* (Vol. 1). (Oak Harbor, WA: Logos Research Systems, Inc., 1997), Psalm 119:48.

[853] Swanson, J. *Dictionary of Biblical Languages with Semantic Domains: Hebrew (Old Testament)* (electronic ed.). (Oak Harbor: Logos Research Systems, Inc., 1997).

[854] Plumer, W. S. *Studies in the Book of Psalms: Being a Critical and Expository Commentary, with Doctrinal and Practical Remarks on the Entire Psalter.* (Philadelphia; Edinburgh: J. B. Lippincott Company; A & C Black, 1872), 1039.

[855] Ibid.

[856] Ibid.

[857] Bridges, C. *Exposition of Psalm 119: As Illustrative of the Character and Exercises of Christian Experience* (Seventeenth Edition). (New York: Robert Carter and Brothers, 1861), 70.

[858] Plumer, W. S. *Studies in the Book of Psalms: Being a Critical and Expository Commentary, with Doctrinal and Practical Remarks on the Entire Psalter.* (Philadelphia; Edinburgh: J. B. Lippincott Company; A & C Black, 1872), 1041.

[859] Spurgeon, C. H. *The Treasury of David.* (Grand Rapids, Michigan: Kregel Publications, 2004), Psalm 119:44.

[860] Kirkpatrick, A. F. (Ed.). *The Cambridge Bible for Schools and Colleges,* Psalms. (Cambridge: Cambridge University Press, 1914), Psalm 119:45.

[861] Barnes, Albert. Notes on the Psalms, Critical, Explanatory and Practical. (New York: Harper & Brothers, 1868), Psalm 119:45.

[862] Plumer, W. S. *Studies in the Book of Psalms: Being a Critical and Expository Commentary, with Doctrinal and Practical Remarks on the Entire Psalter.* (Philadelphia; Edinburgh: J. B. Lippincott Company; A & C Black, 1872), 1040.

[863] Simeon, C. *Horae Homileticae: Psalms, LXXIII–CL* (Vol. 6). (London: Samuel Holdsworth, 1836), 326.

[864] Spurgeon, C. H. *The Treasury of David.* (Grand Rapids, Michigan: Kregel Publications, 2004), Psalm 119:45.

[865] Alexander, J. A. *The Psalms Translated and Explained.* (Edinburgh: Andrew Elliot; James Thin, 1864), 488.

[866] Gill, John. *The John Gill Exposition of the Entire Bible,* Psalm 119:46.

[867] Lockyer, Herbert, Sr. *Psalms: A Devotional Commentary*. (Grand Rapids: Kregel Publications, 1993), 552.

[868] Bridges, C. *Exposition of Psalm 119: As Illustrative of the Character and Exercises of Christian Experience* (Seventeenth Edition). (New York: Robert Carter and Brothers, 1861), Psalm 119:46.

[869] Alexander, J. A. *The Psalms Translated and Explained.* (Edinburgh: Andrew Elliot; James Thin, 1864), 488.

[870] "I Am Not Ashamed" Lyrics. Retrieved December 3, 2018, from https://www.lyrics.com/lyric/5213611/Janet+Paschal.

[871] Henry, M. *Matthew Henry's Commentary on the Whole Bible: Complete and Unabridged in One Volume.* (Peabody: Hendrickson, 1994), 918.

[872] Alexander, J. A. *The Psalms Translated and Explained.* (Edinburgh: Andrew Elliot; James Thin, 1864), 488.

873 Bridges, C. *Exposition of Psalm 119: As Illustrative of the Character and Exercises of Christian Experience* (Seventeenth Edition). (New York: Robert Carter and Brothers, 1861), Psalm 119:47.

874 Perowne, J. J. S. *The Book of Psalms; A New Translation, with Introductions and Notes, Explanatory and Critical* (Fifth Edition, Revised, Vol. 1). (London; Cambridge: George Bell and Sons; Deighton Bell and Co., 1883), 354.

875 Bridges, C. *Exposition of Psalm 119: As Illustrative of the Character and Exercises of Christian Experience* (Seventeenth Edition). (New York: Robert Carter and Brothers, 1861), Psalm 119:48.

876 Kidner, Derek. *Psalms 73–150: A Commentary on Books III–V of the Psalms.* (Downers Grove, Ill.: InterVarsity, 1975), 461.

877 Gill, John. *The John Gill Exposition of the Entire Bible,* Psalm 119:48.

878 Alexander, J. A. *The Psalms Translated and Explained.* (Edinburgh: Andrew Elliot; James Thin, 1864), 488.

879 Plumer, W. S. *Studies in the Book of Psalms: Being a Critical and Expository Commentary, with Doctrinal and Practical Remarks on the Entire Psalter.* (Philadelphia; Edinburgh: J. B. Lippincott Company; A & C Black, 1872), 1040.

880 Pierson, A. T. *George Mueller of Bristol.* (Grand Rapids: Fleming Revell Company, 1899), .

881 Bridges, C. *Exposition of Psalm 119: As Illustrative of the Character and Exercises of Christian Experience* (Seventeenth Edition). (New York: Robert Carter and Brothers, 1861), Psalm 119:48

882 Henry, M. *Matthew Henry's Commentary on the Whole Bible: Complete and Unabridged in One Volume.* (Peabody: Hendrickson, 1994), 918.

883 Plumer, W. S. *Studies in the Book of Psalms: Being a Critical and Expository Commentary, with Doctrinal and Practical Remarks on the Entire Psalter.* (Philadelphia; Edinburgh: J. B. Lippincott Company; A & C Black, 1872), 1042.

884 Cowman, L. B. *Streams in the Desert,* (Grand Rapids: Zondervan, 1999), May 15.

885 Gesenius, W., and S. P. Tregelles. *Gesenius' Hebrew and Chaldee Lexicon to the Old Testament Scriptures.* (Bellingham, WA: Logos Bible Software, 2003), 187.

886 Harman, A. *Psalms: A Mentor Commentary (Vol. 1–2).* (Ross-shire, Great Britain: Mentor, 2011), 855.

887 Swanson, J. *Dictionary of Biblical Languages with Semantic Domains: Hebrew (Old Testament)* (electronic ed.). (Oak Harbor: Logos Research Systems, Inc., 1997).

888 Ibid.

889 Landes, G. M. *Building Your Biblical Hebrew Vocabulary: Learning Words by Frequency and Cognate* (Vol. 41). (Atlanta, GA: Society of Biblical Literature, 2001), 74.

[890] Kirkpatrick, A. F. (Ed.). *The Cambridge Bible for Schools and Colleges,* Psalms. (Cambridge: Cambridge University Press, 1914), Psalm119:50.

[891] Holladay, W. L., and L. Köhler. A Concise Hebrew and Aramaic Lexicon of the Old Testament. (Leiden: Brill, 2000), 102.

[892] Brown, F., S. R. Driver, and C. A. Briggs. *Enhanced Brown-Driver-Briggs Hebrew and English Lexicon.* (Oxford: Clarendon Press, 1977), 267.

[893] Holladay, W. L., and L. Köhler. A Concise Hebrew and Aramaic Lexicon of the Old Testament. (Leiden: Brill, 2000), 176.

[894] Brown, F., S. R. Driver, and C. A. Briggs. *Enhanced Brown-Driver-Briggs Hebrew and English Lexicon.* (Oxford: Clarendon Press, 1977), 435.

[895] Simeon, C. *Horae Homileticae: Psalms, LXXIII–CL* (Vol. 6). (London: Samuel Holdsworth, 1836), 330.

[896] Thomas, R. L. *New American Standard Hebrew-Aramaic and Greek Dictionaries: updated edition.* (Anaheim: Foundation Publications, Inc., 1998).

[897] Barnes, Albert. Notes on the Psalms, Critical, Explanatory and Practical. (New York: Harper & Brothers, 1868), Psalm 119:53.

[898] Henry, M. *Matthew Henry's Commentary on the Whole Bible: Complete and Unabridged in One Volume.* (Peabody: Hendrickson, 1994), 919.

[899] Landes, G. M. *Building Your Biblical Hebrew Vocabulary: Learning Words by Frequency and Cognate* (Vol. 41). (Atlanta, GA: Society of Biblical Literature, 2001), 163.

[900] Spurgeon, C. H. *The Treasury of David.* (Grand Rapids, Michigan: Kregel Publications, 2004), Psalm 119:49.

[901] Plumer, W. S. *Studies in the Book of Psalms: Being a Critical and Expository Commentary, with Doctrinal and Practical Remarks on the Entire Psalter.* (Philadelphia; Edinburgh: J. B. Lippincott Company; A & C Black, 1872), 1042.

[902] Henry, M. *Matthew Henry's Commentary on the Whole Bible: Complete and Unabridged in One Volume.* (Peabody: Hendrickson, 1994), 918.

[903] Spurgeon, C. H. *The Treasury of David.* (Grand Rapids, Michigan: Kregel Publications, 2004), Psalm 119:49.

[904] Plumer, W. S. *Studies in the Book of Psalms: Being a Critical and Expository Commentary, with Doctrinal and Practical Remarks on the Entire Psalter.* (Philadelphia; Edinburgh: J. B. Lippincott Company; A & C Black, 1872), 1043.

[905] Bridges, C. *Exposition of Psalm 119: As Illustrative of the Character and Exercises of Christian Experience* (Seventeenth Edition). (New York: Robert Carter and Brothers, 1861), 82.

[906] Spurgeon, C. H. *The Treasury of David.* (Grand Rapids, Michigan: Kregel Publications, 2004), Psalm 119:50.

[907] Courson, Jon. *Jon Courson's Application Commentary.* (Nashville, TN: Thomas Nelson, 2003), 1472.

[908] Blackwood, Andrew W. *The Funeral.* (Grand Rapids, Michigan: Baker Book House, 1942), 140.

[909] Moody, D. L. *The Seven "I Will's" of Christ.* www.jesus-is-savior.com/Books, accessed, May 22, 2013.

[910] Spurgeon, C. H. *The Treasury of David.* (Grand Rapids, Michigan: Kregel Publications, 2004), Psalm 119:50.

[911] Plumer, W. S. *Studies in the Book of Psalms: Being a Critical and Expository Commentary, with Doctrinal and Practical Remarks on the Entire Psalter.* (Philadelphia; Edinburgh: J. B. Lippincott Company; A & C Black, 1872), 1043.

[912] Pink, Arthur W. "The Power of God's Word to Convict Men of Sin." The Divine Inspiration of the Bible. http://biblehub.com/library/pink/the_divine_inspiration_of_the_bible/i_the_power_of_gods.htm, accessed July 16, 2018.

[913] Bridges, C. *Exposition of Psalm 119: As Illustrative of the Character and Exercises of Christian Experience* (Seventeenth Edition). (New York: Robert Carter and Brothers, 1861), Psalm 119:50.

[914] Henry, M. *Matthew Henry's Commentary on the Whole Bible: Complete and Unabridged in One Volume.* (Peabody: Hendrickson, 1994), 918.

[915] Plumer, W. S. *Studies in the Book of Psalms: Being a Critical and Expository Commentary, with Doctrinal and Practical Remarks on the Entire Psalter.* (Philadelphia; Edinburgh: J. B. Lippincott Company; A & C Black, 1872), 1044.

[916] Ibid., 1045.

[917] Henry, M. *Matthew Henry's Commentary on the Whole Bible: Complete and Unabridged in One Volume.* (Peabody: Hendrickson, 1994), 918.

[918] Simeon, C. *Horae Homileticae: Psalms, LXXIII–CL* (Vol. 6). (London: Samuel Holdsworth, 1836), 333.

[919] Barnes, Albert. Notes on the Psalms, Critical, Explanatory and Practical. (New York: Harper & Brothers, 1868), Psalm 119:52.

[920] Kirkpatrick, A. F. (Ed.). *The Cambridge Bible for Schools and Colleges,* Psalms. (Cambridge: Cambridge University Press, 1914), Psalm 119:54.

[921] Jamieson, R., A. R. Fausset, & D. Brown. *Commentary Critical and Explanatory on the Whole Bible* (Vol. 1). (Oak Harbor, WA: Logos Research Systems, Inc., 1997), Psalm 119:54.

[922] Plumer, W. S. *Studies in the Book of Psalms: Being a Critical and Expository Commentary, with Doctrinal and Practical Remarks on the Entire Psalter.* (Philadelphia; Edinburgh: J. B. Lippincott Company; A & C Black, 1872), 1043.

[923] Ibid.

[924] Ibid.

[925] Ibid.

[926] Ibid.

[927] Ibid.

[928] Spurgeon, C. H. *Morning and Evening,* November 2 (Evening).

[929] https://biblehub.com/commentaries/psalms/119-55.htm.

[930] Gill, John. *The John Gill Exposition of the Entire Bible,* Psalm 119:55.

[931] Spurgeon, C. H. *Morning and Evening,* April 28 (Morning).

[932] Swanson, J. *Dictionary of Biblical Languages with Semantic Domains: Hebrew (Old Testament)* (electronic ed.). (Oak Harbor: Logos Research Systems, Inc., 1997).

[933] Alexander, J. A. *The Psalms Translated and Explained.* (Edinburgh: Andrew Elliot; James Thin, 1864), 491.

[934] Vine, W. E., M. F. Unger, and W. White, Jr. *Vine's Complete Expository Dictionary of Old and New Testament Words* (Vol. 1). (Nashville: T. Nelson, 1996), 79.

[935] Holladay, W. L., and L. Köhler. A Concise Hebrew and Aramaic Lexicon of the Old Testament. (Leiden: Brill, 2000), 296.

[936] Harman, A. *Psalms: A Mentor Commentary (Vol. 1–2).* (Ross-shire, Great Britain: Mentor, 2011), 859.

[937] Henry, M. *Matthew Henry's Commentary on the Whole Bible: Complete and Unabridged in One Volume.* (Peabody: Hendrickson, 1994), 919.

[938] Barnes, Albert. Notes on the Psalms, Critical, Explanatory and Practical. (New York: Harper & Brothers, 1868), Psalm 119:63.

[939] Bridges, C. *Exposition of Psalm 119: As Illustrative of the Character and Exercises of Christian Experience* (Seventeenth Edition). (New York: Robert Carter and Brothers, 1861), 100.

[940] Ibid., Psalm 119:63.

[941] Plumer, W. S. *Studies in the Book of Psalms: Being a Critical and Expository Commentary, with Doctrinal and Practical Remarks on the Entire Psalter.* (Philadelphia; Edinburgh: J. B. Lippincott Company; A & C Black, 1872), 1047.

[942] Ibid., 1049.

[943] Coppes, L. J., R. L. Harris, G. L. Archer Jr., and B. K. Waltke (Eds.). *Theological Wordbook of the Old Testament,* 1652 עָנָה, (electronic ed.). (Chicago: Moody Press, 1999, 682.

[944] Ross, A. P. In Walvoord, J. F. and R. B. Zuck (Eds.). *The Bible Knowledge Commentary: An Exposition of the Scriptures* (Vol. 1, Psalms). (Wheaton, IL: Victor Books, 1985), 881.

[945] Harman, A. *Psalms: A Mentor Commentary (Vol. 1–2).* (Ross-shire, Great Britain: Mentor, 2011), 860.

[946] Swanson, J. *Dictionary of Biblical Languages with Semantic Domains: Hebrew (Old Testament)* (electronic ed.). (Oak Harbor: Logos Research Systems, Inc., 1997).

947 Landes, G. M. *Building Your Biblical Hebrew Vocabulary: Learning Words by Frequency and Cognate* (Vol. 41). (Atlanta, GA: Society of Biblical Literature, 2001), 58.

948 Alexander, J. A. *The Psalms Translated and Explained.* (Edinburgh: Andrew Elliot; James Thin, 1864), 492.

949 Swanson, J. *Dictionary of Biblical Languages with Semantic Domains: Hebrew (Old Testament)* (electronic ed.). (Oak Harbor: Logos Research Systems, Inc., 1997).

950 Alexander, J. A. *The Psalms Translated and Explained.* (Edinburgh: Andrew Elliot; James Thin, 1864), 492.

951 Vine, W. E., M. F. Unger, and W. White, Jr. *Vine's Complete Expository Dictionary of Old and New Testament Words* (Vol. 1). (Nashville: T. Nelson, 1996), 256.

952 Holladay, W. L., and L. Köhler. A Concise Hebrew and Aramaic Lexicon of the Old Testament. (Leiden: Brill, 2000), 86.

953 Brown, F., S. R. Driver, and C. A. Briggs. *Enhanced Brown-Driver-Briggs Hebrew and English Lexicon.* (Oxford: Clarendon Press, 1977), 381.

954 Holladay, W. L., and L. Köhler. A Concise Hebrew and Aramaic Lexicon of the Old Testament. (Leiden: Brill, 2000), 383.

955 Ibid., 156.

956 Swanson, J. *Dictionary of Biblical Languages with Semantic Domains: Hebrew (Old Testament)* (electronic ed.). (Oak Harbor: Logos Research Systems, Inc., 1997).

957 https://biblehub.com/psalms/119-70.htm.

958 Spurgeon, C. H. *The Treasury of David.* (Grand Rapids, Michigan: Kregel Publications, 2004), Psalm 119:70.

959 Alexander, J. A. *The Psalms Translated and Explained.* (Edinburgh: Andrew Elliot; James Thin, 1864), 492.

960 Holladay, W. L., and L. Köhler. A Concise Hebrew and Aramaic Lexicon of the Old Testament. (Leiden: Brill, 2000), 122.

961 Spence-Jones, H. D. M. (Ed.). *Psalms,* (Vol. 3). (London; New York: Funk & Wagnalls Company, 1909), 107.

962 Benson, Joseph. *The Holy Bible With Notes, Critical, Explanatory and Practical.* (London: J. Kershaw, 1825), Psalm 119:71.

963 Spence-Jones, H. D. M. (Ed.). *Psalms,* (Vol. 3). (London; New York: Funk & Wagnalls Company, 1909), 107.

964 Simeon, C. *Horae Homileticae: Psalms, LXXIII–CL* (Vol. 6). (London: Samuel Holdsworth, 1836), 339.

965 Coppes, L. J., R. L. Harris, G. L. Archer Jr., and B. K. Waltke (Eds.). *Theological Wordbook of the Old Testament,* 1652 עָנָה, (electronic ed.). (Chicago: Moody Press, 1999), 682.

966 Henry, M. *Matthew Henry's Commentary on the Whole Bible: Complete and Unabridged in One Volume.* (Peabody: Hendrickson, 1994), 919.

967 Gill, John. *The John Gill Exposition of the Entire Bible,* Psalm 119:67.

968 Bridges, C. *Exposition of Psalm 119: As Illustrative of the Character and Exercises of Christian Experience* (Seventeenth Edition). (New York: Robert Carter and Brothers, 1861), 110.

969 Spurgeon, C. H. *The Treasury of David.* (Grand Rapids, Michigan: Kregel Publications, 2004), Psalm 119:68.

970 Henry, M. *Matthew Henry's Commentary on the Whole Bible: Complete and Unabridged in One Volume.* (Peabody: Hendrickson, 1994), 920.

971 Bridges, C. *Exposition of Psalm 119: As Illustrative of the Character and Exercises of Christian Experience* (Seventeenth Edition). (New York: Robert Carter and Brothers, 1861), Psalm 119:67.

972 Jamieson, R., A. R. Fausset, & D. Brown. *Commentary Critical and Explanatory on the Whole Bible* (Vol. 1). (Oak Harbor, WA: Logos Research Systems, Inc., 1997), Psalm 119:71–72.

973 Gill, John. *The John Gill Exposition of the Entire Bible,* Psalm 119:71.

974 Vine, W. E., M. F. Unger, and W. White, Jr. *Vine's Complete Expository Dictionary of Old and New Testament Words* (Vol. 1). (Nashville: T. Nelson, 1996), 176.

975 Swanson, J. *Dictionary of Biblical Languages with Semantic Domains: Hebrew (Old Testament)* (electronic ed.). (Oak Harbor: Logos Research Systems, Inc., 1997).

976 Bridges, C. *Exposition of Psalm 119: As Illustrative of the Character and Exercises of Christian Experience* (Seventeenth Edition). (New York: Robert Carter and Brothers, 1861), 131.

977 Ibid., 133.

978 Benson, Joseph. *The Holy Bible With Notes, Critical, Explanatory and Practical.* (London: J. Kershaw, 1825), Psalm 119:80.

979 Barnes, Albert. Notes on the Psalms, Critical, Explanatory and Practical. (New York: Harper & Brothers, 1868), Psalm 119:80.

980 Spurgeon, C. H. *The Treasury of David.* (Grand Rapids, Michigan: Kregel Publications, 2004), Psalm 119:80.

981 Contributed by Dr. Nina Gunter who got it from veteran missionary Louise Robinson Chapman (Africa: 1920–1940).

982 Macrae, A. A., R. L. Harris, G. L. Archer Jr., and B. K. Waltke (Eds.). *Theological Wordbook of the Old Testament,* 1631 עלם, (electronic ed.). (Chicago: Moody Press, 1999), 672.

983 Swanson, J. *Dictionary of Biblical Languages with Semantic Domains: Hebrew (Old Testament)* (electronic ed.). (Oak Harbor: Logos Research Systems, Inc., 1997).

984 Kirkpatrick, A. F. (Ed.). *The Cambridge Bible for Schools and Colleges,* Psalms. (Cambridge: Cambridge University Press, 1914), Psalm 119:90.

985 Spurgeon, C. H. *The Treasury of David.* (Grand Rapids, Michigan: Kregel Publications, 2004), Psalm 119:91.

986 Henry, M. *Matthew Henry's Commentary on the Whole Bible: Complete and Unabridged in One Volume.* (Peabody: Hendrickson, 1994), 921.

987 Alexander, J. A. *The Psalms Translated and Explained.* (Edinburgh: Andrew Elliot; James Thin, 1864), 495.

988 Benson, Joseph. *The Holy Bible With Notes, Critical, Explanatory and Practical.* (London: J. Kershaw, 1825), Psalm 119:89.

989 Allen, L. C. *Psalms 101–150* (Revised) (Vol. 21). (Dallas: Word, Incorporated, 2002), 189.

990 Spence-Jones, H. D. M. (Ed.). *Psalms,* (Vol. 3). (London; New York: Funk & Wagnalls Company, 1909), 108.

991 Dictionary.com.

992 Spurgeon, C. H. *The Treasury of David.* (Grand Rapids, Michigan: Kregel Publications, 2004), Psalm 119:91 (Hints to Preachers).

993 Harman, A. *Psalms: A Mentor Commentary (Vol. 1–2).* (Ross-shire, Great Britain: Mentor, 2011), 865.

994 Barnes, Albert. Notes on the Psalms, Critical, Explanatory and Practical. (New York: Harper & Brothers, 1868), Psalm 119:96.

995 Ibid.

996 Benson, Joseph. *The Holy Bible With Notes, Critical, Explanatory and Practical.* (London: J. Kershaw, 1825), Psalm 119:96.

997 Jamieson, R., A. R. Fausset, & D. Brown. *Commentary Critical and Explanatory on the Whole Bible* (Vol. 1). (Oak Harbor, WA: Logos Research Systems, Inc., 1997), Psalm 119:96.

998 Barnes, Albert. Notes on the Psalms, Critical, Explanatory and Practical. (New York: Harper & Brothers, 1868), Psalm 119:96.

999 https://biblehub.com/commentaries/psalms/119-96.htm.

1000 Moody, D. L. *Pleasures and Profit in Bible Study.* (Grand Rapids: Fleming Revell Publishers, 1895), 32–33.

1001 Strong, J. *A Concise Dictionary of the Words in the Greek Testament and the Hebrew Bible.* (Vol. 2). (Bellingham, WA: Logos Bible Software, 2009), 55.

¹⁰⁰² Swanson, J. *Dictionary of Biblical Languages with Semantic Domains: Hebrew (Old Testament)* (electronic ed.). (Oak Harbor: Logos Research Systems, Inc., 1997).

¹⁰⁰³ Strong, J. *A Concise Dictionary of the Words in the Greek Testament and the Hebrew Bible.* (Vol. 2). (Bellingham, WA: Logos Bible Software, 2009), 118.

¹⁰⁰⁴ Landes, G. M. *Building Your Biblical Hebrew Vocabulary: Learning Words by Frequency and Cognate* (Vol. 41). (Atlanta, GA: Society of Biblical Literature, 2001), 57.

¹⁰⁰⁵ Gesenius, W., and S. P. Tregelles. *Gesenius' Hebrew and Chaldee Lexicon to the Old Testament Scriptures.* (Bellingham, WA: Logos Bible Software, 2003), 366.

¹⁰⁰⁶ Ibid.

¹⁰⁰⁷ Swanson, J. *Dictionary of Biblical Languages with Semantic Domains: Hebrew (Old Testament)* (electronic ed.). (Oak Harbor: Logos Research Systems, Inc., 1997).

¹⁰⁰⁸ Gesenius, W., and S. P. Tregelles. *Gesenius' Hebrew and Chaldee Lexicon to the Old Testament Scriptures.* (Bellingham, WA: Logos Bible Software, 2003), 113.

¹⁰⁰⁹ Holladay, W. L., and L. Köhler. A Concise Hebrew and Aramaic Lexicon of the Old Testament. (Leiden: Brill, 2000), 353.

¹⁰¹⁰ Ibid., 383.

¹⁰¹¹ Vine, W. E., M. F. Unger, and W. White, Jr. *Vine's Complete Expository Dictionary of Old and New Testament Words* (Vol. 1). (Nashville: T. Nelson, 1996), 77.

¹⁰¹² Barnes, Albert. Notes on the Psalms, Critical, Explanatory and Practical. (New York: Harper & Brothers, 1868), Psalm 119:101.

¹⁰¹³ Ibid.

¹⁰¹⁴ Spurgeon, C. H. *The Treasury of David.* (Grand Rapids, Michigan: Kregel Publications, 2004), Psalm 119:101.

¹⁰¹⁵ Bridges, C. *Exposition of Psalm 119: As Illustrative of the Character and Exercises of Christian Experience* (Seventeenth Edition). (New York: Robert Carter and Brothers, 1861), Psalm 119:102.

¹⁰¹⁶ Kirkpatrick, A. F. (Ed.). *The Cambridge Bible for Schools and Colleges, Psalms.* (Cambridge: Cambridge University Press, 1914), Psalm 119:104.

¹⁰¹⁷ Plumer, W. S. *Studies in the Book of Psalms: Being a Critical and Expository Commentary, with Doctrinal and Practical Remarks on the Entire Psalter.* (Philadelphia; Edinburgh: J. B. Lippincott Company; A & C Black, 1872), 1064.

¹⁰¹⁸ Henry, M. *Matthew Henry's Commentary on the Whole Bible: Complete and Unabridged in One Volume.* (Peabody: Hendrickson, 1994), 923.

¹⁰¹⁹ Plumer, W. S. *Studies in the Book of Psalms: Being a Critical and Expository Commentary, with Doctrinal and Practical Remarks on the Entire Psalter.* (Philadelphia; Edinburgh: J. B. Lippincott Company; A & C Black, 1872), 1064–1065.

[1020] Swanson, J. *Dictionary of Biblical Languages with Semantic Domains: Hebrew (Old Testament)* (electronic ed.). (Oak Harbor: Logos Research Systems, Inc., 1997).

[1021] Landes, G. M. *Building Your Biblical Hebrew Vocabulary: Learning Words by Frequency and Cognate* (Vol. 41). (Atlanta, GA: Society of Biblical Literature, 2001), 173.

[1022] Jamieson, R., A. R. Fausset, & D. Brown. *Commentary Critical and Explanatory on the Whole Bible* (Vol. 1). (Oak Harbor, WA: Logos Research Systems, Inc., 1997), Psalm 119:105.

[1023] Barnes, Albert. Notes on the Psalms, Critical, Explanatory and Practical. (New York: Harper & Brothers, 1868), Psalm 119:105.

[1024] Strong, J. *The New Strong's Dictionary of Hebrew and Greek Words.* (Nashville: Thomas Nelson, 1996).

[1025] Whitaker, R., F. Brown, S. R. Driver, and C. A. Briggs. *The Abridged Brown-Driver-Briggs Hebrew-English Lexicon of the Old Testament.* (New York: Houghton, Mifflin and Company, 1906).

[1026] Barnes, Albert. Notes on the Psalms, Critical, Explanatory and Practical. (New York: Harper & Brothers, 1868), Psalm 119:105.

[1027] Gill, John. *The John Gill Exposition of the Entire Bible,* Psalm 119:105.

[1028] Bridges, C. *Exposition of Psalm 119: As Illustrative of the Character and Exercises of Christian Experience* (Seventeenth Edition). (New York: Robert Carter and Brothers, 1861), Psalm 119:105.

[1029] Gill, John. *The John Gill Exposition of the Entire Bible,* Psalm 119:105.

[1030] Henry, M. *Matthew Henry's Commentary on the Whole Bible: Complete and Unabridged in One Volume.* (Peabody: Hendrickson, 1994), 923.

[1031] Ibid.

[1032] Plumer, W. S. *Studies in the Book of Psalms: Being a Critical and Expository Commentary, with Doctrinal and Practical Remarks on the Entire Psalter.* (Philadelphia; Edinburgh: J. B. Lippincott Company; A & C Black, 1872), 1066.

[1033] Gesenius, W., and S. P. Tregelles. *Gesenius' Hebrew and Chaldee Lexicon to the Old Testament Scriptures.* (Bellingham, WA: Logos Bible Software, 2003), 661.

[1034] Swanson, J. *Dictionary of Biblical Languages with Semantic Domains: Hebrew (Old Testament)* (electronic ed.). (Oak Harbor: Logos Research Systems, Inc., 1997).

[1035] Barnes, Albert. Notes on the Psalms, Critical, Explanatory and Practical. (New York: Harper & Brothers, 1868), Psalm 119:126.

[1036] Holladay, W. L., and L. Köhler. A Concise Hebrew and Aramaic Lexicon of the Old Testament. (Leiden: Brill, 2000), 299.

[1037] Henry, M. *Matthew Henry's Commentary on the Whole Bible: Complete and Unabridged in One Volume.* (Peabody: Hendrickson, 1994), Psalms 119:126.

[1038] Mellor, E. "The Hem of Christ's Garment," 19. As cited in the Sermon Bible Commentary.

[1039] Bridges, C. *Exposition of Psalm 119: As Illustrative of the Character and Exercises of Christian Experience* (Seventeenth Edition). (New York: Robert Carter and Brothers, 1861), Psalm 119:126.

[1040] Ogilvie, Lloyd J. (General Editor). *The Preacher's Commentary: Psalms 73 – 150.* (Nashville: Thomas Nelson Publishers, 1989), 349.

[1041] Hanegraaff, Hank. "The Counterfeit Revival Revisited," CRI Statement DP245. http://www.equip.org/PDF/DP245.pdf, accessed November 21, 2018.

[1042] Hamilton, William W. *Sermons on the Books of the Bible,* (Vol. 5), 116.

[1043] Ibid., 186.

[1044] Spurgeon, C. H. *The Treasury of David.* (Grand Rapids, Michigan: Kregel Publications, 2004), Psalm 119:126.

[1045] Barnes, Albert. Notes on the Psalms, Critical, Explanatory and Practical. (New York: Harper & Brothers, 1868), Psalm 119:126.

[1046] Bridges, C. *Exposition of Psalm 119: As Illustrative of the Character and Exercises of Christian Experience* (Seventeenth Edition). (New York: Robert Carter and Brothers, 1861), Psalm 119:126.

[1047] Coke, Thomas. *A Commentary on the Holy Bible.* (London: G. Whitfield, 1801), 119:126.

[1048] Henry, M. *Matthew Henry's Commentary on the Whole Bible: Complete and Unabridged in One Volume.* (Peabody: Hendrickson, 1994), 803.

[1049] Spurgeon, C. H. *The Treasury of David.* (Grand Rapids, Michigan: Kregel Publications, 2004), Psalm 119:126.

[1050] Henry, M. *Matthew Henry's Commentary on the Whole Bible: Complete and Unabridged in One Volume.* (Peabody: Hendrickson, 1994), 924.

[1051] Spurgeon, C. H. *The Treasury of David.* (Grand Rapids, Michigan: Kregel Publications, 2004), Psalm 119:126.

[1052] Kirkpatrick, A. F. (Ed.). *The Cambridge Bible for Schools and Colleges,* Psalms. (Cambridge: Cambridge University Press, 1914), Psalm 119:129.

[1053] Harman, A. *Psalms: A Mentor Commentary (Vol. 1–2).* (Ross-shire, Great Britain: Mentor, 2011), 873.

[1054] Spence-Jones, H. D. M. (Ed.). *Psalms,* (Vol. 3). (London; New York: Funk & Wagnalls Company, 1909), 110.

[1055] Barnes, Albert. Notes on the Psalms, Critical, Explanatory and Practical. (New York: Harper & Brothers, 1868), Psalm 119:129.

[1056] Gill, John. *The John Gill Exposition of the Entire Bible,* Psalm 119:129.

[1057] Plumer, W. S. *Studies in the Book of Psalms: Being a Critical and Expository Commentary, with Doctrinal and Practical Remarks on the Entire Psalter.* (Philadelphia; Edinburgh: J. B. Lippincott Company; A & C Black, 1872), 1075.

[1058] Spurgeon, C. H. *The Treasury of David.* (Grand Rapids, Michigan: Kregel Publications, 2004), Psalm 119:129.

[1059] Henry, M. *Matthew Henry's Commentary on the Whole Bible: Complete and Unabridged in One Volume.* (Peabody: Hendrickson, 1994), 925.

[1060] Spurgeon, C. H. *The Treasury of David.* (Grand Rapids, Michigan: Kregel Publications, 2004), Psalm 119:129.

[1061] Henry, M. *Matthew Henry's Commentary on the Whole Bible: Complete and Unabridged in One Volume.* (Peabody: Hendrickson, 1994), 925.

[1062] Spurgeon, C. H. *The Treasury of David.* (Grand Rapids, Michigan: Kregel Publications, 2004), Psalm 119:129.

[1063] Jamieson, R., A. R. Fausset, & D. Brown. *Commentary Critical and Explanatory on the Whole Bible* (Vol. 1). (Oak Harbor, WA: Logos Research Systems, Inc., 1997), Psalm 119:130.

[1064] Kirkpatrick, A. F. (Ed.). *The Cambridge Bible for Schools and Colleges, Psalms.* (Cambridge: Cambridge University Press, 1914), Psalm 119:130.

[1065] Gesenius, W., and S. P. Tregelles. *Gesenius' Hebrew and Chaldee Lexicon to the Old Testament Scriptures.* (Bellingham, WA: Logos Bible Software, 2003), 697.

[1066] Strong, J. *Enhanced Strong's Lexicon.* (Ontario: Woodside Bible Fellowship, 1995).

[1067] Gesenius, W., and S. P. Tregelles. *Gesenius' Hebrew and Chaldee Lexicon to the Old Testament Scriptures.* (Bellingham, WA: Logos Bible Software, 2003), 23.

[1068] Swanson, J. *Dictionary of Biblical Languages with Semantic Domains: Hebrew (Old Testament)* (electronic ed.). (Oak Harbor: Logos Research Systems, Inc., 1997).

[1069] Alexander, J. A. *The Psalms Translated and Explained.* (Edinburgh: Andrew Elliot; James Thin, 1864), 89.

[1070] Spurgeon, C. H. *The Treasury of David.* (Grand Rapids, Michigan: Kregel Publications, 2004), Psalm 119:130.

[1071] Henry, M. *Matthew Henry's Commentary on the Whole Bible: Complete and Unabridged in One Volume.* (Peabody: Hendrickson, 1994), 925.

[1072] Ibid.

[1073] Bridges, C. *Exposition of Psalm 119: As Illustrative of the Character and Exercises of Christian Experience* (Seventeenth Edition). (New York: Robert Carter and Brothers, 1861), 208.

[1074] Henry, M. *Matthew Henry's Commentary on the Whole Bible: Complete and Unabridged in One Volume.* (Peabody: Hendrickson, 1994), 925.

[1075] Spurgeon, C. H. *The Treasury of David.* (Grand Rapids, Michigan: Kregel Publications, 2004), Psalm 119:130.

[1076] Bridges, C. *Exposition of Psalm 119: As Illustrative of the Character and Exercises of Christian Experience* (Seventeenth Edition). (New York: Robert Carter and Brothers, 1861), Psalm 119:130.

[1077] Gesenius, W., and S. P. Tregelles. *Gesenius' Hebrew and Chaldee Lexicon to the Old Testament Scriptures.* (Bellingham, WA: Logos Bible Software, 2003), 678.

[1078] Swanson, J. *Dictionary of Biblical Languages with Semantic Domains: Hebrew (Old Testament)* (electronic ed.). (Oak Harbor: Logos Research Systems, Inc., 1997).

[1079] Benson, Joseph. *The Holy Bible With Notes, Critical, Explanatory and Practical.* (London: J. Kershaw, 1825), Psalm 119:132.

[1080] Barnes, Albert. Notes on the Psalms, Critical, Explanatory and Practical. (New York: Harper & Brothers, 1868), Psalm 119:132.

[1081] Kirkpatrick, A. F. (Ed.). *The Cambridge Bible for Schools and Colleges, Psalms.* (Cambridge: Cambridge University Press, 1914), Psalm 119:132.

[1082] Vine, W. E., M. F. Unger, and W. White, Jr. *Vine's Complete Expository Dictionary of Old and New Testament Words* (Vol. 1). (Nashville: T. Nelson, 1996), 186.

[1083] Swanson, J. *Dictionary of Biblical Languages with Semantic Domains: Hebrew (Old Testament)* (electronic ed.). (Oak Harbor: Logos Research Systems, Inc., 1997).

[1084] Livingston, G. H., R. L. Harris, G. L. Archer Jr., and B. K. Waltke (Eds.). *Theological Wordbook of the Old Testament,* 48 אין, (electronic ed.). (Chicago: Moody Press, 1999), 23.

[1085] Strong, J. *A Concise Dictionary of the Words in the Greek Testament and the Hebrew Bible.* (Vol. 2). (Bellingham, WA: Logos Bible Software, 2009), 117.

[1086] Exell, Joseph S. Ed. *The Biblical Illustrator,* Psalm 118:1–4. T. DeWitt Talmage.

[1087] Henry, M. *Matthew Henry's Commentary on the Whole Bible: Complete and Unabridged in One Volume.* (Peabody: Hendrickson, 1994), 925.

[1088] Spurgeon, C. H. *The Treasury of David.* (Grand Rapids, Michigan: Kregel Publications, 2004), Psalm 119:133.

[1089] Bridges, C. *Exposition of Psalm 119: As Illustrative of the Character and Exercises of Christian Experience* (Seventeenth Edition). (New York: Robert Carter and Brothers, 1861), Psalm 119:33.

[1090] Benson, Joseph. *The Holy Bible With Notes, Critical, Explanatory and Practical.* (London: J. Kershaw, 1825), Psalm 119:133.

[1091] Clarke, Adam. *Clarkes' Commentary and Critical Notes,* Psalm 119:133.

[1092] Plumer, W. S. *Studies in the Book of Psalms: Being a Critical and Expository Commentary, with Doctrinal and Practical Remarks on the Entire Psalter.* (Philadelphia; Edinburgh: J. B. Lippincott Company; A & C Black, 1872), 1075.

1093 Barnes, Albert. Notes on the Psalms, Critical, Explanatory and Practical. (New York: Harper & Brothers, 1868), Psalm 119:136.
1094 Sanders, Oswald J. *The Revival We Need*. (New York: The Christian Alliance Publishing Company, 1925), Chapter 3.
1095 E. M. Harrison. *How to Win Souls*. (Wheaton: Van Kamper Press, 1952), 23.
1096 Plumer, W. S. *Studies in the Book of Psalms: Being a Critical and Expository Commentary, with Doctrinal and Practical Remarks on the Entire Psalter*. (Philadelphia; Edinburgh: J. B. Lippincott Company; A & C Black, 1872), 1076.
1097 Spurgeon, C. H. *The Treasury of David*. (Grand Rapids, Michigan: Kregel Publications, 2004), Psalm 119:136.
1098 https://biblehub.com/commentaries/psalms/119-136.htm.
1099 Appelman, Hymen J. *The Savior's Invitation and Other Evangelistic Sermons*. (Grand Rapids: Baker Book House, 1981), 35–42.
1100 Barnes, Albert. Notes on the Psalms, Critical, Explanatory and Practical. (New York: Harper & Brothers, 1868), Psalm 119:136.
1101 Bridges, C. *Exposition of Psalm 119: As Illustrative of the Character and Exercises of Christian Experience* (Seventeenth Edition). (New York: Robert Carter and Brothers, 1861), Psalm 119:136.
1102 Plumer, W. S. *Studies in the Book of Psalms: Being a Critical and Expository Commentary, with Doctrinal and Practical Remarks on the Entire Psalter*. (Philadelphia; Edinburgh: J. B. Lippincott Company; A & C Black, 1872), 1077.
1103 Henry, M. *Matthew Henry's Commentary on the Whole Bible: Complete and Unabridged in One Volume*. (Peabody: Hendrickson, 1994), 925.
1104 Plumer, W. S. *Studies in the Book of Psalms: Being a Critical and Expository Commentary, with Doctrinal and Practical Remarks on the Entire Psalter*. (Philadelphia; Edinburgh: J. B. Lippincott Company; A & C Black, 1872), 1077.
1105 Simeon, C. *Horae Homileticae: Psalms, LXXIII–CL* (Vol. 6). (London: Samuel Holdsworth, 1836), 369.
1106 Bridges, C. *Exposition of Psalm 119: As Illustrative of the Character and Exercises of Christian Experience* (Seventeenth Edition). (New York: Robert Carter and Brothers, 1861), Psalm 119:136.
1107 Gesenius, W., and S. P. Tregelles. *Gesenius' Hebrew and Chaldee Lexicon to the Old Testament Scriptures*. (Bellingham, WA: Logos Bible Software, 2003), 870.
1108 Ibid., 3.
1109 Barnes, Albert. Notes on the Psalms, Critical, Explanatory and Practical. (New York: Harper & Brothers, 1868), Psalm 119:176.
1110 Ibid.
1111 Perowne, J. J. S. *The Book of Psalms; A New Translation, with Introductions and Notes, Explanatory and Critical* (Fifth Edition, Revised, Vol. 1). (London; Cambridge: George Bell and Sons; Deighton Bell and Co., 1883), 367.

[1112] Plumer, W. S. *Studies in the Book of Psalms: Being a Critical and Expository Commentary, with Doctrinal and Practical Remarks on the Entire Psalter.* (Philadelphia; Edinburgh: J. B. Lippincott Company; A & C Black, 1872), 1090.

[1113] Barnes, Albert. Notes on the Psalms, Critical, Explanatory and Practical. (New York: Harper & Brothers, 1868), Psalm 119:176.

[1114] Ibid.

[1115] Spurgeon, C. H. *The Treasury of David.* (Grand Rapids, Michigan: Kregel Publications, 2004), Psalm 119:176.

[1116] Spurgeon, C. H. *Morning and Evening,* October 22 (Morning).

[1117] Strong, J. *The New Strong's Dictionary of Hebrew and Greek Words.* (Nashville: Thomas Nelson, 1996).

[1118] Landes, G. M. *Building Your Biblical Hebrew Vocabulary: Learning Words by Frequency and Cognate* (Vol. 41). (Atlanta, GA: Society of Biblical Literature, 2001), 51.

[1119] Swanson, J. *Dictionary of Biblical Languages with Semantic Domains: Hebrew (Old Testament)* (electronic ed.). (Oak Harbor: Logos Research Systems, Inc., 1997).

[1120] Brown, F., S. R. Driver, and C. A. Briggs. *Enhanced Brown-Driver-Briggs Hebrew and English Lexicon.* (Oxford: Clarendon Press, 1977), 1055.

[1121] Swanson, J. *Dictionary of Biblical Languages with Semantic Domains: Hebrew (Old Testament)* (electronic ed.). (Oak Harbor: Logos Research Systems, Inc., 1997).

[1122] https://biblehub.com/commentaries/psalms/120-2.htm.

[1123] Kirkpatrick, A. F. (Ed.). *The Cambridge Bible for Schools and Colleges, Psalms.* (Cambridge: Cambridge University Press, 1914), Psalm 120:3-4.

[1124] Ibid.

[1125] Jamieson, R., A. R. Fausset, & D. Brown. *Commentary Critical and Explanatory on the Whole Bible* (Vol. 1). (Oak Harbor, WA: Logos Research Systems, Inc., 1997), Psalm 120:1.

[1126] Ibid.

[1127] Spence-Jones, H. D. M. (Ed.). *Psalms,* (Vol. 3). (London; New York: Funk & Wagnalls Company, 1909), 213.

[1128] Kirkpatrick, A. F. (Ed.). *The Cambridge Bible for Schools and Colleges, Psalms.* (Cambridge: Cambridge University Press, 1914), Psalm 120 (Introduction).

[1129] Henry, M. *Matthew Henry's Commentary on the Whole Bible: Complete and Unabridged in One Volume.* (Peabody: Hendrickson, 1994), 929.

[1130] Plumer, W. S. *Studies in the Book of Psalms: Being a Critical and Expository Commentary, with Doctrinal and Practical Remarks on the Entire Psalter.* (Philadelphia; Edinburgh: J. B. Lippincott Company; A & C Black, 1872), 1093.

[1131] Dixon, Francis. "Seven Things God Hates." (Bournemouth, England: Lansdowne Bible School and Postal Fellowship, October 29, 1974).

[1132] Barclay, W. (Ed.). The Letters to Timothy, Titus, and Philemon. (Philadelphia: Westminster John Knox Press, 1975), 189.

[1133] Spurgeon, C. H. *Faith's Checkbook,* November 16.

[1134] Barclay, W. (Ed.). The Letters to Timothy, Titus, and Philemon. (Philadelphia: Westminster John Knox Press, 1975), 189.

[1135] Horne, G. *A Commentary on the Book of Psalms.* (New York: Robert Carter & Brothers, 1856), 465.

[1136] Alexander, J. A. *The Psalms Translated and Explained.* (Edinburgh: Andrew Elliot; James Thin, 1864), 508.

[1137] Plumer, W. S. *Studies in the Book of Psalms: Being a Critical and Expository Commentary, with Doctrinal and Practical Remarks on the Entire Psalter.* (Philadelphia; Edinburgh: J. B. Lippincott Company; A & C Black, 1872), 1094.

[1138] Spurgeon, C. H. *Psalms.* (Wheaton, IL: Crossway Books, 1993), 253.

[1139] Henry, M. *Matthew Henry's Commentary on the Whole Bible: Complete and Unabridged in One Volume.* (Peabody: Hendrickson, 1994), 929.

[1140] Torrey, R. A. *How to Work for Christ: A Compendium of Effective Methods.* (Chicago; New York: James Nisbet & Company, 1901), 457–458.

[1141] Spence-Jones, H. D. M. (Ed.). *Proverbs.* (London; New York: Funk & Wagnalls Company, 1909), 492.

[1142] Exell, Joseph S. Ed. *The Biblical Illustrator,* Psalm 120:2. R. Newton ("Lying Lips").

[1143] Gill, John. *The John Gill Exposition of the Entire Bible,* Psalm 121:1.

[1144] Simeon, C. *Horae Homileticae: Psalms, LXXIII–CL* (Vol. 6). (London: Samuel Holdsworth, 1836), 380.

[1145] Spence-Jones, H. D. M. (Ed.). *Psalms,* (Vol. 3). (London; New York: Funk & Wagnalls Company, 1909), 184.

[1146] Gill, John. *The John Gill Exposition of the Entire Bible,* Psalm 121:1.

[1147] Jamieson, R., A. R. Fausset, & D. Brown. *Commentary Critical and Explanatory on the Whole Bible* (Vol. 1). (Oak Harbor, WA: Logos Research Systems, Inc., 1997), Psalm 121:1.

[1148] Spence-Jones, H. D. M. (Ed.). *Psalms,* (Vol. 3). (London; New York: Funk & Wagnalls Company, 1909), 184.

[1149] Kirkpatrick, A. F. (Ed.). *The Cambridge Bible for Schools and Colleges,* Psalms. (Cambridge: Cambridge University Press, 1914), Psalm 121:1.

[1150] Swanson, J. *Dictionary of Biblical Languages with Semantic Domains: Hebrew (Old Testament)* (electronic ed.). (Oak Harbor: Logos Research Systems, Inc., 1997).

[1151] https://biblehub.com/psalms/121-2.htm.

[1152] Kirkpatrick, A. F. (Ed.). *The Cambridge Bible for Schools and Colleges,*
Psalms. (Cambridge: Cambridge University Press, 1914), Psalm 121:2.

[1153] Brown, F., S. R. Driver, and C. A. Briggs. *Enhanced Brown-Driver-Briggs
Hebrew and English Lexicon.* (Oxford: Clarendon Press, 1977), 556.

[1154] Barnes, Albert. Notes on the Psalms, Critical, Explanatory and Practical.
(New York: Harper & Brothers, 1868),Psalm 121:3.

[1155] MacArthur, J., Jr. (Ed.). *The MacArthur Study Bible,* (electronic ed.).
(Nashville, TN: Word Pub, 1997), 856.

[1156] Landes, G. M. *Building Your Biblical Hebrew Vocabulary: Learning Words by
Frequency and Cognate* (Vol. 41). (Atlanta, GA: Society of Biblical Literature,
2001), 58.

[1157] Barnes, Albert. Notes on the Psalms, Critical, Explanatory and Practical.
(New York: Harper & Brothers, 1868),Psalm 121:4.

[1158] Kirkpatrick, A. F. (Ed.). *The Cambridge Bible for Schools and Colleges,*
Psalms. (Cambridge: Cambridge University Press, 1914), Psalm 121:5.

[1159] Spence-Jones, H. D. M. (Ed.). *Psalms,* (Vol. 3). (London; New York: Funk &
Wagnalls Company, 1909), 185.

[1160] Ibid.

[1161] Vine, W. E., M. F. Unger, and W. White, Jr. *Vine's Complete Expository
Dictionary of Old and New Testament Words* (Vol. 1). (Nashville: T. Nelson,
1996), 204.

[1162] Jennings, A. C., and W. H. Lowe. *The Psalms, with Introductions and Critical
Notes* (Second Edition, Vol. 2). (London: Macmillan and Co., 1885), 302.

[1163] Barnes, Albert. Notes on the Psalms, Critical, Explanatory and Practical.
(New York: Harper & Brothers, 1868),Psalm 121:6.

[1164] Jennings, A. C., and W. H. Lowe. *The Psalms, with Introductions and Critical
Notes* (Second Edition, Vol. 2). (London: Macmillan and Co., 1885), 303.

[1165] Clarke, Adam. *Clarkes' Commentary and Critical Notes*, Psalm 121:6.

[1166] Barnes, Albert. Notes on the Psalms, Critical, Explanatory and Practical.
(New York: Harper & Brothers, 1868),Psalm 121:6.

[1167] Gesenius, W., and S. P. Tregelles. *Gesenius' Hebrew and Chaldee Lexicon to
the Old Testament Scriptures.* (Bellingham, WA: Logos Bible Software, 2003), 837.

[1168] Swanson, J. *Dictionary of Biblical Languages with Semantic Domains:
Hebrew (Old Testament)* (electronic ed.). (Oak Harbor: Logos Research Systems,
Inc., 1997).

[1169] Henry, M. *Matthew Henry's Commentary on the Whole Bible: Complete and
Unabridged in One Volume.* (Peabody: Hendrickson, 1994), 930.

[1170] Kirkpatrick, A. F. (Ed.). *The Cambridge Bible for Schools and Colleges,*
Psalms. (Cambridge: Cambridge University Press, 1914), Psalm 121:8.

[1171] Jennings, A. C., and W. H. Lowe. *The Psalms, with Introductions and Critical Notes* (Second Edition, Vol. 2). (London: Macmillan and Co., 1885), 303.

[1172] Alexander, J. A. *The Psalms Translated and Explained.* (Edinburgh: Andrew Elliot; James Thin, 1864), 509.

[1173] Simeon, C. *Horae Homileticae: Psalms, LXXIII–CL* (Vol. 6). (London: Samuel Holdsworth, 1836), 380–381.

[1174] Henry, Matthew. *Matthew Henry's Concise Bible Commentary,* Psalm 121:2.

[1175] Henry, M. *Matthew Henry's Commentary on the Whole Bible: Complete and Unabridged in One Volume.* (Peabody: Hendrickson, 1994), 930.

[1176] Gill, John. *The John Gill Exposition of the Entire Bible,* Psalm 121:2.

[1177] Plumer, W. S. *Studies in the Book of Psalms: Being a Critical and Expository Commentary, with Doctrinal and Practical Remarks on the Entire Psalter.* (Philadelphia; Edinburgh: J. B. Lippincott Company; A & C Black, 1872), 1096.

[1178] Ibid.

[1179] Ibid., 1097.

[1180] Perowne, J. J. S. *The Book of Psalms; A New Translation, with Introductions and Notes, Explanatory and Critical* (Fifth Edition, Revised, Vol. 1). (London; Cambridge: George Bell and Sons; Deighton Bell and Co., 1883), 375.

[1181] Alexander, J. A. *The Psalms Translated and Explained.* (Edinburgh: Andrew Elliot; James Thin, 1864), 510.

[1182] Kirkpatrick, A. F. (Ed.). *The Cambridge Bible for Schools and Colleges,* Psalms. (Cambridge: Cambridge University Press, 1914), Psalm 121:8.

[1183] Horne, G. *A Commentary on the Book of Psalms.* (New York: Robert Carter & Brothers, 1856), 467.

[1184] The author heard something similar in a sermon.

[1185] Simeon, C. *Horae Homileticae: Psalms, LXXIII–CL* (Vol. 6). (London: Samuel Holdsworth, 1836), 384.

[1186] Truett, George W. *A Quest For Souls.* (New York: Harper & Brothers Publishers, 1917), 265.

[1187] Boice, J. M. *Psalms 107–150: An Expositional Commentary.* (Grand Rapids, MI: Baker Books, 2005), 1079.

[1188] Spurgeon, C. H. *Psalms.* (Wheaton, IL: Crossway Books, 1993), 257.

[1189] Swanson, J. *Dictionary of Biblical Languages with Semantic Domains: Hebrew (Old Testament)* (electronic ed.). (Oak Harbor: Logos Research Systems, Inc., 1997).

[1190] Jennings, A. C., and W. H. Lowe. *The Psalms, with Introductions and Critical Notes* (Second Edition, Vol. 2). (London: Macmillan and Co., 1885), 304.

[1191] Benson, Joseph. *The Holy Bible With Notes, Critical, Explanatory and Practical.* (London: J. Kershaw, 1825), Psalm 122:1.

[1192] Plumer, W. S. *Studies in the Book of Psalms: Being a Critical and Expository Commentary, with Doctrinal and Practical Remarks on the Entire Psalter.* (Philadelphia; Edinburgh: J. B. Lippincott Company; A & C Black, 1872), 1099.

[1193] Barnes, Albert. Notes on the Psalms, Critical, Explanatory and Practical. (New York: Harper & Brothers, 1868),Psalm 122:1.

[1194] Henry, M. *Matthew Henry's Commentary on the Whole Bible: Complete and Unabridged in One Volume.* (Peabody: Hendrickson, 1994), 930.

[1195] Plumer, W. S. *Studies in the Book of Psalms: Being a Critical and Expository Commentary, with Doctrinal and Practical Remarks on the Entire Psalter.* (Philadelphia; Edinburgh: J. B. Lippincott Company; A & C Black, 1872), 1101.

[1196] Ibid.

[1197] Spurgeon, C. H. *The Treasury of David.* (Grand Rapids, Michigan: Kregel Publications, 2004), Psalm 122:1.

[1198] Plumer, W. S. *Studies in the Book of Psalms: Being a Critical and Expository Commentary, with Doctrinal and Practical Remarks on the Entire Psalter.* (Philadelphia; Edinburgh: J. B. Lippincott Company; A & C Black, 1872), 1101.

[1199] Harris, R. L., G. L. Archer Jr., and B. K. Waltke (Eds.). *Theological Wordbook of the Old Testament,* (electronic ed.). (Chicago: Moody Press, 1999), 891.

[1200] Plumer, W. S. *Studies in the Book of Psalms: Being a Critical and Expository Commentary, with Doctrinal and Practical Remarks on the Entire Psalter.* (Philadelphia; Edinburgh: J. B. Lippincott Company; A & C Black, 1872), 1100.

[1201] Kirkpatrick, A. F. (Ed.). *The Cambridge Bible for Schools and Colleges,* Psalms. (Cambridge: Cambridge University Press, 1914), Psalm 122:6.

[1202] Landes, G. M. *Building Your Biblical Hebrew Vocabulary: Learning Words by Frequency and Cognate* (Vol. 41). (Atlanta, GA: Society of Biblical Literature, 2001), 70.

[1203] Whitaker, R., F. Brown, S. R. Driver, and C. A. Briggs. *The Abridged Brown-Driver-Briggs Hebrew-English Lexicon of the Old Testament*. (New York: Houghton, Mifflin and Company, 1906).

[1204] Perowne, J. J. S. *The Book of Psalms; A New Translation, with Introductions and Notes, Explanatory and Critical* (Fifth Edition, Revised, Vol. 1). (London; Cambridge: George Bell and Sons; Deighton Bell and Co., 1883), 380.

[1205] Swanson, J. *Dictionary of Biblical Languages with Semantic Domains: Hebrew (Old Testament)* (electronic ed.). (Oak Harbor: Logos Research Systems, Inc., 1997).

[1206] Gesenius, W., and S. P. Tregelles. *Gesenius' Hebrew and Chaldee Lexicon to the Old Testament Scriptures.* (Bellingham, WA: Logos Bible Software, 2003), 15.

[1207] Barnes, Albert. Notes on the Psalms, Critical, Explanatory and Practical. (New York: Harper & Brothers, 1868),Psalm 122:7.

[1208] Jamieson, R., A. R. Fausset, & D. Brown. *Commentary Critical and Explanatory on the Whole Bible* (Vol. 1). (Oak Harbor, WA: Logos Research Systems, Inc., 1997), Psalm 122:6–7.

[1209] Plumer, W. S. *Studies in the Book of Psalms: Being a Critical and Expository Commentary, with Doctrinal and Practical Remarks on the Entire Psalter.* (Philadelphia; Edinburgh: J. B. Lippincott Company; A & C Black, 1872), 1100.

[1210] Gesenius, W., and S. P. Tregelles. *Gesenius' Hebrew and Chaldee Lexicon to the Old Testament Scriptures.* (Bellingham, WA: Logos Bible Software, 2003), 825.

[1211] https://biblehub.com/commentaries/psalms/122-7.htm.

[1212] Boice, J. M. *Psalms 107–150: An Expositional Commentary.* (Grand Rapids, MI: Baker Books, 2005), 1083.

[1213] Spence-Jones, H. D. M. (Ed.). *Psalms,* (Vol. 3). (London; New York: Funk & Wagnalls Company, 1909), 193.

[1214] Keil & Delitzsch. Commentary on the Old Testament: Volume 5. (Peabody, Massachusetts: Hendrickson Publishers, 2006), 765.

[1215] A mosaic with the inscription *Shalom al Yisrael* may be seen at https://www.pinterest.com/pin/216665432051496357/.

[1216] Barnes, Albert. Notes on the Psalms, Critical, Explanatory and Practical. (New York: Harper & Brothers, 1868),Psalm 122:6.

[1217] Boice, J. M. *Psalms 107–150: An Expositional Commentary.* (Grand Rapids, MI: Baker Books, 2005), 1085.

[1218] Boice, J. M. *Psalms 107–150: An Expositional Commentary.* (Grand Rapids, MI: Baker Books, 2005), 1086.

[1219] Spurgeon, C. H. *Psalms.* (Wheaton, IL: Crossway Books, 1993), 261.

[1220] Horne, G. *A Commentary on the Book of Psalms.* (New York: Robert Carter & Brothers, 1856), 469.

[1221] Spence-Jones, H. D. M. (Ed.). *Psalms,* (Vol. 3). (London; New York: Funk & Wagnalls Company, 1909), 202.

[1222] Jamieson, R., A. R. Fausset, & D. Brown. *Commentary Critical and Explanatory on the Whole Bible* (Vol. 1). (Oak Harbor, WA: Logos Research Systems, Inc., 1997), Psalm 123:2.

[1223] Spurgeon, C. H. *Psalms.* (Wheaton, IL: Crossway Books, 1993), 262–263.

[1224] Holladay, W. L., and L. Köhler. A Concise Hebrew and Aramaic Lexicon of the Old Testament. (Leiden: Brill, 2000), 380.

[1225] Spence-Jones, H. D. M. (Ed.). *Psalms,* (Vol. 3). (London; New York: Funk & Wagnalls Company, 1909), 202.

[1226] Swanson, J. *Dictionary of Biblical Languages with Semantic Domains: Hebrew (Old Testament)* (electronic ed.). (Oak Harbor: Logos Research Systems, Inc., 1997).

[1227] Henry, M. *Matthew Henry's Commentary on the Whole Bible: Complete and Unabridged in One Volume.* (Peabody: Hendrickson, 1994), 931.

[1228] Vine, W. E., M. F. Unger, and W. White, Jr. *Vine's Complete Expository Dictionary of Old and New Testament Words* (Vol. 1). (Nashville: T. Nelson, 1996), 100.

[1229] Dilday, R. H., Jr., and J. H. Kennedy. *Psalms.* In H. F. Paschall and H. H. Hobbs (Eds.). *The Teacher's Bible Commentary.* (Nashville: Broadman and Holman Publishers, 1972), 345.

[1230] Alexander, J. A. *The Psalms Translated and Explained.* (Edinburgh: Andrew Elliot; James Thin, 1864), 512.

[1231] Perowne, J. J. S. *The Book of Psalms; A New Translation, with Introductions and Notes, Explanatory and Critical* (Fifth Edition, Revised, Vol. 1). (London; Cambridge: George Bell and Sons; Deighton Bell and Co., 1883), 383.

[1232] Henry, M. *Matthew Henry's Commentary on the Whole Bible: Complete and Unabridged in One Volume.* (Peabody: Hendrickson, 1994), 931.

[1233] Spurgeon, C. H. *Psalms.* (Wheaton, IL: Crossway Books, 1993), 264.

[1234] Chambers, Oswald. *My Utmost For His Highest,* November 23.

[1235] Henry, M. *Matthew Henry's Commentary on the Whole Bible: Complete and Unabridged in One Volume.* (Peabody: Hendrickson, 1994), 931.

[1236] Kirkpatrick, A. F. (Ed.). *The Cambridge Bible for Schools and Colleges,* Psalms. (Cambridge: Cambridge University Press, 1914), Psalm 123 (Introduction).

[1237] Barnes, Albert. Notes on the Psalms, Critical, Explanatory and Practical. (New York: Harper & Brothers, 1868),Psalm 123:2.

[1238] Plumer, W. S. *Studies in the Book of Psalms: Being a Critical and Expository Commentary, with Doctrinal and Practical Remarks on the Entire Psalter.* (Philadelphia; Edinburgh: J. B. Lippincott Company; A & C Black, 1872), 1103.

[1239] Spurgeon, C. H. *The Treasury of David.* (Grand Rapids, Michigan: Kregel Publications, 2004), Psalm 123:2.

[1240] Jamieson, R., A. R. Fausset, & D. Brown. *Commentary Critical and Explanatory on the Whole Bible* (Vol. 1). (Oak Harbor, WA: Logos Research Systems, Inc., 1997), Psalm 123:2.

[1241] Henry, M. *Matthew Henry's Commentary on the Whole Bible: Complete and Unabridged in One Volume.* (Peabody: Hendrickson, 1994), 931.

[1242] Manton, Thomas. *One Hundred and Ninety Sermons on the Hundred and Nineteenth Psalm,* Vol. 2. (London: William Brown, 1845), 585–586.

[1243] Spurgeon, C. H. *The Treasury of David.* (Grand Rapids, Michigan: Kregel Publications, 2004), Psalm 123:1.

[1244] Maclaren, Alexander in Nicholl, W. Robertson (ed.). *The Expositor's Bible, The Psalms* (Vol. III. Psalms XC-CL). (London: Hodder and Stoughton, 1894), 308.

[1245] Spurgeon, C. H. *The Treasury of David.* (Grand Rapids, Michigan: Kregel Publications, 2004), Psalm 123:1.

[1246] Chambers, Oswald. *My Utmost For His Highest,* November 24.

[1247] Barnes, Albert. Notes on the Psalms, Critical, Explanatory and Practical. (New York: Harper & Brothers, 1868),Psalm 124:1.

[1248] Swanson, J. *Dictionary of Biblical Languages with Semantic Domains: Hebrew (Old Testament)* (electronic ed.). (Oak Harbor: Logos Research Systems, Inc., 1997).

[1249] Barnes, Albert. Notes on the Psalms, Critical, Explanatory and Practical. (New York: Harper & Brothers, 1868),Psalm 124:3.

[1250] Spence-Jones, H. D. M. (Ed.). *Psalms,* (Vol. 3). (London; New York: Funk & Wagnalls Company, 1909), 205.

[1251] Swanson, J. *Dictionary of Biblical Languages with Semantic Domains: Hebrew (Old Testament)* (electronic ed.). (Oak Harbor: Logos Research Systems, Inc., 1997).

[1252] Brown, F., S. R. Driver, and C. A. Briggs. *Enhanced Brown-Driver-Briggs Hebrew and English Lexicon.* (Oxford: Clarendon Press, 1977), 636.

[1253] Kirkpatrick, A. F. (Ed.). *The Cambridge Bible for Schools and Colleges,* Psalms. (Cambridge: Cambridge University Press, 1914), Psalm 124:4.

[1254] Barnes, Albert. Notes on the Psalms, Critical, Explanatory and Practical. (New York: Harper & Brothers, 1868),Psalm 124:5.

[1255] Jamieson, R., A. R. Fausset, & D. Brown. *Commentary Critical and Explanatory on the Whole Bible* (Vol. 1). (Oak Harbor, WA: Logos Research Systems, Inc., 1997), Psalm 124:5.

[1256] Thomas, R. L. *New American Standard Hebrew-Aramaic and Greek Dictionaries: updated edition.* (Anaheim: Foundation Publications, Inc., 1998).

[1257] Barnes, Albert. Notes on the Psalms, Critical, Explanatory and Practical. (New York: Harper & Brothers, 1868),Psalm 124:6.

[1258] Jamieson, R., A. R. Fausset, & D. Brown. *Commentary Critical and Explanatory on the Whole Bible* (Vol. 1). (Oak Harbor, WA: Logos Research Systems, Inc., 1997), Psalm 124:6–7.

[1259] Swanson, J. *Dictionary of Biblical Languages with Semantic Domains: Hebrew (Old Testament)* (electronic ed.). (Oak Harbor: Logos Research Systems, Inc., 1997).

[1260] Gesenius, W., and S. P. Tregelles. *Gesenius' Hebrew and Chaldee Lexicon to the Old Testament Scriptures.* (Bellingham, WA: Logos Bible Software, 2003), 671.

[1261] Swanson, J. *Dictionary of Biblical Languages with Semantic Domains: Hebrew (Old Testament)* (electronic ed.). (Oak Harbor: Logos Research Systems, Inc., 1997).

[1262] Landes, G. M. *Building Your Biblical Hebrew Vocabulary: Learning Words by Frequency and Cognate* (Vol. 41). (Atlanta, GA: Society of Biblical Literature, 2001), 73.

[1263] Spence-Jones, H. D. M. (Ed.). *Psalms,* (Vol. 3). (London; New York: Funk & Wagnalls Company, 1909), 206.

[1264] Jamieson, R., A. R. Fausset, & D. Brown. *Commentary Critical and Explanatory on the Whole Bible* (Vol. 1). (Oak Harbor, WA: Logos Research Systems, Inc., 1997), Psalm 124:8.

[1265] Spence-Jones, H. D. M. (Ed.). *Psalms,* (Vol. 3). (London; New York: Funk & Wagnalls Company, 1909), 206.

[1266] Spurgeon, C. H. *The Treasury of David.* (Grand Rapids, Michigan: Kregel Publications, 2004), Psalm 124:8.

[1267] Henry, M. *Matthew Henry's Commentary on the Whole Bible: Complete and Unabridged in One Volume.* (Peabody: Hendrickson, 1994), 931.

[1268] Boice, J. M. *Psalms 107–150: An Expositional Commentary.* (Grand Rapids, MI: Baker Books, 2005), 1096.

[1269] Kirkpatrick, A. F. (Ed.). *The Cambridge Bible for Schools and Colleges, Psalms.* (Cambridge: Cambridge University Press, 1914), Psalm 124 (Introduction).

[1270] Dilday, R. H., Jr., and J. H. Kennedy. *Psalms.* In H. F. Paschall and H. H. Hobbs (Eds.). *The Teacher's Bible Commentary.* (Nashville: Broadman and Holman Publishers, 1972), 345.

[1271] Exell, Joseph S. Ed. *The Biblical Illustrator,* Psalm 124:1–8. S. Davies ("Ifs and Thens").

[1272] Alexander, J. A. *The Psalms Translated and Explained.* (Edinburgh: Andrew Elliot; James Thin, 1864), 512.

[1273] Spurgeon, C. H. *The Treasury of David.* (Grand Rapids, Michigan: Kregel Publications, 2004), Psalm 124:1.

[1274] Hamilton, William W. *Sermons on the Books of the Bible,* (Vol. 4), 166.

[1275] Spurgeon, C. H. *The Treasury of David.* (Grand Rapids, Michigan: Kregel Publications, 2004), Psalm 124:1.

[1276] https://www.crosswalk.com/faith/spiritual-life/inspiring-quotes/30-christian-quotes-about-thankfulness.html, accessed July 29, 2018.

[1277] https://www.brainyquote.com/quotes/abraham_lincoln_388944, accessed December 3, 2018.

[1278] Swanson, J. *Dictionary of Biblical Languages with Semantic Domains: Hebrew (Old Testament)* (electronic ed.). (Oak Harbor: Logos Research Systems, Inc., 1997).

[1279] Simeon, C. *Horae Homileticae: Psalms, LXXIII–CL* (Vol. 6). (London: Samuel Holdsworth, 1836), 392.

[1280] Barnes, Albert. Notes on the Psalms, Critical, Explanatory and Practical. (New York: Harper & Brothers, 1868),Psalm 125:1.

[1281] Jamieson, R., A. R. Fausset, & D. Brown. *Commentary Critical and Explanatory on the Whole Bible* (Vol. 1). (Oak Harbor, WA: Logos Research Systems, Inc., 1997), Psalm 125:1.

[1282] Kirkpatrick, A. F. (Ed.). *The Cambridge Bible for Schools and Colleges, Psalms.* (Cambridge: Cambridge University Press, 1914), Psalm 125:1.

[1283] Ibid.

[1284] Plumer, W. S. *Studies in the Book of Psalms: Being a Critical and Expository Commentary, with Doctrinal and Practical Remarks on the Entire Psalter.* (Philadelphia; Edinburgh: J. B. Lippincott Company; A & C Black, 1872), 1108.

[1285] Gill, John. *The John Gill Exposition of the Entire Bible,* Psalm 125:2.

[1286] Benson, Joseph. *The Holy Bible With Notes, Critical, Explanatory and Practical.* (London: J. Kershaw, 1825), Psalm 125:2.

[1287] Maclaren, Alexander. *The Expositor's Bible:* The Psalms. (New York: Scriptura Press, 2015), Psalm 125.

[1288] Jennings, A. C., and W. H. Lowe. *The Psalms, with Introductions and Critical Notes* (Second Edition, Vol. 2). (London: Macmillan and Co., 1885), 310.

[1289] Maclaren, Alexander. *The Expositor's Bible:* The Psalms. (New York: Scriptura Press, 2015), Psalm 125.

[1290] Henry, M. *Matthew Henry's Commentary on the Whole Bible: Complete and Unabridged in One Volume.* (Peabody: Hendrickson, 1994), 932.

[1291] VanGemeren, Willem A. *The Expositor's Bible Commentary,* Psalms. (Grand Rapids: Zondervan, 1991), Psalm 125:1–5.

[1292] Horne, G. *A Commentary on the Book of Psalms.* (New York: Robert Carter & Brothers, 1856), 474.

[1293] Simeon, C. *Horae Homileticae: Psalms, LXXIII–CL* (Vol. 6). (London: Samuel Holdsworth, 1836), 392–393.

[1294] Plumer, W. S. *Studies in the Book of Psalms: Being a Critical and Expository Commentary, with Doctrinal and Practical Remarks on the Entire Psalter.* (Philadelphia; Edinburgh: J. B. Lippincott Company; A & C Black, 1872), 1108.

[1295] Henry, M. *Matthew Henry's Commentary on the Whole Bible: Complete and Unabridged in One Volume.* (Peabody: Hendrickson, 1994), 932.

[1296] Gill, John. *The John Gill Exposition of the Entire Bible,* Psalm 125:1.

[1297] Kirkpatrick, A. F. (Ed.). *The Cambridge Bible for Schools and Colleges, Psalms.* (Cambridge: Cambridge University Press, 1914), Psalm 125:2.

[1298] Alexander, J. A. *The Psalms Translated and Explained.* (Edinburgh: Andrew Elliot; James Thin, 1864), 514.

[1299] Spurgeon, C. H. *Psalms.* (Wheaton, IL: Crossway Books, 1993), 268.

[1300] Clarke, Adam. *Clarkes' Commentary and Critical Notes,* Psalm 125:2.

[1301] Plumer, W. S. *Studies in the Book of Psalms: Being a Critical and Expository Commentary, with Doctrinal and Practical Remarks on the Entire Psalter.* (Philadelphia; Edinburgh: J. B. Lippincott Company; A & C Black, 1872), 1109.

[1302] Spurgeon, C. H. *The Treasury of David.* (Grand Rapids, Michigan: Kregel Publications, 2004), Psalm 125. Explanatory notes and quaint sayings.

[1303] Bonar, A. A. *Christ and His Church in the Book of Psalms.* (New York: Robert Carter & Brothers, 1860), 227.

[1304] Kaiser, W. C., R. L. Harris, G. L. Archer Jr., and B. K. Waltke (Eds.). *Theological Wordbook of the Old Testament,* 582 רָעַע, (electronic ed.). (Chicago: Moody Press, 1999), 252.

[1305] Holladay, W. L., and L. Köhler. A Concise Hebrew and Aramaic Lexicon of the Old Testament. (Leiden: Brill, 2000), 322.

[1306] Strong, J. *A Concise Dictionary of the Words in the Greek Testament and the Hebrew Bible.* (Vol. 2). (Bellingham, WA: Logos Bible Software, 2009), 109.

[1307] Brown, F., S. R. Driver, and C. A. Briggs. *Enhanced Brown-Driver-Briggs Hebrew and English Lexicon.* (Oxford: Clarendon Press, 1977), 669.

[1308] Harman, A. *Psalms: A Mentor Commentary (Vol. 1–2).* (Ross-shire, Great Britain: Mentor, 2011), 911.

[1309] Henry, M. *Matthew Henry's Commentary on the Whole Bible: Complete and Unabridged in One Volume.* (Peabody: Hendrickson, 1994), 932.

[1310] Ibid.

[1311] Simeon, C. *Horae Homileticae: Psalms, LXXIII–CL* (Vol. 6). (London: Samuel Holdsworth, 1836), 397–398.

[1312] Plumer, W. S. *Studies in the Book of Psalms: Being a Critical and Expository Commentary, with Doctrinal and Practical Remarks on the Entire Psalter.* (Philadelphia; Edinburgh: J. B. Lippincott Company; A & C Black, 1872), 1110.

[1313] Ibid., 1113.

[1314] Appelman, Hymen J. *The Savior's Invitation and Other Evangelistic Sermons.* (Grand Rapids: Baker Book House, 1981), 35.

[1315] Spurgeon, C. H. *Psalms.* (Wheaton, IL: Crossway Books, 1993), 271.

[1316] MacDonald, W. *Believer's Bible Commentary: Old and New Testaments,* (A. Farstad, Ed.) (Nashville: Thomas Nelson, 1995), 755.

[1317] Benson, Joseph. *The Holy Bible With Notes, Critical, Explanatory and Practical.* (London: J. Kershaw, 1825), Psalm 126:5-6.

[1318] Henry, Matthew. *Concise Commentary on the Bible.* Psalm 125:5–6.

[1319] Henry, M. *Matthew Henry's Commentary on the Whole Bible: Complete and Unabridged in One Volume.* (Peabody: Hendrickson, 1994), 933.

[1320] Simeon, C. *Horae Homileticae: Psalms, LXXIII–CL* (Vol. 6). (London: Samuel Holdsworth, 1836), 407.

[1321] Swanson, J. *Dictionary of Biblical Languages with Semantic Domains: Hebrew (Old Testament)* (electronic ed.). (Oak Harbor: Logos Research Systems, Inc., 1997).

[1322] Futato, M. D. *Beginning Biblical Hebrew.* (Winona Lake, IN: Eisenbrauns, 2003), 283.

[1323] Spence-Jones, H. D. M. (Ed.). *Psalms,* (Vol. 3). (London; New York: Funk & Wagnalls Company, 1909), 227.

[1324] Harman, A. *Psalms: A Mentor Commentary (Vol. 1–2).* (Ross-shire, Great Britain: Mentor, 2011), 915.

[1325] Carroll, B. H. *An Interpretation of the English Bible: The Poetical Books of the Bible.* (Nashville: Broadman Press, 1948), 121.

[1326] Henry, M. *Matthew Henry's Commentary on the Whole Bible: Complete and Unabridged in One Volume.* (Peabody: Hendrickson, 1994), 934.

[1327] Criswell, W. A., P. Patterson, E. R. Clendenen, D. L. Akin, M. Chamberlin, D. K. Patterson, and J. Pogue (Eds.). Believer's Study Bible, (electronic ed.). (Nashville: Thomas Nelson, 1991), Ps. 127:3.

[1328] Exell, Joseph S. Ed. *The Biblical Illustrator,* Psalm 124:4. N. McMichael ("Children as Arrows").

[1329] Carroll, B. H. *An Interpretation of the English Bible: The Poetical Books of the Bible.* (Nashville: Broadman Press, 1948), 121.

[1330] Plumer, W. S. *Studies in the Book of Psalms: Being a Critical and Expository Commentary, with Doctrinal and Practical Remarks on the Entire Psalter.* (Philadelphia; Edinburgh: J. B. Lippincott Company; A & C Black, 1872), 1115.

[1331] Henry, M. *Matthew Henry's Commentary on the Whole Bible: Complete and Unabridged in One Volume.* (Peabody: Hendrickson, 1994), 934.

[1332] Harman, A. *Psalms: A Mentor Commentary (Vol. 1–2).* (Ross-shire, Great Britain: Mentor, 2011), 917–918.

[1333] Henry, M. *Matthew Henry's Commentary on the Whole Bible: Complete and Unabridged in One Volume.* (Peabody: Hendrickson, 1994), 934.

[1334] Dilday, R. H., Jr., and J. H. Kennedy. *Psalms.* In H. F. Paschall and H. H. Hobbs (Eds.). *The Teacher's Bible Commentary.* (Nashville: Broadman and Holman Publishers, 1972), 347.

[1335] Jennings, A. C., and W. H. Lowe. *The Psalms, with Introductions and Critical Notes* (Second Edition, Vol. 2). (London: Macmillan and Co., 1885), 319.

[1336] Futato, M. D. *Beginning Biblical Hebrew.* (Winona Lake, IN: Eisenbrauns, 2003), 284.

[1337] Barnes, Albert. Notes on the Psalms, Critical, Explanatory and Practical. (New York: Harper & Brothers, 1868),Psalm 128:1.

[1338] Harman, A. *Psalms: A Mentor Commentary (Vol. 1–2).* (Ross-shire, Great Britain: Mentor, 2011), 917.

[1339] Spence-Jones, H. D. M. (Ed.). *Psalms,* (Vol. 3). (London; New York: Funk & Wagnalls Company, 1909), 235.

[1340] Jennings, A. C., and W. H. Lowe. *The Psalms, with Introductions and Critical Notes* (Second Edition, Vol. 2). (London: Macmillan and Co., 1885), 319.

[1341] Brown, F., S. R. Driver, and C. A. Briggs. *Enhanced Brown-Driver-Briggs Hebrew and English Lexicon.* (Oxford: Clarendon Press, 1977), 373.

[1342] Harman, A. *Psalms: A Mentor Commentary (Vol. 1–2).* (Ross-shire, Great Britain: Mentor, 2011), 918.

[1343] https://biblehub.com/commentaries/psalms/128-3.htm.

[1344] Jennings, A. C., and W. H. Lowe. *The Psalms, with Introductions and Critical Notes* (Second Edition, Vol. 2). (London: Macmillan and Co., 1885), 319–320.

[1345] Plumer, W. S. *Studies in the Book of Psalms: Being a Critical and Expository Commentary, with Doctrinal and Practical Remarks on the Entire Psalter.* (Philadelphia; Edinburgh: J. B. Lippincott Company; A & C Black, 1872), 1117.

[1346] Henry, M. *Matthew Henry's Commentary on the Whole Bible: Complete and Unabridged in One Volume.* (Peabody: Hendrickson, 1994), 934.

[1347] Kirkpatrick, A. F. (Ed.). *The Cambridge Bible for Schools and Colleges, Psalms.* (Cambridge: Cambridge University Press, 1914), Psalm 128 (Introduction).

[1348] Alexander, J. A. *The Psalms Translated and Explained.* (Edinburgh: Andrew Elliot; James Thin, 1864), 518.

[1349] Spence-Jones, H. D. M. (Ed.). *Psalms,* (Vol. 3). (London; New York: Funk & Wagnalls Company, 1909), 235.

[1350] Henry, M. *Matthew Henry's Commentary on the Whole Bible: Complete and Unabridged in One Volume.* (Peabody: Hendrickson, 1994), 934.

[1351] Spurgeon, C. H. *Psalms.* (Wheaton, IL: Crossway Books, 1993), 276.

[1352] Spence-Jones, H. D. M. (Ed.). *Psalms,* (Vol. 3). (London; New York: Funk & Wagnalls Company, 1909), 236.

[1353] Benson, Joseph. *The Holy Bible With Notes, Critical, Explanatory and Practical.* (London: J. Kershaw, 1825), Psalm 128:2.

[1354] Spurgeon, C. H. *Psalms.* (Wheaton, IL: Crossway Books, 1993), 276–277.

[1355] Holladay, W. L., and L. Köhler. A Concise Hebrew and Aramaic Lexicon of the Old Testament. (Leiden: Brill, 2000), 311.

[1356] Benson, Joseph. *The Holy Bible With Notes, Critical, Explanatory and Practical.* (London: J. Kershaw, 1825), Psalm 129:1.

[1357] Kirkpatrick, A. F. (Ed.). *The Cambridge Bible for Schools and Colleges, Psalms.* (Cambridge: Cambridge University Press, 1914), Psalm 129:1.

[1358] Ibid.

[1359] Barnes, Albert. Notes on the Psalms, Critical, Explanatory and Practical. (New York: Harper & Brothers, 1868),Psalm 129:2.

[1360] Spence-Jones, H. D. M. (Ed.). *Psalms,* (Vol. 3). (London; New York: Funk & Wagnalls Company, 1909), 241.

[1361] Brown, F., S. R. Driver, and C. A. Briggs. *Enhanced Brown-Driver-Briggs Hebrew and English Lexicon.* (Oxford: Clarendon Press, 1977), 360.

[1362] Swanson, J. *Dictionary of Biblical Languages with Semantic Domains: Hebrew (Old Testament)* (electronic ed.). (Oak Harbor: Logos Research Systems, Inc., 1997).

[1363] Jamieson, R., A. R. Fausset, & D. Brown. *Commentary Critical and Explanatory on the Whole Bible* (Vol. 1). (Oak Harbor, WA: Logos Research Systems, Inc., 1997), Psalm 129:4.

[1364] Swanson, J. *Dictionary of Biblical Languages with Semantic Domains: Hebrew (Old Testament)* (electronic ed.). (Oak Harbor: Logos Research Systems, Inc., 1997).

[1365] Holladay, W. L., and L. Köhler. A Concise Hebrew and Aramaic Lexicon of the Old Testament. (Leiden: Brill, 2000), 253.

[1366] Kirkpatrick, A. F. (Ed.). *The Cambridge Bible for Schools and Colleges,* Psalms. (Cambridge: Cambridge University Press, 1914), Psalm 129:6.

[1367] Jamieson, R., A. R. Fausset, & D. Brown. *Commentary Critical and Explanatory on the Whole Bible* (Vol. 1). (Oak Harbor, WA: Logos Research Systems, Inc., 1997), Psalm 129:6.

[1368] Gill, John. *The John Gill Exposition of the Entire Bible,* Psalm 129:7.

[1369] Perowne, J. J. S. *The Book of Psalms; A New Translation, with Introductions and Notes, Explanatory and Critical* (Fifth Edition, Revised, Vol. 1). (London; Cambridge: George Bell and Sons; Deighton Bell and Co., 1883), 401.

[1370] Swanson, J. *Dictionary of Biblical Languages with Semantic Domains: Hebrew (Old Testament)* (electronic ed.). (Oak Harbor: Logos Research Systems, Inc., 1997).

[1371] Jennings, A. C., and W. H. Lowe. *The Psalms, with Introductions and Critical Notes* (Second Edition, Vol. 2). (London: Macmillan and Co., 1885), 320.

[1372] Henry, M. *Matthew Henry's Commentary on the Whole Bible: Complete and Unabridged in One Volume.* (Peabody: Hendrickson, 1994), 934.

[1373] Plumer, W. S. *Studies in the Book of Psalms: Being a Critical and Expository Commentary, with Doctrinal and Practical Remarks on the Entire Psalter.* (Philadelphia; Edinburgh: J. B. Lippincott Company; A & C Black, 1872), 1121.

[1374] Harman, A. *Psalms: A Mentor Commentary (Vol. 1–2).* (Ross-shire, Great Britain: Mentor, 2011), 922.

[1375] https://biblehub.com/commentaries/psalms/129-3.htm.

[1376] Spurgeon, C. H. *Psalms.* (Wheaton, IL: Crossway Books, 1993), 278–279.

[1377] Plumer, W. S. *Studies in the Book of Psalms: Being a Critical and Expository Commentary, with Doctrinal and Practical Remarks on the Entire Psalter.* (Philadelphia; Edinburgh: J. B. Lippincott Company; A & C Black, 1872), 1122.

[1378] Perowne, J. J. S. *The Book of Psalms; A New Translation, with Introductions and Notes, Explanatory and Critical* (Fifth Edition, Revised, Vol. 1). (London; Cambridge: George Bell and Sons; Deighton Bell and Co., 1883), 400.

[1379] Spurgeon, C. H. *Psalms.* (Wheaton, IL: Crossway Books, 1993), 278–279.

[1380] Swindoll, Chuck. "Facets of Integrity." Insight for Today, February 6, 2018.

[1381] Ibid.

[1382] https://www.christianquotes.info/quotes-by-topic/quotes-about-gossip/#ixzz5MqXjWyQy, accessed July 31, 2018.

[1383] Spence-Jones, H. D. M. (Ed.). *Psalms,* (Vol. 3). (London; New York: Funk & Wagnalls Company, 1909), 246.

[1384] Swanson, J. *Dictionary of Biblical Languages with Semantic Domains: Hebrew (Old Testament)* (electronic ed.). (Oak Harbor: Logos Research Systems, Inc., 1997).

[1385] Benson, Joseph. *The Holy Bible With Notes, Critical, Explanatory and Practical.* (London: J. Kershaw, 1825), Psalm 130:3.

[1386] Holladay, W. L., and L. Köhler. A Concise Hebrew and Aramaic Lexicon of the Old Testament. (Leiden: Brill, 2000), 268.

[1387] Gesenius, W., and S. P. Tregelles. *Gesenius' Hebrew and Chaldee Lexicon to the Old Testament Scriptures.* (Bellingham, WA: Logos Bible Software, 2003), 614.

[1388] Benson, Joseph. *The Holy Bible With Notes, Critical, Explanatory and Practical.* (London: J. Kershaw, 1825), Psalm 130:3.

[1389] Jamieson, R., A. R. Fausset, & D. Brown. *Commentary Critical and Explanatory on the Whole Bible* (Vol. 1). (Oak Harbor, WA: Logos Research Systems, Inc., 1997), Psalm 130:3.

[1390] Strong, J. *A Concise Dictionary of the Words in the Greek Testament and the Hebrew Bible.* (Vol. 2). (Bellingham, WA: Logos Bible Software, 2009), 83.

[1391] Simeon, C. *Horae Homileticae: Psalms, LXXIII–CL* (Vol. 6). (London: Samuel Holdsworth, 1836), 412.

[1392] Lockyer, Herbert, Sr. *Psalms: A Devotional Commentary.* (Grand Rapids: Kregel Publications, 1993), 667.

[1393] Ibid.

[1394] Boice, J. M. *Psalms 107–150: An Expositional Commentary.* (Grand Rapids, MI: Baker Books, 2005), 1138.

[1395] Lockyer, Herbert, Sr. *Psalms: A Devotional Commentary.* (Grand Rapids: Kregel Publications, 1993), 667.

[1396] Barnes, Albert. Notes on the Psalms, Critical, Explanatory and Practical. (New York: Harper & Brothers, 1868), Psalm 130:3.

[1397] Exell, Joseph S. Ed. *The Biblical Illustrator,* Psalm 130:4. Charles Spurgeon ("There Is Forgiveness").

[1398] Ibid.

[1399] Plumer, W. S. *Studies in the Book of Psalms: Being a Critical and Expository Commentary, with Doctrinal and Practical Remarks on the Entire Psalter.* (Philadelphia; Edinburgh: J. B. Lippincott Company; A & C Black, 1872), 1125.

[1400] Barnes, Albert. Notes on the Psalms, Critical, Explanatory and Practical. (New York: Harper & Brothers, 1868),Psalm 130:4.

[1401] Spurgeon, C. H. *The Treasury of David.* (Grand Rapids, Michigan: Kregel Publications, 2004), Psalm 130: 4.

[1402] Benson, Joseph. *The Holy Bible With Notes, Critical, Explanatory and Practical.* (London: J. Kershaw, 1825), Psalm 130:7.

[1403] Spurgeon, C. H. *The Treasury of David.* (Grand Rapids, Michigan: Kregel Publications, 2004), Psalm 130: 4.

[1404] Henry, Matthew. *Matthew Henry's Concise Bible Commentary,* Psalm 130:3.

[1405] Spurgeon, C. H. *The Treasury of David.* (Grand Rapids, Michigan: Kregel Publications, 2004), Psalm 131. Explanatory notes and quaint sayings.

[1406] Henry, M. *Matthew Henry's Commentary on the Whole Bible: Complete and Unabridged in One Volume.* (Peabody: Hendrickson, 1994), 935.

[1407] Strong, J. *A Concise Dictionary of the Words in the Greek Testament and the Hebrew Bible.* (Vol. 2). (Bellingham, WA: Logos Bible Software, 2009), 25.

[1408] Benson, Joseph. *The Holy Bible With Notes, Critical, Explanatory and Practical.* (London: J. Kershaw, 1825), Psalm 131:1.

[1409] Spurgeon, C. H. *The Treasury of David.* (Grand Rapids, Michigan: Kregel Publications, 2004), Psalm 131:1.

[1410] Plumer, W. S. *Studies in the Book of Psalms: Being a Critical and Expository Commentary, with Doctrinal and Practical Remarks on the Entire Psalter.* (Philadelphia; Edinburgh: J. B. Lippincott Company; A & C Black, 1872), 1128.

[1411] Horne, G. *A Commentary on the Book of Psalms.* (New York: Robert Carter & Brothers, 1856), 486.

[1412] Jamieson, R., A. R. Fausset, & D. Brown. *Commentary Critical and Explanatory on the Whole Bible* (Vol. 1). (Oak Harbor, WA: Logos Research Systems, Inc., 1997), Psalm 131:1–3.

[1413] Spurgeon, C. H. *The Treasury of David.* (Grand Rapids, Michigan: Kregel Publications, 2004), Psalm 131, Introduction.

[1414] Perowne, J. J. S. *The Book of Psalms; A New Translation, with Introductions and Notes, Explanatory and Critical* (Fifth Edition, Revised, Vol. 1). (London; Cambridge: George Bell and Sons; Deighton Bell and Co., 1883), 407.

[1415] Spurgeon, C. H. *The Treasury of David.* (Grand Rapids, Michigan: Kregel Publications, 2004), Psalm 131. Explanatory notes and quaint sayings

1416 Ibid.

1417 Ibid.

1418 Murray, Andrew. *Humility: The Beauty of Holiness*. (Aneko Christian Classics), chapter 8.

1419 B. E. B. *Holy Meditations for Every Day*. (London: Frederick Warne & Co., 1867), 15.

1420 Lockyer, Herbert, Sr. *Psalms: A Devotional Commentary*. (Grand Rapids: Kregel Publications, 1993), 675.

1421 Murray, Andrew. *Humility: The Beauty of Holiness*. (Aneko Christian Classics), chapter 2.

1422 De Burgh, W. *A Commentary on the Book of Psalms; Critical, Devotional, and Prophetical*. (Dublin; London; Edinburgh: Hodges, Smith and Co.; Hamilton, Adams & Co.; John Menzies, 1858), 927.

1423 McKane, William. *Proverbs*. Old Testament Library, 490 cited in The NET Bible Notes First Edition. (Biblical Studies Press, 2006), Pr. 16:18.

1424 Plumer, W. S. *Studies in the Book of Psalms: Being a Critical and Expository Commentary, with Doctrinal and Practical Remarks on the Entire Psalter*. (Philadelphia; Edinburgh: J. B. Lippincott Company; A & C Black, 1872), 1129.

1425 http://www.cslewisinstitute.org/Pride_and_Humility_Page1, accessed September 3, 2017.

1426 Plumer, W. S. *Studies in the Book of Psalms: Being a Critical and Expository Commentary, with Doctrinal and Practical Remarks on the Entire Psalter*. (Philadelphia; Edinburgh: J. B. Lippincott Company; A & C Black, 1872), 1129.

1427 https://gracequotes.org/quote/you-can-have-no-greater-sign-of-confirmed-pride-th/, accessed August 30, 2018.

1428 Henry, M. *Matthew Henry's Commentary on the Whole Bible: Complete and Unabridged in One Volume*. (Peabody: Hendrickson, 1994), 936.

1429 Spence-Jones, H. D. M. (Ed.). *Psalms,* (Vol. 3). (London; New York: Funk & Wagnalls Company, 1909), 253.

1430 Ross, A. P. In Walvoord, J. F. and R. B. Zuck (Eds.). *The Bible Knowledge Commentary: An Exposition of the Scriptures* (Vol. 1, Psalms). (Wheaton, IL: Victor Books, 1985), 887.

1431 Strong, J. *The New Strong's Dictionary of Hebrew and Greek Words*. (Nashville: Thomas Nelson, 1996).

1432 Spence-Jones, H. D. M. (Ed.). *Psalms,* (Vol. 3). (London; New York: Funk & Wagnalls Company, 1909), 253.

1433 Dilday, R. H., Jr., and J. H. Kennedy. *Psalms*. In H. F. Paschall and H. H. Hobbs (Eds.). *The Teacher's Bible Commentary*. (Nashville: Broadman and Holman Publishers, 1972), 348.

[1434] Benson, Joseph. *The Holy Bible With Notes, Critical, Explanatory and Practical.* (London: J. Kershaw, 1825), Psalm 131:2.

[1435] Plumer, W. S. *Studies in the Book of Psalms: Being a Critical and Expository Commentary, with Doctrinal and Practical Remarks on the Entire Psalter.* (Philadelphia; Edinburgh: J. B. Lippincott Company; A & C Black, 1872), 1129.

[1436] https://biblehub.com/commentaries/psalms/131-3.htm.

[1437] Henry, M. *Matthew Henry's Commentary on the Whole Bible: Complete and Unabridged in One Volume.* (Peabody: Hendrickson, 1994), 935–936.

[1438] Gill, John. *The John Gill Exposition of the Entire Bible,* Psalm 131:2.

[1439] Spurgeon, C. H. *Psalms.* (Wheaton, IL: Crossway Books, 1993), 286.

[1440] Kirkpatrick, A. F. (Ed.). *The Cambridge Bible for Schools and Colleges, Psalms.* (Cambridge: Cambridge University Press, 1914), Psalm 131:2.

[1441] Perowne, J. J. S. *The Book of Psalms; A New Translation, with Introductions and Notes, Explanatory and Critical* (Fifth Edition, Revised, Vol. 1). (London; Cambridge: George Bell and Sons; Deighton Bell and Co., 1883), 407.

[1442] Horne, G. *A Commentary on the Book of Psalms.* (New York: Robert Carter & Brothers, 1856), 486.

[1443] Spurgeon, C. H. *Psalms.* (Wheaton, IL: Crossway Books, 1993), 287.

[1444] Spurgeon, C. H. "The Weaned Child" (Sermon # 1210). https://www.spurgeongems.org/vols19-21/chs1210.pdf, accessed August 3, 2018. The sermon is well worth the read.

[1445] Henry, M. *Matthew Henry's Commentary on the Whole Bible: Complete and Unabridged in One Volume.* (Peabody: Hendrickson, 1994), 936.

[1446] Simeon, C. *Horae Homileticae: Psalms, LXXIII–CL* (Vol. 6). (London: Samuel Holdsworth, 1836), 423.

[1447] Swanson, J. *Dictionary of Biblical Languages with Semantic Domains: Hebrew (Old Testament)* (electronic ed.). (Oak Harbor: Logos Research Systems, Inc., 1997).

[1448] Gesenius, W., and S. P. Tregelles. *Gesenius' Hebrew and Chaldee Lexicon to the Old Testament Scriptures.* (Bellingham, WA: Logos Bible Software, 2003), 430.

[1449] Vine, W. E., M. F. Unger, and W. White, Jr. *Vine's Complete Expository Dictionary of Old and New Testament Words* (Vol. 1). (Nashville: T. Nelson, 1996), 205.

[1450] Thomas, R. L. *New American Standard Hebrew-Aramaic and Greek Dictionaries: updated edition.* (Anaheim: Foundation Publications, Inc., 1998).

[1451] Vine, W. E., M. F. Unger, and W. White, Jr. *Vine's Complete Expository Dictionary of Old and New Testament Words* (Vol. 1). (Nashville: T. Nelson, 1996), 234.

[1452] Harman, A. *Psalms: A Mentor Commentary (Vol. 1–2).* (Ross-shire, Great Britain: Mentor, 2011), 934.

[1453] Spurgeon, C. H. *Psalms.* (Wheaton, IL: Crossway Books, 1993), 292.

[1454] Scarborough, L. R. *With Christ after the Lost.* (Nashville: Broadman Press, 1952), 12–13.

[1455] Barclay, William. *The Letters to the Corinthians.* Daily Study Bible Series. (Philadelphia: The Westminster Press, 2000), 208.

[1456] Cave, Doy. "Olford: Preaching Is Much More Than Just Giving a Sermon." Baptist Press. http://www.jmm.aaa.net.au/articles/8407.htm, accessed June 23, 2009.

[1457] Spurgeon, C. H. Lectures to My Students. (Grand Rapids: Zondervan, 1970), 197.

[1458] Rosscup, James E. (John MacArthur and the Master's Seminary Faculty). *Preaching: How to Preach Biblically.* (Nashville: Thomas Nelson, 2005), 64, 67.

[1459] Criswell, W. A. *Criswell's Guidebook for Pastors.* (Nashville: Broadman Press, 1980), 235.

[1460] Spurgeon, C. H. *Morning and Evening,* June 27.

[1461] Spence-Jones, H. D. M. (Ed.). *Psalms,* (Vol. 3). (London; New York: Funk & Wagnalls Company, 1909), 260.

[1462] Merriam-Webster.

[1463] Hamilton, William W. *Sermons on the Books of the Bible,* (Vol. 3), 258.

[1464] Spurgeon, C. H. *Psalms.* (Wheaton, IL: Crossway Books, 1993), 298.

[1465] Thomas, R. L. *New American Standard Hebrew-Aramaic and Greek Dictionaries: updated edition.* (Anaheim: Foundation Publications, Inc., 1998).

[1466] Swanson, J. *Dictionary of Biblical Languages with Semantic Domains: Hebrew (Old Testament)* (electronic ed.). (Oak Harbor: Logos Research Systems, Inc., 1997).

[1467] Barnes, Albert. Notes on the Psalms, Critical, Explanatory and Practical. (New York: Harper & Brothers, 1868), Psalm 133:1.

[1468] Plumer, W. S. *Studies in the Book of Psalms: Being a Critical and Expository Commentary, with Doctrinal and Practical Remarks on the Entire Psalter.* (Philadelphia; Edinburgh: J. B. Lippincott Company; A & C Black, 1872), 1137.

[1469] Vine, W. E., M. F. Unger, and W. White, Jr. *Vine's Complete Expository Dictionary of Old and New Testament Words* (Vol. 1). (Nashville: T. Nelson, 1996), 64.

[1470] Swanson, J. *Dictionary of Biblical Languages with Semantic Domains: Hebrew (Old Testament)* (electronic ed.). (Oak Harbor: Logos Research Systems, Inc., 1997).

[1471] Spence-Jones, H. D. M. (Ed.). *Psalms,* (Vol. 3). (London; New York: Funk & Wagnalls Company, 1909), 270.

[1472] Simeon, C. *Horae Homileticae: Psalms, LXXIII–CL* (Vol. 6). (London: Samuel Holdsworth, 1836), 430.

[1473] Benson, Joseph. *The Holy Bible With Notes, Critical, Explanatory and Practical.* (London: J. Kershaw, 1825), Psalm 133:2.

[1474] Kirkpatrick, A. F. (Ed.). *The Cambridge Bible for Schools and Colleges, Psalms.* (Cambridge: Cambridge University Press, 1914), Psalm 133:2.

[1475] Barnes, Albert. Notes on the Psalms, Critical, Explanatory and Practical. (New York: Harper & Brothers, 1868), Psalm 133:2.

[1476] Spurgeon, C. H. *Psalms.* (Wheaton, IL: Crossway Books, 1993), 300.

[1477] Benson, Joseph. *The Holy Bible With Notes, Critical, Explanatory and Practical.* (London: J. Kershaw, 1825), Psalm 133:3.

[1478] Ibid.

[1479] Jamieson, R., A. R. Fausset, & D. Brown. *Commentary Critical and Explanatory on the Whole Bible* (Vol. 1). (Oak Harbor, WA: Logos Research Systems, Inc., 1997), Psalm 133:3.

[1480] https://biblehub.com/commentaries/psalms/133-3.htm.

[1481] Gill, John. *The John Gill Exposition of the Entire Bible,* Psalm 133:3.

[1482] Harman, A. *Psalms: A Mentor Commentary (Vol. 1–2).* (Ross-shire, Great Britain: Mentor, 2011), 937.

[1483] Perowne, J. J. S. *The Book of Psalms; A New Translation, with Introductions and Notes, Explanatory and Critical* (Fifth Edition, Revised, Vol. 1). (London; Cambridge: George Bell and Sons; Deighton Bell and Co., 1883), 417.

[1484] Plumer, W. S. *Studies in the Book of Psalms: Being a Critical and Expository Commentary, with Doctrinal and Practical Remarks on the Entire Psalter.* (Philadelphia; Edinburgh: J. B. Lippincott Company; A & C Black, 1872), 1137.

[1485] https://www.christianquotes.info/quotes-by-topic/quotes-about-unity/#ixzz5NDnmejoX, accessed August 4, 2018.

[1486] https://www.christianquotes.info/quotes-by-topic/quotes-about-unity/#ixzz5NDoqiAzP, accessed August 4, 2018.

[1487] Spence-Jones, H. D. M. (Ed.). *Psalms,* (Vol. 3). (London; New York: Funk & Wagnalls Company, 1909), 271.

[1488] Horne, G. *A Commentary on the Book of Psalms.* (New York: Robert Carter & Brothers, 1856), 492.

[1489] https://www.christianquotes.info/quotes-by-topic/quotes-about-unity/#ixzz5NDsF61dv, accessed August 4, 2018.

[1490] https://www.christianquotes.info/quotes-by-topic/quotes-about-unity/#ixzz5NDqqHsLo, accessed August 4, 2018.

[1491] Horne, G. *A Commentary on the Book of Psalms.* (New York: Robert Carter & Brothers, 1856), 491.

[1492] Rogers, Adrian. "Reconciliation Leads to Revival!", Love Worth Finding Daily Devotional, January 8.

[1493] Burke, Edmund. https://www.christianquotes.info/quotes-by-topic/quotes-about-unity/#ixzz5NDslTV84, accessed August 4, 2018.

[1494] Plumer, W. S. *Studies in the Book of Psalms: Being a Critical and Expository Commentary, with Doctrinal and Practical Remarks on the Entire Psalter.* (Philadelphia; Edinburgh: J. B. Lippincott Company; A & C Black, 1872), 1141.

[1495] Brown, F., S. R. Driver, and C. A. Briggs. *Enhanced Brown-Driver-Briggs Hebrew and English Lexicon.* (Oxford: Clarendon Press, 1977), 138.

[1496] Plumer, W. S. *Studies in the Book of Psalms: Being a Critical and Expository Commentary, with Doctrinal and Practical Remarks on the Entire Psalter.* (Philadelphia; Edinburgh: J. B. Lippincott Company; A & C Black, 1872), 1141.

[1497] Maclaren, Alexander. *The Expositor's Bible:* The Psalms. (New York: Scriptura Press, 2015), Psalm 134:1–3.

[1498] Barnes, Albert. Notes on the Psalms, Critical, Explanatory and Practical. (New York: Harper & Brothers, 1868), Psalm 134:1.

[1499] Plumer, W. S. *Studies in the Book of Psalms: Being a Critical and Expository Commentary, with Doctrinal and Practical Remarks on the Entire Psalter.* (Philadelphia; Edinburgh: J. B. Lippincott Company; A & C Black, 1872), 1141–1142. See 1 Chronicles 9:33.

[1500] Perowne, J. J. S. *The Book of Psalms; A New Translation, with Introductions and Notes, Explanatory and Critical* (Fifth Edition, Revised, Vol. 1). (London; Cambridge: George Bell and Sons; Deighton Bell and Co., 1883), 422.

[1501] Barnes, Albert. Notes on the Psalms, Critical, Explanatory and Practical. (New York: Harper & Brothers, 1868), Psalm 134:2.

[1502] https://biblehub.com/commentaries/psalms/134-2.htm.

[1503] Gill, John. *The John Gill Exposition of the Entire Bible,* Psalm 134:2.

[1504] Spurgeon, C. H. *Psalms.* (Wheaton, IL: Crossway Books, 1993), 302.

[1505] Barnes, Albert. Notes on the Psalms, Critical, Explanatory and Practical. (New York: Harper & Brothers, 1868), Psalm 134:3.

[1506] Keil & Delitzsch. Commentary on the Old Testament: Volume 5. (Peabody, Massachusetts: Hendrickson Publishers, 2006), 791.

[1507] Perowne, J. J. S. *The Book of Psalms; A New Translation, with Introductions and Notes, Explanatory and Critical* (Fifth Edition, Revised, Vol. 1). (London; Cambridge: George Bell and Sons; Deighton Bell and Co., 1883), 421.

[1508] Horne, G. *A Commentary on the Book of Psalms.* (New York: Robert Carter & Brothers, 1856), 493.

[1509] Hill, Junior. "He oft refreshed me." (a sermon). http://media.sermonaudio.com, accessed March 26, 2014. Parenthesis content added by author from the body of the sermon.

[1510] Swanson, J. *Dictionary of Biblical Languages with Semantic Domains: Hebrew (Old Testament)* (electronic ed.). (Oak Harbor: Logos Research Systems, Inc., 1997).

[1511] https://biblehub.com/commentaries/psalms/135-13.htm.

[1512] Plumer, W. S. *Studies in the Book of Psalms: Being a Critical and Expository Commentary, with Doctrinal and Practical Remarks on the Entire Psalter.* (Philadelphia; Edinburgh: J. B. Lippincott Company; A & C Black, 1872), 1146.

[1513] Spurgeon, C. H. *Psalms.* (Wheaton, IL: Crossway Books, 1993), 308.

[1514] Plumer, W. S. *Studies in the Book of Psalms: Being a Critical and Expository Commentary, with Doctrinal and Practical Remarks on the Entire Psalter.* (Philadelphia; Edinburgh: J. B. Lippincott Company; A & C Black, 1872), 1144.

[1515] Perowne, J. J. S. *The Book of Psalms; A New Translation, with Introductions and Notes, Explanatory and Critical* (Fifth Edition, Revised, Vol. 1). (London; Cambridge: George Bell and Sons; Deighton Bell and Co., 1883), 423.

[1516] Jennings, A. C., and W. H. Lowe. *The Psalms, with Introductions and Critical Notes* (Second Edition, Vol. 2). (London: Macmillan and Co., 1885), 336.

[1517] Spurgeon, C. H. *Psalms.* (Wheaton, IL: Crossway Books, 1993), 308.

[1518] Kirkpatrick, A. F. (Ed.). *The Cambridge Bible for Schools and Colleges,* Psalms. (Cambridge: Cambridge University Press, 1914), Psalm 135:13.

[1519] Henry, M. *Matthew Henry's Commentary on the Whole Bible: Complete and Unabridged in One Volume.* (Peabody: Hendrickson, 1994), 939.

[1520] Gill, John. *The John Gill Exposition of the Entire Bible,* Psalm 135:12.

[1521] Smith, Shelton L. (Ed.). *Great Preaching on Christ.* (Murfreesboro, TN: The Sword of the Lord Publishers, 2002), 65–66. Italics added.

[1522] Ibid. Italics added.

[1523] Spurgeon, C. H. *Psalms.* (Wheaton, IL: Crossway Books, 1993), 308.

[1524] Smith, Shelton L. (Ed.). *Great Preaching on Christ.* (Murfreesboro, TN: The Sword of the Lord Publishers, 2002), 66.

[1525] Horne, G. *A Commentary on the Book of Psalms.* (New York: Robert Carter & Brothers, 1856), 496.

[1526] Vine, W. E., M. F. Unger, and W. White, Jr. *Vine's Complete Expository Dictionary of Old and New Testament Words* (Vol. 1). (Nashville: T. Nelson, 1996), 44.

[1527] Holladay, W. L., and L. Köhler. A Concise Hebrew and Aramaic Lexicon of the Old Testament. (Leiden: Brill, 2000), 122.

[1528] Vine, W. E., M. F. Unger, and W. White, Jr. *Vine's Complete Expository Dictionary of Old and New Testament Words* (Vol. 1). (Nashville: T. Nelson, 1996), 142.

[1529] Jennings, A. C., and W. H. Lowe. *The Psalms, with Introductions and Critical Notes* (Second Edition, Vol. 2). (London: Macmillan and Co., 1885), 339.

[1530] Perowne, J. J. S. *The Book of Psalms; A New Translation, with Introductions and Notes, Explanatory and Critical* (Fifth Edition, Revised, Vol. 1). (London; Cambridge: George Bell and Sons; Deighton Bell and Co., 1883), 427.

[1531] Plumer, W. S. *Studies in the Book of Psalms: Being a Critical and Expository Commentary, with Doctrinal and Practical Remarks on the Entire Psalter.* (Philadelphia; Edinburgh: J. B. Lippincott Company; A & C Black, 1872), 1149.

[1532] Horne, G. *A Commentary on the Book of Psalms.* (New York: Robert Carter & Brothers, 1856), 497.

[1533] Spurgeon, C. H. *Psalms.* (Wheaton, IL: Crossway Books, 1993), 311.

[1534] Henry, M. *Matthew Henry's Commentary on the Whole Bible: Complete and Unabridged in One Volume.* (Peabody: Hendrickson, 1994), 939.

[1535] Plumer, W. S. *Studies in the Book of Psalms: Being a Critical and Expository Commentary, with Doctrinal and Practical Remarks on the Entire Psalter.* (Philadelphia; Edinburgh: J. B. Lippincott Company; A & C Black, 1872), 1149.

[1536] Ibid.

[1537] Henry, Matthew. *Matthew Henry's Concise Bible Commentary,* Psalm 136:1–9.

[1538] https://www.christianquotes.info/quotes-by-topic/quotes-about-mercy/#ixzz5NL41HX6u, accessed August 5, 2018.

[1539] Kirkpatrick, A. F. (Ed.). *The Cambridge Bible for Schools and Colleges,* Psalms. (Cambridge: Cambridge University Press, 1914), Psalm 137:1.

[1540] Spurgeon, C. H. *The Treasury of David.* (Grand Rapids, Michigan: Kregel Publications, 2004), Psalm 137:1. Explanatory notes and quaint sayings. From Joseph Addison's Dialogues on Medals.

[1541] Benson, Joseph. *The Holy Bible With Notes, Critical, Explanatory and Practical.* (London: J. Kershaw, 1825), Psalm 137:1.

[1542] Spence-Jones, H. D. M. (Ed.). *Psalms,* (Vol. 3). (London; New York: Funk & Wagnalls Company, 1909), 296.

[1543] Brown, F., S. R. Driver, and C. A. Briggs. *Enhanced Brown-Driver-Briggs Hebrew and English Lexicon.* (Oxford: Clarendon Press, 1977), 113.

[1544] Benson, Joseph. *The Holy Bible With Notes, Critical, Explanatory and Practical.* (London: J. Kershaw, 1825), Psalm 137:1.

[1545] Gill, John. *The John Gill Exposition of the Entire Bible,* Psalm 137:1.

[1546] Swanson, J. *Dictionary of Biblical Languages with Semantic Domains: Hebrew (Old Testament)* (electronic ed.). (Oak Harbor: Logos Research Systems, Inc., 1997).

[1547] Barnes, Albert. Notes on the Psalms, Critical, Explanatory and Practical. (New York: Harper & Brothers, 1868), Psalm 137:2.

[1548] Ibid. Note: Barnes states he actually saw a transplanted willow tree from ancient Babylon in London, giving evidence to the correctness of the text.

[1549] Gesenius, W., and S. P. Tregelles. *Gesenius' Hebrew and Chaldee Lexicon to the Old Testament Scriptures.* (Bellingham, WA: Logos Bible Software, 2003), 798.

[1550] Swanson, J. *Dictionary of Biblical Languages with Semantic Domains: Hebrew (Old Testament)* (electronic ed.). (Oak Harbor: Logos Research Systems, Inc., 1997).

[1551] Gesenius, W., and S. P. Tregelles. *Gesenius' Hebrew and Chaldee Lexicon to the Old Testament Scriptures.* (Bellingham, WA: Logos Bible Software, 2003), 859.

[1552] Spence-Jones, H. D. M. (Ed.). *Psalms,* (Vol. 3). (London; New York: Funk & Wagnalls Company, 1909), 296.

[1553] Brown, F., S. R. Driver, and C. A. Briggs. *Enhanced Brown-Driver-Briggs Hebrew and English Lexicon.* (Oxford: Clarendon Press, 1977), 970.

[1554] Gill, John. *The John Gill Exposition of the Entire Bible,* Psalm 137:3.

[1555] https://biblehub.com/commentaries/psalms/137-4.htm.

[1556] Spurgeon, C. H. *Psalms.* (Wheaton, IL: Crossway Books, 1993), 321.

[1557] Perowne, J. J. S. *The Book of Psalms; A New Translation, with Introductions and Notes, Explanatory and Critical* (Fifth Edition, Revised, Vol. 1). (London; Cambridge: George Bell and Sons; Deighton Bell and Co., 1883), 430.

[1558] Plumer, W. S. *Studies in the Book of Psalms: Being a Critical and Expository Commentary, with Doctrinal and Practical Remarks on the Entire Psalter.* (Philadelphia; Edinburgh: J. B. Lippincott Company; A & C Black, 1872), 1153.

[1559] Spurgeon, C. H. *The Treasury of David.* (Grand Rapids, Michigan: Kregel Publications, 2004), Psalm 137:1.

[1560] Henry, M. *Matthew Henry's Commentary on the Whole Bible: Complete and Unabridged in One Volume.* (Peabody: Hendrickson, 1994), 940.

[1561] Simeon, C. *Horae Homileticae: Psalms, LXXIII–CL* (Vol. 6). (London: Samuel Holdsworth, 1836), 437.

[1562] Henry, M. *Matthew Henry's Commentary on the Whole Bible: Complete and Unabridged in One Volume.* (Peabody: Hendrickson, 1994), 941.

[1563] Barnes, Albert. Notes on the Psalms, Critical, Explanatory and Practical. (New York: Harper & Brothers, 1868), Psalm 138:2.

[1564] Gill, John. *The John Gill Exposition of the Entire Bible,* Psalm 138:3.

[1565] Landes, G. M. *Building Your Biblical Hebrew Vocabulary: Learning Words by Frequency and Cognate* (Vol. 41). (Atlanta, GA: Society of Biblical Literature, 2001), 51.

[1566] Ibid., 57.

[1567] Spence-Jones, H. D. M. (Ed.). *Psalms,* (Vol. 3). (London; New York: Funk & Wagnalls Company, 1909), 303.

[1568] Barnes, Albert. Notes on the Psalms, Critical, Explanatory and Practical. (New York: Harper & Brothers, 1868), Psalm 138:3.

[1569] Ibid.

[1570] Kirkpatrick, A. F. (Ed.). *The Cambridge Bible for Schools and Colleges, Psalms.* (Cambridge: Cambridge University Press, 1914), Psalm 138:3.

[1571] Jamieson, R., A. R. Fausset, & D. Brown. *Commentary Critical and Explanatory on the Whole Bible* (Vol. 1). (Oak Harbor, WA: Logos Research Systems, Inc., 1997), Psalm 138:3–5.

[1572] Plumer, W. S. *Studies in the Book of Psalms: Being a Critical and Expository Commentary, with Doctrinal and Practical Remarks on the Entire Psalter.* (Philadelphia; Edinburgh: J. B. Lippincott Company; A & C Black, 1872), 1158.

[1573] Ibid.

[1574] Ibid.

[1575] Ibid.

[1576] Ibid.

[1577] Ibid.

[1578] Ibid.

[1579] Spurgeon, C. H. *Psalms.* (Wheaton, IL: Crossway Books, 1993), 324.

[1580] Henry, M. *Matthew Henry's Commentary on the Whole Bible: Complete and Unabridged in One Volume.* (Peabody: Hendrickson, 1994), 941.

[1581] Ibid.

[1582] Spurgeon, C. H. *Psalms.* (Wheaton, IL: Crossway Books, 1993), 324–325.

[1583] Plumer, W. S. *Studies in the Book of Psalms: Being a Critical and Expository Commentary, with Doctrinal and Practical Remarks on the Entire Psalter.* (Philadelphia; Edinburgh: J. B. Lippincott Company; A & C Black, 1872), 1158.

[1584] Hutson, Curtis. (Ed.), *Great Preaching on Prayer.* (Murfreesboro, Tenn.: Sword of the Lord Publishers, 1988), 45.

[1585] Barnes, Albert. Notes on the Psalms, Critical, Explanatory and Practical. (New York: Harper & Brothers, 1868), Psalm 138:7.

[1586] Cowman, L. B. *Streams in the Desert,* (Grand Rapids: Zondervan, 1999), April 23.

[1587] Horne, G. *A Commentary on the Book of Psalms.* (New York: Robert Carter & Brothers, 1856), 503.

[1588] Spurgeon, C. H. *The Treasury of David.* (Grand Rapids, Michigan: Kregel Publications, 2004), Psalm 137:8.

[1589] Spurgeon, C. H. "Faith in Perfection" (Sermon #231), January 2, 1859. Delivered at the Music Hall, Royal Surrey Gardens.

[1590] Keller, Timothy J. *Prayer: Experiencing Awe and Intimacy with God.* (New York: Penguin Books, 2016), 32.

[1591] Bounds, E.M. *The Weapon of Prayer.* (Radford, VA: Wilder Publications, 2008), 25.

[1592] Gesenius, W., and S. P. Tregelles. *Gesenius' Hebrew and Chaldee Lexicon to the Old Testament Scriptures.* (Bellingham, WA: Logos Bible Software, 2003), 301.

[1593] Plumer, W. S. *Studies in the Book of Psalms: Being a Critical and Expository Commentary, with Doctrinal and Practical Remarks on the Entire Psalter.* (Philadelphia; Edinburgh: J. B. Lippincott Company; A & C Black, 1872), 1165.

1594 Vine, W. E., M. F. Unger, and W. White, Jr. *Vine's Complete Expository Dictionary of Old and New Testament Words* (Vol. 1). (Nashville: T. Nelson, 1996), 130.

1595 Swanson, J. *Dictionary of Biblical Languages with Semantic Domains: Hebrew (Old Testament)* (electronic ed.). (Oak Harbor: Logos Research Systems, Inc., 1997).

1596 Barnes, Albert. Notes on the Psalms, Critical, Explanatory and Practical. (New York: Harper & Brothers, 1868), Psalm 139:23.

1597 Gill, John. *The John Gill Exposition of the Entire Bible,* Psalm 139:23.

1598 Bratcher, R. G. and W. D. Reyburn. *A Translator's Handbook on the Book of Psalms.* (New York: United Bible Societies, 1991), 1132.

1599 Plumer, W. S. *Studies in the Book of Psalms: Being a Critical and Expository Commentary, with Doctrinal and Practical Remarks on the Entire Psalter.* (Philadelphia; Edinburgh: J. B. Lippincott Company; A & C Black, 1872), 1165.

1600 Gill, John. *The John Gill Exposition of the Entire Bible,* Psalm 139:24.

1601 Bratcher, R. G. and W. D. Reyburn. *A Translator's Handbook on the Book of Psalms.* (New York: United Bible Societies, 1991), 1133.

1602 Barnes, Albert. Notes on the Psalms, Critical, Explanatory and Practical. (New York: Harper & Brothers, 1868), Psalm 139:24.

1603 Swanson, J. *Dictionary of Biblical Languages with Semantic Domains: Hebrew (Old Testament)* (electronic ed.). (Oak Harbor: Logos Research Systems, Inc., 1997).

1604 Williams, D., and L. J. Ogilvie. *Psalms 73–150* (Vol. 14). (Nashville: Thomas Nelson Inc., 1989), 476.

1605 Plumer, W. S. *Studies in the Book of Psalms: Being a Critical and Expository Commentary, with Doctrinal and Practical Remarks on the Entire Psalter.* (Philadelphia; Edinburgh: J. B. Lippincott Company; A & C Black, 1872), 1165.

1606 Barnes, Albert. Notes on the Psalms, Critical, Explanatory and Practical. (New York: Harper & Brothers, 1868), Psalm 139:24.

1607 Kirkpatrick, A. F. (Ed.). *The Cambridge Bible for Schools and Colleges,* Psalms. (Cambridge: Cambridge University Press, 1914), Psalm 139:23.

1608 Maclaren, Alexander. *The Expositor's Bible:* The Psalms. (New York: Scriptura Press, 2015), Psalm 139:23–4.

1609 Horne, G. *A Commentary on the Book of Psalms.* (New York: Robert Carter & Brothers, 1856), 508.

1610 Williams, D., and L. J. Ogilvie. *Psalms 73–150* (Vol. 14). (Nashville: Thomas Nelson Inc., 1989), 476.

1611 Plumer, W. S. *Studies in the Book of Psalms: Being a Critical and Expository Commentary, with Doctrinal and Practical Remarks on the Entire Psalter.* (Philadelphia; Edinburgh: J. B. Lippincott Company; A & C Black, 1872), 1166.

[1612] Perowne, J. J. S. *The Book of Psalms; A New Translation, with Introductions and Notes, Explanatory and Critical* (Fifth Edition, Revised, Vol. 1). (London; Cambridge: George Bell and Sons; Deighton Bell and Co., 1883), 443.

[1613] Maclaren, Alexander. *The Expositor's Bible:* The Psalms. (New York: Scriptura Press, 2015), Psalm 139:23–24.

[1614] Spence-Jones, H. D. M. (Ed.). *Psalms,* (Vol. 3). (London; New York: Funk & Wagnalls Company, 1909), 321.

[1615] Plumer, W. S. *Studies in the Book of Psalms: Being a Critical and Expository Commentary, with Doctrinal and Practical Remarks on the Entire Psalter.* (Philadelphia; Edinburgh: J. B. Lippincott Company; A & C Black, 1872), 1165.

[1616] Ibid., 1166.

[1617] Bratcher, R. G. and W. D. Reyburn. *A Translator's Handbook on the Book of Psalms.* (New York: United Bible Societies, 1991), 1133.

[1618] Spurgeon, C. H. *Psalms.* (Wheaton, IL: Crossway Books, 1993), 332.

[1619] Henry, M. *Matthew Henry's Commentary on the Whole Bible: Complete and Unabridged in One Volume.* (Peabody: Hendrickson, 1994), 943.

[1620] Harman, A. *Psalms: A Mentor Commentary (Vol. 1–2).* (Ross-shire, Great Britain: Mentor, 2011), 961–962.

[1621] Williams, D., and L. J. Ogilvie. *Psalms 73–150* (Vol. 14). (Nashville: Thomas Nelson Inc., 1989), 476.

[1622] Google Dictionary.

[1623] *The Spurgeon Study Bible.* (Nashville: Holman Bible Publishers, 2017), 746.

[1624] Chambers, Oswald. *My Utmost For His Highest,* February 6.

[1625] Maclaren, Alexander. *The Expositor's Bible:* The Psalms. (New York: Scriptura Press, 2015), Psalm 139:23–24.

[1626] Spurgeon, C. H. *Psalms.* (Wheaton, IL: Crossway Books, 1993), 331–332.

[1627] Maclaren, Alexander. *The Expositor's Bible:* The Psalms. (New York: Scriptura Press, 2015), Psalm 139:23–24.

[1628] Plumer, W. S. *Studies in the Book of Psalms: Being a Critical and Expository Commentary, with Doctrinal and Practical Remarks on the Entire Psalter.* (Philadelphia; Edinburgh: J. B. Lippincott Company; A & C Black, 1872), 1169.

[1629] Dilday, R. H., Jr., and J. H. Kennedy. *Psalms.* In H. F. Paschall and H. H. Hobbs (Eds.). *The Teacher's Bible Commentary.* (Nashville: Broadman and Holman Publishers, 1972), 352.

[1630] Barnes, Albert. Notes on the Psalms, Critical, Explanatory and Practical. (New York: Harper & Brothers, 1868), Psalm 140:11.

[1631] Spurgeon, C. H. *Psalms.* (Wheaton, IL: Crossway Books, 1993), 335.

[1632] Brown, F., S. R. Driver, and C. A. Briggs. *Enhanced Brown-Driver-Briggs Hebrew and English Lexicon.* (Oxford: Clarendon Press, 1977), 948.

[1633] Spurgeon, C. H. *The Treasury of David.* (Grand Rapids, Michigan: Kregel Publications, 2004), Psalm 140 (Introduction).

[1634] Gill, John. *The John Gill Exposition of the Entire Bible,* Psalm 140:11.

[1635] Jennings, A. C., and W. H. Lowe. *The Psalms, with Introductions and Critical Notes* (Second Edition, Vol. 2). (London: Macmillan and Co., 1885), 361.

[1636] Talmage, T. DeWitt. *The New Tabernacle Sermons.* (New York: George Munro,1886), 368–371.

[1637] Jennings, A. C., and W. H. Lowe. *The Psalms, with Introductions and Critical Notes* (Second Edition, Vol. 2). (London: Macmillan and Co., 1885), 361.

[1638] Henry, M. *Matthew Henry's Commentary on the Whole Bible: Complete and Unabridged in One Volume.* (Peabody: Hendrickson, 1994), 943–944.

[1639] Horne, G. *A Commentary on the Book of Psalms.* (New York: Robert Carter & Brothers, 1856), 509.

[1640] Spurgeon, C. H. *The Treasury of David.* (Grand Rapids, Michigan: Kregel Publications, 2004), Psalm 140:11.

[1641] Henry, Matthew. *Matthew Henry's Concise Bible Commentary,* Psalm 140:11.

[1642] Vine, W. E., M. F. Unger, and W. White, Jr. *Vine's Complete Expository Dictionary of Old and New Testament Words* (Vol. 1). (Nashville: T. Nelson, 1996), 29.

[1643] Gesenius, W., and S. P. Tregelles. *Gesenius' Hebrew and Chaldee Lexicon to the Old Testament Scriptures.* (Bellingham, WA: Logos Bible Software, 2003), 267.

[1644] Barnes, Albert. Notes on the Psalms, Critical, Explanatory and Practical. (New York: Harper & Brothers, 1868), Psalm 105:1.

[1645] Vine, W. E., M. F. Unger, and W. White, Jr. *Vine's Complete Expository Dictionary of Old and New Testament Words* (Vol. 1). (Nashville: T. Nelson, 1996), 186.

[1646] Alexander, J. A. *The Psalms Translated and Explained.* (Edinburgh: Andrew Elliot; James Thin, 1864), 545.

[1647] Swanson, J. *Dictionary of Biblical Languages with Semantic Domains: Hebrew (Old Testament)* (electronic ed.). (Oak Harbor: Logos Research Systems, Inc., 1997).

[1648] Ibid.

[1649] Spence-Jones, H. D. M. (Ed.). *Psalms,* (Vol. 3). (London; New York: Funk & Wagnalls Company, 1909), 333.

[1650] Kirkpatrick, A. F. (Ed.). *The Cambridge Bible for Schools and Colleges,* Psalms. (Cambridge: Cambridge University Press, 1914), Psalm 141:2.

[1651] Perowne, J. J. S. *The Book of Psalms; A New Translation, with Introductions and Notes, Explanatory and Critical* (Fifth Edition, Revised, Vol. 1). (London; Cambridge: George Bell and Sons; Deighton Bell and Co., 1883), 452.

[1652] Alexander, J. A. *The Psalms Translated and Explained.* (Edinburgh: Andrew Elliot; James Thin, 1864), 545.

[1653] https://biblehub.com/psalms/141-3.htm.

[1654] Spence-Jones, H. D. M. (Ed.). *Psalms,* (Vol. 3). (London; New York: Funk & Wagnalls Company, 1909), 333.

[1655] Spurgeon, C. H. *The Treasury of David.* (Grand Rapids, Michigan: Kregel Publications, 2004), Psalm 141:4.

[1656] Barnes, Albert. Notes on the Psalms, Critical, Explanatory and Practical. (New York: Harper & Brothers, 1868), Psalm 141:4.

[1657] Ibid.

[1658] Swanson, J. *Dictionary of Biblical Languages with Semantic Domains: Hebrew (Old Testament)* (electronic ed.). (Oak Harbor: Logos Research Systems, Inc., 1997).

[1659] Spence-Jones, H. D. M. (Ed.). *Psalms,* (Vol. 3). (London; New York: Funk & Wagnalls Company, 1909), 333.

[1660] Brown, F., S. R. Driver, and C. A. Briggs. *Enhanced Brown-Driver-Briggs Hebrew and English Lexicon.* (Oxford: Clarendon Press, 1977), 1036.

[1661] Jennings, A. C., and W. H. Lowe. *The Psalms, with Introductions and Critical Notes* (Second Edition, Vol. 2). (London: Macmillan and Co., 1885), 366.

[1662] Harris, R. L., G. L. Archer Jr., and B. K. Waltke (Eds.). *Theological Wordbook of the Old Testament,* (electronic ed.). (Chicago: Moody Press, 1999), 722.

[1663] Holladay, W. L., and L. Köhler. A Concise Hebrew and Aramaic Lexicon of the Old Testament. (Leiden: Brill, 2000), 142.

[1664] Whitaker, R., F. Brown, S. R. Driver, and C. A. Briggs. *The Abridged Brown-Driver-Briggs Hebrew-English Lexicon of the Old Testament.* (New York: Houghton, Mifflin and Company, 1906).

[1665] Swanson, J. *Dictionary of Biblical Languages with Semantic Domains: Hebrew (Old Testament)* (electronic ed.). (Oak Harbor: Logos Research Systems, Inc., 1997).

[1666] Gesenius, W., and S. P. Tregelles. *Gesenius' Hebrew and Chaldee Lexicon to the Old Testament Scriptures.* (Bellingham, WA: Logos Bible Software, 2003), 557.

[1667] Holladay, W. L., and L. Köhler. A Concise Hebrew and Aramaic Lexicon of the Old Testament. (Leiden: Brill, 2000), 242.

[1668] Swanson, J. *Dictionary of Biblical Languages with Semantic Domains: Hebrew (Old Testament)* (electronic ed.). (Oak Harbor: Logos Research Systems, Inc., 1997).

[1669] Alexander, J. A. *The Psalms Translated and Explained.* (Edinburgh: Andrew Elliot; James Thin, 1864), 547.

[1670] Henry, M. *Matthew Henry's Commentary on the Whole Bible: Complete and Unabridged in One Volume.* (Peabody: Hendrickson, 1994), 944.

[1671] Spurgeon, C. H. *The Treasury of David.* (Grand Rapids, Michigan: Kregel Publications, 2004), Psalm 141:1.

[1672] Henry, M. *Matthew Henry's Commentary on the Whole Bible: Complete and Unabridged in One Volume.* (Peabody: Hendrickson, 1994), 944.

[1673] Kirkpatrick, A. F. (Ed.). *The Cambridge Bible for Schools and Colleges, Psalms.* (Cambridge: Cambridge University Press, 1914), Psalm 141:3.

[1674] Barnes, Albert. Notes on the Psalms, Critical, Explanatory and Practical. (New York: Harper & Brothers, 1868), Psalm 141:4.

[1675] Spurgeon, C. H. *The Treasury of David.* (Grand Rapids, Michigan: Kregel Publications, 2004), Psalm 141:4.

[1676] Benson, Joseph. *The Holy Bible With Notes, Critical, Explanatory and Practical.* (London: J. Kershaw, 1825), Psalm 141:9.

[1677] Henry, M. *Matthew Henry's Commentary on the Whole Bible: Complete and Unabridged in One Volume.* (Peabody: Hendrickson, 1994), 944.

[1678] Spurgeon, C. H. *Psalms.* (Wheaton, IL: Crossway Books, 1993), 338.

[1679] Spurgeon, C. H. *Morning and Evening,* August 19 (Evening).

[1680] Horne, G. *A Commentary on the Book of Psalms.* (New York: Robert Carter & Brothers, 1856), 510–511.

[1681] https://www.brainyquote.com/topics/snare, accessed September 9, 2018.

[1682] Strong, J. *The New Strong's Dictionary of Hebrew and Greek Words.* (Nashville: Thomas Nelson, 1996).

[1683] Plumer, W. S. *Studies in the Book of Psalms: Being a Critical and Expository Commentary, with Doctrinal and Practical Remarks on the Entire Psalter.* (Philadelphia; Edinburgh: J. B. Lippincott Company; A & C Black, 1872), 1176.

[1684] Barnes, Albert. Notes on the Psalms, Critical, Explanatory and Practical. (New York: Harper & Brothers, 1868), Psalm 142:4.

[1685] Kirkpatrick, A. F. (Ed.). *The Cambridge Bible for Schools and Colleges, Psalms.* (Cambridge: Cambridge University Press, 1914), Psalm 142:4.

[1686] Perowne, J. J. S. *The Book of Psalms; A New Translation, with Introductions and Notes, Explanatory and Critical* (Fifth Edition, Revised, Vol. 1). (London; Cambridge: George Bell and Sons; Deighton Bell and Co., 1883), 457.

[1687] Strong, J. *The New Strong's Dictionary of Hebrew and Greek Words.* (Nashville: Thomas Nelson, 1996).

[1688] Swanson, J. *Dictionary of Biblical Languages with Semantic Domains: Hebrew (Old Testament)* (electronic ed.). (Oak Harbor: Logos Research Systems, Inc., 1997).

[1689] Plumer, W. S. *Studies in the Book of Psalms: Being a Critical and Expository Commentary, with Doctrinal and Practical Remarks on the Entire Psalter.* (Philadelphia; Edinburgh: J. B. Lippincott Company; A & C Black, 1872), 1176.

[1690] Landes, G. M. *Building Your Biblical Hebrew Vocabulary: Learning Words by Frequency and Cognate* (Vol. 41). (Atlanta, GA: Society of Biblical Literature, 2001), 61.

[1691] Barnes, Albert. Notes on the Psalms, Critical, Explanatory and Practical. (New York: Harper & Brothers, 1868), Psalm 142:4.

[1692] Plumer, W. S. *Studies in the Book of Psalms: Being a Critical and Expository Commentary, with Doctrinal and Practical Remarks on the Entire Psalter.* (Philadelphia; Edinburgh: J. B. Lippincott Company; A & C Black, 1872), 1176.

[1693] Wiersbe, W. W. *With the Word Bible Commentary.* (Nashville: Thomas Nelson, 1991), Ps. 57:1.

[1694] Spurgeon, C. H. *The Treasury of David.* (Grand Rapids, Michigan: Kregel Publications, 2004), Psalm 142:4.

[1695] Ibid.

[1696] Henry, M. *Matthew Henry's Commentary on the Whole Bible: Complete and Unabridged in One Volume.* (Peabody: Hendrickson, 1994), 945.

[1697] Gill, John. *The John Gill Exposition of the Entire Bible,* Psalm 142:4.

[1698] Criswell, W. A. "Ready to Witness," Daily Word, December 9.

[1699] Bales, Porter M. *Revival Sermons.* (Nashville: Broadman Press, 1938), 1937.

[1700] Dixon, Francis. Francis Dixon Bible Studies. *"How Much Do We Care For Souls?,"* (Psalm 142: 4). August, 1968.

[1701] Henry, M. *Matthew Henry's Commentary on the Whole Bible: Complete and Unabridged in One Volume.* (Peabody: Hendrickson, 1994), 945.

[1702] Plumer, W. S. *Studies in the Book of Psalms: Being a Critical and Expository Commentary, with Doctrinal and Practical Remarks on the Entire Psalter.* (Philadelphia; Edinburgh: J. B. Lippincott Company; A & C Black, 1872), 1179.

[1703] Vine, W. E., M. F. Unger, and W. White, Jr. *Vine's Complete Expository Dictionary of Old and New Testament Words* (Vol. 1). (Nashville: T. Nelson, 1996), 142.

[1704] Gesenius, W., and S. P. Tregelles. *Gesenius' Hebrew and Chaldee Lexicon to the Old Testament Scriptures.* (Bellingham, WA: Logos Bible Software, 2003), 137.

[1705] Oswalt, J. N., R. L. Harris, G. L. Archer Jr., and B. K. Waltke (Eds.). *Theological Wordbook of the Old Testament,* 233 נבט, (electronic ed.). (Chicago: Moody Press, 1999), 101.

[1706] Thomas, R. L. *New American Standard Hebrew-Aramaic and Greek Dictionaries: updated edition.* (Anaheim: Foundation Publications, Inc., 1998).

[1707] Vine, W. E., M. F. Unger, and W. White, Jr. *Vine's Complete Expository Dictionary of Old and New Testament Words* (Vol. 1). (Nashville: T. Nelson, 1996), 279.

[1708] Alexander, J. A. *The Psalms Translated and Explained.* (Edinburgh: Andrew Elliot; James Thin, 1864), 549.

1709 https://biblehub.com/psalms/143-8.htm.

1710 Gill, John. *The John Gill Exposition of the Entire Bible,* Psalm 143:8.

1711 Swanson, J. *Dictionary of Biblical Languages with Semantic Domains: Hebrew (Old Testament)* (electronic ed.). (Oak Harbor: Logos Research Systems, Inc., 1997).

1712 Barnes, Albert. Notes on the Psalms, Critical, Explanatory and Practical. (New York: Harper & Brothers, 1868), Psalm 143:9.

1713 Ibid., Psalm 143:10.

1714 Ibid.

1715 Spurgeon, C. H. *Psalms.* (Wheaton, IL: Crossway Books, 1993), 346.

1716 Holladay, W. L., and L. Köhler. A Concise Hebrew and Aramaic Lexicon of the Old Testament. (Leiden: Brill, 2000), 193.

1717 Spurgeon, C. H. *The Treasury of David.* (Grand Rapids, Michigan: Kregel Publications, 2004), Psalm 143:10.

1718 Simeon, C. *Horae Homileticae: Psalms, LXXIII–CL* (Vol. 6). (London: Samuel Holdsworth, 1836), 475.

1719 Henry, M. *Matthew Henry's Commentary on the Whole Bible: Complete and Unabridged in One Volume.* (Peabody: Hendrickson, 1994), 946.

1720 Raleigh, A. "From Dawn to the Perfect Day," 190. Cited in The Sermon Bible.

1721 Maclaren, Alexander. *The Expositor's Bible:* The Psalms. (New York: Scriptura Press, 2015), Psalm 143:10.

1722 Spurgeon, C. H. *The Treasury of David.* (Grand Rapids, Michigan: Kregel Publications, 2004), Psalm 143:10.

1723 Horne, G. *A Commentary on the Book of Psalms.* (New York: Robert Carter & Brothers, 1856), 516–517.

1724 Ravenhill, Leonard. *Why Revival Tarries.* (Grand Rapids: Bethany House Publishers, 2004), 54.

1725 https://www.christianquotes.info/quotes-by-topic/quotes-about-the-holy-spirit/#ixzz5Nh7vRyCr, accessed August 9, 2018.

1726 https://www.brainyquote.com/topics/holy_spirit, accessed August 9, 2018.

1727 Spurgeon, C. H. *Psalms.* (Wheaton, IL: Crossway Books, 1993), 346.

1728 Oswalt, J. N., R. L. Harris, G. L. Archer Jr., and B. K. Waltke (Eds.). *Theological Wordbook of the Old Testament,* 285 בָּרַךְ, (electronic ed.). (Chicago: Moody Press, 1999), 132.

1729 Barnes, Albert. Notes on the Psalms, Critical, Explanatory and Practical. (New York: Harper & Brothers, 1868), Psalm 144:1.

1730 Vine, W. E., M. F. Unger, and W. White, Jr. *Vine's Complete Expository Dictionary of Old and New Testament Words* (Vol. 1). (Nashville: T. Nelson, 1996), 142.

[1731] Swanson, J. *Dictionary of Biblical Languages with Semantic Domains: Hebrew (Old Testament)* (electronic ed.). (Oak Harbor: Logos Research Systems, Inc., 1997).

[1732] Landes, G. M. *Building Your Biblical Hebrew Vocabulary: Learning Words by Frequency and Cognate* (Vol. 41). (Atlanta, GA: Society of Biblical Literature, 2001), 107.

[1733] Barnes, Albert. Notes on the Psalms, Critical, Explanatory and Practical. (New York: Harper & Brothers, 1868), Psalm 144:2.

[1734] Plumer, W. S. *Studies in the Book of Psalms: Being a Critical and Expository Commentary, with Doctrinal and Practical Remarks on the Entire Psalter.* (Philadelphia; Edinburgh: J. B. Lippincott Company; A & C Black, 1872), 1183.

[1735] Barnes, Albert. Notes on the Psalms, Critical, Explanatory and Practical. (New York: Harper & Brothers, 1868), Psalm 144:3.

[1736] Ibid.

[1737] Swanson, J. *Dictionary of Biblical Languages with Semantic Domains: Hebrew (Old Testament)* (electronic ed.). (Oak Harbor: Logos Research Systems, Inc., 1997).

[1738] https://biblehub.com/commentaries/psalms/144-4.htm.

[1739] Jennings, A. C., and W. H. Lowe. *The Psalms, with Introductions and Critical Notes* (Second Edition, Vol. 2). (London: Macmillan and Co., 1885), 374.

[1740] Clarke, Adam. *Clarkes' Commentary and Critical Notes*, Psalm 144 (Introduction).

[1741] Alexander, J. A. *The Psalms Translated and Explained.* (Edinburgh: Andrew Elliot; James Thin, 1864), 550.

[1742] Jennings, A. C., and W. H. Lowe. *The Psalms, with Introductions and Critical Notes* (Second Edition, Vol. 2). (London: Macmillan and Co., 1885), 372.

[1743] Lockyer, Herbert, Sr. *Psalms: A Devotional Commentary,* Psalm 119. (Grand Rapids: Kregel Publications, 1993), 755.

[1744] Jennings, A. C., and W. H. Lowe. *The Psalms, with Introductions and Critical Notes* (Second Edition, Vol. 2). (London: Macmillan and Co., 1885), 374.

[1745] Spurgeon, C. H. *The Treasury of David.* (Grand Rapids, Michigan: Kregel Publications, 2004), Psalm 144:3.

[1746] Henry, Matthew. *Matthew Henry's Concise Bible Commentary,* Psalm 144:1–8.

[1747] Google Dictionary.

[1748] Plumer, W. S. *Studies in the Book of Psalms: Being a Critical and Expository Commentary, with Doctrinal and Practical Remarks on the Entire Psalter.* (Philadelphia; Edinburgh: J. B. Lippincott Company; A & C Black, 1872), 1183.

[1749] Spurgeon, C. H. *The Treasury of David.* (Grand Rapids, Michigan: Kregel Publications, 2004), Psalm 144:4. Explanatory notes and quaint sayings.

[1750] Barnes, Albert. Notes on the Psalms, Critical, Explanatory and Practical. (New York: Harper & Brothers, 1868), Psalm 144:4.

[1751] Henry, Matthew. *Matthew Henry's Concise Bible Commentary,* Psalm 144:1–8.

[1752] Barnes, Albert. Notes on the Psalms, Critical, Explanatory and Practical. (New York: Harper & Brothers, 1868), James 4:14.

[1753] Ibid.

[1754] The author discovered the outline while in seminary and adapted it.

[1755] Swanson, J. *Dictionary of Biblical Languages with Semantic Domains: Hebrew (Old Testament)* (electronic ed.). (Oak Harbor: Logos Research Systems, Inc., 1997).

[1756] Strong, J. *A Concise Dictionary of the Words in the Greek Testament and the Hebrew Bible.* (Vol. 2). (Bellingham, WA: Logos Bible Software, 2009), 108.

[1757] Plumer, W. S. *Studies in the Book of Psalms: Being a Critical and Expository Commentary, with Doctrinal and Practical Remarks on the Entire Psalter.* (Philadelphia; Edinburgh: J. B. Lippincott Company; A & C Black, 1872), 1188.

[1758] Gesenius, W., and S. P. Tregelles. *Gesenius' Hebrew and Chaldee Lexicon to the Old Testament Scriptures.* (Bellingham, WA: Logos Bible Software, 2003), 158.

[1759] Barnes, Albert. Notes on the Psalms, Critical, Explanatory and Practical. (New York: Harper & Brothers, 1868), Psalm 145:8.

[1760] Landes, G. M. *Building Your Biblical Hebrew Vocabulary: Learning Words by Frequency and Cognate* (Vol. 41). (Atlanta, GA: Society of Biblical Literature, 2001), 72.

[1761] Holladay, W. L., and L. Köhler. A Concise Hebrew and Aramaic Lexicon of the Old Testament. (Leiden: Brill, 2000), 337.

[1762] Landes, G. M. *Building Your Biblical Hebrew Vocabulary: Learning Words by Frequency and Cognate* (Vol. 41). (Atlanta, GA: Society of Biblical Literature, 2001), 51.

[1763] Alexander, R. H., R. L. Harris, G. L. Archer Jr., and B. K. Waltke (Eds.). *Theological Wordbook of the Old Testament,* 847 יָדָה , (electronic ed.). (Chicago: Moody Press, 1999), 364.

[1764] Swanson, J. *Dictionary of Biblical Languages with Semantic Domains: Hebrew (Old Testament)* (electronic ed.). (Oak Harbor: Logos Research Systems, Inc., 1997).

[1765] Benson, Joseph. *The Holy Bible With Notes, Critical, Explanatory and Practical.* (London: J. Kershaw, 1825), Psalm 145:11.

[1766] Alexander, J. A. *The Psalms Translated and Explained.* (Edinburgh: Andrew Elliot; James Thin, 1864), 554.

1767 Plumer, W. S. *Studies in the Book of Psalms: Being a Critical and Expository Commentary, with Doctrinal and Practical Remarks on the Entire Psalter.* (Philadelphia; Edinburgh: J. B. Lippincott Company; A & C Black, 1872), 1189.

1768 Ibid.

1769 Ibid., 1187.

1770 Henry, M. *Matthew Henry's Commentary on the Whole Bible: Complete and Unabridged in One Volume.* (Peabody: Hendrickson, 1994), 948.

1771 https://www.thegospelcoalition.org/blogs/trevin-wax/quotes-on-the-goodness-and-mercy-of-god/, accessed August 11, 2018.

1772 Spence-Jones, H. D. M. (Ed.). *Psalms,* (Vol. 3). (London; New York: Funk & Wagnalls Company, 1909), 374.

1773 Henry, M. *Matthew Henry's Commentary on the Whole Bible: Complete and Unabridged in One Volume.* (Peabody: Hendrickson, 1994), 948.

1774 Spence-Jones, H. D. M. (Ed.). *Psalms,* (Vol. 3). (London; New York: Funk & Wagnalls Company, 1909), 378.

1775 Pink, A. W. *The Attributes of God.* (Grand Rapids: Baker Book House, 1975), 77.

1776 Ibid.

1777 https://biblehub.com/commentaries/romans/2-4.htm.

1778 Barnes, Albert. Notes on the Psalms, Critical, Explanatory and Practical. (New York: Harper & Brothers, 1868), Romans 2:4.

1779 Ibid.

1780 https://biblehub.com/commentaries/romans/2-4.htm.

1781 Plumer, W. S. *Studies in the Book of Psalms: Being a Critical and Expository Commentary, with Doctrinal and Practical Remarks on the Entire Psalter.* (Philadelphia; Edinburgh: J. B. Lippincott Company; A & C Black, 1872), 1188.

1782 https://biblehub.com/commentaries/psalms/145-4.htm.

1783 Plumer, W. S. *Studies in the Book of Psalms: Being a Critical and Expository Commentary, with Doctrinal and Practical Remarks on the Entire Psalter.* (Philadelphia; Edinburgh: J. B. Lippincott Company; A & C Black, 1872), 1188.

1784 Horne, G. *A Commentary on the Book of Psalms.* (New York: Robert Carter & Brothers, 1856), 521.

1785 Henry, M. *Matthew Henry's Commentary on the Whole Bible: Complete and Unabridged in One Volume.* (Peabody: Hendrickson, 1994), 948.

1786 Landes, G. M. *Building Your Biblical Hebrew Vocabulary: Learning Words by Frequency and Cognate* (Vol. 41). (Atlanta, GA: Society of Biblical Literature, 2001), 58.

1787 Alexander, J. A. *The Psalms Translated and Explained.* (Edinburgh: Andrew Elliot; James Thin, 1864), 557.

[1788] Gesenius, W., and S. P. Tregelles. *Gesenius' Hebrew and Chaldee Lexicon to the Old Testament Scriptures.* (Bellingham, WA: Logos Bible Software, 2003), 178.

[1789] Plumer, W. S. *Studies in the Book of Psalms: Being a Critical and Expository Commentary, with Doctrinal and Practical Remarks on the Entire Psalter.* (Philadelphia; Edinburgh: J. B. Lippincott Company; A & C Black, 1872), 1194.

[1790] Jennings, A. C., and W. H. Lowe. *The Psalms, with Introductions and Critical Notes* (Second Edition, Vol. 2). (London: Macmillan and Co., 1885), 384.

[1791] Barnes, Albert. Notes on the Psalms, Critical, Explanatory and Practical. (New York: Harper & Brothers, 1868), Psalm 146:9.

[1792] Jennings, A. C., and W. H. Lowe. *The Psalms, with Introductions and Critical Notes* (Second Edition, Vol. 2). (London: Macmillan and Co., 1885), 384.

[1793] Clarke, Adam. *Clarkes' Commentary and Critical Notes,* Psalm 146. (Introduction)

[1794] Jennings, A. C., and W. H. Lowe. *The Psalms, with Introductions and Critical Notes* (Second Edition, Vol. 2). (London: Macmillan and Co., 1885), 382.

[1795] Perowne, J. J. S. *The Book of Psalms; A New Translation, with Introductions and Notes, Explanatory and Critical* (Fifth Edition, Revised, Vol. 1). (London; Cambridge: George Bell and Sons; Deighton Bell and Co., 1883), 474.

[1796] Kirkpatrick, A. F. (Ed.). *The Cambridge Bible for Schools and Colleges, Psalms.* (Cambridge: Cambridge University Press, 1914), Psalm 146:9.

[1797] Plumer, W. S. *Studies in the Book of Psalms: Being a Critical and Expository Commentary, with Doctrinal and Practical Remarks on the Entire Psalter.* (Philadelphia; Edinburgh: J. B. Lippincott Company; A & C Black, 1872), 1194.

[1798] Alexander, J. A. *The Psalms Translated and Explained.* (Edinburgh: Andrew Elliot; James Thin, 1864), 557.

[1799] Henry, M. *Matthew Henry's Commentary on the Whole Bible: Complete and Unabridged in One Volume.* (Peabody: Hendrickson, 1994), 950.

[1800] Barnes, Albert. Notes on the Psalms, Critical, Explanatory and Practical. (New York: Harper & Brothers, 1868), Psalm 146:9.

[1801] Gill, John. *The John Gill Exposition of the Entire Bible,* Psalm 146:9.

[1802] Henry, M. *Matthew Henry's Commentary on the Whole Bible: Complete and Unabridged in One Volume.* (Peabody: Hendrickson, 1994), 1007.

[1803] McGee, J. V. *Thru the Bible Commentary:* The Epistles (1 and 2 Timothy/Titus/Philemon) (electronic ed.), Vol. 50. (Nashville: Thomas Nelson, 1991), 70–71.

[1804] Mounce, W. D. *Pastoral Epistles* (Vol. 46). (Dallas: Word, Incorporated, 2000), 278.

[1805] https://biblehub.com/psalms/146-9.htm.

[1806] Spence-Jones, H. D. M. (Ed.). *Psalms,* (Vol. 3). (London; New York: Funk & Wagnalls Company, 1909), 390.

[1807] Plumer, W. S. *Studies in the Book of Psalms: Being a Critical and Expository Commentary, with Doctrinal and Practical Remarks on the Entire Psalter.* (Philadelphia; Edinburgh: J. B. Lippincott Company; A & C Black, 1872), 1194.

[1808] Barnes, Albert. Notes on the Psalms, Critical, Explanatory and Practical. (New York: Harper & Brothers, 1868), Psalm 146:9.

[1809] Cowman, L. B. *Streams in the Desert,* (Grand Rapids: Zondervan, 1999), January 18.

[1810] Vine, W. E., M. F. Unger, and W. White, Jr. *Vine's Complete Expository Dictionary of Old and New Testament Words* (Vol. 1). (Nashville: T. Nelson, 1996), 250.

[1811] Kirkpatrick, A. F. (Ed.). *The Cambridge Bible for Schools and Colleges,* Psalms. (Cambridge: Cambridge University Press, 1914), Psalm 147:13.

[1812] Barnes, Albert. Notes on the Psalms, Critical, Explanatory and Practical. (New York: Harper & Brothers, 1868), Psalm 147:13.

[1813] Perowne, J. J. S. *The Book of Psalms; A New Translation, with Introductions and Notes, Explanatory and Critical* (Fifth Edition, Revised, Vol. 1). (London; Cambridge: George Bell and Sons; Deighton Bell and Co., 1883), 477.

[1814] Barnes, Albert. Notes on the Psalms, Critical, Explanatory and Practical. (New York: Harper & Brothers, 1868), Psalm 147:13.

[1815] Spence-Jones, H. D. M. (Ed.). *Psalms,* (Vol. 3). (London; New York: Funk & Wagnalls Company, 1909), 400.

[1816] Clarke, Adam. *Clarkes' Commentary and Critical Notes*, Psalm 147 (Introduction).

[1817] Jennings, A. C., and W. H. Lowe. *The Psalms, with Introductions and Critical Notes* (Second Edition, Vol. 2). (London: Macmillan and Co., 1885), 384–385.

[1818] Spurgeon, C. H. *Morning and Evening,* November 15 (Morning).

[1819] Spurgeon, C. H. *Psalms.* (Wheaton, IL: Crossway Books, 1993), 363.

[1820] Swanson, J. *Dictionary of Biblical Languages with Semantic Domains: Hebrew (Old Testament)* (electronic ed.). (Oak Harbor: Logos Research Systems, Inc., 1997).

[1821] Spence-Jones, H. D. M. (Ed.). *Psalms,* (Vol. 3). (London; New York: Funk & Wagnalls Company, 1909), 407.

[1822] Ibid.

[1823] Holladay, W. L., and L. Köhler. A Concise Hebrew and Aramaic Lexicon of the Old Testament. (Leiden: Brill, 2000), 302.

[1824] Plumer, W. S. *Studies in the Book of Psalms: Being a Critical and Expository Commentary, with Doctrinal and Practical Remarks on the Entire Psalter.* (Philadelphia; Edinburgh: J. B. Lippincott Company; A & C Black, 1872), 1202.

[1825] Horne, G. *A Commentary on the Book of Psalms.* (New York: Robert Carter & Brothers, 1856), 530.

1826 Plumer, W. S. *Studies in the Book of Psalms: Being a Critical and Expository Commentary, with Doctrinal and Practical Remarks on the Entire Psalter.* (Philadelphia; Edinburgh: J. B. Lippincott Company; A & C Black, 1872), 1202.

1827 Ibid.

1828 Ibid.

1829 Jamieson, R., A. R. Fausset, & D. Brown. *Commentary Critical and Explanatory on the Whole Bible* (Vol. 1). (Oak Harbor, WA: Logos Research Systems, Inc., 1997), Psalm 148:5.

1830 Ibid.

1831 Benson, Joseph. *The Holy Bible With Notes, Critical, Explanatory and Practical.* (London: J. Kershaw, 1825), Psalm 148:5.

1832 Gesenius, W., and S. P. Tregelles. *Gesenius' Hebrew and Chaldee Lexicon to the Old Testament Scriptures.* (Bellingham, WA: Logos Bible Software, 2003), 637.

1833 Barnes, Albert. Notes on the Psalms, Critical, Explanatory and Practical. (New York: Harper & Brothers, 1868), Psalm 148:6.

1834 Jamieson, R., A. R. Fausset, & D. Brown. *Commentary Critical and Explanatory on the Whole Bible* (Vol. 1). (Oak Harbor, WA: Logos Research Systems, Inc., 1997), Psalm 148:6.

1835 https://biblehub.com/commentaries/psalms/148-6.htm.

1836 Henry, M. *Matthew Henry's Commentary on the Whole Bible: Complete and Unabridged in One Volume.* (Peabody: Hendrickson, 1994), 952.

1837 Brown, F., S. R. Driver, and C. A. Briggs. *Enhanced Brown-Driver-Briggs Hebrew and English Lexicon.* (Oxford: Clarendon Press, 1977), 349.

1838 https://biblehub.com/commentaries/psalms/148-6.htm.

1839 Swanson, J. *Dictionary of Biblical Languages with Semantic Domains: Hebrew (Old Testament)* (electronic ed.). (Oak Harbor: Logos Research Systems, Inc., 1997).

1840 Barnes, Albert. Notes on the Psalms, Critical, Explanatory and Practical. (New York: Harper & Brothers, 1868), Psalm 148:7.

1841 Plumer, W. S. *Studies in the Book of Psalms: Being a Critical and Expository Commentary, with Doctrinal and Practical Remarks on the Entire Psalter.* (Philadelphia; Edinburgh: J. B. Lippincott Company; A & C Black, 1872), 1202–1203.

1842 Spence-Jones, H. D. M. (Ed.). *Psalms,* (Vol. 3). (London; New York: Funk & Wagnalls Company, 1909), 407.

1843 Spurgeon, C. H. *Psalms.* (Wheaton, IL: Crossway Books, 1993), 367.

1844 Benson, Joseph. *The Holy Bible With Notes, Critical, Explanatory and Practical.* (London: J. Kershaw, 1825), Psalm 148:9.

1845 Jamieson, R., A. R. Fausset, & D. Brown. *Commentary Critical and Explanatory on the Whole Bible* (Vol. 1). (Oak Harbor, WA: Logos Research Systems, Inc., 1997), Psalm 148:9.

[1846] Spurgeon, C. H. *Psalms*. (Wheaton, IL: Crossway Books, 1993), 367.

[1847] Jamieson, R., A. R. Fausset, & D. Brown. *Commentary Critical and Explanatory on the Whole Bible* (Vol. 1). (Oak Harbor, WA: Logos Research Systems, Inc., 1997), Psalm 148:11–12.

[1848] Horne, G. *A Commentary on the Book of Psalms*. (New York: Robert Carter & Brothers, 1856), 531.

[1849] Henry, M. *Matthew Henry's Commentary on the Whole Bible: Complete and Unabridged in One Volume*. (Peabody: Hendrickson, 1994), 952.

[1850] Benson, Joseph. *The Holy Bible With Notes, Critical, Explanatory and Practical*. (London: J. Kershaw, 1825), Psalm 148:13.

[1851] Gill, John. *The John Gill Exposition of the Entire Bible,* Psalm 148:13.

[1852] Ibid.

[1853] Clarke, Adam. *Clarkes' Commentary and Critical Notes*, Psalm 148 (Introduction).

[1854] Perowne, J. J. S. *The Book of Psalms; A New Translation, with Introductions and Notes, Explanatory and Critical* (Fifth Edition, Revised, Vol. 1). (London; Cambridge: George Bell and Sons; Deighton Bell and Co., 1883), 479.

[1855] Horne, G. *A Commentary on the Book of Psalms*. (New York: Robert Carter & Brothers, 1856), 530.

[1856] Henry, M. *Matthew Henry's Commentary on the Whole Bible: Complete and Unabridged in One Volume*. (Peabody: Hendrickson, 1994), 951.

[1857] Spence-Jones, H. D. M. (Ed.). *Psalms,* (Vol. 3). (London; New York: Funk & Wagnalls Company, 1909), 408.

[1858] Horne, G. *A Commentary on the Book of Psalms*. (New York: Robert Carter & Brothers, 1856), 530.

[1859] Gill, John. *The John Gill Exposition of the Entire Bible,* Psalm 148:9.

[1860] Ibid.

[1861] Plumer, W. S. *Studies in the Book of Psalms: Being a Critical and Expository Commentary, with Doctrinal and Practical Remarks on the Entire Psalter*. (Philadelphia; Edinburgh: J. B. Lippincott Company; A & C Black, 1872), 1203.

[1862] Henry, M. *Matthew Henry's Commentary on the Whole Bible: Complete and Unabridged in One Volume*. (Peabody: Hendrickson, 1994), 952.

[1863] Horne, G. *A Commentary on the Book of Psalms*. (New York: Robert Carter & Brothers, 1856), 532.

[1864] Swanson, J. *Dictionary of Biblical Languages with Semantic Domains: Hebrew (Old Testament)* (electronic ed.). (Oak Harbor: Logos Research Systems, Inc., 1997).

[1865] Gill, John. *The John Gill Exposition of the Entire Bible,* Psalm 149:4.

[1866] Barnes, Albert. Notes on the Psalms, Critical, Explanatory and Practical. (New York: Harper & Brothers, 1868), Psalm 149:4.

[1867] Holladay, W. L., and L. Köhler. A Concise Hebrew and Aramaic Lexicon of the Old Testament. (Leiden: Brill, 2000), 278.

[1868] Spurgeon, C. H. *Psalms.* (Wheaton, IL: Crossway Books, 1993), 370.

[1869] Kirkpatrick, A. F. (Ed.). *The Cambridge Bible for Schools and Colleges,* Psalms. (Cambridge: Cambridge University Press, 1914), Psalm 149:4.

[1870] https://biblehub.com/commentaries/psalms/149-4.htm.

[1871] Henry, M. *Matthew Henry's Commentary on the Whole Bible: Complete and Unabridged in One Volume.* (Peabody: Hendrickson, 1994), 953.

[1872] Plumer, W. S. *Studies in the Book of Psalms: Being a Critical and Expository Commentary, with Doctrinal and Practical Remarks on the Entire Psalter.* (Philadelphia; Edinburgh: J. B. Lippincott Company; A & C Black, 1872), 1205.

[1873] Henry, M. *Matthew Henry's Commentary on the Whole Bible: Complete and Unabridged in One Volume.* (Peabody: Hendrickson, 1994), 952.

[1874] Plumer, W. S. *Studies in the Book of Psalms: Being a Critical and Expository Commentary, with Doctrinal and Practical Remarks on the Entire Psalter.* (Philadelphia; Edinburgh: J. B. Lippincott Company; A & C Black, 1872), 1206.

[1875] Exell, Joseph S. Ed. *The Biblical Illustrator,* Psalm 149:4.

[1876] Spurgeon, C. H. "Hallelujah! Hallelujah!" (Sermon #2421), Delivered at the Metropolitan Tabernacle, Newington, on Lord's Day evening, June 19, 1887.

[1877] Spurgeon, C. H. *Psalms.* (Wheaton, IL: Crossway Books, 1993), 370.

[1878] Boice, J. M. *Psalms 107–150: An Expositional Commentary.* (Grand Rapids, MI: Baker Books, 2005), 1283.

[1879] Dilday, R. H., Jr., and J. H. Kennedy. *Psalms.* In H. F. Paschall and H. H. Hobbs (Eds.). *The Teacher's Bible Commentary.* (Nashville: Broadman and Holman Publishers, 1972), 356.

[1880] Spurgeon, C. H. "Hallelujah! Hallelujah!" (Sermon #2421), Delivered at the Metropolitan Tabernacle, Newington, on Lord's Day evening, June 19, 1887.

[1881] Ibid.

[1882] Swanson, J. *Dictionary of Biblical Languages with Semantic Domains: Hebrew (Old Testament)* (electronic ed.). (Oak Harbor: Logos Research Systems, Inc., 1997).

[1883] Futato, M. D. *Beginning Biblical Hebrew.* (Winona Lake, IN: Eisenbrauns, 2003), 288.

[1884] Spence-Jones, H. D. M. (Ed.). *Psalms,* (Vol. 3). (London; New York: Funk & Wagnalls Company, 1909), 417.

[1885] Dilday, R. H., Jr., and J. H. Kennedy. *Psalms.* In H. F. Paschall and H. H. Hobbs (Eds.). *The Teacher's Bible Commentary.* (Nashville: Broadman and Holman Publishers, 1972), 357.

[1886] Barnes, Albert. Notes on the Psalms, Critical, Explanatory and Practical. (New York: Harper & Brothers, 1868), Psalm 150:1.

[1887] Benson, Joseph. *The Holy Bible With Notes, Critical, Explanatory and Practical.* (London: J. Kershaw, 1825), Psalm 150:2.

[1888] Barnes, Albert. Notes on the Psalms, Critical, Explanatory and Practical. (New York: Harper & Brothers, 1868), Psalm 150:2.

[1889] Kirkpatrick, A. F. (Ed.). *The Cambridge Bible for Schools and Colleges, Psalms.* (Cambridge: Cambridge University Press, 1914), Psalm 150:2.

[1890] Gill, John. *The John Gill Exposition of the Entire Bible,* Psalm 150:2.

[1891] Alexander, J. A. *The Psalms Translated and Explained.* (Edinburgh: Andrew Elliot; James Thin, 1864), 564.

[1892] Swanson, J. *Dictionary of Biblical Languages with Semantic Domains: Hebrew (Old Testament)* (electronic ed.). (Oak Harbor: Logos Research Systems, Inc., 1997).

[1893] Plumer, W. S. *Studies in the Book of Psalms: Being a Critical and Expository Commentary, with Doctrinal and Practical Remarks on the Entire Psalter.* (Philadelphia; Edinburgh: J. B. Lippincott Company; A & C Black, 1872), 1209.

[1894] Swanson, J. *Dictionary of Biblical Languages with Semantic Domains: Hebrew (Old Testament)* (electronic ed.). (Oak Harbor: Logos Research Systems, Inc., 1997).

[1895] Holladay, W. L., and L. Köhler. A Concise Hebrew and Aramaic Lexicon of the Old Testament. (Leiden: Brill, 2000), 393.

[1896] Swanson, J. *Dictionary of Biblical Languages with Semantic Domains: Hebrew (Old Testament)* (electronic ed.). (Oak Harbor: Logos Research Systems, Inc., 1997).

[1897] Plumer, W. S. *Studies in the Book of Psalms: Being a Critical and Expository Commentary, with Doctrinal and Practical Remarks on the Entire Psalter.* (Philadelphia; Edinburgh: J. B. Lippincott Company; A & C Black, 1872), 1209.

[1898] Harris, R. L., G. L. Archer Jr., and B. K. Waltke (Eds.). *Theological Wordbook of the Old Testament,* (electronic ed.). (Chicago: Moody Press, 1999), 644.

[1899] Plumer, W. S. *Studies in the Book of Psalms: Being a Critical and Expository Commentary, with Doctrinal and Practical Remarks on the Entire Psalter.* (Philadelphia; Edinburgh: J. B. Lippincott Company; A & C Black, 1872), 1210.

[1900] Benson, Joseph. *The Holy Bible With Notes, Critical, Explanatory and Practical.* (London: J. Kershaw, 1825), Psalm 150:6.

[1901] Jamieson, R., A. R. Fausset, & D. Brown. *Commentary Critical and Explanatory on the Whole Bible* (Vol. 1). (Oak Harbor, WA: Logos Research Systems, Inc., 1997), Psalm 150:1–6.

[1902] Jennings, A. C., and W. H. Lowe. *The Psalms, with Introductions and Critical Notes* (Second Edition, Vol. 2). (London: Macmillan and Co., 1885), 391.

[1903] Simeon, C. *Horae Homileticae: Psalms, LXXIII–CL* (Vol. 6). (London: Samuel Holdsworth, 1836), 527.

[1904] Hamilton, William W. *Sermons on Books of the Bible: Vol. 2.* (Nashville: Broadman Press, 1925), 36.

[1905] Ellsworth, R. *Opening Up Psalms.* (Leominster: Day One Publications, 2006), 129.

[1906] MacArthur, J., Jr. (Ed.). *The MacArthur Study Bible,* (electronic ed.). (Nashville, TN: Word Pub, 1997), 872.

[1907] Spurgeon, C. H. *The Treasury of David.* (Grand Rapids, Michigan: Kregel Publications, 2004), Psalm 150:1.

[1908] Spence-Jones, H. D. M. (Ed.). *Psalms,* (Vol. 3). (London; New York: Funk & Wagnalls Company, 1909), 418.

[1909] Henry, M. *Matthew Henry's Commentary on the Whole Bible: Complete and Unabridged in One Volume.* (Peabody: Hendrickson, 1994), 954.

[1910] Ellsworth, R. *Opening Up Psalms.* (Leominster: Day One Publications, 2006), 130.

[1911] Benson, Joseph. *The Holy Bible With Notes, Critical, Explanatory and Practical.* (London: J. Kershaw, 1825), Psalm 150:2.

[1912] Henry, M. *Matthew Henry's Commentary on the Whole Bible: Complete and Unabridged in One Volume.* (Peabody: Hendrickson, 1994), 954.

[1913] Kett, Henry. *The Flowers of Wit.* (London: Weybridge Press, 1814), 177.

[1914] MacArthur, John. *MacArthur Bible Commentary.* (Nashville: Thomas Nelson, 2005), Ephesians 5:19.

[1915] Exell, Joseph S. Ed. *The Biblical Illustrator,* Psalm 150:3–5.

[1916] Criswell, W. A., P. Patterson, E. R. Clendenen, D. L. Akin, M. Chamberlin, D. K. Patterson, and J. Pogue (Eds.). Believer's Study Bible, (electronic ed.). (Nashville: Thomas Nelson, 1991), Ps. 150:3–5.

[1917] Barnes, Albert. Notes on the Psalms, Critical, Explanatory and Practical. (New York: Harper & Brothers, 1868), Psalm 150:6.

[1918] Spurgeon, C. H. *Psalms.* (Wheaton, IL: Crossway Books, 1993), 373.

[1919] Jamieson, R., A. R. Fausset, & D. Brown. *Commentary Critical and Explanatory on the Whole Bible* (Vol. 1). (Oak Harbor, WA: Logos Research Systems, Inc., 1997), Psalm 150:6.

[1920] Henry, M. *Matthew Henry's Commentary on the Whole Bible: Complete and Unabridged in One Volume.* (Peabody: Hendrickson, 1994), 954.

[1921] Ibid.

[1922] Ibid.